Howard Walters: Through The Years

DISCLAIMER

The recommendations on the use of pesticides made in this book in no way constitute an endorsement to use those pesticides by the American Rose Society, The recommendations made herein were solely made by Howard Walters as he understood their proper and legal use at the time the articles were published. The American Rose Society recognizes that the proper use and registration of pesticides is constantly under review by national and state agencies. Before using any pesticide, the user should consult current labeling for that pesticide for appropriate plant species, varieties, use rates, and application timings. Use of pesticides outside their labeled uses is strictly prohibited.

For the duration that Howard Walters's column appeared in *American Rose*, the magazine mainly printed black-and-white photographs. In an attempt to remain historically accurate and to retain the true spirit of Rambling Rosarian, we used black-and-white photographs exclusively in this publication. Additionally, Walters's columns appear exactly as they did in their original publications, during which time *American Rose* had numerous different style guidelines.

American Rose Society
P. O. Box 30,000 • Shreveport, LA 71130-0010 • www.ars.org

Director of Publications, Managing Editor: Beth Smiley
Associate Editor/Graphic Designer: Lisa Butler
Associate Editor: Kelly Phelan
*With special thanks to Maria Scott, Peggy Spivey, Carol Spiers and Bradlee Robertson
for their help in compiling columns for publication.*

TABLE OF CONTENTS

FOREWARD

Howard Walters served the American Rose Society and its membership for decades, most notably as its President, President Emeritus, author, and lecturer. He received the highest commendations of the Society – the ARS Gold Medal and the Joseph and Marion Klima Gold Medal for Rose Education.

This volume is a compilation of the thirty-two years of his columns bearing the title *Rosarian Ramblings* that were published in the *American Rose* for the first time in September 1970 and continuously until the April 2003 issue, just a month before his death. It earned for him the sobriquet, the Rambler, which he proudly accepted. The column was his gift to rosarians and an edifice to his commitment to rose education. In the column he was forever teaching, promoting the old tried and true methods, introducing the reader to new products, new technologies, new garden tools, and spicing his down-to-earth, even humorous, writing style with such philosophical observations as "advice is like manure; it's only good when spread around" or "the best thing about spring is that it always comes when it's most needed."

The reader will find his writings to be as much fun to read as they are informative. Although he readily accepted the use of chemical pesticides and fertilizers, he insisted on their proper use and hammered home the injunction to "read and follow the label directions." At the same time he was a serious advocate of organic gardening. He is famous for the promotion of the elixir of the rose gods, "cow tea" and "alfalfa tea," the recipes for which can be found scattered throughout the columns. He acknowledged the role of science in rose culture, but never burdened the reader with its complicated details.

Howard writes from experience. His advice is based on results he has achieved in his garden. It is not simply folklore that has been passed down from rosarian to rosarian without validation. Enjoy this book for the information it imparts and for the entertainment it provides. And remember this wise saying that you will run across as you peruse the pages — "With roses, it's what you learn after you know it all that counts."

Dr. John T. Dickman

Rambling is perhaps the best description of this new ARS column, as I can't claim to be much of a rosarian. So ramble we will, over and through a number of rose subjects, watching and hoping for comments and contributions from you faithful rose readers. Have something you want to contribute??? Send it along. This is a great spot to swap ideas and comments, the more the merrier. Just in case you read something you really like in these sketchy columns, we would like to hear about that, too. Meantime, read on.

I'm a great fan of rose publications, as are most rosarians, novice and pro. If you have a rose bulletin you would like to exchange, put us on your list and we will reply with monthly issues of THE ROSE-ETTE, modestly described as the sprightly and informative publication of the Houston Rose Society. It's a good way to trade information as I have always believed that a good publication is essential to a vigorous and enthusiastic rose society. Maybe one of these days we can compile a list of newsletters around the country and get a new round of exchanges going. If you have been reading these bulletins, you have probably noticed some rather strange names for the columnists, maybe coined to avoid responsibility for their advice. A couple that amuse me are "Gertie Gopher's Gardening Guesses" and "Around the Sepals With the Aphid". The Aphid even has his own letterhead. These Texas scribes are competing with the "Rose Bug" and "Petal Pusher". What other entries do we have in this elite group?

Ran on to some sound advice the other day from "Slats" Wathen that bears repeating. He reminds us that we often ignore a great many tried and true rose products, varieties and gardening practices for "newer" things or "miracle" applications to cure all of our rose troubles. We'll take any miracles we can get; but in the meantime we have fungicides, insecticides, equipment and cultivars that stagger the imagination. Regular use and less wishful thinking can fill your place with roses and trophies. Slats is from the Golden Triangle of Southeast Texas, has a house full of hardware, and won the Nicholson Bowl in 1969. Enough said.

Plenty of enthusiasm for the new ARS Headquarters at Shreveport, Louisiana, was noted during the Denver Convention in June. A visit to the rolling, piney hills just west of Shreveport will convince anyone that this is an ideal spot for roses. It's beautiful country with a long growing season and hospitable people. Typical of the area is genial John Lawhon, lawyer-rosarian who put together the land donation for ARS. This was quite a promotion job, and you can be sure that Shreveport is behind the rose center all the way. The whole city is rose minded, and has been for years. Rose plantings in the parkways, on the street corners and around public buildings are glowing with color nine months of the year. Mrs. Lawhon (Gladys) is doing her part, too. In the last month she has signed up 92 new ARS members and says she could have done better if the land promotion hadn't taken so much time. Make it a point to meet the Lawhons at the Kansas City meeting this month. They are sure to be there with some pictures and promotional material. Ya'll come, heah??

You rosarians who like formulas will go for this: a recipe for making artificial manure, guaranteed to be better than the real stuff and less expensive, too. Visit your local feed store. Take 100 pounds each of cottonseed hulls, rough cut alfalfa meal, and fish meal. Mix with about a yard of partially decomposed leaves or other organic matter, moisten and stir about every other day. If all is working well, a sharp ammonia odor will escape when you stir. Let pile heat and work about two weeks. You will have the best organic fertilizer available. If you're a gourmet, add some other trace materials such as seaweed, bloodmeal, rock phosphate, etc. Use 1 shovelful per bush. Do Not get the mixture too wet (or use cottonseed meal) or you will get some odors you didn't plan to have.

Another good tip for novice or pro is as simple as shaking a bottle. If you want to get a wettable powder like Phaltan or Manzate into solution without lumps, measure the powder into a large dry jar (with a tight lid), add HOT water, shake a couple of times... and no more lumps or straining. Makes a good mixture every time. Add insecticides with aromatic bases to the mixture later. If you use a clear glass jar to shake up the mix you can also observe the compatibility of the ingredients before pouring into your sprayer.

A fashion note for rosarians — the in thing this year is matching stay-pressed coveralls (both his and hers) with appropriate rose society and ARS insignia. Some of the styles are really attractive, and cause a lot of comment and enthusiasm. There's something about a uniform that just adds to the feeling of participation. The things are very practical, too. Jump into the coveralls at 4 a.m., zip the zipper, enter roses until deadline time, recover over coffee, have picture made with winners, and still be stylish and welcome at the judge's luncheon. Coverall-clad rosarians just seem to be more friendly and approachable to visitors at the show. It might be worth a try in your society.

OCT. 1970

THOUGHT FOR THE MONTH: It matters not what goal you seek, It's secret here reposes; You've got to dig from week to week To get results or roses. ~ Edgar A. Guest

These rose ramblings have already run into some sticky (and smelly) questions about the formula for artificial manure. Remember the caution that the mixture must not get too wet, otherwise a slime forms and you have some odors that can't be mistaken for ammonia. It's a great formula... imagine good manure without having to put up with a cow. Just in case you broadcast fish meal in the rose beds (use about two cups per bush), stir it up in the mulch a couple of times to mix with other organic material. Result: Little or no smell, other than that good growing odor of nitrogen. If you are bothered with cats and dogs after fish meal, try broadcasting a pound or two of cayenne pepper on top of the mulch. You might say it adds spice to the mixture.

Some of the gourmet mixtures recommended in these columns may seem a bit on the novice side to the old pros, but we hope that some of the beginners will give these ideas a try. We all know, for example, that most sprays and chemicals have a limited shelf life, and rapidly lose their effectiveness when kept for long periods on a garage shelf that is alternately hot and then freezing. But how many of us bother to DATE the package, or to repackage wettable powders in a glass jar with a tight lid? Big mayonnaise jars are good for this, and you can also tape the label on the outside. Another good trick is to note your favorite mixture proportions on the jar with a grease pencil so you won't have to figure it out again. Just these two ideas can save you some blackspot or mildew problems sometimes due to spraying with old materials, or maybe head off leaf burn because of a spray concentration that was too strong. One last thought in this line... have you tried the small medicine glass for measuring your spray materials. Many garden shops have them, about 25 cents each, with easy-to-read markings for teaspoons, tablespoons and ounces.

On the fashion scene for rosarians, I am reminded that many clubs now have nylon rain jackets with appropriate rose insignia, names and so forth on them. Golfers found these jackets useful first, and most have some kind of golf patch on the pocket. Of course you'll want to take the golf deal off... who ever heard of a rosarian who also had enough time to play golf? This extra form of identification can pay big dividends in reaching visitors at your shows, and makes us seem a bit more informal and fun. I haven't noticed many suit and tie characters in the rose garden lately, have you? Had a chance to visit the Shreveport site for our new ARS headquarters the other day, and I'm even more impressed with the land selection. The gently rolling land is covered with piney woods, many of them specimen trees. The soil is sandy and well-drained and the overall feeling is one of natural beauty. As you walk through the pines and over the slopes, it isn't hard to imagine the natural settings for roses that will be developed. It's a warm experience just to visit Shreveport, their rose plantings throughout the city are beautiful, and the residents are justifiably proud of them. You'll never find a friendlier place, and most conversations end with locally-flavored hospitality to the effect, "Ya'll come back, heah?"

Had an interesting question last week. A garden visitor noticed the reinforcing bar stakes securing the rosebushes and remarked that this was certainly an unusual way to get iron to the plants. It took some tact to advise that the stakes were really just to keep the roses from blowing over, but it also reminded me that sometimes the obvious is not so obvious. Reinforcing bar (about 3/8 inch diameter) cut into two-foot lengths will secure most rose plants that are planted high. Use about two bars to each bush, cross and bind the canes by driving the bars well into the soil. It's a trick used in the Houston Municipal Rose Garden and has helped very tall bushes through heavy rains and hurricane strength winds. Little or no additional tie material is needed if the bars are used right.

Every grower has a favorite kind of rose bed mulch, to which he attributes much of his success. But it might just pay to consider two fairly new mulches now generally available in most parts of the country. A great disadvantage of most organic mixtures is the constant replacement and sometimes unsightly appearance of the rose beds. If you have a rose location you want to look especially well groomed, take minimum care and still do the job that a good mulch should, consider a deep application of pine or redwood bark chunks or the even newer calcined clay jumbos. The bark should be at least medium sized (1/2 inch to 2 1/2 inch) and liberally used. It lasts a long time, has good appearance, water percolates through the covering easily, smothers weeds and seems to promote that delicate humus balance in the top layers of the actual growing soil. The soil stays moist, friable and seems full of bacterial life. Calcined clay chunks (marketed under a number of different names) are also very decorative and beneficial. One rose bed I have observed (along a concrete driveway exposed to full sun) has been mulched with three inches of medium sized pieces for some four years and the roses are thriving. A check of the soil underneath shows everything in good order. It can't blow, wash away or decompose and holds great quantities of water like a sponge.

Nov. 1970

THOUGHT FOR THE MONTH: Some people are always grumbling because roses have thorns. I am thankful that thorns have roses.

To you rose faithful, a deliverance! *Benlate* is finally cleared for home garden use and the DuPont folks can now save our rose gardens from blackspot and mildew... at least that's what we have all been led to believe. The tests to date have been great --spraying every two weeks has given excellent control of both fungus problems, and some claim has been made that spider mites also find it offensive. That's almost too good to be true. But *Benlate*, like all other insecticides and fungicides, has to be applied before it can do any good. The same rosarian who forgot or skipped his weekly fungicide control will also slip up on *Benlate*. Regularity is still the answer for fungus control, even if the material is systemic in action. On the systemic qualities of *Benlate*, here's how a Doctor of Plant Pathology explained it to me, using small words that I can understand: *Benlate* sprayed on the leaves will actually enter the cells in those leaves and will kill the multiplying fungus spores as they attempt to invade the leaf structure. The fungicide in the cell system of the plant will only move UP as the plant grows. In short, spray the lower leaves well since spray on the top of the plant will not go down.

While we are on sprays, I have to pass this one along. We have all heard the stories of how unusual mixtures seem to kill spider mites, scourge of the rose grower. Like the lady rosarian who mixed up flour and water, sprayed the leaves and claimed no more mites. But this one is even better — an enthusiastic rosarian of scientific nature (he is really a Medical Doctor with a non-green thumb who will go unnamed) thought that if flour paste was good, a stronger glue would be even better. Since he also builds guitars as a hobby, he had on hand some old-fashioned hoof and horn glue. Carefully mixing this compound at just the right temperature, he sprayed his mite infested 'Margo Kosters' and ... no more mites. Pressing on with this scientific breakthrough, he examined the leaves under a microscope and found that at least one leg of the mite was firmly' stuck to the leaf and had met death by starvation. Believe it or not.

Now to more serious matters... like a testimonial for intelligent organic soil improvement from a good grower in Texas. "...I've been using several good organic recommendations in my yard, and

they have helped a lot. Best of all, started composting shredded oak leaves and have applied this to my rose bed, digging some in, also a layer of compost on the surface under the mulch. I can proudly report I have lots of earthworms now and the roses are doing fine". This is a good time to be thinking about compost and saving the leaves that are falling in the yard. Don't waste a leaf if you can avoid it... we'll give you a couple of simple composting ideas in these rambling columns next month.

Since the holiday season will soon be with us (comes soon after the rose catalogs arrive) how about remembering your gardening friends with rose gift certificates?? It's a great idea, and he is remembered again when the bushes are delivered for planting. The catalog folks or your own nurseryman can give you a hand... for a special touch, specify the cultivars you think he might enjoy. If the green-thumber is just beginning, a membership in ARS will make you a friend for life.

Speaking of cultivars, the newest introductions are great and attract plenty of attention. But don't forget that there are scores of beautiful roses selling for much less than the near $5 tab for the latest thing. Non-patents that sell for about $1.50 each for No. 1's, are good gifts for beginners; you know they have to be good in some respects or they wouldn't still be around. Besides, what garden can do without 'Peace', 'Charlotte Armstrong', 'Crimson Glory', 'Eclipse', 'Else Poulsen', 'K. T. Marshall', 'Show Girl', 'The Doctor', or 'Vogue'?? All are off patent; all are good. Look in the back pages of the catalog and order plenty; there's always room for one more.

Add little known but ought to be noted facts: That Shreveport has some 300 separate rose plantings scattered around the city, tucked into traffic islands, ornamenting boulevards. Nearly 20,000 rose plants are in bloom there some nine months of the year... That most rose growers do not make enough use of mass plantings of Floribundas for landscape effects. Take 'Valentine' for example — a good, free-flowering red that will seldom win a show trophy, but one that cleans itself, needs almost no maintenance other than water and occasional feeding. It gives beauty season-long in colorful displays, winning friends for roses. After all, isn't that what this rose business is all about??

By this time all but the balmiest areas of the country have set aside their rose worries and are planning for the garden that will match or exceed the catalog claims. This fireside euphoria is great, but plans and schedules will pay off with blooms you can cut. Check the local Proof of the Pudding, sketch a new area in the garden, get the compost pile heating under the snow... get ready for a very rosy 1971. Here are a few ideas you might like to try...

How about a "Sattelite" garden?? That is, a garden of roses of any description not actually on your property. You would be surprised how rewarding this off-premises garden can be, making new friends for roses, more room for your own rose efforts and a chance to use some new growing ideas. There is plenty of unclaimed territory for such efforts... a vacant lot close by, a shut-in neighbor who can't keep up with yard work anymore, your church or a home for senior citizens. With a little help and your experience, surprising things can happen. Sometimes the roses do better when we don't worry over them so much, and the average viewer of a "Rose Sattelite" spot doesn't know a split center from a sepal. But he does know this is a big improvement over the bare lawn and sick bushes. Once the beds are built, a couple of hours a week will do the trick, and I am speaking from experience. The hose-on sprayer works fine, overhead watering (set and forget type) percolates down through slow-acting organic fertilizer, and the spent blooms are taken care of earlier by giving away lots of bouquets. And the best added plus of all... it just makes you FEEL GOOD.

This brings us to a friendly reference, the Golden Triangle rose folks of Southeast Texas, the guys who "Grow 'Em, Show 'Em, Share 'Em." That is their motto and they live up to every word: Sample a little of this strong brew and your rose people will put the FUN back into rose growing. Caught a quote from one of the rose nuts from this group last week. He allowed, "When rose growing isn't fun anymore and the rules and ribbons are more important than blooms, I'll go back to grass."

Here is a good idea on composting, especially for the city lot gardener, because even the smallest homesite can use it. If you have room for a conventional twenty gallon metal garbage can in your back yard, you've got it made! Just do this: Cut out the bottom of a large garbage em (a can that needs replacing because the bottom is rusted out will do just fine). Select a convenient spot and spade up an area the width of the can. Then with both hands firmly work the can a few inches into the ground until you feel sure it is firmly in place. It is preferable if the lid is tight fitting. Now you are ready to start.

As often as you wish, dump your garbage into your new composter and sprinkle a little dirt over the new additions. Once every week or two reach in with any handy garden tool and stir the compost a bit and add some water (just keep it moist). When it appears that you have filled the container, let it rest a week or two — examine it — and then you will find there is room for more. The product you thus manufacture will be rich in food content -and depending on your table — you will have twenty gallons of a mixture as beautiful as any potting soil you can buy.

Something for the ladies (and gentlemen arrangers, too)... The detergent makers have one redeeming quality... almost enough to overcome the sick feeling left from their commercials and the phosphate residue left in our water. They package their products in colorful plastic containers similar to the old syrup bottles; a large container below and a small container above with a handle. Cut the soft plastic at midline and fill the bottom with roses for friends. The colorful containers are not only good looking, but also hold roses well and don't have to be returned. Add this good thought to get them to the friend safely: Take a sturdy cardboard box, punch holes in the sides of the box to accommodate plant ties which will hold the containers firmly against the side of the box. Add padding as necessary to keep the floral materials from being crushed. Several containers can be carried in a single box — safely without tipping.

This light-hearted recommendation is passed along just to remind you that rose growing after all is a hobby, for fun and satisfaction. An experienced rosarian who was pressed with questions on yellow leaves, sagely replied that he had finally reduced the perplexing problem of yellow leaves on roses to a very simple explanation: Leaves on roses are just naturally yellow — the green just covers it sometimes.

How many New Year's resolutions for roses have you made so far??... or have you taken stock of what roses have done for you and what you have done for roses this past year? If we balanced our efforts against what our roses have produced for us in the way of beauty, satisfaction and friendship, the roses in our gardens would come out ahead about three to one. How about improving these odds in '71... and here are a few ideas you might like to try...

Have you thought about making available "rose lists" of the most popular and productive roses in your area. Something less expansive than a formal proof of the pudding is needed, a simple list of the ten favorite Hybrid Teas, Grandifloras and Floribundas and their color descriptions.

Put these out through the nurseries handling roses... you will be doing them a favor and helping a good many beginning rose growers. This brings us back to an old theme... that rose growing ought to be made easy and fun. Your local society can also get some mileage out of the project by identifying the source of the list and advising the: "when, where and why of rose society meetings."

If you are REALLY anxious to make friends for roses, write up a two-page brief on rose care for your area; identify your rose society, and put these sheets out through the nurseries and at your rose shows. This is not as easy as it sounds, as it is a tough job to keep the suggestions simple and brief. But it is a cheap and reliable way to attract new rose growers, and it will payoff in blooms and friends all season. The Texas Rose Research Foundation has a great single sheet giveaway of Rose Growing Suggestions, and The Houston Rose Society has given away some 20,000 copies of similar advice. If you would like copies of these hints to start you off, drop me a line.

We have talked a lot about composting lately, but few growers have the grinder equipment to speed up the process. Now that you have plenty of leaves to work with, here is an idea to get the bacteria working in record time. Rake up the leaves in a sort of windrow in an open space of lawn. The windrow can be three feet or so wide and a foot high. Dampen the leaves with a spray from the hose. Fire up your rotary lawn mower; leave off the catching bag; and run the mower in one direction down the row of leaves. Repeat the chopping process a couple of times until shredding is complete. The result will be a neat row of well-chopped, organic material ready for composting on some garden area. The secret is to dampen the leaves before running the mower. The leaves and other materials chop better and do not blow all over the yard. If you are anxious for very fast compost, add some cheap source of nitrogen to the composting piles, dampen slightly and even cover with some plastic material to conserve heat. The products you make will probably be superior to the expensive bagged material you buy at the garden shop.

If you are planning a new rosebed, give some extra thought to the edging material around the bed and also to the height of the bed above the level of the lawn or other growing areas. A good, neat edging can do much more than improve the appearance of the bed; it can also improve drainage, keep out grass and keep your growing medium just the way you want it. A favorite around here is redwood about 1 x 8 inches, nailed securely into redwood corner posts. Redwood is easy to cut, lasts a long time, can be stained and even bent into some graceful shapes. To make the 1 x 8 boards look heavier, nail a cap piece of redwood on top, that is a 1 x 4 cut down the middle. The cap piece also covers up your nailing mistakes. Red cedar also works well. The whole idea is to allow good drainage for the rosebushes and makes fertilizers, water and air more readily available to the roots.

Another suggestion that may sound like heresy to you growers in the North is to plant some of your rosebushes with the bud unions well above ground level, NOT buried as is the common practice. Extensive field trials and experiment stations report more vigorous bushes, better production of basal breaks and no appreciable winterkill, provided some winter protection is added. Note that last statement... PROVIDED that some winter protection is added. Most cold climate rosarians add winter protection as a matter of good growing practice to save as much cane as possible. Give this suggestion your own field trial with a few bushes this year. Compare bush results. Provide some extra winter cover, and you might be surprised to find that rosebushes do not have to be buried under the soil, making good pruning and bush development next to impossible.

Strolled through the new ARS property at Shreveport in November, and was overwhelmed at the fall beauty of the trees and shrubs. It was a woodlands scene to challenge a poet. How could roses go wrong with nature's backdrop to finish the picture.

February is a great rose month, and real rose nuts are already thinking about how to frame and hang those rose certificates they are sure to win in the spring shows. The Queen of the Show blooms to come don't suffer the indignities of competition and criticism… great splashes of color brighten the landscape design without having to lift a shovel. With the ever-faithful promise of the rose catalogs, who needs more? Free from the demands of the garden, the rose gardener can devote his ample energies to thinking, planning and just plain dreaming of things to come, and that is a worthwhile occupation once in a while. These light-hearted ramblings are passed along here just to remind you again that rose growing after all is just a hobby and ought to be easy and fun. Try a couple of these ideas on for size in your garden…

Afraid to try some of the new and different? Reluctant to dig up and throwaway those bushes that "might take another year to get established"? There is an old rosarian saying, "Those that don't put out, pull out". To make the conscience feel better, offer the bushes you want to replace to another rosarian, or have a plant exchange. It is a good way to get a friend started in roses; it may take a little spade work as well as free bushes, but the rewards in the long run will be great. The "Grow 'Em, Show 'Em, Share 'Em" philosophy has a satisfaction way beyond polishing up some silver trophy. A new rose grower has to start somewhere, and the bushes that didn't quite please your critical eye can dazzle a beginner.

Winter is also a good time for rose competitors to sharpen up their showing tricks and get some enthusiasm going for the approaching show season. One of the most fun things I have seen is a *U-Haul* trailer rolling down the highway with GOLDEN TRIANGLE ROSE SOCIETY boldly lettered on both sides. On arrival at an out-of-town show, every exhibitor knows who is there, and the fun begins. Here is how it works: It is a cooperative effort. Several growers get together to rent the trailer on the basis of the space required to haul their insulated garbage cans, or other means of rose transport. They usually add some extra ice to the trailer, in addition to the materials in their containers. During the early morning hours before a major show, the trailer makes the rounds of the growers, picks up the containers and sets out for the big event. Before long a caravan is formed and takes off in high spirits. The rosarians not only have a great time, but their roses also get to the show in good shape. Can you imagine the shock if YOUR rose society rolled up to a distant show with a trailer load of roses?? Try it sometime soon; you will make friends for roses and fun for yourself.

Another good use of a trailer is to haul rose show supplies, or to take staging materials to an exhibit. It may also be used to take ten or fifteen rosebushes to a pruning demonstration, or some program props to a special garden show or meeting. There is something about the showmanship that adds interest far beyond the modest cost.

How about a program suggestion for late winter? In line with "It's easy to grow roses"; this program will involve all your members and has many variations to suit your situation. The whole idea is to get your members to swap ideas and experiences with roses. It is a type of workshop; breaking the members present down into groups of eight to ten per group. Worktables are better than auditorium type seating. Set up four or five different groups. Call them: Rose Testers, Bug Fighters, Soil Scientists, Trophy Chasers, Catalog Consultants, etc. Make up small identifying signs from some old catalogs. Appoint an experienced and talkative moderator for each table. As your members come in, each may choose the table that interests him most. For example, the Rose Testers are going to discuss varieties and performance; the Soil Scientists will talk about fertilizers and rose bed preparation and on and on. The trick is to write up a short outline with some leading questions for each group to cover. EVERY member at the table can contribute something. The leading question for the Bug Fighters might include: Do you use a spreader sticker? What kind?… What type sprayer do you use?… Any experience with systemics?… What concentration is best for *Phaltan*?… What is a typical spray program for our area? Then turn the groups loose on their questions and ask the moderator to jot down some of the conclusions, in preparation for a five-minute summary to the whole audience later. You will find the only problem is to get all of the "Workshop Experts" to be quiet. If you can use a set of outlines, drop me a line.

Speaking of "Rambling Rosarians", how long has it been since your rose society exec committee got together with other exhibitors, workers and just plain dirt gardeners interested in making your rose growing hobby more fun?? Call it a brainstorming session or whatever, it's a good idea occasionally to review where you have been, where you are going, with some new thoughts of how to get there. Remember the secret of brainstorming is to list EVERY idea fired off in rapid succession without rejecting or criticizing anything. When the idea well has temporarily run dry, go over the schemes again and match up the best points of each. You'll be surprised how many good programs and approaches can come out of this mixture. The executive committee is the logical place to start since this group sets the pace and tone of local rose activities, good or bad. They are in a position to do the work for the rose growers, letting the fun and pleasure of roses come through at the meetings.

One of my pet peeves is to attend a rose society meeting (no names mentioned — if the shoe fits, wear it) and be bored through thirty minutes of listless minutes, nit-picking discussions over the cost of refreshment cookies, droning recitations of finances, motions, seconds, rephrasing and discussions of things that have nothing to do with growing and enjoying better roses. Rose people get together to be entertained and informed, not to sit as a judicial body. Membership grows when roses are fun. Put the plus of pleasure back into your rose meeting and insist that the exec committee do 99% of the work and decision making. It's like enjoying the first warm breath of spring after a long, long winter.

Enough editorial comment... now to something positive on roses and growers from here and there. This one is just too good to escape without note as it honors and describes one of our top rose authorities and gives us some food for thought in our own daily contacts. The subject was Dr. Eldon Lyle, Vice President of ARS and likely successor to the top spot. This genial, down-to-earth rose man had just finished a detailed discussion of fungicide tests for a large and attentive group. The applause was warm and enthusiastic, but the most rewarding response came from a comment overheard in the back of the room, "Even when he is talking in front of a group, I always have the feeling that he is talking just to me." This is the way to get involvement in roses. Try it sometime.

And a special thanks for Melvin Wyant's reminder that I should qualify the statement that No.1, non-patent varieties are available at $1.50 each. Some growers do have No. 1's at this price (if purchased in quantity), but most do not. However, we agree that there's a lot of rose pleasure in the older standards without paying the price of the latest introductions. The worst buy of all is the cheap rose (usually packaged in a store window for who knows how long) that has a very slim chance for survival. The standards from a reliable grower or local nursery are your best buys for color and production all season long.

As for planting those new roses, how about the old saying "Never plant a $5.00 bush in a 50 cent hole." We have all heard it, but sometimes forget. Nothing pays off in future blooms like a well prepared rose bed. A few extra hours of spade work in the spring saves many more hours of sweat-producing labor in the summer. Check other local rosarians for their favorite mixtures and get out the fork and shovel. If it is an existing bed, take up the old bushes and heel in or put them in cold storage until the soil can be worked over. In our mild climate where roses seldom become really dormant, a favorite trick is to dig and prune bushes in January, moisten with sphagnum moss, wrap in heavy plastic, box and place in the cold storage warehouse. Cold storage for up to 100 bushes won't cost more than $5.00 per month, provided you compact the pruned bushes about like the bare root roses you get in the mail. While your roses enjoy a good dormancy, you have plenty of time to work on the new rose beds. Bushes that have been in cold storage come out with a vigor that has to be seen to be believed. Just sorry that I don't have a suggestion for your growers in the north on how to keep the bushes warm.

The Shreveport ARS site is the scene of lots of activity these days with note taking, measuring, walking and retracing the wooded paths that criss-cross the rolling slopes. Object of all this site study is to come up with the best natural use of the terrain features. It's quite a job to provide for test and display gardens, old rose and miniature gardens, landscaping demonstrations, nature trails, picnic and shelter areas. Of one thing we can be sure, ARS will have a woodland garden unique in the world, a natural facility for the benefit of every rosarian.

Do you know one of the most important things that sets spring apart as compared to the other seasons?? I think it's the SHOWMANSHIP of springtime; that bold, colorful, new, fresh, emerging, time-to-start-over feeling that cones over us with warm weather. Does your rose society have the same kind of Showmanship to match the season? Maybe its time to mulch and add a little food to your rose society diet, turn the planting medium a bit, try some new formulas and varieties. You might be surprised what happens.

As a starter for spring, how about setting up a schedule and a couple of workers to have a small rose show at the monthly meetings. Many societies do this very successfully. The old-timers as well as the newcomers enjoy it and adds some of the color and flair so often missing at our meetings. A good small show is proof of accomplishment in our rose growing efforts. Around these parts, this part of the program is called the Six-Pack Show, the Continuing Show, and Practice Show. The Six-Pack name is very appropriate; usually entries are limited to no more than six per exhibitor and can be carried in your favorite beverage carrier — by the way, did you know that beer on potted Miniature roses produces great bloom and growth?? Anyway, a limited number of color classes can be set up and the Best of Show determined using standard ARS judging rules. If you want real competition, set up a point system for a major prize at the end of the season. Talk about competition... growers who never enter a regular show will come in with outstanding blooms, and to my way of thinking, that's what this rose hobby business is all about. I have some copies of an excellent show schedule and rules for small shows... I'll be glad to send you a copy. This activity might be just the thing to get your group out of dormancy this year...

Talking about dormancy, here's a good way to break dormancy on a bare root rose bush that may have dried out in shipment. Lightly prune the bush according to your taste and soak in water or planting solution at least overnight. When ready to plant, make up a loose-fitting hood or cover of medium weight, plastic material securing the edges of the plastic with staples so that the hood closes rather securely around the shank of the bush. If you want a little extra humidity, add a handful of wet sphagnum moss inside the bag. Plant the bush as usual, "mud" the roots in. After the first warm day of sunshine, you'll see condensed moisture inside the plastic. Leave the hood in place for a week or ten days, or until the bush is well budded out. Then gradually cut some air holes in the plastic to reduce the temperature. Take the hood off when strong shoots and leaves begin to appear. This also works for tree roses. Make sure some wet moss is added to a tree rose hood. They will be off to the best start ever; in fact, I always start a tree rose this way, and I've never had a failure.

A short hint for you folks in the North still pruning. If you want to paint the large pruning cuts, use some orange shellac in an old liquid shoe polish bottle. The dauber gives good neat coverage of the material and is very convenient. In our area, orange shellac seems to work better than the asphalt tree paints. If you are cutting large, woody canes, be sure to use a small keyhole saw rather than the crushing blade of a lopper. The cut will heal faster, particularly around the bud union.

It's time to set up the fungus disease control program for the year, and repeat again and again that an early start and regular schedule are essential. Trials by the Texas Rose Research Foundation strongly indicate that early season beginning of fungicide spray treatments are advantageous. Start with a soaking fungicidal cleanup spray immediately after pruning. Add a miticide if you have problems.

One of the most successful tests recently reported involved beds of 'Tropicana' and 'Spartan' in a public location in East Texas. *Benlate* fungicide was used for three full seasons. In 1969 the beds were-relatively free of blackspot and mildew. In 1970, *Benlate* fungicidal spray was started in early February, used at 1 tablespoon per two gallons of water, directed to both the under and upper sides of the leaves. There were 20 applications through October and at that time there was yet to be any sign of blackspot, mildew, fungicide burn, unsightly spray residue or damage to the growth of the bushes. *Cygon 2E* (I teaspoon per gallon) was added four times during the season. Spider mite was never seen. Untreated test plots in the area were badly defoliated with blackspot and mildew.

One more thought. Make this the year to start

a garden record book, jotting down the dates and spray formulations you use. I use a small calendar diary and note pruning times, feeding times, rainfall, temperatures, planting dates and so on. If you are an exhibitor, a good diary is a must.

SHOW TIME is here... your golden opportunity to have more fun with roses and win more friends for roses at the same time. Besides the competition and the trophies, what are your rose shows doing for roses??

One important thing a rose show should be doing is attracting more gardeners to roses and showing interested green-thumbers just how easy rose growing can be. An educational exhibit at the rose show can do more to attract and interest people than the trophy table. Few visitors expect to grow roses like the show winners, but they do have a strong desire to be able to grow some nice blooms to cut for themselves and their friends.

What should an Educational Exhibit have?? First of all, friendly hosts who know a little something about roses, followed with simple, understandable exhibits that offer the basics without controversy. In short, keep it simple and make the information easy to remember. One of the best educational displays I have seen was used year after year, in a major city, and was a pet project of a rose grower who had never challenged anyone at the show table. He had painstakingly made up the signs, the simple instructions, gathered the materials, and carefully stored and updated the display between shows. The display had simple charts on planting, samples of typical soils, samples of typical mulches, containers of commonly used fungicides and insecticides, sprayers, lists of varieties that did well in the area, some well-groomed, healthy roses growing in containers... all made attractive with trimmed and mounted rose pictures taken from the catalogs. The display was set up somewhat away from the rose show so that it would not compete for space or attention. However, during most of the day the educational area was more crowded than the trophy table. The hosts in the area pushed three things: the fun of growing roses, a copy of printed rose growing suggestions, and information on rose society activities with an invitation to join. If your society is not doing as much, it's a great time to start, however modestly. If you need a start on preparing a rose growing suggestions sheet, drop me a line and I will be happy to send you a tried and proven giveaway. When rose shows attract, interest and encourage just plain dirt gardeners, you are doing a good job. New growers are the lifeblood of any rose society. Give your society a transfusion of enthusiastic novices this spring.

Now that we are on the subject of lifeblood, how about some bloodmeal for your roses just before show time. Whether you are an organic gardener or not, you will be surprised at the· invigorating effect bloodmeal has on stem, foliage and especially color. Growers around here use about one-half cup of bloodmeal per bush, broadcast evenly over the root zone about fifteen days before a show. Scratch in lightly and water heavily. Continue to give the bush all the water it can tolerate. All kinds of undesirable things can happen if you fail to water thoroughly. There are many sources of bloodmeal or beef-blood mixtures, which are usually inexpensive. Buy directly from a stockyard-packinghouse if you can, otherwise deal through a custom feeds-fertilizer dealer.

Check up on your hose-on sprayer before you get too far into the season. The Hayes and similar hose-ons are usually quite reliable, but can get stopped up slightly and produce a spray mixture that is several times more concentrated than planned. Run a simple test of your sprayer by filling the concentrate bottle of the sprayer with plain water and measure the output in a container of known size. Use the same hose and water connection you usually do for actual spraying. If your mixture results are very far off, you had better buy a new sprayer, clean out the old one if you can, or cut the dilution of the concentrate. Another thing, a 5/8-inch diameter hose on a water line with good pressure will give more reliable results. Hose-on sprayers have sometimes been downgraded by growers without a sound basis. In a test I performed last year, I sprayed my own garden with an engine-driven centrifugal pump sprayer working from a carefully measured tank. I used an ordinary hose-on 6-gallon sprayer at a satellite garden of similar size. Both gardens were sprayed on the same days with the same concentrations. I had just as effective blackspot, mildew, and insect control with the hose-on as with the mechanical pump putting out 125 pounds of pressure. I also had about the same amount of leaf burn (when I made a mistake) with each method. The hose-on required about one-third more spray materials, but it would take a lot of *Manzate* and *Cygon 2E* to make up the $125 cost of the power sprayer. This is not to make a case for the hose sprayer, as I will continue to use the power equipment since it definitely gives a better leaf coverage with less chance of burn. However, you can rely on the cheap, easy-to-use, quick clean-up hose sprayer and get good control.

JUN. 1971

THOUGHT FOR THE MONTH: Moon trips and space spectaculars are ho-hum compared to the pictures and promises of the guys who make up the rose catalogs.

Have you ever wondered what an "average" rosarian is like? Had an interesting program not long ago that sketched (or maybe made up a caricature) of an ordinary rose society member… and his rose facts of life are varied. You salesmen, membership chairmen, hybridizers and other assorted rose folk ought to take note of what this "everyday" rose nut is all about.

Just over 100 rose folks participated in the workshop type program, and information was swapped freely, as some informal polls were taken. It was a fun type approach, and rewarding from many standpoints. Obviously this was a small sample of a regional nature, but I suspect that the basic facts probably apply to most rose societies.

In the first place, most of the members had at least 75 rose bushes, representing all types. A surprising number had tree roses, and Miniatures seemed to be increasingly popular. Hybrid Teas were still by far the most popular, with Floribundas a poor second, followed by Grandifloras. However, about half of those polled said they planned to use more Floribundas in mass planting (all one variety) for landscape features. On an average the members had purchased fifteen new rose bushes this spring, about half of them bare root and about half potted in one way or another. Some thirty percent had purchased twenty-five or more new bushes, and twenty percent had invested in fifty or more (I told you these were rose nuts). At an average price of $4.00 per plant, this rose society had exercised a sizeable financial punch. No member had bought fewer than five new plants. When asked how much they usually expected to spend for new plants each year, the most common answer was, "about $100". Obviously many spent much, much more than that.

Hybridizers please note… an attempt to make up a "most popular ten varieties" list resulted in a list of nearly thirty, and it was still growing when the discussion was cut off. It seems that there is a place for most everything in someone's garden. 'First Prize' was considered the best new rose in many, many seasons; most of the growers had three or more plants. Some "dark horses" in the race for popularity on the show table included Carla, Bel Ange, Old Smoothie and Red Devil. AARS winners came out very well. Nine out of ten growers had bought at least one of the 1971 winners, and most had two or more. 'Command Performance' attracted more purchasers than 'Red Gold' or 'Aquarius'.

Most of the growers fed both organics and chemical fertilizers on a monthly basis. Eight out of ten used foliar feedings on an every-other-week basis. *Ra-Pid-Gro* led in popularity, followed by *Ortho Liquid Rose Food* (perhaps because of a recent one cent sale). Fish meal and fish emulsion fertilizers were used by half of the growers, and most everyone wanted a cheap, weed free source of animal manures that "hadn't been heat treated and all the good stuff taken out" Readily soluble chemical fertilizers generally followed a 1-2-1 analysis ratio.

Manzate and *Phaltan* still lead in popularity for blackspot control, but *Benlate*, in spite of its price, is gaining rapidly. *Acti-dion PM* was the universal choice for control and eradication of mildew, pending more experience with *Benlate*. *Isotox* and liquid formulations of malathion were the most popular insect controls. Hose-on sprayer fans take heart; you are still in the majority. Seven out of ten rosarians use hose sprayers, and the rest have invested in tank types and various power-driven sprayers.

Only two out of ten members seem interested in rose show competition; most of the members grew roses to give away as cut flowers for friends, enjoy themselves or to just give them something beautiful to work with. Most liked to go to the shows, but only a few wanted to: prune, disbud, spray, shelter, groom, store and agonize over show winners. Membership in the rose society was primarily for rose culture information, second as a pleasant social thing, and way down the list was interest in competitive growing.

Rose bulletins were very popular, and some members joined primarily to receive up-to-date information. Growers appear to be serious in their efforts to have better roses and want more and more facts and formulas to try in their gardens. Variety discussions, lists of new materials and what-to-do-this-month advice were high on the list of most-wanted subjects.

As a rose grower, maybe you fit this sketch. Anyway, I think: it is important for us to understand that most rose-hobby people are in it for fun and beauty and are willing to spend money and participate along these lines. Program Chairmen ... take note: your members might be trying to tell you something.

Summer is finally here with promises of great things to come with roses, marred only a little by the usual hot-weather problems of eager rosarians. We will touch on the good and the bad in these rambling columns and hope that your rose vases are overflowing in a sweepstakes of color.

To begin with, your second full bloom should be more colorful, longer stemmed and complemented with better foliage than the first spring flush of bloom. You can cut more freely, shape the bushes and generally control the production of your bushes — something not always possible with cold-warm-cold turns of springtime weather. If you aren't getting these results, you should check signals with some other rose folks to see how they are doing. It has been obvious to me, over many years of rose growing, that the most successful growers have a very definite routine for all of their rose activities; their spray program has a regular schedule; feeding is done on a careful program; watering, grooming, etc. is done at the right time every time. The deep soaking that was skipped; the spraying that was missed because of "hot weather," or the rose food that never got to the rose bed… all make a big difference in rose pleasure. Our roses will tolerate a heap of abuse, but give rewards all out of proportion when we use a little judgement.

I like to feed roses lightly every four to six weeks during the growing season, beginning with a top dressing of manure or compost early in the spring. After two weeks follow with one cup of fish meal per bush. One month after pruning add a handful of balanced rose food with trace elements. Every four weeks thereafter I use a rose fertilizer with a 1-2-1 analysis watered in thoroughly. In our mild climate (we have good bloom through November) I use another cup or so of fish meal about September I and *Ra-Pid-Gro* or *Ortho Gro* about October I. I also like to use a foliar feeding every two weeks except when the thermometer goes over 90 degrees. Blood meal and Epsom Salts are added extras about two weeks before major show dates. This formula may not work for you, but the idea is to get a mixture and program going for your area and stick with it.

Water is probably our toughest problem when the weather really gets hot. Nothing good can hap-

pen to a rose bush without plenty of water. We tend to overrate the summer showers, and need to take care of the deep soaking ourselves. First thing — buy an accurate rain gauge so that you will know just how much help the weatherman is giving, then consider installing a pipe-soaker system of some kind or other. You don't have to be a master plumber (they all have gardeners) as this is a do-it-yourself project with polyethylene pipe. There is no threading, hard cutting or special tools needed. You can buy all of the connections, pipe and cement for joints and get free advice at most any farm store. Use 1/2 to 5/8-inch pipe if available. Layout the pipe in the rose bed and mark for length and location of watering holes. I like small water holes about every twelve inches, either drilled in the pipe with a 3/32-inch bit or pushed through with a hot ice pick. Line up the water holes on one side of the pipe only and install down so that all of the water goes into the ground and mulch. The plastic pipe rig can be buried an inch or two, laid on top of the mulch, or covered with mulch. I like a covering of mulch best. The results are fantastic — better growth, less spray burn, less waste of water, and best of all… less work. Some pre-fab water systems are available, but few are as reliable and as economical as the polyethylene pipe.

If you haven't mulched your rose beds already, you are in trouble. If yours isn't working too well, try a mixture of cheap, locally-available materials that will stay loose for insulation and percolation and will break down slowly. Sugar cane pulp, shredded pine bark, pine needles and oak leaves are popular here. Each one is good when used alone; mixed together they seem unbeatable. The differences in the sizes and textures let water and air reach the soil so that all kinds of good organic things happen.

A thought for Program Chairmen everywhere — July is a great month for: watermelon parties (in a rose garden, of course), garden tours, open gardens, ice cream socials and informal gatherings of all kinds for members and friends. No need to fade with the summer heat, just combine it with fun. The Hospitality Ladies, bless them through with a rose-picnic-party long remembered.

AUG.
1971

THOUGHT FOR THE MONTH:
When the glass is at ninety a man is a fool, Who directs not his efforts to try to keep cool.

The hot August sun will soon be separating the rose growers from the rose wishers, and the biggest loser of all will be the new grower who just doesn't know how to cope with hot, dry weather, spider mites and spray burn. Here is a good chance for rose societies to get into the thick of things with programs slanted toward hot weather problems and a helping hand from some of the more experienced growers. Has your society made up a list of young men (or maintenance firms) who can handle a good rose garden for a week or a month while the owner is vacationing?? I know several young men who learned something about roses at an early age who are now cashing in on this experience during the summer months. It is good for the rose folks and for the college bank account also. You will be doing your members a real favor with some spade work along this line — might even make some new friends for the rose society.

Since we are on service, you may recall that these pages carried a long list of Consulting Rosarians a few months ago, complete with addresses. The list was great, but all too often that is where it stops. The consultants have a certificate to hang up; their names appear on a list here and there, and then we promptly forget about them. For the most part, these are enthusiastic and informed people, ready and willing to assist wherever and whenever they can. Most of them are too modest to insist that their services be used, and so they wait for the call that seldom comes. Put YOUR Consulting Rosarian to work. If he (or she) is worth anything at all, he ought to be worked. Set aside a part of your program every month for the consulting rosarian. Assign a definite topic each month. Assign responsibility for the "Question Box" — one of the most popular features of a rose society meeting. Your members (newer ones in particular) can get more from this part of the program than from most of the program speakers I have had to sit through. More rose growers rust out than wear out, so make sure that they have something to do.

Another thing that bothers me is that too many writers, speakers, consulting rosarians and various other "rose experts" are reluctant to name specific products, sprayers, fertilizers or what have you. If he has found through experience that something works (or perhaps doesn't work) he needs enough backbone to stand up and be counted. He should at least be courageous enough to say, "It does a good job for me; try it if you like". It makes the expert weigh his words a little more carefully and gives some practical facts to the less experienced. One of the greatest things my co-columnist, "Uncle Charlie" Dawson has done over the years has been to list and give details about various things he has tried. I still have a faded column by Uncle Charlie taped to the inside of the storage cabinet where I keep my sprays. It must be six or eight years old at least, but I still refer to it on certain items. Not that I always agree with his conclusions, but he at least gives me a place to start.

And you had better get a head start on the spider mite problem if you live in a hot, dry area. More questions are probably being asked about these tenacious pests than any other rose problem. And you can probably come up with just as many answers. My answer is very simple and very old... wash 'em off with water. Greenhouse men were washing mites years and years before the exotic chemicals came from the test tubes. I personally like the water wand advertised in these pages. Or it isn't too hard to build one yourself. The fine, high pressure water breaks up the webbing on the undersides of the leaves and sends the spiders... I don't know where. Anyway, it seems to break up the reproductive cycle of the mites and the plants begin to grow again. A good washing two or three times a week when you first notice spiders will probably get you out of trouble, and a weekly washing after that will maintain control. If you also want to use an insecticide (and run the risk of leaf burn) wash the leaves first and follow with a drenching spray on the undersides. Apply three times at five-day intervals. Another trick that reduces burn is to spray late in the evening, and then wash off the tops of the leaves with a fine water mist early the next morning. Of course, basic to any spray program is to soak the rose beds before spraying and avoid spraying during the hottest part of the day. In spite of all these precautions, it is sometimes hard to tell whether more leaf damage is done by the mites or by the spray. I also believe that overhead watering of roses helps control mites, and I make it a regular practice to set a cone-spray lawn sprinkler under the plants and soak the beds. Anyway, one of these ideas may help you get through the summer with some green leaves.

SEPT. 1971

THOUGHT FOR THE MONTH:
A bit of fragrance always clings to the hand that gives roses. Old Chinese Proverb

These Rambling Rosarian columns have been running for a year now, and it seems only last week that I was jotting down some ideas for that first issue. With a year gone by and twelve issues wiser, I have concluded that it is, after all, worth the time and effort to come up with some rose thoughts for whatever they are worth. The real reward is the letters and cards from rose fans all over the country. Keep up the letters... and the questions... and I will do my best to answer them as soon as possible.

While we are on the subject of rambling rose advice, how is your local rose society publication doing?? Quite often the local society is about as lively as its publication, which puts quite a burden on the editor. Jack Lauer commented recently in his "President's Message" column that the publication staff (and that is usually just one person) is largely unsung and deserves all the help it can get.

I agree with HELP THE EDITOR 100 percent. He has a lot to take care of without much help but has plenty of "suggestions." If he can turn some of these "suggestions" into real assistance, he is something of a salesman as well as a diplomat. If YOU sincerely want to help, jot down some thoughts on any kind of rose subject and pass it on ... he is usually so desperate that he will take anything. Just say it in your own words in your own way; with a little editing and punctuation thrown in here and there, your observations will reach a good many rose growers... and that is the whole idea.

Just a couple of thoughts for you editors... WORK at getting those short articles in for publication. You will seldom get a contribution (money or material) without some sales work. If you insist on doing the whole job yourself, you are simply depriving your society and burdening yourself.

A little more attention to the general look and "quality" of your newsletter will help you with your readers. We are all prone to rate a publication on first impressions, and if those impressions are poor or negative we tend to rate the material in the same way. There are so many excellent reproduction methods available now that there is no excuse for a poorly printed, cheap looking newsletter. There is very little cost difference between

the best and the worst; in fact, you can't afford to send a shabby bulletin to your members. They are expecting a worthwhile, attractive, newsy letter for their membership money... and it is up to you to give it to them. I like the litho-offset method the best myself. If you have access to an offset press (many businesses have them), you can simply type a paper master yourself and have it run for about 1.5 cents per sheet. Or the "Quick-Copy" letter shops can take your typewritten (and pasted up) material and print copies directly from a photo image. The photo-offset routine will cost about two cents per sheet.

One last note that every editor knows, but still needs to be reminded from time to time... use NAMES. Everyone likes to see his name in print, and this makes him more a part of the rose scene. Talk about rose growers and their roses; give a pat on the back from time to time; name the people who are doing the work; furnish the names, addresses and telephone numbers of consulting rosarians and accredited judges... in short let your readers know who is doing what in the rose business. Your publication will be livelier, and your readers more interested as they become involved in roses.

While we are on the subject of names, have you properly named (labeled) your roses for the benefit of your garden visitors? A good labeling system adds pleasure for them, and the grower unconsciously becomes better acquainted with his cultivars through constant repetition. Don't leave the wire tag on the bush; I am convinced that all sorts of unsatisfactory things happen when you do. A good rose label is inexpensive; Harlane (advertised in these pages) is excellent and attractive, and *Everlast* makes a fine label. I use and recommend both of them. The Harlane is complete and ready to go. The *Everlast* label can be printed with a weatherproof crayon, but I prefer to apply a "*Dymotape*" label to the blank name plate. The tape sticks well and is good for at least two seasons. Then it is a simple job to punch out a new one; the tapes come in a variety of colors. Another good idea is to write the year you planted each cultivar on the back of the name plate; it helps when you are trying to decide which roses to replace. I use the *Dymo-Everlast* combination labels on other plant materials, and my memory is getting sharper all the time as I tour the garden with visitors. Amaze your friends with a storehouse of garden information... read the labels first.

Autumn is upon us, and I hope you are enjoying a cornucopia of roses on these mild sunny days that so appropriately end the season. For you readers who do not have much to do with flower arrangers, cornucopia means an abundance of roses (bushels in fact) — like a horn of plenty. Anyway, if you are not getting your bushels of roses, now is the time to do something about it for next year. Try a couple of these ideas.

It is a good time to begin building those new rose beds, or revamping the old ones. Started now, the beds will have a chance to mix, mellow and compost a little before planting time. Rose bushes planted in new, hot mixtures are off to a very rough start and are risky at best. Like good wines, rose beds get better with age. When you begin working on the new beds, remember that a healthy growing medium is made up of soil, humus, water and air. All kinds of healthy things happen when the micro-organisms, so essential to soil productivity, have this kind of medium in which to work.

No one formula can be applied to all of the soils mixtures scattered across the country, but the basic requirements are always the same. If the soil is heavy, loosen with sharp sand, gypsum and humus. If the soil is sandy and lacking in water holding capacity, add humus and composted matter. The best growing medium always has a good balance of soil, humus, water and air. Do whatever is necessary to get nutrients, water and air into the root zone. If the balance is any good at all, the roses are going to grow.

Here on the Gulf Coast, our soils are primarily tight, heavy and on the alkaline side. We sometimes find it hard to understand how roses can be commercially grown in the sandy soils of East Texas. The sand just seems too light to support growth. But the heavy soils (properly prepared) and the sandy loams have two very important things in common: friability, good drainage and free movement of air and water.

Good drainage is essential, and throws all the other factors out of balance if it is not present. I had a classic example in a rose bed last year. A good soil mixture 18 inches deep was used in a bed 12 feet in diameter, bordered with a 3 foot concrete walk. All of this was on top of a tight gumbo soil. The new bushes started off fine in the spring, but

after heavy rains or overwatering, the leaves began to yellow. Growth gradually slowed and the plants showed no vigor. The soil had a sour odor, and attempts to loosen the soil in the mucky 28 bathtub didn't last very long. This spring the bushes were removed, some sharp sand added to the mixture, and a tile drain line laid from a bed of gravel to an outlet 25 feet away with a drop of about I foot. Twenty 'Europeana' were then planted in the bed, bordered with twenty 'Summer Snow'. The result, season-long, has been outstanding. The bushes are vigorous, constantly blooming, and have never yellowed even after the heaviest rains (5 inches in one day); and the soil is sweet-smelling and friable. The bed has not been cultivated since application of 4 inches of partially composted pine bark mulch; and the soil underneath is still loose enough to run your fingers through easily. Now THAT'S the way to grow roses.

When you are building these live, well drained rose beds for your own enjoyment, add a rose bed to your front yard for the enjoyment of others. A mass display of one colorful variety in a single bed is probably the most eye-catching. Floribundas are my favorites for this kind of planting, and I have had great results with 'Europeana', 'Valentine' and 'Redgold'. You can see the roses a block away. Plant them close together for a really massed effect. In my opinion the beds are even attractive in the winter when the leaves have fallen. A neat edging for the raised beds adds considerably to the year-round landscape feature. You will soon be known as "the house with the beautiful roses all the time". And that is a nice position to be in.

Tried another new watering device this year that works fine. It is called the Water-Hole. Simply described, it is a flared piece of plastic pipe about 2 1/2 inches in diameter and about IS inches long. About fifteen 3/8-inch holes are drilled in the sides of the pipe. The short perforated pipe is buried in the rose bed between two bushes with just a little of the flared top showing. Let the hose run slowly into the pipe and the perforations distribute the water slowly and without waste into the root zone. It is something like a well casing in reverse. Water-Hole is particularly good for small circular beds that are hard to keep moist. They are inexpensive and available through many garden magazines and shops… or make some of your own. Good luck.

Where did the rose season go? It seems like I was pruning back only a few weeks ago. Since the rose nuts in most parts of the country are now resting from their more active outside labors, we might reflect a little on the season's performance and offer a rose idea or two gathered during the year. And many thanks to you readers who have taken time to write and pass along a suggestion. Sometimes we pass up obvious ideas that can really help a good many growers.

Stay away from severely root pruned roses when planting next spring. Too many careless nurseries and packagers prune the roots way back so that they fit the container. The root half of the bush is more important than the top, because roses won't grow and develop without a decent root system. The cheap packaged rose is seldom a bargain, and it has no value at all if the roots have been chopped. Short roots have a delayed reaction, brought home to me dramatically this season. Three full-caned, No.1, packaged 'Mister Lincoln' bushes were given to me for a satellite garden last spring. The multiflora root stock was cut to about 3 inches. I also had on hand three other 'Mister Lincoln's' with 15 -18 inches of roots. All six roses were planted bare root, trimming the root ends slightly on the longer version. All six started well, bloomed about equally in seven weeks and appeared healthy. However, after the first bloom out the long-root bushes moved ahead much more rapidly with new canes, better leaves and general size. The real difference was demonstrated in August when both temperature and humidity were high. New top growth on the short pruned bushes Wilted, burned and showed definite leaf scalding. Bloom seldom developed on this growth. New growth would break and develop only a few inches. Meanwhile, the well-rooted bushes in the same beds were Vigorous, bloomed well and had no significant wilt or scald. The short-root roses just did not have the capacity to move enough water and nutrients. Dug up this fall, the short roots had developed very little... only a few rootlets extended from the stubs. Moral: Good roses don't come in small packages.

Another observation which was proved again this season (and reported from many sources) is that even the best fungicide must have regular COVERAGE to be effective. It is not so much the amount of material that you put into the sprayer but how much of the spray actually COVERS the leaves, top and bottom. The Texas Rose Research Foundation ran tests over several years showing conclusively that good coverage was the biggest single factor in controlling fungus diseases. If you haven't been getting control, don't increase the amount of fungicide per gallon or double up with another check out the amount of spray that is actually getting on the leaves. I have always sprayed from below to the dripping point and have had good control with *Phaltan, Manzate* or *Benlate*. The lesson: spray regularly, drench thoroughly.

Take care of the left-over sprays this winter. Discard small amounts of odds and ends rather than carry over. And dispose of PROPERLY. Spray materials are potent in concentrated form. Keep wettable powders in tightly sealed glass containers rather than in sacks or boxes. Use a china pencil to DATE the material, identify and note unusual formulation. Large mouth mayonnaise or pickle jars are ideal. Age, cold, heat and sunlight affect sprays. If in doubt, discard. Some spray materials have an expiration date, others give the grower some warning when the mixtures don't blend just right. It is a poor gamble to risk the leaves of a rose garden for a couple of dollars worth of old spray.

Hope you are not wasting any of those fall leaves and other garden vegetation. A garden's biggest boon is COMPOST. It is one of nature's products that we haven't been able to improve on. And because it is natural, we ought to take advantage of it. I am not so enthusiastic about garbage, egg shells and what have you, but I do know that leaves, clippings, and vegetable materials combined with soil and a source of nitrogen can make the greatest soil restorer ever. Get a couple piles or bins going. Use materials of different textures, throw in some soil as a source of bacteria and feed the process with nitrogen from manure, cottonseed or alfalfa meal. Moisten but don't soak. Get air into the mixture. Staggered slates like old corn crib give good aeration. If all is working well, the pile will heat in just a few days and the process will in about six to eight weeks, depending on the temperature.

What better start for a budding rose gardener

than a membership in ARS? We are getting better all the time... your gift membership will be remembered for a long time, paying off in fun and roses. Along this same line is a thought for the month...

A Reason for Roses: Would you rather have 'Tropicana' or tranquilizers??

Since weary rosarians have retired from their beds, while visions of trophies dance in their heads; it is time to take stock of the blooms that were not, and order show winners instead. Grant this writer just a bit of poetic license and I think you will see the point. Fireside euphoria in December is a pleasant pastime, but thoughtful planning for the year to come will pay off with more blooms and rose fun. Start with the local or regional Proof of the Pudding report. Check over the ratings and comments from growers just like you. Order those cultivars (I still prefer to say "varieties") that have performed well for others, and then spice your rose efforts with a few long shots. If your local group doesn't have a Proof of the Pudding, start one. It can be the subject of an entire meeting with everyone participating. You will be surprised at the enthusiasm generated by such a workshop. If you would like to have a suggested workshop outline on varieties, drop me a line… I might even give you my list of favorites… sure winners every time.

Except for a few fortunate Gulf Coast Texans, Californians and Floridians, rose blooms right now are a thing fondly remembered from last season… but it doesn't have to be that way. For some year-round fun, try a few Miniature roses in pots grown in the house. Potted Miniatures are becoming more and more popular, and quite a few enterprising florists are now furnishing blooming Miniature roses in place of the usual fare of azaleas, chrysanthemums, poinsettias and what have you. Roses make great gifts for the shut-in, furnishing lots of bloom with little care and no complaint. And they are easy for you to grow indoors, also.

Miniatures in pots thrive under *Gro-Lux* fluorescents. The special Violet-tinted light enhances both the bloom and the foliage, and seems to furnish everything the diminutive plants need. It is easy to build your own fluorescent fixture, mounted over a growing stand. But I would advise that you look into some kind of indoor light setup similar to the Flora-Cart arrangement, which is advertised in many of the garden magazines. This is a tubular frame, mounted on wheels, with either two or three plastic (growing) trays. The fluorescent fixtures are hung appropriately in the frame, and each contains two Gro-Lux tubes and two incandescent sockets, in which I have used 2S-watt, soft-light bulbs.

The light balance seems to be ideal. Some plants seem to do better without the incandescents, but this is probably also dependent on the amount of natural light that is available to the growing area. I have seen these indoor lighting systems used in a completely dark basement, with incredible results. If the lady of the house wants something besides Miniatures, some African violets, gloxinias and certain blooming begonias make good companions.

There are several good books available on growing plants indoors under artificial lights. Get one when you start. As far as Miniatures are concerned, remember that they do best in a high-humus, well-aerated soil with good drainage. Several good soluble foods are available. And it is easy to get good Miniature rooted cuttings any time of year. Ernest Williams, of Mini-Roses in Dallas, and Ralph Moore of Sequoia Nursery in Visalia, California, are perhaps best known to ARS members. Both of these fine grower-hybridizers have been active in developing and promoting Miniatures for many years. Whether you live in Minnesota or Sarasota, you will enjoy growing Miniatures indoors. A few favorites?? I like: Toy Clown, Starina, Tiny Flame, Jeanie Williams, Gold Coin and Chipper. Try just a few for winter rose fun.

Have to pass on this story about the "War of the Roses", written up in the Oklahoma Orbit Sunday supplement in early October. Seems that there is a traditional football rivalry between the Oklahoma "Sooners" and the Texas "Longhorns", fought out in the Cotton Bowl every fall with some 65,000 rabid fans in attendance. This year, by sheer coincidence, the South Central District Rose Show was held in Oklahoma City on the same day as the game with a parallel rivalry, Oklahoma vs Texas. The headline read, "It will be third down and a cloud of rose dust this weekend as Oklahoma's best growers take on the powerful Texas Long-Thorns in their annual showdown for regional supremacy". The pun-filled (and fun-filled) article continued with such observations as "Arkansas is also hip-deep (rose hips, please) in the competition, but the Golden Triangle fighters from Texas have been digging in for months". The results?? Oklahoma won the football game, but Texas swept the rose trophies with Golden Triangle quarterback Vic

LaRocca leading the way. Appropriately, Sooner Ewing Gafford showed the best 'Oklahoma'. Who says growing roses isn't fun??

As you read this, the fund campaign in Shreveport for The American Rose Center will be in full swing. The response in Shreveport makes you feel good all over… in fact a description of the enthusiasm sounds more like a "Tall Texas Tale" than the truth. The business people are giving their time and their money in a way that's hard for a big-city dweller to understand. Without a doubt, these folks want The American Rose Center to be the best in the world. As ARS members, can we want any less??

Don't worry, ARS members will have plenty of opportunity to have a hand in the rose center. The nationwide campaign will get underway this spring, and you will be hearing more and more about the features of The American Rose Center as the months go by. Hope you have noticed the special news insert in the magazine this month… it will be a monthly feature talking about people and projects related to our new home. At first you will hear a lot about Frank Terry, the ARS fund drive consultant; and Carson Scoggins, the Gulf Coast District Director from Shreveport. They are doing a great job. Carson is a retired DuPont sales rep who moved to Shreveport after a lifetime career in Chicago. He stirred up so much notice about The American Rose Center that the Shreveport Chamber of Commerce said they had to have him on their staff. So that's how it stands now, Carson promotes Shreveport half the time and roses the other half, or maybe roses come out a little ahead.

Wish all of you could meet John D. Caruthers, Jr., Campaign General Chairman for Shreveport. He things big, works hard, has pride in his city, and attracts good workers around him. His banking interests put him in touch with most everyone in the area, and he sells roses just as hard as banking. John is a blue-ribbon winner in every way.

Blue ribbons take us to roses and even in January some rose work needs to be done. Most rose societies are beginning a new year… is your rose society going to have a better year than last?? Organization and finances plague most rose groups, but both problems can be solved with common sense. Most of us make a mistake by not working out a smooth transition from one set of officers to another. Sounds simple, but usually overlooked. Some good work in January and an extra informal meeting or two pays off all season. How about invoices to your members for their dues?? We are all used to paying bills. Make it easy to pay local and national dues with a simple invoice form. You can expect prompt, businesslike payment. And let me repeat my favorite advice on business: keep rose society business in the Executive Committee where it belongs. They were elected to do the work, not run a debating society. The same goes for recitation of the minutes of the last meeting. Minutes ought to go. What you did last month is old hat, what you are doing NOW is important. Keep your members informed with a breezy newsletter. Entertain and inform the rose nuts on roses when you get together. Rose growers come back when you talk about roses.

Following our own advice, here are some odds and ends on roses. Believe it or not, some of our rose growers will be pruning on February 15; and that is the best time to start a fungus control program. As soon as you prune, DRENCH the canes and bud union with full-strength fungicide mixture. Some like oil-sulfur dormant sprays. Others prefer to use *Phaltan, Manzate* or *Benlate* with a favorite broad-spectrum insecticide. I like a *Benlate-Diazinon* mixture as a cleanup spray, following with *Benlate* alone every two weeks thereafter. I'll add *Cygon* or *Isotox* to the fungicide when new leaves and aphids appear. This program has kept the three rose gardens that I take care of completely free of blackspot and mildew for the past two seasons. I can't offer a better testimonial.

If you are still building a rose bed, don't forget that a raised bed has more good things going for it than lawn-level plantings. Drainage, aeration and control of all growing factors are improved with elevated beds. For a fast layout, try "L" shaped concrete blocks. Straights combined with outside and inside curves make almost any shape bed possible. The "foot" part of the L curb makes a good edge for the lawnmower wheel. Creeping grasses find it tough to jump. If you are good with bricks, a vertical row of bricks with squashed mortar is very attractive. For an extra touch, run a course lengthwise at lawn level for a neat edge and a course for the lawnmower. If you have a power edger, it's easy to have a manicured look all season.

For most of our rosarians right now, looking at the world through rose-colored glasses only makes the snow a different tint... certainly no warmer. But good rosarians know that now is the time to plan and dream a little... perhaps following these sage words: "The smart gardener does his weeding before he plants." Top exhibitors get that way because they start working on the show winner in February... more often than not it is the February of the previous year. But that is part of the fun of rose growing. There is always something to look forward to and something to improve upon.

If you want to improve your performance with Miniatures, particularly newly-rooted cuttings, you will want to follow this soil formula.

MINI-ROSE POTTING SOIL

Three bales of Canadian Peat Moss (6 cu. ft. bales); 4 bags of No.6 Perlite (4 cu. ft. bags); 6 bags of Pine Bark mulch, screened through W' screen (Net recovery about 3 bags, 3 cu. ft. each); 1 cubic yard of Plaster sand (approximately); six 4-inch pots of 48% Phosphate; 10 pounds of Cottonseed Meal; two 4-inch pots 5-10-5 Pelleted Fertilizer; three 4-inch pots Sulfa-Soil; 1 gallon of Carl Pool Root Activator Concentrate; 50 pounds of Steer Manure (heat treated).

All of the ingredients are spread in a pile and turned three times, covering with a plastic sheet. Turn twice a week for about two weeks; this not only mixes but also controls the heating of the mixture as the bacteria in the Root Activator is working. If the soil is to be stored for any length of time, omit the 5-10-5 and add just before use. The mix is used not only in small pots but in gallon cans, seed flats and even as potting soil for geraniums, begonias and in terrariums.

Ernest Williams further comments that the humus content of the mix will hold up for about three years. Home growers can readily break the formula down for smaller quantities, and may want to substitute a good garden soil for part of the sand. Plaster sand is preferable to "sharp" sand, as it is finer, is free flowing and contains no clay. It is important to note that this soil is formulated for use with soluble fertilizers. The acidifier indicates that alkaline water will be used, neutralized in part by the acid balance of the soluble fertilizers.

The formulation listed here has been evolved over about a fifteen-year period, with an accurate record kept of each mixture... and that is a lot of mixtures. From time to time the proportions are adjusted to "feel" as the peat moss bulk will vary, depending mostly on the compactness of the bale. Older bales are generally broken down a bit more and have smaller particles. The brown peat seems to be superior to the black or activated peat for this mixture.

Apparently there are a number of enthusiastic Miniature fans as this reporter was swamped with requests for more information after a December column on growing Miniatures under lights. When the requests piled up, it was obvious that an expert ought to be called in. Fortunately, you won't find anyone much more expert on Miniatures in Texas than Ernest Williams of Dallas, owner-operator-hybridizer of MINI-ROSES. And just to be fair and give equal time to two of the top mini-rose growers of the country, here are their addresses: Ernest Williams, MINI-ROSES, P. O. Box 4255 Station A, Dallas, Texas 75208; and Ralph Moore, SEQUOIA, 2519 E. Noble Ave., Visalia, California 93227. Both of them have extensive lists of Miniature cultivars for sale, and both are mighty fine folks to deal with.

Miniatures under lights can keep you in roses year-round with fewer problems than most house plants. Growers in cold climates with dry furnace heat should consider draping a plastic sheet over the growing stand at night to raise the humidity. Flora-Cart plant stands have fiberglass trays suitable for moist perlite bedding material, or a number of other humidity releasing tricks can be used. Anyway, try some indoor beauty... and enjoy your roses.

Has the spring planting fever spread to your area yet?? We are having an epidemic of such fevers here on the Gulf Coast, and it is good to be outdoors working in the roses again. For most of our readers, March is starting and planting time, so here are a couple of suggestions that can make your rose garden more colorful than ever.

How about some tree roses this year?? Maybe it is too cold in your area to successfully maintain tree roses without a lot of hard work and winter protection. But here is a way to have trees without much winter problem. Some of the most impressive tree roses I have ever seen have been grown in redwood tubs or large earthen pots, enjoying a prominent accent place on the patio or garden walk in the summer and moved into the garage or garden shed in the winter. Some extra care in selection of the planting medium makes all the difference in growing good tree roses in tubs season after season without winterkill.

Tree roses in planters will thrive in the temperatures of Utah and Colorado, as well as in the heat and humidity of Texas and Louisiana. The formula for growth and hardiness is: good drainage, access of air to the root zone, and ability to retain moisture. If the formula is in good balance, a 22-inch diameter redwood planter requires a good watering only twice a week, even during very hot conditions. There are many variables in the watering program, but the point is that tree roses in planters do not take any more care or water than roses in conventional beds.

I like a mixture of I part organic soil, I part Canadian peat moss and 1 part calcined clay granules. If you are not familiar with calcined clay, you can find it marketed in most parts of the country under the trade name *TERRA-GREEN*. This is a product of the Oil-Dri Corporation, originally developed as a floor sweep to pick up oil and grease on garage floors. Calcined clay granules are extremely porous, something like a microscopic honeycomb. The material has the ability to take in moisture for slow release on demand of the feeder roots. The granules can become almost instantly saturated, hold the moisture for long periods and release without souring, packing or decomposing. I have observed calcined clay granules in rose beds and pots five years after mixing, and have seen no breakdown or change in composition whatsoever.

The results described here are supported by experiments by the Michigan State University Agricultural Experiment Station. The experiments concerned roses grown in various potting mixtures, including various combinations of peat, calcined clay, soil and perlite. The pots were watered daily throughout the season and were fertilized weekly with soluble fertilizer. Growth response was recorded three times during the season.

The following is abstracted from the Michigan State report:

"Commercial growers of potted roses use granular materials incorporated with soil in potting mixtures as a standard to insure good drainage and the access of air to the root zone. The quantity of oxygen available to the roots has been definitely shown to be correlated to the amount of top growth produced by the rose plants.

"All the lots containing calcined clay showed superior growth throughout the season to those in soil only, in peat only, or in mixtures with perlite. Also mixtures in which peat was a component showed greater growth than those in which peat was not used. The increased growth of rose plants in the calcined clay mixtures with both soil and peat, ranging from I part to 4 parts of the material, show that growers may benefit by adding calcined clay to their potting mixtures."

Mixtures with the best growth rate were: 1 part peat, 1 part clay, 1 part soil; 1 peat to 1 clay; 2 organic soil to 1 clay; and 3 peat to 1 clay. If you would like a copy of the table rating the 10 different mixtures, I would be glad to mail you one.

Since some readers are bound to ask, here are the tree roses I have enjoyed the most: Ole, Helen Traubel, Tiffany, Duet, Oklahoma, Lemon Spice, and Sea Foam. You can't imagine the amount of fragrance that one 'Lemon Spice' can lend to a patio, or the color that 'Ole' can give to plain brick walls. Try 'em; you'll like 'em.

Spring and sprained backs go hand in hand... but that's the lot of the eager rosarian. Most of us go at rose growing in enthusiastic bursts, even though we know that a regular schedule will pay off with more roses for less work. Resolution for April: Set a schedule; keep a schedule. These ramblings will try to pass on a few starters to make it easier.

First off... what better way to start the rose season than taking in the ARS National Convention and Rose Show, April 26-29 in Dallas?? If you haven't been to a national program, you just don't know what you have missed. It's fun and serious at the same time, and the rosarians you run into there are just as anxious to swap rose stories as you are. One of the greatest pleasures is making new friends across the country, opening up new gardens to visit. It's a good feeling to know that there is a rose fan in almost any corner of the country you may choose to visit.

The Dallas meeting is typically TEXAS-BIG. The entertainments are on a grand scale; and the educational programs cover topics as diverse as cytogenetic research, far-out rose arrangements, hybridizing, judging guidelines and how to run a better rose society. Another feature is presentation of the long range plans for The American Rose Center in Shreveport. And you'll have to go a long way to find better roses in a national show. The "Golden Triangle" team from Southeast Texas will be in "Big D" in force. Dallas is the "Time of Your Life City." Try it, you'll like it.

And if you haven't tried EARLY fungus control, do it this year. Carefully controlled tests show without a doubt that a DRENCHING spray immediately after pruning is important to good fungus control all season. It makes good sense to me to use a good fungicide combined with a broad-spectrum insecticide rather than an oil-sulfur mixture. Modern fungicides are specifics for blackspot-mildew problems. I like a *Manzate-Spectracide* or *Benlate-Spectracide* mixture during the early part of the season. Another favorite around here is *Phaltan-Isotox*. Use these products at full strength, drenching canes, bud union and general rosebed area. Later in the spring, a favorite switch is to *Benlate-Cygon*. Spray every ten days during the vigorous spring growth. Follow a REGULAR pattern. When the really hot weather hits Texas, we use *Benlate* alone since it produces practically no residue or leaf burn. Insecticides are used very sparingly and only for SPECIFIC problems. Another word about *Benlate*. The latest Texas Rose Research report advises that *Benlate* does not have the lasting or residual effect in prevention of blackspot that some of the older fungicides have demonstrated. *Benlate* MUST be used on a regular basis, starting with a garden free of blackspot. It is effective for both blackspot and mildew when used as a preventative. It's a real boon in HOT weather.

When planting in April remember that new bushes need to be FLOODED in and kept well watered until the roots have become established. Springtime conditions can dry out roses very rapidly... keep them moist. It's a good idea to mound up soil and mulch material over the bud union and well up on the canes of new bushes to conserve moisture. Gradually remove the loose material over a two-to-three week period until the bud union is exposed to sunshine. Mounding new bushes also gives some protection from late frosts. Conditions and problems vary throughout the country, but in much of our area field hay or sugar cane pulp are popular insulators. The insulator then becomes part of the mulch with many benefits during the season.

Here's another idea passed on to me from Curtis Amox in San Antonio. Curtis has a severe alkali problem, complicated with salty water and very porous drainage. Elevated beds become alkaline very quickly, and the nutrients were leached out. Last year the bushes were left in 3-gallon metal cans sunk into the usual rosebed. Each rose can was fed and watered individually. The roses in the cans considerably outproduced the bushes planted in the beds at the same time. This year Curtis will try sinking plastic cans in an effort to control the planting medium conditions. If you have a similar problem, you might want to try it.

MAY 1972

THOUGHT FOR THE MONTH: *Never invite a rosarian for an evening of wine, women and roses. He'll want to know what kind of roses.*

Pardon this intrusion of your garden privacy, but are you growing more roses and enjoying it less?? Maybe you are just taking yourself too seriously. These columns have always maintained that most anyone can grow roses, and that roses are fun. This is what attracts new rose people; and when growers and rose societies realize the easy-fun aspect of rose beauty we won't be able to handle all of the membership applications. It's something like the old salesman's line... "Don't sell the steak, sell the sizzle." As rose salesmen, we have the world's greatest product, provided we don't complicate the sale with our expertise. In short, make it easy and make it fun. For the most part, growing roses is just common sense.

For a few common sense reminders, read on. Like how to mix wettable powders and oil-based insecticides into a compatible mixture. HOT water is the answer. Use a glass mixing container with a tight lid. Carefully mark the outside of the container for the amount of concentrated mixture that fits your sprayer. Measure the wettable powders into the container first. Then slowly add hot tap water, swirling the mixture into a thick paste. Continue to add water up to the right concentration. Swirling the mixture seems to mix best without foam and suds. The glass container makes it easy to see what's going on. Aromatic-based ingredients (*Isotox, Cygon, Spectracide*) are added next, swirling gently. Add any spreader-sticker last. The concentrated spray is now ready to use, WITHOUT any straining or stirring. And don't miss the obvious advantage of the glass container — you can always see how the mixture is doing. The danger of a glass container?? Very little, since any rosarian with garden sense is wearing gloves and handling the mixture with care.

Another common sense idea you might want to return to is SPECIFIC spraying for insects. Specific insecticide use means to spray for a particular insect problem when it occurs. Too many anxious rosarians load up spray mixtures with insecticides when they are not needed. It's not only wasteful but does the plant no good either. When aphids are present (and they will appear in hatching cycles), spray for aphids. The same routine follows for thrips. Insect overkill with broad-spectrum insecticides (*Sevin* is an example) leads to nothing but

trouble for most rosarians. When the hard-to-kill beetles move in, get out the *Sevin* and spray specifically for the problem. It's safe to say that more rosarians have lost more leaves to spray problems than they have to bugs. And have you ever seen any blooms on a bush without leaves??

It's dangerous to make a recommendation without clearly stating the EXCEPTIONS. Specific spraying applies ONLY to insecticides. Fungus control is best obtained through prevention rather than by eradication after the infection becomes evident. In simplest terms, keep rosebushes free of fungus by REGULAR spraying with a reliable fungicide as a preventative. When conditions are conducive to blackspot, for example, spray every seven to ten days for good control. Use a good mildewcide when conditions are right for this problem. But even this regular fungus control routine has some exceptions. If the roses are free of infection, spray intervals during the hot, dry part of the summer can be extended up to twenty-one days. Several garden plots observed during the past two years were free of blackspot and mildew throughout the season even though *Benlate* application was extended to every three weeks during late June, July and August.

Many rosarians throughout the country will be doing their "fingernail pruning" about this time; a very useful follow-up of their springtime pruning-grooming routine. Fingernail pruning refers to the deft removal of unwanted growth, buds or eyes while the growth is still small. Disbudding is really a form of fingernail pruning to get rid of side buds on Hybrid Teas and Grandifloras and also terminal buds on Floribundas. Fingernail pruning can also take care of the blind shoots and "rosette leaves" that will never do anything for the plant except invite fungus infection and spider mites. This growth is usually in the center of the bush and hard to reach with the sprayer. Flick it out while small, letting the sunshine get in for vigorous new growth and bloom.

How about disbudding by the hobbyist-gardener who just wants color in the yard and all the bloom he can get? Although disbudding will produce the biggest and best specimen roses, a well-groomed and cared-for plant will thrive without disbudding and make bushels of roses. Full blooming without disbudding does not "weaken" the plant, it simply is performing its natural function. Groom a multiple-bloom spray by cutting spent blooms as they occur, then cut back to the first five-leaflet when all the blooms are spent to encourage faster new growth and another bloom crop. Patient rosarians do perform a good service, however, when the terminal bud of a new cane on a new bush is pinched out. This gives a new bush a chance to become established before producing a crop of roses. It's the same reason that an old-time rose grower will usually cut very short stems on a newly-planted bush. Call it common sense or garden sense, it makes more fun... and roses.

Have you ever been worried over the "old rosarian's tales" about roses that usually promised dire consequences if some particular practice was followed?? For example, every rose grower has heard at one time or another that crown gall and root gall would certainly strangle any rose so infected. We were not only encouraged to pull that rose up promptly but also to burn the remains and haul away all of the "infected" soil in the rosebed. As in many old tales, the stories had some substance in fact. But the problem was blown completely out of proportion. Carefully observed test plots (and your own garden experience) show that roses with crown gall can live and produce for many years, and that clean bushes can be planted in infected beds without infection. In one test at the Tyler (Texas) municipal rose garden, bushes with crown gall were transplanted to one bed for observation and produced nearly as many roses as the "new" bushes planted nearby. The only treatment the infected bushes received was replanting at a higher level so that sunlight could get to the gall area. Now, nearly five years later, the "Doomed" roses are still doing quite well. You probably observed the same thing with some of your old rosebushes.

And how about the old adage: "Never wet the leaves"? This makes no more sense than trying to eliminate rainfall. Overhead watering is not bad. In fact, in many cases, overhead watering offers some substantial benefits that all of the soaking systems combined cannot match. The effectiveness of fungicides, today, eliminates worry of wet foliage. This is not to suggest that growers wet down the leaves each evening; but no harm can come from regular overhead watering, provided that the grower follows a systematic fungicide spray program. Many growers set a cone-type lawn sprinkler directly in the rosebeds and let the water spray up under the rosebushes. This accomplishes two things: it washes off the spider mites and effectively prevents old spray buildup.

Rosebeds with soaker systems completely underground should also get the overhead, underneath, water-all-over-the-place watering about once a week. Spider mites simply do not like all that water, but the roses do. An old grower, highly respected in this area, often advised that hosing down healthy rosebushes after a very hot day was just like the gardener having some refreshments after a long dry spell. And he had tremendous success with roses. The foliage from his garden was always healthy, always clean and invariably free of mildew. Moral of the story: roses like to be clean and cool just like rosarians. And with the junk floating in the air these days, most everything can stand a washing from time to time.

Another warning served on rose newcomers declared that all spraying must cover rose leaves over, under, sideways and crossways. This is good advice, if you are spraying for fungus diseases or spider mites under the leaves, but is wasteful and useless if your problem is thrips. A good rose competitor knows that a good misting of the tops of the rosebushes every other day with a specific for thrips will do all the good that is necessary. Around here, *Cygan 2E* is the most popular. For show blooms, start spraying with *Cygon* just as soon as any color is showing, or when the sepals first begin to come down. Thoroughly mist the bloom area every other day, even when the bloom is 1/3 to 1/2 open. Shake off any excess spray if the bloom is a real show winner. *Cygan* does not seem to damage the bloom, particularly if the spraying is done in the evening. You have to hit the thrips to kill them. And don't forget other host plants for thrips: lilies, amaryllis, gladiolas and other light colored, fragrant flowers.

Have you burned your bed mulch lately?? If you did, it was a waste. Aside from the need for normal neatness and bed cleanup, leave the mulch material in the rosebeds year after year. The gradual breakdown of organic mulch materials restores the humus balance in the soil and adds something to the soil processes that the chemical men have never been able to duplicate. Growers used to think that spores of all kinds of dread rose diseases lurked in the bed mulch, and they faithfully raked up and destroyed this material just as it was beginning to do some good. Instead, after pruning and normal debris removal in the spring, use a good cleanup spray (broad spectrum insecticide plus a good fungicide) and drench the rose canes and the leftover mulch materials. Sunlight, air and the good bugs will do the rest for you. You might want to add a little nitrogen to speed up the decomposition process and replace nitrogen leached during the winter. Blackspot spores live on green, live tissue, not on cellulose materials in the process of decomposition. Good growers have been happily enjoying the benefits of mulch for years by following this simple routine. It works with pine straw, leaf mixes, bark mixes — what have you. Proves again that nature probably knows best.

These rambling columns have recently been treating the "rose facts of life" somewhat irreverently... Just another way of saying that all of the old stories about roses are not true and that growing roses isn't really so hard after all. Let's review just a few rose basics for the beginner... and for the old-timer with an open mind.

Organic vs. inorganic gardening will raise the temperature of most any rose society meeting, and each side crusades to defeat the opposition once and for all when they meet. This is foolish and costly in roses, as both points of view have merit. Use the best of both schools and enjoy really fine roses. Take fertilization, for example. Good organic foods in a properly prepared bed will help any grower produce good roses consistently. Manure, cottonseed meal, rock phosphate and so on will help any soil achieve a good working balance; and the stability lasts year after year. On the other hand, inorganics from the chemist's workshop can correct a deficiency, spur along some new growth or provide the nitrogen boost needed in the spring. A deficiency of available iron is easy to correct with the chelates now available; it's a much slower process organically. Why pass up all those good roses in the meantime? Take the best from both schools.

The same reasoning follows in insect control. Keep the bushes healthy and vigorous with good growing practices and give up a few blooms to the insects once in a while. A few aphids and beetles are not worth contaminating the whole garden with broad spectrum insecticides. And some of the broad spectrum materials will kill off the natural predators, causing an even greater insect problem. Take on spider mites with a water wand. But when show time arrives or a particular insect persists, spray with a SPECIFIC insecticide for that problem, using only the amount of material absolutely necessary. An example: for corn earworms and certain beetles that bore into new buds, dust ONLY the bud areas of the plant with a 5% Sevin dust. Get the dust on the buds you want to protect. The same thinking applies to thrip control. Use *Cygon 2E* as a mist spray on buds and opening blooms. Why drench the whole bush when the thrips are on the blooms? Try this SPECIFIC approach and find that there is a happy middle ground of common

sense that's good for roses.

The benefits of various types of mulching materials have also been argued for years. Unless you happen to be blessed with that "perfect" soil and have everything going for you with water, drainage, aeration, humus balance and what have you, a good rosebed mulch is a natural essential for good rose culture. In deciding what to use, consider what a good mulch is supposed to do. A mulch should let air and water through freely, should not pack, decompose slowly, add humus to the soil, have a pleasing appearance, not harbor bugs and generally provide a good soil insulation to keep the feeder roots cool and moisture level high. This is a good-sized order, but one many mulch materials can fill. Usually a combination of materials is more effective than just one. For example, pine needles, shredded pine bark and partially composted leaves in' combination work better than anyone used alone. Oak leaves and some kind of coarse bark or woody material are good. A shredder that chops up all kinds of organic matter makes the best combination of all. Favorites along the Gulf Coast are medium coarse pine bark mulch, a former "waste" product from paper production; and bagasse or sugar cane pulp, a leftover from sugar mills. Use a minimum of two to three inches of mulch, enjoy all the good things that happen to the soil and soil processes. An old rosarian around here quips that a good mulch is worth its weight in gold... and in roses. Weigh some out for yourself this season.

A word on summer feeding. While roses are heavy feeders, they respond best to frequent, light feedings rather than massive fertilization. Whatever your favorite food might be, try half the quantity twice as often. You'll get more blooms for your money. And don't neglect WATER, WATER, WATER. The best soils and rose foods can't do any good until available to the plant in solution. Light sprinkling is wasteful, deep soaking is best. If a rosebed is well constructed and has good drainage, it is almost impossible to overwater. Depending on the soil and temperature, use two inches of water per week. And be sure to consult a reliable rain gauge; don't guess that the summer shower took care of the roses. If you are watering overhead, set the rain gauge within the irrigated area and check the water actually getting to the roses.

A good trick is to set several coffee cans in the bed area to be watered and check the amount of water they catch.

Another good summer practice is to cut roses in the morning when they are fresher and have more substance. Take a bucket of warm water to the rose garden and plunge the stems in as soon as cut. Keep in this conditioning water for at least 30 minutes before refrigeration or other uses. The roses will last longer and look better. Several good preservative and conditioning formulas are available and commonly used; but early cutting and warm water are most important.

You will notice two kinds of rose growers this month: those in the garden and those in the house. Any doubt in your mind which one will have the most roses in the cooler days of September? It is just common sense that roses MUST have care during the hottest parts of the summer to put out the "Indian Summer" harvest blooms that often are the finest of the season. Roses don't want to take a vacation in the summer; they want to eat and drink regularly just like rosarians. Light regular feedings with plenty of water are still best. For growers in the north, mid-August should be the last application of 1-2-1 fertilizer that encourages new green growth. The fall and winter conditioning process is best served by use of foods high in phosphate and potash with NO nitrogen. A well conditioned rose will survive winter cold much more readily than a plant constantly forced for more and more production. In commercial growing, good rose plants are the important product, and most growers stop fertilization about August 1 to prepare the plants for natural dormancy and winter. But the bloom production is still good in these fields in the fall, because roses will invariably bloom if they have a good crop of leaves. There is a lesson to be learned here by home gardeners.

Another lesson that needs to be taught over and over again in midsummer is common sense control of spider mites. More questions are probably asked about these tenacious pests than any other rose problem; and more solutions are offered. As far as I know, no miracle spray has yet come along to eliminate the pests; but a common sense approach and the sprays we do have will control them. In the hot, dry south and southwest, water is still the best answer. Just wash 'em off with water — no leaf burn, no spray residue, almost no mites. Greenhouse men were washing mites years and years before exotic chemicals came from the test tubes.

The water wand advertised in these pages works fine, or you can build one yourself. The fine spray of high pressure water breaks up the webbing on the undersides of the leaves and sends the spiders into orbit. Anyway, the water washing breaks up the reproduction cycle of the mites and the plants begin to green up and grow again. You will know you have spiders when leaves turn a gray-green, then dried-brown and then fall off. At the first sign of gray-green, check the undersides of lower leaves for a whitish webbing and tiny reddish-brown specks. If in doubt, shake a few of the critters off on a white sheet of paper and watch them move. IMMEDIATELY get out the water wand and wash two or three times the first week. A weekly washing after that will probably maintain control. If you also want to use a miticide (and run the risk of leaf burn), wash the leaves first and follow with a drenching spray on the undersides. Apply three times at five-day intervals.

Basic to any spray program is to soak the rosebeds first and avoid spraying in the hottest part of the day. Some rosarians use insecticides in the evening, then wash off the tops of the leaves with a fine water mist early the next morning. In spite of all precautions, it is sometimes hard to tell whether more leaf damage is done by mites or by spray. In the hot, dry summer, the name of the rose game is LEAVES. Do everything possible to keep a good, healthy leaf system. As reported earlier, well maintained plants can't help but produce roses. Whether leaves are lost because of mites, blackspot, mildew, spray burn or dehydration, the results are still the same — no roses.

Foliar feeding is another practice to be approached with caution during the hottest part of the summer, if leaves are to stay green. The combination of foliar foods, a summer sprinkle and scalding sun will generally result in burned leaves, just opposite the intended result. If summer temperatures are moderate in your area, foliar feed cautiously; if it is hot, wait until daytime temps drop below 85 degrees.

Rose garden visits around the country show that Miniatures are spreading like crabgrass, and that is a lot of growth. Colorful and easy to care for, Miniatures are the best buys in the rose world today. If you are not enjoying at least 20 or 25 of these diminutive beauties, you are missing a real treat. Used in a dozen different ways, minis put out bloom and are attractive plants when other roses are in a summer slump or shivering in the cold. Border beds of nothing but Miniatures are probably the most attractive; but planter boxes and large tubs can also be masses of color. I recently saw some minis in a rock garden, and they looked right at home. A Salt Lake City small-rose fan told me that some of the Miniatures there even bloomed under the snow. A Chipper emerging through the snow may be too much to expect, but there is no doubt that Miniatures are far more winter hardy than bush roses. They deserve a place of their own that is in proportion to their size. And since their low, dense growing habit is a natural haven for mites, plant where it will be easy to wash with water. Water-wash Miniatures as a weekly routine and mites will never become a problem. Your biggest problem will be to find space to plant some more.

Harvest month for rosarians has finally arrived... and your buckets of roses should be overflowing. Except for that first, fresh spring bloom, fall roses are usually the best of all. If this doesn't seem to be the case in your garden, make a check list of rose events during the season and see if you can't come up with some plans and practices that will payoff next year. Right NOW you should be planning (and even doing some digging) of new beds for the future. Good roses aren't grown by accident; rosebed preparation is the first (and probably most important) step in rose production.

Within the next month or so most growers will have plenty of leaves and other composting materials available. Make these materials REALLY available for your roses with some kind of compost pile even if you can't handle all of your leafy production. Once you have experienced the benefits of good compost, you'll find space for more leaves next year. If no space at all is available for a compost pile or rack, use a vegetable garden area or maybe the new rosebed under construction. Turn and dig the soil in the bed area making a sort of wind-row of soil. Pile leaves, clippings etc. in the depressed trench and add some of the excess soil on top as a dressing. If you have a good source of nitrogen like manure or cottonseed meal, add to the leaves to make the whole process work faster. Keep moist and turn lightly about every two weeks. Add some more leaves as the pile goes down. Before hard-freeze time the composting material should be broken down enough to add directly to other bed areas. Be sure to partially compost leaves before adding to a new rosebed. Composting first gives better, faster results with less work.

A universal formula for rosebeds is almost an impossibility; but certain basics must be accomplished by one means or another. A good soil process must have available water, nutrients and oxygen. A heavy soil will need sandy components as well as humus to permit air and water to reach the root zone. A sandy soil will need greater quantities of humus to retain water in the root zone. Check some rosebeds of others in your area to come up with a formula that's just right.

Your Consulting Rosarian should be able to make specific recommendations; and make sure the recommendations are SPECIFIC. Addition of a LITTLE superphosphate might be a cup or a pound. Some "rose experts" with misguided modesty are reluctant to name specific products, fertilizers or formulas.

Growing experience ought to be passed on. Any rose reference ought to be able to say "It does a good job for me, try it if you like." This makes the rose talker weigh the recommendation a little more carefully and gives practical facts to the inexperienced.

Here's a thought that always brings some rebuttal: cultivate rosebeds lightly from time to time to assist movement of air and water in the soil. Most rosarians will benefit from this practice if done with a little common sense. Mulches and some soils tend to pack from rainfall and sunshine. Breaking up the crust lets air and water through again and physically mixes some of the humus product of the mulch with the topsoil. A three-finger cultivator scratching an inch deep is just about right. If the mulch has been properly applied this loosening should not damage the feeder roots. Another good trick for tight soils is to make some small holes around the rosebush with a spading fork, the four-prong kind that is about six inches long. Spade in all the way and work the handle back and forth a few times. Fertilizers can get into the root zone faster if some is dropped into the holes. Fish meal works great this way, and slow moving rock phosphate (or superphosphate) can also get to where the work is. Keep the spading fork at least a foot away from the rose shank or bud union, and give each bush three or four good jabs; once a month is not too often.

Many of these bits of advice appear to be so simple that they are likely to be ignored. There is a need for a Question Box session at EVERY rose society meeting. The newcomer learns more from these "give and take" sessions than from most of the formal programs presented. A Consulting Rosarian or other experienced rose nut should take on this job at every meeting, fielding all kinds of everyday rose questions with down-to-earth answers. Have the questions written; then no one is embarrassed by lack of knowledge (except maybe the attending rose expert). If the Question Box is working right, you'll have a tough time turning off the discussion in the 15-20 minutes allotted for the session. It's a good idea to have a couple of "planted" questions in the box in case the listeners are slow to get the idea. Have a few "sick rose" samples on hand for demonstration; you'll be surprised how many rose people are not sure what a blackspot leaf looks like, or the difference between powdery mildew and spider mite webbing. If a picture is worth a thousand words, a sample must be worth a good deal more.

OCT. 1972

THOUGHT FOR THE MONTH: Smart rosarians learn by the mistakes of others. You don't have time to make them all yourself.

Rose season is growing short in most parts of the country now, and it is a good time to think a bit about the successes and shortcomings of your roses. This is the time to do something about next year, particularly in soil and rose bed preparation, taking advantage of the mounds of organic materials waiting to be composted.

I am not foolish enough to recommend a soil mixture that is EXACTLY right for your rose situation. But I do know that every good rose medium strikes a healthy balance of soil, humus, water and air. All of the exotic additions ever recommended for rose beds are intended to accomplish these very simple basics. Work toward these fundamentals, temper with a little common sense and you will have a rose bed mixture in which roses just to grow.

For example, if your soil is a tight clay, add sharp sand and humus. Some gypsum is also a good idea. Sandy loams welcome the addition of humus-composted materials. In both cases, the soil modifications have introduced friability for air movement and have also made water readily available to carry soluble nutrients. All kinds of good things happen when water, air, soil and a humus bacteria source get together. Get busy now. Like good wines, rose beds get better with age.

If you MUST have a formula for rose beds, here is one that has worked well in Houston for years (beginning with a heavy black gumbo that is slightly alkaline). For 100 square feet of rose bed elevated four to six inches above yard level, mix up the following:

ROSE BEDS WITH HEAVY BLACK GUMBO

1 bale brown peat moss or 1/2 yard pine bark mulch
1/2 yard of sharp sand or builders sand
1/2 yard compost
1/2 yard composted barnyard manure
25 pounds agricultural gypsum
10 pounds rock phosphate
10 pounds 5-10-5 complete rose food

Mix in well with existing soil to a depth of about 10 inches. Let new bed settle and compost for two weeks, then use a spading fork to mix again. Stir and mix several more times for best results. Allow 6 to 8 weeks of settling, mixing, and composting time before planting.

For rose folks interested in the newest of the new, here is a condensation of a July, 1972 report on *Triarimol* (Eli Lilly No.273) by the Texas Rose Research Foundation. The product has been under test in Tyler, Texas for four years.

"One of the leading new fungicides continues to be *Triarimol*, especially good as a control and preventative of powdery mildew. The liquid formulation of *Triarimol* is a 7.2 percent active material applied at very low concentrations of as little as 2.0 cc per gallon (equivalent to 24 ppm) and has proved to be safe at more than twice that amount. It has been proved safe and beneficial in control of powdery mildew when used at weekly intervals; it also has benefit and about 80 percent control in preventing mildew when used at monthly intervals on varieties of roses known to be susceptible to the disease. The result of the monthly test schedule is evidence that the compound has enough systemic action to prevent the disease on new growth that has occurred between the periods of spraying.

"In trials this year, *Benlate* (fungicide) at normal dosage (1/2 tablespoon per gallon) has been added to *Triarimol* to furnish control of blackspot also. No added spreader has been found necessary. Trials combining *Triarimol* and *maneb* and *folpet* fungicides have also proved to be safe combinations, limited only by the amount of toxicity from the added materials during periods of hot and dry weather.

"Using the rose variety 'Else Poulsen', there is nearly perfect control of blackspot and powdery mildew with a seven-day spray frequency of *Triarimol* in combination with either *Benlate* or *folpet*; this degree of control is evident within three feet of untreated check plants which at the present time (July) have more than 70 percent powdery mildew and 10 percent blackspot.

"Difference in bush size is already evident between the treated and untreated plots, and with hot and humid conditions it is expected that defoliation from blackspot will increase rapidly in the check plants.

"Spraying at 14-day intervals is quite effective, but not nearly so good as weekly treatment where check plants are so near as to furnish spores for spread of both powdery mildew and blackspot.

Rust is not a factor nor has it ever been noted in the test garden."

Editor's Note: Triarimol has not yet been released by USDA for home use. However, it is expected to be cleared soon for ornamentals.

Another rose season is at an end for most of us, and it's a good time to make up a rose score sheet of our efforts. Memories are short, and when the rose catalog fever hits in January most every rosarian forgets some of the failures of certain cultivars (I still prefer the term varieties) and the shortcomings of several of the rose beds. It's been said many times before, but the Queen of the Show begins to grow the winter before the exhibition. Good garden plans payoff in blue ribbons.

Proof of the Pudding has now been turned over to the Consulting Rosarians, but we'll have to wait until the Annual is published in February to know just how much good these reports can do for our particular situations. A very worthwhile rose society project would be to compile a "Performance Chart" of favorite and new cultivars in your area and make this information available to all your members. The local rating is worth far more than a generalization. Even if only 100 varieties are rated, newcomers and old pros will benefit. In fact, limiting the number of roses to be rated makes the job easier and gives a better chance for each rose to be rated by several individuals. Another suggestion: rate the roses on the basis of 1 thru 10 rather than on A thru D technique. Many growers are likely to give a favorite rose an "A" rating, which would give it 10 points or a "perfect" rose. Since there is no perfect rose YET, a graduated scale of points makes more sense. Program Chairmen, pay attention. A "Performance Chart" workshop night will make a great program and involve some members who have never been seen or heard.

Last month these columns offered a formula for rose beds. Continuing in this sure-to-be criticized practice, here's a GREAT formula for Miniature roses. It is good for pots, tubs, boxes or elevated Miniature rose beds. In making an elevated bed, make sure that the top six or eight inches of soil has been worked up and tilled in about the same way an ordinary garden bed would be prepared. This recipe will make up enough Miniature rose bed mix for about 100 square feet of bed elevated 4 to 6 inches above yard level. Miniatures MUST have good drainage; a built-up bed is important. Mix up the following:

MINIATURE ROSE BED MIXTURE

1 Bale Canadian Peat Moss (6 cu. ft. bale)
2 Bags No.6 Perlite (4 cu. ft. bag)
2 Bags Pine Bark Mulch (screen thru 14-in. screen)
1 Barrow Load Sharp Sand or Plaster's Sand (large wheelbarrow)
1 Barrow Load Light Garden Soil
3 Cups 48% Phosphate
5 Pounds Cottonseed Meal
25 Pounds Steer Manure (kiln run)
1 Cup Sulfasoil
1 Cup 5-10-5 Pelleted Fertilizer
1 Quart Carl Pool Root Activator

Mix the ingredients in a large pile, moisten and cover with plastic sheeting. Turn mixture weekly for three weeks. Composting and heating will blend ingredients and mix can be used immediately. If making a new bed, distribute mixture 4 inches deep in lightly tilled bed area and work in slightly. Let the new bed settle before planting. The soil is formulated for use with soluble fertilizers, such as *Carl Pool, Peter's Special Soluble Plant Food* or *Ra-Pid-Gro*. The acidifier is included to overcome the use of alkaline water. The humus content will hold up about 3 years. An experienced grower may want to substitute additional soil, sand or humus to get the right light "feel" to the mixture. The best mix is light, very friable and full of tiny air spaces so that the fine, hairy roots of Miniatures can develop and spread easily. Miniature cuttings should root readily in the formula.

Every get-together of rose folks raises the same question: How do we get more rose society members active in the affairs of the society? Or, How do we get newer members to become officers? Obviously there is no simple answer to these problems, but some recent workshop sessions brought up some suggestions so simple that they are usually ignored. For example, how many rose groups make it a policy to have a sort of "understudy" for each officer; that is to require the "irreplaceable" officer to groom his own successor. It's a very simple thought, but a management practice employed by major corporations the country over. Another good break-in technique is to urge newly elected chairmen to work with and meet with the former leaders for a month or two before taking over. This assures some degree of continuity. If interested rosarians have had some kind of involvement, they are likely to respond when asked. "Asked" is an important word. We are all inclined to say "No" for our prospect when he should have the chance to answer for himself. Another human frailty that influences all too many of us is the conviction that we cannot be replaced; no one can do the job as well as we can. How do we know if a newcomer never has a chance? If your exec group has this kind of weakening fungus, spade up some new ground, try out some new cuttings. They will likely take better than you think.

Here's some new ground that all ARS folks ought to turn. Harry Wheatcroft, the Rose Ambassador from Nottingham, England, said in Pittsburgh that 50 million rose plants are sold in England alone each year, and 40% of them are Floribundas. It's no wonder that the whole of England seems to be in bloom — a land of gardeners.

Where have all the roses gone?? And the too-short rose season. Seems like only a few weeks ago that the roses had to be pruned. If there's a moral here, it must be that rose business goes on year-round and it's time to start working on the blue ribbon winners for next season.

The regular show winners have already made up order lists for new roses next year· and you should be working on yours. Many of the best exhibition roses are sold out early, and new introductions are sometimes in short supply. Place an order n ow and make up another next spring for winterkill replacements. What to order is up to you, but it's an easy job if the Proof of the Pudding Committee has been working. If you don't have a local rating program for roses, get one started NOW. Even casual study of show results helps. In the South Central District in 1972 several roses invariably showed up in the top trophy collections. The show winners have been using 'First Prize', 'Swarthmore', 'Anne Letts', 'Christian Dior' and 'Granada' time after time. We are also seeing more and more of 'Big Ben', 'White Masterpiece' and 'Century Two'. If you're a serious exhibitor, get two or three of each variety.

And if you want to save some money, watch for these roses which are either off patent or about to be off patent. You just can't go wrong with: Chrysler Imperial, Tiffany, Peace, Anne Letts, Confidence or Queen Elizabeth. There are many fine, non-patent varieties to encourage a new grower to expand a garden.

Picked up several good ideas at the rose shows this fall to pass on to you loyal readers. Proves again that there's always something new. Application of liquid fertilizer has always been a job -mixing the concentrate with water in a big trash barrel and then pouring a bucketful around each plant. A SMART rosarian told me that he puts the concentrate (like *Orth-Gro*) in an *Ortho Hose-On Lawn Feeder*, turns on the hose, and lets the water pressure do the work. Hold your thumb over the application bypass for about ten seconds and about 2 gallons of the right mix is in the rose bed. Take your thumb off and soak in with plain water while washing off the foliage. The same trick can be used with concentrations of *Ra-Pid-Gro*, *Carl Pool* or any other completely soluble rose preparation or acidifier.

Also looked into several new plantings of roses in five-gallon cans that were buried in a conventional rose bed. This was reported last year as a way to control alkalinity and leaching on a limestone hillside garden. After two years the roses are still performing very well, show no signs of chlorosis and have replaced all of the original canes. Digging around the buried cans shows that the metal is nearly rusted through, but is apparently barrier enough to hold most of the water and liquid food applied to the plant. The can is full of small, hairy roots. Bakeries and restaurants are good sources of metal cans as shortening is packed this way.

Here's a good winter project for a rosarian group. Since Miniature roses are becoming more and more popular, better containers to display roses at home or in a show are a problem for rosarians. Miniatures deserve something better than an odd-lot assortment of test tubes stuck into metal washers or wooden blocks. A very attractive base and tube for single bloom or spray Miniatures can be made for less than six cents each, just about the cost of a conventional rose vase. Styrofoam balls 2lh inches in diameter make very stable bases by cutting in half. The cut can be made on a hot-wire machine commonly available at a florist supply wholesaler or on an ordinary jig or band saw. With a little practice, the halves will come out just-right every time.

Use No. 400 *Aqua-Piks* (commonly used for orchids etc.) for the containers. Insert the *Aqua-Pik* in the round top of the half-ball. Makes a stable, attractive display. If the white Styrofoam gets dirty with use, spray paint with some neutral color. The supplies are available from any florist supply wholesaler; *Aqua-Piks* cost about $2.40 per 100 and foam balls about 80 cents per dozen.

You may have mixed feelings about this idea, but it has been a very popular money-maker in this area for several years. Several rose societies sell the rose blooms that are not entered during a show, or else sell blooms that are in good condition at the conclusion of a one-day show. Obviously this can only be done when visitors in a buying mood are present, such as a show held in a shopping mall. Tastefully done, the rose sale is good for the society and the rose buyer. A collection of six nice roses for $1.00 finds more buyers than roses. One area society holds a Saturday-Sunday rose show on Mother's Day weekend in a popular shopping mall. The society routinely sells several hundred rose blooms in standard rose show vases trimmed off with a bit of appropriate ribbon. The $1.00 donation is at least 85 cents profit. Every buyer also gets a short promotional note about the rose society, and where additional information on roses is available. A good many friends have been made for roses through this promotion. Variations on this theme can help out financially-ailing rose societies in many parts of the country.

Another December chore besides ordering ARS memberships for gardening friends is new rose bed preparation. Get after it NOW if you possibly can. Early winter work pays off in bushels of roses next spring. However, exercise caution. See the warning printed below.

JAN. 1973

THOUGHT FOR THE MONTH: The widespread occurrence of backaches will continue as long as postal laws permit the mailing of rose catalogs.

Noticed any spider mites these cold nights?? This just proves again that every rose problem has some kind of solution sometime. When our roses don't have a problem, we create one. It's been said time and time again and it's still true; roses are the most popular and productive flower in the world in spite of rosarians — not because of them. And all of this long preamble is just a come-on to wish all reader-rosarians a VERY ROSY NEW YEAR with plenty of FUN and roses. And thanks again for the cards and comments directed this way from all over the country — rose folks are the greatest in the world.

If you need a first-of-the-year rose problem or project, try this one on for size. It's time to plan your spray schedule. For those of you with blowing snow and frozen ground this may seem ridiculous, but many sections will soon be starting a new rose year. Fungus control is a matter of prevention. Field trials and carefully controlled tests in gardens just like yours show that a fungus control program should START immediately after pruning, drenching the canes and bud union thoroughly. Use a combination of a broad spectrum insecticide (*Diazinon* is a good one) and your favorite fungicide (*phaltan, maneb* or *Benlate*) at full strength. Control over-wintering spores on the canes before temperature and humidity multiply and spread the infection. An insecticide-fungicide combination is generally more effective than an oil-sulfur combination, and is less likely to burn. Don't wait for new leaves to appear. Prune and spray the same day. Spray again in two weeks with the same combination. Then set up your usual control program. And don't forget to spray the Climbers and Shrub roses at the same time --an infected host plant can spread blackspot spores like wildfire when conditions are right. A CLEAN start helps make a clean garden season-long.

Some thoughtful rose society planning is in order in January to make sure that new (and old) members take part in practical educational programs before the serious rose season begins. It's amazing how many rose growers can't identify the shank, or the bud union, or find a bud eye on a year-old cane. They have heard the terms over and over again, but don't connect the words with the real thing. Try a program on planting in January.

Make a simulated rose bed on top of a large formica-top table. Build the sides of I-inch by 8-inch redwood to resemble a built-up rose bed and fill the box with a large bag of bark mulch material_ Bring several well-pruned rosebushes to the meeting (preferably discards) and actually plant the bushes in the box. It's also a good idea to show how a canned rosebush should be planted --that is by carefully cutting the sides of the tarpaper container and gently spreading the roots in much the same way as a bareroot rosebush. These practical demonstrations can help most any rose grower.

A good pruning demonstration can be managed in much the same way. Provide an instructor and helper with at least eight or ten rosebushes of various types, just as they are dug from the yard. Use ordinary pruning tools available to everyone and properly prune the bushes while offering a running commentary on "why and how."

How about a timely program built around cultivars to help new rosarians place orders for rosebushes. Local ratings and popularity lists are most useful to beginners; and even the oldtimers are sometimes surprised how popular and productive the old favorites are. Make up a short questionnaire to be given each member. Provide plenty of space to write.

Try these questions: list five favorite Hybrid Tea roses; most productive rose, best show rose, best rose in several color classes, most fragrant, disease resistant roses, best new introduction; list five "must-have" Miniatures, and on and on. While a consulting rosarian talks about what to look for in a good rosebush, quickly summarize the answer sheets and pass the information on to your group. A more complete listing can be printed in the next monthly publication. A good summary from many growers is worth the price of a year's membership to a novice.

Last but not least, plan a rose bed for your front yard this year. Plant it with just one variety if possible for a massed color effect. Floribundas are ideal for a planting of this type and some excellent varieties are available. We sometimes talk about beautification and then keep the beauty to ourselves. If you want to sell roses, show the product. Besides, sharing is half the fun of having a rose garden. A real attention-getter is a bed or a border

of Miniature roses to add color to a front planting. Most casual visitors don't even know what
they are. I have a round bed with twelve 'Chipper'
Miniatures that has outbloomed and outperformed
every annual ever tried in the same location. Think
small and colorful — you won't be disappointed.

February is a FUN month for roses — too early for the really HARD work to begin, and yet late enough for the memories of last season to get better and better. Or have you noticed that the good roses of last season have more form, color, size and what have you when snow is on the ground? In the north, the Queen-of-the-Show winners are safely dormant under their cones, surely to emerge even better this season. In the south, the pleasant job of pruning will begin shortly and even the old stand-bys promise great things with swelling new buds. It's one of the great things about roses — a rosarian just can't wait to get the new season going.

How about some of those sentimental old favorites? Are they really putting out all they should? Most rosarians are reluctant to dig up and throw-away those bushes that "seem to be going downhill." Or the newer variety that "might need another year to get established." There's an old rosarian saying to the effect that, "Those that don't put out, pull out." Or another rose friend says, "Prune the weak ones with a spade." It takes even longer to take care of a poor rosebush than a productive one. To ease rosarian pangs of conscience, offer the bushes you want to replace to another rosarian, or have a plant exchange. It's a good way to get a friend started in roses; with a little spade work and free roses, the rose rewards in the long run will be great. For some reason known only to nature, a transplanted bush will often take a new lease on life — maybe just to confound the grower. Shared rosebushes can get someone started; and the roses that didn't quite please your critical eye can dazzle a beginner.

If you haven't finished building your rose beds yet, don't forget that a raised bed has more good things going for it than lawn-level plantings. A raised bed provides much more than just good drainage, although this is an important factor. Every good soil medium strikes a healthy balance of soil, humus, water and air. All of the exotic additions ever recommended for rose beds are intended to make these basics work. The raised bed takes care of the water and air; and in turn water and air make the nutrients in the soil available to the plant. Simple. All kinds of good things happen when water, air, soil and a humus bacteria source get together. Let nature do the work. The rosarian

should enjoy the roses.

Some good materials are available to make attractive built-up beds. Available most places and gaining in popularity are "L" shaped concrete blocks. Concrete in this form is perfectly safe to use around roses. Set a lawn level, it's easy to pick up 6 or 8 inches of elevation. "L" curb usually comes in 24-inch, 12-inch, and 6-inch straight lengths; combined with inside and outside curves almost any shape bed is possible. A round bed 6 feet in diameter is available with 12 inside curves set together. Set the blocks in a tamped sandy base; no concrete footing or foundation is usually necessary. Although it's hands-and-knees work, laying "L" block doesn't take much skill and goes fast. Another bonus of "L" curb is the foot portion of the L that makes a good edge for the lawnmower wheel. Creeping grasses can't jump it, and the edger blade follows the edge for a very neat layout.

Even if you aren't much good with bricks, a vertical row of bricks or blocks with "squashed" mortar makes an attractive rose bed edging. However, this kind of installation usually takes some kind of light foundation. This shapes up to be work. If you are going to this kind of trouble, be sure to run an extra course lengthwise at lawn level for the mower wheel — and don't forget the drainage holes in the mortar. Bathtubs are for rosarians, not for roses.

Redwood and cedar are also easy to use, last a long time and blend in with most any garden plan. If you can use a handsaw, you can build rose beds with redwood. Be sure to use redwood posts and braces for long life. My preference is I-inch by 8-inch redwood capped with a I x 2-inch redwood finishing strip to cover up any alignment or nailing mistakes. Wood can be stained to match the trim on a house or can be left to weather naturally. Again, drill a few drainage holes for best performance. Heavy construction is not necessary; the edging only retains the soil mixture which has no tendency to burst out of bounds.

It seems early to talk about spray schedules, but for many this is the time to start. Begin the season with a CLEAN garden. As soon as the bushes have been pruned, drench the canes, bud union and immediate soil area with a spray of fungicide-insecticide to kill overwintering spores and insects.

A Phaltan-Isotox or Benlate-Spectracide mixture seems more effective than oil-sulfur dormant sprays and is less likely to burn. Spray IMMEDI-ATELY. Repeat in a week. Then follow a normal every-ten-day routine. It works.

MAR. 1973

THOUGHT FOR THE MONTH: *There are three kinds of rosarians: those who make things happen, those who watch things happen, and those who don't know what happened.*

Rambling through my "research library" — which is really a collection of junk, clippings, notes and stolen items from other publications — it's obvious that rosarians are the targets of dozens of new "miracle" formulations and preparations every year that promise to make roses grow bigger, better and easier. But very few of these "amazing" discoveries enjoy popularity more than a year or two. Roses and rosarians know better and are only temporarily distracted by the claims. For the most part it's innocent puffery, but rose faddists can also drop a good piece of money and lose rosebushes in the process. Discount the claims with a heavy application of common sense — and then check with some other growers for trial results. It's fun to experiment, but only when a grower can afford the loss — a little like betting on the horses.

After this preamble on the dangers of "miracle" cures, let me recommend a really miraculous product that has been around for a long time but largely overlooked. Agricultural gypsum (Calcium Sulfate) makes growing worthwhile again for rosarians cursed with heavy, alkaline soils. Gypsum has been used for centuries, and many rosarians routinely add gypsum to a rose bed mixture, without a clear understanding of just how it works. A scientific discussion is beyond this reporter's scope, but these personal observations may help rosarians decide if gypsum can help their gardens. Dr. John Gannon of Houston is credited with painstaking investigation of the properties of gypsum, publishing an extensive report in the *1971 American Rose Annual*, Page 75.

Gypsum helps break up heavy, alkaline soils and reduces the toxic effect of sodium on plants, especially when irrigating water contains relatively large amounts of sodium. Under proper circumstances, gypsum reacts chemically with clay soil particles and humus, removing excess sodium and reducing the tendency of the soil to "puddle" and subsequently pack. Sodium is a very reactive element and forms "salts" very readily; and in the case of clay soils becomes firmly attached to the particles causing an increase in the soil pH, giving an alkaline reaction. The absorbed sodium makes soils heavy, wet and retards plant growth.

The sodium atom attached to the clay has a very strong attraction for water, reaching a point where the particle attracts water more than another clay particle. The rosarian knows this as slimy mud. The particles can remain suspended in water for long periods; and when the water does drain away, the clay bits settle into a tightly packed condition. The air space remaining in the soil is very small, resulting in hard soil with poor aeration and drainage -hardly a good condition for roses. It's easy for this same condition to develop in potted plants through use of alkaline water --and many city water supplies contain substantial amounts of sodium salts.

Roses will not thrive in tight, alkaline soils. Application of gypsum will help relieve both conditions and restore good growth and bloom. Gypsum does the job by exchanging calcium ions for sodium ions attached to the soil particles, and manages the trick without any toxicity to the rosebushes. Gypsum is applied as a powder and worked into the soil, or leached downward through the soil by rain or irrigation. It is slow to dissolve and the benefits last for a long time. An application of from 10 to 20 pounds per 100 square feet is recommended for a long effective period. Growers in the Southwest who are plagued with very alkaline water, commonly treat rose beds with a surface application of 10 pounds of gypsum per 100 square feet each spring. Several things must happen for gypsum to do the job. Enough gypsum must dissolve for the chemical reaction to take place, producing sodium sulfate. The sodium sulfate is then leached from the soil by adequate drainage. Since the soil is still very tight, mechanical loosening of the soil is then in order, although natural processes will eventually do the job. The process works from the top down until the leaching process is complete and the soil opened up. Even after the soil is cleared of excess sodium, enough gypsum must be kept in the path of irrigation water to offset any buildup of the alkaline condition. Rose beds, potted roses and especially potted Miniature roses will respond vigorously and dramatically to treatment with gypsum. Water, plant nutrients and air again can reach the rose feeding zone. Since gypsum is neutral, it will not affect the pH reading of the soil by its application. If in doubt, use gypsum. Work a good supply of gypsum into any new rose bed under construction. For roses already established, add gypsum to the top few inches of soil with careful cultivation. Rain and regular watering will move the beneficial qualities downward. This easy-to-use, cheap, safe, non-toxic, proven, available-everywhere miracle really works!

Spring is here — and has been for most rosarians for some time. It's quite a fever that drives a rosarian to build new beds, exceed the budget and work in the cold and wet for some new blooms this spring. Has your rose society broken dormancy yet, or is there a lot of winterkill? Spring is the time for the new and renewal... early season program activities will largely determine membership and enthusiasm all year. How about a Rose Quiz program — questions and answers from all directions? Properly planned — with the answers fielded by someone fast on his (or her) feet — the program can involve many members and get things moving. Here are some typical questions the RAMBLING ROSARIAN has received... just something to get started... the rest is up to you. My new rosebushes are either dead or dormant. How do I get them started? Bare root roses sometimes dry out in shipment and are reluctant to start. To begin the recovery process, lightly prune the bush and soak in water or planting solution at least overnight. Before planting, make a loose-fitting hood or cover of medium weight clear plastic material. Secure the edges of the plastic with staples so the hood closes rather securely around the shank of the bush. Add a handful of wet sphagnum moss inside the bag for extra humidity. Plant the bush and "mud" in with plenty of water. Moisture will condense inside the plastic assuring that the process is working. Leave the hood in place for a week or ten days, or until the bush is breaking good eyes. Then gradually cut some air holes in the plastic to reduce the temperature. Take the hood off entirely in about a week. Is "heat treated" or "sterilized" manure any good? Is the real thing better? It's VERY GOOD, although I still prefer the old fashioned kind. The analysis on the manure sack doesn't begin to tell the benefits of manure in rose beds or mixed with the mulch. Manure is a fair source of nitrogen, a good source of humus and an excellent culture for the micro-organisms that make all soil processes work. Micro-biologists still haven't unlocked all of the miracles performed by these soil workers. Heat treated manure from feed lots needs to be mixed with soil or other mulches to become "wetted" and in contact with soil bacteria. Sack manure tends to shed water rather than absorb. If you have a cow-lot friend, by all means keep him

as a friend. The product he has, even with weed seeds, is the greatest ever for all-around rose growing. Are cane sealers worth the time and effort? In wet climates or where borers are around, cane sealers are very useful. Rosarians here prefer shellac, painting all large pruning cuts, especially around the bud union. Use an old liquid shoe polish bottle. The dauber gives neat coverage, is convenient and the dauber doesn't dry out. *Elmer's Glue* is another good sealer, complete with an applicator. Asphalt is the least popular here. In cutting large, woody canes use a small keyhole saw (*Stanley* has an inexpensive one) rather than the crushing blade of a lopper. The cut will heal much faster, particularly around the bud union. I thought that salts were bad for roses. Why do you recommend *Epsom Salts*? The word "salt" can be applied to a thousand very common chemical combinations, not all of them bad, with table salt the most generally known. *Epsom Salts* is really magnesium sulfate, and this particular salt can do more for roses than for rosarians in the springtime. Used with discretion, magnesium sulfate will promote basal breaks and put on a surge of new green growth. It's most effective when a slightly alkaline condition exists in the rose bed, but seems to do no harm even when an acid condition exists. Available at most feed stores for about 15 cents per pound, magnesium sulfate can be applied at about 1/4 cup (2 ounces) per bush broadcast around the root perimeter. Water in thoroughly, it's very soluble. If the soil is deficient in magnesium, surprising things will happen -all good. If the soil has enough magnesium, no harm will be done by this light application. Are you still sold on *Benlate*? Is it really a miracle? *Benlate* is no miracle, but I am still sold on it as an excellent and safe fungicide. Perhaps too much was expected of *Benlate* from the beginning, attributing properties to it that were never deserved or claimed. After several years of use myself, rather broad observation and lots of letters from blackspot distributors all over the country, I still rely on *Benlate* as a blackspot-mildew fungicide without use of any other material. *Benlate* seems best when used alone, without a spreader-sticker or aroma tic-base insecticide. Start protection program at pruning time, continue every 10 days until hot, dry weather prevails. Stretch period to two weeks or so in hot weather. Resume every-10 days routine in the fall. Use 1 tablespoon to two gallons of water. When insect control is NECESSARY, use the appropriate control separately. Result: A clean garden season-long.

If your rose society is like most throughout the country, you are scoring more points at the rose shows than with new members, particularly the "young" ones that we all talk about but fail to recruit and hold. Maybe you are selling the wrong thing. When rosarians get together, talk usually dwells on problems with roses — diseases, insects, winterkill, and the necessity for magic potions for all occasions. Have you talked about the FUN of roses — and then done something about it? The easy-fun aspect of rose growing attracts members. A good salesman sells benefits, not difficulties. As rose salesmen we have the world's greatest product, provided we don't talk ourselves out of the sale. Growing roses is just common sense. Make roses easy and fun and you won't be able to handle all of the memberships.

"Service after the sale" holds rose members. This service is more than getting up some kind of rose program each month that's announced by a non-information bulletin. A rose novice wants rose information; he thrives on it — and so will your old members. This is a pretty big order, but most societies are sitting on a wealth of information about roses that's just waiting to be tapped. I'm referring to the growers in your society who want to share rose experience with others but who are frustrated in their attempts. Solution: a local Proof of the Pudding evaluation of roses available to every member, visitor or garden shop interested enough to read it. Local evaluation has everything going for it with few of the complexities of national and regional rating systems.

Local rose rating is easy, and it involves many members. For a list of roses to be rated, begin with the named varieties in your show schedule. Expand this with some study of popular rose catalogs and then review the varieties that routinely appear in the color class sections of the show. With very little effort, you'll have a list of 200-250 roses widely grown in the area. It's a good project for Consulting Rosarians and Judges. Separate Hybrid Teas, Grandifloras, Floribundas, etc. This helps a novice identify the roses. Prepare a report sheet for each member, typewritten and double spaced. Allow space for name of the variety, number of plants grown, number of years grown and ALL the space possible for comments. Carefully done, the

report can be a self-fold envelope with the return address of the project chairman.

What about a scale for rating the roses? You have probably heard that a national committee has been appointed to come up with recommendations for a better system. This is long overdue and a subject of considerable interest throughout the country. No problem. Your local society doesn't have to wait for some final decision. Here's a rating system that will work until something better comes along:

A 9 points Excellent rose. Highly recommended. A must.

B 7 points Very good. Recommend for most growers.

C 5 points Good. Will keep. Might recommend.

D 3 points Fair. Will replace.

E 1 point Poor. Throwaway.

Compile the reports, note the most pertinent comments and reproduce for the benefit of all members. And do it BEFORE rose order season. This is the kind of service that makes your members happy.

If you have comments or suggestions on Proof of the Pudding nationally (or locally), drop a note to Francis Dollinger, 3255 Blackmon Lane, Beaumont, Texas 77703. He is working hard on recommendations to make rose ratings have more meaning for every rosarian. A member of the infamous Golden Triangle exhibitor gang, Francis knows roses and how to report them.

Here's an unscientific report that's worth passing on to rose fans — the same kind of observation that you can make and pass on to your members. For what it is worth, rose beds prepared with vermiculite (about 25% by volume) produce root systems on roses that have to be seen to be believed. The rose beds were prepared four years ago with 1/3 clay-loam garden soil, 1/3 humus (peat moss, manure, compost), 1/4 vermiculite and the balance sharp sand. Other incidentals included rock phosphate and gypsum. Roses growing in the mix were dug this spring and the root systems were at least 1/3 more fibrous and extensive than roses grown in a bed without vermiculite. The root systems were healthy, had many tiny new feeders, and had obviously matured and expanded considerably since planting. Rose notes show the only significant difference was the addition of vermiculite. This doesn't prove that this product is the greatest thing ever for roses, but it confirms again that soil additions supporting better aeration and friability help grow better roses. It's worth a try, anyway.

JUN. 1973

THOUGHT FOR THE MONTH: *the curious thing about grass is that it grows greener on the other side of the fence, but faster on your side.*

The Consulting Rosarian business is a tough one these days as old-time remedies are declared "ecologically unacceptable," new products are introduced in amazing quantities and newly-minted rose nuts swear that a favorite formula will pay off with "bushels" of blooms immediately. It's all part of the fun of roses, but we must present a very contradictory picture to the newcomer as the old-pro is confused and the novice is positive. Re-read the "Roses Coast to Coast" section sometime and note that the worthy columnists all too frequently contradict each other, and even more often offer advice without qualifying statements. It proves again that roses must be the hardiest of plants to survive all this abuse. Please, rose fans, if you are going to give advice, make sure that the instructions are SPECIFIC and ACCURATE, and that ALL of the qualifying statements are included. Then if something goes wrong, at least you'll know what caused it. This rosarian is as guilty as the next in this department, and promises to do better.

How about a specific for spider mites? Water, just plain water, is still the best and safest. The old dangers of water on rose foliage just aren't true anymore. If you have a water wand, use it. If you don't have, make one or set a cone-type lawn sprinkler under the plants and water away the mites. Any water-spray head that directs a pattern of water droplets over a broad area will do.

And overhead watering is NOT bad. Soaking systems are great, but even these need to be supplemented with overhead-underneath drenchings on a regular basis. The effectiveness of fungicides today eliminates the worry of wet foliage. Overhead irrigation works best in the early morning hours so that the leaves have a chance to dry before evening, or before the HOT noon sun scalds the leaves. This practice is safe even in the high-humidity areas. Around here, the foliage is wet from dew every morning anyway. A good drenching with the hose washes off the excess spray residue, cools the plant and makes the roots happy, too. It makes sense that roses like to be clean.

One old rosarian in this area invariably hosed down healthy rosebushes after a very hot day, reasoning that roses need refreshments just like the rosarian. He usually held the hose in one hand and a beer can in the other. The foliage in his garden was healthy, always clean and COMPLETELY FREE of mildew and blackspot.

Obviously, overhead watering is not in order the week before a big rose show. Sun and moisture will ruin any bloom.

Slow soaking or a careful hand irrigation is better then. One rose grower near here plants roses in the middle of a three-foot barrel ring, forming a kind of dam around the bush. All liquid fertilizer and hand watering goes into the ring as a supplement to rainfall and other irrigation. These bushes are over eight feet tall.

Whatever irrigation method you use, SOAK the rose bed, don't sprinkle. Put down at least an inch of water at a time. If the rose beds are properly drained, it's almost impossible to over-water. Roses in the heavy soils of the Gulf Coast take about two inches of water per week during the summer, plus additional summer rains. Porous, sandy soils can take much more. If you are not sure of application rate with a lawn sprinkler, set out a couple of coffee cans around the sprayer and turn off the hose when the cans have an inch of water. And if you don't have an accurate rain gauge, get one. Know how much water your roses are actually receiving.

With Miniature roses gaining in popularity every season and attracting more attention at the rose shows, rose keepers for these tiny beauties are very much in order. Keepers are easy to make and local exhibitors report excellent keeping results up to eight days. The materials are cheap and easy to come by. Take two six-ounce frozen orange juice cans, some old X-ray film or light weight plastic carpet runner and a bit of sealing tape or plastic cement. Make a tube about seven inches long by wrapping the plastic around both cans, placed end to end. Seal or tape an overlapped edge. Then squeeze the plastic material and insert into one of the cans. Add about an inch of water to the can. Slide the second can over the top of the plastic material and the sealed tube is complete. This makes an airtight container about eight inches long that is easy to unload and takes up very little room in the transport box or refrigerator. Two or three Miniature specimens fit beautifully and arrive at the show in great shape.

At last, a use for ice cream cartons. Both quart

and half-gallon sizes make good rose Cones for shading. Tack or staple the carton to a wooden stake and place over the bloom. They will last longer if sprayed or brushed with varnish, but even with no spray are good for a season. Besides, the cartons add interest to the garden. Be sure to use a strawberry-flavor carton over 'Strawberry Blonde'.

Been on a garden tour lately? If you haven't, you are missing one of the best parts of rose growing. The tour can be formal, informal, or on the spur of the moment -just dropping by to visit with a couple of rosarians to swap stories. You will be surprised how much you can learn... and have some rose fun at the same time.

Spring tours around here turned up a number of good ideas. You may want to try some. A real eye-catcher was a long bed of 'Europeana' along a driveway with a row of 'Summer Snow' in the foreground. This rosarian could be spotted from two blocks away. The two varieties make an outstanding combination planted for mass display. Another traffic-stopper was a bed of about 30 'Leprechaun' planted for mass effect in a front yard. These multi-color Floribundas show dense foliage, huge floret sprays of yellow, cerise, pink and cream and are absolutely uniform in bush form. The bushes were planted about 18 inches apart, and each plant had at least eight good canes. Center of attention in another yard was a round bed of 'Chipper', a beautiful, free-flowering Miniature that grows like a Polyantha. About ten plants filled the bed (5 feet in diameter) with a mound of color. Another good use of Miniatures was a planting of 'Jet Trail' around the base of a black gas light-house number feature. The Miniatures were partially trained up the pole. The contrast was excellent.

Prettiest patio had a combination of Miniatures in pots and some of the new "patio" tree roses in 5-gallon redwood tubs. The patio roses are on 18 to 24-inch standards and are kept groomed to stay in proper proportion. Several Miniature trees were also doing well. Double redwood "splints" helped support the 10-inch standards and the bundle of blooms from double budding. They looked like colorful lollipops.

Saw an "old fashioned" garden that is somewhat unusual for this part of the country. Most roses here are grown in formal beds of one kind or another. This garden had Hybrid Teas toward the back, Floribundas mixed in here and there in the middle, and Miniatures toward the front. The colors were all mixed, and no apparent planting pattern was followed. Some stepping stones were added for maintenance access. About 75 roses of all kinds were planted in a corner and along a fence, making a rainbow of color. The grower follows a fertilization schedule based on square feet, much like the formula by John van Barneveld at Rose Hills in California. All of the roses were doing well with no suggestion of incompatibility. In early spring the grower has tulips and spring bulbs in front, later giving way to alyssum, ageratum and portulaca. The overall effect was beautiful.

One garden built on a small acreage used old railroad ties (very weathered) for edging built-up beds. The rustic effect was softened even more with some violets and portulaca. Spotted here and there on the edge were some begonias and coleus. Another grower had access to some imperfect cinder-cement blocks, the kind with two large holes for airspace. The blocks were laid in a bed of sand just like laying a course for a foundation. The single row of blocks effectively built up the bed about six inches, and the holes were filled with ordinary garden soil. Small summer annuals were planted in the holes for one of the brightest borders I have ever seen. The raw concrete look was softened by staining the blocks with a mixture of redwood stain and ordinary solvent. The solvent carried the pigment in the pores of the block, leaving behind a soft, red-brown patina, rather than a painted look.

How about "slag" for a mulch? This porous byproduct resembles volcanic rock and is usually red-brown in color. The grower stockpiled the material for several months after hauling from an old industrial slag dump, leaching away any acids with plenty of water. Water percolated through the 2-inch layer readily; the beds were weed-free and the soil cool and moist. The effect was most attractive.

Visited with many growers on spray equipment and techniques. Equipment ranged from the *Atomist* to *Hayes Hose-On*. Several used the *Hudson* pump," tank, and one had a jet pump powered with a gasoline engine. All had two things in common -a regular spraying program and no disease.

One grower reported a new approach to spider mite control that may be worth trying. His mites had built up an immunity to most insecticides and the infestation Was too much for the water wand. Something drastic had to be done. Remembering the controls used by camellia growers here, the rosarian used the water wand first and followed up with an under-leaf drenching of Volck, 2 table-spoons per gallon of water. The process was re-peated in four days, even though the temperatures were in the low 90s. Only a few plants showed leaf damage; none was severe. Some leaf drop may have been due to mite damage. The mites appeared to be under control, and the bushes were growing vigorously. This control has been used by organic gardeners for years, but usually avoided by rosar-ians except during dormant periods. It would be interesting to know if other growers have safely used this material during hot weather. All of which proves again that rosarians can be as resourceful as the bugs.

Everybody loves a giveaway... we're all suckers for "Fill in the Coupon" directions and regularly send away for catalogs, bulletins, price lists and free offers by the dozens. That's good, because it shows real interest. Offers mentioned in these columns usually attract lots of mail. In case you missed some of these "timely and worthwhile" offerings, here's a repeat of some of the more popular that drew many inquiries. As they say in other magazines, it's all "Free of Cost or Obligation."

To get rose growers to show and enjoy roses more, how about scheduling a small rose show at monthly meetings. The old timers as well as the newcomers enjoy it and adds some color and flair so often missed at our meetings. Show and compare is good advice anytime. Around here, the small show is called the Six-Pack Show or the Continuing Show. The Six Pack name is very appropriate as entries are usually limited to no more than six per exhibitor and can be carried in your favorite beverage carrier. A limited number of color classes are set up and the Best of Show awarded using standard ARS rules. For real competition, set up a major prize for the end of the season. Talk about competition, growers who never enter regular shows will bring in outstanding blooms and become better participants in all of the activities of the group. That's what this rose hobby business is all about. I have copies of an excellent show schedule and rules for small shows. Send for one.

Want a great program to break your group out of a summer slump? How about a workshop with EVERYONE participating? The program says again and again that "It's easy and fun to grow roses." It has many variations to suit your situation and gets your members to swap ideas and experience with roses. Break your members down into groups of 8; worktables are better than auditorium type seating. Set up four or five different groups. Call them Rose Testers, Bug Fighters, Soil Scientists, Trophy Chasers, Catalog Consultants or Program Planners... just to name a few. Make up small identifying signs from old rose catalogs. Appoint an experienced and talkative moderator for each group, furnish each panel member with a short outline of the items to be covered. As your members come into the meeting, they can select tables that interest them most. For example, Rose Testers

are going to discuss varieties and performance; the Soil Scientists will talk about fertilizers and rose bed preparation... and on and on. The trick is to write up a short outline with leading questions for each group to answer. EVERY member can contribute something. Turn the groups loose on their questions and ask the moderator to note the conclusions for a five minute summary to the whole audience later. The biggest problem is to get the "workshop experts" to quit talking. If you need an outline to get started, drop me a line.

Rose bulletins are important to the life of a rose society. Good communications are always popular and many members join just to receive up-to-date information. Growers and just plain hobbyists are serious in their efforts to have better roses and want more facts and formulas to try in their gardens. Specific what-to-do advice, list of new materials, variety discussions and features on roses are high on the list of most-wanted subjects. If your bulletin isn't doing the job, perhaps you need to measure it against a new standard... maybe you are just in a rut. A Bulletin Workshop Outline is available along with a publication scoring sheet. If you'll send along a couple of stamped, self-addressed envelopes, I'll also return a few issues of the *Houston ROSE-ETTE* just for comparison and maybe some new ideas.

Have you tried tree roses in redwood tubs? They are a pleasure to grow, even in cold climates. Extra care in the selection of a planting medium makes all the difference in growing good tree roses in tubs season after season without winterkill. A well-established tree rose can be moved into the garage for winter and back onto the patio for color in the summer. The formula for growth and hardiness is good drainage, access of air to the root zone and ability to retain moisture and nutrients. An ideal mixture is I part organic soil, I part Canadian peat moss and I part calcined clay. Calcined clay is marketed around the country as *TERRA-GREEN*, a product of the Oil-Dri Corporation. A report by Michigan State details experiments with various mixtures. If you want one, write. The cost is just a comment or two on how well your tree roses are doing.

Rosarians are thinking small these days, and Miniatures are climbing in popularity. Beds, pots, planters, tubs and what have you can handle these little beauties if you have the right soil mix. They do NOT grow like their big brothers. Miniatures perform better in a medium prepared for their needs. Ernest Williams of MINI-ROSES has a dandy soil formula that I have cut down for the average grower. For the formula and fun with Miniatures, drop a letter with a few words on your Miniature efforts. How many growers have Miniatures under lights? Maybe some of your experiences can be passed along. Write when you can, and keep the following in mind.

The Rambling Rosarian is three years old, thirty-six issues wiser, and still convinced that roses and rose folks make up the greatest combination anywhere. With your indulgence, these rose thoughts will continue with some old, new, and borrowed odds and ends that make rose growing fun.

You might have more fun (and information, too) in your rose society meetings if you follow the example of a Texas group I know. Two regular features have been added to make the overall program more interesting and varied. A Consulting Rosarian presents a ROSE REPORT on some aspect of rose growing each month, briefly discussing such things as spray equipment, how to water, conditioning roses or even yellow leaves. Five or ten minutes is the limit, only one topic, no wandering. The results are great; newcomers and old pros have something new to discuss and it keeps the Consulting Rosarians on their toes. It's a tougher job than you think to get a clear meaning across in just five minutes. Lots of rose people can (and do) wander through a rose topic for a half an hour and say less. The ROSE REPORT should add some spice to the program, not run in competition. Assign a definite topic each month, swap the job around for variety. More rose growers rust out than wear out, so make sure your resident rose experts' have something to do.

Another monthly feature is called the SIDE BUD, a brief review of what's new and interesting in publications on roses. This might be a check list of books and periodicals available, a "borrowed" article from a rose bulletin, a brief on a new rose topic or a collection of thoughts that pertain to the major program for the evening. In many cases, the Side Bud is suitable for reprinting in the bulletin. Again, the basis of Side Bud is brevity. Tell the facts in a way to make the listener want more. You'll reach a good many rose people this way.

Environmental protection is a popular rose topic now since every rose grower had a shelf-load of potions and preventions. Protecting the environment is great, but we should be even more interested in protecting the rosarian and the rose foliage. Poor labeling and storage are common. The product gets the blame more often than the rosarian. If you're going to spray, use fresh materials that are accurately labeled. We all know, for example, that most sprays have a limited shelf life and rapidly lose their effectiveness when kept for long periods on a shelf that's alternately hot and freezing. But how many of us bother to DATE the package or to repackage the wettable powders in a glass jar with a tight lid? Big mayonnaise jars are good for this, and you can tape the label to the outside. Another good trick is to note your favorite mixture proportions on the jar with a grease pencil so that you won't have to figure them out again. These two ideas can save you some blackspot or mildew due to spraying with old materials or head off leaf burn because a spray concentration was too strong. A MUST for the spray shelf is a small medicine glass for measuring spray materials. Most garden shops have them for about 25 cents each with easy-to-read markings for teaspoons, tablespoons and ounces.

Common sense tells us that a good spray mixture is important, but few rosarians know how to blend wettable powders and oil-based insecticides into a compatible mixture. HOT water is the answer. Use a glass mixing container with a tight lid. Carefully mark the outside of the container for the amount of concentrated mixture that fits your sprayer. Measure the wettable powders in the container first. Then slowly add HOT tap water, swirling the mixture into a thick paste. Continue to add warm water to the right concentration. Swirling the mixture seems to work best without foam and suds. The glass container makes it easy to see what's going on. Aromatic-based ingredients are added next, swirling gently. Add any spreader-sticker last. The spray mixture is now ready to use WITHOUT any straining. The large glass container is obvious -you can always see what the mixture is doing. The danger of a glass container is very small since any rosarian with garden sense is wearing gloves and handling the mixture with care. If one of the ingredients precipitates out, safely dispose of the whole batch and try to identify the product that makes the problem. For example, over-age *Cygon* will cause *Benlate* to precipitate out immediately. Result: no protection and a clogged sprayer.

If you haven't tried the Water Hole yet, buy some or make some to install in your new rose beds this fall. The Water Hole is a short piece of plastic pipe that works like a well casing in reverse. About 15 inches long, 3 inches in diameter and drilled with a dozen 3/8-inch holes in the sides, the pipe is buried in the rose bed with just a little of the flared top showing. Let the water hose run slowly into the pipe; the perforations distribute water without waste into the root zone. Good for small circular beds that are hard to keep moist, the pipes are inexpensive and available thru garden magazines or shops -or make your own. They'll be surrounded by rose roots in less than a season.

Oct.
1973

THOUGHT FOR THE MONTH: Have you noticed that grass is greener on the other side of the fence, but grows faster on your side?

It had been a particularly frustrating day in the garden… nothing seemed to go right. If sheer will power could produce a Queen of Show, then the yard should have been overflowing with trophies. Something was wrong with everything but the resident rosarian. About this time my Texas Aggie son, uninhibited with rose rules and doctrine, observed that most things are very simple when you know the solution; we just tend to miss the keys along the way. And that's probably true for rose nuts of all ages; we insist that we can force a solution and forget to watch for the easy clues.

For example, have you ever noticed that an ample helping of manure used before other rose foods seems to make the whole formula work better? We don't have to understand it to appreciate the results. A good spring starter or rose show feeding schedule should always include manure a week or two before the soluble applications. Another way to accomplish the same thing is to add about 10 pounds of bloodmeal to the typical 40-pound sack of organic based rose food. Work the mix in a bit with the soil bacteria and watch the results.

Maybe your sharp rosarian eye has noted that spraying just after a rain gives better leaf coverage (better wetting) and seems to stick longer. It's not a bad practice to wash off the plants after a long, dry spell, then spray. Another good reason to water overhead at least some of the time. And you've certainly seen that organic material, earthworms and healthy rose bushes go together. And doesn't the soil smell good when organics, soil and sand are working together? Nature must be trying to tell us something.

Of course you know that *Acti-Dione PM* works better when used alone, and that you only have to worry about new, nitrogen-lush growth. But have you learned that this excellent fungicide works even better if the powdery spores are washed off before spraying? Or you might want to move the plant with chronic mildew to a spot with better air circulation. Some growers use a "sacrificial lamb" technique to good advantage. Keep a mildewer like 'Orange Flame' or 'Fire King' in the garden; either will tell you right away when mildew conditions are right. The rose 'Day Dream' has always been a good spray tester for me. The leaves always burn at the slightest mistake.

If you have been around very many rose gardens, you've noticed that a casual garden visitor will always show more interest in and ask more questions about the "sick" rose in the garden than the other 100 that are performing well Obviously, if I knew what the problem might be I would do something about it. Since no one wants to admit lack of expertise, I usually confide that the bush in question has been left for the bugs so that they won't bother the rest of the roses. My good rose friend Carson Scoggins has another put-down. He tells the visitor that the rose needs to be pruned… with a spade.

Here's something you should look for: roses growing in a "strawberry pyramid" style planting. The Miniatures are spectacular in such a setting. You older rosarians will remember how you built a series of rectangular boxes, each about a foot smaller than the others and then filled the pyramid with sandy soil spiced with plenty of manure. This old time idea grows Miniatures as rewarding as the red-ripe strawberries that used to cascade over the sides.

Have you noticed what Miniatures are doing in the rose shows now? If you aren't growing 20 or 25 varieties, you are missing a lot of fun. A 1000-bloom show in this area will have nearly 250 miniatures represented. Miniatures don't compete with the big roses, they complement them. Minis can bring enjoyment to many rose growers who do not have the space or the physical ability to handle the larger types.

I'm sure you know the rose grower who "always seems to have plenty" of roses for the house, his neighbors, church or rose arranger friends. Check the garage and you'll find that he has a refrigerator for nothing but roses; and that most of the good blooms are harvested on a regular basis, conditioned and then refrigerated for use later. The also-ran blooms are left in the yard, and still make a great display. This same grower is probably a good exhibitor because he knows how to cut and hold his blooms rather than relying on "good luck" the day of the show.

Last but not least, I've noticed that most good gardens have a compost pile hidden away somewhere in the yard. Some are scientific, production-line affairs; and others are simply heaps of clippings, soil and what-have-you. The results are the same in the rose bed... better aeration, better root growth, better bushes, better blooms. No yard is too small. Even an old garbage can (no bottom, tight lid) can convert kitchen scraps, clippings, soil and moisture into the richest plant food that nature can produce. The recipe is simple: add, stir, sprinkle, settle. Then add, stir, sprinkle, etc. It beats anything you can buy in a sack or can.

November is a great rose month... the successful rose nuts are framing the certificates won during the past season and the not-quite-so-successful are ordering the sure winners for next season and planning shelf space for the silverware. Queen of the Show blooms don't suffer the indignities of competition and criticism in November; and rose garden plans are alive with color without having to lift a shovel. Living with the ever-faithful promises of the rose catalogs, who needs more? For some fun ideas with roses that aren't too much work, read on.

How about some manure without having to put up with a cow? There's something better than the heat treated, seed free, sterilized, screened (and sometimes nutrient free) kind that comes in the convenient sack with the picture of a cow on the front. Enjoy the benefits without having to pitch hay. Besides, that stuff in the sacks just doesn't seem like manure to me. Amaze your friends at the next rose society meeting with this secret recipe for artificial manure... it's guaranteed to be better than the sack stuff and a lot less expensive.

ARTIFICIAL MANURE
3 yards of leaves or compost mix
100 pounds of cottonseed hulls
100 pounds of cottonseed meal
100 pounds rough cut alfalfa me al
50 pounds bone meal
50 pounds fish meal

All of the ingredients (except the leaves from your trees) can be bought at your local feed store. Use any area suitable for composting, maybe the spot where you grew vegetables last year. Pile the leaves, clippings, compost or what have you about 2 feet deep to conserve heat. Add the ingredients a little at a time and turn with a garden fork. Moisten LIGHTLY and turn every few days. Cover with plastic for faster results. If all is working well, a sharp ammonia odor will escape as you stir. If you make a mistake, a different smell (dead) will not only escape but fill the neighborhood. It probably means that the cottonseed meal got too wet (it turns into a slime) or that you do not have enough coarse organic material. In 3 weeks you'll have the best organic fertilizer made. Cold winter weather will stop the process; in the spring use 2 good garden shovels of mix per bush as a starter. If you're a manure gourmet, add some trace materials such as seaweed, rock phosphate or decomposed granite. You'll want to be first on your block with such a distinction.

Stumbled into some rather useless information the other day but thought it might be worth passing on. We have all heard about chelated minerals that are supposed to work immediate miracles. "Chelated" usually meant to me that the stuff was going to be expensive. The word "chelate" comes from the Greek word for claw, especially the claw of a crustacean, like a lobster. In fertilizer terms, this claw becomes a ring around a central metallic ion held in a sort of coordination complex. To you and me, it means that the chelate structure makes the mineral more readily available to the feeder roots. You might say that the ring protects and unlocks at the same time. Don't try to discuss chelates with your chemist friends, but use chelates when you need quick and reliable action.

I hope this is YOUR year for a "Satellite" garden... that is a garden of roses away from home that you plan, plant and care for just like your own. You'll be surprised how rewarding this off-premises garden can be, making new friends for roses and more room for your own rose experiences. There's plenty of unclaimed territory for such efforts... a vacant lot close by, an elderly neighbor's yard, a church, a home for senior citizens or a school. Get the interest and cooperation of someone at the site. Set realistic goals. These roses are not for show competition. The admirer of a "rose satellite" doesn't know a split center from a sepal. But he does know that this is a big improvement over bare lawn and sick bushes.

Once the beds are built, a few hours a week will do the trick, and I'm speaking from experience. A hose-on sprayer works fine, overhead watering (set and forget type) is good, edging for the beds saves time weeding. Rosesbushes are easy to come by. A local nurseryman will usually help. Plant inexpensive off-patent varieties. With some common sense and a little sweat, $100 will plant and maintain a fair-sized garden for a year. A good start might be a bed of 25 'Valentine' roses adding color to the lawn at church with an accenting planting of 'Summer Snow' for interest. I like masses of Floribundas best for public plantings; but use your own imagination. Make 1974 YOUR year to feel good with roses.

There's no such thing as a dormant rosarian, even at the end the rose year. If there's a "hot stove" league for baseball fans, there must be "compost committee" meetings to keep rosarians busy, as these columns get rose problems well after the rose cones are covered with snow. Sharing some of these thorny questions here may fuel your "compost committee" discussions while waiting for the snow to melt.

Dear Rosarian: Where do you recommend I buy roses?

That's a tough question, and the wrong answer can lose a lot of friends (and readers). I have always recommended that rosarians, serous and not-so-serious, buy only Number 1 bushes from reputable nurserymen who specialize in roses or who handle enough roses to know what it's all about. Packaged roses in the grocery story are a waste of time and money if you want really good blooms. There are many good rose growers throughout the country who describe their products well, take care in packaging and stand behind their sales. They may grow in Ohio, Pennsylvania, Texas, California or Oregon (or even Canada). They have one thing in common: they want rosarians to be happy and order more bushes next season.

Can you tell me what I should plant?

Not unless you tell me what you expect to get from your garden. What I consider to be a great rose may not appeal to you at all, or may not grow well for you. You may be looking for lots of cut flowers in the house; your fellow-rosarian may be interest in Queen of the Show. Every rosarian has a list of favorites, and usually likes to talk about them. Rose people have many sources of information; the handbook for Selecting Roses is a good place to start. ARS also provides a great service with the *American Rose Annual*. Many rose societies also publish regional Proof-of-the-Pudding reports. If your group isn't doing something like this, get them going. It's one of the best services they can perform. Also makes an excellent topic for a winter program. I like a workshop style program in which comments and suggestions from many growers can be combined for the benefit of all.

Rambler, do you prefer bare root or potted roses?

I'll take bare root roses every time, because I like to see the root systems I am planting. If bare root roses have been properly stored and shipped, you'll probably be happier with the results. The nurseryman pots roses for the convenience of the gardener and also to protect his investment. He cannot hold a bare root rose any length of time. Most rose pots are too small and the bushes are carelessly pruned and planted. The gardener already has plenty of dirt; he wants to buy a good rosebush. See what your are getting; if at all possible. When I do have to buy a potted rose (or if I have had to pot a bush to hold it), I replant the rose in much the same way a bare root bush is handled. This can be dangerous late in the season, but still works best most of the time.

Are California grown roses better than Texas grown?

That's a loaded question to ask a Texan (even a transplanted one from Colorado). In my opinion, a good Texas grower can turn out just as good a bush as a good California grower. I can't see any difference in performance in my own garden. A better test might be the Houston Rose Garden planted some 10 years ago with roses from both major growing areas. Some 3000 bushes were involved, about 150 varieties. By mid-season, even the most experienced rosarian could not distinguish between California and Texas-grown plants. Some beds had plants of the same variety from both areas. For all practical purposes, performance was identical. It makes much more sense to look into who you buy from rather than where you buy roses.

Doesn't overhead watering give you a lot of blackspot?

No, not at all. In fact, I believe that overhead watering is good for roses, provided that the watering program calls for deep soaking. A regular fungicide program gives a rosarian all the protection he will ever nee. The secret is, and always has been, regular schedule, good coverage and an early start on a spray program. Obviously a rosarian does not water overhead and risk water spots on blooms just before a show. But most of the time, watering with an everyday lawn sprinkler is as convenient and effective as any method yet devised.

I have a very small garden. Can a hose-on sprayer doe the job?

A hose-on sprayer (*Hayes* or what have you)

can not only do the job, but do it very well. It's convenient, fast, cheap and effective. Although a hose-on does waste some materials and perhaps adds to the overall insecticide problem, it is the answer for many gardeners. I have cared for a 250-bush garden in Houston for 2 years using a hose-on exclusively, with no blackspot or mildew. Also no spider mites (overhead watering). This kind of convenience made the garden possible.

Howard Walters with Dr. R. C. Allen in 1974.

How about a couple of rose resolutions for 1974?? Roses are hardly any fun unless there are some rules to break, so try out your will power on some of these...

THIS ROSARIAN RESOLUTELY RESOLVES TO:

1. Spray on schedule in spite of fishing trips
2. Show restraint in reading of rose catalogs
3. Order only 10 bushes more than the garden will hold
4. Save money by ordering three of a kind
5. Refrain from telling Queen of Show story again
6. Turn away from miracle rose cures
7. Let weatherman handle rainfall without help
8. Consider bugs as part of nature's balance
9. Permit limited cutting of roses for the house
10. Come in from garden for supper on time
11. Let roses grow without swearing
12. USE SOME COMMON ROSE SENSE

Now that we're off to a good start with roses, try on this first-of-the-year project for size. It's time to plan your spray schedule. For those of you with frozen ground and blowing snow, this may sound ridiculous, but many sections will soon be starting a new rose year. Fungus control is a matter of prevention. Field trials and the experiences of growers in gardens just like yours show that a fungus control program must start IMMEDIATELY after pruning, drenching the canes and bud union thoroughly. Use a broad spectrum insecticide (*Diazinon* is a good one) combined with your favorite fungicide (*Benlate, Phaltan, Manzate*). Use both at full strength and add a spreader-sticker to encourage penetration into the cracks and crevices of the bud union and older canes. The whole idea is to control over-wintering spores on the canes BEFORE temperature and humidity are right for growth of these organisms. An insecticide-fungicide combination is generally more effective than an oil-sulfur combination, and less likely to burn. Don't wait for new leaves to appear. Prune and spray the same day; spray again in two weeks with the same combination. Then follow usual program REGULARLY. And don't forget to spray the climbers and shrub roses at the same time. An in-fected host plant can spread blackspot spores like wildfire when conditions are right. A CLEAN start will go a long way toward a clean garden season-long.

If you are still building a new rose bed, don't forget that a raised bed has more good things going for it than lawn-level plantings. Drainage, aeration, fertilization and ease of maintenance are greatly improved with elevated beds. For a fast layout, concrete blocks are good, especially the 4-in. thick cinder block kind with air space in the center. They are easy to lay and need no foundation. An L-shaped concrete curb is available in this part of the country and is very popular. The "foot" part of the L curb makes a good path for the lawnmower wheel. Creeping grasses find it hard to jump.

If you are good with bricks, a vertical row of bricks with squashed mortar is attractive. For an extra touch, run a course lengthwise at lawn level for a neat edge and guide for the lawnmower. A tamped footing of sand is usually enough foundation. Lay the bricks in about 3-ft. sections and leave a half-inch crack for drainage. If you need to tie in the whole brick edging, allow several good weep holes so that excess water can drain freely.

If you run into a bargain on redwood or western cedar, these materials make a very handsome edging for rose beds. Both are easy to use and last indefinitely. Two-inch material is the most stable, although 1-in. works all right. I prefer a height of from six to eight inches for built up beds, as we average 80 or more inches of rain per year, usually in 4-in. downpours. Drier areas can use less buildup and still get good results.

Ever thought about having a rose tour in VERY early spring? If rose pruning demonstrations are useful, how about some demonstrations on planting and layout and early season care? It seems to me that this is the place we can help more novice rosarians rather than offering free (and non-tiring) advice on the problem later in the year. It's very hard to duplicate yard conditions for a demonstration during a rose society meeting. Some advance planning by the program chairman can help many beginners.

For a fun project in '74, make up a "How to Grow Roses" giveaway sheet with some specific information for your area. The hardest part of the job is keeping the advice SIMPLE and EASY. Roses ought to be fun, and they can be. Novices drop like 61ackspot leaves when advice gets complicated by "experts". If you would like a starter sheet to use for a guide, drop me a card and ask for "How To Grow Roses In Houston". It is now in its fifth printing totaling some 40,000 copies. It's a cheap and easy way to reach gardeners who can turn into rosarians.

FEB.
1974

THOUGHT FOR THE MONTH: When offering suggestions, Keep them soft and sweet.
You never know from day to day Which words you'll have to eat.

Looking at the world through rose-colored glasses is a good February pastime. For one thing, it makes the snow look warmer; and even the rose cones hold a promise of better things to come this season. Mid-winter can be a fun time for roses because the really hard work is yet to come... I've never known a rosarian to wear out looking at rose catalogs. But if your eyes are tired from catalog overkill, try out a couple of items...

Every rosarian likes to plant new bushes, and most think that they do the job fairly well. But if rosebushes could talk, some sad tales of mishandling and sick soil would surely be told. We've all heard the old saying about "Never plant a $5 bush in a 50 cent hole" Maybe we just forgot that "nothing in rose growing pays off like a well-prepared rose bed." A few extra hours of spade work in the spring (or winter) saves sweat-producing labor in the summer. Check with some local rosarians for their favorite formulas and get out the fork and shovel. New bed or old, follow the formula.

If it is an existing bed, take up the old bushes and heel in or put in cold storage until the soil can be worked over. In our mild climate where roses seldom become really dormant, a good practice is to dig and prune bushes in January, pack with moist sphagnum moss, wrap in heavy plastic, box and place in a cold storage warehouse. Store about 35 degrees. Cold storage for up to about 100 bushes will cost about $10 for a month, provided that the bushes are pruned and compact. If you live in a mild climate, make SURE that the bushes are not in active growth and show definite signs of dormancy. Remember that growing practices affect dormancy almost as much as weather. Late fertilizing is a common mistake. Even cutting spent blooms encourages new growth. If you tried for late blooms, don't try to store.

I attempted to store a number of roses last season that were not in dormancy. The results were disastrous. Only about 5 bushes out of 100 survived storage. The effect was the same as exposing fresh, green growth to sudden cold. Dormant storage is still a good idea, if used with common sense. Roses properly stored bud out and grow with a vigor that has to been seen to be believed. And for some reason, apparently known only to roses, transplanted bushes often take a new lease on life and perform better than ever.

Another suggestion that may sound like insanity to growers in the north is to plant new roses this year with the bud unions well above bed level, NOT buried as is the common practice. Extensive field trials, experiment stations and home garden test report more vigorous bushes, better production of basal breaks and no appreciable difference in winterkill provided winter protection is given. Note that the last statement... PROVIDED that winter protection is given. Most cold climate rosarians add winter protection as a matter of good growing practice to save as much as cane as possible. Give this suggestion your own field trial with some bushes this year. Compare bush results. Provide some extra winter cover (there are lots of good ways) and you'll be pleasantly surprised that roses do not have to be buried to survive.

There are all kinds of myths and old rosarian tales about planting roses. Fortunately most of them aren't true. Some oldtimers maintain that a grower must "stomp" on the roots during planting to "get rid of the air". It gets rid of the air and breaks the roots and compacts the soil so tight that water and air (both essential to soil processes) don't have a chance. The best planting tool is PLENTY of water. Using the pyramid technique in the hole to support the root system properly, add some soil and gently fill in around the roots. With the hose running at a slow trickle, thoroughly soak the entire root system and soil, then add more soil and repeat the process. Keep your feet OUT of the hole... if you are planting properly you'll just get your boots full of mud. I usually soak one newly planted bush while digging and planting the next one; then move the hose while backfilling. An expression commonly used around here is to "mud" roses in; that is to have the whole bed area deeply soaked after planting.

Make sure that the bush is planted high enough to leave room for mulch later on. Roses will invariably sink a bit as the beds settle. Allow for this in the beginning. Cover the bud union and several inches of cane with soil or mulch (maybe a combination of both) when planting. Conserve moisture in the canes and protect new buds from sudden drops in temperature. As new buds start and weather moderates, gradually remove the mound so that sunshine can get to the bud union. Don't probe with a fork or stick; gradually wash off the cover with a stream from the hose. It's gentle and helps keep the bed moist too. Water and sun are your best friends in the springtime-or anytime. Use them.

Rosarians need to be on the alert for a now-dormant virus that's certain to infect most gardens during the next 30 days or so. It's near-epidemic on the Gulf Coast now and will move north with warm weather. Called Springtime Rose Fever, it sets in with housecleaning side effects and lingers until the resident rosarian has definitely broken dormancy. Only known eradicant is to get outdoors and work in the roses again... and here are some ways to begin...

Speaking of dormancy, here's a good way to break dormancy on a bare root rose that may have dried out in shipment. Lightly prune the bush according to your taste and soak in water or root activator solution at least overnight. When ready to plant, make up a loose-fitting hood or cover of medium weight plastic material, securing the edges of the plastic with staples so that the hood closes rather securely around the shank of the bush. If you want a little extra humidity, add a handful of wet sphagnum moss inside the bag. Plant the bush as usual, "mud" the roots in, and be sure to keep the planting area well soaked for the next two weeks. After the first warm day of sunshine, you'll see condensed moisture inside the plastic. Leave the hood in place for the next week or 10 days, or until the bush is well budded out. Then gradually cut some air holes in the plastic to reduce the temperature. Take the hood off when strong shoots and leaves begin to appear. This plastic "hot cap" also works for tree roses: Make sure some wet moss is added to a tree rose hood. They will be off to the best start ever; in fact, I always start a tree rose this way and have never had a failure.

For you folks in the north who are still pruning (assuming that there is something left to prune), make painting new cuts a little easier with this simple suggestion. Use some shellac in an old liquid shoe polish bottle. The dauber gives a good neat coverage of the material and is very convenient. In our area, shellac or even Elmer's Glue seems to work better than the asphalt tree paints. I like to paint the end of any cane larger than my thumb, and all cuts made at the bud union. If you are cutting large, woody canes, be sure to use a small keyhole saw rather than the crushing blade of a lopper. The cut will heal faster, particularly around the bud union.

Another good idea is to clean up the bud union, either above or below the ground level. Trim off the old cane stubs so that the bud union can heal and rejuvenate itself. Be careful that in the cleaning process you don't damage new buds. A handy cleaning tool that's safe and readily available is a short length of rose cane about as big around as your little finger. Use the cut end of the cane like a wood rasp and knock off the old corky bark and expose stubs that need more trimming. A clean bud union exposed to the warmth of the sun will reward you with many more basal breaks... and eventually more bush and better roses. Your rose society may need to break out for spring, too. As a starter, set up a schedule and a couple of workers to have a small rose show at the monthly meetings. Many societies do this very successfully. The old-timers as well as the newcomers enjoy it and it adds some color and flair so often missing at our meetings. A good small show is proof of accomplishment in our rose growing efforts. Around here, the competition is called the Six-Pack Show, because the entries are usually carried in your favorite beverage carrier. It's also wise to limit exhibitors to six or eight entries; make the exhibitor judge his own roses before he brings them. Use standard ARS rules; award points so that a winner for the evening can be declared, and an accumulated total can be the basis for a major award at the end of the season. Talk about competition; growers who never enter a regular show will come in with outstanding blooms. To my way of thinking, that's what this rose hobby business is all about. I have some copies of an excellent show schedule and rules for small shows; I'll be glad to send you a copy. The activity might be just the thing to get your group alive and growing this year. Spring is also a good time for a dose of salts for your established roses. Of course, I mean Epsom Salts (really magnesium sulfate), which can do more for roses than for rosarians. Used with discretion, magnesium sulfate will promote basal breaks and encourage production of green, healthy leaves. It's most effective when an alkaline condition exists in the rose bed, but seems to do no harm even when an acid condition prevails. Available at most feed stores at about 15c per pound (or in bulk at the drug store), magnesium sulfate can be applied at a rate of about two ounces per bush broadcast around the root perimeter. Water in thoroughly; it is completely soluble. If the soil is deficient in magnesium, good and surprising things will happen. If the soil has sufficient magnesium, no harm will be done by this light application. Incidentally, the two-ounce medicine glass used for measuring sprays makes an excellent applicator... a great tool for the garden.

Eavesdropping near the coffee urn at a midwinter rose workshop, a visitor gets the idea that rose growing is largely a painstaking hobby — usually in the small of the back. A rosarian in another think session was overheard saying that another of life's rose ironies is to have house cleaning, gardening and spring fever all come at the same time. Anyway, it's plain to see that rose folks are having a good time at these sessions... learning and telling rose stories at the same time. These April Ramblings pass on some of these rose cuttings (or are they spent blooms) from several of these sessions...

By the way, if your area is not sponsoring some workshop activities during the off months, you are missing some of the best events in the rose season. Some areas have all-day sessions with good speakers, demonstrations, panels, luncheons and what have you — almost like a small district meeting. Many others have pruning demonstrations or planting practices. Sponsoring groups around here easily make $100 or more just by getting the rose gals together for a covered dish luncheon and charging the participants a dollar or so each. Gets everyone involved.

During one pruning demonstration, a speaker advised beginners to keep the blade of the pruning shears DOWN because the anvil part of the shears bruises the cane. A questioner allowed that it didn't make any difference since the anvil was going to bruise regardless of its position... until a trial cut or two convinced him that the bruised portion occurred on the part of the cane to be thrown away.

You'll hear lots of talk about Miniatures at rose get-togethers. Apparently we are going to see more and more grown this year. Let's hope that Miniature growers (small roses, not small growers) and show chairmen remember that rose growing is supposed to be fun and not the makings of an argument. An easy way to accommodate Miniatures (and they are an important part of the show) is to set up a couple of trophies for Miniatures, including a Miniatures sweepstakes trophy. From what I hear, we'll see 'Windy City', 'Starglo', 'Magic Carrousel' and 'Toy Clown' on the winner's table this year. And don't overlook 'Over the Rainbow', 'Janna' and 'Mary Marshall' if you want to compete. I like all of them and have had good success

both in pots and in open beds.

Some societies are now adding a show class for Miniatures in pots. It's a very attractive section of the show and gets attention from all the visitors. Collections of Miniatures (5 specimen, 5 varieties or 3 reds, etc.) are popular; a Miniature English box class also draws exhibitors. Of course, set up separate classes for single specimen and spray exhibits. The attractiveness of Miniatures is very dependent on appropriate staging; multi-level shelves or a carrousel-shelf arrangement is very worthwhile. .

There's always talk about what roses will be winning this year. A promising entry is 'Toro'; every serious exhibitor seems to want a pair. 'White Masterpiece' gets some votes, looks like the best white exhibition type yet for hot climates. Didn't talk to a rosarian who hadn't ordered at least two 'Perfume Delight'. What it doesn't win on the show table it can surely win in the garden with its great fragrance and color. By the way, you serious exhibitors know already that to win you'll need at least two plants of a variety, preferably more. Another plus is the strong accent a pair makes in the landscape plan. 'Oldtimer' is popular now in the southwest, it opens well under dry conditions in spite of its size. 'Red Lion' is also appearing more often. In my opinion, a great show rose with rich color. A terrific, talked-about Floribunda for landscape, cutting or even drying is 'Apache Tears', I believe available only from Fred Edmunds. A favorite of mine is 'Leprechaun', a multi-color Floribunda from Kimbrew Roses that takes care of itself, makes a fabulous color display and is perfect for a landscape bedding rose. (A perfect rose?)

Every rosarian likes lists of roses; and at one meeting some pretty good (and experienced) rose judges and exhibitors were asked to name the IS best AARS roses introduced in the LAST 10 YEARS. After much discussion and switching votes (like politicians) here's the result (NOT in order of preference): Royal Highness, First Prize, Miss All American Beauty, Mister Lincoln, Granada, Europeana, Medallion, Gene Boerner, Tropicana, Apricot Nectar, Scarlet Knight, Electron, American Heritage, Aquarius and Angel Face. Another list of ALL TIME AARS winners added these old favorites (it seemed impossible to cull the group to IS winners): Sarabande, Queen Elizabeth, Tiffany, Chrysler Imperial, Peace and Ivory Fashion. Also in the running were 'Starfire', 'Fashion' and 'Duet'. Everyone in the workshop enjoyed the lively vote-casting and it proves again that there are lots of good roses available, even though the newest introductions catch most of the attention.

Finally, if you REALLY want to be with it in the rose world for '74, use roses in the landscape, out in front where people can enjoy their beauty. A mass of 'Europeana' along the drive will set you off as "the house with the beautiful roses all the time". It's a great way to live.

Leafing through the catalogs and horticulture magazines, it's interesting to note that common sense is about the only thing not being advertised. Just a small "trial packet" of this miracle ingredient would fill our gardens with flowers. Some plain dirt gardening can put the fun back into roses, and that's what it is all about. When we convince ourselves that roses are easy and fun (and then tell others), we won't be able to handle all of the applications for our rose societies. They'll all want to be there showing off their roses.

You might want to show off your common sense with a formula for "liquid compost". This is more commonly known as "cow tea". Remember how the really good old gardeners always had a barrel or two of tea steeping behind the garage? It was a good practice then, and still is. Roses (and most other plants) just jump out of the ground with an application or two of tea. Besides, it's cheap and easy to brew. Plastic garbage cans are good; keep two or three brewing in various stages to have a constant supply. Onion, potato or two sacks make good tea bags; fill with six or eight dried cow chunks and tie with a long piece of wire or rope. This is where the common sense comes in — the tie needs to be long enough to hang outside the barrel. Steep in a barrelful of water for about 10 days, sloshing the bag around once in a while. Use about two gallons of tea per bush for really great results. One tea bag is good for about two brews. Dried chunks are best; dehydrated, sterilized stuff from bags is something like instant coffee-it just isn't the real thing. Try it; your roses will like it.

Here's a common sense way to use an old garbage can as a composter. It's good for the city gardener because even the smallest homesite can use it. If you have room for a 20-gal. garbage can in your back yard, you've got it made. Here's how: cut out the bottom of a large garbage can (a can that's rusting out and needs replacing will do just fine). Get an out-of-the-way spot and spade up an area the width of the can. Work the can a few inches into the soil until it is firmly in place. Make sure it has a tight-fitting lid. Now you're ready to go.

Whenever you have kitchen garbage, dump into the composter and sprinkle a little dirt over the new entries. Stir the compost about once a week and add just enough water to keep the mixture moist. When it appears that the container is full, let the batch rest a week or so, check the can, and you'll find that there's room for more. The compost you make has just about everything a plant can use-and depending on your table, you'll soon have 20 gallons of potting soil or soil conditioner that's better than anything you can buy.

Don't throw away old coffee cans. They're good for much more than holding nails and stuff in the garage. Use the cans for rain and irrigating gauges so that you'll always know just how much water the rose beds are getting. Good for lawn care, too. Set the cans in the beds, turn on the hose, and when the cans have an inch or so of water in them, turn the hose off. Like the old gardener says, "Soak, don't sprinkle."

Want to be a smart gardener? Label roses and other plants and become an instant expert. A good labeling system adds pleasure for garden visitors, and a grower unconsciously becomes better acquainted with his cultivars through constant repetition. A good rose label is inexpensive; *Harlane* is excellent and attractive, and *Everlast* makes a fine label with a wire stake (both are advertised in this magazine). I use both and can recommend either. The *Harlane* is complete and ready to go (and also costs a little more). *Everlast* can be printed with a weatherproof crayon, but I like to apply a "*Dymotype*" strip to the blank plate. The tape sticks well and is good for one season. Then peel off and apply a new one. It's also a good idea to print the year each cultivar is planted on the back of the label. It helps when trying' to decide which roses to replace. Other plants can use the same system. Surprise your friends with a storehouse of garden information... read the label first.

Another good tip for novice or pro is as simple as shaking a bottle. To get a wettable powder like *Phaltan, Manzate* or *Benlate* into solution without lumps, measure the powder into a large dry jar (with a tight lid), add HOT water and swirl or shake a couple of times. No more lumps or straining. Makes a good mix every time. Insecticides with a petroleum distillate base should be added after the powders are in solution, then add spreader-sticker if needed. With a clear glass jar the rosarian can check the compatibility of the ingredients before pouring in to the sprayer. One last, cheap suggestion: use a small medicine glass to measure spray materials. Most garden shops have them for about 25c each, with easy-to-read markings for teaspoons, tablespoons and ounces.

OPINION... The man who never changes his mind never corrects his mistakes. And that's what this Rambling is all about: some ideas and opinions you may want to explore in your own garden.

THRIPS AND *CYGON 2E*... *Cygon 2E* still seems to be the best pre-show control for thrips. Although some *Cygon*-fungicide combinations may cause leaf and cane damage, *Cygon* used alone is safe and effective. When spraying for thrips, remember that the entire bush does NOT have to be drenched for control. Use alone with water (no spreader-sticker) at two teaspoons per gallon and lightly mist the bloom and bud areas two or three times a week when the thrips migration is on. For spot control, mix up a small amount of FRESH *Cygon* and spray selected buds with a *Windex*-type sprayer. Begin control before the sepals come down. Properly used, *Cygon* will not damage even the light-colored blooms and will definitely control thrips. Leftover spray should be used on thrip host plants like lilies, iris and gladioli.

BENLATE... Since this boon for rosarians is still cussed and discussed any time rose folks get together, here's a timely report from Texas Rose Research Foundation Trial Notes March 1974, written by Dr. E. W. Lyle, Plant Pathologist:

"Certain reports have come to our attention that the fungicide *Benlate* might not be as effective now as when first introduced. Our results are contrary to that; and again in the 1973 season it was evident that good control of black spot on roses could be obtained with *Benlate* (1/2 tablespoon per gallon), if the spray treatments were made every seven days. This was true even with untreated check plants severely infected with black spot and powdery mildew next to those sprayed with *Benlate*. There were thirty applications of *Benlate* during the season, showing the safety of weekly spraying even during the summer months, as well as the overall effectiveness of this fungicide.

"Again, *Phaltan* and *Manzate* sprays had a longer residual action, holding the foliage into January, 1974 while the *Benlate* treated plants began to defoliate soon after discontinuing spraying on November 7, 1973. The main variety was the rose Else Poulsen. Demonstration trials of mixtures of *Benlate* with either *Phaltan* or *Manzate* for use in the cool weather of spring and fall have shown advantage without the risk of burn during the hot summer months."

WETTABLE MALATHION... This may be the answer for a safe insecticide for use with *Benlate*. Most parts of the country have a formulator who supplies 25WP Malathion, although it may be available only in bulk quantities. A 20-lb. package can be split for use by several rosarians during the season. Application of 1 tbsp. per gallon is safe and effective even during hot weather. It mixes well and is definitely compatible with *Benlate* and a bio-degradable spreader-sticker. Trials in this area have shown no leaf or cane damage and good control of aphids, thrips and other common chewing-sucking insects. Ecologically speaking, Malathion is an acceptable product widely used as a mosquito spray and in general agriculture. It is one of the safer sprays for home use. Of course, use an insecticide ONLY when specifically needed. Don't add insecticide to regular fungicide control when no problem exists. Maintain natural predator control whenever you can.

SAFELY DISPOSE OF OLD SPRAY MATERIALS... Do this before the rose season is one day older. Many materials lose effectiveness with age or will give some most unexpected results. If you have old, uncertain materials, discard immediately in a safe manner. Read the instructions on the container. A few dollars worth of old spray is certainly not worth risking a rose garden.

A NEW TROPHY IDEA... An unusual trophy now being offered in the South Central District is the ACHING BACK TROPHY, open to "senior" exhibitors over 60 years old. They compete in a class for two exhibition roses in one vase. The rules are simple: anyone attaining a seniority of 60 or over any time during the year can enter the fun for a sterling serving bowl. "Red" Huff of San Antonio came up with this idea ... but failed to win it himself the first time.

HOW ABOUT ROSEBUSHES... instead of the usual small silver keeper awards? Exhibitors really go for certificates good for two rosebushes of THEIR CHOICE for delivery the following season. This seems more appropriate than silver knickknacks that need polishing, take up shelf space and eventually wind up in the closet. Besides, the price of silver makes such awards almost prohibitive these days. You can probably work out some special arrangements with a local rose supplier. Everyone wins. The rose supplier likes the business and the winner likes a practical award for a change. Those not so fortunate at the show table get to see some more good roses grown.

JUL. 1974	*No column printed this month.*

These rambling columns have, from time to time, offered some rather good advice on roses. And none was better than the common sense approach to growing roses; let the "miracle" products endure a critical trial before upsetting a home gardener's routine. Followed my own advice for a change last year, producing more and better roses with less work. Roses will just naturally grow if we don't interfere too much.

For example, a "natural" organic approach can make living easy and roses beautiful if used with a little, common sense. As any rosarian knows, the advocates of organic vs. inorganic gardening can raise the temperature of a rose society meeting in a matter of minutes as each side crusades to defeat the opposition once and for all. This is costly in roses and foolish, as both points of view have merit. You'll enjoy really fine roses by using the best from both schools. Fertilization is a good example. Good organic materials in a properly prepared rose bed will help any grower produce good roses consistently. Composts, manure, cottonseed meal, rock phosphate and so on will help soil achieve a good working balance; and the stability and results last year after year.

On the other hand, inorganics from the chemist's workshop can correct a deficiency, strengthen new growth or provide a nitrogen boost needed in the spring. A deficiency in iron is easy to correct with the chelates now available; it's a much slower process organically. What's the point in passing up all those good roses in the meantime? Take the best from both schools,

Mulching materials and their benefits have also been argued for years. You have visited fine gardens which used mulch; and equally good gardens that had no r1mlch at all. Harold Weaver's prize-winning garden is an excellent example of fine roses consistently... and no mulch. Frank Benardella uses a "water and scratch" system to keep the soil loose and aerated. But unless you happen to be blessed with that "perfect" soil and have everything going for you with water, drainage, aeration, humus balance and what have you, a good rose bed mulch is a natural asset for good rose culture.

Consider what a good mulch is supposed to do in deciding what material to use. A mulch should let air and water through freely, should not pack, decompose slowly, add humus to the soil, have a pleasing appearance, not harbor bugs and generally provide a good soil insulation to keep the soil and feeder roots cool and moisture level high. This is a good sized order, but one that many mulch materials can fill. Usually, a combination of materials is more effective than just one. For example, pine needles, shredded pine bark and partially composted leaves work better than anyone used alone. A shredder that chops up all kinds of organic matter is the best of all. Oak leaves and some kind of coarse bark and woody material are good. Samuel Grande Park in Dallas uses about four inches of wood chips throughout their extensive rose plantings, using the product of their tree chipper for garden paths as well. The garden is attractive, weed-free and growing vigorously.

Favorite mulches along the Gulf Coast are medium-coarse pine bark mulch, a former "waste" product from paper production; and bagasse (sugar cane pulp), a leftover from sugar mills. Redwood bark chips are also growing in popularity. If you are going to use a mulch, use enough to do some good. Use a minimum of two or three inches of your favorite material to enjoy all the good things that can happen to the soil and soil processes. An old rosarian I admire greatly quips that a good mulch is worth its weight in gold... and in roses. Weigh some out for yourself this season.

Rose feeding should also come naturally. While roses are heavy feeders, they respond best to frequent, light feedings rather than massive fertilization. An overdose of rose food might be compared to the Thanksgiving dinner of the rosarian... both of them are going to be under the weather for a while until nature takes its course. Whatever your favorite formula is, try half the quantity twice as often. You'll get more blooms for the money. And don't forget to WATER, WATER, WATER. The best soils and fertilizers can't do a bit of good until available to the plant in solution. Light sprinkling is wasteful; deep soaking is best. If a rose bed is well constructed and has good drainage, it's almost impossible to overwater. Depending on the soil and the temperature, roses need about two inches per week. Don't guess that a summer shower soaked the roses, consult a reliable rain gauge. If you are watering overhead, set the rain gauge within the irrigated area and check the water actually getting to the roses. A cheap way of measuring is to set several coffee cans in the bed area to be watered and check the amount of water they catch.

SEPT. 1974

THOUGHT FOR THE MONTH:
Some people die rich, others live rich. It's a good thing that rosarians know the difference.

Having a terrific rose year... modestly noting that the Rambler's roses are bigger, better, more productive and vigorous-just plain more enjoyable-than they have been in years. But there's a problem in every garden; mine happens to be that I don't know why the roses are so much better. This may sound like looking for something to worry about; wouldn't it be great to know if some kind of green key opened up this great box of roses? A few new touches have been added this past year... an under-mulch soaker hose system, heavy organic feeding (artificial manure) early in the season, a shovelful of sewage sludge per bush after the first bloomout, a "snack" of organic food between regular feedings, only occasional use of insecticide... or maybe it's less concern with pruning, grooming, pulling and generally bothering the bushes all the time. Choose any reason you like ... I'll take the results because it's all part of the fun of growing roses.

Common sense is probably the best rose formula... and this applies to insect control for most growers. Keep the bushes healthy and vigorous with good growing practices and give up a few blooms to the bugs once in a while. A few aphids and thrips are not worth contaminating the whole garden with broad spectrum insecticides. Kill off the natural predators and you'll have an even greater insect problem. This is especially true of the "kill-everything" sprays that some overeager rosarians use to fight spider mites. Obviously, when showtime arrives or a particular insect persists, spray with a SPECIFIC insecticide for the problem, using only that amount of material absolutely necessary.

And how about some restraint in what we do for Miniatures? These little beauties can tolerate almost everything except the rosarian. For the most part we overfeed, overspray and generally fuss over Miniatures until it is a wonder they grow at all. Give Miniatures a VERY LIGHT feeding every two weeks or so; availability and regularity are the keys to success. And don't drown Miniature plants with spray. More leaves have been knocked off with spray than by spider mites and blackspot combined. Miniatures can also be grown in the same beds as the big roses... a good example is Rose Hills in California... put out fertilizer on a square footage basis; Miniatures occupy fewer square feet, therefore get less fertilizer. And unless you just have a lot of time to waste, meticulous grooming and trimming won't produce better Miniature blooms than a hedge-shears approach. If I have upset your favorite practice, sorry about that... but it works for me.

Enjoyed the "plants can't tell the difference" during the discussion of organic gardening at the ARS. Albuquerque meeting, referring to the desirability of chemical nutrients vs. nutrients from organic sources. Again, common rose sense will grow the best roses. Nutrients are absorbed the same way, regardless of source. Nature just works a little harder to make foods available organically. But' keep in mind that organic matter plays four important roles in the soil: as a direct plant nutrient, as a nutrient for micro-organisms, as a soil structure and as a water reservoir. Animal manures, green manures and crop residues make these good things in the soil possible. Try it, you and your roses will like it.

As it is for the sports fan, there's always next year for the rose grower. You'll be getting some winners if you grow a few of these... 'Alec's Red' is a must, one of the most brilliant, eye-catching colors in a long time; 'Red Lion' and 'Norman Hartnell' are championship types, as evidenced by Harold Weaver's sweep of the major trophies at Albuquerque; 'Toro' or 'Uncle Joe' is/are also essential if you are a serious exhibitor. I don't know if it is the same rose or not, and I don't care. This kind of red beauty belongs in every garden.

Also get a couple of plants of 'Peach Beauty', exquisite form and lovely color like a ripe Alberta peach. It's a color every hybridizer is talking about and introducing. They are also excited over "orange-pink". 'Nantucket' is a fine peach blend HT; 'Twinkie' is a peach-pink Miniature that has a good many uses in the garden. Good Floribundas are 'Cupid's Charm', a delicate pink blend, and 'Jolly Good', a happy pink that blooms all the time in mass plantings. 'Lemon Sherbet', just like its name, is delicious. And watch for 'Benjamin Franklin', a profuse blooming pink HT; 'Angel Girl', orange-pink HT with real class. To catch your visual imagination get 'Summer Wine', bright pink HT, or 'Red Reflection', a brilliant color with facets like a diamond. Buy 'em all if you can. Just save a few dollars for some more good ones yet to come.

Looking through my extensive technical library (mostly odds and ends of junk) for something new and exciting for you anxious rosarians, it struck me that the old time religion of rose growing probably worked the best after all. Remember when a "feeding schedule" amounted to nothing more than a couple of shovelfuls of manure in the spring and maybe a little more in the summer if it wasn't too hot to haul it? The watering system came from the sky or from the hose stuck in a tin can and laid in the rose garden. Rose gardens even smelled better then-I suspect we didn't mask the fragrance with sprays of all kinds. Winter protection was easier then, too. All of the leaves that fell from the trees were piled into the rose bed to be reduced to the world's best compost by spring. Snow and sun did their jobs in a natural way, and the roses were just naturally better. This is not to suggest that we throw away our sprayers, but that some old gardener approaches haven't worn out over the years.

An old idea that still works in modern gardens is the "strawberry pyramid" or barrel for Miniature roses. The strawberry box is usually associated with cascades of red strawberries or perhaps some ferns and rock garden flowers. The Minis thrive under these same conditions; and the design of the planter can be as modern as you want to make it. A simple method is to build a series of rectangular boxes each about a foot smaller than the previous box and fill the resulting pyramid with sandy garden soil liberally spiced with manure. Redwood or cedar make good construction materials; even old fence posts can be erected around a frame to make a rustic, multi-level box. Not long ago I saw a three-level Mini planting made from old railroad cross ties and bridge timbers. The effect was spectacular. Miniatures are very effective when used at levels other than around the lawn. If you are really old-fashioned, you might want to slip a few strawberry plants into the overall planting to furnish refreshment to the rosarian at his labors.

Another good planting idea uses cinder or cement blocks (the block with the five-inch square openings in the middle) set at random in a Miniature rose bed or planting to give the garden another dimension. Many of the smaller growing Miniatures do very well under these conditions, and are a lot cheaper than Minis on tree standards. Take care of the raw concrete look by painting or spraying the blocks with any color shingle stain, cut in half with petroleum solvent. The mixture soaks into the blocks like water into a sponge, leaving behind a soft patina of color. Work the blocks into the soil about three inches, then fill with good potting soil mixture and plant like any other pot. The blocks can be arranged into some interesting patterns and even moved around later if you are careful. These same blocks make good rose bed edges, too. Built-up beds work best in most areas, and this approach is fairly cheap and easy compared to laying bricks. Plant some Minis in the blocks along the edge, or add some color with portulaca, lobelia, or alyssum. This added touch brings out the beauty of roses without adding much to maintenance. Incidentally, as the demonstration gardens are developed at the American Rose Center, you'll see many uses of other flowers with roses in the landscape. The overall effect is colorful and finished.

If you have some leftover cinder blocks, build a compost pile by laying the blocks so that air space is horizontal. Air and the right balance of moisture are essential to a good compost pile. These blocks help provide both. You have probably noticed that most good gardens have a compost pile hidden away somewhere in the yard. Some are fancy production-line affairs; and others may simply be piles of clippings, dirt, and what-have-you. The results are the same when the compost gets to the rose bed (or strawberry box)... better aeration, better root growth, better bushes and, therefore, better blooms. No yard is too small. And if you use the old garbage can (no bottom, tight lid) technique, you can convert kitchen scraps, clippings, dirt and leftovers into the best plant food that nature can produce. It still beats anything you can buy in a sack or can.

And I have to pass on one other "old-fashioned" bit of rose fun that I was honored to participate in not long ago. It was called "Dr. Lyle Night" honoring our good friend Eldon Lyle and his gracious wife, Clara. The event was sponsored by the Golden Triangle Rose Society of Southeast Texas and attracted 100 rosarians from five states. I've attended District meetings with poorer attendance. About 500 good roses decorated the tables and a heap of 60 door prizes filled the end of the meeting room. The steaks were good (and cheap), the rose talk was sparkling, and the program nostalgic as Dr. Lyle shared photo reminiscences of rose people around the country. The fun ran over into the next day (Saturday) as the meeting adjourned to the beach for an all-day picnic, swim party and rose conference. More good rose information was swapped between barbeque, beans and trimmings than at most rose conferences. Who says that rose growing can't be fun??

For you reporters across the country, Dr. Lyle won the swimming contest with no close competition and was awarded an extra spray of sunburn lotion.

Whatever happened to the rose-growing season?? It seems like I was spring pruning just a few weeks ago. November is a good time to prune away at your list of roses for '75 — some of the old ones that aren't putting out much any more as well as a careful look at the "I've got to have that one" list that has accumulated over the season. Your own observation is good, but the observations of a good many growers are even better. Local ratings by all kinds of growers are best yet.

Which says again that a local or regional Proof of the Pudding is the most valuable information we can pass on to rose growers, old and new. A great rose society project might be to compile a "Performance Chart" of favorite and new cultivars in the area for all your members. Even if only 100 roses are rated, the chart will probably cover 90% of the roses grown in the area. Limiting the number of roses to be rated makes the job easier and gives a better chance for each rose to be rated by several individuals. A single rating has limited value; the mere ratings the better.

For better ratings, break away from the generalized A through D method used on the national level; rate the roses on a I to 10 scale instead. A graduated scale of points makes more sense to me. If you program chairmen are looking for "something interesting", try a Performance Chart workshop and follow up with a written recap available to all members. It's a great program and involves members who have never been seen or heard. Besides, it makes spring seem a little closer.

Along the same line, here's a tip of the gardener's cap to the Golden Triangle Rose Society of Southeast Texas. These well known busy rosarians have done it again by compiling a five-year tabulation of the top exhibition roses in the South Central District (1969-1973). These are the guys in the golden coveralls who put together the Top Roses in The United States article published annually in these pages. This time they compare district performance with national performance for the past five years; and they also record points received by various cultivars in spring vs fall shows. For example, they found that 'First Prize' is No.1 in the US and also No.1 in the district. As a show rose it does better in the fall. 'Royal Highness' is No.2 in the US, and No.5 in the South Central District.

Does much better in the spring. Anyway, this tabulation is a must for rosaholics who want to win at the shows. I'll send you a copy of the six-page report if you drop me a line.

And here's a repeat of the "Artificial Manure" formula that enjoyed some heady success around the country last year. The judges have virtually been able to smell out a winner. Pun-making aside, this mixture is far superior to the sanitized and dehydrated stuff that comes in a sack. Its nearest claim to manure is the cow picture on the front. This formula lets you have all the benefits without a cow or pitching hay. Guaranteed to be better and a lot less expensive.

ARTIFICIAL MANURE
3 ample yards of leaves or compost mix
100 lbs. of cottonseed hulls *(or something coarse)*
100 lbs. of cottonseed meal
100 lbs. rough-cut alfalfa meal
50 lbs. bone meal
50 lbs. fish meal

Your local feed store will probably have all of the ingredients except the leaves. Use any area OK for composting — maybe on top of the old vegetable bed. Pile the leaves and what-have-you about two feet deep to conserve heat. Add the ingredients a little at a time and turn with a garden fork. Moisten LIGHTLY and turn twice a week for about a month. Cover with plastic if you are in a hurry or if it gets very cold. When all is working well, a sharp ammonia odor will leak out. If the pile is too wet, a dead smell will crawl across the neighborhood. The reason-cottonseed meal that is too wet turns into a slime; or maybe you did not use enough coarse organic material. Cold weather can stop the process, but usually in about a month you'll have the best organic fertilizer available. In the spring, use two garden shovels of mix per bush as a starter. If you are a manure gourmet, you may want to add some other trace materials such as seaweed, rock phosphate or decomposed granite. Be the first on your block.

Also, for your wintertime reading pleasure, I'll share with you a new kind of show schedule that lets single bloom Hybrid Teas, Floribundas, Grandifloras, Flora-teas or what have you compete on an equal basis. Also multiple bloom HT, FL, GF, etc., cultivars compete with one another much to the delight of the viewing public. As an added extra, there's even an understandable (to me, anyway) explanation of what a rose show is all about, for the casual visitor or novice. If you want a copy, drop me a note... and promise to send me any comments you may have.

With snow on the ground and the rose year winding down, it seems a good time to check off some of the better rose ideas noted around the country. And it's an interesting sidelight to note that the casual gardener scores in this competition as often as the big show winner.

Here's a good one. A northern state rosarian with a tired back saw no reason to wheel tons of dirt from behind the garage each year to give his roses winter protection. And it was just as tiresome to wheel it back. Instead, the mound of dirt and humus was set up right in the middle of the rose garden, making a pile 18 inches high and covering an area of 4x20 feet. (He has a lot of roses.) In the summertime the mound is planted with petunias that perform with a blaze of color. When frost arrives the covering soil goes back to the rose beds. Simple... and easier.

Another rose grower saw no sense in trying to change the basic characteristics of the soil already there, so he decided to raise the rose beds and use the materials that he had on hand-composted manure and pine bark mulch. Raising the beds about 18 inches with cinder blocks, he filled with half manure and half mulch, alternately adding several inches of ingredients and then mixing with a tiller. Some leftover builder's sand was added for good measure, but no soil of any kind was used. When seen in early October, first-year bushes in the planting averaged over six feet, had six or more excellent new canes and were loaded with show-quality blooms. Foliage was perfect from bottom to top. Only one light feeding with fish emulsion was used. The mixture soaks up water like a sponge, but never seems wet. It is loose enough to easily run your fingers six inches deep into the bed. Common sense worked again. If you think this is a Texas-type story, stop by to see Joe and Charlotte Gould just north of Shreveport (he's our new ARS Treasurer) and see for yourself. It's a great demonstration of practical gardening.

Rosarians in Florida and along the Mississippi Gulf coast have also learned to use available materials. They have mostly sand, and it is estimated to reach China. No problem with drainage here. The problem was how to keep water and nutrients available in the root zone. Humus was added to the sand but the rose beds were not elevated. Fertilizer was added in the form of fish meal and even rough-cut trash fish were buried 18 inches away from the shank of the bush. A cylinder of soil was taken up with a tool something like a bulb planter and the hole filled with a half-cup of fish meal. Then the sand was replaced. Four or five perimeter feedings of this kind produced gigantic results-rosebushes of eight feet in a single season with eight or ten canes. The success seems to come from the concentration of food which released slowly and encouraged broad root growth. The interchange of water and air in the soil was perfectly balanced with organic nutrients. Simple.

A rose bed on the rainy Gulf Coast was plagued with poor drainage. The round bed, ten feet in diameter, was circled with a concrete walk. Efforts to build up the bed did not work. Finally the bed was dug out 18 inches and the soil laid aside. A two-inch drain tile was laid at a low point, covered with gravel, and run to a sump hole beyond the perimeter of the planting. Total drop of the drain line was" less than one foot. But one foot made all the difference in the growth of the roses. The same soil was replaced and the bed planted with 'Europeana'. The bushes are now five feet tall, very bushy and vigorous, and stay in continuous bloom. Two weeks of nearly continuous rain (18-20 inches) didn't produce a yellow leaf.

A rosarian in the temperate south needed to save a number of rosebushes that had been growing in peat pots for most of a season-gradually going downhill. The pots simply could not hold enough moisture during hot summer weather to support the bushes. Leaf burn chlorosis and poor growth resulted. When rose beds were finished in September, the bushes were knocked out of the pots, root pruned and severely top pruned. They were planted as bare root roses. Watering overhead several times each day until the bushes started, the grower approximated a misting propagation system. Within a month the bushes were growing again, throwing new basals and showing vigor nearly equal to plants fresh from storage. Pruning produced a false dormancy and started a new growth cycle. Less than ten percent of the planting was lost. Not bad for plants that were given up as hopeless.

JAN. 1975

THOUGHT FOR THE MONTH: If a rosarian were to enter the Garden of Eden, he would probably order fertilizers right away.

Looking back at this Rambler's Rose Resolutions for '74, one seems to be worth repeating: USE SOME COMMON ROSE SENSE. It's an ingredient a good many rosarians leave on the shelf in the garage as they apply secret potions and miracle cures to rosebushes already afflicted with "Sunday Syndrome". For the benefit of rose novices, "Sunday Syndrome" describes a rosebush worn out from pruning, grooming, pulling, pinching, feeding, scratching, watering, spraying and fussing... not necessarily in that order. Most rosebushes are relieved to see the rosarian go back to work on Monday morning. The symptoms commonly appear on Thursday of each week-yellow leaves, burned leaves, limp foliage and so on — only to go through another ordeal on Sunday. Since Common Rose Sense and Sunday Syndrome may well be present in the rose garden at the same time, this Rambler set out on a scientific research project in '74 that certainly will be a significant addition to rose literature. The trial notes are written on the wall in the tool house, on various bits of note paper in the spray cabinet, and are available for inspection by serious researchers.

On a positive note, it was discovered that half as much fertilizer applied twice as often worked much better than a heap of food all at once. A light feeding every two weeks produced better bushes and more blooms than a once-a-month schedule. Taking some liberties with the common sense resolution produced less favorable results. On the urging of an organic gardener, about 100 earthworms were added (at considerable expense and trouble) to a rose bed about five feet square. Nothing much happened to the roses, and digging in the area two months later showed no more earthworms than in untreated parts of the rose garden. Thinking about it later, it was obvious that the worms were introduced into an area not particularly high in humus and organic material. Apparently they either moved on to better organic pastures or died. A bed area about half compost was alive with worms and very well aerated. And new rosebushes were thriving.

Common sense tells us not to create a problem where none exists, but nagging suspicion of nematodes prompted planting some cantaloupe seeds to find out. Old-timers say that if nematodes are in the soil small cantaloupe plants will not develop and will show substantial evidence on the roots. The melons grew like weeds in the rose bed, bloomed and set fruit nearly overnight. Since it seemed like a waste to pull the melons, the vines were left for a while. Then the roses began to go downhill. A choice had to be made: ripening cantaloupes or roses. The roses won. It is now well established that cantaloupes and roses do not mix. Two feedings of *Ra-Pid-Gro* with a trace of *Epsom Salts* got the roses going again and the fear of nematodes was forgotten.

A local grower recommended a springtime addition of ordinary sugar (about a quarter-cup per bush) to rose beds to feed and encourage micro-organisms. The whole soil process was supposed to speed up. However, the fastest thing in the garden turned out to be flies, insects and tiny, hard-shelled beetles. So much for sugar, especially at today's prices.

Several sources of "stabilized micro-organisms" are on the market in this area and promise to "make dead soils alive again" and generally put billions of nature's microscopic workers on the side of the gardener. Some serious tests of three of these products produced no significant results. Roses in the check beds did just as well as bushes in beds treated according to directions. However, in all fairness to the formulators, the additives were used on rose beds already in excellent condition with good balance of humus, soil, air and water. Again, the rose bed with plenty of humus and manure produced the best roses more consistently than tighter soils or soils low in organic matter. Most rosarians would have to conclude that nature works best when given a good balance of air, friable soil and water.

Your best move for '75 is to plan a spray schedule NOW. Fungus control is a matter of prevention. Start a program IMMEDIATELY after pruning, drenching the canes and bud union thoroughly. Use a broad spectrum insecticide (*Diazinon* is a good one) combined with your favorite fungicide (*Benlate, Phaltan* or *Manzate*). Use at full strength and add a spreader-sticker to encourage penetration into the cracks and crevices of the bud union and older canes. The object is to control over-wintering spores on the canes BEFORE temperature and humidity are right for growth of these organisms. Do NOT wait for new leaves to appear. And don't forget to spray the climbers and shrub roses at the same time. An infected host plant can spread spores like wildfire when conditions are right. Prune and spray the same day; spray again in two weeks with the same combination. Then follow your regular spray program. A CLEAN start will go a long way toward a clean garden season-long.

FEB. 1975

No column printed this month.

Have you noticed that the snow looks better when seen through colored glasses? Warms the heart of the ice-bound rosarian to know that the promises of the rose catalogs will come true one of these days. So pull up a rose catalog and start making some plans for the season just ahead. Trophies are won by the serious rosarian in February and March. There's always something to look forward to and something to improve on.

Floribundas in the landscape plan should be on your winter list of things to do. So many really good Floribundas are on the market now that it's a real loss to beauty if they aren't used to add color, form and accent to the home landscape. This rambler thinks that Floribundas are used best when planted together to take advantage of their overall flower displays. A good-sized rose bed with nothing but Floribundas can produce more flowers and stay colorful longer than combinations of rose types. In warm sections of the country, landscapers use mass plantings of azaleas for dramatic effects-lots of color and shape. Their beauty lasts only a few weeks at most. Floribundas can produce the same effect-only better and longer. And it's another good reason for bringing roses out of the back yard and into the public areas where everyone can enjoy them.

Some plantings call for a half-dozen plants of the same variety, or even more. Other less formal beds can use three or four plants of one Floribunda to blend into a planting with other varieties of similar growth habits and colors. Contrasting colors can be very interesting (combine Summer Snow and Europeana), but have to be carefully used. Make up your own combinations of favorites, but use plenty of plants, plant close together, and bring rose color and impact into the open again.

Miniatures are also more effective when planted together. Somehow their appeal is lost to me when they are tucked in as an afterthought around the tall-growing Hybrid Teas. Some great effects can be created with accent beds, elevated beds, planters, pots, containers, baskets and what-have-you that are in scale with their diminutive growth habits. Although it seems that Miniatures are getting bigger and bigger all the time, even this can be used by a smart grower to add variety to his layout. The climbers and half-climbers can be very attrac-

tive. Minis in hanging baskets are fun, too. Candy Cane is one of the best; Cl. Baby Darling is also good. And I understand that a Cl. Baby Masquerade will soon be introduced. When I saw it, every bloom was covered with a gorgeous combination of yellow, orange and red-rose double flowers.

If you enjoy Minis, your Minis will enjoy blooming more for you if given a soil or potting combination that's just right for their fine root systems. The formula offered here is good for pots, tubs, boxes or elevated Miniature rose beds. In making up an elevated Mini bed, make sure that the top six or eight inches of good garden soil has been worked up and is loose and friable for good drainage. This recipe will make up enough mix for about 100 square feet of bed that's four to six inches above yard level. Some can also be set aside for pots and planters. Mix up the following:

Mini-Miracle Rose Bed Mix
1 bale Canadian peat moss (6 cu. ft. bale)
2 bags No.6 Perlite (4 cu. fl. bags)
3 bags Pine Bark Mulch (3 cu. fl. bags, screened)
liz yard sharp sand or plaster sand
liz yard light garden soil
3 cups 48% phosphate
5 pounds cottonseed meal
25 pounds steer manure (kiln run)
1 cup Sulfasoil
1 cup 5-10-5 rose food
1 quart organic activator solution

Mix the ingredients in large pile, moisten and cover with plastic. Turn weekly for about three weeks. Composting and heating will blend ingredients and mix can be used right away. If making a new bed, spread the mix about four inches deep over tilled area and work in lightly. Let the bed settle before planting. The mix is formulated for use with soluble fertilizers like *Carl Pool, Peter's* or *Ra-Pid-Gro*. The acidifier anticipates the use of alkaline water. The humus content will hold up three years or so. You may want to add additional soil, sand or humus to get the right "feel" to the mixture. The best mix is light, very friable and full of tiny air spaces so that the fine, hairy roots of

Miniature can develop and spread easily. Mini cuttings can also root easily in the mix. For hanging baskets, add more humus. Use less garden soil if the mix is primarily for pots and planters. You and your Miniature will enjoy life more by doing what comes naturally.

Maybe your rose society needs a spring tonic to break dormancy… just a little something different to put on some new growth. How about trying some "one-liners" at your next meeting, briefly touching on some ideas for roses without interfering with the regular program. It's a good assignment for a Consulting Rosarian, one who may have become a little sluggish during the winter. A "one-liner" takes only a minute or two but can do more good than many a lengthy program I've heard. In case you need some suggestions, here are a couple to try out…

A SPRING TONIC FOR TIRED ROSE BEDS… Most rose beds can use a gypsum treatment in the spring. Gypsum can't burn, helps drainage, reduces salt buildup and is a source of calcium. After pruning, broadcast gypsum (Calcium Sulfate) at about 10 lbs. per 100 square feet and work in lightly with a spading fork. Push the fork into the soil and work back and forth. The fork trick is also good to get rock phosphate or superphosphate into the root zone of the rose. Phosphate moves very slowly in the soil and only under ideal conditions.

A DOSE OF SALTS FOR A TOUCH OF GREEN… Established bushes slow to break new basal canes can be encouraged with a tonic of *Epsom Salts* (Magnesium Sulfate). About two or three tablespoons of *Epsom Salts* broadcast in the drip zone of each bush will often help and certainly will do no harm. Water in thoroughly. Get it in bulk from a feed store or drugstore. Plants will green up and put on new growth almost immediately.

PLANT ROSES WITH WATER (and a little soil)… Water, water, water. That's the name of the game when planting new rosebushes. The description "mud 'em in" tells it like it should be. Make sure that bare root roses (and canned plants, too) are deep-soaked when planted and regularly thereafter. Don't sprinkle, SOAK. Until established, new bushes dry out very quickly. Mound up bud union and canes with sailor mulch to conserve moisture.

HOT CAPS FOR ROSEBUSHES… If you have a new rosebush slow to start, clean the soil away from the bud union (assuming you are a GOOD rosarian and plant the bud union ABOVE the soil level), add a handful of very wet sphag-num moss, slip a clear plastic bag or tent over the pruned canes and tie with string around the shank of the bush. It makes a high-humidity forcing greenhouse. After about a week, gradually cut away the bag a little at a time to let cooler air in. Remove entirely in about two weeks. This "air-layering" bag is especially good with tree roses, even if they are beginning to break slightly. They get off to a better start, are protected in case of a cold snap and almost guarantee a robust, healthy tree rose that will not die back.

LET A LITTLE SUNSHINE IN… On the bud union, of course. This grower is still convinced that, except under the most EXTREME weather conditions, roses do best when the bud union is planted at soil level or above. Sunshine can do wonders for a bud union, promoting more canes and heavier canes, PROVIDED that the bushes have good winter protection. In the winter, cover 'em up. In the spring, open 'em up. Prove this practice for yourself. Plant some roses high and some roses low in the same bed. Next spring you'll want to lift the low growers.

IF FISH MEAL SOUNDS FISHY, TRY SOME… Peruvian anchovies must be Swimming again. Anyway, many feed stores now have a delightful odor that brings joy to the rosarian and blooms to the roses. It's an expensive smell, about $20 per 100 lbs. on the Gulf Coast. But 100 pounds goes a long way. Fish meal is easy and nearly odorless to use PROVIDED you handle it the right way. If you bring it home in the car, handle carefully. A light dusting in the seams of the trunk will produce many carsful of smell. Use a heaping cupful per established bush right after pruning. Get fish meal into the soil. Burying is better than broadcasting and scratching. Use a bulb planter tool and take three soil cores (five to six inches deep) in the active root zone of the bush. Pour fish meal into the core holes. Replace soil. Result is no smell, no cat, dog or neighbor problems. And GOOD roses. Use twice a year.

FIX FUNGUS NOW… Fungus control is a matter of PREVENTION, not eradication when blackspot appears. Field trials and experiences of everyday growers conclusively show that a fungus control program should start IMMEDIATELY after pruning, drenching the canes and bud union.

Use a broad spectrum insecticide (Diazinon, Iso-tox, Cygan) combined with your favorite fungi-cide (Phaltan, Manzate, Benlate). Use both at full strength and add a spreader-sticker to encourage penetration into crevices of old canes. Control over-wintering spores on canes BEFORE temper-ature and humidity are right for growth of these organisms.

If you have some snappy one-liners, send 'em along. Maybe we can expand on them in future Ramblings.

These Ramblings haven't discussed rose shows lately... those springtime rituals which turn usually-normal gardeners into fanatic trophy seekers. If too much of this seasonal madness is getting to you, take a look at what rose shows are all about. Besides competition and trophies, it's a great chance to have more fun with roses and win more friends for roses at the same time.

WE SHOULD BE ATTRACTING MORE "PLAIN DIRT" GARDENERS to roses and showing them just how easy rose growing can be. Educational exhibits attract and interest more people than the trophy table. Few visitors expect to grow roses like the show winners, but they do have an outside hope that they can grow some nice blooms for themselves and their friends.

There's nothing tough about setting up an educational section. Most important, provide some friendly hosts who know a little something about roses. Then set up some simple, understandable exhibits that offer the basics without controversy and endless exceptions. Beginners learn the rules first, then the exceptions. Keep it short; make rose information easy to remember and follow.

Rose folks around here still fondly remember the grower who took on the educational display as his pet project. He never challenged anyone at the show table, but he knew roses. This rose teacher made up display signs (used rub-on letters), wrote simple instructions, gathered materials and carefully stored and updated the display between shows. His charts were easy to follow; typical soils and mulches were shown in pie tins. The display had containers of commonly used fungicides and insecticides, sprayers and tools, lists of good varieties for the area... all made more attractive with some healthy, well-grown roses in containers. Set up somewhat away from the rose show, it did not compete for space or attention. However, the "teaching" area was usually more crowded than the winners' circle. When rose shows attract, interest and encourage backyard growers, you are doing a good job. New growers are the lifeblood of any rose society. Give your group a transfusion of enthusiastic novices this spring.

ROSES CAN USE BLOOD, TOO. Bloodmeal, that is. Whether you are an organic gardener or not, you'll be surprised at the invigorating ef-

fect bloodmeal has on stem, foliage and especially color. Gulf Coast growers use about a half cup of bloodmeal per BIG, well-established bush 15 days before a show. Scratch in lightly and WATER heavily. Continue to give the bush all the water it can tolerate. All kinds of bad things happen if you fail to water thoroughly. There are many sources of bloodmeal or beef-blood mixtures, usually inexpensive. Buy directly from stockyards if you can; otherwise, buy from a custom feeds-fertilizer dealer.

FOLLOWING THIS MEDICAL LINE OF ADVICE, try "splinting" tree roses for support rather than using stakes, loose ties and what-have-you. Tree roses must have support, even in protected locations. Splint a tree standard just like a broken arm: bind the standard to a cushioned support. Use 3/8-in reinforcing bar or 1/2-in. electrical conduit. Cut long enough to drive 12-18 inches into the soil. The top should be just under the bud unions (trees are double-budded). Cushion the splint with a length of old rubber or plastic hose. Fit the covered splint on the straight side of the standard. It's easier to do when planting a new rose, but can be located anytime by carefully probing to miss large roots. Wrap the standard and splint with friction tape or electrician's plastic tape in several places.

In areas where trees get very large, special metal rods with welded bars or hoops to support canes may be needed. The idea is to keep both the canes and the standard from whipping around in the wind, chafing and breaking canes and buds. This Rambler once helped doctor an ailing Granada tree rose that was well over five feet in diameter. The canes and bud unions were very heavy and had split the standard down the middle. A piece of pipe was wrapped and taped to the standard; then two holes were drilled through the pipe, bud unions and standard to fit a lightweight U-bolt. A couple of washers and nuts completed the job, pinning the tree together... and it thrived for a good many more years.

AS THEY SAY ON TELEVISION: "A COMBINATION OF INGREDIENTS WORKS BETTER"... for headaches or blackspot. If blackspot has been your headache, try a combination of *Manzate* (*Maneb*) at 1/2 tablespoon each per gal-

lon of water! No spreader-sticker required. Spray
every two weeks to dripping stage. It's fast, fast,
fast relief... and lasts a long time, too.

HAVE YOU EVER WONDERED where the "Old Rosarian's Tales" come from? Or why they live on from season to season, faithfully repeated by rosarians who ought to know better? You know what I'm talking about... those dire warnings that water on the leaves causes blackspot; that crown gall infects a whole bed; that mulch must be burned because of diseases hiding in there... or maybe the perennial favorite that prescribes drenching rosebushes with insecticide every spraying. If you have been around roses very long, you know that these tales discourage and mislead new growers... when we should be making our favorite hobby fun and easy.

IF YOU ARE GOING TO GIVE ADVICE, tell it like it is. For example, crown gall and root gall are really not so bad. Galls seldom "strangle" roses. We used to be told to pull up roses with gall, burn the remains and haul away the infected soil in the rose bed. As in many old tales, the stories had some basis of fact, but were blown completely out of proportion.

Your own garden experience tells you that roses with crown gall can live and produce for many years, and that "clean" bushes can be planted directly in beds previously infected without transmission. In a test in the Tyler (Texas) municipal rose garden, bushes with crown gall were transplanted to one bed for observation and produced nearly as well as "new" bushes planted in the same bed. The infected bushes were replanted at a higher level so that sunshine could get to the gall area. No other treatment was used. Six years later the bushes are still doing well.

"NEVER WET THE LEAVES" makes about as much sense as trying to eliminate rainfall. Overhead watering is not bad. In fact, overhead watering offers some substantial benefits that the soaking systems can't match. The reason: today's effective fungicides virtually eliminate the worry of wet foliage. This is not to suggest that growers wet down the leaves each evening; but not harm will come from regular overhead watering PROVIDED a systematic fungicide spray program is followed. Many good growers set a cone-type lawn sprinkler directly in the rose beds and let the water spray up under the rosebushes. This accomplishes two things: it washes off the spider mites

and effectively prevents old spray buildup.

ROSE BEDS WITH UNDERGROUND or soaker systems should also get the overhead, underneath, water-all-over method about once a week. Spider mites just do not like all that water, and roses do. An old grower told me a long time ago that hosing down healthy rosebushes after a very hot day was just like the gardener having some refreshments after a long dry spell. And he enjoyed tremendous success with roses. The foliage in his garden was always clean, healthy, disease free. Moral: roses like to be clean and cool just like rosarians. With all the junk floating in the air these days, most everything can stand a washing from time to time.

HOPE YOU HAVEN'T BURNED YOUR OVER-WINTERED MULCH LATELY. If you did, it was a waste. Aside from the need for normal neatness, leave mulch material in the rose beds year after year. Gradual breakdown of organic mulches restores the humus balance in the soil and adds an ingredient to soil processes that the chemical men have never been able to duplicate. Rosarians used to think that spores of all kinds of rose diseases lurked in the mulch and they faithfully raked up and destroyed this material just when it was beginning to do some good. Instead, after normal debris removal, use a good cleanup spray and drench the rose canes and leftover mulch. Blackspot spores live on green, live tissue, not on cellulose materials in the process of decomposition. Let sunlight, air, good bugs and nature put the mulch to work. Maybe add a little nitrogen to replace that leached out during the winter and speed up the decomposition process.

ANOTHER WARNING SERVED ON NEWCOMERS claims that spraying must always cover rose leaves over, under, sideways and crossways. It's GOOD advice when spraying for fungus diseases or spider *mites* under the leaves, but is wasteful and useless if the problem is thrips. Good rose competitors know that misting the tops of the plants every other day with *Cygon 2E* will do all the good that is necessary. For show blooms, start spraying with *Cygon* just as soon as color shows. Continue misting bloom areas every other day even when blooms are one-third to one-half open. *Cygon* does not seem to damage the bloom, particularly if sprayed in the evening.

More rose leaves are probably lost from too much spraying than too little. And how many roses have you seen on bushes with no leaves? Use insecticides for SPECIFIC problems only. Constant use of broad spectrum insecticides can do more harm than good. When an insect problem appears, get after it with a specific spray material. Otherwise let nature and the rosebush alone. They are more experienced than you are.

If you are taking yourself and your roses too seriously these days, how about some rose resolutions for 1976?? These timely thoughts have been offered by rosarians from across the country, indicating that the same kind of rose madness exists everywhere. Roses are hardly any fun unless there are some rules to break, so tryout your will power on some of these...

POTPOURRI... a jar of flower petals or spices used for scent; a miscellaneous collection, perhaps a medley... That's what Webster might call these odds and ends of rose petals filled with observation and advice. Hopefully, you trusting readers will find this jar pleasantly fragrant and in harmony with your rose garden.

TUB GROWN ROSES are big this year, and probably will continue to decorate more patios, balconies and odd corners in the future. Some new roses that are sized just right for tub use are coming into the market. Tub roses are somewhere between the Floribundas and the Polyanthas. Free blooming, compact growth habit, indifferent to pruning, grooming and general neglect. Just make sure that the soil mixture has enough humus to retain moisture on a hot patio for a couple of days. Fertilize with one of the balanced liquids, about half strength. If you can't wait for one of the new tub varieties, use a Floribunda or even a small-growing Hybrid Tea. They will add a good bit of pleasure for any grower.

MINIS IN HANGING BASKETS should also be on your garden schedule. The baskets are easy to prepare; just add more humus to your regular Mini-mix. Use sphagnum moss around the mesh or fiber basket for evaporation and cooling; besides, it makes the whole basket more attractive. Most of the bushy types of Miniature roses make very good hanging baskets. When climbers are used, cut back the canes to the desired length and force the laterals. Bush type Miniatures usually have to be topped to force side growth, Half-climbers are probably the best for most baskets or urns. Some good varieties are Over the Rainbow, Beauty Secret, Baby Darling, Nancy Hall, Coral Treasure and Jeanie Williams. Candy Cane (pink with white stripes in clusters) is a real favorite. Hi Ho (coral red, excellent form) is also showy. Canes and laterals can be trained to hang down by add-ing weights, something like a small fishing sinker. Once trained, the weights can be removed.

WHAT'S AHEAD IN ROSES is always a topic of conversation. Rosarians at the San Diego ARS convention were talking about an Austrian Copper rose without blackspot, called EYEPAINT. It will be introduced by Fred Edmunds. Says it will be as big, bushy, colorful and productive as Austrian Cooper, AND will cycle several times a season. NIGHTIME was described by Ollie Weeks as a very dark, dark red Hybrid Tea that he will be introducing next year. Or how about a climbing sport of FIRST PRIZE? Bill Warriner of J&P reported that the sport is very vigorous, more winter hardy than the parent and is a profuse bloomer. A large vase of SEASHELL (AARS-1976) he displayed had all of the transparent iridescence of pink seashells. Not to be outdone, Jack Christensen of Armstrong described INFERNO (how's that for a name?) as an orange-white bi-color, very tall, that looks like the base of a flame. Anyway, we are in line for some great roses next year... save your money.

CONTROLLED RELEASE fertilizers should be attractive to many rose growers in the next year or two as distribution of these fine products widens. *OSMOCOTE* and *PRECISE* are the only two used and known in the Gulf Coast area and the reports have been consistently good. *Osmocote* (18-6-12) has a feeding life of about 8 months. Precise (8-14-2) will feed about 4 months. Feeding cost per plant is low. These approaches to rose feeding should be especially attractive to growers with small gardens or with limited maintenance time. Florists have been using timed release materials for a long time. It will be interesting to see how it works for rose nuts.

DRAINAGE POOR without much chance for relief?? Here's an easy method to help the situation passed on by Dr. Eldon Lyle, Plant Pathologist and great roseman from Tyler, Texas. Dr. Lyle observed that roses planted near the top of a furrow performed better even though the overall bed was not elevated above lawn level and the general area poorly drained. Movement of air in the soil was apparently encouraged by ditching between the rows of roses thereby elevating the rosebushes several inches above the usual level of the bed. Something like planting a hill of corn or mound of cucumbers. Believe it or not, this Rambler saw one rose bed that was built inside a shallow concrete pool that had held water lilies the season before. The pool was filled with soil (sandy-humus garden soil), ditched and furrowed and the roses planted at the highest points of the furrows.

The ditch part of the V-furrow was filled with insulating mulch and, to the casual observer, the bed was level, conventional and attractive. Most attractive was the fact that the roses were thriving in spite of very heavy rains.

MULCH IS NOT MYSTERIOUS; it simply works on the rose bed in a natural way to conserve moisture, lower soil temperature and add humus gradually. Think of mulch as an insulator through which water, air and nutrients can percolate. If insulation is too thin, it doesn't work well. You and your roses will be happier if you add a couple of inches of good living (mulch) to the rose beds.

AUG. 1975	*No column printed this month.*

SEPT. 1975

THOUGHT FOR THE MONTH: One thing I've noticed about the rose season... by the time your back gets used to it, your enthusiasm is gone.

There's an old saying that goes, "There's nothing so blind as the man (rosarian) who won't see." Most rose problems are really quite simple when we think about them later; we just tend to miss the keys to the problem along the way. And just maybe you have forgotten to notice these easy clues...

FOR EXAMPLE, YOUR SHARP ROSARIAN EYE SHOULD have noted that spraying just after a rain gives better leaf coverage (better wetting) and seems to stick longer. It's not a bad practice to wash off the plants after a long, dry spell, then spray. Another good reason to water overhead at least some of the time. And you've certainly seen that organic material, earthworms and healthy rosebushes go together. And doesn't the soil smell good when organics, soil and sand are working together? Nature must be trying to tell us something. Are you listening??

Have you ever noticed that an ample helping of manure used before other rose foods seems to make the whole formula work better? We don't have to understand it to appreciate the results. A good spring starter or rose show feeding schedule should always include manure a week or two before the soluble applications. Another way to accomplish the same thing is to add about 10 pounds of bloodmeal to the typical 40-lb. sack of organic-based rose food. Work the mix in a bit with the soil bacteria and watch the results.

OF COURSE YOU KNOW THAT *ACTI-DIONE PM* WORKS better when used alone, and that you only have to worry about new, nitrogen-lush growth. But have you learned that this excellent fungicide works even better if the powdery spores are washed off before spraying? Or you might want to move the plant with chronic mildew to a spot with better air circulation. Some growers use a "sacrificial lamb" technique to good advantage. Keep a mildewer like Orange Flame or Fire King in the garden; either one will tell you right away when mildew conditions are right. The rose Oldtimer has always been a good spray tester for me. The leaves burn at the slightest mistake.

IF YOU'VE GROWN ROSES VERY LONG, you know that some garden visitors will show more interest in and ask more questions about the "sick" rose in the garden then the other 100 that are performing well. Obviously, if I knew the answer I would do something about it. Since no one wants to admit lack of expertise, I usually confide that the bush in question has been left for the bugs so that they won't bother the rest of the roses. Another good rosarian I know confides that the rose needs to be pruned... with a space.

COMMON SENSE TELLS US THAT A GOOD SPRAY MIXTURE IS IMPORTANT, but few rosarians know how to blend wettable powders and oil-based insecticides into a compatible mixture. HOT water is the answer. Use a glass mixing container with a tight lid. Carefully mark the outside of the container for the amount of concentrated mixture that fits your sprayer. Measure the wettable powders in the container first. Then slowly add HOT tap water, swirling the mixture into a thick paste. Continue to add warm water to the right concentration. Swirling the mixture seems to work best without foam and suds. The glass container makes it easy to see what's going on. Aromatic-based ingredients are added next, swirling gently. Add any spreader-sticker last. The spray mixture is now ready 11 to use WITHOUT any straining. The large glass container is obvious-you can always see what the mixture is doing. The danger of a glass container is very small, since any 11 rosarian with garden sense is wearing gloves and handling the mixture with care. If one of the ingredients precipitates out, safely dispose of the whole batch and try to identify the product that makes the problem. For example, old *Cygon* will cause *Benlate* to precipitate out immediately. Result: no protection and a clogged sprayer.

ENVIRONMENTAL PROTECTION is a popular rose topic, since every rose grower has a shelf-load of potions. Protecting the environment is great, but we should be even more interested in protecting the rosarian and the rose foliage. Poor labeling and storage are common. The product gets the blame more often than the rosarian. If you're going to spray, use fresh materials that are accurately labeled. We all know that most sprays have a limited shelf life and rapidly lose effectiveness when kept for long periods on a shelf that's alternately hot and freezing. But how many of us bother to DATE the package or to repackage the wettable powders in a glass jar with a tight lid? Big mayonnaise jars are good for this, and you can tape the label to the outside. Another good trick is to note your favorite mixture proportions on the jar with a grease pencil so that you won't have to figure them out again. These two ideas can save you some blackspot or mildew due to spraying with old materials, or head off leaf burn because a spray concentration was too strong. A MUST for the spray shelf is a small medicine glass for measuring spray materials. Most garden shops have them for about 25 cents each with easy-to-read markings. Get a couple.

Permit these Ramblings a bit of nostalgia to take another look at some "old time religion" rose suggestions previously noted in these columns. Are they still working?? One unqualified success can be claimed... the hose stuck in a tin can and laid in the rose bed still works and is still popular. Bubbler-soaker manufacturers take note. Water and lots of it still makes roses grow.

"THEY LAUGHED WHEN I FILLED MY ROSE PIT WITH MANURE AND PINE BARK," Joe Gould of Shreveport reported last year. But Joe had the last laugh as his roses average eight feet tall, boast six to eight very sturdy canes, have the healthiest leaves you have ever seen and produce show winners consistently PLUS loads of roses for the house and friends. After two full years, the results have not dropped off at all. His rose beds are about 5 feet wide and built up about 18 inches above lawn level with cinder blocks. The bed (or pit) was filled with equal parts of rotted manure and pine mulch and mixed with a tiller. A little sharp sand was worked in to keep the mix loose. NO soil was used. The mix soaks up water like a sponge and is as light and friable today as it was two years ago. A little fish emulsion is used about six weeks before a rose show. Nothing else is needed. A great demonstration of practical rose gardening.

ANOTHER SOUTH TEXAS ROSE GROWER, Howard Turner, has a twist to this rose recipe for built up rose beds. He used equal parts of horse manure, sewage sludge, compost and light soil. Mixes with a tiller in a bed about three bricks high. Adds 10 pounds of rock phosphate and a pound of Epsom salt per 100 square feet of rose bed to look scientific. The roses look great with very vigorous growth, leaves from top to bottom and more bloom production (almost) than he can give away. Organic balance is doing the job as nature intended.

MORE AND MORE ROSARIANS IN ALL PARTS OF THE COUNTRY ARE USING BUILT UP ROSE BEDS. And they are getting great results. A built up rose area does not have to be a foot high to be effective. Even a few inches above lawn level helps drainage and aeration. If you don't have an elevated rose bed, build one this winter for sure. Compare the results with ordinary plantings and you'll be making new beds as fast as you can lay bricks, cinder blocks, weathered timbers or what-have-you. Get the very best from the bed with a high organic mix cut with just enough sand or light soil to keep the air spaces open. And since the roots have such a great environment, how about planting new bushes with the bud union above ground level (or at least no lower than ground level) in the sunshine and air to produce those basal breaks with show winners? With proper winter protection, bud unions can be planted above ground except under the most severe weather conditions. It's worth a try.

THESE COLUMNS HAVE HAD THE SMELL OF FISH MEAL FOR SOME SEASONS NOW. Is it still good? Absolutely. Fish meal is easier to get now and the price has dropped a little. The Rambler got this observation from Karl Envoldsen of Tampa, Florida: "When I plant a new rose bush (container grown, Fortuniana root stock), I make a hole 15" by 15" by 18" deep and put in two pounds of fish meal. Cover with 5 or 6 inches of dirt (everything here is sandy). Plant the bush with mix of calcined clay, composted cow manure and soil from the hole in equal volume. No need to feed again for two years, except a half inch of cow manure twice a year to encourage roots other than under the bush.

"On a Montezuma after six months I get 75 to 100 blossoms each flush. To keep in continuous bloom, I usually use two bushes and cut spent blooms on one bush about 3/4 inch above the bud at the leaf axil to delay bloom for about 10 days. Therefore I have blooms nearly all the time. After the bushes are grown (about 9 feet), I apply about two pounds of fish meal a year."

IS A COMPOST PILE TOO "OLD-FASHIONED" FOR YOU?? Just remember that the fancy organic mixes for sale at the nursery are simply commercial applications of nature's own recipe, return everything to the soil. Fall is a great time to start a compost pile as all the raw materials are available. If you have a few cinder blocks or even some old lumber, fashion some kind of loose fitting enclosure so that air and water can feed nature's process. Air and the right balance of moisture are essential. Most good rose gardens have compost piles hidden away somewhere in the yard. Some are fancy affairs; others are piles of clippings, dirt and what-not. The results are the same when compost gets to the rose bed or garden… better aeration, better root growth, better bushes and therefore better blooms. No yard is too small. With a little effort, anyone can -convert organic material into the best plant food that nature can produce. It still beats anything that comes in a sack or can.

Add some old-fashioned sweat to these formulas and you'll be surprised at the results. The old gardener approaches haven't worn out over the years, just the gardeners.

Since another rose season is at the end for most of us, it's a good time to make up a rose score sheet for our efforts. Memories are short, and when the rose catalog fever hits in January most every rosarian forgets about the failures of some cultivars (I still like to call them varieties) and the shortcomings of several of the rose beds. It's been said many times before, but the Queen of the Show begins to grow the winter before the exhibition. Good garden plans pay off in good roses and blue ribbons. What's your point score in planning?

FIRST OF ALL, WHAT'S PRODUCING CONSISTENTLY GOOD ROSES IN YOUR AREA? Not just the show winners, but the varieties that put out year after year... the roses that please every rose nut, not just the hardware hounds. Proof of the Pudding as operated by ARS is undergoing its annual revision, and we'll have to wait and see how much good the "new approach" can do for our particular situations. But there's no need to wait on the local level... a very worthwhile rose society project might be to compile a "Performance Chart" of favorite and new varieties in your area and to make this information available to all your members. Even if only 100 varieties are rated, newcomers and old pros will benefit. A local rating is worth far more than a generalization or average. Limiting the number of roses to be rated makes the job easier and gives a better chance for each rose to be rated by several individuals.

ANOTHER IDEA: rate the roses on a basis of 1 through 10 rather than on an A through D averaging technique. A graduated scale of points makes much more sense. Since there is no perfect rose yet, hope you won't find too many 10s submitted by over-enthusiastic growers. Penn-Jersey District publishes a Proof of the Pudding based on observations by a dozen or more big growers who offer very candid comments on the merits of each rose. It's so good that they charge $1.00 per copy and sell out every year. Program Chairman, pay attention. A "Performance Chart" night can make a great program and involve some members who have never been seen or heard. The results will help attract new members; too.

HOW'S YOUR SCORE ON MEMBERSHIP?? Every get-together of rose folks raises the same questions: How do we get new members? How do we get more rose society members active in the affairs of the society? Or, how do we get newer members to become officers? Obviously there's no single answer to these problems, but recent workshop sessions made some suggestions so simple that they are usually overlooked. For example, how many rose societies make it a policy to have a sort of "understudy" for each officer; that is, to require the "irreplaceable" officer to groom his own successor. It's a simple thought, but a management practice employed by most major businesses. Another good break-in technique is to insist that newly-elected chiefs work with the former leaders for a month or so before taking over. This gives some degree of continuity. If interested rosarians have had some kind of involvement they are more likely to respond favorably when asked.

"Asked" is an important word. We are all inclined to say no for a prospect when he should have a chance to answer for himself. And all too many of us have the notion that we can't be replaced, no one can do the job as well as we can. How do we know, if the newcomer never has had a chance? If your exec group has this kind of fungus, spade up some new ground, tryout some new cuttings. They will likely take better than you think.

IF BLACKSPOT IS SCORING MORE POINTS than roses in your garden, check your signals, as you are doing something very wrong. Dr. Eldon Lyle of the Texas Rose Research Foundation confirms again that nearly perfect control of blackspot is safely available to rosarians through regular spraying. Reporting on his work in 1975, Dr. Lyle found that *Benlate-Manzate* or *Benlate-Phaltan* (I/2 tb./gal. and also 1/2 tb./gal. of either *Manzate* or *Phaltan 75W*) weekly sprays gave nearly perfect control of blackspot in eight demonstration locations. Spraying of all locations began the same week as pruning back (February 19-25). Also noticed: spreader-sticker has not been beneficial in Tyler tests for extending lasting effects of fungicide sprays, for either blackspot or mildew. An estimated one gallon of spray per 40 bushes was used each time. Unsprayed checks showed incidence of 40% to 50% blackspot infection during the 74-day spring test period. An unusual number of days of rain contributed to the high incidence of blackspot. The frequency of rain during the test was 13 out of 25 days in March; 12 out of 30 in April, and 12 out of 19 in May for a total of 37 days with a trace of rain during the 74-day test. Dr. Lyle's test reports consistently recommend spraying at time of pruning, weekly applications and thorough leaf coverage with fungicide spray. The results': "nearly perfect" control. Now it's your turn.

Weary rosarians have retired from their beds,
While visions of trophies dance in their heads;
It's time to take stock of the blooms that were not,
And order show winners instead.

Grant the Rambler just a bit of poetic rose license and you'll see the point. Fireside fantasies in December are great, but thoughtful planning for the year ahead will payoff in more blooms and rose fun. The regular show winners have already made up order lists for new roses for next year, and you should be working on yours. Many of the best exhibition roses are sold out early, and new introductions are sometimes in short supply. Make up an order now and then place another next spring for winterkill replacements. What to order is up to you, but the job is a lot easier if your local Proof of the Pudding committee has done its job.

Except for a few fortunate rosarians in the warmer climates, rose blooms right now are a thing fondly remembered from last season... but it doesn't have to be that way. For some year 'round fun, try some Miniature roses in pots in the house. Potted Miniatures are getting more and more popular, and some of the enterprising florists are now offering blooming Miniature roses in place of the usual fare of azaleas, chrysanthemums and what-have-you. Roses make great gifts for the shut-in, giving lots of bloom without much care. And they are easy to grow inside, yourself.

Miniatures in pots thrive under plant-light fluorescents. The special violet-tinted light seems to provide everything the diminutive bushes need. If you are a do-it-yourselfer, build your own fixture mounted over a growing stand. For a bit fancier setup, look into the Flora-Cart arrangement advertised in many of the garden magazines. It's a tubular frame mounted on wheels with either two or three plastic growing trays. The plant-light fixtures are hung in the frame (adjustable) and have two fluorescent tubes and two incandescent sockets in each. The light balance seems to be ideal. Some plants seem to do better without the incandescents, but this is probably affected by the amount of natural light available. The systems work even in a completely dark basement. And if the lady of the house wants something besides Miniatures, African violets, gloxinias and certain blooming begonias make good companions.

There are several good books available on growing indoors under lights. Get one when you start. For Minis, remember that they do best in a high-humus, well aerated soil with good drainage. Harmon Saville of Nor-East Roses offered some ideas during a panel program (ARS 1975 fall meeting) that make good sense. He suggests a soilless mix of peat, perlite and vermiculite with just a touch of 18-6-12 Osmocote for steady reeding. Perlite scores high as a growing medium since it holds air and water, actually having 20% air space by volume. Harmon suggests about 16 hours of light per day, with the fixtures about 6 inches above the plants. The secret for Minis indoors is a careful, regular feeding program. In short, Mini growers feed, feed, feed at low, low concentration.

Spider mites find their way to Miniature roses indoors just like they do outdoors. But the control is also the same-strong water spray. If you have a laundry tub, put the pot in the tub and spray the undersides of the leaves with plenty of water. Repeat about three times at three-day intervals. Water-wash again at the first sign of mite damage. Water gets rid of mites and makes the plants healthier, too. And water is certainly safer to use and apply than miticides indoors.

Minis prefer high humidity. If you have dry furnace heat, you'll have to come up with some way to add moisture to the air. A plastic sheet over the growing frame or Flora-Cart will help; moist gravel or perlite in the tray also releases moisture. And take it easy on the heat. A range of 55 to about 70 degrees is fine; but check the temperature UNDER the lights. They generate lots of heat.

Even ice and snow can't cool rose interest in the winter. The Penn-Jersey rose nuts had a Miniature rose show in January as part of a rose conference. Had lots of blooms as well as Minis in pots. It's a great idea to brighten a long winter.

Picked up another good idea that makes roses fun for more people from the Syracuse (New York) Rose Society. Syracuse says that evening garden tours have attracted and involved more members (and others interested in roses) than the formal week-end affairs ever did. They scheduled two rose gardens per evening, beginning about 6 PM. With two or more hours of good light left, the summer evening garden visits accommodated many people who just could not take part in a Saturday-Sunday tour. Another plus: both the rosarians and roses stayed cooler. The society set aside several evenings for gardens during the summer so that 'most everyone could participate. Program chairmen take note... this is a way to get participation.

If you are taking yourself and your roses too seriously these days, how about some rose resolutions for 1976?? These timely thoughts have been offered by rosarians from across the country, indicating that the same kind of rose madness exists everywhere. Roses are hardly any fun unless there are some rules to break, so tryout your will power on some of these...

THIS ROSARIAN RESOLUTELY RESOLVES TO:

1. Tell Queen of The Show story only when asked.

2. Restrict Reading of rose catalogs to one hour per week.

3. Order only ten more roses than the garden, will hold.

4. Save money by ordering three of everything.

5. Dig up no more than 10% of lawn area per year for roses.

6. Buy only two miracle rose cures for "testing".

7. Let weather man handle rainfall without help.

8. Think of bugs as part of nature's balance.

9. Allow limited cutting of roses for the house.

10. Come in from garden for supper on time.

11. Wear clean shirt for Sunday rose garden work.

12. Encourage rose growth without swearing.

13. USE SOME COMMON ROSE SENSE

Now that these important resolutions have been made, it's time to take on another New Year's Tradition... predictions of what's ahead. This is easy for a rosarian, as he knows that next year's garden is going to be bigger and better than ever before. What will this rose garden of the future look like?

THIS RAMBLER THINKS that the rosarian of the future will be planting more Floribundas in a landscape plan, taking advantage of the good new varieties coming on the market. Roses will appear in many front yards, where they should have been all the time. Roses will be used more and more for massed effect rather than as specimen plantings. Hybridizers are working in this direction, introducing varieties that are heavy flowering, have

Hybrid Tea form, stay in bloom most of the time and are suitable for cutting. And this is what MOST ordinary rose growers and backyard gardeners are interested in. TORO and UNCLE JOE may be the rage for rose nuts, but roses like CATHEDRAL, BAHIA, ROSE PARADE, GENE BOERNER and EUROPEANA will bring more people pleasure in rose growing.

And before long, we're confident that a lucky hybridizer will introduce red, pink and yellow versions of SEAFOAM, one of the most versatile landscape roses ever developed. Many hybridizers are working toward these colors, it's just a matter of time.

TIMED RELEASE FERTILIZERS like Osmocote and Precise will be more and more popular with rosarians and formulations with various combinations of trace minerals will be marketed. For many growers, it will be the best thing since Benlate.

Like Benlate, timed release fertilizer will not work miracles with roses, but will help many growers who otherwise might give up. Biological insect control will also come into its own very soon, hastened by a dwindling assortment of insecticides. Rose people and gardeners in general are ecology conscious; and they will pay the price for safe, effective controls of pests in the garden.

THE RAMBLER'S CRYSTAL BALL also sees less emphasis on competitive rose showing, at least in the way we know it now. More rose exhibitions will be staged; more shopping malls will be filled with roses and rose hobbyists anxious to encourage others to grow roses. Rose societies will tend toward small monthly competitions at regular meetings, encouraging ALL the members (not just the trophy winners) to participate. Such an arrangement might be called two-level competition; the big growers can come on strong at the annual or district rose show. The American Rose Society has an interest in this development if it is to attract some 10,000 new members needed for an active, healthy society. These new members will be looking for cultural information, landscape help and rose fun. The groups that provide this kind of rose package will have lots of members.

ROSE SHOW SCHEDULES will be more simple in the future, making it easy for anyone to enter roses without being an expert. The alphabetical system will expand to most parts of the country. If you haven't seen this kind of schedule, drop me a line and you'll get a copy by return mail. Try it, you'll like it.

You may see the future through rose-colored glasses of a different hue; but all of us have to make roses more interesting, more fun and more widely used by more people... with whatever skills we have. The Rambler wishes you a very Rosy 1976.

WINTER IS A GREAT TIME FOR ROSES... the real rose nuts are already thinking about how to frame rose certificates that are sure to be won in the spring shows. Besides, it's too early for the really HARD work to begin in the garden and yet late enough for the memories of last summer to get better and better. You are certain to have noted that good roses from last season always have more form, color, size and what-have-you when snow is on the ground. This is called "looking at the world through rose-colored glasses". So if your eyes are tired from rose visions or just plain old catalog overkill, tryout a couple of these ideas for more fun with roses in the coming season...

ALL ROSARIANS LIKE TO PLANT NEW BUSHES, and most think that they do a pretty fair job. But if roses could talk, some sad tales of mishandling would surely be told. Obviously, it makes no sense to put a $5 bush in a 50c hole. Most cases are not this extreme, but a good grower knows that a well-prepared rose bed pays off in roses. A few extra hours of spade work in the winter saves sweat-producing labor in the summer. Check out some local rose bed formulas and get out the fork and shovel. New bed or old, follow the formula.

There are all kinds of old-rosarian tales about planting roses. Fortunately, most of them are not true. Some old timers maintain that a grower has to "stomp" on the roots to "get rid of the air". This not only gets rid of the air, it also breaks the roots and compacts the soil so tight that water and air (both essential to soil processes) don't have a chance. The best planting tool is PLENTY of water.

Using the pyramid method in the hole to support the roots and stabilize the shank, add some soil and gently fill in around the roots. With the hose running at a slow trickle, thoroughly soak the entire root system and soil. Then add more soil and repeat the process. Keep your feet OUT of the hole... if you are planting properly you'll just get your boots full of mud. I usually soak one newly planted bush while digging and planting the next one; then move the hose while backfilling. An expression commonly used around here is to "mud" the roses in. Then soak the whole bed area again after planting.

Hope you are not guilty of a common mis-take when planting... roots drying out in the sun and wind while the "rosarian" decides on spacing, location, takes a coffee break, etc. Soak bare root roses overnight in water, and keep them in water until just before final pruning and planting. Dry roots and dehydrated bushes just don't start. The commercial nurseryman takes great pains to deliver a fresh bush. It can all be undone with careless handling.

SPEAKING OF DEHYDRATED ROSES, don't be taken in by "new crop" packaged roses at the supermarket, drugstore, garden shop or street corner, no matter what bargains they appear to be. Supermarkets should sell groceries, nurseries should sell roses. Packaged roses with chopped roots, waxed tops and a handful of wood shavings are never bargains... and they are totally worthless after a few days in a hot store window. If you are interested in roses, plant good rosebushes in the first place.

Continuing the planting process, plant high enough to leave room for mulch later in the season. Roses will invariably sink a little as beds settle. Allow for this in the beginning. Cover the bud union and several inches of cane with soil or mulch (or maybe a combination of both) when planting. This conserves moisture in the canes and protects new buds from sudden drops in temperature. As new buds start and weather moderates, gradually remove the mound so that sunshine can get to the bud union. Don't probe with a fork or stick; gradually wash off the cover with a stream from the hose. It's gentle and keeps the bed moist, too. Water and sun are your best friends in the springtime-or anytime. Use them.

ANOTHER SUGGESTION — considered radical by growers in the north — is to plant roses with bud unions above bed level, NOT buried as is the common practice in colder climates. Field trials with bud unions no lower than bed level report more vigorous bushes, better production of basal breaks and no appreciable difference in winterkill, provided winter protection is given. Note that last statement... PROVIDED winter protection is given. Most cold climate rosarians use winter protection as a matter of good growing practice to save as much cane as possible. Give this suggestion your own field trial this year with a few bushes.

Compare bush results. Provide some extra winter cover (there are lots of good ways) and you'll be pleasantly surprised that roses do not have to be buried to survive. Your reward: more bush and therefore more bloom.

HAS THE SPRING PLANTING FEVER SPREAD TO YOUR AREA YET?? An epidemic of such fevers is spreading on the Gulf Coast, brought under control with liberal doses of time outdoors with the roses again. But for many of our readers, March is a time for plans and orders... a particularly dangerous time for rosarians weakened by months of cold and snow. They're so anxious to get going in the garden again that they fall prey to the old garden con game called "miracle formulations" or sometimes revealed as "amazing discoveries". Rosarians are favorite targets of these maladies... for the most part it's innocent puffery but rose faddists can drop a good piece of money and lose rosebushes in the process. Healthy roses and rosarians know better. Discount the claims with a heavy application of common sense. Experiments are fun, but only when a grower can afford the loss... a little like betting on horses.

After this warning about "miracles", permit the Rambler to brief you again about a REALLY miraculous aid for gardeners that has been around a long time but largely overlooked. Agricultural gypsum (calcium sulfate) makes growing worthwhile again for rosarians cursed with heavy, alkaline soils. And early spring is a good time to take the cure. Gypsum has been used since the time of the Romans, and many growers routinely add it to a rose bed mixture without a clear understanding of just how it works. A scientific discussion is beyond the Rambler's scope, but these personal observations may help rosarians decide if gypsum can help their gardens.

GYPSUM helps break up heavy, alkaline, clay soils and reduces the toxic effect of sodium on plants, especially when irrigating water contains substantial amounts of sodium. Under proper circumstances, gypsum reacts chemically with clay soil particles and organic matter, removing excess sodium and reducing the tendency of the soil to "puddle" and later pack. Sodium is a very reactive element and forms "salts" very readily; and in the case of clay soils becomes firmly attached to the particles, causing an increase in soil pH, giving an alkaline reaction. The adsorbed sodium makes soils heavy, wet and unsuitable for roses (and a good many other plants).

SODIUM atoms attached to clay particles have a very strong attraction for water, reaching a point where the particle attracts water more than another clay particle. We know this as slimy mud. The particles can remain suspended in water for long periods; and when the water does drain away, the clay bits settle into a tight mass. Among other things, rosarians call this gumbo. The air space remaining in the soil is very small, resulting in a hard soil with poor aeration and drainage. This same condition develops in potted plants through use of alkaline water, and many city water supplies contain substantial amounts of sodium salts.

Roses will not thrive in tight, alkaline soils. Application of gypsum will help relieve both conditions and restore good health and bloom. Gypsum works by exchanging calcium ions for sodium ions attached to the soil particles, and performs this "miracle" without toxicity to rosebushes. It works best when mechanically mixed into the soil (making a new rose bed); but also leaches downward through the soil by rainfall or irrigation (existing plantings). Gypsum is slow to dissolve, and the benefits last a long time. An application of from 10 to 20 pounds per 100 square feet is recommended for a long effective period. Southwest growers plagued with very alkaline water commonly treat rose beds with a surface application of 10 pounds of gypsum per 100 square feet each spring.

Several things must happen for 'gypsum to do the job. Enough gypsum must dissolve for the chemical reaction to take place, producing sodium sulfate... The sodium sulfate is then leached from the soil by adequate drainage.

MECHANICAL LOOSENING HELPS DRAINAGE, although natural processes will eventually work. The process works from the top down until the leaching process is complete and the soil opened up. Even after the soil is cleared of excess sodium, enough gypsum must be kept in the path of irrigation water to offset any buildup of the alkaline condition.

ROSE BEDS (especially built-up beds) and container grown roses will respond vigorously and dramatically to treatment with gypsum. Water, plant nutrients and air can again reach the rose feeding zone. Gypsum is neutral and will not affect the pH reading of the soil by its application.

Work a good supply of gypsum into any new rose bed under construction if salts or alkaline problems are suspected. For roses already established, add gypsum to the top few inches of soil with careful cultivation. Rain and regular watering will move the beneficial qualities downward. This is one easy-to-use, safe, cheap, non-toxic, proven, available-anywhere MIRACLE that really works.

Dropped in on a rose society "workshop" program the other day… it just turned out that way because the program speaker didn't show up. But the resourceful rose folks there turned the evening into a real rose winner and had a good time in the process… learning and telling rose stories at the same time. Each Consulting Rosarian took on a rose topic or two and visited about his experiences for a few minutes, then asked for comments from the group. These "real rose happenings" did a lot more good than many lengthy programs I've heard. In case your group would like to have a "live" session, here are some rose cuttings (or are they spent blooms?) to get you started…

MANURE IS LIKE MONEY… It's only good when spread around. If you have a good source of manure get out the shovel and start spreading. Even the dehydrated, sterilized, weed-free homogenized kind can do some good when it comes into contact with micro-organisms in the soil. The nutrient value of manure is really very low, but it makes all kinds of good things happen in the soil. It's more of a soil conditioner than a fertilizer; use generously without fear. Old-time rose growers know that a good top dressing of manure applied FIRST in the spring gets the soil ready for pelletized formulas later. If you have a good source, use it-and let your friends in on the treat, too.

DORMANT SPRAYS ARE NOT SO DORMANT… They often burn. Especially the lime-sulfur petroleum mixtures that smell, stain and gum up sprayers. If rose plants are REALLY dormant, and the weather is REALLY cool, "dormant" mixtures can be used. But why take a chance, when it's easy to get BETTER protection from rose preparations we use all the time? A *Manzate-Diazinon* or *Phaltan-Isotox* full-strength mixture carefully applied will take care of the overwintering insects, fungus spores or other troubles that plague roses in the spring. Use the spray mix at pruning time, thoroughly drenching canes and bud union. Add a little spreader-sticker to make sure that the spray gets into all the crevices. It's the first step in a fungus disease prevention program for a new season. The most important spraying of the season is the first spraying, controlling problems before they get out of hand. And don't forget to spray fungus hosts like green canes on ramblers that are "too big to work with". Spores are on green plant material just waiting for the right combination of temperature and humidity to multiply and infect everything within range.

FISHERMEN AND ROSES LIKE FISH… Fishmeal is preferable for roses, worked into the soil at pruning time. This isn't a product carried by most garden shops, but smart rosarians know the feed stores who make up mixes for poultry raisers. Fishmeal is commonly used in specialty feeds, and accommodating "farm type" stores can get it for you. On the Gulf Coast, fishmeal is selling for $20 per 100 pounds. Use a heaping cupful per established bush right after pruning. To keep down the smell, get it in contact with the soil. Scratch in and then water. If you have a very sensitive nose (or sensitive neighbors) eliminate ALL the smell by burying it in core holes in the active root zone of the plant. Pour into the core holes, replace soil. The only smell will be gorgeous roses. Use twice a season.

A SPRINGTIME REMINDER… Plain dirt gardeners (and especially those who use manure) should get a Tetanus booster shot. It's common sense to maintain this protection if you work in the soil. It's also smart to check over rubber gloves and other protective equipment you'll be using during the spray season. Spraying is safer and easier if you have an orderly procedure using equipment that is intended for the job.

CANE SEALERS-BOON OR BANE? The right cane sealer applied at the right time can do some good, but most of the results are highly overrated. Too many sealers contribute to dieback and hinder rather than help a plant reseal a wound. Rosarians around here like shellac, painting all the large pruning cuts, especially around the bud union. An old liquid shoe polish bottle with a dauber is very handy, neat and doesn't dry out. Elmer's Glue is another good sealer, believe it or not. It does the job just long enough for the plant to seal naturally. Bud unions carefully pruned and then sealed with Elmer's seem to heal over faster than with other materials. Asphalt-base tree paint is probably the worst sealer for roses. If the weather turns hot, the petroleum base appears to burn green tissue, making another wound. Cutting tools affect sealing, too. For large, woody canes, use a small keyhole saw rather than the crushing blade of a lopper. Cuts heal much taster, especially around the bud union.

NEW ROSES NEED SPRING BLANKETS... Hill up and protect newly planted rosebushes; not only to keep from freezing but also to conserve moisture until the roots are established. Cover the bud union and several inches of cane with soil. For a hard freeze, hill up a little higher and protect with a good insulator like field hay or shredded leaves. A water-soaked burlap sack (we call them tow-sacks here) also helps new bushes start and protects, too.

Stealing the title from a sensational best seller a few years ago, these Ramblings might be called "What You Always Wanted to Know About Roses But Were Afraid to Ask". It's surprising how many rose society meetings drone on and on talking about everything except common sense ways to grow and have fun with roses. Some plain dirt gardening with a free swap of ideas can put the fun back into roses and roses into more backyards. When we convince ourselves that roses are easy and fun (and then tell others) we won't be able to handle all the applications. Make it easy to ask questions without embarrassment; throw out a couple of simple thoughts and watch the meeting warm up. For a starter, here are repeats of some questions asked the Rambler time after time…

COW TEA… Where do you get it? Cow tea isn't bought, it's brewed. Organic growers call it "organic compost" these days, but old timers remember when people with good flowers and vegetables always had a barrel of tea steeping behind the garage. Roses and other plants jumped out of the ground with an application or two. Six or eight dried cow chunks will make a whole barrelful. Plastic garbage cans work fine; keep two or three brewing in various stages for a constant supply. Onion or potato sacks make good tea bags. Fill with cow chunks and tie with a long piece of wire or rope (make sure it's long enough). Steep in a barrelful of water about ten days, sloshing the bag around once in a while. One tea bag is good for about two brews. Dried chunks are best; dehydrated stuff in bags is something like instant coffee-it's not the real thing. Use about two gallons of tea per bush for great results. By the way, rainwater or well water makes better tea than the chlorinated city stuff. It's the REAL thing.

DO MY ROSES GET ENOUGH WATER? Use a rain gauge to find out; a plain old coffee can set in the rose bed (or beds). You'll always know just how much water the rose beds are getting, not just guessing. Set the cans in the beds, turn on the hose, and when the cans have an inch or so of water in them, turn the hose off. Follow the Old Gardener Adage, "Soak, don't sprinkle". And don't be afraid to get the foliage wet. Leaves were meant to be washed… provided a fungicide spray program is on schedule. If fungus control is hit and miss, it won't make any difference if the leaves are wet or not… you'll have blackspot and mildew.

SPRAY MATERIALS DON'T SEEM TO MIX… and lumps will clog many sprayers until rosarians learn to use HOT water to make a gravy-like paste before diluting. To get a wettable powder into solution without lumps, measure the powder into a large glass jar (a wide-mouth, gallon-size mayonnaise jar is great), add a cup or so of HOT water and swirl or shake a couple of times. No lumps or straining. Insecticides with petroleum distillate base should be added AFTER wettable powders are in solution and diluted; add spreader-sticker last if needed. Using a clear glass jar, the rosarian can check the compatibility of ingredients before pouring into the sprayer. You can see what you are doing. For example, you'll find that old *Cygon 2E* will cause *Benlate* or *Manzate* to precipitate out of solution, making a gummy mess if poured into a sprayer.

I'D LIKE TO MAKE SOME COMPOST… It's easy even for a small-lot, city gardener. If there's room for a 20-gallon garbage can in the back yard, you're in business. Cut out the bottom of a large garbage can. A can that's rusting out and needs replacing will do just fine. Get an out-of-the-way spot and spade up an area the width of the can. Work the can into the soil a few inches until it's firmly in place. Make sure it has a tight fitting lid. Whenever there's some kitchen garbage or some leftover leaves, dump into the composter and sprinkle a little dirt over the new entries. Stir about once a week and add just enough water to keep mixture moist. When the can seems to be full, let the batch rest a week and you'll find there's room for more. The compost you make has just about everything a plant can use; and depending on your table, you11 have 20 gallons of potting soil or soil conditioner that's better than anything you can buy.

MY ROSES NEED TO BE CHELATED… Referring, of course, to chelated minerals that are touted by the marketers to work instant miracles. It also usually means expensive. The word "chelate" comes from the Greek word for claw, such as the claw of a lobster. In fertilizer terms, the claw becomes a ring around a central metallic ion. To ordinary rosarians like you and me, it means that a chelated structure makes a mineral more readily available to the feeder roots. It could be said that the ring protects and unlocks at the same time. Don't try to discuss chelates with your chemist friends, but use when a quick, reliable action is needed, like a quick shot of iron when the leaves lose color.

It's a tough job to give rose advice these days… old time remedies are being declared "ecologically unacceptable", new products are coming into the market in bewildering quantities and freshly-sprouted rose nuts swear that a secret formula makes roses put out "loads" of blooms every time. This is all a part of the fun of roses, but we must appear to be very strange to the newcomer. The old pro comes on as confused and the novice seems positive. For real confusion, re-read the "Roses Coast to Coast" carefully and note that the worthy columnists frequently contradict each other and offer advice without qualifying statements. It proves again that roses must be the hardiest of plants to survive all this abuse.

IF YOU WANT TO GIVE ADVICE, make sure that the instructions are specific and accurate, and that all of the qualifying statements are included. If something goes wrong, at least you'll have some idea what caused it. This Rambler is as guilty as the next in this department, and promises to do better… (starting soon).

AN OLD-TIMER SPOKE UP in a recent issue of the San Francisco ROSARIAN and his philosophy is worth passing along. "He is Esper Parish, author of *Notes of a Self Taught Rosarian*. He is strictly a no-nonsense rosarian. He's sincere, direct, earthy and as sound as the dollar was in 1880, the year Esper was born (that's a lot of "rose experience). He is delightful to listen to and to read. Among other things, Esper says, "There are frequent instances where good results are secured through some method entirely apart from accepted practices." He also advocates"… the simplest methods that will give good results if we are to interest more people in roses." To which the Rambler adds, "AMEN."

A SIMPLE ANSWER FOR SPIDER MITES?? Water, just plain water, is still the best and the safest. The old problems of water on rose foliage are not problems any more. If you have a water wand, use it. If you don't have one, make one or set a cone-type lawn sprinkler under the plants and water away the mites. Any kind of water-spray head that will direct a pattern of water droplets over a fairly wide area will do the job. Use a water wand as part of a regular garden routine. Start BEFORE mites get the upper hand.

OVERHEAD WATERING IS NOT BAD. Soaking systems are great (and the Rambler uses one), but even these need to be supplemented with overhead-underneath drenchings on a regular BASIS. Today's effective fungicides eliminate the worry of wet foliage. Overhead irrigation works best in the morning so that the leaves have a chance to dry off before evening or hot sun scalds the leaves. It's safe even in high humidity areas. Around here, the foliage is wet with dew every morning anyway. A good drenching washes off excess spray residue, cools the plant and makes the roots happy. It makes sense that a clean leaf works better.

ROSES NEED REFRESHMENTS, just like rosarians. One old (and very successful) rosarian in this area invariably hosed down healthy rosebushes after a very hot day. He usually held the hose in one hand and a beer can in the other. The foliage in his garden was invariably healthy, always clean and

COMPLETELY FREE of blackspot and mildew. He shared his refreshments with visiting rosarians, too.

BEFORE A BIG ROSE SHOW, slow soak or hand irrigate roses. Overhead watering and sun can ruin show blooms. A trophy-wise rosarian near here plants roses in the middle of a three-foot barrel ring, forming a sort of dam around the bush. All liquid feeding and hand watering goes into the ring as a supplement to rainfall and other irrigation. The roses are over eight feet tall.

SOAK, DON'T SPRINKLE. Whatever irrigation you use, SOAK the rose bed. Put down at least an inch of water at a time. Well drained rose beds are almost impossible to over-water. Roses in heavy soils (and built up beds) on the Gulf Coast take about two inches of water per week during the summer, in addition to summer rains. Porous, sandy soils take much more. To check the amount of water roses are getting, set out a couple of coffee cans in the rose beds and turn off the hose when the cans have an inch of water. It's the cheapest rain gauge ever made.

ICE CREAM FOR ROSES? Feed contents to the rosarian, save cartons for roses. Half-gallon ice cream cartons make good rose cones for shading show blooms. Tack or staple the carton to a wooden stake and place over the bloom. And cartons add interest to the garden. Careful growers are reported to use Cherry-Vanilla flavor over CHERRY VANILLA. Anyway, it's an interesting idea and no more strange than others I've heard.

The nostalgic theme for the month prompts some clips from previous Rambler columns and other writings… ideas that brought the most response (pro and con) from you good readers. Good rose ideas may mildew a bit… but they never die. Try out some of these.

ANOTHER LESSON that needs to be taught over and over again in mid-summer is common sense control of spider mites. More questions are probably being asked about these tenacious pests than any other rose problem; and more solutions are being offered. As far as I know, no miracle spray has yet come along to eliminate the pests; but a common sense approach and the sprays we do have will control them. In the hot, dry south and southwest, water is still the best answer. Just wash 'em off with water-no leaf burn, no spray residue, almost no mites. Greenhouse men were washing mites years and years before exotic chemicals came from the test tubes.

BENLATE is no miracle, but I am still sold on it as an excellent and safe fungicide. Perhaps too much was expected of *Benlate* from the beginning, attributing properties to it that were never deserved or claimed. After several years of use myself, rather broad observation and lots of letters from blackspot distributors all over the country, I still rely on *Benlate* as a blackspot-mildew fungicide without use of any other material. Benlate seems best when used alone, without a spreader-sticker or aromatic-base insecticide. Start protection program at pruning time, continue every 10 days.

SAVE THE LEAVES… It's sometimes hard to tell if more leaf damage is done by spray or by insects. Especially during the summer, the name of the rose game is LEAVES. Do everything possible to maintain a good, healthy leaf system. If you MUST spray, soak the rose beds first and spray during cooler hours. Some rosarians use insecticides in the evenings, then wash off the tops of the leaves with a fine water mist the next morning before the sun gets hot. To repeat what every good rosarian knows: well maintained plants can't help but produce roses. Whether leaves are lost because of mites, blackspot, mildew, spray burn or dehydration, the results are still the same: no roses.

A WARNING served on newcomers claims that spraying must always cover rose leaves over, under, sideways and crossways. It's GOOD advice when spraying for fungus diseases or spider mites under the leaves, but is wasteful and useless if the problem is thrips. Good rose competitors know that misting the tops of the plants every other day with *Cygan 2E* will do all the good that is necessary. For show blooms, start spraying with *Cygon* just as soon as color shows. Continue misting bloom areas every other day even when blooms are one-third to one-half open. *Cygan* does not seem to damage the bloom, particularly if sprayed in the evening.

STABILIZED MICRO-ORGANISMS are on the market that promise to "make dead soils alive again" and generally put billions of nature's microscopic workers on the side of the gardener. Some serious tests of three of these products produced no significant results. Roses in the check beds did just as well as bushes in beds treated according to directions. However, in all fairness to the formulators, the additives were used on rose beds already in excellent condition with good balance of humus, soil, air and water. Again, the rose bed with plenty of humus and manure produced the best roses more consistently than tighter soils or soils low in organic matter. Most rosarians would have to conclude that nature works best when given a good balance of air, friable soil and water.

COMMON SENSE is probably the best rose formula… and this applies to insect control for most growers. Keep the bushes healthy and vigorous with good growing practices and give up a few blooms to the bugs once in a while. A few aphids and thrips are not worth contaminating the whole garden with broad spectrum insecticides. Kill off the natural predators and you'll have an even greater insect problem. This is especially true of the "kill-everything" sprays that some overeager rosarians use to fight spider mites.

FAVORITE THOUGHTS FOR THE MONTH:

Faith will never die as long as there are rose catalogs.

Don't make the rose garden too big if your wife tires easily.

Roses like a lot of water, mostly in the form of sweat.

When everything else fails, read the directions.

From time to time these rambling columns have offered some rather good advice on roses. And none was better than the common sense approach to growing roses; let the new "wonders of science" mature for a season or two before upsetting a routine that works. Following a routine, you'll produce more and better roses with less work. Roses just naturally grow if we don't interfere too much.

ROSE FEEDING needs some common sense. Just do what comes naturally. While roses are heavy feeders, they respond to light, frequent feedings rather than massive fertilization. An overdose of rose food might be compared to the Thanksgiving Dinner of the rosarian... both will be under the weather until nature takes its course. Whatever your favorite formula, try half the quantity twice as often. You'll get more blooms for the money.

OSMOCOTE fits ideally into the natural scheme of things. A time-release material, it makes plant food available as factor of soil temperature. When the soil is warm, nutrients are released to a growing plant. Why is the plant growing?? Because the soil is warm. *PRECISE* and other products of this type do the same thing with minor variations. A supplement of trace elements has to be added to some of the timed-release formulas, but the overall program is appropriate for many rosarians around the country show that these fertilizers, properly applied, maintain good growth throughout the season and then shut off at the right time, permitting the plants to go dormant. You may want to consider slow release in your program next season.

WATER AND MORE WATER is still the name of the game for roses. The best soils and fertilizers can't do a bit of good until available to the plant in solution. Light sprinkling is wasteful; deep soaking is best. Depending on the soil and the temperature, roses need two inches of water per week. Don't guess; use a reliable rain gauge. If you water overhead, set the rain gauge in the irrigated area and check the amount actually getting to the roses. Overheard Fred Edmunds quoting a rose sage who said, "The hand that holds the hose grows roses." Not bad advice.

BUILT UP ROSE BEDS make a natural setting for roses. Although roses will tolerate many soils, poor drainage and lack of aeration will slowly but surely weaken plants. Many new growers enjoy an excellent first flush of bloom, progressively dropping off until the newcomer gives up in disgust, usually by the end of the first year. A major cause is poor soil aeration; roots are highly intolerant of waterlogged soil. Most growers do not realize that drainage of soil is both external and internal.

EXTERNAL or SURFACE DRAINAGE is generally understood, and most rosarians take care of it with slopes and ditches. Many believe that the problem is solved if water does not stand on the soil after heavy rains. Water moves through the soil in direct proportion to the size of soil particles. Heavy solid like clays and fine silts hold more water than soils with larger particles. Heavy soils inhibit downward movement of water. When the interparticle spaces of the soil are filled with water, an insufficient amount of air (oxygen) is available to the roots for normal respiration and growth. Active, new roots suffer most.

TENDER, YOUNG ROSE ROOTS can be damaged or destroyed if submerged in water for more than a few hours. Most damage occurs during prolonged rains in the growing season if the soil has poor drainage. Digging out a deep bed and replacing the soil does not correct the internal drainage problem, because the surrounding soil will not permit excess water to drain away rapidly. Soil water must escape from the soil below and surrounding it.

HIGH ROSE BEDS are common practice on the Gulf Coast, and should be used in many other parts of the country with poor drainage. They are easy to make. The existing soil is not disturbed except to scrape off the grass. Beds are then built above the ground line with soil that has been mixed just for that purpose. Build high enough so that the tops of the beds are 10 to 12 inches above the surrounding ground after settling. A common mix is 1/3 loamy topsoil, 1/3 peat or compost (leaves, shredded bark, plant residues) and 1/3 sharp sand. If the topsoil brought in is sandy, use about 1/2 topsoil and 1/2 peat or compost. For a REALLY productive bed, incorporate some animal manure or fishmeal. Mix two or three times with a rototiller and allow to settle and "work" for a month or two. Superphosphate, gypsum, Epsom salt, and what-have-you can be added "to taste". Anyway, roses love it and will thrive for many years in the bed without major problems.

The **RAMBLING ROSARIAN** is now six years old, seventy-two issues wiser, and still convinced that roses and rose people make up the greatest combination anywhere. With your indulgence, these Ramblings will continue with some old, new, borrowed and true odds and ends that make rose growing fun.

PICKED OFF ANY BLACKSPOT LEAVES LATELY? You are wasting your time. This has been the Rambler's experience, with no less authority than Dr. Eldon W. Lyle, Plant Pathologist of the Texas Rose Research Foundation. In brief, Dr. Lyle says to forget about the leaves and concentrate on It good spray program. It is a waste of time to pick off blackspot leaves except to make the bushes appear more tidy. Unseen infection supplies all the spores necessary to create fast spread of the disease. While infected leaves remain on the canes or stems, they put food and substance into the bushes. The main thing is to get a good spray program going on a weekly basis. Use *Benlate* at full strength (1 tbs. per 2 gallons) combined with *Phaltan* or *Manzate* at half strength (1 tbs. per 2 gallons of water). Use enough spray to reach the dripping stage from the leaves.

BEGIN A FUNGUS CONTROL PROGRAM the same week as pruning back the bushes in the spring. This is the best control of blackspot spores originating from cane infections where fungus over-winters, thus preventing spread to tender leaves as they start to form. It's more effective and less damaging to bushes than "dormant" sprays.

DEFOLIATION, whether from blackspot or hand picking of leaves, lessens the vitality of the bushes in proportion to the amount of leaves removed. If only 10% of the leaves are shed, not much harm is done to the bushes. Anything over 50% defoliation is very weakening. Rosebushes without leaves just do not have roses.

FALLEN LEAVES on the ground or on top of the mulch are not a source of carryover of the disease, although this is a very common belief. As soon as a diseased leaf falls and begins to decay, the blackspot disease also begins to decay. There is no need to remove the mulch that remains at the end of the season; just add more as needed for the next season.

EVERYBODY TELLS YOU HOW TO PREVENT BLACKSPOT, but no one wants to go out on a limb about curing it. Karl Envoldsen (K&E Research) is a concise, straight-to-the-point kind of note writer. Karl says, "If you have blackspot you must spray twice a week to keep new leaves clean; do this four times and your troubles are almost over." Karl E. also fired the Rambler another note, taking him to task for advising hot water as an assist in mixing wettable powders. He points out that a hot mix can separate oils from the mixture. The Rambler should have been more precise and advised WARM water for spray mixes, never having observed ANY separation with this method.

WANT A NEAT, EFFECTIVE MULCH? Pine bark chunks may be the answer you are looking for. Pine bark chunks (and even wood chips and chunks) are available in most parts of the country now, arid are rather inexpensive. In the long run, pine bark is very cheap because it lasts season after season. About two inches of chunks on top of a well-prepared rose bed lets air water and nutrients through, even if manure is used. And, even after several years, even if manure is used. And, even after several years, the soil in the rose bed appears to be as well aerated and alive as the first season. Wood chips may take a bit more nitrogen to make up for a soil loss in decomposition, but this is easily remedied. Chunks keep down the weeds, won't blow away and are quite attractive. What more could a rosarian want??

CHUNKS AND MINIS get along well, too. Recently visited an extensive miniature rose garden, completely mulched with pine bark chunks. The soil was moist and cool under the bark, ideal conditions for tiny feeder roots. Besides, the beds LOOKED good. The grower (in addition to liquid mixes) broadcasts fish meal in the beds or else feeds with a half-inch of ground manure. Water carries the organic fertilizer right to the soil where it begins to work. A half-inch difference in about three weeks.

LANDSCAPE TIMBERS will probably be in your future rose garden. Thanks to pressure treating with decay-retarding chemicals, timbers of all sizes can be used to construct many garden features easier and cheaper than most of the brick and mortar approaches. You have probably heard of "Wolmanized" timbers, and there are other process names that offer similar results. They are good for terracing, edging, elevating and general construction in most any shape a saw can cut or a rosarian imagine. Your local lumberman has a "how to" folder on landscape timbers. Makes a great project for fall or winter.

Indian Summer has arrived for most of us, and as defined by Webster it is "a happy and flourishing period occurring toward the end of something." Hope you have noticed that roses ARE happier this time of year, putting out a harvest that's bigger, better and more colorful. But it is not an end, just a pleasant time for rose planning... and here are a few thoughts to get you started...

How about a "Satellite Garden"... that is a rose garden of any description that doesn't actually belong to you?? You'll be surprised how rewarding an off-premises garden can be, making new friends for roses, more room for your own rose efforts and a chance to use some new gardening ideas. There's plenty of unclaimed territory just right for roses... a parkway or parking strip close by, a shut-in neighbor who can't keep up with a yard any more, your church or library, a home for senior citizens. With a little help and your experience, surprising things can happen. Sometimes roses do better when we don't worry over them so much, and the average viewer of a "rose satellite" spot doesn't know a split center from a sepal. But he does know that this is a big improvement over bare lawn and sick shrubbery. Once the rose beds are built, a few minutes a week will do the trick, and I'm speaking from experience.

Visited a beautiful planting of Tropicana roses just last week outside the small air terminal at Tyler, Texas. Our good friend Dr. Lyle looks after these roses and he says he averages about 20 minutes per week spraying, cutting spent blooms, *etc.* Overhead watering of the lawn areas also takes care of the roses. The bushes were 6 to 7 feet tall, averaged 8 to 10 canes per plant, and were covered with blooms. No blackspot, no mildew. The planting is accented with an offset of a half dozen tree roses, also very large and loaded with blooms. What a great way to be greeted on arrival. You just know this has to be a pleasant city. How about exploring some opportunities in your area, making it a better place to live?? And, best of all, it makes YOU feel good.

It's popular to talk about composting these days, but not many rosarians have grinding equipment to speed up the process, or at least you don't THINK you have. But the rotary lawnmower in the garage is a satisfactory substitute to at least get started. Now that there are lots of leaves to work with, here's an idea to get bacteria working in record time. Rake up tree leaves in a sort of windrow on an open space of lawn. The row can be 3 or 4 feet wide and several inches deep. Dampen the leaves with a spray from the hose. Fire up the rotary lawnmower, leave off the catching bag, and run the mower in a U-shaped pattern around the row of leaves. Repeat the chopping process a couple of times until shredding is complete. The result will be two neat rows of well-chopped organic material ready for composting in some garden area. The trick is to dampen the leaves, because they cut better and don't blow all over the yard. If you're anxious for some very fast compost, add a cheap source of nitrogen to the pile, dampen slightly and even cover with plastic to conserve heat. The mix you make is better than anything you can buy.

Mulches are also big with most growers, and everyone seems to have a favorite. Although it seems like the wrong time of year to talk about mulch, off-season bargains are usually available from nurseries that do not want to carryover bulky items. Two new materials are coming up in popularity and are worth considering. If you have a rose location you want to look exceptionally well groomed, require minimum care and still do the job a good mulch should, look into an application of pine or other bark chunks or even the newer calcined clay jumbos. The bark should be at least a medium-sized (1 inch to 2 1/2 inches) and liberally used (2 inches minimum).

A disadvantage of many organic mixtures is the constant replacement and sometimes unsightly appearance of the rose beds, particularly in the fall and winter. Bark chunks last a long time, have good appearance, allow water to percolate through easily, smother weeds and seem to promote a delicate humus balance in the top layers of the actual growing soil. The soil stays moist, friable, and seems full of bacterial life. Obviously, the soil must have good organic content in the first place, as bark chunks won't add much. However, even manure or well-rotted compost will filter through the chunks and help the humus balance.

Calcined clay chunks (marketed under a number of different names) are also very decorative and beneficial. Have been watching one large rose bed (along a concrete driveway exposed to full sun) that has been mulched with medium-sized pieces for nearly five years and the roses are thriving. A check of soil underneath shows everything in good order. It can't blow, wash away or decompose, and holds great quantities of water like a sponge. Looks good all winter, too.

From time to time the Rambler wonders just how many of these rose ideas are catching on; or to put it another way, which ideas will catch the Rambler. But rose nuts are great people; they are as moved to write about successes as to complain about failures. The Rambler is happy to report a success story this month, a testimonial for not just one but several rose ideas these columns have offered in various forms. Might be worth trying in your garden next year.

You'll perhaps recall that the Rambler likes tree roses, particularly in tubs and planters. To overcome some conditions which seem to be drawbacks, particularly in the North, it was recommended that a special mix be used in the planters, that the trees be started. with a plastic-bag "greenhouse" technique, fed regularly with organic fish emulsion, and, finally, wheeled into the garage for winter dormancy in areas with severe winter climates. Also, trees should be supported with a "splint" technique, for beauty as well as practical reasons.

Sandie Morris, Central District Director-elect, reported some "tree rose trials" she performed, in an enthusiastic series of letters with pictures. Since Sandie is from Missouri (St. Joseph), the photos were apparently to show the Rambler just how well the trees performed. In spite of the whims of the Missouri weather (described as the hottest, coldest, driest, windiest and most humid anywhere), actual statistics as of the end of August (third bloom cycle) were:

CHICAGO PEACE — 12 canes, maximum length 34 inches, 18 buds and blooms on the bush.

ANGEL FACE — 18 canes, maximum length 30 inches, 37 buds and blooms on the bush.

ELECTRON — 19 canes, maximum length 37 inches, 20 buds and blooms on the bush.

Sandie's comments (edited somewhat for believability) tell how it was done. "I used exactly what you recommended — 1/3 peat and compost, 1/3 Kitty Litter, and 1/3 good old Missouri dirt. The trees were planted in 22-in. redwood tubs the first week in March and treated as recommended — i.e., the lollipop plastic 'greenhouse'. They have been fed at approximately four-week intervals with 1 gallon (1 tbs. per gallon) of fish emul-

sion per tub and 1 feeding in early July of granular 12-12-8 with trace elements.

"I water the tubs every other day in 80-90° weather, although I'm sure they could go much longer. The **basal** breaks have been unbelievable, making me think we all plant our roses much too deep around here. The basals come out, go down, curve back up and make terrific canes, particularly the Chicago Peace.

"All of the trees in the tubs have produced probably twice the number of blooms as their counterparts growing in the ground (although double budding on the trees is a factor). They have been completely disease free and I spray with *Isotox* (as needed) and either *Maneb* or *Phaltan* (depending on the temperature, which was near 100 for several weeks). They have been washed periodically for red spider and have been sprayed twice with *Plictran* for same? Compared to trees planted in the ground at the same time, the trees in tubs look considerably better. I just couldn't be happier with my trees. I even grow my miniatures in tubs — just can't keep them clean (spider mites) in the ground, but they do great in redwood. Besides, they just look good."

Why did the trees in tubs perform so well? Probably because the soil mix provided an ideal medium for feeder roots (air, water and nutrients) and warmed up quickly in the spring for faster root development. This is just a guess (educated?) on the part of the Rambler, but it's obvious that these conditions were ideal. Also, it's well known that roses perform only as well as development of the roots permits. Good feeder root systems mean good roses.

The Kitty Litter (calcined clay granules) is essential in the mix. The granules have hundreds of microscopic air and water spaces, absorbing and releasing moisture as needed. This is the storage and exchange that supports soil processes to make plant nutrients available. Feed stores (and even grocery stores) have kitty litter available in 50-lb. sacks at very low cost. Make sure that the Litter has no additives or deodorizers... use just plain granules.

Fish emulsion fertilizer completes the natural soil process chain, providing organic, non-burning support for soil microorganisms. When these tiny workers are busy converting nutrients into forms available to plants, roses grow and rosarians are happy. It's a great way to enjoy roses.

Although it's the end of another rose year, it's not a time for dormant rosarians. Baseball fans used to have a "hot stove" league in the winter season; rosarians should be forming up "compost committees" to break down some good ideas while the bushes are covered with snow. If your compost group needs a starter, here are some rose clippings to add to the pile.

ROSE BLOOMS IN DECEMBER don't have to be something fondly remembered from last season; miniature roses in pots can add color year-round. Some of the sharper florists are beginning to offer blooming miniatures in place of the usual fare of plants that flower for a few days and are thrown away. You can be your own florist; roses make great gifts for a shut-in, giving lots of bloom without much care. And they do something for the rosarian, too.

PLANT-LIGHT FLUORESCENTS have made mini growing easy, providing everything the plants need. Build your own plant stands if you're handy with tools; or, if you want something a bit fancier, get a Flora-Cart setup that's advertised in many of the garden magazines. It's a tubular frame mounted on wheels with plastic growing trays. The plant light fixtures are hung in the frame (adjustable) and have two fluorescent tubes and two incandescent sockets in each. In any indoor setup, it's important that the fixtures be adjustable, as the distance from light source to plants is critical. Miniatures seem to do better without the incandescents, but this is probably tied in with the amount of natural light available. African violets, gloxinias and many blooming begonias like the same conditions as minis and make good companions. About 12 to 16 hours of light per day (use an automatic timer) with the fixtures about six inches above the plants works for most growers.

MINIS DO BEST IN HIGH-HUMUS, well aerated soil with good drainage. Credit Harmon Saville of Nor'East roses for a mini formula that's easy to make up and lasts for several seasons. He suggests a soilless mix of peat, perlite and vermiculite, with just a bit of *18-6-12 Osmocote* for slow-release feeding. *Perlite* is a good growing medium because it retains air and water, having about 20% air space by volume. The plants will tolerate considerable differences in potting mixtures, but must have a very careful, regular feeding program. Good mini growers use soluble foods in very low concentrations at two-to three-week intervals. As a start, try your favorite formulation at one-quarter strength. Add or subtract as needed. I like Atlas Fish Emulsion.

WATER SPRAY WILL TAKE CARE OF SPIDER MITES. Put the mini pot in a laundry tub and spray the undersides of the leaves with plenty of water. Water-wash even before mites show up; the extra water cleans the leaves and makes the whole system work better. Mites can usually be cleared up with three washings at three-day intervals. Minis also prefer high humidity. Add some moisture to the air if you have dry furnace heat. A plastic sheet over the growing frame will help; moist gravel or perlite in the growing tray also releases moisture. And watch the heat. A range of 50° to about 70° is ideal. Check the temperature UNDER the lights and near the plants, as lamps generate considerable heat.

WHILE ENJOYING MINIATURES inside this winter, keep an eye on what's happening outside as well. Watch for some clues as to the effectiveness of your winter protection system. Is it able to keep up with changes in the weather? The best methods handle a broad range of conditions and, in the Rambler's observations, usually use natural materials. It seems that Mother Nature isn't often fooled; soil and leaves have been nature's way to protect living things since time began. Whether you mound, cover, bank, tip or otherwise insulate rose canes, dirt and leaves seem to be able to handle the changes in the weather best. In simple terms, just do what comes naturally.

A FAVORITE "COMPOST COMMITTEE" TOPIC concerns the merits of California-grown vs. Texas-grown rosebushes (or other states, for that matter). This is a delicate subject for a Texan to discuss, even a transplanted one from Colorado. But it is the Rambler's observation that good growers in California and good growers in Texas turn out equally good bushes for most parts of the country. When planted side by side, the same varieties of roses from both major growing areas perform about the same. Even a critical observer can't tell one from the other. It makes much more sense to look into WHO you buy from rather than

WHERE you buy roses.

Bill Homan of the Maine RS shares a good rose-grower story that proves that all the nuts in the world don't necessarily come from trees. Bill reports that Star Roses grew and sold some unusually large rose plants last year. Would you believe that one customer returned his order saying that they were so large that they had to be old bushes?? All this just as he had concluded that rose people represented the last bastion of sanity in this old world.

It's traditional for columnists to review and reflect on the year just ended, arriving at carefully-qualified conclusions about whether the year was good or bad. The Rambler is afflicted with the same strain of hindsight wisdom and herewith passes on some ideas from here and there... you can make your own conclusions. But one thing comes through strong and clear... rosarians are beginning to use more COMMON ROSE SENSE, making both roses and rosarians happier. Anyway, here are some bits of rose research that are certain to be significant additions to rose literature. The trial notes are available to serious researchers... on the walls of the tool shed, scraps of paper in the spray cabinet, and carefully catalogued somewhere in the clipboard that won't hold any more junk.

More manure in the soil mix does not necessarily produce more roses. A mixture of half finely-ground barnyard manure and half pine bark (ground and composted) looked good but gave poor results. The excessive organic material appeared to be too tight for good air space, although water penetrated freely. Another bed of 1/3 manure, 1/3 compost and 1/3 sand and soil performed much better. Except for the planting mix, both beds were treated identically. Conclusion: if a little is good, more isn't necessarily better.

But don't give up on manure. A mix of horse manure and sawdust (composted) applied in early spring got roses off to a flying start. Two beds with two inches of horse mix just after pruning started faster, produced more canes and better blooms than beds started with 12-24-12. The rest of the feeding program was the same. And the organic fed plants tolerated hot midsummer much better. Roses fed fishmeal also out-performed plants fed only with inorganics. A technical breakthrough was noted in the fishmeal experiment: it doesn't smell when poured into holes punched around the perimeter of rose bushes. Top off the holes with soil and water thoroughly. Even dogs and cats leave ill1planted fishmeal alone.

Some other odds and ends learned the hard way. Single rows of roses do not seem to get bigger or bloom better than roses planted in double rows, even in climates that commonly produce huge roses. The single rows are also less attractive, lacking something in balance and proportion or

mass or something. Anyway, all the Rambler's roses go back to double rows next year... Too impatient to root miniature cuttings? Then dig up some miniature clumps and split the plants, replanting each with plenty of room to grow. Many mini varieties are much more productive after digging and splitting. Since new growth produces blooms, it makes sense to open up a miniature rose plant so that it can break and spread... Patio-size rose standards are easier to grow and maintain than most rosarians think. A good soil mix with plenty of organic material makes these accent plants perform on the hottest patio. Redwood or clay pots work fine, at least 12 inches in diameter. Water every-other day and enjoy the beauty.

Tree roses and miniatures mix very well. Trees are beautiful because they add another dimension to the landscape; but the effect is hidden if floribundas or other large roses are planted in the same bed. Miniatures planted under tree roses are like an accenting carpet in a well-appointed room. Color mixtures don't make much difference, either. Just be a bit careful in feeding tree roses so that the minis won't burn. Use less food more often — a good piece of advice for other roses, too... It seemed like a good idea at the time to plant Red Cascade (climbing mini) in a brick foundation planter exposed to full sun. The plants started very well, producing two- and three-foot runners in less than 60 days. Soon the planter bed was a solid mass of lush foliage and a few blooms (on the tips of the canes). Then the spider mites moved into what must have been mite heaven. The thick, tangled foliage and canes (about five inches deep) kept the water wand, sprays and even friendly insects from the undersides of the leaves. Mites multiplied by the millions in the hospitable environment. Sprays burned up the leaves the mites didn't like. Moral: use Red Cascade in a hanging basket, on a low trellis, or in a manner where mite controls can work.

Benlate-Manzate combinations worked better than *Benlate-Phaltan* in controlling fungus diseases for the Rambler. Both kept blackspot in check, but the *Phaltan* mix seemed to toughen and burn foliage more. Leaf damage has several stages; coarse, tough foliage is an early sign of trouble. Like sunburn, repeated exposures aggravate cell damage… Highly alkaline water makes a better spray mix if neutralized first with 1 tablespoon of ordinary vinegar per gallon of water. Fungicides work better with less burn. Rainwater is best, but not many of us have a rainbarrel these days. Come to think of it, that's COMMON ROSE SENSE.

In case you haven't noticed, February is a GOOD month for roses-too early for the really hard work to begin and yet late enough for the roses of last season to get better and better. There's something about snow on the ground that makes last season's roses have more form, color, size (and winners). Now that Queen-of-the-Show winners are safely dormant under cones or leaves, rosarians in the north can spend full time with catalogs and the *American Rose Annual*. In the south, pruning will begin shortly as even the old standbys promise great things with swelling new buds. It's great to be a rosarian... you just can't wait to get the new season started.

Sap begins to rise in roses and rosarians at about the same time... the first warm day. But this season, how about some common rose sense? Nature and roses perform best gradually; crash spring programs usually crash with the first cold snap. It's similar to the "Sunday Syndrome" that occurs in the summertime. Sunday Syndrome is a rose affliction caused by the rosarian: a rosebush worn out from pruning, grooming, pulling, pinching, feeding, scratching, watering, spraying and fussing (not necessarily in that order). In the spring it takes the form of uncovering, digging, probing, feeding, cutting and drenching with gunk before the soil is warm enough to support growth. Let spring and rose work come on gradually; you'll get better results.

It's the Rambler's opinion that "dormant" sprays are overdone and overrated, often causing more cane damage than good. The lime-sulfur-oil concoctions are hard to use (particularly when it's cold and the plants are really dormant) and do not offer the safe and effective control of overwintering disease and insects that specific fungicides and insecticides do. These controls are already on the rosarian's shelf. Trials over the last seven years by the Texas Rose Research Foundation conclusively show that a cleanup spray of *Phaltan-Isotox, Manzate-Spectracide* or similar mix applied immediately after pruning establishes a sound control program for the season. Use *Phaltan-Isotox* at full strength as directed on the package. Thoroughly drench the canes, bud union and immediate surrounding area. Spray the same day the bushes are pruned. Fungus spores overwinter on green canes;

insects hide out in corky tissue. The name of the game for fungus is control. Start early and enjoy roses more.

Roses start better when planted the right way, too. If there is a key step in planting, it's water. Thorough, deep soaking for all steps of the planting process. The Rambler is a "cone type" planter, supporting the root system with a cone of well-prepared soil. Cover the roots lightly and begin to run water slowly into the hole. Add some more soil; water will fill in the voids. While one bush is soaking, plant the next one. Then come back with more soil, more water, etc. Don't stomp on the roots to "tamp" the soil in place. Let water do the work. It makes a rosarian cringe to see a 200-lb. enthusiast breaking and displacing rose roots with size 12 boots.

And don't forget to hill up canes of new bushes with all the soil, mulch or other insulating material available. This not only protects from the cold, but keeps canes from drying out. Until roots are well established, canes are very vulnerable to sun and wind. Constant temperature and moist conditions help roses start. It's the same principle with plastic tents over plants slow to start. Throw a handful of wet sphagnum moss over the bud union, form a tent of clear plastic material (like the plastic roses are shipped in) over the bush and secure at the shank. The result is a high humidity, warm greenhouse that encourages breaks. When the bushes have started, gradually cut holes in the plastic to lower the temperature. Remove in about two weeks, depending on the weather.

Some rose society programs may need a spring tonic, too. For example, has your group thought seriously about a shopping mall rose show or exhibition where roses can be sold (call it a donation)? A Houston area show last fall netted $725 and made lots of friends for roses at the same time. Besides the money, the group handed out several thousand information sheets on roses. Signed up new members and made roses fun. Surplus roses of fair quality were placed in *Water Piks* and inserted into a *Styrofoam* display block. These brought a $1 donation. Better roses in 26-cent display vases produced $2 each. Winners and collections went for $3 to $4. Not a bloom went to waste.

Ray Golden of Sacramento, California, passes on this thought that has lots of merit. Why not have more rose "Festivals" and "Fairs" instead of shows? Rose competition can still be there, but the overall event can be broadened to attract more people. When exhibition halls and shopping malls are filled with roses, rose societies are going to have more people as well. Prospective rosarians are looking for cultural information, landscape help and rose fun. The groups that provide this kind of rose package will grow and prosper. And ARS has an interest in this development, if it is to attract some 10,000 new members needed for an active, healthy society. It's common rose sense to appeal to and build on a broad base... people who like roses.

MAR. 1977

THOUGHT FOR THE MONTH: When you think you have graduated from the school of experience, someone thinks up a new course.

Roses Coast to Coast has failed to alert rosarians to a serious rose virus that is now epidemic in the South and seems sure to spread north in the next month or so. It's called Spring Rose Fever, an infection brought on by rose catalogs (dormant when snow is on the ground) that erupts with fever and light-headedness on the first warm day of spring. The condition persists until the resident rosarian breaks dormancy and gets outdoors to work in the roses again. Here are some cures…

How about some tree roses this season? If it's too cold in your area to have good tree roses without considerable work and winter protection, try a few in tubs and planters. Some of the most impressive tree roses you'll ever see are grown in redwood tubs, used as garden or patio accents during the summer and moved into the garage or garden shed in the winter. Or, if you are skeptical about winter hardiness in planters, trees can be pulled from the planters (they form a big ball of roots) and protected with a Minnesota Tip method. Either way will produce loads of roses.

Extra care in the selection of the planting medium makes all the difference in growing good roses in tubs season after season. Roses in tubs will thrive in the temperatures of Missouri, Minnesota and New York as well as in the heat and humidity of Texas and Louisiana. The formula for growth and survival is good drainage, air in the root zone, and ability to retain moisture. A 22-inch tub requires watering about twice a week if the formula is in good balance, even during hot weather. There are many variables in the watering program, but roses in planters seldom require any more care or water than roses in conventional beds.

The mix that seems to work best has 1/3 garden soil, 1/3 Canadian peat moss and 1/3 calcined clay granules (Kitty Litter). Use granules without additives. It's inexpensive and available in 50-lb. bags at most feed stores. Calcined clay granules are extremely porous, something like a microscopic honeycomb. The material has the ability to take in moisture for slow release to feeder roots without souring, packing or decomposing. If you still have doubts about this strange mix, check the success of Sandie Morris in the November, 1976, Rambler column. Her experience is shared by rosarians all over the country.

These simple suggestions may help cold-climate rosarians who will soon be pruning (assuming there is something left to prune). Painting new cuts is fast and easy with shellac in an old liquid shoe polish bottle. The dauber gives good, neat coverage of your favorite material and is very convenient. Shellac or even *Elmer's White Glue* seems to work better than asphalt-base paints in our area. The Rambler likes to paint the end of any cane thumb-size or larger and all cuts made at the bud union. Unless you just have lots of time for pruning and painting, don't bother painting very light canes; they heal quickly without help. Painting is like any other would treatment, stops bleeding and keeps foreign matter out. As far as fungus infection is concerned, a drenching cleanup spray of *Phaltan-Isotox* or *Manzate-Spectracide* gives all the protection needed.

The Rambler thinks it is impractical and a waste of time to attempt to disinfect pruning tools with Lysol, alcohol or what-have-you between rosebushes. It's hard to imagine rose pruning under antiseptic condition. Thousands of rosebushes pruned over some 20 years have never shown any signs of cross-infection. A careful rosarian with clean, SHARP tools can do a good job without worry.

There's some technique involved in pruning that can make a difference in die-back, healing of cuts and a vigorous spring start. For large, woody canes, use a small keyhole saw instead of the crushing jaws of a lopper. Cuts will heal faster, particularly on the bud union. And make it a regular habit to keep the BLADE of the pruning shear DOWN so that the opposing jaw of the shear does not bruise good rose cane. To say it another way, let the jaw bruise the cane material that is cut off. Use pruners that are large enough and sharp enough to make cuts smooth and clean. If the cut isn't smooth and easy, you are using the wrong tool. Another good idea is to clean up the bud union, either above or below ground. Use a small pruning saw with fine teeth to trim off old stubs flush with the bud union so that it can completely heal over. Be careful of new buds. A short length of rose cane used like a wood rasp works fine.

Everyone likes a giveaway, so the Rambler has reproduced and will pass on Rose Guide

Sheets written by The Minnesota Rose Society. This material is great for cold-climate rosarians; written in simple garden languages, with sketches. The "Spring Set" consists of Pruning, Spring Care, Miniature Roses, Tree Roses and Old Garden Roses. Dorothy Campbell and a host of other Minnesota Rose Society folks have done an excellent job and their work deserves to be shared. If you would like a set, drop the Rambler a note; and the next time the hat is passed for the American Rose Center, drop in an extra dollar. Roses and rosarians will benefit. PS: A "Summer Set" will be available later.

With the "Winter of '77" beginning to melt, it's time for rosarians to talk about spider mites again. Every rose season has a new kind of problem: and when our roses don't have a problem, we create one. It's been said time and time again and it's still true, roses are the most popular and productive flower in the world in spit of rosarians, not because of them. Of course it doesn't really hurt anything to hope that the hard winter froze the mites once and for all... but we'll probably just come up with a meaner strain. All this long preamble is just to remind you again that roses are supposed to be fun; and that rose folks are the greatest in the world.

If you need an early-in-the-season rose problem or project, try this one on for size. Get your rose spray schedule going. For those of you just finding your roses under the snow, this may seem ridiculous; but in our part of the country we have been spraying since Valentine's Day. Fungus control is a matter of prevention. Field trials and carefully controlled tests in gardens just like yours show that a fungus control program should be started IMMEDIATELY after pruning, drenching the canes and bud union thoroughly. Even if there's only a little live wood left, drench it. Use a combination of a broad spectrum insecticide (*Diazinon* is a good one) with your favorite fungicide (*Phaltan* or *Manzate*) at full strength. Control over-wintering spores on the canes before temperature and humidity multiply and spread the infection. Blackspot spores are still there on the green cane material, in spite of the winter cold.

An insecticide-fungicide combination is a more effective fungus control than an oil-sulfur combination, and less likely to burn. Don't wait for new leaves to appear. Prune and spray the same day. Spray again in two weeks with the same combination then set up your usual control program. And don't forget to spray climbers and shrub roses at the same time. An infected plant can spread blackspot spores like wildfire when conditions are right. A clean start is the best way to have a clean garden all season.

If you have some plants that are a little winter-sluggish; or a bare root rose that might have dried out in shipment; here's a way to break dormancy that's fast and easy. Prune the bush to taste; and

for bare-root roses, soak in water or planting solution at least overnight. Make up a loose fitting hood of clear plastic material and secure the edges of the plastic with staples or a loose tie so that the hood closes rather securely around the shank of the bush. For some extra humidity, add a handful of wet sphagnum moss inside the bag. Plant the bush as usual; mud in the roots. After the first warm day or two, you'll see condensed moisture inside the hood. Leave the hood in place for a week or so; them cut some air holes to reduce temperature. Take the hood off (gradually) when strong shoots and leaves begin to appear. Works great for tree roses, too.

Rose societies need to break winter dormancy, too. See to it that your rose activities reflect the same freshness, thought, effort and imagination as the roses you plant. One of my pet peeves is to attend a rose society meeting (no names mentioned) and be bored through thirty minutes of listless minutes, nit-picking discussions over the cost of refreshment cookies, droning recitations of finances, motions, seconds, rephrasing and discussions of things that have nothing to do with growing and enjoying better roses. Rose people get together to be entertained and informed, not to sit as a judicial body. Membership grows when roses are fun. Put the plus of pleasure back into your rose meeting and insist that the exec committee do 99% of the work and the decision making. It's like enjoying the first warm breath of spring after a long winter.

One more thought to turn on rose participation. How about awarding rose bushes instead of silver keeper-trophies?? Exhibitors of all persuasions really go for certificates good for two rose bushes of their choice for delivery the following season. Roses are more appropriate than silver knick-knacks that need polishing. You can work out special discounts with local suppliers (and many of the national mail-order growers). The rose supplier likes the business and the winner likes a practical award for a change.

Another giveaway. You may have noted last month that the Rambler will pass on Rose Guide Sheets written by the Minnesota Rose Society (Spring Set). Some more guides are now ready for rosarians, called the Summer Set. It includes Correcting Nutritional Deficiencies, Summer Care of

Roses, Keeping Roses Healthy, Grow and Show, and... for late in the season... The Minnesota Tip. The Minnesota Rose Society people have worked hard on these guides, and they are useful for rosarians in every part of the country. If you would like to have either set, drop the Rambler a note... no cost or postage. But it would be good for roses and rosarians if you would drop in an extra dollar for The American Rose Center at your next fund event.

MAY 1977

THOUGHT FOR THE MONTH: *Prayer Of The Rosarian: Please, Lord, give me a little patience... and give it to me right away.*

Have you ever thought about the market potential for common garden sense? It's about the only thing not advertised in our favorite garden magazines; just a small "trial packet" of this miracle ingredient would fill our gardens with flowers. Some plain dirt gardening makes roses fun, and that's what it's all about. As ARS members, we have the world's greatest produce... when we convince ourselves and others that roses are easy and fun, we won't be able to handle all of the applications for our rose societies. Have you sold your share lately?

Here's an idea that's easy to sell, and the roses will sell themselves. Plain dirt gardeners know that an ample helping of manure used before other rose foods will make the whole formula work better. We don't have to understand it to appreciate the results. An early season starter or rose show feeding schedule should always include manure a week or two before soluble applications. Another way to accomplish the same thing is to add about 20 lbs. of bloodmeal to a typical 40-lb. sack of organic based rose food. Work the mix with soil bacteria and watch the results.

Sacked manure has been getting a bad press lately, primarily charged with adding too much salt to the soil. This may well be the case with manure from feed lot applications, but don't condemn well-composted barnyard products. Straight from the farm, manure is nature's own soil conditioner... and you can't fool Mother Nature.

But just in case you don't have a farm friend for the real thing, how about making up a batch of artificial manure? It's just as good (maybe better, because it releases more nutrients) and can be produced on any city lot. You get all the benefits without the cow. Here's the formula:

ARTIFICIAL MANURE

3 ample yards of leaves or compost materials
100 lbs. of cottonseed hulls (or something coarse)
100 lbs. of cottonseed meal
100 lbs. rough cut alfalfa meal
50 lbs. of bone meal
50 lbs. of fish meal

The local feed store will have all the ingredients except the leaves. Use any area OK for composting, may on top of the old vegetable bed. Pile the leaves and coarse materials about two feet deep. Add the ingredients a little at a time and turn with a garden fork. Moisten LIGHTLY; turn with a fork twice a week for two weeks. Cover with plastic if you are in a hurry. When the pile is working properly, a sharp ammonia odor will leak out. Don't get the pile too wet, or a very different odor win fill the neighborhood. When cottonseed meal gets too wet (and if there is not enough coarse composting material) it turns into a slime with a dead smell that crawls along the ground like fog.

In about three weeks you'll have the best organic fertilizer available. Use about two garden shovelfuls of artificial manure per established bush; repeat in late summer with about one shovelful. If you are a manure gourmet, you may want to add other trace materials such as seaweed, rock phosphate or decomposed granite. Be the first on your block.

Sydney Maxfield, Director of the Tyler (Texas) Municipal Rose Garden, passes on some experiences he has had with replacement rosebushes in an established rose bed. If you have ever tried to add new plants to beds with existing large bushes, you know that it takes a very long time for the new plants to catch up... and some of them never do. Maxfield's trials show that it is more a matter of root competition than competition for sunlight. He found that new bushes started in containers made the transition better and caught up with the old bushes much faster. Trial bushes were planted in containers about one month before the usual bare root planting time and placed in a protected location. When the container bushes were growing to the point of good leaves, they were transferred to the established rose beds by cutting off the pots, for minimum root disturbance. By early summer the new plants had caught up. For northern rose growers, it is important to remember that the old plants were pruned to approximately 18 inches and had at least three good canes. A close check of the pots shows why it works. The warmer (and probably better) soil of the container encouraged root development, and the roots in turn were able to compete and support top growth. It's worth a try in many gardens.

Another note along the same line which would seem to discount the shading theory. A number of rose beds were oriented east and west, making a row of roses on the north and a row of roses on the south. Most growers would assume that roses in the south (sunny) row would out-perform the roses in the north (shady) row. However, by minimizing root competition, even new plants in the north row kept up with older plants in the south. If there's a moral here, it must be that good root systems make good roses. Might be called common garden sense.

The best roses in the world are probably grown while standing around the coffeepot after a rose meeting. Coffee and cookies bring out the best in rosarians... the best and most practical advice on how to grow better roses. Which makes me wonder why we don't have more workshop sessions for growers to share their experiences. If rose talk over coffee is good, wouldn't rose talk with everyone be even better? Anyway, here are some ideas to talk about at your next meeting.

Why do we use so many insecticides? For the most part they are not necessary. Nature has a built-in balance, and the less we disturb it the better off we are. Use specific controls for specific insects, ONLY when needed. The habit of adding insecticides to fungicides on a weekly basis is wasteful and addictive. Once started, the practice is hard to stop. Most gardens can get along very well with two or three general insecticide sprayings a season (using spot controls for thrips, corn ear worms and so forth) as needed. Use a specific insecticide by itself. Spray only those parts of the rose that are affected. Thrips don't live under the leaves at the bottom of the plant; why spray there? Mist the buds and blooms, that's where thrips are busy. *Orthene* or *Cygon* offer good control without overkill. The same conservative practice applies to spider mites. Too many poisons contribute to the spider mite problem rather than eliminate it. Spray addicts who have kicked the habit are telling about better roses... mostly because the rosebushes are able to grow as nature intended. Moral of the spider mite story: If you don't have a water wand, get one.

There's a watering system now available to ordinary rose growers that deserves to be shared. It is so simple to build that 'most anyone (with a helper or two) can have a system running over a week-end. The *Dramm Nozzle* makes it all possible. It's a two-piece nozzle of hard plastic with a threaded connection. A pin diffuser sprays water in a circle parallel to the rose bed. In other words, the water sprays out, not up. Pull the pin out of the top of the nozzle and a thin stream of water shoots straight up (and clears out any junk in the water line). For a serious blockage, unscrew the top half of the nozzle and the whole system can be flushed out. The flushing process can be done while the system is turned on~almost without getting wet.

The water distribution system is made from 1/2-in. Schedule 40 PVC pipe. This is the rigid type plastic pipe; and connections, elbows, tees and adapters are available at most lumber yards, hardware stores or plumbing shops. The pipe cuts easily with a hacksaw, and all connections are made with epoxy glue. If you make a mistake, cut out the section and glue up another one. The plastic pipe system is laid on the surface of the rose bed and can be attached permanently to a water source or connected to a garden hose with a quick-coupler (cheap and easy). Ordinary water pressure from a 5/8-in. hose will supply an irrigating line 40 feet long with IS to 18 nozzles. Each nozzle will spray an area three to four feet in diameter, depending on the pressure. Control the pressure at the house tap or install a valve at the head of each line.

Dramm nozzles are inserted into PVC pipe with a tapered neoprene washer. Drill holes (11 132-in.) in the pipe. Clean out any bits of shavings. Insert a tapered washer (fits like a saddle) and screw in the nozzle. The nozzle is threaded and tapered; screw in two or three turns for a tight fit. All the connections can be made without tools, ordinary grip like threading a hose connection is all that's necessary.

Best of all, it's cheap. At retail, each nozzle costs about 30 cents; each tapered washer about 10 cents. They are available from most greenhouse supply houses and come in three delivery rates; mix and match to suit the need. It's a good idea to use nozzles with less deliverability at the head of the line (where pressure is greater), graduating to sizes with more deliverability near the end of the line. Water distribution is very even, easily controlled and less wasteful. A rose bed 40 feet long and five feet wide can be watered thoroughly in 20 minutes. It's a time-saving answer for a rosarian with formal rose beds.

This RAMBLER column began with some comments about sharing, so here are some sharing offers you might like to get. Giveaway 1: The Editor's Workshop, an outline for anyone working with rose society publications. Giveaway 2: Rosarian's Workshop, a four-page guide for conducting a general participation rose workshop.

It has been used many times and is a sure-fire winner. Giveaway 3: Alphabetical Show Schedule, a simple show schedule (even an artistic schedule) that makes rose shows so easy that they are almost fun. The alphabetical system is universally used in the South Central District with great results. If you could use any of this material, the Rambler is glad to share it… no cost or postage. But it would help roses if you would drop in an extra dollar for the Rose Center at your next fund event.

JUL.
1977

THOUGHT FOR THE MONTH:
Nature is an original artist. That's why she never copies the pictures in the rose catalog.

This Rambler collection of roses (or maybe spent blooms) touches on the old and the new... some ideas to provoke discussion and a few old rose tips to help you remember just how much fun growing roses used to be... and still is.

Tree Roses used alone in an accent planting are attractive and different. Build a rose bed in the usual way, but plant a dozen or more tree roses with the same spacing as normal bush roses. Mix and match varieties to taste. The planting is attractive even when the roses are not blooming. Natural looking ground cover like pine bark chunks or composted material with Ajuga ground cover makes a pleasant break in an expanse of lawn. In moderate climates, tree roses are easy to grow and less likely to have the common problems of bush roses. Carefully staked (use the "splinting method") with electrical conduit pipe, the trees add a whole new dimension to the landscape. Select varieties that repeat well with medium-size blooms rather than "show winner" types. Europeana, Ole, The Fairy, Ginger, Sea Foam and Tiffany are excellent examples of varieties suitable for trees in the landscape.

Miniature roses would seem to be lost in a bed mulched with medium to large chunks of pine bark, but just the opposite is true. The soft, weathered look of bark accents green leaves and small blooms. Besides making a good mulch, bark chunks keep foliage cleaner with less splash of soil and sand from heavy rains. No weeds either. Since water percolates easily through the two-inch cover, pelletized or liquid fertilizers can be used. No need to disturb the cover during the season; just enjoy the roses.

The hose-on sprayer is a luxury few rose growers can afford any more. Even though it seems cheap in the beginning, wasted spray materials run up the cost. Aside from the handling and ecological hazards, hose-on sprayers use two or three times as much spray material to do the same job as a good tank-type sprayer. The Rambler was a fan of hose-ons for a long time, primarily because they were simple and easy to use... and the once-in-a-while type gardener would spray instead of putting it off. But in a time of rising costs and spray controls, it makes good sense to invest in a tank sprayer with sufficient size and pressure to deliver the right mix to rose plants every time.

Miniatures are coming up in the world in fence baskets something like the half-planters that orchid fanciers use. Fence baskets are made just like regular hanging baskets, but are flat on one side so that they can hang on a fence (or a post). Some have interesting shapes and are formed from various materials... wire, pottery, peatboard or what-have-you. Line and fill the containers just like any other hanging basket; use plenty of organic material to hold the moisture. Hang on a sunny fence and enjoy miniatures close up. The American Rose Center will have a "post" garden made of landscape timbers with fence baskets of miniatures. In this planting, a capillary tube watering system will water and feed all of the baskets at one time. It's a technique that many growers can use. Use garden type minis that cascade and are free flowering; there are a good many available.

Some of the old time religion of rose growing may be missing from meetings these days, but they'll know you are an old-pro grower when you tell how your watering system used to be a hose poked into an old time can. Move the hose and can once in a while and the whole bed was soaked rather than sprinkled. A feeding program for the rose faithful was a shovelful of manure whenever it wasn't too hot to shovel, which suited roses about right. A manure pile behind the garage was the badge of a good gardener. Unlike the chemical potions today, a few shovelfuls more or less couldn't do any harm; roses were supposed to grow that way.

Roses smelled better some years ago, probably because the grower didn't cover up the fragrance with sprays of every description. A little less pollution probably helped, too. COW TEA was a faithful remedy for a sick plant, brewed from rainwater caught in a barrel. It made a sick plant well, and a well plant even better. Our rain barrel had a secret ingredient; several pounds of rusting nails in the bottom. Hydrangeas (and roses) got a regular treatment.

Winter protection consisted of leaves from the trees, carefully raked from the lawn and piled high in the rose beds. The rose bed looked like a brown snow bank before winter arrived. By spring the leaves had settled and composted (and a few had blown away) but snows and thaws and wind and sun hadn't done much damage. When new breaks began to come up through the woodsy mulch, it was time to add some more manure and start the whole process over again.

But enough of the old... today we'll take the benefits of Benlate, Osmocote, Orthene, Phaltan, Cygon, Diazinon and all the rest. The lab has given even the old-time rosarian the tools to enjoy roses more, grow more roses easier and better than ever before... provided he uses some rose sense. So if you'll excuse me, I have to go out and load my power sprayer with a systemic insecticide and fungicide... as soon as the sprinkling system cuts off.

Now and then the Rambler responds with clips from previous columns, ideas that have brought the most reaction (pro and can) from you good readers. Good rose ideas may fade a bit, but they don't die back. You may want to rate some of these with your own scale of points...

SAVE THE LEAVES. It's sometimes hard to tell if more leaf damage is done by spray or by insects. Especially during the summer, the name of the rose game is LEAVES. Do everything possible to maintain a good, healthy leaf system. If you MUST spray, soak the rose beds first and spray during cooler hours. Some rosarians use insecticides in the evenings, then wash off the tops of the leaves with a fine water mist the next morning before the sun gets hot. To repeat what every good rosarian knows: well maintained plants can't help but produce roses. Whether leaves are lost because of mites, blackspot, mildew, spray burn or dehydration, the results are still the same: no roses.

MULCH IS NOT MYSTERIOUS, it simply works in the rose bed in a natural way to conserve moisture, lower soil temperature and add humus gradually. Think of mulch as an insulator through which water, air and nutrients can percolate. If insulation is too thin, it doesn't work well. You and your roses will be happier if you add a couple of inches of good living (mulch) to the rose beds.

SOME "ROSE AUTHORITIES" claim that sprays must always cover rose leaves over, under, sideways and crossways. It's GOOD advice when spraying for fungus diseases or spider mites under the leaves, but is wasteful and useless if the problem is thrips. Good rose competitors know that misting the tops of the plants with *Cygan 2E* or *Orthene* will do all the good that is necessary. For show blooms, start spraying just as soon as color shows. Continue misting bloom areas twice a week even when blooms are one-third to one-half open.

"NEVER WET THE LEAVES" makes about as much sense as trying to eliminate rainfall. Overhead watering is not bad. In fact, overhead watering offers some substantial benefits that soaking systems can't match. The reason: today's effective fungicides virtually eliminate the worry of wet foliage. This is not to suggest that growers wet down the leaves each evening, but no harm will come from regular overhead watering PROVIDED a systematic fungicide spray program is followed. Many growers set a cone-type lawn sprinkler directly in the rose bed and let the water spray up under the rosebushes. This accomplishes two things: it washes off the spider mites and effectively prevents old spray buildup.

Rose beds with irrigation systems should also get the overhead, underneath, water-all-over method about once a week. Spider mites just do not like all that water, and roses do. An old grower told me a long time ago that hosing down healthy rosebushes after a very hot day was just like the gardener having some refreshments after a long dry spell. And he enjoyed tremendous success with roses. The foliage in his garden was always clean, healthy, disease free. Moral: roses like to be clean and cool just like rosarians. With all the junk floating in the air these days, 'most everything can stand a washing from time to time.

BUILT UP ROSE BEDS make a natural growing medium for roses. Although roses will tolerate many soils, poor drainage and lack of aeration will slowly but surely weaken plants. Many new growers enjoy an excellent first flush of bloom, progressively dropping off until the newcomer gives up in disgust, usually by the end of the first year. A major cause is poor soil aeration; roots are highly intolerant of waterlogged soil. Most growers do not realize that drainage of soil is both external and internal, and a good rose bed should provide both.

EXTERNAL OR SURFACE DRAINAGE is generally understood, and most rosarians take care of it with slopes and ditches. Many believe that the problem is solved if water does not stand on the soil after heavy rains; but internal drainage is even more important. Water moves through the soil in direct proportion to the size of soil particles. Heavy soils like clays and fine silts hold more water than soils with larger particles, and inhibit downward movement of water. When the interparticle spaces of the soil are filled with water, an insufficient amount of air (oxygen) is available to the roots for normal respiration and growth. Active, new roots suffer most.

FEEDER ROOTS GRADUALLY SUFFOCATE in waterlogged soil. Most damage occurs during prolonged rains in the growing season; feeder roots cannot keep up with plant demand. Digging out a deep bed and replacing the soil does not necessarily correct an internal drainage problem, because the surrounding soil will not permit excess water to drain away rapidly. Soil water must escape from the soil below and surrounding the bed area. Nature, roots (and roses) work best when given a good balance of air, friable soil and water.

THERE'S AN OLD SAYING that goes, "There's nothing so blind as the man [rosarian] who won't see." Most rose problems are quite simple when we think about them later; we just tend to miss the keys to the problem along the way.

Happy Rose Anniversary! Seven years older and 84 issues wiser, the RAMBLING ROSARIAN still thinks that roses and rose folks are the greatest. We'll begin a new season with some typical reader questions...

WHAT'S A SPLINT FOR A ROSE TREE? Tree roses, like broken arms, need support. Stakes and loose ties won't do the job. To splint a tree rose, use a 3/8-inch reinforcing bar or a 1/2-inch electrical conduit. Cut the splint long enough to drive 12 to 18 inches into the ground. Top of the splint should be higher than the bud unions (trees are double budded). Cushion the splint with a length or sections of rubber or plastic hose. Fit the covered splint to the side of the standard which is the straightest. It's easiest to do when planting the tree, but can also be located by careful probing to miss large roots. Then wrap the standard and splint with friction tape or plastic electrician tape in several places... exactly like splinting a broken arm.

NUMBERS ON FERTILIZER BAGS CONFUSE ME. Here's how to read the numbers on a fertilizer bag (also read the directions). In most states, fertilizers must show the analysis of nitrogen, phosphorus and potash in the package, in that order, expressed as a percentage of weight. For example, a 100-pound bag of 10-6-4 contains 10 pounds of available nitrogen, 6 pounds of phosphorus and four pounds of potassium (compounded in various ways). When comparing costs of fertilizers, do so on the basis of actual pounds of available material, rather than on the weight of the bag. A bag of 12-24-12 at $8.00 for 50 pounds is a much better buy than a 50-pound bag of 5-10-5 at $6.00. Keep the percentage analysis in mind when applying the material, as well. A 12-24-12 formulation is more than twice as strong as 5-10-5. Read the directions!

DO YOU HAVE ANY GOOD PROGRAM IDEAS? Short, interesting features add variety to programs and are popular with newcomers and old pros. Try a ROSE REPORT from a different Consulting Rosarian each month; briefly discussing a timely topic such as spray equipment, how to water, conditioning roses... even yellow leaves. Five or ten minutes is the limit; only ONE topic, no wandering. It's a tougher job than you think to get the point across in five minutes. The Rose Re-port should add spice to the program, not run in competition. Assign a definite topic each month, swap the job around for variety. The SIDE BUD is another feature, reviewing what's new in rose publications. It might be a "borrowed" article from a rose bulletin, a brief on a new rose topic, or sources of materials that expand on the major program of the evening. The basis of Side Bud is brevity. Tell the facts in a way to make the member want more. You'll reach a good many rose people this way.

WHAT'S PRUNING AND WHAT'S GROOMING? There's really not much difference in pruning or grooming roses for fall blooms, at least in the milder climates. It's mostly a matter of degree. Pruning generally means more severe cutting back of rose canes; grooming is commonly accepted as removal of twiggy growth and trimming back to healthy bud eyes on canes and laterals the size of a pencil. A plant is "groomed" every time a bloom is cut. In the fall, GROOM bushes so that the strength and vigor of the plant can be concentrated for good bloom production.

IS THERE AN EASY WAY TO USE LIQUID FERTILIZERS? If your back is tired and you don't want to lug buckets of diluted liquids around the rose garden, get out the easy and reliable lawn sprayer that *Ortho* has marketed for many years. *Ortho's* lawn sprayer is a device that fits on the hose and puts out a coarse spray, metering from ajar just like a hose-on sprayer. It works the same, just puts out more volume. Before mixing up anything, attach the sprayer to the hose, start the syphon process and count how many seconds it takes to put out a gallon of mix. My sprayer takes about six seconds. Mix up the right concentration of fertilizer to fill the syphon jar. Dole out a gallon of formula mix for each plant (with the hose doing the work) and then give each plant another gallon of plain water by taking your thumb off the syphon tube. The plain water also washes off any fertilizer mix that may have gotten on the foliage. Remember that the mix is a soil-soak, NOT a foliar spray. The lawn sprayer will cover 150 plants in about an hour, if you move fast.

HIGH COSTS FOR MATERIALS? BUILD A COMPOST PILE. Nature supplies the raw materials. You supply some rose sense. Use some leftover bricks, blocks or boards to contain the pile. Lay or fit so that air can reach the composting materials. Air and the right balance of moisture are essential for a good compost pile. Most good gardens have a compost heap (bin, rick, frame, etc.) hidden away somewhere in the yard. Some are fancy affairs, others are just piles of clippings, leaves, dirt and what-have-you. The results are the same when compost gets to the rose bed... better aeration, better root growth, better bushes and therefore better blooms. No yard is too small. Convert leaves and clippings into the best plant food that nature can produce. It beats anything you can buy in a sack or can.

OCT. 1977

THOUGHT FOR THE MONTH:
Don't envy your neighbor whose grass is greener. His water bill is higher, too.

If there's such a thing as a rose harvest, now's the time. The sun is not quite as hot, the nights are a bit cooler and roses respond with better color, better form, larger size IF the resident rosarian has been doing his homework earlier in the season. Anyway, if you aren't harvesting bushels of roses, now is the time to do something about it for next year.

Nothing much happens with roses without a good growing mixture. Now's the time to begin building new rose beds, or revamping old ones. Started now, the beds have a chance to mix, mellow and compost a bit before planting time. Winter is like an extra gardener, alternately freezing and thawing to mechanically blend the ingredients. Roses planted in fresh, hot mixtures are off to a rough start and are risky at best. Like good wines, carefully blended rose beds get better with age. There's no universal formula for rose beds, but the basic requirements are always the same. A good growing medium ALWAYS has a balance of soil, humus, water and air. All of the exotic additions ever recommended for rose beds were intended to accomplish these simple basics.

It's hard to go wrong with a mix of about 1/3 soil, 1/3 sand and 1/3 humus or compost. Use whatever humus additive is cheap and available. Peat moss, composted bark, home-made compost, manure, leaves or mixtures of all of these will do the job. If the soil is on the heavy side, add some more sand. If the soil is sandy, use more manure or compost. Mixtures work the best; particles of different sizes give a planting medium friability... that is, the ability of water and air to move freely through the soil so that all of the soil processes work. When soils are working, roses grow.

It's a good time to build a "Satellite Garden", too... a rose garden of any type that doesn't actually belong to you. An off-premises rose garden makes new friends for roses as well as more room for your own rose efforts and a chance to try some new gardening ideas. There's plenty of unclaimed ground just right for roses... a parkway or parking strip nearby, a disabled neighbor who can't keep up with a yard any more, your church or library, a home for senior citizens. With a little help and your experience, surprising things can happen. Enlist the help of someone close by to do the watering... almost any kind of personal involvement. And don't worry about the "quality" of individual blooms. Sometimes roses do better when we don't worry over them so much; the average viewer of a "rose satellite" spot doesn't know a split center from a sepal. But he does know that the rose planting is a big improvement over bare lawn or sick shrubs. Once the beds are built, a few minutes a week for spraying and spent blooms will do the trick. It's a great way to promote roses.

Following up on built-up rose beds, it's obvious that elevated beds produce more, last longer, require less care and consistently provide more pleasure for rosarians than conventional lawn-level plantings. This is not to say that level plantings do not have a place (and are sometimes required) in certain situations. But when the landscape plan permits, elevated beds do a better job. The beds don't have to be a foot high to be effective; even a few inches above lawn level helps drainage and aeration. If you're skeptical, build one elevated bed this winter and compare results next season. By year-end you'll be making new beds as fast as you can lay bricks, cinder blocks, weathered timbers or what-have-you. Get the very best from the bed with a high organic mix with just enough sand and light soil to keep the air spaces open. And with the roots in such a great environment, go the rest of the way by planting new bushes with the bud union at ground level so that sunshine and air will produce basal breaks for show winners. With appropriate winter protection, bud unions can be planted above ground except under the most severe winter conditions. The same insulation that protects buried roses protects ground-level roses.

Winter protection may not seem to be an appropriate subject for a Gulf Coast rosarian, but experience, observation and common sense might offer an idea or two. After growing roses in Colorado (and learning the hard way) for many years, it seemed that the natural approaches worked best for winter protection, The best protection from cold Wind, hot sun, thawing, drying, blowing snow, low temperatures (to -25°), dry soil and sand storms came from the trees... free for the raking. Leaves piled high in the rose bed and weighted a bit with soil or manure made the plantings look like a brown snow bank before winter arrived. By spring the leaves had settled a bit, partially composted (and a few had blown away). Snows, thaws and wind hadn't done much damage. New breaks began to come up through the woodsy mulch at the right time… just in time for some more manure to start the whole process over again. Excess soil and leaves were added to the vegetable patch or beds for annuals. It seemed that everything grew better, naturally.

Nov. 1977

THOUGHT FOR THE MONTH: (particularly for incoming rose society officers)
When in charge, ponder. When in trouble, delegate. When in doubt, mumble.

Whatever happened to the rose season? Strange how time flies when you're having fun. And part of the fun of rose growing is sharing ideas and experiences... so here are some clippings and cuttings from rosarians around the country. Many thanks to you faithful readers who have taken time to write and pass on a suggestion or make a comment.

The event may not change the rose world, but the "Weekend With The Lyles" hosted by the Golden Triangle RS (of Southeast Texas) annually attracts rose nuts from everywhere. The crowd came from five states this year to share a dinner evening with Dr. and Mrs. Eldon Lyle (he's a past president of ARS and probably the best-known rose pathologist in the world). Like pictures at home, Dr. Lyle had a little bit of everything... some rose friends, rose gardens, rose practices... with common sense comments for more roses with less work. He set the stage for the beach party on Saturday, an all-day event with heaps of good food, swimming, sunning and plenty of rose talk. Every rose problem seems to have a solution at the beach party.

Here's a report from the Rose Triangle on just one of the events: "Dr. Lyle foolishly believed the *Texaco* advertisement: 'Trust your car to the man who wears the star' by riding to the beach with 40-year *Texaco* veteran Horace Burdett, who ran out of gas on the way. When Dr. Lyle finally did get to the beach, he was already four miles behind in his swimming and kinda got carried away. He swam out to one of the drilling platforms where he was stopped by the Coast Guard and politely told that he would have to return to the three-mile limit or install running lights as he was a navigational hazard." Now THAT'S a fun rose event.

Overheard at the beach party... the proposal to give ARS Mini Certificates on the basis of Gold to a spray, Silver to a one bloom specimen and Bronze to a spray was buried in the sand and left for dead. They liked direct competition between the best one bloom per stem and best spray specimens with the certificates, awarded to the top three roses regardless of type. Another topic concerned roses produced commercially on their own roots (rather than budded). J&P is supposed to be doing extensive field trials in this area. Hope they share some of their findings with serious rosarians. Last but not least, it was agreed that show sections for miniature roses will soon be as large as sections for large roses. Is it time to have rose shows for miniatures only?

Here's a well-deserved plug for the Rose Hybridizers Association. If you are serious about roses, you ought to join RHA, even if you never plan to cross anything. Their quarterly bulletins contain a wealth of information, edited by Bob Harvey, the "Okie from Muskogee". Dues are just $4 per year, a real bargain. Give them a try in '78 with $4 to Don Nielson, Treasurer, 508 S. Juniper, Toppenish, WA 98948.

Roses in pots, tubs and planters need some winter protection in most areas, but make sure that the protection "breathes". A tub-grown rose goes through a dormancy in the same way a ground-planted rose does. If possible, move tubs and planters into an unheated garage after the first good frost. Wrap tree rose standards and bud unions with loose insulating material like feed sacks or old blankets. Don't cover with plastic. Let dormancy occur as naturally as possible; avoid sharp changes in temperature. When the tubs get too dry, add some water. Roses are woody plants that will tolerate a wide temperature range if permitted to adjust naturally. Rosarians (and roses) get into trouble when nature is left out of the formula.

Rose workshops around the country are beginning to discuss why soils work rather than "secret formulas". And that's a good sign, because every local soil condition is different and may need a slightly different treatment. For most of us, an ideal planting medium has about 1/3 sand, 1/3 soil and 1/3 organic material. The medium accommodates air, water and nutrients in balance so that feeder roots can develop and support the plant. Roses perform only as well as the roots permit. Good feeder-root systems mean good roses.

Friability is the essential ingredient, providing millions of microscopic air and water spaces in the soil, absorbing and releasing moisture as needed. This is the storage and exchange that supports soil processes to make plant nutrients available. The natural soil process chain is completed with food support for soil microorganisms. When these tiny workers are busy converting nutrients into forms available to plants, roses grow and rosarians are happy. You'll enjoy roses more if you think about this and do what comes naturally when building a new rose bed or rejuvenating an old one. Let nature and the rosebush alone as much as you can; they are much more experienced than you are.

As surely as the "hot stove league" plots strategy for baseball, "compost committee" meetings of rosarians turn out some mellow ideas while rose cones are covered with snow. Since there is no such thing as a dormant rosarian, here's some fuel for your composting sessions...

MINIATURES IN POTS AND BASKETS are gaining in popularity around the country and are attracting rose show visitors. A spot in your next show schedule might be in order; check the scale of points used by the Men's Garden Club, since ARS has no guideline in this area. Anything that will ADD to the attractiveness or educational aspect of a show is worthwhile. You'll get lots of attention with a pipe rack hung with five or six baskets of minis.

HELP A BEGINNER at container-grown minis with suggestions for a high organic mix, preferably one that's home-made. Just make sure that the mix has enough sand to breathe and that the composted organic matter is coarse enough to prevent packing. An assortment of organic materials is best; stems, leaves, manure and what-have-you will stay loose and encourage root growth. Some Osmocote (timed release fertilizer) is also good; it saves repeated liquid food applications and keeps something on the menu for the plants all the time.

THERE'S A GOOD STORY ABOUT *Osmocote*. It seems that one of our larger mini growers got a letter back from a customer who advised that the plants had arrived in good shape but that it had taken quite a while to pick out all of the insect eggs in the planting mixture. Now that the eggs were destroyed the plants seemed to be doing fine. The customer suggested a more careful check of future shipments. Note for the neophyte: *Osmocote* is a tiny, tan pellet that looks like an egg.

MINI GROWERS around here report a correlation between high nitrogen feeding and spider mites. It seems that the soft, green growth brought on by nitrogen is much more likely to be infested with mites; more mature growth less likely. And the tender leaves are easily burned with miticides, too. Best results are generally obtained with water soluble, low nitrogen, high phosphorus formulations like *Peter's* (9-45-15) or *Carl Pool* (9-56-8). Another tip: cut off the terminals of climbing or basket-type miniatures for better branching and more blooms. This is particularly important for a rampant grower like *Red Cascade*. Growers are also talking about better guidelines for the "open" or decorative type miniatures. More and more shows have classes for "fully open" blooms; but don't fall into the trap by calling for "stamens must show" like the big roses. Instead, specify something like "one bloom per stem, fully open, taking into consideration configuration of the bloom". One more mini idea... how about rose shows for miniatures only, no large roses shown or permitted? They are easy to stage and there's no shortage of friendly malls, commercial buildings or garden centers as hosts.

HERBICIDES AND ROSES ordinarily do not get along, but a new product called ROUND-UP promises to be a real help to rosarians. It's great for edging rose beds, walkways or other plantings; almost any place where weed or grass control is needed. Roundup works on green plant material only, translocating in the plant to kill the root as well as the top. It dissipates very quickly without soil contamination. It handles creeping grasses (Bermuda, Centipede, etc.), most common weeds, even nutgrass.

APPLICATION RATE FOR Roundup is 3 tablespoons per gallon of water; use in a plastic pump-type sprayer as the material is highly corrosive. A fan-shape spray nozzle that covers a band two or three inches wide safely controls application so that no spray touches rose leaves or canes. Stay 18 inches or so away from canes or bud union. Most farm supply stores will have *Roundup*; it is a *Monsanto* product and retails for about $65 per gallon. Buy a gallon and break it into pints for rose friends; that's enough for the average grower for a year or so.

ROSES CAN BE PLANTED in Roundup-treated areas shortly after application. In an extreme case, Roundup was used to kill a healthy stand of Bermuda grass for a new rose planting. Five days after application, forms were set for a built-up bed and soil added without disturbing the old lawn area. Roses were planted the following day and are thriving. More conservative applicators advise a delay of two weeks before working or planting a treated area, but it is still the easiest way ever to clean up an area for new rose plantings.

ANOTHER PLUG for built-up rose beds. In a carefully controlled trial in the Tyler (TX) Rose Garden, established, edged beds at lawn level were raised by adding a single 2x4 curbing, soil and humus added to the new level, and roses replanted with bud unions exposed. The performance of roses in the "new" beds was substantially better than roses of the same varieties in adjacent plantings at lawn level. Roses simply do better with good drainage.

January is the month for semi-dormant rosarians... it's too early for really hard work to begin in the garden and yet late enough for last summer's roses to get better and better. The story about the Queen of the Show is told more often when snow is on the ground; it's the only rose that has more form, color, size and character with old age. So if you're tired of rose stories and eyes are weak from catalog overkill and rose visions, look out on the snow with rose-colored glasses and think about a couple of these ideas for more fun with roses in the coming season...

FOLLOWING UP on a Rambler report from '76, it can safely be reported that more manure in the soil mix does not always produce more roses. The '76 example described a new rose bed that had a mixture of half finely-ground barnyard manure and half pine bark (also ground and composted) that looked good but gave poor results. The excessive amounts of organic material tended to pack; the overall mix lacked air space although water disappeared like pouring through sand. Rose performance was very poor in the mixture, probably due to two factors. In addition to the obvious lack of air space, decomposition of the organic matter produced excessive amounts of carbon dioxide which in turn inhibited root development. The decomposition factor paralleled the experience of Dr. Eldon Lyle, Plant Pathologist for the Texas Rose Research Foundation. Dr. Lyle tried organic planting medium from commercial mushroom operations as a mix for packaged roses. The mushroom medium appeared to be ideal; it was light in weight, retained moisture and was easy to handle. However, rose roots were severely retarded by measurable excesses of carbon dioxide.

THE HIGH ORGANIC PROBLEM was easily corrected by adding sharp sand and garden soil, resulting in a final mix of about 1/3 manure, 1/3 compost and 1/3 sand and soil. Roses in this mix responded quickly, produced well and were easily maintained. At the end of the first season, some roses dug from this bed had masses of feeder roots (on *multiflora* understock) and no evidence of galls or root dieback. The plants transplanted very successfully. At the end of the second full season, the results are the same: good vigor and full production in spite of a very dry season. No

additional organics were added other than a two-inch mulch; a feeding program of fish meal and 12-24-12 kept the whole process going. Conclusion: if a little is good, more isn't necessarily better.

ROSE CATALOGS ARE GREAT in the winter, but keep an eye on what's happening outside as well. Watch for some clues on the effectiveness of your winter protection system. Does the system keep up with changes in the weather? The best methods handle a broad range of conditions and, in the Rambler's observations, usually use natural materials. Mother Nature isn't often fooled; soil and leaves have been nature's way to protect things since time began. Whether you mound, cover, bank, tip or otherwise insulate rose canes, dirt and leaves seem to be able to handle changes in the weather best. If you are using something other than nature's way, check to see how well the materials parallel nature. In simple terms, just do what comes naturally.

WHAT'S THE BEST ROSE SOURCE?! The best source is the grower-outlet who is able to deliver a fresh No.1 plant, will stand behind it and will make you happy. The source may be mail order or local nursery, California or Texas, bare-root or potted. Check with some other rose growers in your area about their sources. Inquire about how roses are handled and shipped; does the local nurseryman know how to hold roses? If a source has been taking good care of you, let him know. If a problem needs correcting, let him know about that, too. It makes sense to KNOW your source.

ROSARIANS MAKE MISTAKES, TOO; it may not be the grower's fault. Hope you aren't guilty of the *most* common mistake in handling a new rose... roots drying out in the sun while the "rosarian" decides on spacing, location, takes a coffee break, *etc*. Soak bare-root roses overnight in water, and keep them in water until just before final pruning and planting. Dry roots and dehydrated bushes just won't start. The commercial nurseryman takes great pains to deliver a fresh plant. It can all be undone with careless handling.

ON THE SUBJECT OF DEHYDRATED ROSES, don't be taken by "new crop" packaged roses at the supermarket, drugstore, garden shop or street comer peddler, no matter what kind of bargain it appears to be. Supermarkets should sell groceries, nurseries should sell roses. Packaged roses with chopped roots, butchered tops and a handful of wood shavings are seldom bargains... and they are totally worthless after a few days in a sunny store window. If you are interested in roses, plant good roses in the first place. It takes a good deal more time and effort to try to grow a poor than to grow a healthy plant... and the results can't be compared. The same advice applies to non-performers in your present garden... those that don't put out, PULL OUT.

With that note, the Rambler wishes you a Very Rosy 1978.

With snow on the ground or winter rains turning rose beds to mud holes, the real rose nuts are already thinking about how to frame and hang those rose certificates sure to be won in the spring shows... show winners to come don't suffer the indignities of competition and criticism... splashes of color and promises of catalogs brighten the landscape design without having to lift a shovel. Thinking, planning and just plain dreaming of things to come are worthwhile occupations once in a while and good reminders that roses are a hobby and ought to be easy and fun.

ROSES ARE MORE FUN if you try some new ideas. Reluctant to dig up and replace those bushes that "might need another year to get established"? Good rose advice says, "Those that don't put out, pull out." But to make the conscience feel better, offer the plants you don't want at a plant exchange. An exchange takes a little spade work and extra care, but it's a good way to get someone started in roses. A new grower has to start somewhere, and the bushes that don't quite make the show table can dazzle a beginner. 'Most everyone has had the experience of giving away a less-than-successful plant only to have it come on with a vigor that amazes the donor.

TRANSPLANTING ROSES ought to be at the design discretion of the grower, too. If the plant doesn't seem to be doing well in a particular location or if the color is "all wrong", move it somewhere else. Roses are surprisingly resilient, and transplanting often seems to give them a new lease on life. For whatever reason, it's worth a try.

ROSE BEDS NEED A NEW LEASE ON LIFE once in a while, too... in spite of some "show winners" still growing there. Organic matter in the soil is gradually depleted, and additions of mulch and other materials on top won't perform quite the same job that bacteria-supporting organics will do in the root zone. Some rose beds last longer than others; but heavy feedings of nitrogen are definitely a factor in using up the materials that bring life to the soil. Soil organisms thrive in a medium of organic matter, air and water. As materials are broken down, soils become tighter and less able to support root systems. Rose production gradually declines; more fertilizer won't reverse the process. Rebuilding the whole bed produces the best results

with the least effort. It's a chance to start over, even with established plants.

THE BEST TIME TO REBUILD is when roses are dormant, preferably just before breaking in early spring. Dig the roses carefully with a spading fork; do not prune or otherwise encourage new growth. Bury or cover with soil, sacks, straw or any other material that will keep bushes cool and damp while the bed is being rebuilt. Try to preserve dormancy if at all possible. It's safe to hold roses in this way for a week or more, if necessary. Rebuild a bed in much the same way as making a new bed: a final mixture of 1/3 compost or manure, 1/3 loamy soil and 1/3 sand is about right in most areas. Add bone meal, rock phosphate or superphosphate (your choice) and work thoroughly into the bed and future root zone. Phosphate does not move readily in the soil; place it where it will do some good. Don't add soluble rose fertilizers if the beds are to be replanted in a short time. It's safer to feed from the top when bushes are established and growing. Local soil conditions may call for other additives, such as gypsum for loosening heavy clays. Turn the whole mixture several times with a fork, shovel or tiller. Deep cultivation with a three-prong fork is also good. Wet down the bed area, turn again the next day; two or three times is usually enough. Finally, allow the bed to settle (wetting helps) before attempting to plant. DORMANT ROSES can be handled like bare-root plants when replanting. Prune canes according to the usual practice for your climate. Wash the soil off the roots and trim out any dead or broken parts. Trim root ends lightly to encourage callousing and new feeder roots. Also trim out any root galls or gall growths on the shank or bud union. Some growers claim that disinfecting cut galls with *Lysol* or *Clorox* retards recurrence, but this has never been demonstrated in field trials. Similarly, soils in which galled plants have grown do not transmit infection from plant to plant. Most growers have lived with root gall for a long time, have enjoyed fine roses and will continue to do so. When very large galls girdle the shank or bud union and restrict growth, it's time to pull out and start over. But this doesn't happen very often in the normal garden. PLANT ON A SOIL CONE that supports roots, cover roots with a layer of soil and flood in with plenty of water. Then add more soil, more water. Don't "tamp" with size 12 boots. Water, and plenty of it, will do all the settling needed. Finally, mound up the canes to hold moisture and protect from cold. Gradually uncover as the weather moderates, in much the same way as a bare-root, new plant. Begin regular feeding routine when strong growth appears. Result: A rose bed and roses almost as good as new.

Rambling through my "research library"... which is really a collection of clippings, junk, notes and stolen items from rose publications and talks... it's obvious that rosarians are turned on by a variety of rose ideas that promise to make roses grow bigger, better and easier. Some of the nostrums are old; some of them are "miracle" formulations with "amazing" results. But rose folks like to hear and read about what others are doing with roses, even if they have been over the same ground time after time. Old and new, here are some rose cuttings worth a thought or two...

PLANT ROSES WITH WATER (and a little soil). Water, water, water... that's the name of the game when planting new roses. "Mud 'em in" tells it like it should be. "Make sure that bare-root roses (and canned plants, too) are deep soaked when planted and regularly thereafter. Don't sprinkle, SOAK.

OLD ROSARIAN TALES seem to live forever, particularly stories about how to plant roses. Fortunately most of them are not true. Some old-timers maintain that a grower has to "stomp" on the roots with backfilling to "get rid of the air" This not only gets rid of air but also breaks roots and compacts the soil so tightly that air and water (both essential to the soil process) don't have a chance. The best planting tool is PLENTY of water.

USE A CONE OF SOIL in the planting hole to support the roots and stabilize the shank. Then carefully add prepared soil and gently fill in around the roots. With the hose running at a slow trickle, thoroughly soak the root area and soil. Then add more soil and repeat the process. Keep your feet OUT of the hole... if you are doing the right thing you'll just get your boots full of mud. Soak one newly planted bush while digging and planting the next one; then move the hose while backfilling. Mound up soil and mulch around the canes; set the lawn sprinkler and soak again.

FIX FUNGUS FAST AND FIRST. Disease control is a matter of prevention, not eradication when blackspot appears. Years of field trials and backyard experience conclusively show that a disease control spray program should start immediately after pruning, drenching the canes and bud union. Use a broad spectrum insecticide (*Diazinon, Cygon, Orthene, Isotox*) combined with a favorite fungicide (*Phaltan, Benlate, Manzate*). Use both at full strength and add a spreader-sticker to encourage penetration into crevices of old canes. Disease spores are carried over on live plant tissue, just waiting until temperature and humidity are right for growth of these organisms. By reducing numbers early, control is easier later. Unless a scale problem is evident, an insecticide-fungicide combination does more good than an oil-sulfur mixture. Oil-sulfur stains, smells, burns, plugs sprayers and generally refuses to cooperate with the rosarian. Advice: use the same controls for disease all year long.

MINI GREENHOUSE FOR ROSES... New rosebushes slow to start respond quickly to a high-humidity situation that's easy to make. Clean soil and mulch away from the bud union (assuming you are an enlightened rosarian and plant with the bud union above soil level) so that a "hot cap" or tent can be secured around the shank. The same idea also works for roses planted deeper, but the tent has to be held in place with soil. Anyway, after clearing away, add a handful of very wet sphagnum moss over the bud union area, slip a clear plastic bag over the pruned canes and tie with a string around the shank. It becomes a small forcing greenhouse. After about a week, depending on the temperature, gradually cut away the bag a little at a time to let cooler air in. Remove entirely in about two weeks. This "air layering" bag is especially good with tree roses, even if they are beginning to break. They get off to a better start by insuring adequate moisture in the canes until the root system can support growth. The bag also protects in case of a cold snap and almost guarantees a robust, healthy tree rose that will not die back.

SPREAD A LITTLE SUNSHINE... and make roses grow by opening up the bud union. The Rambler is still convinced that except under the most EXTREME weather conditions, roses do best when the bud union is planted at soil level or above. Sunshine can do wonders for a bud union, promoting more and heavier canes, PROVIDED that the plants have good winter protection. In the winter, cover 'em up; in the spring, open 'em up. How about a small field trial in your own garden? Plant some roses high and some roses low in the same bed. Next spring you'll want to lift the buried plants. You'll be glad you tried it.

SOIL MOUNDS PROTECT new roses, or roses that have been transplanted. Use soil and mulch to hill up canes as high as the material will go. Soil acts as an insulator, conserving ˙ moisture and maintaining a moderate temperature. Hot sun and cold winds don't help new rose canes. When good growth starts and frost danger is past, gradually uncover over a period of a week or two with a gentle stream of water. Poking and scratching snaps off new breaks. Let water do the job… good for the roots, too.

Took part in a unique workshop program the other day... "one-liners" from the audience that covered a wide range of rose topics. Instead of the usual speaker, members (and visitors) spoke for a minute or two on any rose subject that came to mind and then asked for comments. Everyone had a good time in the process, learning and telling rose stories at the same time. They discussed real rose happenings and offered practical advice... and probably did more good than with more formal approaches. It's an example of a "life" rose session rather than a canned package that neatly takes 45 minutes of program time. It's worth a try in your rose society... here are a few topics to get started:

FOR A TOUCH OF GREEN, try a dose of salts... Epsom salt (magnesium sulfate). Established plants slow to break new basal canes may need a spring tonic. About two or three tablespoons of Epsom salt broadcast within the drip zone of each bush will often help and certainly do no harm. Water in thoroughly. If soil is deficient in magnesium (essential to leaf production), plants will green up and put on new growth almost immediately. Get it in bulk from a feed store or drugstore.

FERTILIZER MUST GET INTO SOLUTION. Rose foods do no good until in solution and in the root zone of the plant. Dry, pelletized fertilizers on top of the soil are fine IF there is a regular, ample supply of water to dissolve the nutrients and carry them to the roots. For a faster spring start, use fertilizer already in solution and soak the roots. Old-timers also know that deep soaking BEFORE using liquid foods also speeds up the process. For a real surprise, try dissolving your favorite dry rose food in water. It may be less soluble than you think.

SPRING TONICS FOR TIRED ROSES. Most rose beds, particularly in clay soils, can use a gypsum treatment in the spring. Gypsum can't burn, helps drainage, reduces salt build-up and is a source of calcium. After pruning, broadcast gypsum (calcium sulfate) at about 10 lbs. per square feet and work in lightly with a spading fork. The fork trick is also good to get rock phosphate or superphosphate into the root zone. Phosphate moves very slowly in the soil and only under ideal conditions.

ACCENT THE POSITIVE. Too many rose "experts" insist on talking about all the bad things that can happen with roses. What rose beginner would want to take up a hobby that emphasizes fungus diseases, cankers, viruses, galls, nematodes and various other afflictions that threaten garden and gardener? Roses were grown and enjoyed a good many years before these problems were even identified. To attract gardeners to roses, talk about blooms and color and length of growing season. And the fact that regular care with safe and readily available materials makes roses a most rewarding garden experience.

IT'S NOT A FISH STORY. Fish meal really works. Although not available everywhere, many feed stores (fish meal is carried in poultry feeds) have that delightful odor that brings joy to rosarians and blooms to roses. It's an expensive smell, about $22 per 100 lbs. on the Gulf Coast. But 100 pounds goes a long way. It's easy and odorless if used properly. Use a heaping cupful per bush as soon as the soil warms up. Covered with soil there's no smell. Use a bulb planter or similar tool to take three or four cores about five or six inches deep within the drip zone of the bush. Put fish meal into the holes. Replace soil. The result is no smell; no cat, dog or neighbor problems. And really GOOD roses if used twice a year.

REMEMBER COW TEA? Call it "liquid compost" or whatever, but brew up a batch for good roses. Back in BC (Before Chemicals), gardeners always had a barrel or two steeping behind the garage. It was a good practice then and still is. Although there's not much direct nutrient value, the boost given soil organisms makes everything else work better. Use several plastic garbage cans; keep two or three brewing all the time (rainwater is best). Onion or potato sacks make good tea bags; fill with some dried cow chips and tie with a long piece of wire or rope. Steep for about 10 days, sloshing around once in a while. Use about two gallons of tea per bush for fantastic results.

SPEAKING OF MANURE... it seems that manure is getting a bad press, and it is mostly undeserved. Feed lot, sacked manure CAN have excessive salts. But even that can be easily leached by adding to a compost pile with other organic materials and let rain, nature (and maybe a little gypsum) do what comes naturally. Manure is a growing medium for microorganisms in the soil; more of a soil conditioner than a fertilizer. Use generously without worrying. If you have a good source of the real thing, get out the shovel and start spreading. A few weeks is a small price to pay for an active, working soil that produces bushels of roses. Makes a good mulch, too.

If you have taken the ledge to try no more than on one "miracle" for roses this year, allow the Rambler to offer a pair for your consideration. Both make growing roses easier and more fun; and that's what this hobby is all about. Previous mentions in these columns brought a flood of mail... so here's an up-to-date recap:

THE *DRAMM NOZZLE IRRIGATION SYSTEM* is definitely the way to go for most backyard rosarians. It's the best (and cheapest) thing to come along in a long, long time. And it is so simple to build that most anyone (maybe with a helper) can have a complete garden system running over a weekend. The *Dramm Nozzle* makes it all possible. A pin diffuser sprays water in a full circle parallel to the rose bed. In other words, the water sprays out, not up. Water distribution is very even, easily controlled and with less waste. A time-saver also, the system can thoroughly water a rose bed 40 feet long and 5 feet wide in less than twenty minutes. Miniatures thrive with a *Dramm* system; the flat, fine spray washes off mites and creates 100% humidity.

THE SYSTEM IS MADE from 6-inch Schedule 40 PVC pipe. This is the rigid-type plastic pipe; connections, elbows, tees and adapters are available at most lumber yards, hardware stores or plumbing shops. The pipe cuts easily with a hacksaw and all connections are made with PVC cement. If you make a mistake, cut out the section and glue up another one. The plastic pipe system is laid on the surface of the rose bed (on top of any mulch) and can be attached permanently to a water source or connected to a water hose with a quick coupler (cheap and easy). Ordinary water pressure from a 5/8-inch garden hose will supply a 40-foot irrigating line with 16 to 18 nozzles. Each nozzle will spray an area from three to four feet in diameter, depending on pressure. Control volume (and size of spray) at the house tap or install a valve at the head of each line. Runs longer than 40 feet may require 5/8-inch pipe to deliver enough volume for consistent four-foot watering patterns.

DRAMM nozzles are inserted into PVC pipe with a tapered neoprene washer. Drill holes (15/32-inch) at nozzle locations in the pipe; be careful with alignment. Clean out any bits of shavings. Insert a tapered washer (fits like a saddle) and screw in the nozzle. The nozzle is also threaded and tapered; screw in two or three turns for a tight fit. All the connections can be made without tools, ordinary grip like threading a hose connection is all that is necessary.

MAINTENANCE IS EASY. If a nozzle does not have an even spray or stops up, pull the deflecting pin out of the nozzle and a thin stream of water shoots straight up and clears out any junk in the water line. For a serious blockage, unscrew the top half of the nozzle and the whole system can be flushed out. The flushing process can be done while the system is on... almost without getting wet.

Best of all, it's cheap. Each nozzle-washer set costs about 50 cents. They are available from many greenhouse supply companies (who also have many other good things for rosarians). If you can find a local source, try mail order from ROSE KEEPERS or from KIMBREW-WALTER ROSES, both regular advertisers in this magazine. If you install *Dramm* in just one bed, you'll soon convert the whole garden.

ROSES AND HERBICIDES ordinarily do not get along, but relatively new product called *ROUNDUP* offers real help to rosarians. Use Roundup any place where weed or grass control is needed; it's great for edging rose beds, walkways, or for killing grass and weeds in an area to be planted. *Roundup* works on GREEN plant material only, translocating in the plant to kill the root as well as the top. It dissipates in the soil very quickly WITHOUT contamination. Crops can be planted in treated areas in just a few days. It handles creeping grasses (Bermuda, Centipede, *etc.),* most common weeds, even nutgrass.

Application rate for *Roundup* is 3 tablespoons per gallon of water. Use in a plastic, pump-type sprayer as the material is highly corrosive. A fan-shaped spray nozzle that covers a band two or three inches wide safely controls application so that no spray touches rose leaves. Stay about six inches away from rose canes or bud unions. Many farm supply stores have *Roundup*; it is a *Monsanto* product and sells for about $65 per gallon. Buy a gallon and break it into smaller lots for friends. A pint lasts an average grower a year or more.

ROSES CAN BE PLANTED in *Roundup-*

treated areas shortly after application. A healthy stand of Bermuda grass was sprayed for a new rose planting. Five days later, forms were set for a built-up bed and soil added without disturbing the lawn area. Potted roses in full leaf and bloom were planted the following day. The new bushes hardly wilted, even though taken from pots and planted in mid-summer. You can expect the same results for miniatures. It's the easiest way to clean up an area for new rose plantings or to keep grass out of the existing beds.

JUN. 1978

THOUGHT FOR THE MONTH: Don't boast about your rose growing ability…
just show us your roses. ~Harry Roberts Hendersonville, NC

Listening-in by the coffee urn, it seems that the best roses in the world are grown around the rose society hospitality table. Wouldn't it be great to share this hands-on experience with everyone at a workshop session? Call it a "Garden Collection" program of personal know-how… and it might go something like this…

OVERFED ROSES can be saved. You know the feeling, new leaves turn crisp and brown and the bush looks like it is going into a crisis. Just flush the excess out of the root zone with lots of water, assuming there's someplace for the water to go. Water is the best and only treatment; flood generously and often and let nature take its course. If a clay soil is too tight for drainage, add some gypsum to help the process along. The same advice applies to excess foliar food and spray combinations. Wash off the leaves and let the sun-leaf process work again.

CHARISMA is going to be a sensational border for landscapers. It's colorful, with mannerly growth and blooms that hang on in spite of wind and sun. It won't make much for exhibitors at a rose show, but it makes a great show along a driveway. Which reminds us again that roses deserve to be in the front yard as well the back. Many fine varieties are coming on the market now that belong in the landscape plan. Many miniatures also need to be used in general plantings. They are good in rock gardens, along borders, banks and steps. Select a type with the color and shape needed. Most of them get along well with other plant materials since they aren't as particular about feeding (unless grossly overfed). And some growers overlook the fact that miniatures can be planted almost anytime, including midsummer, with some reasonable care and protection.

LOOK OUT for pressure-treated wood products around miniatures or immature plants. Most lumberyard products are fresh from the mill, and preservative treated posts and planks leach a gas that bums tender leaves. A rosarian using short-cut sections of treated posts for a Japanese effect around a miniature planting had burned leaves almost like spray burn. In about three months, the posts dried out and the minis began to grow again. If in doubt, stack treated lumber in the sun for a while, like the mill should have done in the first place. Old railroad cross ties are OK, but freshly creosoted ties are bad news for plants.

FOUNTAINS AND POOLS are finally beginning to find a place in the rose garden. For a good many years rosarians avoided water features, fearing mildew and blackspot problems. But, with effective fungicides available today, roses and water get along very well. Pools, splashing fountains, streams in rock gardens, as well as other treatments, make a fine background or feature setting for roses, particularly miniatures and Floribundas. But remember that pool water requires chlorine treatment, and that's not good if drained off into the rose bed. Drain to the street or storm sewer.

ALTERNATE FUNGICIDES for better blackspot-mildew control. That's the practice of many rosarians; using *Manzate* the first week, *Benlate* the second and following up with *Phaltan*. If it's near showtime, adjust the schedule to use *Benlate* to cut down on spray residue. Rosarians along the Gulf Coast like a combination spray, which seems to accomplish the same thing. In the spring during cooler weather, combine one tablespoon of *Benlate* and one tablespoon of *Phaltan* per two gallons of water and spray weekly. During very hot weather, use *Benlate* alone; or for hot, muggy conditions, use *Benlate/Manzate*, one tablespoon each per two gallons of water. There's somewhat more residue with *Manzate*, but it will help give longer and better control if blackspot breaks out.

TAKE IT EASY with insecticides. More and more rose growers are reporting that LESS insecticide will do a better job. Don't add an insecticide every time the garden is sprayed. Use specific controls for specific insect problems, ONLY when needed. The habit of adding insecticides to fungicides on a weekly basis is wasteful and addictive. Nature had a built-in balance, and the less we disturb it the better. Thrips require a different treatment; mist the bud and bloom areas with *Orthene* or *Cygon* when they are a problem. There's no point in spraying the whole bush. And when spray mixtures build up on the leaves, wash them off. Water and lots of it can't hurt a healthy rose bush. The same treatment applies to spider mites; wash the undersides of the leaves as well as the tops. For hot climate rosarians, the water wand makes rose growing fun again.

ROSARIANS USING TIME RELEASE FERTILIZERS (Osmocote, Precise, *etc.*) have been keeping it quiet for one reason or another, probably to enjoy a competitive edge a little longer. It's the easy way to feed roses the right amount all the time. With some do-it-yourself supplements, roses will thrive. Choose a shorter release time for short growing seasons, longer release for warmer climates. Gives a rose grower more time to enjoy roses… and that's what this is all about.

THESE RAMBLING COLUMNS treat the "rose facts of life" somewhat irreverently from time to time, but growing good roses really hasn't changed much over the years. Here are some of old clips and quotes from the RAMBLER (a bit yellow and mildewed) that are just as good today as they were ten years ago...

PLAIN ROSE SENSE tells us that roses must have consistent care during the hottest part of the summer in order to put out a harvest of blooms in the fall. Roses don't vacation during the summer; they want to eat and drink regularly just like rosarians. Hot-climate summer blooms may be small, open too fast and lack a little something in color; but at least some blooms are being produced, an evidence that the bush is vigorous and healthy. Stay on a summer schedule of light, regular feedings with plenty of water to keep the whole process going.

SPIDER MITES... Common sense control of spider mites needs to be reviewed over and over again in mid-summer. No miracle spray has yet come along to eliminate these pests... at least not one available to the backyard rosarian. But, quick action and plain water will do the job. Just wash 'em off with water; no leaf burn, no spray residue, almost no mites. Greenhouse people have been washing off mites for years and years, long before exotic chemicals. Buy a Water Wand (advertised in these pages) or build one yourself. Just direct a fine spray of water under pressure to break up webbing on the undersides of rose leaves and send mites to a watery grave. Roses will green up and begin to grow as mites are controlled. Spider mites have arrived when leaves turn gray-green, then yellow-brown, then drop off. When leaves lose color, check the undersides of the leaves for threads of white webbing and specks that look like salt and pepper. If in doubt, shake off a few of the specks on a white sheet of paper and watch them move. Get out the water wand immediately and wash two or three times the first week. A weekly washing after that will maintain control. If you MUST use a miticide (and run the risk of leaf burn) wash the leaves first and follow with a drenching spray on the undersides. Apply three times at five-day intervals.

BENEFITS OF MULCHING MATERIALS

have been discussed for years. Unless a garden has that "perfect" soil with water retention, drainage, aeration, humus balance and what-have-you, a good mulch will add roses with less work. Consider what a good mulch is supposed to do. If it's working right, a mulch lets water and air pass freely (along with nutrients), does not pack, decomposes slowly, adds humus to the soil, has a pleasing appearance, does not harbor bugs and generally provides a good soil insulation to keep the soil feeder roots cool and moisture level high. This is a good-sized order, but one which many mulches can fill.

Usually a combination of materials is more effective than just one. For example, pine needles, shredded pine bark and partially composted leaves in combination work better than anyone used alone. Oak leaves and some kind of coarse bark or woody material are good. A shredder that chops up all kinds of organic matter makes the best combination of all. Use a minimum of two or three inches of mulch, enjoy all the good things that happen to the soil and soil processes. An old rosarian around here quips that mulch is worth its weight in gold... and in roses. Weigh some for yourself this season.

SUMMER FEEDING. While roses are heavy feeders, they respond best to frequent, light feedings rather than massive fertilization. Whatever your favorite food might be, try half the quantity twice as often. You'll get more blooms for your money. And, of course, WATER. The best soils and rose foods can't do any good until available to the plant in solution. Light sprinkling is wasteful; deep soaking is best. A well-constructed rose bed with good drainage is almost impossible to overwater. Depending on the soil and the temperature, use two inches per week. And, be sure to consult a reliable rain gauge; don't guess the amount of a summer shower. If you are watering overhead, set the rain gauge within the irrigated area and check the amount of water actually reaching the roses. A good trick is to set several coffee cans in the bed area to be watered and check the amount of water they can catch.

SAVE THE LEAVES. It's sometimes hard to tell if more leaf damage is done by spray or by diseases and insects. Particularly during the summer, the name of rose game is LEAVES. Do everything possible to maintain a good, healthy leaf system. When you MUST spray, soak the rose beds first and spray during the cooler hours. To repeat what every good rosarian knows, well maintained plants can't help but produce roses. Whether leaves are lost because of mites, blackspot, mildew, spray burn or dehydration, the result is the same: no roses.

It's amazing how much good rose sense is available when rosarians get together in a non-competitive situation... like the Region VII Rose Conference held in Tyler, Texas, in June. Rose nuts from allover came to talk about roses, spin some yarns about how well their roses were doing and take in the Tyler Rose Garden and commercial fields. Here are just a few of the "rose breaks" worth repeating...

PLANTING SHOCK takes quite a toll when miniatures are set out during the summer. One grower plants anytime (without loss) by first planting the new miniature in a gallon container and placing in a shaded, protected location for about two weeks. When the plant shows signs of starting, slit the container and set out the plant and soil with minimum disturbance. Make sure that the container soil and final planting area are approximately the same mix.

WEATHERED WOOD makes an attractive trellis or background for climbing miniatures. And, it does not have to be in a rock garden or other informal planting. Wood fences and brick walls are softened with driftwood or other naturally-aged material.

ROCK GARDENS and miniatures just naturally go together. Since minis come in all sizes, colors, and shapes, there's hardly a nook or area that can't use a bit of small rose beauty. Other annuals and perennials mix well with minis, too. While the maintenance job is a little more difficult, the overall effect is striking. A mound, terrace or slope gives any rosarian a chance to show some creative landscape talent; a one-of-a-kind rose garden that no one else can duplicate.

THE TYLER ROSE GARDEN has added some 300 new rose trees, using them very effectively for backgrounds, entrance ways, accents and dividers. No bush roses are planted under the trees; the planting is made in regular raised beds and heavily mulched. Tree roses have considerable flair... and could add to the driveway edge or long fence that's hard to landscape. Except in the most extreme climates, tree roses are very rewarding.

HAVE SPIDER MITES? Here's a quote from someone who HAD them. "When *Orthene* first came out, we sprayed the whole plant every two weeks and for the first time in years had no thrips and the most beautiful light-colored roses you have ever seen. However, in about sixty days spider mites burned through the plantings like wildfire, something we had never had before. We discontinued *Orthene*, began washing with water twice a week and made one application of *Plictran*. Then more water. The mites are now under control and we use *Orthene* on the bud and bloom areas ONLY. The thrips are under control and the plants have leaves again."

EXHIBITORS can teach the backyard rose grower something, too. For example, you'll enjoy cut roses longer if they are conditioned in hot water immediately after cutting. Immerse in deep hot water (a bit hotter than washing your hands) and let stand in a cool dark place until the water has cooled. Another trick is to further stabilize these conditioned blooms in the refrigerator overnight so that you'll always have some good blooms to give away, enjoy in the house or maybe enter in a small rose society show. And, the flower arrangers will love you, too.

ROSE FOLIAGE can be dry cleaned with a piece of cheesecloth or an old T-shirt. In fact, the dry method seems to bring out more sheen in the leaves than the water, water-detergent combinations or what-have-you. Spray residue comes right off without streaking. Just be careful not to tear the leaves. If you are an exhibitor, another obvious help (wish I had thought of it) is to make out an entry tag BEFORE the show for EACH named variety. Then when that tag is gone, you'll know that the entry is in and you won't duplicate it. For challenge classes, set up the correct number of tags for the competition and fix with a paper clip. Enter the names of the varieties when the final selection has been made.

OVERHEAD WATERING is still popular even with those rosarians fortunate to have other, more automatic systems. Exhibition-minded growers avoid getting blooms wet just before shows; but they attribute better foliage and overall growth to the washing, cooling action of water and lots of it. Effective fungicides have virtually eliminated the old problems of blackspot and mildew.

CAREFREE roses are really not so carefree, on no less authority than Dr. Griffith Buck who hybridized CAREFREE BEAUTY. Even the carefree series needs fungicide protection on a monthly basis. But this Iowa State rosarian has been able to transmit the winter hardiness of Siberian roses to progeny that are quite attractive, prolific in bloom and a rose landscaper's delight in the cold country.

SIMPLE AS A, B, C... That's the alphabetical rose schedule. More and more rose societies are going to the alphabetical schedule to make it easy to show and easy to judge. And that's what this rose FUN is all about. If you would like a sample alphabetical schedule (there's one for miniatures-only shows, too), just drop the Rambler a note. You'll get a copy as fast as spider mites strike.

SEPT.
1978

THOUGHT FOR THE MONTH:
Don't be in a hurry to use new insecticides. Wait until they get the bugs out.

An old-timer rosarian remarked to me recently that "a smart rosarian knows what to do with what he knows"… which is another way of saying that most rose problems have rather simple solutions when we think them through. Here are some thoughts on using what you already know to enjoy roses more…

MOST ALL of us have noticed that an ample helping of manure used before other rose foods seems to make the whole formula work better. And, we don't have to understand it to appreciate the results. A good routine program or rose show feeding schedule ought to include manure about two weeks before the soluble applications. Manure seems to be an appetizer for the micro-organisms that convert nutrients into forms actually available to plants. In case you are short on manure… adapt. Add about ten pounds of blood meal (or fish meal) to the typical forty pound sack of organic based rose food. Work the mix in wit a bit of soil bacteria and watch the results.

AND SHARP ROSARIAN eyes have picked up that spraying just after rain gives better leaf coverage (better wetting) and seems to stick longer. If rain is in short supply, it's not a bad idea to wash off the plants after a long, dry spell and then spray. It's another good reason to water overhead at least some of the time. And, you have certainly seen that organic material, earthworms and healthy rose bushes, go together. Doesn't the soil smell good when organics, soil and sand, are working together?? Nature must be trying to tell us something. Are we listening?

SOME ROSE FOLKS know (or have read the directions) that *Acti-Dione PM* works better when used alone and that new, nitrogen-lush leaves should be sprayed until dripping. But have you also learned that this excellent fungicide works even better if the powdery spores are washed off before spraying? Ordinary baking soda (1 tablespoon per gallon of water) sprayed about twice a week also helps control mildew, probably due to the washing action.

ANOTHER COMMON sense idea is to move a plant with chronic mildew to a spot with better air circulation. Some growers even use a "sacrificial lamb" technique. Keep a mildewer like ORANGE FLAME or FIREKING (you may want to nominate other varieties) in the garden; either one that will tell you right away when mildew conditions are right. The double up on control efforts for a while to keep the rest of the garden clean. A good test rose for spray materials is OLDTIMER. The leaves burn at the slightest mistake. You may be able to catch yourself in a careless practice before burning up the whole garden.

COMMON SENSE tells us that good spray mixtures are important, but not many rosarians know how to blend wettable powders (WP) and oil-based insecticides (EC) into compatible mixtures. Warm water is the answer. Use a large glass mixing container with a tight lid; this way you can always see what's going on. Measure wettable powders into the container first; then slowly add warm water, swirling the mixture into a thick paste. Continue to add warm water to a thin consistency. Swirling seems to work best without foam or suds. For very alkaline water, add one tablespoon of vinegar per gallon. Ingredients with aromatic distillates are added next, swirling gently. Add any spreader-sticker last. The spray mixture is now ready to use WITHOUT straining, even in a sprayer with the smallest nozzle.

ANY ROSARIAN with garden sense is wearing gloves and handling spray mixtures with care so that the danger of using a glass container is very small. If one of the spray materials precipitates out, safely dispose of the whole batch and try to identify the product that caused the problem. For example, old *Cygon* will cause *Benlate* to precipitate out immediately. Result: no protection and clogged sprayer.

ENVIRONMENTAL PROTECTION is an important rose topic since every rose grower has a shelf-load of potions. This means protecting the rosarians, the foliage AND the environment. Careless handling and storage create most of the problems; and the product gets the blame more often than the rosarian. READ THE DIRECTIONS. When sprays are necessary, use fresh materials that are accurately labeled. Follow the precautions carefully. Read ALL of the directions before you start.

MOST SPRAY MATERIALS have limited shelf life and lose effectiveness (or sometimes become more potent) when kept too long in environments that are alternately hot and cold. It is important to know just how old spray materials are, but not many rose people bother to DATE packages or to repackage wettable powders in containers that can be sealed. Large glass jars with tight lids are good for this: and a label can be taped to the outside.

ANOTHER GOOD TRICK is to note your favorite mixture proportions on the jar with a grease pencil so that you won't have to figure them out again. These two precautions can save roses from blackspot and mildew due to spraying with old materials or head off leaf burn because a spray concentration was too strong. And, a must for every spray shelf is a small medicine glass used exclusively for measuring spray materials. Most garden shops have them for about 25 cents each with easy-to-read markings. Get a couple. Use them wisely for best results.

Call it "summer madness" or just being out in the hot, Texas sun too long, but the Walters family has moved to a new home… leaving behind several hundred roses and twenty some years of landscaping effort. It was a hard decision to make, particularly in mid-summer when roses can't be moved. There's considerably more space for roses in the new location and the Rambler will be sharing some of the trials (and triumphs?) of starting all over again in these columns in the months to come. Hope that some of these observations will be useful to you good readers who may be in the process of moving, expanding, changing, or just looking for a new project.

AIR POLLUTION was a major factor in the relocation decision. Traffic had increased like spider mites over the last five years, leaving behind a greasy residue on leaves, walks, sills, pools and people. Overhead watering helped some, but the roses seemed less and less productive. And it was easier to bum the leaves, even with plain water, unless washed down on a regular basis. Periodic spraying with ordinary baking soda (1 tablespoon per gallon of water) also seemed to help and cleaned up traces of powdery mildew at the same time. Leaf coarseness and traces of bum are early signs of toxic reaction to air pollutants.

MINIATURES can be moved, even in 100 degree, mid-August. Select the plants to be moved carefully; the smaller, less mature plants shock least. Trim back moderately so that the root system has less to support and lift from rose bed to pot or can with soil and roots intact. Keep in a shaded location for about two weeks, then gradually move to more sun and begin light feeding. When new rose beds are ready, reverse the operation and have an established miniature planting overnight. Some fifty miniatures (including some mini trees) survived the move with little more than a few yellow leaves.

A WELL-ESTABLISHED miniature rose planting can be the source of several more miniature rose beds with just a little effort. Since most mini blooms come from newer wood and new breaks, removal of old wood and dead material encourages growth. An easy way to clean up large miniature plants is to dig them while dormant (or just before breaking dormancy in cold climates)

and gently break up the clumps, usually finishing up two or three plants with good roots. Prune out old wood, trim the roots a little and replant. They will usually respond with better growth and more blooms than before… plus another garden. Gulf Coast rose folks usually dig minis about every three years, and its a good time to rejuvenate the beds, too. It's on the Rambler's calendar for spring next year (back at the old beds) and worthwhile for you to consider as well.

MASSES OF FLORIBUNDAS are high on the list of priorities in the Rambler's new plantings. They are great for color, growth and landscape accent. In some areas, five or ten plants of the same variety will be a landscape feature. Another less formal area will have several different varieties, although the growth habits will be similar. Floribundas look best when planted close together for a mass of leaves and color. Depth of the beds needs to be considered, too. A front-lawn planting (on 15-inch centers) of twenty CHARISMA at our old location was a traffic stopper. It's going to be used again to accent a contemporary home of Mexican brick with brownstained cedar trim. GINGERSNAP and TRAILBLAZER are also going to be used as both have outstanding color. EUROPEANA will fill an area between the driveway and fence with beautiful foliage as well as blooms. BON BON and ROSE PARADE will be used in foundation and entrance plantings.

ROSE SPACING is also important. Many exhibitors maintain that wide spacing produces better show blooms, but close planting gives a better "rose bed" effect. Beds with lots of rose plants seem to look greener, maybe because they shade one another. Individual rose plants are not very attractive, particularly if permitted to grow tall. Tall growing varieties are used more effectively if Floribundas or even tall growing miniatures are planted in front to screen and fill in the gaps left by long, heavy canes. Of course, this all depends on climate, length of growing season and many other factors. But as a general rule, Hybrid Teas, Floribundas and even Miniatures can be used in a common bed to create a mass of roses.

GOOD IDEAS are not a bit particular about who has them, and Keith and Enola Collins of Beaumont, Texas, figured that miniatures would do better in a hot climate if the soil could be kept cooler. Most of the common mulches wouldn't do the job, so they switched to large chunks of pine bark (two or three inches) and filled in all the spaces between miniature plants about three inches deep. The results over the last three years have been outstanding. On a recent visit during a 100° day, the soil under the bark checked out to be cool and moist, the roses were thriving, overall effect was most pleasing... and there were NO spider mites. The Collins' family believes in fish meal, broadcasting generously and washing in. In contact with the soil, it goes to work to produce the finest minis you'll ever see. You'll see plenty of pine chunks in the Rambler's mini beds next year.

Nov. 1978

THOUGHT FOR THE MONTH: Advice for the novice (and some others):
Roses are supposed to have yellow leaves; they just turn green sometimes.

There's a respected old-timer in this area who makes a lot of rose sense. In a recent talk, he advised that "the really GOOD roses are grown in November and December when rose nuts aren't distracted by the blooms." Which seems like a contradiction, but he is right on target as usual. Late fall calls for winter protection (if you need it), rose bed preparation and variety planning. A poor job now usually means poor roses in the spring.

WINTER PROTECTION doesn't have to be fancy, just do what comes naturally. Nature conditions plants for cold, storing strength for the spring that's sure to come. The natural way to protect is with soil and leaves or combinations of materials that breathe and adjust to changing conditions. Cones, wraps, baskets and barriers are not in the same league as Mother Nature. Whatever method you like, think a bit about how nature might use the materials to best advantage.

NEW OR REBUILT rose beds need some time to settle and mellow before spring planting. Some freezing and thawing, settling and draining, washing and blowing for a few months can tell a good deal about how a bed will perform under growing conditions. It's better to find out early that the drainage is no good and not after the new plants have turned yellow. A poor winter bed is an even poorer spring bed.

VARIETIES (called cultivars by the pro-types) deserves some careful thought away from the excitement of the rose show. What are you trying to achieve?? Lots of roses to cut for the house, something leafy and colorful to hide the foundation, a landscape accent, a collection requiring less care or a garden to make the exhibitor's heart beat faster?? Here's where the local Proof of the Pudding comes in. Check garden AND exhibition ratings;, visit with several different growers. And after all this, THEN make out the order for spring.

CUTTING TO A FIVE-LEAFLET is gospel to most rose people. It is supposed to reduce dieback, make a new bud develop faster, encourage plant vigor and generally give more blooms per season. But such grooming isn't ALWAYS in the best interest of the plant. Some studies in public gardens show that simply cutting off a spent bloom resulted in just as many breaks that came on as fast or faster than canes trimmed to a lower, heavier five-leaflet. The stem dried up and the plant put out new stems and leaves without hesitation. Best of all, mass plantings with light trimming had many leaves throughout the season and considerably less winterkill. It follows that healthy, vigorous plants with more leaves (the food producer for the plant) will be in better condition to take on whatever nature has to offer. You might want to keep an eye on some leafy plants in your own garden and see if there's a relationship between plant size this year and a start next spring. Of course, if you are an exhibitor, you'll want to direct all the strength of the plant to a few canes and blooms. But in the long run, there's a price to pay

HYBRIDIZERS at the Boston ARS meeting came up with some good hot-stove topics. Discussing a blue rose, the pros (Sam McGredy and Bill Warriner) told the hobbyists on the panel (Frank Benardella, Vince Gioia and Dale Martin) that there would be a tremendous market for a really blue rose but that it wasn't likely in our day. McGredy offered some hope with the observation that there were no orange-colored roses before 1950 and now we accept them as usual. McGredy saw the prospect as a "two-headed cow reversal" or mutation and asked "but will anyone see it?" Roses growing in spikes like gladiolas or delphinium may also be in our future. McGredy has a seven-foot shrub now that blooms at least every leaf axil… but all the blooms are single. It may take fifty years to breed in good blooms. Anyway, it's different, the attribute that sells roses everywhere.

THE RAMBLER'S NEW GARDEN DIARY recorded plenty of digging, grubbing, and tree work this month (September) but not much real progress for the roses. Pool excavation produced about four truckloads of dirt worth saving (sand/clay mix) for filling and leveling. The rest had to be hauled out, compacting a future rose garden area like the base for a freeway. But restoration is already underway. Excess sharp sand (left over from the gunite crew) and an equal volume of pine mulch were laid down in a windrow about eight inches deep in top of the compacted clay. Following a general rain, two hours work with a *Rototiller* blended a good mixture that incorporated about eight inches of clay base. Some very heavy rains followed, but the raised soil (about five feet wide) drained very well, stayed loose and could be worked easily the following day. With the addition of four or five inches of barnyard manure and ten pounds each of Gypsum and Superphosphate (per 100 square feet of bed) plus some more work with the tiller, the new bed should be ready for edging roses in the spring. The mix is roughly a 1/3 soil. 1/3 sand, and 1/3 organic matter combination that has been successfully growing roses in flood or drought for many years. You may want to try it in your own raised bed preparation this fall.

With snow on the ground and the rose year winding down, it seems a good time for rose reflection to enjoy last year's garden just a little more. While fireside fantasies in December are great, it's thoughtful planning for the year ahead that pays off in more blooms. The year-in-year-out show winners have already made up order lists for new roses, and you should be working on yours. Many of the best exhibition roses are sold out early. Make up an order now and then place another next spring to replace those that don't make it through the winter.

FOR A MAJOR LANDSCAPE PROJECT, consider buying 1-grade plants on a wholesale basis. With a little extra care, 1Ws will catch up with No. 1's by the end of the first season. Plant the smaller bushes a little closer together (close spacing usually looks better anyway) and enjoy a good many more roses than you might have otherwise been able to afford. It's a great way to plant a whole driveway or fenceline. The 1Ws come in bundles of ten, and you can usually get your local nurseryman to order them (EARLY) from his supplier. He's even more likely to help if several rose folks pool their orders for 100 or more plants at a time. Even with a markup, these smaller plants will turn out to be real bargains.

MINIATURE-ONLY ROSE SHOWS last year turned out to be very popular in many parts of the country, resulting in new members for sponsoring rose societies and a whole new range of interest for gardeners. For societies that usually have just one rose show a year, a mini-only show is another chance to have fun and get more people into roses with minimum effort. They are easy to stage and there's no shortage of friendly malls or garden centers as hosts. Now's the time to line up a host location and sketch out a schedule. Or the Rambler will be glad to send along a mini-schedule that has worked very well in Houston.

LESS SPRAY MEANS LESS MITES, at least that's what reports from all over the country are saying. These are ordinary rose people who switched from saturation miticide spraying to infrequent applications of insecticides for SPECIFIC insect problems only. Apparently Mother Nature got the good and bad insects into balance again for the benefit of all. Washing off mites with water IS a valid miticide alternative. Many rose writers report general use of insecticide only two or three times a season; something like Malathion or Orthene. Spot controls of thrips or worms were used only when needed and ONLY on the affected areas. It is worth a try in your garden plan next season.

BETTER DRAINAGE YIELDS DRAMATIC RESULTS but is commonly overlooked by rosarians who otherwise go to great lengths to make sure that the rose bed is "just right."

Some gardens are blessed with good drainage, but most are not. If you don't have it, make it. Agricultural drain line is the way to go in most gardens. Relatively inexpensive, it comes in rolls, is corrugated for strength and flexibility and can be laid in, over, under and around garden problems. To make a new bed or rejuvenate an old one, dig a trench the length of the rose bed and about a foot below the normal root level, gradually sloping down to a drain, ditch or even a gravel leaching pit. Use an inch or so of gravel or sand in the bottom of the ditch, lay the drain line, cover the line with tar paper to keep drain holes open and backfill with some sand if you have it or garden soil from the ditch. You11 enjoy dramatic rose results in the first season.

FROM THE RAMBLER'S GARDEN DIARY... October has been a slow month as far as new rose bed construction is concerned, but most of the layout work and planning decisions has been made. Several heavy rains confirmed that the yard drains were working (very important on the wet Gulf Coast), paths to the rose beds were fairly dry and no major low spots appeared. Fill sand and garden soil are settling all right but it seems like another truckload or so will be needed, most of it to be spread by hand. Cultivating with a tiller (borrowed) makes leveling and grading easier, rains do most of the work.

LANDSCAPE TIMBERS will be used for most of the Rambler's new beds in the back yard, three timbers high except on slopes. They are easy to work with ordinary hand tools, can be spiked together for stability and don't require any sort of footing or foundation if secured in place with reinforcing rod pegs. Just drill through the timbers and drive the rod about a foot into the ground. Like building a log house, the sides of the bed are more stable and attractive if the timbers are arranged to overlap joints. More formal plantings in front will use "soldier course" bricks; that is bricks standing on end along the edge of a cement walk or stable border. In most cases, the bricks will be set in sand side-by-side, with no mortar. The result is good drainage (build up bed), an attractive outline and a project that can be done by an ordinary gardener with some time, a short-handled shovel and a level. For a really professional job, mash bricks into soft concrete in the trench; they are more stable and will last a long, long time.

With important Rose Resolutions out of the way, (Example: Order only ten more roses than the garden will hold), it's time to take on another New Year's tradition… predictions of what's ahead. This is easy for the rosarian because he knows that the garden next year is bound to be bigger and better than ever. Let's take a look at what the '79 garden will have.

FLORIBUNDAS will appear in showy masses in more gardens this year, taking advantage of some good new varieties on the market. And you'll see more roses in the front yard where they should have been all the time. Roses will be used more often for massed-effect rather than as specimen plantings. Shrubs and landscape varieties that will tolerate low temperatures and now-and-then care will win new gardening friends. Hybridizers are working hard in this direction, introducing roses that have good form, stay in bloom most of the time and can be cut for the house. This is what MOST ordinary rose growers and backyard gardeners are interested in. Queen-of-the-Show types may be great for the rose nuts, but roses like GENE BOERNER, ROSE PARADE, MERCI, ACCENT, EUROPEANA, SUNSPRITE and CHARISMA will bring more people pleasure in rose growing. Best of all, these roses will do well in most climates.

TIMED-RELEASE FERTILIZERS like *Osmocote* and Precise will be used in large and small gardens. Used in combination with organics and trace-mineral supplements, the hard work and guess work of fertilizing all season can be forgotten. For the backyard grower, timed-release fertilizers mean more roses with less work. Like Benlate, these new fertilizers will not work miracles, but will help many growers who might otherwise give up.

ROSE COMPETITION, at least the way we know it now, will have less emphasis in the future. More rose exhibitions will be staged and more shopping malls will be filled with roses and rosarians anxious to encourage others to grow roses. Rose societies will tend toward small monthly competitions at the variation of particles in the mix. Sharp sand helps "open up" regular meetings, encouraging ALL the members (not just the just trophy chasers) to participate. This might be called a two-level competition; the big growers can come on strong at the annual and district shows while the less experienced enjoy sharing while learning.

CONSULTING ROSARIANS will be doing their thing at local nurseries and at workshops, promoting roses and easy rose care. ARS has a big interest in this grass-roots growth if the society is to attract some 10,000 new members for a healthy, active organization. These are the same people essential to a local society, potential growers who are looking for cultural information, landscape help and rose fun. The groups that provide this kind of rose package will have lots of members. Although you may see the future through rose colored glasses of a different hue, all of us have to make roses more interesting, more fun and more widely used by more people… with whatever skills we have.

FROM THE RAMBLER'S GARDEN DIARY… A completely new landscape plan and rose garden in just one season seems more like wishful, rose-catalog thinking all the time. The optimism of October has been replaced with mud, cold and a work schedule that's way behind by November. During dry weather, drainage and leveling looked promising. Now, some 75 yards of river sand later, we still have low spots and water that won't run the right direction. But there's one bright spot, at least the problems are showing up now rather than next spring when the rose beds are planted. Just another good reason for starting early so that nature can do its thing. But both of us are going to have to hurry, because the Rambler's yard will be on the garden tour during the ARS National Convention in Houston in April 1979, ready or not.

A MOUND OF MINI ROSES is now underway. It's not exactly a rock garden or a terraced bank, but more of an elevated area in an otherwise flat landscape. There's some weathered wood, a few native rocks and odds and ends of other plant materials for variety. Short timbers hold the soil and give a natural look. The idea came from the garden of Harlan Clark of Denver, Colorado, an outstanding grower and do-it-yourself landscaper. Harlan has a great program on the development of his garden that he'll share with rose folks attending the ARS meeting in Houston. It remains to be seen if the copy (mine) is as good as the real thing (Harlan's).

MIXTURES OF MATERIALS are working best in the Rambler's new beds. Sand, soil and organic matter in roughly equal proportions make a bed friable enough to work easily within a few hours after a heavy rain. The secret seems to be in the variation of particles in the mix. Sharp sand helps "open up" the soil; coarse Perlite will do almost the same thing. Calcined clay (sold as Terra Green in many places) is also a good soil conditioner. When water and air move easily through the soil with organic matter to feed bacteria, roses are bound to grow. If manure isn't available use compost or peat moss. Just make sure that the three basic elements, (soil, sand and organics), are working for you and for your roses.

February is a great time for roses. It's too early for the really hard work to begin in the garden and yet late enough for the memories of last summer to get better and better. There's something about snow on the ground that makes last season's roses have more form, color and size. It's called "looking at the world through rose-colored glasses." So if your eyes are tired from rose visions or catalog overkill, think about some of these old-but-new ideas for the coming season.

SAP RISES in roses and rosarians about the same time... the first warm day. How about some common rose sense this season? Nature and roses perform best gradually; crash spring programs usually crash with the first cold snap. In the summertime it's called Sunday Syndrome, a rose affliction caused by the anxious rosarian who prunes, pulls, grooms, feeds, scratches, waters, sprays and fusses over the plants, (not necessarily in that order). In the spring it takes the form of uncovering, digging, probing, feeding, cutting and drenching with gunk before the soil is warm enough to support growth. Let spring and roses come on gradually, you'll get better results.

ALL ROSARIANS like to plant to new roses and most think they do a pretty fair job. But if roses could talk, some sad tales of mishandling would be told. Obviously it makes no sense to put a $5 bush in a 50-cent hole. Most cases are not this bad, but a good grower knows that a well-prepared rose bed pays off in roses. A few extra hours of spade work in the winter saves sweat-producing labor in the summer. Check out a local rose bed formula and get out the fork and shovel.

OLD ROSARIAN TALES are commonly passed along on how to plant roses and some often are cruel to plant and planter alike. For example, some old-timers claim that a grower has to "stomp" on the roots to "get rid of the air." This not only gets rid of the air but also breaks the roots and compacts the soil so that water and air, which are both essential to soil processes, don't have a chance.

The best planting tool is plenty of water. Thorough, deep soaking is the key. The Rambler is a "cone type" planter, supporting the root system with a cone of well-prepared soil. Cover the roots lightly and begin to run water slowly into the hole.

Add some more soil, water will fill in the voids. While one bush is soaking, plant the next one. Then come back with soil, more water, etc. Don't tamp the soil in place. Let water do the work. It makes a rosarian cringe to see a 200-pound gardener breaking and displacing rose roots with size 12 boots.

DORMANT SPRAYS are overdone and overrated in the Rambler's opinion, often causing more cane damage than good. The lime-sulfur-oil combinations are hard to use, particularly when it's cold and the plants are really dormant. They don't offer the safe and effective control of overwintering insects and diseases that specific insecticides and fungicides do. These controls are already on the rosarian's shelf.

Field and home tests conclusively show that a cleanup spray of Phaltan-Isotox, Manzate-Spectracide or similar mix applied IMMEDIATELY after pruning establishes a sound control program for the season. Use favorite mixture at full strength as shown on the label. Thoroughly drench the canes and bud union. Spray the same day that bushes are pruned. Fungus spores carryover on green canes; insects hide out in corky tissue. The name of the game for fungus is CONTROL. Start early and enjoy roses more.

HILL UP CANES of new bushes with all the soil, mulch or other insulating material available. This not only protects from the cold but keeps canes from drying out. Until roots are well established, canes are very vulnerable to sun and wind. Constant temperature and moist conditions help roses start. It's the same principle with plastic tents over plants slow to start. Throw a handful of wet sphagnum moss over the bud union; form a tent of clear plastic material, (like the plastic roses are shipped in,) over the bush and secure at the shank. The result is a moist, warm greenhouse that encourages breaks. Gradually uncover when plants have started.

FROM THE RAMBLER'S GARDEN DIARY... December has been a tough month for new rose beds and transplanting shrubs because of one heavy rain after another. But, the rains did prove one thing: agricultural drain lines really work. The flexible, corrugated plastic type is easy to lay and inexpensive. The Rambler's installation is about a foot below the bed level, gradually draining to a storm sewer. Lay some tar paper over the line, add a little gravel or sand and backfill with ordinary soil. Drained beds can be worked within hours after a heavy rain.

LANDSCAPE TIMBERS have been a very pleasant surprise. They are easy to work, shape, cut and fit with ordinary hand tools. They make most attractive bed edging. A Roto-Tiller is another boon to the gardener. It really takes the work out of bed mixing as well as general yard leveling. Borrow or rent one for your next project.

Spring rose fever is epidemic about now, brought on by rose catalogs and evidenced by light-headedness on the first warm day of spring. It's likely to hang on until the resident rosarian breaks dormancy and gets outdoors again. Here are a couple of dormancy, also back, breakers to open up a new season. GET A JUMP on spring by making up a mound of potting and planter mix out on the driveway or in a frozen corner of the yard. Then you'll be ready to try some tree roses in redwood tubs or brighten up the patio with floribundas in cedar, clay or redwood planters. Ordinary garden soil just doesn't work in planters. A little extra care in the selection of a planting medium makes all the difference in growing roses in containers season after season. The formula for growth and survival is good drainage, air in the root zone and the ability to retain moisture.

THE MIX THAT WORKS BEST has about 1/3 garden soil, 1/3 Canadian peat moss and 1/3 calcined clay granules (kitty litter). Use granules without additives. It's cheap and available in feed stores in 50-pound bags. Calcined clay granules are extremely porous, something like microscopic honeycomb. The material has the ability to take in moisture for slow release to feeder roots without souring, packing or breaking down. You may want to add some Osmocote for feeding or maybe some sharp sand for better porosity. Pile up the ingredients on the driveway, mix, sift and mix again. Moisten and let stand about a week. Mix again and you're ready for planting.

PRUNING TECHNIQUE can make a big difference in die back, healing of cuts and a vigorous spring start. For large, woody canes, use a small keyhole saw instead of the crushing jaws of a lopper. Cuts will heal fast, particularly on the bud union. Make it a regular habit to keep the BLADE of the pruning saw DOWN so that the opposing jaw of the shear does not bruise good rose cane. To say it another way, let the jaw bruise the cane material that is cut off. Use pruners large and sharp' enough to make smooth and clean cuts. If it isn't easy, you're using the wrong tool. Clean up the bud union whenever you can. Use a small pruning saw with fine teeth to trim off old stubs flush with the bud union so that it can heal over. Just be careful of new buds.

A NEW PRODUCT you may want to look into before cleaning and edging beds is called *EDGE GARD*, a plastic edging material shaped like a "T". Visualize a T on its side. One part of the T top is imbedded in the soil as a stabilizer; the other half of the top acts as a mulch and soil retainer. The long leg of the T on the grass side of the edging acts as a runner for the lawnmower wheel. It is flexible, easy to install, nearly indestructible and fairly inexpensive. An ARS member from North Carolina came up with the idea; he got tired of lawn trimming. *Edge Gard* is shipped direct in 8 and 10 foot lengths. For an illustrated folder write to *Edge Gard*, 1327 Burtonwood Circle, Charlotte, North Carolina, 28212.

ELMER'S GLUE has found another use... sealing rose canes. Even the plastic applicator bottle is useful, or, if that doesn't feel handy, put some into an old shoe polish bottle and use the dauber. The Rambler likes to paint the end of any cane thumb-size or larger and all cuts made at the bud union. Unless you have problems with borers in your area, don't bother sealing very light canes as they heal quickly without help. Painting is like any other wound treatment, the point is to stop bleeding and keep foreign matter out.

I MAY BE WRONG but the Rambler thinks that it is impractical and a waste of time to attempt to disinfect pruning tools with *Lysol*, alcohol or what-have-you between rose bushes. It's hard to imagine rose pruning under antiseptic conditions. Thousands of rose bushes pruned by the Rambler over some twenty years have never shown signs of cross infection. A careful rosarian with clean, SHARP tools can do a good job without worry.

FROM THE RAMBLER'S GARDEN DIARY... January's rains have smoothed out the newly built planting mounds to something natural looking. It remains to be seen if the floribundas to be planted there will have that made-by-nature look. Variety selection was tough. The large mound by the mailbox will have Gingersnap and Playboy; Sunsprite for a smaller mound and Trailblazer along the fence. Another large and informal area of mixed floribundas will have several plants each of Little Darling, Picnic, Accent, Apache Tears, Faberge, Angel Face and some very attractive new singles named Dusky Maiden, Sweet Vivien and

Dairy Maid. We're looking for great masses of color.

A ROSE FRIEND pointed out that landscape timbers are even easier to use with framing angles and plates like those used in rafter construction. Sure enough, structural wood fasteners of galvanized steel make a backyard hammer guy look like a pro. If you're using timbers, check with your local builders for some TECO fasteners. Make rose bed building easier. That's the name of the game!

How about some Garden Gems this month… the kind of rose comments heard around the refreshments table? Speakers seldom mention them, apparently assuming that everyone already knows them, but, a gem or two can make rose growing easier and that's what this is all about.

IF POTS ARE A PUZZLE, try to outsmart them. Rose roots are meant to be spread into the general soil medium of a rose bed. Accomplish this the best way you can. Unless potted roses are in full leaf, they can be handled almost like a bare root rose, carefully arranging roots and soil with minimum disturbance. The roots of MOST potted roses are cramped and twisted in the container, depriving the plant of a broad area in which to feed and a firm foundation for future growth. "Disappearing" pots really don't disappear in the soil either; years later the roots still tend to be in the same tight ball. Leafed-out plants in containers need to be CAREFULLY removed by cutting the pot and shifting the roots into a more natural planting condition. Pot bound roses in cans for a long time will respond well to cutting the outside root ball in several places with a sharp knife; new feeder roots will spread out into the planting medium.

FOR BARE ROOT ROSES, make a "mound" shape with planting soil to support the root system as well as the shank of the bush. Spread the roots out, not down, making a much more stable foundation for the rose plant. Don't forget to allow for some mulch later. Bud unions respond to sunshine and soil warmth, not burial. Another mound helps get roses started. Hill up soil, mulch or what-have-you around new canes to hold moisture until roots are established. A mound is a good insulation from heat or cold. After the plant is growing well, uncover slowly; water from the hose does less damage than poking around with a cultivator. The plant probably needs the water anyway. Water makes everything happen. If a rose bed is properly prepared, it is hard to use too much water. Make sure that bare root roses, (and canned plants, too), are deep soaked when planted and regularly thereafter. Don't sprinkle, SOAK!

ORGANICS are always a good choice for a first feeding. Manure, fish meal, sludge or other organics can be applied right after pruning. As the soil warms up, the food (and micro-organisms) are ready to go to work. Fast acting fertilizers seem to work better after soil has had an organic tonic. For a fast start, dissolve a tablespoon or so of 12-24-12 or 13-13-13 in a gallon of water and soak the root zone. However, you must remember that this feeding won't do much good until the soil has warmed up and the roots are working. Most of the effect is lost in cold, rainy weather. Use some judgement in the amounts of high nitrogen foods applied. Light, more frequent feedings do more good than heavy applications. Large plants can handle more than small roses. Whatever fertilizing formula you like, use it ONLY on established plants, not new bushes.

TREE ROSES need support, even in protected locations. Stakes and loose ties are used by many rosarians but are not as effective as splints, properly applied. To splint a tree rose, use a 3/8-inch reinforcing bar or 1/2-inch electrical conduit. Cut the splint long enough to drive 12-28 inches into the· soil. The top should be just under the bud unions (tree roses are double-budded.) Cushion the splint with a length of plastic or rubber hose· slipped over the entire length of the pipe. Fix the covered splint on the side of the tree standard that is the straightest. It is easiest to do when planting a new rose, but can also be done by carefully probing to miss large roots. Then wrap the standard and splint with friction tape or electrician's plastic tape in several places, exactly like splinting a broken arm.

LIKE ROSARIANS, most rose beds can use a spring tonic, an early-season treatment with gypsum (Calcium Carbonate). Gypsum can't bum, helps drainage in clay soils, curbs salt buildup and is a source of calcium. After pruning, broadcast gypsum at about 20 pounds per 100 square feet, work it in lightly with a spading fork. Push the fork into the soil and work back and forth. The fork trick is also good to get rock phosphate or superphosphate into the root zone of the rose. Phosphate moves very slowly in the soil and only under ideal conditions. All kinds of good things happen when air, water and food are present in the root zone. Don't disturb the roots, but open up the soil a bit for better action.

FROM THE RAMBLER'S GARDEN

DIARY... It's mid-February (at writing time) and the new rose beds are finally planted. The formula went something like this: 1/3 sharp sand (gritty), 1/3 light soil and 1/3 organic matter (about half horse manure and half ground pine bark). For every 100 square feet of planting area, there's about 25 pounds of gypsum, 15 pounds of superphosphate (0-20-0) and 25 pounds of roughcut alfalfa meal. Each bed was tilled four times, watered down after each mix. The result is a light, friable mix that can be scooped up by hand. It looks great; now we'll see if it grows roses! Come to Houston Rosetime '79 and see for yourself! The all-new rose garden will be on tour April 22. Come see us.

The Rambler hasn't discussed rose shows lately... those springtime rituals that turn usually normal gardeners into fanatic trophy-seekers. In the event that you have a touch of this seasonal madness, check your personal schedule on what rose shows are all about. Besides competition and trophies, it's a great time to win friends for roses and have fun, too.

PLAIN DIRT gardeners should be a rose show trophy goal. We need to attract these backyard folks and show them just how easy rose growing can be. Educational exhibits attract and interest more people than the trophy table. Few rose show visitors expect to grow roses like the show winners, but they do have an outside hope that they can grow some nice blooms for themselves and their friends.

EDUCATIONAL stations do not have to be works of art or major productions. It's most important to provide some friendly hosts who know a little something about roses. Just set up some simple, understandable exhibits that offer the basics without controversy and endless qualifications. Beginners learn the rules first, then the exceptions. Keep it short; make rose information easy to remember and follow. Rose folks around here still fondly remember the grower who annually volunteered to take on the educational display as his pet project. He never challenged anyone at the show table, but he knew roses. He grew some fine ones and wanted to share. This rose teacher made up display signs, (used rub-on letters), wrote some simple guidelines, gathered materials and carefully stored and updated the display between shows.

HIS ROSE CHARTS were easy to follow and typical soils and mulches were shown in pie tins where visitors could feel and sift and identify with their own situations. The displays had containers (empty) of commonly used fungicides and insecticides, sprayers and tools, lists of good varieties for the area... all made more attractive with some healthy, well groomed roses growing in containers. Set up away from the rose show, the display didn't compete for space or attention. However, the "teaching" area was often more crowded than the winner's circle. When rose shows attract, interest and encourage backyard growers, you are doing a good job.

NEED A STARTER? The Houston Rose Society offers a beginner's guide called "Suggestions for Growing Roses in Houston" to all show visitors (and in many other places, too). The handout costs about two cents, just about as cheap as you can get, but invaluable to the beginner. Any rose society can do the same thing. If you would like a sample to get your good intentions started, write to the Rambler and a copy will be on its way by return mail. But don't wait... rose show season is now!

PLANTS CAN'T TELL THE DIFFERENCE... a favorite quote from a discussion on organic vs. inorganic gardening, a reference to the desirability of chemical nutrients vs. nutrients from organic sources. It's a no-win discussion, particularly with someone just getting into gardening. Nutrients are absorbed in the same way, regardless of source. Nature just works a little harder to make food available organically. But keep in mind that organic matter plays four important roles in the soil: as a direct plant nutrient, as a nutrient for microorganisms, as a soil structure and as a water reservoir. Animal manures, green manures and crop residues make these good things in the soil possible. Try it, you and your roses will like it.

ROSE BED MULCH is another no-win subject. Many fine rose growers don't use mulch. Other equally good growers use tons of the stuff. In deciding for yourself, consider what a good mulch is supposed to do. A good mulch should let water and air through freely, decompose slowly, conserve moisture, add humus to the soil, aid in the fertilizing process, have a pleasing appearance and, in general, provide a good soil insulation to keep the feeder roots cool and moisture level in a constant range. That's a good sized order, but one that many materials can fill. If you need help in one of these areas, try a mulch program for a while. Usually, a combination of materials is more effective than just one. For example, pine needles, shredded pine bark and partially composted leaves work better than anyone ingredient used alone. A shredder that chops up all kinds of organic matter is the best of all. Oak leaves and some kind of coarse bark or woody material are also good. If it's loose, friable and easy to handle, it's got to be good. Old rosarians on the hot Gulf Coast say that a good mulch is worth its weight in gold... and in roses.

FROM THE RAMBLER'S GARDEN DIARY... Well, the roses are in, spray programs started, watering routines set up... now all they have to do is grow. It's a great temptation to feed "just a little" to hurry the process, but so far I have resisted the temptation. The results will be in on April 22. I'll tell you all about it in June.

JUN.
1979

THOUGHT FOR THE MONTH: Rose experience is a wonderful thing.
It lets you recognize a mistake when you make it again.

Overheard at a rose society meeting the other day was the remark that "Rose people are really great about sharing experiences, but they don't talk enough about ordinary things in the yard… guess they assume we already know." Most of us have to plead guilty to this charge; but, in our own defense, we have probably just forgotten some lessons learned the hard way. Have you heard the story about the rose guy who…

SNAPPED OFF the new basal breaks thinking they were sucker growths? Or the one who pruned with a sharp shovel so more growth would go to the tops? None of YOU have ever done such a thing, but, maybe our mistakes were just as bad; like doubling the strength of a spray mix to "clean up those bugs;" or adding an extra handful of fertilizer to hurry the plants along. If patience is a virtue, most rosarians aren't very virtuous.

PASS ALONG some positive things from time to time. A rose friend shares an idea to add red food coloring to Elmer's Glue (used as a cane sealer) to keep track where he has been. Nearly everyone has some Elmer's on the shelf; it's a thought worth trying. Another is to break up the soil ball a bit when transplanting potted roses. If they have been in pots any time at all, the roots are almost certainly pot-bound. Loosen up the root mass and soil just a little, maybe even slice the outer mass with a sharp knife, in much the way an azalea root ball is encouraged to develop new roots and expand into new soil.

WHAT'S A ROSETTE? It's easy to identify this kind of blind growth once you have seen it, but hard to describe to a newcomer. Show a beginner by snapping off a rosette and point out that no terminal bud has developed. Leaf production is great but productive new canes produce blooms. Have you ever pointed out the immature bud at the axil of a five-leaflet? I know it took me a long time to figure out why people talked about "cut back the stem to five leaves." Pass along WHY something is good for roses.

ROSE PURISTS may object to having other plants mixed with roses, but many flowering as well as ground cover materials go well with roses. Unless the setting is just right, formal beds of roses can be unattractive with thorny canes (sans leaves) sticking up out of the soil One way to create a mass

of green is to plant roses closer together so that they will fill in. The visitor's eye then sees pleasant shapes of green with loads of blooms on top. Or soften the picture with portulaca a border; petunias also do well; dwarf marigolds are okay too… might even keep a few insects away. Alyssum adds even more fragrance to a rose garden; ageratum is attractive too. If you do add some annuals to the rose bed, don't forget to spray these plants as many are hosts for a variety of pests. There's an absolutely TRUE story of the rose grower who was so proud of his outstanding crop of violets planted around his rose beds, but by mid-season the roses were all defoliated by spider mites in spite of every spray material he could find. Checking the violets, the undersides of the leaves were alive with mites, supplying a new batch every time the old ones died. When the violets left, so did the mites.

BREAK AWAY from the same types of roses for a change. There are some new singles coming on the market that are beautiful Dairy Maid is something of a golden Dainty Bess. Along a similar line, Sweet Vivien is a gorgeous rose with good form, not many petals, but in bloom most of the time. Patio Patty is a good newcomer, too. It's classed as a floribunda, but grows and blooms like a polyantha; great for a border or pot and not a bit particular about how it is handled. Why not more miniatures in general plantings? They are good along borders, banks, steps and in rock gardens. Just select _a type of the color and shape needed. Most minis get along well with other plant materials as they aren't as fussy about feeding (unless grossly overfed). Another plus is that miniatures can be planted almost anytime, including midsummer, with some reasonable care and protection.

FROM THE RAMBLER'S GARDEN DIARY… How did the garden tour in April turn out? As this is written (April 10) the garden has ten more days to come into bloom and it appears promising. The minis will be out first with floribundas not far behind. Except for some heavy-petaled hybrid teas, we'll have lots of roses. Only wish that the mass plantings of floribundas had been planted closer together. Even though they will spread out, better and closer placement would have created a more pleasing effect. A side note, roses in pots for the patio came into bloom ten days ahead of those in beds; same varieties, same shipment. Warm soil just gets roots off to a faster start. Anyway, it's a great feeling to have springtime and roses in bloom. Hope the fever hits you, too.

When offering suggestions, keep them soft and sweet.

You never know from day to day, which words you'll have to eat.

If you're hungry for suggestions, here are some to chew on... sometimes called the "Old Time Religion" for growing roses. You have been growing roses a long time if you can remember when...

A FEEDING SCHEDULE was no more than a shovelful or two of manure applied when it wasn't too hot, (too hot in the pile and too hot to shovel.) It did wonders for roses, not only fed the plants but cooled the soil, encouraged the good bugs and never seemed to throw nature out of balance. And remember when water systems meant a little ditching plus a hose in a can or with a rag tied over the end? We were doing the right thing without knowing it: deep watering, slow soaking, happy plants. Or sometimes the lawn sprinkler was set in the rose bed, turned on and forgotten for a half-hour or so. The result: fresh leaves and roses, well watered beds.

ROSES SMELLED BETTER in the old days, probably because they weren't covered with insecticides. A few roses and leaves were lost to bugs, but plants weren't defoliated with spray burn. Obviously there's a happy medium in all this; careful spraying for specific problems will help bring fragrance back to the garden. This may seem like heresy to the insecticide addicts, but roses get along quite well with an insecticide application or two per season. Mist the tops with *Orthene* or *Cygon* as needed for thrips, but otherwise let nature do her job.

WINTER PROTECTION was simple then, too. Leaves and pine needles and leftover straw piled in the rose bed did a good job, working all winter to moderate temperature and moisture. By spring, a good part of the protection had broken down into good humus that fed and conditioned. Some of the excess went to the compost pile to build summer conditioner. Every garden had a compost or manure pile (or a combination) that was a steady source of good things for the garden. Better ,gardeners had a barrel for cow tea, patiently brewed and applied to plants that needed a boost. So far, no miracle in a package has been able to come up to the performance of cow tea.

HORSE MANURE was popular, too. It was great for a warming layer under beds of cuttings, (remember the old cold frame?) About five inches of manure under a couple inches of river sand would steam up glass frames with humidity as favorite roses, geraniums and begonias took root; kept the frames safe and warm, (covered with gunny sacks,) during the coldest spring. Rhubarb came right on in the spring by setting an apple crate over the clump, adding a shovel or two of horse manure and covering the top with a piece of glass; it was certain to produce the earliest, freshest and sweetest rhubarb around.

ORIGINAL, GENUINE MANURE is hard to come by these days, but all is not lost. For just a touch of the good old days, try some artificial manure. It has enjoyed heady success around the country and is far better than anything that comes in a sack... all the benefits without the cow or pitching hay.

The Fragrant Formula

3 ample yards of leaves or rough compost mix

100 pounds of rice hulls (or something course)

100 pounds of cottonseed meal

100 pounds of rough cut alfalfa meal

50 pounds of bone meal

50 pounds of fish meal

Use any area okay for composting. Pile the leaves about two feet deep and add dry ingredients, turn with a fork. Moisten LIGHTLY: turn with a fork twice a week for three weeks. Do NOT get too wet. Cottonseed meal turns into a slime when wet, (with an awful dead smell, too.) The mix is done when it looks like real manure. Use about two shovelfuls per rosebush anytime after soil warms up; throw on another shovel if rose production lags. An application feeds for about three months. You may want to add some other seasoning, (such as copper or rock phosphate), as needed; but the Fragrant Formula is a great organic mix and not too expensive. It won't change the pH of the soil appreciably and releases gradually and naturally. It's good for young or old plants, something like Grandmother's tonic.

FROM THE RAMBLER'S GARDEN DIARY... How did the April garden tour for Houston

Rosetime '79 turn out? Both roses and rosarians survived eight inches of rain just two days before the tour and ducked for shelter from thunder-showers on the tour/breakfast morning. Heavy mulch, (four to five inches of horse manure and wood chips), on the beds stayed in place, drained well and presented a natural, attractive look. For a totally new garden, that's quite an accomplishment. The roses responded with good bloom, lots of new leaves and low breaks to spare. Nature appeared to be working. Anyway, we had a great time feeding some 250 rosarians; greeting and showing the garden to another 250 rose folks… convinced more than ever that rose people are the greatest in the world.

CUTTING SOME SPENT BLOOMS the other day, (sounds better than dead-heading), it occurred to me that repetition can be a good thing in giving advice as well as in the rose garden. Weekly grooming helps a rosarian keep up with what's going on by directing attention to individual bushes and canes; a review of the basics from time to time rechecks rose habits. You may want to recheck some of these spent blooms (or new breaks, as the case may be) in your garden.

LEAF COVERAGE is the name of the game in fungicide application and control. A once-over-lightly will not do the job. While regularity of a fungicide program is essential, it won't do a bit of good unless the tops and undersides of the leaves are thoroughly wetted. Begin spraying from underneath, fall-out will usually take care of the tops. Leaves should be near-dripping on completion... and knock off any excess with a rap of the spray wand on the canes.·

YELLOW LEAVES are really not so bad. They often appear in the center of the bush after about the second bloom-out, indicating a very natural replacement process. These leaves have gone through a maturity cycle and will yellow and drop off. This should happen only to the leaves which first appeared on the bush in the spring. If more yellow replaces green, check for poor drainage, spider mites or spray burn. A rose leaf that is naturally ageing will GRADUALLY turn yellow and drop off. Other causes are more dramatic.

PLAIN WATER will scald rose leaves when temperatures are in the 90's. Add some spray materials, a bit of spreader-sticker and the result can be leaves burned to a crisp. How many roses have you seen on bushes without leaves? If this is your problem, try a "Cool Rosarian Spray Routine". Thoroughly soak beds with water in the morning or afternoon to make sure ample moisture reaches the leaves. About sundown, wash down the bushes with lots of water from the hose. Wash first, then spray. Result: No burn, better protection. Spray material covers clean leaves better. If you are a morning person or really worried about black spot, soak beds in the evening (without wetting leaves), get up early... wash bushes, spray... all before breakfast and hot sunshine.

ROSE ADVICE is often conflicting; an ex-ample is frequency of fungicide spraying during hot weather. Standard advice is to use *Benlate* on a weekly basis, adding *Maneb* if some black spot is evident. But old-timers know that a CLEAN garden without infection can go for two or three weeks without spraying when the weather is hot and dry. But they ALSO know that summer thundershowers will bring black spot on again and a need for more frequent spraying.

ALKALINE WATER can play tricks in the sprayer and is thought to reduce the effectiveness of *Benlate* and other fungicides. If your water is highly alkaline, you may want to try two teaspoons of plain white vinegar per gallon of water in the spray mix. Add vinegar to water BEFORE mixing in *Benlate*. The mist seems to wet leaves better without adding a spreader-sticker.

TAKE IT EASY WITH INSECTICIDES is being echoed in rose bulletins all over the country. Here's a quote from one, "Last year I used the least insecticides ever and had the least insects." The common theme is "use insecticides sparingly for specific problems." There's no point at all in killing everything in the garden that crawls, jumps, flies or drifts in. Once that routine is started, you're an insecticide junkie for the rest of the season. Nature will work with you if you'll let her. Mist the bud and bloom areas lightly with *Orthene* or *Cygon* if thrips get too bad, but DON'T drench the leaves. Let the good bugs and nature take care' of the bush and leaves while you take care of the blooms. It's a fair exchange.

ROSES AND PEOPLE thrive on a steady diet... a well balanced availability all the time. Too much rose food is about like too much people food during the holidays; both will suffer from the consequences. Good availability levels and lots of water will do the trick with roses. A light feeding every four to six weeks does considerably more good than an overdose now and then. And the main ingredient in any feeding program is water. Plants take up nutrients in the solution, not dry feed. Every thorough watering is a feeding as well. If the rose beds are well drained, it's almost impossible to over water.

FROM THE RAMBLER'S GARDEN DIARY... The new bushes are doing great; and it would take more than an expert rosarian to pick out the 1 1/2 grade roses from the No. 1's. All of them have from four to five canes, lots of foliage and are coming into a third cycle of bloom (June 10). It's hard to pinpoint anyone factor that produced this growth, but two new practices for the Rambler are a very light, sandy soil mix and addition of alfalfa meal to the beds before planting. That's always a problem when things are going right, you don't know what caused it. Moral: If you are getting good roses with what you are doing, don't change.

LIGHT, SANDY SOIL helps roots spread out. While trenching through a new bed for a drain line about two weeks ago, some fine feeder roots were exposed that extended from six to eight inches long in all directions from the mature roots. Even though some roots were cut in the trenching operation, the bushes involved didn't slow down; evidently there were more than enough roots to support vigorous growth.

CHANGE ANYTHING? In a two-row planting of a rose bed five feet Wide, it appears that planting on closer centers would be more attractive. Presently spaced on 30-inch centers and staggered, the bushes' would be better on 24-inch centers allowing growth to the outside and inside of the bed. In a two-row system it is still easy to reach in to spray and groom. Otherwise, the layout looks great.

HOW ABOUT SHARING? The Rambler could use some Thoughts for the Month. If you have a good one you're willing to share, send it along. Please give credit if you know the source.

SEPT. 1979

THOUGHT FOR THE MONTH: Even the poorest rosarian isn't completely worthless. He can always serve as a bad example.

Harvest month for rosarians has finally arrived… and your buckets of roses should be overflowing. Except for that first spring bloom, fall roses should be the best of all. If your buckets are less than full, make a check list of rose happenings during the past season and see if you can't come up with plans and practices that will payoff next year. Right NOW you should be planning (and doing some digging) of new rose beds for the future. Good roses aren't grown by accident; rose bed preparation is the first (and probably the most important) step in rose production.

LEAVES AND OTHER COMPOSTING materials will be plentiful for most growers within the next month or so. It's a rich harvest and should be made available for roses with some sort of compost pile even if all the leafy production can't be used. Experience the benefits of compost just once and you'll find space for more leaves next year. If no space at all is available for a compost pile or rick, use a vegetable garden area or maybe the spot where the new rose garden is to be.

COMPOSTING IN PLACE is easy. Just turn and dig the soil in the bed area making a windrow of soil. Pile leaves, clippings, *etc.* in the depressed trench and add some excess soil on top as a dressing. Add a good source of nitrogen like manure of cottonseed meal to the leaves to make the whole process work faster. Keep moist and turn lightly every two weeks. Add some more leaves as the pile goes down. Before hard freeze time, the composting material should be broken down enough to till and mix in place or add to other bed areas. Composting season can be stretched a bit by covering a trench or pile with black plastic to hold heat. It works even in freezing weather.

ROSE BEDS GET TIRED, too, near the end of a long season. There's a good chance that all they need is a little light cultivation from time to time to help move water and air in the soil. Mulches and some soils tend to pack from rainfall and sunshine. Breaking up the crust lets water and air through again and mechanically mixes some of the humus product of the mulch with the top soil. A four-tine cultivator scratching an inch deep is about right. The sharp, pitchfork-type works best. If mulch has been properly applied, this loosening should not damage feeder roots.

TIGHT SOILS open up with a spading fork, too. Punch some small holes around the drip line of the bush with a fork, the four-prong kind that's about six inches long. Spade in all the way and work back and forth a few times. Fertilizers, water and air can get into the root zone faster; its particularly good for slow-moving rock phosphate or superphosphate to get to where the work is being done. Give each bush three or four good jabs; it's a good practice most anytime.

MIRACLE CURES are seldom miracles. A new crop of "stabilized micro-organisms" hit the market in our area again this season promising to "make dead soils alive again" and put billions of nature's microscopic workers on the side of the gardener. Some serious trials of two of these "miracles" produced no dramatic results. Roses in check beds did just as well as those treated according to directions. However, in all fairness to the formulators, the additives were used in beds already in excellent condition with good balance of humus, air, soil and water. Rose beds with plenty of humus and manure produced the best roses more consistently than tighter soils or soils low in organic matter.

CALCINED CLAY granules make a great soil conditioner in addition to or in place of some organic material. Each granule is like a tiny sponge with air spaces and tremendous water holding capability. It's sold around here as *Terra-Green*, a TM of the Oil-Dri Corporation. A soil mix with one quarter Terra-Green will grow almost anything. Many nursery people use it for rooting cuttings with NO other additives. Available in 50 pound bags, it's worth looking for at greenhouse supply firms.

COARSE *PERLITE* is a great product, too. It's a good conditioner for rose beds and a useful additive for many light potting mixes. Miniature rose potting mixes commonly have *Perlite* as a major component. Here's another use: a wet soggy stretch of lawn that refuses to drain or dry out will respond to an "injection" of *Perlite*. Use a spading fork and aerate the wet area, spading as deep as the prongs will go; rock the fork back and forth. Do a small area; then broadcast Perlite and rake to fill up the holes. The result: better drainage, more air, more lawn. A wet, rotting lawn can be restored in three weeks or less.

FROM THE RAMBLER'S GARDEN DI-ARY... Planting new roses in mid-July sounds next to impossible but not with miniatures. Some twenty miniatures in four-inch pots were set out in full sun without a yellow leaf or sign of stress. Bloom cycle continued without interruption. The four-inch pot method is a good way to reduce shock for newly-rooted minis or plants in very small pots. They seem to grow faster and mature better in four-inch pots compared to direct bed planting. Four to six weeks in the larger pot under controlled conditions is all that it takes. Light feeding, regular watering, vigorous plants. Fifteen large plants of Rise 'n Shine make a beautiful edge planting for a bed of Sunsprite.

Learned a lesson (again) the hard way that rose beds need to be watered thoroughly BEFORE feeding as well as after feeding. Thinking that the soil looked moist enough, about two ounces of 15-5-10 broadcast per plant and then watered in resulted in yellow and burned lower leaves in four days. Similar applications to soaked beds brought on only new growth. As the Thought for the Month once said, "Experience is the name we give to our mistakes."

Webster defines Indian Summer as "a happy and flourishing period occurring toward the end of something." Since this pleasant period has' arrived for most of us, I hope that you have noticed that the roses are happier this time of year, putting out a harvest that's bigger, better and more colorful. But, it is not an end, just a pleasant time for rose planning... maybe you'll include some of these ideas in your plans...

COMPOSTING always comes up this time of year as a solution for the leaves all over the yard. Too many otherwise sharp rose growers pass up this harvest, thinking that they don't have the equipment or the space. The equipment is already in the garage (rotary lawn mower) and the now-cleared garden patch is the place to let nature do its job.

Rake up tree leaves in a sort of wind-row on an open space of lawn. The row can be three or four feet wide and several inches deep. Dampen the leaves with a spray from the hose, (keeps them from blowing all over). Start up the rotary lawn mower, leave off the catcher bag and run the mower in a "U" pattern around the row of leaves. Reverse the direction and repeat the process until shredding is complete. The result will be two neat rows of well-chopped organic material ready for composting in the garden area. If you're anxious for a very fast job, add some cheap source of nitrogen to the pile, dampen slightly and cover with plastic to conserve heat. Turn the pile now and then for a mix that's better than anything you can buy.

"SATELLITE" ROSE GARDENS are catching on and you should catch one for yourself... a rose planting of any description that doesn't actually belong to you. You'll be surprised how rewarding an off-premises garden can be, making new friends for roses, more room for your own rose efforts and a chance to try some new gardening ideas. There's plenty of unclaimed territory just right for roses... a parkway or parking strip, a church or library, a home for senior folks, maybe a neighbor who can't take care of a large yard anymore. With a little help and your experience, surprising things can happen. Sometimes roses do better when we don't worry over them so much; the average visitor to a planting doesn't know a split center from a sepal. But it's obvious that the planting is a big improvement over bare lawn and sick shrubbery. Once the rose beds are built, a half hour per week will do the trick, and I'm speaking from experience.

COLD CLIMATE rosarians have known for a long time that late season feeding means winterkill and dieback. Gradual dormancy is the key to survival, setting the rose clock for cold weather ahead. The same rule applies to growers in more moderate climates as well. A cold snap in December damages green canes, weakens the plant and starts a chain reaction of dieback the following spring. Stop feeding at least eight weeks before cool weather arrives. As the season winds down, leave spent blooms on the bush and gradually reduce the amount of water. The result will be a plant more able to take winter weather... naturally.

WINTER PROTECTION should be a natural thing, too. The Rambler has commented on this from time to time, even though there's no problem or practice here on the Gulf Coast. Growing roses in Colorado, (long before knowing how it was supposed to be done), a soil and compost mound over the bud union and lower canes, plus lots of leaves, kept roses in good shape from minus 20 degrees to plus 50's with cold, dry winds and strong sunshine.

Notes and comments from some really cold places seem to support this natural practice. A typical reader's note says, "I don't have the time or energy to build boxes or bury, so I have always thrown in some dirt and piled on leaves as high as I could go. Even got some leaves from the neighbors. Maybe it's against the rules but my roses always do all right." Maybe nature's rules are the best after all. Except under the most extreme conditions, natural insulation can do the job.

FROM THE RAMBLER'S GARDEN DIARY... Light, regular feedings plus plenty of water have paid off in lots of leaves and blooms this summer, contrary to the "easing off" practice common in our hot climate. While the blooms have not been spectacular, production has been steady and growth vigorous. Roses really don't need a rest period in the summer, just regular care. Some light, green foliage cropped up in late July that greened right up again with *Epsom Salts*. Will use again at about one ounce per plant with the last light feeding on September 1. Heavy rains and use of alkaline city water seem to deplete the availability of magnesium so essential for green leaves and growth.

EARLY SEASON MULCH, all five inches of it, has virtually disappeared from the rose beds, leaving only a loose humus trace. The mulch mix of horse manure and stable shavings did a good job this season./Maybe some material a bit more coarse will extend the life of/future applications. Mixtures of materials ordinarily make the best mulch; coarse and fine materials will break down at different rates.

BUILT UP BEDS do make a difference. In new plantings this year, identical roses planted at the same time performed much better in beds built up 12 inches versus those built up about six inches. The planting mixture was identical, tilling and loosening the sub-soil was the same; only the bed depth varied. Roses in the higher beds are one third to one half larger and more vigorous than those in shallow plantings. Although not very scientific, the conclusion is that higher beds for better aeration and drainage grows better roses, at least on the Gulf Coast. Even less scientific, it worked about the same for me in Colorado, too. Anyway, do your own thing wherever you are and enjoy roses all you can.

Check off November as a great rose month... the show winners are framing their certificates while the contenders are ordering sure winners for next season. Queens-of-the-Show are always more beautiful as recalled in November; color faults and imperfections in form are easily forgotten. Rose garden plans are visualized in full color without lifting a shovel. It's called looking at the world through rose colored glasses. Meantime, rest your eyes on some of these rose ideas...

LATE FALL is a good time to get materials together for new rose beds next year. Last summer's vegetable garden is an ideal spot to stockpile soil, sand, mulch and manure. Mix the pile from time to time as weather permits. Nature helps in the process with rain, snow, freezes and thaws. By springtime, the mix is ready for use anywhere in the yard.

MEANTIME, get some rose bed construction underway before really bad weather hits. Whether you are a built-up or garden-level rose grower, good edging materials help take the work out of yard work. I hope that by this time the Rambler has convinced you to use built-up beds for better drainage and aeration. Growers, in even the coldest areas, are surprising themselves with better growth and no more winter damage than with lawn-level plantings. How about just one raised bed this fall for comparison?

LANDSCAPE TIMBERS make attractive rose beds in many applications. Treated with decay retarding salts (Wolmanized), timbers last indefinitely, are easy to handle and fairly inexpensive.

Anything you used to do as a kid with Lincoln Logs, you can do with landscape timbers. A tamped sand base works fine in most cases; run a concrete or block footing if the level or position is a critical factor. To stabilize timbers, drill through the bottom timber and drive a short length of reinforcing rod into the ground. Most lumberyards have corner and joint plates to tie the sides and ends together. Add a second row of timbers by drilling and nailing with gutter nails. The result is a bed that looks good, drains well and keeps its shape. Penta-treated materials have also been tried, but gradual vaporizations of the petroleum-based preservative can severely burn rose leaves.

Wolmanized material appears to be safe for even the most sensitive bedding plants.

BRICKS stabilized in concrete are easy to use even without bricklaying skills. A "soldier course" of bricks (bricks on end) can be masked into a soft footing of concrete, lining up on a string. Instead of lining up bricks face to face, space each brick with a wood block about an inch thick. Insert a brick in the concrete mix (fairly stiff), line up the edge to the guide string. Fit the wood spacer block to the brick and insert another brick next to it. When lined up, slip the spacer out and keep on going. The spaced bricks look good and drain well. In areas of deep frost or shifting soils, stabilize the concrete footing by adding overlapping lengths of reinforcing bar. Build a few feet of edging at a time using sack-mix concrete. It may not be the cheapest, but it's convenient.

CONCRETE BLOCKS may be the best answer in some areas. They can be set in sand without mortar, although it is best to stabilize the corners in concrete. The raw look of concrete can be softened with a mixture of shingle stain and any cheap petroleum solvent (half and half). The color mix penetrates the blocks leaving behind a soft color that weathers well. In fact, the older it gets, the better it looks.

ON YOUR OWN DEPARTMENT: Here's a solution to the Japanese Beetle problem offered by a very successful exhibitor. In addition to the usual picking off, beetle traps and soil treatment with *Diazinon* granules, this exhibitor places Styrofoam cups over buds with exhibition potential about a week to 10 days before they would ordinarily open. He reports that the beetles will not venture inside the cup to work on the bud; it seems to keep thrips away, too. To keep the cup from blowing away, a light wire secures the cup to a leaflet on the lower parts of the stem. He claims the bud develops normally, has good color and does not bruise. Take the cup off about a half day before cutting for exhibition. For folks with lots of beetles, it may be worth a try.

FROM THE RAMBLER'S GARDEN DIARY... It's amazing the amount of bloom that can come from a floribunda planting in just one season. After planting on March 1, (1-1/2 grade plants), the first good bloom flush began on April

15 and there has been good color ever since. The plants are still fully leafed to the bud union and present a mass of foliage, blooms and developing buds. It's hard to tell where one bush stops and another begins. The miniature plantings are not far behind. Overall, the miniature bed looks like a patchwork quilt of color. If you aren't planning a mass of these free-blooming types for next year, you are missing a real rose experience. Exhibition types are great, but can't compete in the mass color class.

RAINFALL in Houston this year suited water lilies more than roses. But high, well drained beds handled the excess water very well; no yellow leaves, no slowing of growth, no lack of bloom. Rose plantings in the area without good drainage struggled or died. Which tells us again that roses do only as well as their roots. Good, functional root systems mean good roses.

"I've got a problem with my roses. What would you suggest I do about it?" The Rambler's mail has had the same question in a hundred different forms, and the conclusion is usually about the same, too. "What have you been doing in your garden?" So that we'll have a sort of starting spot for next year, here's an outline of what the Rambler has been doing and with pretty good results. You're welcome to try any or all...

FUNGUS DISEASES. *Benlate* and *Manzate* seem to do the best job here. Use one tablespoon each of *Benlate* and *Manzate* per two gallons of water. Start spraying immediately after pruning and continue throughout the season on a seven to ten day schedule. Spray until foliage is dripping; use a spreadersticker like *AG 98*, (a few drops per gallon), for better coverage. For very alkaline water, add about a half tablespoon of vinegar per gallon of water. In early spring or cool weather, *Phaltan-Benlate* combination works better. During hot, dry spells, *Benlate* alone will keep gardens free of black spot. *Funginex, Ortho's* new three-way fungicide (black spot, powdery mildew and rust) may be the answer for the future. Trials with *Triphorine*, (the active ingredient in *Funginex*), have been very encouraging. *Funginex* will definitely be in Rambler's program next season.

POWDERY MILDEW is a tougher problem than black spot. A regular program with *Benlate-Phaltan* combination is usually effective on the Gulf Coast. When conditions are really severe, treat with *Acti-Dione PM*, spraying only the infected and new foliage. It is usually back under control in about a week. *ActiDione PM* is sometimes hard to get, so *Funginex* may be the answer in this area, too.

SPRAY EQUIPMENT The Rambler used a hose-on sprayer for years and years with good results on several hundred roses. But the high cost of chemicals, environmental considerations and a tired back from pulling the hose around finally brought a switch to a Hudson Suburban powered with a gasoline engine. It's a great piece of equipment and I don't know why I didn't switch sooner. I had also used a centrifugal pump previously, but the Hudson seems easier to handle. The Atomist is also a good sprayer, PROVIDED that the leaves get good coverage and wetting.

This qualification is true of ANY sprayer. Wetting is essential for control. Before buying a sprayer, visit some other gardens while spraying is going on, then you'll know if it fits your situation.

THRIPS Use *Orthene* or *Cygon*; *Orthene* seems to have a longer residual, *Cygon* may leave less discoloration. During heavy blooming periods, spray only the bud and bloom areas, lightly misting from the top. Don't saturate the plant. Just before a show, applications about twice a week will control the worst infestation. Use these products alone: Don't mix with fungicide for all-over spraying. Go after the specific problem only. Both insecticides work equally well for aphids. Two or three general insecticide sprayings per season take good care of the Rambler's roses.

CORN EAR WORMS These tiny destroyers are tough to handle. The Rambler has tried *Orthene*, 10% *Sevin* dust, *Thurcide* and *Cygon*... and none of them gave good control. The best approach seems to be control of the moth that lays the eggs on the developing buds. *Diazinon* granules broadcast in the general rose bed area appear to do some good. Those of us who live in the South treat all of the lawn and yard areas with Diazinon for chinch bugs anyway. Incidentally, the same broadcast treatment shows some promise in controlling midge.

The Rambler likes the black-light, bug-zapper that attracts and then electrocutes the moths... and other insects, too. There are many variations of these grid devices and all severely reduce the insect population. They are usually on sale at the end of the season. You might want to drop a hint to Santa Claus that a bug-zapper would just fit in your stocking.

FEEDING Start out the season with an ample helping of manure or some sort of organic mix and then begin regular, light feeding about every six weeks with a balanced, readily soluble fertilizer with trace elements. *Osmocote* is a great product, too. If the once-a-season method fits your schedule, just supplement with trace elements from time to time. A steady, balanced diet readily available makes roses happy. And plenty of water makes the whole process work. Nothing happens to nutrients in the ground until they go into solution and become available to the roots. As Dr. Eldon Lyle so often says, "Every time you water it's like an extra feeding."

ROSE BEDS. The Rambler likes built-up beds for drainage and aeration. Everything seems to work better. Under some conditions, elevation or drainage may have to be modified. The best all-around bed mix has a good, light balance: 1/3 soil, 1/3 sand and 1/3 manure, compost or organic matter. Supplement as needed, but keep this basic formula in mind. If in doubt, add a bit more organic matter. It feeds the whole process.

WHAT ROSES TO PLANT? That's a personal thing. Some like to show, others like to cut for the house, others like a landscape planting. Do your own thing with roses. The Rambler likes them all. And so will you if you give them a chance. Have a very rosey 1980!

JAN. 1980

THOUGHT FOR THE MONTH:
It's easy to spot a smart rosarian. His views are the same as yours.

The January routine for columnists is to review and reflect on the year just ended, arriving at some carefully qualified, conclusions (mostly hindsight) for the benefit of those who haven't caught up on the August magazine yet. To see just1 how good some of these conclusions have been, the RAMBLER checked out advice that appeared in these New Year columns in the early 1970s. It turns out that we are still talking about and doing the same things.

The RAMBLER suggested "rose lists" of popular and productive roses in 1971. Something less than a formal Proof of the Pudding for beginners and ordinary gardeners. Just a simple list of popular and easy-to-grow hybrid teas, garden, floribunda and miniature roses along with their color descriptions. Put out the lists through local nurseries handling roses. You'll be doing them a favor and helping beginners, too. The local society gets some mileage out of the project by identifying the source and advising the when, where and why of rose society meetings.

I TO REALLY MAKE FRIENDS FOR ROSES, write up a two page brief on rose care for the local area. Identify the rose society and broadcast them wherever gardeners congregate. Keep the suggestion brief and simple. Let them get the refinements of rose growing by coming to the meetings. It's still a cheap and reliable way to attract new rose growers and will payoff in roses and friends all season.

THOUGHTFUL PROGRAM PLANNING was a subject in 'f' 1972. Make sure that new and old members take part in I educational programs before the serious rose season begins. It's amazing how many rose growers can't identify the shank, the bud union or find a bud-eye on a year-old cane. They have heard the terms over and over again, but haven't connected the words with the real thing.

TRY A PROGRAM on planting in January or February. Build a simulated rose bed on a formica-top table. Make a three-sided box of 1x 8 redwood to resemble a built-up rose bed and fill with a large bag of bark mulch material. Bring several well-trimmed bushes to the meeting and actually plant in the box. Show how a canned bush ought to be planted by carefully cutting the sides of the container and gently spreading the roots in much the same way as a bare root plant. There's nothing much better than a practical demonstration.

OUT IN FRONT was the advice of the same column. Plan a rose bed for the front yard this year. Use just one variety for a massed color effect or at least roses with the same growth and bloom habit. Floribundas are ideal for plantings of this type. We talk about beautification and then keep the beauty to ourselves. If you want to sell roses, show the product. Besides, sharing is half the fun of having a rose garden. A real attention getter is a bed or border of miniature roses to add color to a front planting. Most casual visitors won't even know what they are. The RAMBLER noted that a round bed with twelve Chipper miniatures outbloomed and outperformed every annual ever tried in the same location. Think small and colorful... you won't be disappointed.

"YOUR BEST SCORE FOR '74" was to plan a spray schedule while snow was still on the ground. Start the spray routine IMMEDIATELY after pruning, drenching the canes and bud union thoroughly. Use a broad spectrum insecticide (*Diazinon* is a good one) combined with your favorite fungicide, (or combination of fungicides like *Benlate*, *Phaltan* or *Manzate*). Use at full strength and add a spreader sticker to encourage penetration into the cracks and crevices of the bud union and older canes.

THE OBJECT IS to control over-wintering spores BEFORE temperature and humidity are right for the growth of these organisms. Do NOT wait for new leaves to appear. Don't forget to spray climbing and shrub roses at the same time. An infected host plant can spread spores like wildfire when conditions are right. Prune and spray the same day. Spray again in two weeks with the same combination. Then follow a regular fungicide protection program without the insecticide for a clean garden all season.

MORE MANURE IN THE SOIL does not always produce more roses. A 1974 example of what not to do related how a mix of one-half finely ground manure, one-half pine bark mulch, also finely ground" and very little soil looked good but gave poor results. The excessive amounts of organic material tended to pack and lacked air space. The high organic problem was easily corrected by adding sharp sand and garden soil resulting in a final mix of about one-third manure, one-third compost and one-third sand and soil. At the end of the first season, roses dug from this bed had masses of feeder roots on multiflora understock with no evidence of gall. The bushes transplanted very successfully. Conclusion: If a little is good, more isn't necessarily better.

HOW ABOUT A ROSE TOUR in very early spring? If rose pruning demonstrations are useful, how about some demonstrations on planting and layout and early season care? It seems to the RAMBLER that this is the place we can help novice rosarians rather than offering free and non-participating advice on problems later in the year. It's very hard to duplicate yard conditions for a demonstration during a rose society meeting. Some advance planning can help many beginners.

TREE ROSES AND MINIS? A perfect combination. Each accents the other. Use the minis as a frame, a backdrop, a filler. They don't compete for attention, they share it. In just one season, you'll wonder why you hadn't thought of it much sooner.

SOUND ADVICE is good ANY year: Make rose growing easy and fun and we won't be able to handle all the memberships.

If you want to look at the world through rose-colored' glasses in 1980, it is time to go to work. For those of us in the milder climates, pruning and planting will soon be underway. The cold-country people have to see roses in the snow just a little longer.

But the point is roses and nature do things on schedule... and rosarians would be wise to stay in step. Whether planting or planning, let nature lend a hand.

COLD, WET WEATHER is considered a blessing in this part of the country. We try to get new roses into the ground just before or even during a rainy spell so the bushes will become established with lots of water. Until feeder roots start, bushes I have to rely on moisture stored in the roots and canes.

Warm, dry weather can cause real stress. Canes dry out before roots are ready to go to work. It is the reason why canes of new plants should be hilled up with soil to hold moisture and maintain a constant, moderate temperature. Around here, a muddy rosarian is probably a smart one... letting nature do part of the work.

ROSES START BETTER when planted the right way. Again, the key is water. Thorough, deep soaking for all steps in the planting process. The Rambler likes to soak bare root bushes in water overnight before planting -there is no chance for them to dry out. This may not be really necessary, but it cannot hurt a thing. When repruning for planting, ALWAYS drop the trimmed plants into a garbage can of water and keep them there until actual planting. As a last step, fish the bush out of the water and put it directly into the hole. Plan first, then plant. Do not scatter the bushes out in the bed waiting for you to get to them. Move from water to soil and everything seems to work better.

THE RAMBLER is a "cone type" planter, supporting the root system of a bare root bush with a cone of well prepared soil. Cover the roots lightly and begin to run water slowly into the hole. Add some more soil. Water will begin to fill in the voids.

While one bush in soaking, plant the next one. Then come back with more soil, more water, etc. There is no need to tamp. Let the water do the work. The result will be a rose supported naturally.

ROOT PRUNING? Probably. The Rambler lightly trims the ends of most of the roots and cuts out broken roots. Root tips are the most prone to dry out. Trimming exposes healthy tissue for new root hairs to develop. In my experience, trimming results in a healthier root system. Others disagree. If it works for you, keep it up.

HILL UP NEW BUSHES with all the soil, mulch or other insulating material that is needed to protect canes until just the tips show. This not only protects from cold, but keeps canes from drying out. A constant temperature and moist conditions help roses start.

When the bushes have started, gradually cut some holes in the plastic to reduce the temperature. Remove entirely in about two weeks, depending on the weather. The tent is a must for tree roses. It is well worth the extra time and effort in better, stronger breaks and canes.

PACKAGED ROSES bring out strong responses from most rosarians... mostly negative. Given a choice, most of us prefer a No.1 bare root rose direct from the grower or good plants potted by a reliable local nurseryman. But we cannot ignore that there are millions of packaged roses sold every year and SOME of them have been carefully handled, shipped and sold at a fair price. It is a turnoff for new rose hobbyists to be told "packaged stuff is junk." Obviously, package roses with chopped roots; broken canes and a handful of wood shavings are not much good... and are totally worthless after a few days in a hot store window. A fresh packaged rose can be trimmed, soaked and planted with the same care as a grower's Jumbo... and can produce as many fine roses. Some roses now come ready to plant, pot and all. If still dormant, good practice suggests that the plant be removed from the pot, trimmed and planted, spreading the roots normally. For advanced growth, leave the plant in the pot, but cut or trim the pot so the roots can expand into the rose bed area.

We are in the business to ENCOURAGE rose growing and we owe something to the newcomer to show him how to get better results. We need all the rose friends we can get, too. The rosarian or society who finds fault with a local nursery supplier who sells packaged roses cannot expect a warm welcome when THEY want something. It will pay us to learn more about packaged roses. Something tells me more and more of our roses are going to be supplied this way and we had better be prepared.

An epidemic of spring planting fever reminds us that when warm weather comes, garden con artists are sure to follow. Rosarians are easy prey, weakened by months of snow and cold. They are so anxious to get going in the garden again that they fall for the old miracle formulation claim or the often used amazing discovery.

For the most part, it is good-natured puffery and about all you will lose is your money. But rosebushes can also be lost in the process, losing a whole season in the process. Healthy rosarians know better. Discount the claims with a heavy application of common sense. Miracles are fun, but only when a grower can take the loss… a little like betting on horses.

DO NOT BET on unproductive plants, even though you may be reluctant to dig up and replace those bushes that may take another year to get established. Prune them with a shovel. But to make the conscience feel better, offer the plants you do not want at a plant exchange. It takes a little extra spade work and care, but it is a good way to get someone going with roses.

A new grower has to start somewhere and the bushes that did not quite meet your expectations can produce blooms to dazzle a beginner. Most everyone has had the experience of giving away a less-than-successful plant only to have it come on with a vigor that amazes the donor.

OLD ROSE BEDS may not die but they can gradually fade away. Even though a few show winners may still be growing in an old bed, it may be better management to rebuild a rose bed before it finally gives up.

Rose beds get old when organic matter in the soil is gradually depleted and additions of mulch and other materials on top will not perform quite the same job as bacteria supporting organics will in the root zone. Some rose beds last longer than others. Heavy feedings of nitrogen are definitely a factor in using up the materials that bring life to the soil. Soil organisms thrive in a medium of organic matter, air and water.

As materials are broken down, soils become tighter and less able to support root systems. Rose production gradually declines and more fertilizer will not reverse the process. Rebuilding the whole bed produces the best results with least effort. It is a chance to start over, even though established plants are involved.

REBUILD BEDS when roses are dormant, preferably just before breaking in early spring. Dig the bushes carefully with a spading fork -do not prune or otherwise encourage new growth. Bury or cover the bushes with soil, sacks, straw or any other material that will keep the plants cool and damp while the bed is being rebuilt. Try to preserve dormancy if at all possible.

Roses can be safely held this way for a week or longer if necessary. Rebuild a bed in much the same way as making a new one -a final mixture, by volume, of 1/3 compost or manure, 1/3 loamy soil and 1/3 sand is about right. Add bonemeal, rock phosphate or superphosphate (your choice) and work thoroughly into the bed and future root zone. Phosphates do not move readily in the soil. Place it where it will do some good.

SOLUBLE FERTILIZERS are too hot to add to a rebuilt bed if the beds are to be replanted in a short time. It is safer to feed from the top when bushes are established and growing. Horse or cow barn manure is probably OK even if it has not had much of a chance to heat or compost. Mixed in the soil, it is not likely to overheat.

Local soil conditions may call for other additives, such as gypsum for loosening clays or an acidifier for alkaline soils. Turn the whole mixture with a fork, shovel or tiller. A tiller does the best job, but deep cultivation with a three-prong fork is also good. Wet down the bed area, turn again the next day -two or three times is usually enough. Finally, allow the bed to settle wetting helps -before attempting to plant.

DORMANT ROSES can be handled like bare root roses when replanting. If it is time for growth to start, prune canes according to the usual practice for your climate. Wash the soil off the roots and trim out any dead or broken parts. Trim root ends lightly to encourage callousing and new feeder roots. Trim up any root galls or gall growths· on the shank or bud union.

Some growers maintain that disinfecting trimmed galls with *Lysol* or *Clorox* retards reoccurrence, but an equal number of growers disagree. Most growers have galls they do not even know about and have had them for a long time. They have also enjoyed fine roses and will continue to do so. When very large galls girdle the shank or bud union and restrict growth, it is time to throwaway and start over. Fortunately this does not happen very often in most gardens.

SPOT REBUILDING can help, but it is not as good as the real thing. If the whole bed cannot be reworked, remove some soil from the planting area and replace with a light, organic mix. Make sure it is well mixed. Blend some of the new soil into the surrounding area so that there is no dramatic soil change.

The greatest problem is to create a tub or hole to collect water. Light, friable soil is much more receptive to water than adjoining tight soil. A little extra blending or building up can make a great deal of difference.

APR. 1980

THOUGHT FOR THE MONTH: The rosarian's prayer: When we are strong, make us willing to change. And when we are right, make us easy to live with.

With the Winter of '80 about to melt, it is time for rosarians to talk about spider mites and crown gall again. Every rose season seems to have some new kind of problem and when our roses do not have a problem, we create one.

It has been talked about over and over again and it is still true — roses are the most popular and productive flower in the world in spite of rosarians, not because of them. This preamble just reminds us that rose folks just have to be the greatest in the world to put up with this kind of abuse.

WHO CAN EXPLAIN why the rose planted in the middle of the lawn without care or concern grows to tremendous size and produces bushels of blooms? The plant is neglected and abused, but still performs against all the rules. This tells us there is no BEST way to grow roses, just lots of good ways.

WE CONFUSE NEW MEMBERS with heaps of scientific mumbo-jumbo about why things happen when we should be talking about results. For example, I cannot explain why root and crown galls seem to disappear when plants are shifted to sandy, friable rose beds.

Maybe more air contributes to the gall decline, maybe the lack of certain humus combinations reduces risk. But it is an observed fact and we ought to pass it along that galled plants will often recover just by trimming up a bit and planting higher in a sandy location.

ROOTS GROW better in sandy, friable soils, too. There should be plenty of humus present, too. Just stay away from the silty, clay combinations that pack and refuse to hold air or water. The soil can be exceedingly rich, but the roots have to be able to grow and take up the nutrients. Sandy, built-up beds have been a revelation to me. I will just enjoy the results without trying to explain all the reasons.

UNDER TEST this season in the Rambler's garden is a rose bed made from bank sand and ground pine bark, built up about 12 inches above the level of the lawn. Bank sand on the Gulf Coast is a silty sand laced with clay. It is deposited by the slow moving rivers of the coastal prairie.

Proportions of sand and bark are about half and half. Additions include 20 pounds of gypsum, 20 pounds of fish meal, 50 pounds of alfalfa meal and 10 pounds of 15-10-5 rose food with trace elements per 100 square feet. Till, water, till and settle for about a month. By the standards set with last year's mix -more sharp sand -this ought to make roses grow.

WHEN ALL GOES WELL, in about three weeks you will have the best organic fertilizer available. Use about two garden shovels of artificial manure per established plant. Repeat in late summer with another shovelful. Use correspondingly smaller amounts for miniatures in beds.

If you are a manure gourmet, you may want to add other trace materials such as seaweed, rock phosphate or decomposed granite. If your soil is on the acid side, skip the cottonseed meal and substitute horse stall manure with wood shavings or some other manure source. You will be glad you tried it.

BY POPULAR DEMAND here is a repeat of the FRAGRANT FORMULA for artificial manure that makes almost anything grow. This is for the rosarian who does not have a farm friend with the real thing. The Fragrant Formula is just as good and probably better because it releases more nutrients and can be produced on any city lot. You will enjoy all the benefits without the cow. Here is the formula: three "ample yards of compost materials or leaves; 100 pounds of cottonseed hulls or something coarse; 100 pounds of cottonseed meal; 100 pounds of rough cut alfalfa meal; 50 pounds of bone meal and 50 pounds of fish meal.

Your local feed store will have all the ingredients except the leaves. Use any area satisfactory for composting. Pile the leaves and coarse materials about two feet deep. Add the ingredients a little at a time and turn with a garden fork. Moisten LIGHTLY. Turn with a fork twice a week for two weeks. Cover with plastic if you are in a real hurry. When the pile is working properly, an ammonia odor will leak out.

A DIFFERENT ODOR will leak if the pile gets too wet or if there is not enough coarse composting material. Wet cottonseed meal turns into a slime that smells dead and crawls along the ground like a fog. If you do have an odor, add more rough materials and turn more frequently.

THERE MUST BE A REASON why an

application of organic manure in the spring makes other fertilizers work better. My guess is that the organics feed the micro-organisms that do all the work converting nutrients into a form that roses can take up. Anyway, you will have live soil, organisms and rosebushes. And that is what produces loads of roses.

MAY 1980

THOUGHT FOR THE MONTH: The trouble with rosarians who talk too fast is that they often say something they haven't thought of yet.

For a really lively rose society meeting, try a two-way discussion. It is a free-for-all of rose opinion, advice, experience and observation moderated — or sometimes refereed by — a program person who stays out of the act and lets the audience conduct its own program.

A good referee will have a few warmup questions as well as some question stoppers, guiding the comments so many topics can be covered. The whole idea is to get many people to participate. Here are a few of the items at a discussion that the Rambler recently attended.

WATER MAKES THINGS GROW. The best fertilizer formulation will not do a bit of good until it is in solution and in the root zone of the plant. Dry, pelletized fertilizers are great if there is a regular, ample water supply to dissolve the material and carry the nutrients to the roots.

For a faster start, get food into solution and soak the roots. Old-timers know that a deep soaking before using liquid foods also speeds up the process. For a real surprise, try dissolving your favorite dry rose food in water. It may be less soluble than you think.

MOUND UP THE CANES. Soil and mulch mounded up to protect the canes of newly planted bushes is not so much for freeze protection, but to conserve moisture. Bright sun and dry air can turn green canes into dry sticks in just a day or two when new roots cannot supply enough moisture. New feeder roots must develop before canes and growth put the system under stress.

Two weeks or so is enough most of the time. Let rainfall or some gentle washing with the hose erode the mound. Do not poke at the soil and covered new breaks with a cultivator or trowel. Gradually uncover.

GREEN MATTER MAKES IT GO. Compost, that is. Green residue in a backyard compost pile supplies the enzymes that do the real work breaking down all forms of organic matter. To say it another way, green stuff makes the pile heat up.

There are other starters available, but grass clippings, yard trimmings and kitchen waste are usually available. Green manure works, too, but is a problem for most backyards. Organic material can be recycle into plant food in just two or three weeks with the right approach.

Start with about six inches of dry leaves at the bottom of the heap, add several inches of green materials, then layer with wood shavings or straw. Some cottonseed meal or manure can be added next with some odds and ends of yard trimmings and dirt on top. Lightly moisten the !\Thole pile. Leave a slight hollow on top so that water will not run off.

In about six days, turn the pile with a fork, working from the outside. This gives a good mix. Turn two more times. If the pile gets too hot, add a bit more water. If it has not heated in three or four days, add more green stuff or manure. If there is no heat, it is not working. The compost produced adds life to soils-and blooms to roses. You will wonder how you ever got along without it.

LIQUID COMPOST, TOO. Also called cow tea, it makes roses respond. Back in BC (before chemicals), gardeners always had a barrel or two steeping behind the garage or fence. It was a good practice then and still is. There is not much direct nutrient value to cow tea, but the boost given soil organisms makes everything work better.

Add some soluble fertilizer if it seems to be needed. Keep several plastic garbage cans of tea brewing all the time, rainwater is best. Onion or potato sacks make good tea bags. Fill with cow chips and tie with a long piece of rope or wire. Steep for about 10 days, sloshing around once in a while. Use about two gallons of tea per bush for some sensational results.

CUT ON A SLANT. It makes sense to trim rose canes on a slant so that water can run off, particularly if no sealer is used. Cane pith breaks down with water. which in turn traps more water. Any opening encourages carpenter ants or cane borers.

For whatever reason, when cane pith is broken down, dieback results. The most common sealer on the Gulf Coast? Elmer's Glue or shellac are preferred, usually applied with a dauber in a show polish bottle. Asphalts are least used.

MANZATE, BENLATE, PHALTAN OR TRIFORINE? All are excellent fungicides and have their advocates. But the discussion consensus seemed to be that alternating fungicides worked best of all. *Triforine* had not been tried by most of the participants, but those who had were very enthusiastic. It is available this season in a 6.5 percent liquid formulation as *Funginex*, a product of *Ortho*.

For the hot, humid Gulf Coast, the most common spray program to use is *Phaltan* in the spring, switching to *Manzate* or *Manzate-Benlate* when temperatures reach 80 degrees and *Benlate* alone during the very hot weather. Weekly sprayings are most common, although some stretch applications to two weeks during very hot, dry weather.

HOW TO FEED A MINI. Miniature roses like everything that the big roses do, only less. Keep this in mind regarding concentration as well as quantity. Use one-fourth or less dry fertilizer for miniatures as compared to large roses — and even this may be too much.

For liquid feedings, watch the concentration. Dilute the regular solution to about one-eighth. Fine feeder roots do not like to be overwhelmed with food. Most miniatures are not attractive when overfed. Gross overfeeding can burn and kill. It is better to feed a little more than risk yellow leaves or gross foliage.

Osmocote is a favorite of the miniature grower, supplemented from time to time with very light applications of *Carl Pool Instant Rose Food*. *Peter's* or *Sterns* soluble foods are also popular. But the Rambler's favorite is still *Atlas Fish Emulsion*, an aromatic and soluble mix that makes leaves green, colors bright and healthy vigorous plants. Fish emulsion is a bit more trouble to use, but has always paid off in good results. A little like cow tea, it makes nature work.

There has been a flurry of rose workshops in the South Central and Gulf District the past few months, encouraging an exchange of ideas on roses and rose events you cannot get anywhere else. Hope that your area is fortunate enough to have some programming like this, too. Here are a few of the subjects that brought out the most response.

SPRAY EQUIPMENT. What is the best sprayer? Obviously, there is no one best sprayer for everyone, if you will accept that as an answer. There are a good many rosarians who think that roses cannot be grown without an Atomist and others who say it does about as much good as a hot wind.

From comments heard around the area, the *Atomist* does an excellent job for the person who makes sure the leaves are thoroughly wetted and who sprays on a regular basis. A once over lightly with a hose just does not do the job. The *Atomist* is ideal for the person who does not want to pull or carry a heavy spray tank around and who has a safe power source available. It is good for large or small gardens, if you want to pay the initial price.

HUDSON'S **PUMP SPRAYER** is probably the most commonly used with a size and model for almost every garden. Some gardens have more than one, using a smaller tank for application of herbicides or spot thrip controls.

The fiberglass tank model is particularly good if you are prone to a quick wash instead of a thorough cleaning after each application. The pump-up tank is good for up to several hundred plants, dispensing materials evenly and effectively. For a larger garden, a Hudson Suburban is a good investment, available in electric or gas engine driven models. It sprays almost anything around the yard with a quick change of spray heads.

Of course there are many other home handiman setups, but they all seek to accomplish one thing — good droplets of consistent strength sprayer material applied in the right places without risk to rose, rosarian or environment. The Rambler used to be a hose-on sprayer fan, mostly because of its ease of application and the results were pretty good. But the system is basically wasteful of spray material, can be risky to the applicator and is woefully inconsistent in strength.

ON THE SUBJECT OF SPRAYS, it is great to have a fungicide in liquid form like *Funginex*. No mixing, no swirling, no lumps, no stopped-up spray nozzle. It also wets foliage very well and leaves no visible residue. In short, it is a snap to use and will do a very good job if used on a consistent, regular schedule. That means every seven to 10 days during the growing season.

A CLASSIC COMMENT came up at one session, "Why cut spent blooms when you could be cutting roses?" Which means we should be cutting more roses for homes, friends and displays and discarding fewer spent blooms in the garbage can. A tour of the garden every morning to cut roses, then a few minutes of conditioning and these roses can be enjoyed and shared by more people. It is worth thinking about.

THE WORD IS GETTING AROUND that less insecticide means more roses in the long run. More and more rosarians are coming around to the fact that nature does have a balance and when we use insecticides indiscriminately, something bad is bound to happen, usually an outbreak of spider mites or burned and harsh looking foliage.

THE *BUG ZAPPER,* that electric grid with the attractive black lights, seems to be catching on in popularity. It attracts all sorts of flying insects, electrocuting and depositing them neatly in a tray. It is particularly effective for the moth that lays the eggs for corn ear worms. Makes the garden a good deal more pleasant, too, without all the mosquitoes and gnats. The initial investment is a little high, but is not too bad if you have a power source near the rose garden. It might be just the thing for your own garden gift this season.

To find out about the real world of roses, go on a garden tour. It is amazing the number of rose topics that are discussed by the hosts, probably the best teaching methods anywhere. Tours can be as casual or as organized as required, provided that broad participation is the result. If tours are not important in your rose society routine, get some going. Here are just a few of the topics you are likely to hear discussed in the gardens.

WORM CASTINGS... Are castings the miracle that the worm people claim? Are castings the perfect plant food? Setting aside these superlatives, it seems castings are very useful and perform well in a number of rose situations. Castings are highly nutritious, relatively soluble and, most important, are in a form available to plants.

As the earthworm ingests organic matter, it excretes castings rich in nitrates, phosphates, potash and calcium. In short, it is a natural plant food. Miniature roses thrive on it, used as a top dressing or in the soil mix for beds or pots. About a half inch of castings broadcast in a mini bed and scratched in with other organic material produces excellent results with healthy, glossy foliage and top blooms. There is no evidence of overfeeding, such as oversized blooms, vegetative centers or lush foliage without blooms.

For potted miniatures, use about one-third castings by volume with usual planting medium, leaving out other foods. Restore sick potted plants too by replacing some of old mix with castings. On the Gulf Coast, castings are marketed as Super Stuff and are relatively inexpensive. The supplier here reports other marketers have a good distribution of castings in other parts of the country. You may want to give castings a try, particularly for container grown or hanging basket miniatures.

ALFALFA MEAL seems to be the "in" food for roses this season, although it has been around and used successfully for many years. The ground or pelletized forms work equally well, although the pellets take longer to break down. High in protein, alfalfa meal breaks down in contact with soil organisms and releases nutrients in forms available to plants.

About two cups per established bush is the most common application rate used about twice during the growing season. Broadcast and scratch in lightly. Most users claim healthier foliage, better stems and more breaks. Feed supply stores have alfalfa meal at about $6 for 50 pounds.

BANK SAND AND PINE BARK make an excellent rose bed mix in the Rambler's experience, outperforming some of the most expensive top soil and organic matter mixtures. Since cost is a consideration in most garden projects, check for a source in your area.

Use about half silty sand and half ground pine bark and enrich with about 20 pounds of fishmeal, 50 pounds of alfalfa meal, 20 pounds of gypsum and 10 pounds of 5-10-5 rose food with trace elements per 100 square feet. Grade 1 roses planted in this mix on March 1 are three feet tall after 90 days, very bushy, are in the second bloom cycle and producing basal breaks without a pause. Whatever it is, it is working.

MULCHES for rose beds seem to be gaining in popularity, particularly materials that break down and add nutrients and humus to the soil. The old worry of acids from pine bark mixtures is mostly forgotten. A little extra nitrogen makes up for loss in the decomposition process.

Almost any organic material can be used as a mulch if it acts as an insulator, permits movement of water, air and nutrients and stays attractively in place. Mixtures of materials work best. Use what is cheap and available in the area.

MINIATURES START BETTER when potted for about one month before planting in garden beds. Use a rich, friable mixture similar to what the newly purchased miniature was originally grown in. Four or five inch plastic pots seem to work the best. Repot even those shipped in two inch pots. Keep in a protected location for several weeks and follow a regular watering routine.

If the pots dry out, the whole advantage is lost. Most of those who practice potting before planting report excellent initial growth without transplant shock, more vigorous new growth and a well-developed root system able to cope and compete in a rose bed.

Some varieties take longer to fill out than others, but when growth is well established, carefully slip from the pot and plant. It will never know it has been moved and will continue growth without pause.

Why does it work? Apparently the more carefully controlled potting mix and the warmer soil temperature in the pot encourage better root growth and therefore better top growth. Cooler, less hospitable soils in the garden slow roots somewhat. A protected location -not too hot or too cold helps some, too. You will be surprised how well the potting technique works, even in mid-summer.

SMART ROSARIANS provide for contingencies, too. Ever wonder how some rosarians always seem to have landscape beds without a gap or color blend plantings that always blend? They usually pot up spares in the spring, just like the pros. If a replacement is needed, it is ready to go.

Replacements can be made late in the season with very little transplant shock if carefully done. Your spare is going to be in much better condition than some leftover at the local nursery. It also helps if a replacement has to be planted among established bushes. The better root system of a potted rose can compete on more even terms.

ANNUALS AND ROSES do mix. Some of the most attractive gardens on tour used other plant materials with roses. Borders of portulaca, ageratum or petunias are especially attractive. Alyssum adds even more fragrance to a rose garden.

It is not too late to try some color touches, even in mid-summer. Your roses will like it too.

There is not much really new in growing roses, just consistent application of sound programs and basics that produce good roses year after year. You readers apparently think so, too, because the Rambler's mailbox regularly receives requests to "repeat that thing you did on thrips" or "explain what you meant about insecticides and fungicides together." Rose basics may fade a bit through familiarity, but they do not die back. Here are some refreshers for summertime.

GROW LEAVES, THEN ROSES. It is sometimes hard to tell if more leaf damage is done by spraying or by fungus diseases. Particularly during the summer months, the name of the rose game is leaves. Do everything possible to maintain a good, healthy leaf system. When you do spray, soak the rose beds first and spray during the cooler hours.

A plant needing water is already under stress, spray materials just compound the problem. Even plain water on the leaves can cause damage when the sun is hot. If at all possible, time spray applications so leaves can dry off before the sun gets really hot.

Leaves can sunburn just like rosarians -with painful results. To repeat what every good rosarian knows -well maintained plants with healthy leaves just cannot help but produce roses. Whether leaves are lost because of mites, blackspot, mildew, spray burn or dehydration, the results are the same -no roses.

"NEVER WET THE LEAVES" makes about as much sense as trying to eliminate rainfall. Overhead watering is not bad. In fact, overhead watering offers some advantages that soaking systems cannot match.

Many good rose growers set a cone type sprinkler directly in the rose bed and let the water spray up under the bushes. This accomplishes two things: it washes off the spider mites and effectively prevents spray buildup. Today's effective fungicides virtually eliminate the worry of wet foliage.

This is not to suggest growers wet down the foliage each evening, but no harm will come from regular overhead watering provided a systematic fungicide spray program is followed.

SPIDER MITES DO *NOT* LIKE WATER, put roses do. It is a good practice to use the overhead, underneath, water allover method about once a week even for rose beds with irrigation systems.

Moral: roses like to be clean and cool just like rosarians. With all the junk floating in the air these days, most anything can stand a washing from time to time.

USE SPRAYS INTELLIGENTLY. Some rose authorities claim sprays must always cover rose leaves over under sideways and crossways. That is good advice when spraying for fungus diseases, but wasteful -sometimes even harmful -when spraying for thrips.

Good rose competitors know that misting the buds and blooms with *Orthene* will do all the good that is necessary. There is no need to saturate the whole plant, thrips are at the top. Use the leftover *Orthene* to spray lily and gladiola host blooms.

For good show blooms, begin misting as soon as color shows and continue misting weekly when thrips migration is on. Better yet, spot spray light colored blooms and buds with a *Windex* or similar pump sprayer.

Insecticides used indiscriminately usually bring on an outbreak of spider mites or burned and harsh looking foliage. Use insecticides only when really needed for specific problems applied where the problem occurs.

BUILT UP ROSE BEDS make a natural growing medium for roses, one in which nature does the work. If you have well drained soil that is easy to work, nature is already working and there is less need to build up .

Or if your climatic conditions are particularly severe -either hot or cold — raised beds may not be practical. Just do whatever is necessary to let air, water and nutrients reach the root zone.

Although roses will tolerate many soils, poor drainage and lack of aeration will slowly but surely weaken plants. Many new growers enjoy a beautiful first flush of blooms, progressively dropping off until the newcomer gives up in disgust, usually by the end of the first year.

A major cause is poor aeration. Rose roots just will not tolerate waterlogged soil. Most rose growers do not realize drainage of soil is both external and internal and a good rose bed should provide both.

EXTERNAL OR SURFACE DRAINAGE is generally understood and most backyard gardeners take care of it with slopes and ditches. Many believe the problem is solved if water does not stand on the soil after heavy rains, but internal drainage is even more important.

Water moves through the soil in direct proportion to the size of soil particles. Heavy soils like clays and fine silts hold more water than soils with larger particles and inhibit downward movement of water.

When the interparticle spaces of the soil are filled with water, an insufficient amount of air is available to the roots for normal respiration and growth. Active, new roots suffer most. In fact, the whole soil process slows down when water, air and nutrients are not present in appropriate proportions to support the work of soil micro-organisms.

FEEDER ROOTS GRADUALLY SUFFOCATE in waterlogged soil. Most damage occurs during prolonged rains in the growing season. Feeder roots cannot keep up with plant demands. Digging out a deep bed and replacing the soil does not necessarily correct an internal drainage problem because the surrounding soil does not permit excess water to drain away rapidly. It holds water like a tub. Water must be able to escape through the soil below and surrounding the bed area. Whatever it takes, do it.

Time after time we are reminded of that best of all rose advice — if what you are doing is getting good results, don't change. These Ramblings and other rose sources are only suggestions. There is no one perfect way to grow and enjoy roses. If you are happy, your roses are probably happy, too.

WHY MAKE A CHOICE between a *Benlate* and *Manzate* mixture and *Funginex* disease control. Both are outstanding fungicides, both have some special applications that may be beneficial. *Benlate* and *Manzate* control blackspot, mildew and rust -if it occurs in your area — but at a somewhat higher cost. It is also a liquid formulation that leaves no residue and can be used in the hottest weather. Frequency for Funginex is every seven days for best control -at least on the hot, humid Gulf Coast. Use the product with the features that do the most for you and apply it consistently. The result: happy roses and rosarian.

DISEASE CONTROL does not have to become a crusade. A good product and regular program will work in most gardens. Here is some down to earth advice from Dr. Eldon W. Lyle, Past President of the ARS and Plant Pathologist at the Texas Rose Research Foundation, which was first published in 1979 and just as good today.

"It is a waste of· time to pick off blackspotted leaves except to make the plants more tidy. Unseen infection can quickly take over and supply enough spores of the fungus to create a fast spread of the disease. While the infected leaves remain attached to the rose stems or canes, they put substance and food into the bushes.

"Defoliation whether from blackspot or from hand picking of leaves will lessen the vitality of the bushes in proportion to the amount of leaves removed. If only 10 percent of the leaves are shed, there would not be much harm to the bushes. Anything over 50 percent defoliation is very weakening. Pruning out of yellowed canes is desirable unless this pruning also takes away good foliage from the plant."

DR. LYLE CONTINUED, "The main thing is to get a good spray program once a week (every seven days) and use materials such as *Benlate* and *Manzate* or *Benlate* and *Phaltan*. The spray should contain one tablespoon of *Benlate* per two gallons of water. Add either *Manzate* or *Phaltan* to this

at the same rate. Use enough spray to reach the dripping stage from the leaves.

"Also, next season start such a spray program the same week as pruning back the bushes in the spring. The spores coming from cane infections where the spores overwinter may be killed before spreading to tender new leaves as they start to form."

Dr. Lyle also reported very favorably on *Funginex* (one tablespoon per gallon) or *Triforine* (an 18 percent formulation used at one teaspoon per gallon) as very effective in control of mildew and blackspot when used weekly.

FALLEN LEAVES. Dr. Lyle concluded, "Fallen leaves on the ground or top of the mulch are not a source of carry over of the disease, even though this is a frequent belief. As soon as the diseased leaves fall and start to rot, the blackspot disease also decays. There is no need for removing the mulch that remains from season to season. Just add more to it as needed."

SPIDER MITE CONTROLS. This enemy that comes with the hot and dry season also brings out the hottest comments from rosarians. Some swear by water, some swear at it. Some have an arsenal of miticides, some let nature take its course. Fortunately, the roses survive in spite of all this.

Vendex is the new favorite miticide for those who advocate spraying. Manufactured by Shell Chemical, *Vendex* is recommended at one teaspoon per gallon, applied to the undersides of the leaves. The product has a long residual action and should be applied only once in 28 days and only then if really necessary.

Vendex kills mites by contact action -chemical stability on the foliage prolongs residual kill of mites in all stages from newly hatched to mature adult. Maximum control may not be observed until a week or two after application.

WATER WASHING for mites has its advocates, too. They feel miticides are nearly as harmful to the leaves as mites. Use a water wand if you are fortunate enough to own one or use a garden hose nozzle adjusted to a fine, hard mist. Wash the plants from the bottom up.

Washing breaks up the webs, knocks off the eggs and drowns the hatched mites in the process. Repeat two or three times a week during mite conditions to get them all. Sometimes even the diehard washing advocate will recommend one application of miticide immediately after the second washing to clean up those remaining mites.

The Rambler just has to share this water washing story picked up in the South Carolina Rose Society newsletter. Tom Estridge, President, wrote, "In the event you are too old to play with a water hose on a hot day, turn it into a fun day for the children or grandchildren."

ANOTHER QUOTE, this time from Erskine Carter, 86 years young and growing roses in Albany, Georgia. Erskine wrote, "I have sprayed only with Triforine. No insecticide at all and so far no insects. One exception, the last time I sprayed I noticed some aphids on the young twigs and resolved to give them a of Spectracide the next day. Bless Fanny, there were none the next day, only white specks of their carcasses.

"Triforine good for aphids, too? Last year I had 256 plants and since I'm 86, I could hardly make it to the house. This year I have 120 and me and the roses both feel better and it seems I have almost as many roses, too."

The Year of the Heat Wave is nearly over and none too soon for many rosarians. As one Dallas rosarian observed after 55 consecutive days of 100 degree plus temperatures, "It's the first time I've ever had miniatures on top of six foot bushes."

He is Luckier than some, at least the plants were still alive. There is something to be learned during a hot spell — thoughtfully considered in an air conditioned house. Here are a few sweaty observations from the Rambler.

MULCH can save the day — and rosebushes — during extended periods of heat and drought. Well mulched rose beds did much better than plantings with just a light covering or no protection at all. All kinds of loose insulating materials did the job. Mixtures of ground pine bark, leaves, clippings and manure seemed to work the best. The bark mix stayed loose, but still in place, allowed air and water 10 percolate through to the soil, decomposed slowly and most importantly kept soil temperatures down even during the hottest days.

In spite of good watering practices, many roses become top feeders, developing fine, hairy root systems near the surface of the rose bed to take in the food and water so carefully laid down by the rosarian. In that good care routine, the rose grower inadvertently encouraged fine roots near the surface, roots of neglected plants spread down and out in order to survive.

For whatever reason, fine feeder roots under stress with heat and drought die very quickly, leaving the bush with a root system that will not support the top properly. In short, keep the root system to keep the leaves, the ultimate food producing system for the plant.

CHUNK BARK works exceptionally well with miniature roses making an attractive cover that is an excellent insulator. Chunk bark, usually sold as decorative bark, can be used about three inches deep completely covering the surface between miniature plants. The soil stays exceptionally cool under the bark and retains moisture well. Liquid fertilizers, fish meal, even composted manure washes through the bark and gets to the soil ready to go to work.

Another plus, no weeds, not even nut grass. Believe it or not, plants of Rise 'n Shine in a direct west exposure against a brick wall grew 15 inches high, stayed in full leaf and continuous bloom during two months of 100 degrees. They were watered every other day, lightly fed every two weeks and mulched with three inches of pine bark chunks. The only problem was the plants got too big and it was painful to groom them back.

FEED ROSES, lightly, even during very hot weather if any water at all is available. Without rainfall, rosarians irrigate and leach out many of the nutrients that would ordinarily be available. These have to be replaced in one form or another.

Rose beds fed at half portion on a monthly basis maintained leaves, vigor and even some fair blooms as compared to those watered only and allowed to rest. After grooming in September, the fed plants responded much more quickly than the plants maintained with water alone. It is doubtful if the somewhat deprived plants will catch up this season.

MINIATURES respond very well to regular, light feedings. In fact, minis ignore heat and keep right on producing attractive plants and blooms provided they receive a regular ration. *Carl Pool* Instant Rose Food is the most popular around here in the summer. *Schultz* and *Peters* are widely used in many parts of the country.

Use at half mini strength about every two or three weeks, depending on how much you want the plants to grow. Water first, apply the liquid formula and water again. There is no reason at all for miniatures to slow down in the summer. The blooms will not last long in very hot sun, but the beds are certainly more attractive than yellow-pale plants with seared leaves.

SPRAY SCHEDULES, particularly for fungus diseases, can be extended during periods of hot, dry weather. The range of temperature and humidity is just not right for propagation of blackspot spores and mildew certainly will not be a problem under these conditions. Even on the high humidity Gulf Coast, most rosarians stretched the usual weekly routine to three weeks, using *Benlate* along with spreader sticker.

The real danger in hot weather is to burn the leaves or in any way reduce the capacity of the leaf to produce food. Sunburned or coarsened leaves do not perform well. Keep leaves clean (water overhead very early in the morning), cooled and fed with lots of deep watering and supported with light feeding. Stay off insecticides unless absolutely necessary. Chances are the bugs will do less damage than the insecticides.

ORGANIC rosarians, or mostly organic, suffer least in hot weather. Nature seems to compensate for weather conditions. Less tinkering with the system is needed by the rose grower. There may be some very good scientific reasons for this, but the results are obvious -well prepared beds with organic matter tolerate conditions and support roses better.

ALFALFA is enjoying a surge of popularity, particularly in hot weather. It is a very effective organic stimulant. Here is a testimonial from Dr. Marvous Mastellar, Deep South District Director from Atlanta, "I am using a pelletized form of alfalfa and it disintegrates well. 1 put it all around my Floribundas and they look better then they ever have. Experimenting with hybrid teas and grandifloras where I have many bushes of the same variety, I have treated half with alfalfa and skipped half. The contrast between the treated and untreated bushes of the same variety is startling. The treated Sonia and Queen Elizabeth plants, for instance, are loaded with multiple bloom sprays." Does that tell you something?

Recalling a Rambler column from some years ago, we reported, "The really good roses are grown in November when roses are not distracted by the blooms." It seems like a contradiction, but actually makes a lot of rose sense. Late fall calls for winter protection (if you need it), rosebed preparation and variety planning. A poor job now usually means poor roses in the spring.

DO WHAT COMES NATURALLY in winter protection. Plants are conditioned by nature for the cold, storing vitality for the spring that is sure to come. Nature's way to protect is with soil, leaves or a combination .of materials that adjust to changing conditions.

When cones, wraps, baskets and barriers offer nature's balance, they work rather well. When we try to trick Mother Nature, we all know what happens, sometimes even worse than on TV. Select the method that is easiest for .you. Try to· approximate a natural situation.

Fortunately, Gulf Coast growers do not have to protect. We have to slowdown growth, keep up a spray program and probably strip the leaves from the plants in February to induce some form of dormancy.

November is also a good time to begin some miniature roses under lights. Hybridizers are now offering some excellent· minis that adapt to artificial light very well. Harm Saville of Nor'East Miniature Roses made minis under lights sound easy at the Buffalo ARS meeting.

Harm said the trick is to provide light intensity. Most of the other factors in the house are suitable for minis. Nor'East offers a pamphlet called *The A-B-C of Indoor Culture*. It is a great way to have roses year around. Contact your favorite supplier and get started this month.

NATURE WILL DO SOME OF THE WORK in building a new rose bed if you start now before the ground is frozen. New or rebuilt beds need some time to settle and mellow before spring planting.

Some freezing and thawing, settling and draining, washing and blowing for a few months can tell a great deal about how a bed will perform under growing conditions. It is better to find out now the drainage is poor and not after the leaves have turned yellow. A poor winter bed makes an even poorer spring bed.

LANDSCAPE WITH MINIATURE ROSES. They are about as versatile a flowering plant as you can find. Minis are at home in the North or in the South. They mix with rock gardens or sidewalk plantings, formal beds or under tree roses, as masses of color or small color accents. For sheer bloom production, minis are hard to beat.

In northern climates, minis mix well with other annuals, usually come into bloom early and offer a change in texture and shape. In hot climates, miniature roses replace flowering annuals like petunias, geraniums, salvia and snapdragons. They thrive in planters, boxes and hanging baskets.

For those of us on the hot and humid Gulf Coast, miniatures' are colorful; controllable perennials that are used instead of flowering annuals. The Rambler suggests you get with the miniature program. You will be glad you did.

ARE FLORIBUNDAS DYING OUT? The demise of the floribunda has been reported and lamented by many writers, but it seems to me these colorful landscape roses are just coming into their own for the general rose growing public.

Hybridizers will soon be introducing and promoting more free flowering plants with good growth habit, disease resistance and ability to grow almost anywhere. That is about what Floribundas have been doing all along. The blooms can be cut and enjoyed or left to, be admired on the plant. As rosarians, we need to be demonstrating how floribundas can be used and we will learn something in the process, too.

Masses of blooms of the same variety are great, but mixed, colors can be attractive if the varieties have about the same growth habit. Floribundas mean abundant flowering and usually show off best when used abundantly.

A plant here and there just does not do the same thing as several plants of the same variety planted close together or as a coordinated design of several varieties and colors. It is what we admire in public gardens. The theme is the same in home gardens.

ROSES COST TOO MUCH, particularly for large displays. I do not agree with this claim at all. Considering color production, length of bloom and hardiness, roses are still one of the best landscape, perennial flowering buys,

Purchased for long term beauty, roses are good investments. Growers are moving to make roses less costly, at least in terms of today's dollar. In the future, we are going to be buying smaller plants and maturing them in our home gardens.

We will also see roses grown in pots and distributed on a regional basis. They may be tip budded and one year plants, but will start in the home garden without hesitation. These methods offer some real cost savings to rose propagators who have suffered from having to care for roses for two years and then pay staggering postal rates only to have the plants frozen or dried out in transit -and later replaced free.

We are going to see more roses introduced that grow well on their own roots. This speeds up the marketable rose process and means less cost. Roses by tissue culture are also in the future. One, thing is certain, rose breeders and growers are working hard to give us our favorite plant at a price we can afford to pay. That is a rosy prospect.

There is an old saying that goes, "There's not much that's new under the sun" and that holds true for roses as well. Consistent application of something that works produces the most roses. To prove the point, let us go back to some Rambler columns from December issues of years past to see what we were recommending and if it still works.

BETTER DRAINAGE YIELDS DRAMATIC RESULTS, but is commonly overlooked by rosarians who otherwise go to great lengths to make sure that the rose bed is just right. Some gardens are blessed with good drainage, but most are not. If you do not have it, make it.

Agricultural drain line is a easy way to go. Relatively inexpensive, it comes in rolls, is corrugated for greater flexibility and can be laid in, over, under and around garden problems.

To make a new bed or rejuvenate an old one, dig a trench the length of the rose bed and about a foot below the normal root level, gradually sloping down to a drain, ditch or even a gravel leaching pit. Use an inch or so of gravel or sand in the bottom of the ditch, lay the line and cover with tar paper to keep drain holes open and backfill with sand or light garden soil. You will enjoy dramatic results the first season. (Good in 1976, even better today.)

POOR DRAINAGE PLAGUED A ROSE BED on the rainy Gulf Coast. The round bed, 10 feet in diameter, was circled with a concrete walk. Efforts to build up the bed did not work. Finally the bed was dug out 18 inches and the soil laid aside.

A two inch drain tile was laid at a low point, covered with gravel and run to a sump hole beyond the perimeter of the planting. Total drop of the drain line was less than a foot, but that foot made all the difference in rose growth.

The same soil was replaced and the bed planted with Europeana. By mid-season, the bushes were five feet tall, very bushy and vigorous and in continuous bloom. Two weeks of nearly continuous rain (19 to 20 inches) did not produce a yellow leaf. (That was in 1974. The bushes are still thriving.)

ROSES AND SAND ARE COMPATIBLE. Rosarians in Florida and along the Mississippi Gulf Coast have learned how to use sand to a good advantage. No problems with drainage here. The problem was how to keep water and nutrients available in the root zone.

Humus was added to the planting area as compost, ground pine bark, peat moss -anything organic. Fertilizer is also organic. Fish meal and even trash fish were generously applied. Cylinders of soil were taken about 18 inches from the shank of the bush and filled with about one-half cup of fish meal. Trash fish were buried in the same manner. Then the sand was replaced.

Four or five perimeter feedings of this kind produced gigantic results — rosebushes eight feet tall with six or eight canes in a single season. The success seems to come from the concentration of food, which releases slowly and encourages broad root growth. The exchange of air and water in the sandy mix was perfectly balanced with organic **nutrients.** (First seen in 1973, plants now look like trees.)

MINIATURES IN POTS thrive under **fluorescents,** regardless of the weather outside. Build your own **plant** stand if you are handy with tools. If you want something a **bit** fancier, get a Flora-Cart advertised in many of the garden magazines. In any indoor setup, it is important that fixtures be adjustable as the distance from light source to plants is critical. Minis need about 16 hours of light each day and lights should be set just above the tops of the plants.

Harm Saville of Nor'East Miniatures Roses suggested a potting mixture of one part good garden soil, one part peat moss or other humus and one part medium coarse sand or perlite. Perlite is a good growing medium as it retains both air and water, having about 20 percent air space by volume.

Minis will tolerate differences in potting mixtures, but must have a regular feeding program. Use soluble foods in low concentrations every two or three weeks. In most cases, dissolve one teaspoon of soluble fertilizer in a quart of water and wet the soil in the pots thoroughly.

WATER TAKES CARE OF SPIDER MITES. Put the mini pot in a laundry tub and spray the undersides of the leaves with plenty of water. Wash even before mites show up. The extra water cleans the leaves and makes the whole system work better. Washing two or three times at three day intervals will usually clean up the problem.

Minis also prefer some humidity. Add some moisture to the air if you have dry furnace heat. A plastic sheet over the growing frame will help. Moist gravel or perlite in the growing tray also releases moisture.

Minis like about the same temperature range as rosarians. If you are comfortable, minis will grow. (Since this first appeared in 1973, minis under lights have greatly increased in popularity. Hybridizers are introducing minis just for pots.)

FOR A MAJOR LANDSCAPE PROJECT, consider buying plants at wholesale or at substantially reduced prices. In most cases, they will catch up with the others by the end of the first season.

Plant the smaller bushes a little closer together -close spacing looks better anyway -and enjoy a good many more roses than you might have otherwise been able to afford. It is a great way to plant a whole fence line or driveway.

They come in bundles of 10 and your local nurseryman can usually get what you need if ordered early. These smaller plants will turn out to be real bargains. (A good idea 10 years ago and coming into common practice today. All of us are going to be buying smaller plants in the future and maturing them in our home gardens).

As our 1981 rose year breaks dormancy, the Rambling Rosarian is 10 years older and 120 rambling columns wiser, which proves again we cannot outgrow roses as a hobby. There is always something new with roses or something that needs repeating. Hope your 1981 is a rosy year and that you will continue to share the world's greatest hobby.

JANUARY may not seem an appropriate time to discuss plant hardiness since there is not much we can do about it now, but this excerpt from an article by Dr. Griffith J. Buck of Iowa State University is worth sharing. Dr. Buck is the leading authority on winter hardiness and hybridizer of a new strain of roses that will survive even the most severe winter conditions.

HEALTHY ROSES LIVE LONGER, to paraphrase Dr. Buck. "Preparation of a plant for winter begins, not in the late summer or fall, but in the early spring. The degree of maturity produced in the plant by the end of the growing season is directly related to the kind and quality of culture it received during the growing season.

"The diligence of the gardener in satisfying the plant's cultural requirements can increase its hardiness to its maximum level, but no farther. However, poor culture can definitely lower the level of a plant's hardiness," he wrote.

"**TO REALIZE A PLANT'S** maximum winter hardiness," Dr. Buck wrote, "gardeners should assess their cultural methods critically as well as their effects on the development of high carbohydrate reserves within the plants. They should work for is a steady growth rate throughout the growing season with a careful cessation from mid August until killing frost. "To do this means careful attention to fertilizing, irrigation and photosynthesis. It also means that violent fluctuation in growth rate such as a mid summer dormancy followed by active growth late in the season as the result of pruning, fertilization or irrigation is to be avoided.

"**NOT THE LEAST OF CULTURAL** operations is pest control. Plants which have been defoliated by disease or insect attack are especially vulnerable to premature fall freezes. Premature defoliation interferes with photosynthesis and, therefore, carbohydrate production, by removing the organs concerned.

"Also, it can lead to the stimulation of late growth, which is not only too immature to survive winter temperatures, but requires carbohydrates for its production thus depleting the plant's carbohydrate reserve and reducing its hardiness."

DR. ELDON W. LYLE, Plant Pathologist with the Texas Rose Research Foundation, reported in his November-December *Notes* that the new fungicide Funginex is recommended for control of blackspot, mildew and rust disease. His trials have shown 100 percent control of blackspot when the spray was started early in the season and continued at seven day intervals throughout the growing season. Another encouraging result was apparently perfect control of blackspot by spraying a combination of *Manzate* at half strength (one-half tablespoon per gallon) and *Funginex* every 14 days instead of weekly. No disease was evident at the beginning of the trials.

Partial control of mildew was effected on the variety Else Poulsen. Dr. Lyle cited *Funginex* (*Triforene 6.5 percent EC*) as giving better control of blackspot and mildew than anything being tested currently, providing it is applied every seven days with enough volume to reach the drip stage on the foliage. It also is important to start the use early in the season before the disease becomes evident.

ALFALFA MEAL continues to be the in food for roses and newly discovered by many rosarians. Actually, alfalfa has been used to revive soils for many years. High in protein, alfalfa meal breaks down in contact with soil organisms and somehow triggers the release of soil nutrients in forms available to plants. Few rosarians knew just how it worked, but enjoyed the results.

Now a report by Polysciences, Inc. (Warrington, PA) said *Triacontanol* is what makes it all work. Polysciences said *Triacontanol* is a naturally occurring straight chain alcohol present in the leaves of many plants, particularly alfalfa. It is cited as an extremely powerful plant growth stimulant, which can be used in very small amounts with dramatic increases in yields.

Coarsely ground alfalfa increased yields of field crops and by careful extraction procedures, researchers were able to establish that the active ingredient was *Triacontanol*. Charles Geiger of Tulsa shared this report and added that other trials of alfalfa were equally encouraging. Small quantities were reported to be most effective, following the general tendency of growth hormones to be effective over a narrow range of low concentration.

Geiger pointed out alfalfa is not a substitute for fertilizer or plant food, but when used in conjunction with sound basic practices of adequate and balanced fertilization, correct pH, good drainage and plenty of water, alfalfa will produce almost amazing results, particularly when used with manures.

HOW MUCH ALFALFA is enough? About two cups of alfalfa meal per established bush is the most common application rate, perhaps used twice in a long growing season. In construction of a new bud, add about SO pounds per *WO* square feet of rose bed.

The Rambler has used rough cut alfalfa meal per bush and in new beds and can report it works, for whatever reason. Healthier foliage, better stems, more breaks and overall vigor and that is what produces better roses. Try some alfalfa in 1981.

If you have misplaced your rose colored glasses for 1981, it is time to get them out, polish them up and go to work. Rose time is almost here. Roses and nature follow a schedule and rosarians get along better when they follow it, too.

REWORK OLD ROSE BEDS any time the soil can be worked. Trying to doctor up planting locations where roses have been removed just will not accomplish the same thing as an overall rejuvenation of the bed.

Even though some show winners are still growing in the old bed, they can easily be dug and transplanted for even better results. Most old rose beds become depleted as organic matter breaks down and the soil becomes tight. Mulch and other materials on the top just will not do the same job as working organics in the root zone. The more we feed, the faster beds wear out.

Heavy applications of nitrogen definitely use up the materials that bring life to the soil. Soils work with a balance of organic matter, air and water. As materials are broken down, soils become tighter and less able to support root systems. Rose growth gradually declines and fertilizer will not reverse the process. Rebuilding the whole bed produces the best results with the least effort.

REBUILD when plants are dormant, preferably just before the soil warms up. Dig the bushes to be saved with a spading fork. Do not prune or otherwise encourage new growth. Bury or cover with soil, sacks, straw or other material that will keep bushes cool and moist while the bed is being reworked. Try to preserve dormancy if at all possible.

It is safe to hold roses this way for two weeks or so if necessary. Rebuilding is just like building a new bed; a mixture of about one-third loamy soil, one-third compost or organic matter and one-third sand is about right for most areas.

Add some bone meal, rock phosphate or superphosphate (your choice) and thoroughly work into the bed and future root zone. Phosphates need to be placed where they will do some good -in the root zone. Add other ingredients sparingly, if at all. A reliable soil test may suggest some modifications, particularly if pH is off. But most of the time, addition of organic matter and sand will make most any soil productive again.

DO NOT ADD soluble fertilizers if the bed is to be replanted in a short time. It is safer to feed from the top when bushes have become established. Thoroughly mix several times with a fork, shovel or tiller. If the area is very large, a tiller is the best rental investment you will ever make. Deep cultivation with a three prong fork is also good. Wet down the bed area, turn again the next day. Two or three times is usually enough if you do a good job. Wet down the bed again to help settling and the rejuvenate rose bed is ready to plant.

TRANSPLANTING ROSES is just like handling bare root roses. Prune canes according to the usual practice for your climate. Wash off the roots and trim out any dead or broken parts. Trim root ends lightly to encourage callousing and new feeder roots. *Also* trim out any root galls or gall growth on the shank or bud union. If very large galls girdle the shank or involve many roots, throw them away and start over. It is more work to grow a sick plant than a good one.

ROSES START BETTER when planted the right way. The key is water. Thorough, deep soaking does the most good. When in doubt, use more water. Soaking overnight may not really be necessary, but it certainly does not seem to hurt. When repruning for planting, always drop the finished plants in a trash barrel of water and keep them there until actual planting. The last step is to fish the bush out of the water and place directly in the planting hole. Plan first, then plant. Do not scatter the bushes out in the bed because they dry out quickly. Move from water to soil and everything seems to work better.

WET WEATHER is a blessing when planting, but a little tough on the rosarian. Try to get new bushes into the ground just before or even during a rainy spell so the bushes become established with lots of water. Until feeder roots start, bushes must rely on moisture stored in the roots and canes. Warm, dry weather causes real stress. Canes can dry out before the roots are ready to go to work. That is the reason that canes of new or transplanted roses should be hilled up with soil to conserve moisture and maintain a constant, moderate temperature. Around here a muddy rosarian is probably a smart one, letting nature do part of the work. Do not be in a hurry to remove this protection either. Let rainfall and irrigation gradually uncover the canes.

CONE TYPE planting is easy. Support the root system with a cone of well prepared soil. Spread out the roots naturally. Cover the roots lightly and begin to run water slowly into the hole. Add some more soil. Water will begin to fill in the voids. While one bush is soaking, plant the next one. Then come back with more soil, water, etc. There is no need to tamp, let water do the work. If the cone or support is shaped properly, the bush will not tip or fall even before adding soil. Rootstocks make a difference, of course. Regardless of what you are planting, though, remember to let the roots do what comes naturally and the bush will have a good foundation.

GOOD PLANTING is a hand-and-knees project. If the soil is right, one hand with a short shovel will form a hole, shape a cone and have a bush in position in no time. It grows better, too, with this extra attention.

MAR. 1981

THOUGHT FOR THE MONTH: A successful rosarian is one who manages to keep plants alive until nature has time to cure them.

There is an old saying that goes "there's nothing that succeeds like success," so here is a collection of success stories that may have applications in your rose patch. The Rambler has picked these up from all over the country and is confident — if there is such a thing as confidence in rose growing — they will work.

Sandy rose beds just have to be the greatest thing for rosarians since reliable fungicides if the results in the Rambler's one-third sharp sand, one-third organic matter and one-third garden soil rose beds are to be believed.

Nothing stays the same in that garden very long, so when a rose bed built in early 1979 had to be removed and reshaped, some 40 very large rosebushes were dug in January to be held in a dormant condition pending a new location.

Dug carefully with a spading fork, the bushes had masses of fine feeder roots that went in all directions. The roots held a substantial amount of soil mix, did not break and none showed signs of root or crown gall. These were 1 grade plants set out in February 1979. Both root production and top production were outstanding. All plants were Multiflora rootstock.

The sandy soil mix has since been moved to a new built-up rose bed, some horse manure-wood shavings added for organic matter and urged along with about 50 pounds of rough cut alfalfa meal per 100 square feet of rose bed. It is light, friable and feels and smells like good soil. Transplants and new bushes should take right off.

Alfalfa meal has definitely become the "in" treatment for roses. It really does encourage growth and good leaf production when used in conjunction with organic matter and a regular feeding program. Check the January 1981 Rambler column for details on just how it works. If you want to try some — about two cups per established plant — check out the feed stores in your area.

Alfalfa meal is used in specialty poultry and horse feed mixes and is generally in 50 pound bags. If they do not have it on hand, most feed stores can order from a regional supplier. If you cannot wait and do not mind paying a little more, alfalfa pellets will work all right, too. Pellets are a fairly common rabbit feed. Pellets take a little longer to break down and should not be applied as generously as meal.

Built-up rose beds do work, even in very severe climates. Held in place by a variety of edgings ranging from bricks to blocks to treated lumber to railroad ties, these beds drained better and consistently grew better roses than their lawn level counterparts.

There are exceptions, of course, such as plantings on hillsides or topsoil over a drained, sandy base. But raised beds generally had fewer problems and were easier to maintain. Winter hardiness of roses in raised beds does not seem to be a problem. They enjoy a survival rate equal to or better than lower plantings, probably because of better overall vigor.

Tree roses in tubs and planters have a place in most gardens, even in severe climates. While a tree rose investment is substantial, it is worth every dollar in beauty. Use tree roses as garden and patio accents during the summer and move into a garage or garden shed during the winter.

For severe climates, trees can be pulled from planters (they form a big ball of roots) and buried something like the Minnesota Tip method. For it really sensational accent, plant some miniature roses around the base of the tree roses.

The planter secret is the soil mix with good drainage, air in the root zone and ability to retain moisture. Reliable and easy to prepare is a mix of one-third garden soil, one-third Canadian peat moss and one-third calcined clay granules (kitty litter). Use the granule kind without additives. Greenhouse and nursery supply stores have it.

Calcined clay is used extensively by greenhouse professionals and groundskeepers. Calcined clay granules are extremely porous, something like a microscopic honeycomb. They take in moisture for slow release to feeder roots without souring, packing or breaking down.

Some growers like to add some sharp sand for even better porosity. Makes a great general purpose potting mix, too. Just pick out a spot in a corner of the yard on some paving bricks or boards. Make a big pile of the ingredients, mix and sift and mix again. Moisten and let stand for a week or so. Mix again lightly and the result is available for most potting jobs.

Success with fungicides seems to vary and

for no apparent reason. Far more gardens show excellent control of blackspot and mildew with regular applications of *Funginex* or *Triforine* than reported failures. Good success has been reported with a combination of full strength *Funginex* and one-half tablespoon per gallon of *Manzate* used every 14 days. Residual protection improved appreciably.

The *Triforene-Funginex* success stories had one theme in common: thorough spray wetting every seven days. No deviation whatsoever in the schedule beginning at time of pruning and continuing until killing frost. The schedule could be extended during very hot, dry conditions in mid-summer but watched carefully.

The fungicide protection program that is not applied will not do much good. Application must be made regularly to the dripping stage. Many kinds of equipment can be used for applying the material. Just make sure the leaves are wetted well. No spreader sticker is ordinarily needed, but if the water is highly alkaline, try adding about a tablespoon of ordinary household vinegar per gallon of water. Wetting is considerably improved. But most importantly, apply weekly and enjoy real success in 1981.

I noticed a quote in a horticultural magazine recently that deserves repeat for rosarians, "People rarely succeed at anything unless they have fun doing it."

These columns have said the same thing over and over — that roses are supposed to be fun. When we lose sight of the fact that this is a hobby, the whole thing becomes a burden. How about a theme Rose Fun in '81? Here are some easy and fun ways to make it happen.

INTENSIVE CARE FOR ROSES? Not a bad idea if a plant is sick, delivered late or just in need of some special consideration. The best way is to pot up those problem roses in five gallon containers and locate them somewhere where they will get lots of attention. You will be surprised how they will perk up. There are several good reasons why it works.

Roses in pots develop masses of roots that are able to take up the water and fertilizer when applied more regularly. The roots developed because the soil warmed up faster and stayed warmer. The pot also had better drainage and hence better aeration to support the roots.

It has been a good trick for years to start new bushes in pots to develop the roots before placing them in rose beds in competition with mature plants. Why not keep some roses in pots all the time for variety as well as practical purposes?

A POTTING SOIL MIX is about the same as that for tree roses in containers -one-third garden soil, one-third humus material sharpened with a little sand and one-third calcined clay granules. If you do not have any calcined clay handy, use more humus and sand. You will have to water a little more often with this lighter mix (every day during hot weather), but you will enjoy great results.

The choice of pots is up to you. Clay pots are more attractive, but heavier to move. Black plastic is good, soil warms up quickly. Even metal cans are good for a season or two. Cedar and redwood are best of all, but are expensive, even when you build the boxes yourself.

For winter protection, pull the rose out of the pot and bury it, just like the Minnesota Tip. Safely covered with six or eight inches of soil and leaves, the pampered plants will be ready to go back into pots, or conventional beds, in the spring. You will enjoy roses on the patio this year if you give them a try.

PROBLEMS WITH GALLS seem to possess some rosarians. Roses have had galls for a long time and will continue to have growths of various kinds, but not necessarily disabling.

All of us have had huge plants that have been masses of galls, but they still grew and had roses. There is no point in getting uptight about infection and all sorts of other things that might happen. When we talk about galls and cankers, we drive away the prospective rose growers we are trying to attract.

Talk about all the rose plants that do not have galls and the bushels of beauty they produce. If a few plants give up the ghost to galls, look at it as a good opportunity to try something new without having to expand the rose beds. Three or four years production from a $7 plant is still a good investment in beauty.

FEWER GALLS are noticed, or are disabling, in light, sandy soils. Bud unions and shanks seem to have fewer galls, or they dry up, when they are exposed to sunlight. High humus, acid soils appear to support more gall-like growth.

If you want to perform a little surgery, trim them off. Paint on some disinfectant if you like, but so far no one has been able to clinically demonstrate that this does any good.

ALL PURPOSE, DO EVERYTHING spray mixture continue to do more harm than good. It is unbelievable the things that some rose people put into one mixture. It seems that some should explode rather than protect leaves and roses from fungus and insects.

The Rambler believes in spraying for specific problems with one thing at a time. Sprays may be compatible, but that does not mean they are good for foliage. One spray material at a time results in less burn and happier roses.

If your plants really need an overall application of insecticide at the same time a fungicide application is due, mix up a batch of *Orthene* and *Funginex* and thoroughly wet the leaves. Then do not use insecticides of any kind again until or unless you have a really serious problem. Then use the recommended material at recommended strength. You will wind up with lots more leaves

-and many more roses -at the end of the season.

PRUNING MINIATURES? THINK SMALL. Start with small pruning shears like the *Corona Mini-Shear No.6*. Cut back all canes and growth to about six inches, or to wherever it is alive, depending on the growth habit and vigor of the plant. Cut out all of the really, old woody canes.

Miniatures are on their own roots and hard pruning is a must for quality blooms and well-shaped plants. New growth keeps miniatures young and blooming.

Some growers even advocate the hedge shear method of pruning. This is essentially the method that commercial propagators use. However, the serious miniature hobbyist can usually take time to selectively groom and prune to the best eyes on the most productive canes.

NEED SOME GOOD HELP? Get into the garden of another rosarian or call one of the Consulting Rosarians in your area for a chance to swap rose stories. We often overlook the very best advice because" we are too close to it. Not that all CR's are always right, but they have had the experience to assist in many ways. You will find that roses are more fun than ever.

Meantime, out in the rose garden, all kinds of good things are happening. It is worthwhile to think through the reason why the roses are doing well. It is the way to make sure that good things continue. Here are some solid rose practices that the Rambler knows will work and that you should find out for yourself.

Water, not fertilizer makes roses grow. The best plant food will not do a bit of good until it is in solution and in the root zone of the plant. Pelletized fertilizers are great if there is a regular, ample supply of water to dissolve the material and carry the nutrients to the roots.

For a faster start, get food into solution and soak the roots. Old timers know deep soaking before using any food, liquid or dry, also speeds up the process. For a real shock, try dissolving your favorite dry rose food in water. It may be less soluble than you think.

Take your choice: *Manzate, Benlate, Phaltan* or *Triforine*, but none of these will do any good unless applied consistently and effectively. Most fungicides get a bad reputation because they are not used, not because they are ineffective products.

Any of the above are excellent fungicides. Use the one that suits your particular needs best. *Triforine*, marketed in a 6.5 percent formulation by *Ortho* as *Funginex*, is probably best for small gardens. It is very easy to use, safe for roses and rosarians and readily available. It is a bit expensive for a large spread. Use on a weekly basis, just like the directions say.

A very large garden might use alternative fungicides like *Phaltan* in the spring when temperatures are lower, switching to *Funginex* for no residue during exhibition time followed by *Manzate-Benlate* or *Benlate* alone when temperatures exceed 80 degrees. In the fall when mildew is more prevalent, switch to Phaltan or *Funginex*. Just make sure that a regular schedule is followed.

Alfalfa meal for roses seems to have caught on. Questions are still coming in about sources, combination materials, pellets vs. meal and how much to use. Here are the basic facts: alfalfa meal, or pellet form, is 17 percent protein from most sources, the balance is fiber and fat. Use a cup or so per established plant and scratch into the soil.

Combination feeds may create a problem. Look for alfalfa feed used for rabbits or horses. A farm feed· supply store will have alfalfa in one form or another and most of them have some other organics that are good for gardens. Just think of alfalfa meal as being a much more convenient source than keeping a horse. The end product is the same.

Last summer's drought made more rosarians aware of watering systems and water conservation. As a starter, back yard rosarians should look into the *Dramm* nozzle irrigation system, a cheap and easy way to put water where it will do some good. It is easy to build, almost anyone can have a system running during a weekend.

It is a two piece nozzle of hard plastic with a tapered thread that screws into rigid plastic pipe. A pin diffuser sprays water in a full circle parallel to the rose bed. Water sprays out, not up. Distribution is even, easily controlled without waste.

Saves time, too. A rose bed 40 feet long and five feet wide can be soaked in about 20 minutes. Miniatures thrive on a *Dramm* system. The flat, fine spray washes off mites and creates 100 percent humidity.

Use schedule 40 PVC pipe, either one-half or five-eighths inch. Connections, elbows, tees and adapters are available at most lumber yards, hardware stores or plumbing shops. PVC pipe cuts easily with a hacksaw. All connections are made with PVC cement.

It is very easy to work with, even for a beginner. Lay the pipe system on the surface of the rose bed, connect to a water hose with a quick coupler. About 45 pounds of house pressure will supply a one-half inch, 40 foot irrigating line with 15 to 18 nozzles. Each nozzle will spray an area from three to four feet in diameter, depending on pressure.

Control volume and spread at the house tap or install a valve at the head of each line. Runs longer than 40 feet may require five-eighths inch pipe to deliver enough volume for consistent patterns.

Dramm nozzles are inserted into PVC pipe with a tapered neoprene washer. Drill holes (15/32 inch) at nozzle locations in the pipe, spacing about two feet apart or custom fit to plants. Clean drilled hole and insert tapered washer and screw in the nozzle. The nozzle is also threaded and tapered, two or three turns by hand will give a tight fit. All the connections can be made without tools, just like a hose connection.

Stabilize the pipe system with sleepers, a leg formed by a tee connection and inserted into the rose bed. A leg on each end, and sometimes in the middle, is good. Maintenance is easy.

If a nozzle has an uneven spray or stops up, pull the deflecting pin and a thin stream of water shoots straight up and clears most junk out of the line. For a serious obstruction, unscrew the top half of the nozzle and the whole system can be flushed out. The flushing process can be done while the water is on, usually without getting wet. Lift and drain during winter months. Take out the nozzles and store.

Cheap, too. Nozzle and washer cost about 75 cents. They are available from many greenhouse supply companies, who also have many other good things for rosarians. It you cannot find a local source, try mail order from *Kimbrew-Walter Roses* or from *Rose Keepers*, both advertisers in *American Rose*. Detailed instructions and diagrams are sent with each order.

If you install a *Dramm* system in just one bed, you will soon covert the whole garden. It really works and saves water too, For a demonstration, stop by the Rambler's garden anytime.

Why is it that the most interesting rose topics are usually discussed during "refreshment time" at rose society meetings rather than during the program? It seems that coffee and rose talk just go together. Wouldn't it be great to share some of this "hands-on" experience with everyone at a workshop session? Call it a "Garden Collection" that might go something like this...

A SPECIFIC FOR SPIDER MITES. Water, just plain water is still the safest and best for most growers. If you have a water wand, use it. If not, make one or use some kind of spray nozzle to direct a strong, fine spray under the leaves and through the plant. Water washes off the mites, breaks up the webs and if used soon enough and often enough will keep a garden clean even during the hottest weather. If water just WON'T work, try *Vendex* (now conveniently available in most areas as *Orthomite*). It has a long residual and Should be used no more often than 28 days. Just remember that insecticide applications tend to be habit-forming; use water if at all possible and let nature handle the problem.

THRIPS, MILLIONS OF THEM. Where do they come from? From the grasses, fields, host plants, from EVERYWHERE during warm spring weather. Thrips come in waves to particularly damage light-colored, fragrant buds and blooms. These tiny, tan insects can be seen moving inside blooms; they do their damage by bruising tender petals as they suck juices from the tissue. Blooms turn brown on the edges; buds sometimes will not open at all. To control thrips, spray where they are; on the buds and blooms. Lightly mist the tops of the bushes only with *Orthene* or *Cygon*. During heavy infestation, twice a week may be necessary. Don't spray ALL the plant. But DO spray other host plants and blooms like lilies, amaryllis, gladiolas and other light colored, fragrant flowers. As the summer heats up, thrips usually move on. Until then, spot control is the best answer.

OVERFED ROSES CAN BE SAVED. Somehow the grower made a mistake... new leaves turn crisp and the bush looks like it is going into a crisis. Just flush the excess out of the root zone with plenty of water, assuming there's some place for the excess water to go. Water is the best and only treatment; flood generously and often and

let nature get things back into balance. If clay soil is too tight for good drainage, add some gypsum to help the process along. The same advice applies to excess foliar food and spray combinations. Wash off the leaves and let the sun-leaf process work again.

MINIATURE ROSES GOT A LATE START? It's not too late to have an outstanding miniature rose display this season since miniatures can be planted almost anytime the temperature is over freezing and under boiling. Mini propagators have come up with some good shipping techniques to make it possible to order and get plants in good condition, even in mid-summer. Once received, some careful handling will help ease the shock. A recently-rooted miniature plant in a 2-inch pot needs to be transferred to a 5-inch or larger pot in a soil mix that's compatible with the final growing spot. Protect the new mini in a shaded spot for two weeks or so, gradually exposing to more sun and higher temperature. When new growth has started well, transfer carefully to the mini bed or planter box. And don't be afraid to trim minis back. The result will be a healthier, bushier plant that will support more blooms.

LETHARGIC MINIS? Maybe yellow leaves and not much new growth? It's fairly common with miniatures in pots. Check drainage first; fine roots in soggy soil can't produce. If water and air move freely through the soil, regular light feedings with an organic fertilizer will usually bring the plants around. Atlas Fish Emulsion is a good one. Seems to make the whole process work better. Another trick; some stale beer on a potted miniature will bring green to the leaves and roses to the stems. Cow tea works, too. Just let nature get things back into balance.

NEED CULTIVAR INFORMATION? Our good friend Beverly Dobson has done a yeoman's job in compiling her new *COMBINED ROSE LIST, 1981*. This booklet includes *Roses in Commerce and Cultivation, Rose Registrations Since MODERN ROSES 8* and *Hard-to-Find Roses and Where to Find Them*. The price of the booklet is a bargain at $3.50. Order from Beverly Dobson, 215 Harriman Road, Irvington, NY 10533.

ROSE HYBRIDIZERS ASSOCIATION. If you are really interested in roses, you'll be interested in the work of the Rose Hybridizers Association. RHA has some 600 members scattered across the country (as well as foreign) and all of them are interested in sharing information on hybridizing, parents, tricks and trials in creating your OWN rose. RHS has a regional organization, chairmen who direct all sorts of services and the very best quarterly Newsletter you'll find anywhere. The contents are of rose annual quality every issue. The Spring, 1981 issue had no less than 18 authors, news and announcements, lists of plant hunters (and providers), places to write for all kinds of rose support materials, and all presented in a lively, readable style. Convinced? To join, annual membership dues in the USA are just $4.00 Send to Beverly Dobson, RHA Secretary-Treasurer, 215 Harriman Road, Irvington, NY 10533. You'll be glad you did.

TIME RELEASE FERTILIZERS. Products like *Osmocote*, *Precise* and others are great for many rosarians. It's the easy way to feed roses the right amount of all the time. With some do-it-yourself supplements, roses will thrive. Choose a shorter release time for short growing seasons; longer release for warmer climates. Gives a rose grower more time to enjoy roses… and that's what this is all about.

JUL. 1981

THOUGHT FOR THE MONTH:
Tell me, I'll forget. Show me, I may remember. Involve me, and I'll understand.

To really know what's going on, get out on a garden tour. You'll be amazed at just how much you don't know about roses. At least that's the Rambler's experience, so here are some odds and ends picked up in the gardens this summer.

MINIATURES GROW... particularly when budded on Fortuniana understock as they are in many parts of Florida. Budding accomplishes two things for those hot-weather growers; it gets the plants up and off the ground for better spider mite control and also produces full, bushy plants up to three feet in diameter. Size alone is not the important thing, but the ability to water-wash or spray the underside of a densely leafed bush is vital. Spider mites apparently live and breed continuously in that frost-free environment so their control is a constant problem. And it is a sight to see a miniature like Chipper or Red Flush the size of a medium-size shrub and covered with blooms.

ROSES IN SAND... another Florida growing requirement. Plenty of good drainage; the trick is to hold the water long enough for the roots to pick up. There are plenty of organic rose growers in Florida, incorporating every form of humus imaginable for rose beds. About half sand 'and half compost, manure, peat moss or whatever seems" to be a common formula. A thick layer of mulch is then added on top of the rose planting area and the whole thing is covered with three or four inches of pine needles for insulation and water conservation. The overall effect is very pleasing and garden visitors can walk in and through the rose bushes without packing or otherwise damaging the bed (the roses are planted on about five-foot centers). Except for having to cut some of the blooms from a step ladder, it's the kind of growing that most any rosarian can enjoy.

HANGING BASKETS... miniature roses in hanging baskets are coming on strong in many parts of the country. They make a striking addition to the garden and are surprisingly easy to maintain once the grower gets the hang of it. With so many good miniatures particularly suited for baskets, it's a shame" more growers don't try a few. The secret is in making up a well drained soil mix that will retain moisture for the fine, hairy roots to pick up. Some soilless mixes work well, but the ordinary grower can make up a batch of 1/3 sand, 1/3 light soil and 1/3 compost that will work quite well. Addition of some vermiculite or *perlite* is all right, too. For a good start, just a touch of *Osmocote* in the mix releases slowly and steadily. Hang the baskets in filtered light in very hot climates; don't let the soil mix dry out at any time. About every two weeks, feed with a dilute soluble rose food like *Carl Pool* or *Peters*. Atlas Fish Emulsion is also good but may add an aroma to the patio that you don't want. Use about three miniature plants for a twelve-inch basket; it will fill out faster and cover more evenly. In cold climates, the baskets can be buried in soil and mulch; they will come through the winter in good shape provided that some moisture is available. The Rambler's favorites are Green Ice and Sugar Elf, but there are many others to choose from.

FEED DURING THE SUMMER even in very hot climates, if any source of water is available at all. Hot climate rosarians have thought for years that roses should rest during very hot weather, but that's really not true. If water is no problem, feed light amounts more frequently and enjoy blooms and foliage all the time. The plants also go into fall better able to produce a bumper crop of show-stoppers. Miniatures particularly thrive on a regular, light diet. It is much harder to bring a miniature out of a slump than to keep it busy all summer.

HOT WEATHER SPRAYING can be a problem, but not if a little rose-sense is applied. There's not much sense in spraying to save the leaves if the spray does the job instead of the blackspot. Water roses thoroughly BEFORE spraying and allow enough time for the roots to move the moisture to the leaves. Dry, limp rose leaves will burn; turgid leaves tolerate spray material better. A good practice is to deep-water in the evening and spray early in the morning. Some prefer to water in the morning and spray during the cool-of evening; but leaves seem to have less substance with this routine, having lost some of the moisture through transpiration during the day. Avoid the middle of the day if possible; even plain water can burn and coarsen leaves in intense heat. One spray material at a time is safer, too. Combinations of otherwise safe materials can create a problem. You'll recognize spray burn when leaves suddenly turn clear yellow about three or four days after spraying. The leaves will hang on the plant for a while and then drop off, pushed off by a new crop ready to go to work.

The appearance of spray burn is entirely different from leaves lost to spider mites. Leaves affected by spiders look dry, sometimes turn gray-brown and when completely dried out, will fall off. Mites suck the moisture out of leaves, an effect something like the drying and ageing of leaves in the fall. If mites are suspected, check the undersides carefully and look for gritty gray, black and white specks, similar to a mix of salt and pepper. Wash and/or spray as you prefer, but do it right away.

ROSES AND ROSARIANS... both enjoy the effects of a "*Bug Zapper*", an electronic light-grid that attracts and electrocutes all manner of flying insects. Bug grids come in various sizes, and some will clear a very large area of flying pests. You'll be surprised at the pile of insects eliminated by a grid in just one evening. And you'll be pleasantly surprised at how good it can be on the patio without mosquitoes. Helps control corn ear worms, too, by eliminating the moth that lays the eggs. Treat yourself to a *Zapper* if you don't have one; it's just like watching Star Wars, as my friend Harm Saville commented recently.

Shared ideas make roses grow... most of them not particularly scientific but practical and adaptable for every part of the country. Perhaps you can make good use of some of these observations (maybe changed just a little) and keep the chain of fun and roses going.

ROSE GARDEN TRIALS. What happens when something new is tried? Was a check (untreated) comparison made? Few rosarians have the space (or patience) to compare methods so we enjoy success without ever knowing just what caused it. Without being too technical, here are some observations made over the past three seasons by the Rambler working with rose beds started from scratch.

ALFALFA MEAL (OR PELLETS) WORKS. However, a high organic, manure-rich rose bed seems to produce about as well. In all comparisons, rose beds for miniatures, hybrid teas or floribundas incorporating alfalfa meal supported better roses with greener leaves and more breaks than beds without it. Alfalfa-enriched beds performed equally well with a number of different feeding programs. Some of the feeding programs used highly soluble inorganics, others used slower acting organic-inorganic combinations. All of the processes seemed to work better when alfalfa meal was used in bed preparation (about 50 pounds per 100 square feet) and then fed in spring and fall at about one cup per established plant. Heavier applications did not seem to help, although no damage was done either. And it does not seem to make any difference if the alfalfa is in meal or pellet form. Pellets are easier to use but just a bit more expensive (easier to find, too). Anyway, make your own comparisons.

ORGANICS WORK WELL, TOO. Maybe it is because the manure mixtures had some alfalfa incorporated. The basic mix used 1/3 existing soil, 1/3 sand or very sandy loam and 1/3 organic matter from a horse stable. The partially composted stable material had wood shavings, straw, hay/grain spills and manure. It really made roses grow... and was useful as a top mulch, too. This bed produced just as much as the bed to which alfalfa was added. And after three years, the overall composition is just as light and friable as at the time originally planted. That's great for roots to spread out and support the plant.

FEEDING. Rose beds fed with an inorganic 15-5-10 formula with trace elements matched or exceeded the performance of specialty 14-12-11 formulas or mixes of the commonly recommended 1-2-1 ratios. Most parts of the country have a regional supplier of lawn formulas, generally high in nitrogen with some trace elements. And at a substantially lower price than "specialty" mixes. The food cited here is a "lawn special" with iron, zinc and magnesium. It is very soluble and is safely used on the Gulf Coast at about two ounces per plant per month. Heavy rainfall leaches nitrogen; this formula restores the ingredients for growth.

SLOWER ACTING ORGANICS are useful in some situations without giving up growth or blooms. A rose bed subject to heavy watering three times a week by a sprinkler system was fed with a 14-12-11 organic base on an every-six-weeks basis and the bushes performed very well. The bed was also mulched with three inches of stable manure and wood shavings... not composted at all. This probably controlled the release of nutrients to some degree?

SELECT FEEDING PROGRAMS that fit your climate and growing conditions. For example, late season use of slow acting fertilizers is not wise in a cold climate. Feeding encourages new growth, and new growth freezes and weakens the bush. Light application of a highly soluble food may be safe since it is less likely to encourage late growth. And light applications of any material are always in order. It gives the rosarian time to make up for a mistake. Liquid applications bring out the most dramatic results; in solution the nutrients reach the root zone immediately and are available for conversion to a form useful to the bush. Buckets of formula are heavy and time consuming, but the plant performance can make up for all the work. There's one easy way to apply liquids with a hose on lawn sprayer. Products like *Ra-Pid-Gro* or *Carl Pool Instant* can be dissolved and used in a syphon jar, measuring out the right amount of diluted mix by counting the number -of seconds required to apply a gallon to the soil. Make a "dry run" first. Fill the syphon jar with plain water and attach to the hose. Turn on the hose full pressure. Put your thumb over the bypass hole, activating the syphon.

Count the number of seconds it takes to meter out a gallon. Use the same timing to meter out the mix and then give each plant some plain water, too. You'll see results in a hurry.

MINIATURES PREFER a light, regular diet, even during very hot weather. Minis will grow all the time if given a chance. They respond very quickly to any treatment. There are a number of specialty, soluble formulas available around the country; the favorite in this area is *Carl Pool*. But *Schultz, Peters* and *Atlas* formulas elsewhere are just as good. The Rambler gets best results with a combination of organic (fish emulsion) and inorganic (*Carl Pool*). To maintain good healthy growth with green leaves and lots of blooms, start with one ounce of fish emulsion in a gallon of water and soil soak about three large minis. Use fish about every six weeks. About two weeks before a rose show, use *Carl Pool* (9-56-8) to bring out color and bloom. Minis don't like to be overfed; watch for vegetative centers and poor form, usually a sign of too much nitrogen... just too much food. If this happens, cut down concentration and perhaps frequency. Your particular growing conditions will control your feeding program.

Harvest month for rosarians has finally arrived… your buckets of roses should be overflowing… Except for that first spring bloom, fall roses can be the best of all. If your buckets are less than full, make a check list of rose happenings during the past season and come up with plans and practices that will payoff next year. Right NOW you should be planning (and doing some digging) of new rose beds for the future. Good roses aren't· grown by accident; rose bed preparation is the first (and probably the most important) step in rose production.

LEAVES AND OTHER COMPOSTING materials will be plentiful for most growers within the next month or so. It's a rich harvest and should be made available for roses with some sort of compost pile even if all the leafy production can't be used. Experience the benefits of compost just once and you'll find space for more leaves next year. If no space at all is available for a compost pile or rick, use a vegetable garden area or maybe the spot where the new rose garden is to be.

COMPOSTING IN PLACE is easy. Just turn and dig the soil in the bed area making a wind-row of soil. Pile leaves, clippings, etc. in the depressed trench and add some excess soil on top as a dressing. Add a good source of nitrogen like manure or cottonseed ·meal to the leaves to make the whole process work faster. Keep moist and turn lightly every two weeks. Add some more leaves as the pile goes down. Before hard-freeze time, the composting material should be broken down enough to till and mix in place or add to other bed areas. Composting season can be stretched a bit by covering trench or pile with black plastic to hold heat. It works even in freezing weather.

MIRACLE CURES are seldom miracles. A new crop of "stabilized micro-organisms" or what-have-you hits the market every season promising to "make dead soils alive again" .and put billions of nature's microscopic workers on the side of the gardener. Serious trials of several of these "miracles" produced no dramatic results. Roses in check beds did just as well as those treated according to directions. However, in all fairness to the formulators, the additives were used in beds already in excellent condition with good balance of humus, air, soil and water. Rose beds with plenty of humus and manure produced the best roses more consistently than tighter soils or soils low in organic matter.

ROSE BEDS GET TIRED, too, near the end of a long season. There's a good chance that all they need is a little light cultivation from time to time to help move water and air in the soil. Mulches and some soils tend to pack from rainfall and sunshine. Breaking up the crust lets water and air through again and mechanically mixes some of the humus product of the mulch with top soil. A four-tine cultivator penetrating an inch or so deep is about right.

TIGHT SOILS open up with a spading fork, too. Punch some small holes around the drip line of the bush with a fork, the four-prong kind that's about six inches long. Spade in all the way and work back and forth a few times. Fertilizers, water and air can get into the root zone faster; it's particularly good for slow-moving rock phosphate or superphosphate to get to where the: work is being done. Give each bush three or four good jabs; it's a good practice most anytime.

CALCINED CLAY granules make a great soil conditioner in addition to or in place or some organic material. Each granule is like a tiny sponge with air spaces and tremendous water holding capability. It's Widely sold as *Terra-Green*, a trademark of the Oil-Dri Corporation. A soil mix with one-quarter *Terra-Green* will grow almost anything. Many nursery people use it for rooting cuttings with NO other additives. Available in 50 pound bags at greenhouse supply firms.

COARSE PERLITE is a great product, too. It's a good conditioner for rose beds and a useful additive for many light potting mixes. Miniature rose potting mixes commonly have *Perlite* as a major component. Here's another use; a wet soggy stretch of lawn that refuses to drain or dry out will respond to an "injection" of *Perlite*. Use a spading fork and aerate the wet area, spading as deep as the prongs will go; rock the fork back and forth. Do a small area; then broadcast *Perlite* and rake to fill up the holes. The result: better drainage, more air, more lawn. A wet, rotting lawn can be restored in a few weeks.

FROM THE RAMBLER'S GARDEN DIARY… Planting new roses in mid-summer sounds next to impossible... but not with miniatures. Miniatures in four-inch pots were set out in full sun without a yellow leaf or sign of stress. Bloom cycle continued without interruption. The four-inch pot method is a good way to reduce shock for newly-rooted minis or plants in very small pots. They seem to grow faster and mature better in four-inch pots compared to direct bed planting. Four to six weeks in the larger pot under controlled conditions is all that it takes. Light feeding, regular watering, vigorous plants.

I learned a lesson (again) the hard way that rose beds need to be watered thoroughly BEFORE feeding as well as after feeding. Thinking that the soil looked moist enough, about two ounces of 15-5-10 broadcast per plant and then watered in resulted in yellow and burned lower leaves in four days. Similar applications to soaked beds brought on only new growth. As the Thought for the Month once said, "Experience is the name we give to our mistakes."

Indian Summer has arrived in most parts of the country, described by Webster as "a happy and flourishing period occurring toward the end of something." With this pleasant period at hand, you should be noticing that roses are happier and somehow more beautiful with a harvest that's bigger, better and more colorful. But Indian Summer is not an end, just a pleasant time to enjoy roses arid plan for the future... maybe you'll include some of these items in your plans.

MOUNDS OF LEAVES become a problem for many rosarians this month... a very pleasant problem to have. Too many otherwise sharp rosarians pass up this harvest, thinking that they don't have the equipment or the space to use nature's bounty. Used for winter protection or for composting, leaves return far more to the garden than the small amount of work required to make them effective.

COMPOSTING is easy. Equipment for the job is already in the garage (the rotary lawnmower) and the now-cleared garden patch is the place to let nature do its job. Just rake up the excess leaves in a sort of wind-row on an open space of lawn. The rows can be three or four feet wide and several inches deep. Dampen the leaves a little with a spray from the hose to keep them from blowing all over and the dust down. Start up the rotary lawnmower, leave off the catcher bag, and run the mower in a "U" pattern around the rows of leaves. Reverse the direction and repeat the process until shredding is complete. The result will be two neat rows of well-chopped organic material ready for composting in the garden area. If you're anxious for fast results (but why hurry) add some cheap source of nitrogen to the pile, dampen slightly and cover with plastic to conserve heat. Turn the pile now and then for a mix that's better than anything you can buy.

LEAVES make great insulating material, too. Winter protection is simply a matter of preventing the freezing-thawing cycle and drying out of rose canes. Leaves can do the job very well. A mound of soil or compost over the bud union and lower canes pills lots of leaves will keep most roses in good shape with temperature ranges from 20 below to 20 above, complicated with cold, dry winds and strong sunshine. Leaves make an ideal insulating material, just devise some means of keeping them in place. Wire baskets, rabbit-wire fences, evergreen boughs or even short snow fence will help keep leaves in place. Some cold-climate rosarians even use a combination of cones and leaves for protection, the leaves serving as a sort of protective insulation for the cones and maintaining a more even temperature.

REALLY COLD CLIMATES may require burying roses in soil where freeze-thaw and drying are eliminated. But most areas do very well with addition of soil over the bud union and an insulating blanket by nature. This note from a reader is typical of comments on natural winter protection reporting, "I don't have the time or energy to build boxes or bury, so I have always thrown on some dirt from the garden area and piled on leaves as high as they would go. Even get some leaves from the neighbors. It's not very fancy, but my roses always do all right."

WINTERKILL should often be called summerkill, because a weakened rose, poorly cared for, is much less likely to make it through a cold winter. The best winter protection can't make up for poor summer care. A very common mistake is feeding late in the season to "get the bushes going again". Late season feeding produces new green growth that is subject to dieback and winterkill. Gradual dormancy is important, setting the rose time clock for cold weather ahead. The same rule applies to growers in moderate climates, too. A cold snap in December damages green canes and starts a chain reaction of dieback the following spring.

STOP FEEDING about eight weeks before cold weather arrives. As the season winds down, leave spent blooms on the bush and gradually reduce water. The result will be a rose bush more able to take winter weather naturally. Given a chance, nature will usually do a good job.

MINIATURES are particularly easy to carry through the winter. Most growers virtually bury the plants with a mix of soil, leaves and compost. The small canes help hold the insulation in place so that the freeze-thaw cycle does not occur. Mixtures of materials work best, allowing some air space. Just be careful not to uncover too early in the spring. Even minis in pots and planters can be protected by storing in a spot out of the wind and covering with leaves. Lath fence or snow fence makes a good barrier for such collections, and is a good idea for free-form beds or rose areas subject to winter winds. Anything that will help nature do its job helps roses.

There's a respected old-timer in this area who makes a lot of rose sense. In a recent talk, he advised that "the really GOOD roses are grown in November and December when rose nuts aren't distracted by the blooms." Which seems like a contradiction, but he is right on target as usual. Late fall calls for winter protection (if you need it), rose bed preparation and variety planning. A poor job now usually means poor roses in the spring.

WINTER PROTECTION doesn't have to be fancy, just do what comes naturally. Nature conditions plants for cold, storing strength for the spring that's sure to come. The natural way to protect is with soil and leaves or combinations of materials that breathe and adjust to changing conditions. Cones, wraps, baskets and barriers are not in the same league as Mother Nature. Whatever method you like, think a bit about how nature might use the materials to best advantage.

ROSES IN POTS, TUBS AND PLANTERS, need some winter protection in most areas, but make sure that the protection "breathes." A tub-grown rose goes through a dormancy in the same way a ground-planted rose does. If possible, move tubs and planters into an unheated garage after the first good frost. Wrap tree rose standards and bud unions with loose insulating material, feed sacks or old blankets. Don't cover with plastic. Let dormancy occur as naturally as possible; avoid sharp changes in temperature. When the tubs get too dry, add some water. Roses are woody plants that will tolerate a wide temperature range if permitted to adjust naturally. Rosarians (and roses) get into trouble when nature is left out of the formula.

NEW OR REBUILT rose beds need some time to settle and mellow before spring planting. Some freezing and thawing, settling and draining, washing and blowing for a few months can tell a good deal about how a bed will perform under growing conditions. It's better to find out early that the drainage is no good and not after the new plants have turned yellow. A poor winter bed is an even poorer spring bed.

HERBICIDES AND ROSES ordinarily do not get along, but a product called *ROUNDUP* promises to be a real help to rosarians. It's great for edging rose beds, walkways or other plantings; almost any place where weed or grass control is needed. *Roundup* works on green plant material only, translocating in the plant to kill the root as well as the top. It dissipates very quickly without soil contamination. It handles creeping grasses (Bermuda, Centipede, etc.), most common weeds, even nutgrass.

ROSES CAN BE PLANTED in *Roundup*-treated areas shortly after application. In an extreme case, *Roundup* was used to kill a healthy stand of Bermuda grass for a new rose planting. Five days after application, forms were set for a built-up bed and soil added without disturbing the old lawn area. Roses were planted the following day and are thriving. More conservative applicators advise a delay of two weeks before working or planting a treated area, but it is still the easiest way ever to clean up an area for new rose plantings.

CUTTING TO A FIVE-LEAFLET is gospel to most rose people. It is supposed to reduce dieback, make a new bud develop faster, encourage plant vigor and generally give more blooms per season. But such grooming isn't always in the best interest of the plant. Some studies in public gardens show that simply cutting off a spent bloom resulted-in just as many breaks that came on as fast or faster than canes trimmed to a lower, heavier five-leaflet. The stem dried up and the plant put out new stems and leaves without hesitation. Best of all, mass plantings with light trimming had many leaves throughout the season and considerably less winterkill. It follows that healthy, vigorous plants with more leaves (the food producer for the plant) will be in better condition to take on whatever nature has to offer. You might want to keep an eye on some leafy plants in your own garden and see if there's a relationship between plant size this year and a start next spring. Of course, if you are an exhibitor, you'11 want to direct all the strength of the plant to a few canes and blooms. But in the long run, there's a price to pay.

VARIETY deserves some careful thought away from the excitement of the rose show. What are you trying to achieve? Lots of roses to cut for the house, something leafy and colorful to hide the foundation, a landscape accent, a collection requiring less care or a garden to make the exhibitor's heart beat faster? Here's where the Proof of the Pudding comes in. Check garden·

AND exhibition ratings; visit with several different growers. And after all this, THEN make out the order for spring.

Taking roses too seriously these days?? How about some Rose Resolutions for 1982… timely tips from diaries of rosarians from across the country, proving again that the same kind of rose madness exists everywhere. Roses are hardly any fun unless there are some rules to break, so try out your will power on some of these…

THIS ROSARIAN RESOLUTELY RESOLVES TO:

1. Tell Queen Of The Show story only when asked.

2. Restrict reading of rose catalogs to one hour per week.

3. Order only ten more roses than the garden will hold.

4. Save money by ordering three of everything.

5. Dig up no more than 10% of lawn area per year for roses.

6. Buy only two miracle rose cures for "testing".

7. Let weather man handle rainfall without help,

8. Think of bugs as part of nature's balance.

9. Allow limited cutting of roses for the house.

10. Come in from garden for supper on time.

11. Wear clean shirt for Sunday rose garden work.

12. Encourage some growth without swearing.

13. USE SOME COMMON ROSE SENSE.

The year-end routine for columnists is to review and reflect on the dwindling days, arriving at some carefully-qualified conclusions (mostly hindsight) for the benefit of those readers who haven't read the summer magazines yet. To see just how good some of the advice has been, the Rambler ran through some old, old columns. It turns out that roses and rosarians haven't really changed very much; we are still talking about and advising on the same things we did ten years ago.

THOUGHTFUL PROGRAM PLANNING was a subject in 1972. Make sure that new (and old) members take part in educational programs before the serious rose season begins. It's amazing how many rose growers can't identify the shank, or the bud union, or find a bud-eye on a year-old cane. They have heard the terms over and over again, but haven't connected the words with the real thing. Try a program on planting in January or February. Build a simulated rose bed on a formica-top table. Make a three-side box of 1 x 8 inch redwood to resemble a built-up rose bed and fill with a large bag of bark mulch material. Bring several well-trimmed rosebushes to the meeting and actually plant the bushes in the box. And show how a caned rosebush should be planted — that is by carefully cutting the sides of the container and gently spreading the roots in much the same way as a bare-root plant. There's nothing much better than a practical demonstration.

OUT IN FRONT was the advice of the same column. Plan a rose bed for the front yard this year. Use just one variety for a massed color effect, or at least roses with the same growth and bloom habit. Floribundas are ideal for plantings of this type. We talk about beautification and then keep the beauty to ourselves. If you want to sell roses, show the product. Besides, sharing is half the fun of having a rose garden. A real attention-getter is a bed or border of miniature roses to add color to a front planting. Most casual visitors don't even know what they are. The RAMBLER noted that a round bed with twelve CHIPPER miniatures outbloomed and outperformed every annual ever tried in the same location. Think small and colorful… you won't be disappointed.

"YOUR BEST SCORE FOR '74" was to plan a spray schedule while the snow was still on the ground. Start the spray routine IMMEDIATELY after pruning, drenching the canes and bud union thoroughly. Use a broad spectrum insecticide (*Diazinon* is a good one) combined with your favorite fungicide (or combination of fungicides) like *Funginex, Phaltan* or *Manzate*. Use a full strength and add a spreader-sticker to encourage penetration into the cracks and crevices of the bud union and older canes. The object is to control over-wintering spores BEFORE temperature and humidity are right for growth of these organisms. Do NOT wait for new leaves to appear. And don't forget to spray shrub and climbing roses at the same time. An infected host plant can spread spores like wildfire when conditions are right.

Prune and spray the same day; spray again in two weeks with the same combination. Then follow a regular fungicide protection program (Without the insecticide) for a clean garden all season.

MORE MANURE IN THE SOIL MIX does not always produce more roses. A 1974 example of what not to do related how a mix of half finely-ground manure, half pine bark (also ground and compost) with very little soil looked good but gave poor results. The excessive amounts of organic material tended to pack and lacked air space. The high organic problem was easily corrected by adding sharp sand and garden soil, resulting in a final mix of 1/3 manure, 1/3 compost and 1/3 sand and soil. At the end of the first season roses dug from this bed had masses of feeder roots (on multiflora understock) with no evidence of gall. The plants transplanted very successfully. Conclusion: If a little is good, more isn't necessarily better.

THE BEST ADVICE still holds for ANY year: Make rose growing easy and fun and we won't be able to handle all the memberships.

With important Rose Resolutions out of the way bloom early and offer a change in texture and shape. (Example: Order three of everything to save money), it's time to wish you a 1982 with a rosy hue and that you'll continue to enjoy the world's greatest hobby.

FLORIBUNDAS are going to brighten up more and more mass plantings this year, showing off some good, new varieties now available. MARINA is a good example; bright, free blooming, beautiful foliage. CHARISMA is a great display rose, too, particularly as a border or foundation planting. If you have ever seen a bed of SUNSPRITE in full bloom you'll be a floribunda fan forever. And you'll see more roses in the front garden where they should have been all the time. We'll also see more shrub and landscape varieties that will tolerate low temperatures and now-and-then care; shrubs with flowers that most anyone can enjoy.

FRONT PLANTINGS of roses need some special staging to make them most effective. An attractive border of natural planting material helps shape a rose bed. Brick, stone, timbers or a non-competing low hedge may be used. Most of these materials require very little special skill, just some imagination. In a modern setting, cement blocks set in sand are attractive; plant portulaca or alyssum in the air spaces of the blocks and let the growth soften the line. For early spring, set blocks with spring bulbs for color and green before the roses get started.

HYBRID TEAS AND FLORIBUNDAS are also set off by planting miniatures as a border. Just choose varieties that are bushy and free-flowering; not necessarily the show winners. Most rosebushes are not particularly attractive when viewed from the side. Leggy canes without many leaves don't add much to the landscape. A better top to bottom look is easy with miniatures as a screen.

Miniatures and big roses get along together very well. Fertilize the big ones in the usual way enough food will leach out to take care of their smaller cousins. A border does not have to be all one variety. Select varieties with the same growth habit and picture is complete. Miniatures are great under tree roses, too. Contrasting colors help set off the dimension that tree roses provide. Tree ros-

es in tubs or planters NEED miniatures at the base. In this case, some cascading types add interest.

MINIATURES are as versatile a flowering plant as you will find. They are at home in the north or in the south. Minis mix with rock gardens or sidewalk plantings, formal beds or under tree roses, as masses of color or small color accents. For sheer bloom production, minis are hard to beat. In northern climates, minis mix well with other annuals, usually come into bloom early and offer a change in texture and shape. In hot climates, miniatures replace flowering annuals like petunias, geraniums and snapdragons. They thrive in hanging baskets, planters, boxes and formal beds. For hot climate rosarians, miniatures are colorful, controllable perennials that are used in place of flowering annuals. Get with the miniature program in '82; you'll be glad you did.

ROSES IN CONTAINERS are not as difficult as they may seem. In fact, containers offer some real advantages. Besides mobility, containers offer more bloom in a small space, color when and where needed, controlled growing conditions, and opportunities for roses where none existed before. Pots, cans, containers, planters, boxes, tubs and tiles can hold roses of varying sizes and types. Their use is limited only by your imagination. A two-wheel dolly or a platform with casters makes container-growns easy to move around. It's a way of bringing the rose garden to the patio.

DEEP IRRIGATION systems made container-grown roses practical. It was always a problem to keep containers moist enough to support steady growth. Containers had too much water or not enough. Fertilizing was another problem. With the advent of the inexpensive, do-it-yourself drip systems, water and fertilizer can be applied in just the right proportions… even while the rosarian is vacationing. The systems are inconspicuous and easy to use; flow rates are available for any size container. In brief, the systems can be made as sophisticated or as simple as the user desires. Even the timer unit is simple to install and use. Suggestion: start with a simple system and grow into the more elaborate applications as you gain experience.

MINIATURES do particularly well in containers. Since the container soon fills with feeder roots, growth rate can be controlled by the amount of fertilizer applied. A good many miniature exhibitors, particularly in the warmer climates, routinely grow exhibition varieties in containers to control color, size and exhibition form through careful feeding practices. It's also easier to control bloom cycle in containers.

FOR SICK PLANTS, containers are like intensive care. Warm soil, the right prescription and some protected sun or shade can often bring the sickest plant back to life. It's interesting to try, anyway. And that's what this new rose season is all about, enjoy roses and try something new for '82.

Roses always look good in February, there's no critical judge around to find fault. Unless you are a mini grower under lights, you won't have to show just how good a grower you are for several months. But now's the time for good growing to start…

PLANTING SOON?? Whatever your weather range, hill up new bushes with all the soil, mulch or insulating material you can find to protect new cane and breaks. Cover until just the tips of the canes show. Protect from cold, keep moist. Even if the weather is mild, keep canes from drying out. More bushes are probably lost to drying wind and sun than from cold.

PLASTIC TENTS encourage a plant to break, but do not offer much protection from cold. A tent forms a miniature greenhouse. After planting and mudding in with plenty of water, put some wet sphagnum moss on the bud union, form a tent of clear plastic over the canes and secure with a plant tie around the shank. Hill up around the edges with some soil or mulch. The result is a high-humidity, warm condition ideal for growth. It's a must for tree roses. When the bushes have started, usually in about two weeks, cut some holes to reduce the temperature. Remove entirely about a week later. The whole procedure gives new roots development time to deliver moisture and nutrients to cells and canes. 'The delivery chain has to work for the plant to grow.

TREE ROSE SPLINTS. A must for tree roses if they get any size at all. At the time of planting, carefully place a length of 3/8-inch reinforcing bar or conduit pipe next to the tree standard so that it does not interfere with the roots. Carefully drive the splint into the ground a foot or so, depending on the stability of the soil. Top of the splint should be just even with the bud unions. Then slip a length of old garden hose over the bar or pipe to ground level. This acts as a cushion or pad so that the bar does not chafe. Then tape the covered bar securely to the tree standard with plastic electrician's tape or friction tape. Tape in three or four places, just like a broken arm. The result is a stable, secure tree able to stand up in the wind. Bud unions can still split from the standard but even this can be helped with some "bandage tie" figure eights linking canes from both bud unions.

SANDY SOIL?? Don't worry. Roses will grow in sand, even pure grit. Add what humus is available; it helps hold the moisture and supports soil processes. When humus is lacking, use plenty of water and soluble fertilizer. Use the sand to hold up the plant; feed a liquid diet. Add some sort of mulch on top to retain moisture and watch the plants grow. A common practice in Florida is to core around the perimeter of the plant in three or four places and add a cup of fish meal in each. Cover over. In less than a season the roots have found the fish meal with a mat of vigorous feeders. As long as water and food are available, roses will thrive in almost any form of grit.

ALFALFA MEAL. Great for a new or reworked bed. Give some a try this season. In addition to (not in place of) your favorite formula, work in about 50 pounds of alfalfa meal per 100 square feet of rose bed. The result will be more breaks, better leaves, more color and an overall healthier plant. For existing beds, use a cup or so per large plant, scratch in lightly before growth starts in the spring. Without going into the scientific details, alfalfa supplies an alcohol-chain hormone that makes the other processes work better. You won't find alfalfa meal in most garden shops. Go to a feed store. Alfalfa meal (rough cut or finely ground) is used in poultry and animal feeds. Pellets are just as good. Pellets cost a little more but are easier to broadcast. In the same feed store you'll probably find calcined clay (Kitty Litter) in large bags. Calcined clay is a great additive for potting mixes, planters; any application that needs air space and moisture retention at the same time. Calcined clay pellets are like miniature sponges with thousands of very tiny air spaces to take and release water and nutrients gradually. Chemically inert, it takes many years to break down.

A MINI-STRAWBERRY BARREL? If strawberry barrels are fun, try one with miniature roses. Select varieties that trail well like GREEN ICE or SUGAR ELF. The trick with a barrel is to keep the top moist enough and the bottom drained enough. Allow plenty of drainage at the bottom. Try a heavier mix at the top and lighter at the bottom. A drip irrigator is ideal. Be sure to add soluble food frequently. A cascading barrel of miniatures can be a beautiful garden feature. You probably have some other unique containers suitable for miniature roses, too. A cast iron cook pot (don't forget to drill some holes), chimney tiles, old bird bath or fountain, an old tub or wooden bucket. You're only limited by your imagination.

MINIATURES TOLERATE SHADE better than the big roses, particularly if the varieties are selected carefully. Micro-minis or miniatures bred for' growing under lights usually do well in semi-shade. Less vigorous growers usually do well also. If miniatures reach for the light too much and become lanky, just trim them down and they will fill back in with new growth in a short time. The larger and more established the plant, the better its chances for growth in the shade. Get the mini established in a pot and then move it. Experiment a little, you may be surprised at the results.

The "Winter of '82" may never melt, but it's time to break dormancy and be ready to take on whatever spring has to offer... probably floods, rains and sudden cold snaps.

TAKE A GOOD LOOK at how your roses came through a tough winter, or maybe the suggestion should be WHY they came through the winter. When the time is right, and please don't hurry Mother Nature, pay particular attention to the amount of good wood left on some plants and the total loss of others. Was the protection a little better in some cases?? Less wind, more moisture, insulation able to breathe, more gradual dormancy... all could be factors in survival. You can learn a great deal for future reference if you pay attention. A Rambler Thought For The Month once said that "Experience is the name we give to our mistakes." Let's learn from them, too.

DON'T BE IN A HURRY for springtime to come, particularly in uncovering roses. More plants are probably lost in the "springtime" when the temperature suddenly drops and new growth and swelling canes are frozen than during the winter. It's a good idea to let Nature proceed at a slow pace; let whatever winter protection you use stay on a little longer than usual. Pruning and probing gives the bush a signal that it's time to grow. Give some natural signals a chance this season. Roses in the spring bloom when it's time to bloom, and early uncovering and pruning seldom speed up the process.

WHEN SPRING REALLY ARRIVES, don't waste time on those plants that have been unproductive for more than one season, even though you may be reluctant to give up on them. Prune them with a shovel. But to make your conscience feel better, offer the plants you don't want at a plant exchange. It takes a little extra spade work and care, but it's a good way to get someone going with roses. The bushes that didn't quite meet your expectations can produce loads of roses for someone else.

MOVE 'EM AROUND if you feel like it, too. If a bush doesn't seem to be doing well in a particular location or if the color is "all wrong", move it somewhere else. Transplanting often seems to give a rosebush a new lease on life. Move them· while they are dormant; trim up and handle like a bare root plant. There are roses to gain and not much to lose. Prune canes according to the usual practice for your climate. Wash off the roots and trim out any dead or broken parts. Trim root ends lightly to encourage callousing and new feeder roots. Also trim out any root galls or gall growths on the shank or bud union. If very large galls girdle the shank or involve many roots, throw them away and start over. It's more work to grow a sick plant than a good one.

TREAT GALLS?? Some respected growers maintain that disinfecting trimmed galls with *Lysol* or *Clorox* retards reoccurrence, but an equal number disagree. Most growers have galls they don't even know about, and have had for a long time. If the gall is on the shank or the bud union, sunshine seems to do the most good. The Rambler suggests that you don't worry too much about infection; nature and a well-drained soil are probably the best remedies.

ROOT STIMULANTS for new or newly-transplanted bushes?? There are a number of products on the market that claim to have hormones and what-have-you to make the roots develop "millions of tiny root hairs" for fast and vigorous growth. Some seem to help, but the Rambler suspects that the grower willing to go to that extra effort and expense probably had put together a pretty good rose bed in the first place. Maybe the extra water in planting helped. Who knows?? If you have a favorite, use it with plenty of water. Just don't add any fertilizer, even though the label says, "Can't burn when used as directed." Some of the best growers the Rambler knows use some "cow tea" for planting special bushes. It's too much trouble to use routinely on a number of plants, but can help in special cases. Cow tea contains very little nitrogen, and it's so diluted that it can't hurt anything. It's the secret ingredient that does the trick.

MOUND UP THE CANES. Soil and mulch mounded up to protect the canes of newly planted bushes is not so much for freeze protection as for conservation of moisture. Bright sun and dry air can turn green canes into dry sticks in just a day or two when new roots can't supply enough moisture. New feeder roots MUST develop BEFORE new growth puts the system under stress. Two weeks or so is enough most of the time. If the rose bed is short on soil and mulch, bring some in. Mound until just the tips of the new canes are sticking out. Let rainfall or some gentle washing with the hose gradually erode the mound; don't poke at the soil (and concealed new breaks) with a cultivator or trowel.

LIQUID COMPOST is a great organic starter. It's also called "cow tea". Back in BC (Before Chemicals), good gardeners always had a barrel or two steeping behind the garage or fence. It was a good practice and still is. There's not much direct nutrient value to cow tea as mentioned earlier, but the boost given soil organisms makes everything work better. Add some soluble fertilizer for ESTABLISHED bushes when danger of frost is passed. Food in an available form brings a fast reaction. Hold off until the soil warms up, then use a half-bucket of cow tea laced with something like Ra-Pid-Gro and stand back. The bushes are going to grow. Keep several plastic garbage cans of tea brewing all the time (rainwater is best). Onion or potato sacks make good tea bags; fill with cow chips and tie with a long piece of rope or wire. Steep for about 10 days, sloshing around once in a while. You'll know when it's ready. And Good Luck!

The best thing about spring is that it always comes when it's most needed. And after the winter of '82, we need it more than ever. Here are a few tips to get your mind off the bad weather…

LEARN BY DOING. Dug some plants from the Rambler's garden that had been in for three years. Root growth was tremendous (in sandy/organic soil) and had a consistent growth pattern — great masses of hair roots had grown around cones of fish meal. In one large planting, three cones of soil were lifted about 18 inches from each rose shank and filled with a cup of fish meal and covered. The developing roots invariable "found" the fish meal and set up a feeding station. When dug, the root system looked like a tripod, and a solid one at that. Apparently the Indians with the fish knew what they were doing all the time. If fish meal is hard to come by in your area, maybe you should make friends with a fisherman.

ANOTHER OBSERVATION. Galls that had been trimmed from the shank (or where the roots joined the shank) and exposed to sun and air had generally healed and dried up. The plants treated this way continued to grow in about the same way as uninfected plants. Not a very scientific observation, but the incidence of galls was not particularly disabling. The treated roses have been replanted in another garden… will come up with another report next year.

SPRING MINI FORMULA. Miniatures don't need a heavy initial feeding, just a steady diet in proportion to their size. A combination of inorganic/organic works fine. Combine *Carl Pool Instant Rose Food* (9-56-8) and a good fish emulsion like Atlas. Use one tablespoon of each to a gallon of water. Use about a quart per mini. If *Carl Pool* is not available in your area, *Schultz* or *Peters* works just as well. Use monthly during the growing season for outstanding bloom and foliage.

A DOSE OF SALTS… *Epsom Salts*, that is. Magnesium Sulfate is a good green growth stimulant. Many growers routinely broadcast about two or three ounces of Epsom Salts per established plant after the soil has warmed up a bit. It seems to encourage basal breaks and green leaves; it can't hurt and may help get your plants off to the fastest start ever. Growers in alkaline soils or using highly alkaline water often use *Epsom Salts* two or three times a season.

A ROSARIAN'S DILEMMA. Who can explain why the rose planted in the middle of a lawn without care or concern grows to tremendous size and produces bushels of blooms? The bush is neglected and abused but still performs against all the rules. This should tell us that there is no BEST way to grow roses, just lots of good ways. Which is another way of saying, "if what you are doing works, stay with it."

THE RAMBLER BUILT two new rose beds this season with bank sand (silty) and ground pine bark, a huge pile of compost and a mix of horse manure and stable hay. Added about 20 pounds of superphosphate (0-18-0) and 50 pounds of alfalfa pellets per 100 square feet. Tilled the mixture three times, watered twice and cultivated to encourage air. The resulting beds are about 12 inches above the lawn level, well drained and soft enough to plant without a shovel. At the end of the third week (ran out of time) planted bare root roses that have taken off without a problem. Lesson: natural ingredients blend and work for the rosarian who is in a hurry. Beds built from approximately the same mix three years ago are still supporting outstanding roses.

SICK BAY FOR ROSES. Particularly important in the spring if a plant is sick, delivered late or in need of some special care. Pot up problem roses in five-gallon containers and locate where they can get some special attention. They usually perk up in a hurry. There are several good reasons why it works. Roses in pots develop masses of roots that are better able to take up water and fertilizer. Roots develop because the soil mix warms up faster and stays warmer; a pot usually has better drainage and aeration to support soil processes. It has been a good trick by old-timer rosarians to start new bushes in containers to develop roots before placing them in rose beds in competition with mature plants. And you may want to keep some roses in pots all the time for variety as well as replacement.

A GOOD CONTAINER MIX is about the same as that for container-grown tree roses: 1/3 garden soil, 1/3 humus material sharpened with a little sand and 1/3 calcined clay granules. If calcined clay is not handy, use more humus and sand. You'll have to water a little more often with this light mix (every day during hot weather,) but you'll enjoy great results. Choice of pots is up to you; clay pots are more attractive but heavier to move around. Black plastic is good, soil warms up quickly. Even metal cans are good for a season or two (restaurants are a good source.) Cedar and redwood are probably best of all but are expensive, even when you build the boxes yourself.

CONTAINER ROSES are easy to winterize. Pull the rose out of the container and bury it, just like the Minnesota tip. Cover with six or eight inches of soil and leaves, and the pampered plants will be ready to go back into pots (or regular beds) in the spring. You still have time to enjoy roses on the patio this season if you get after it. They're certainly worth a try.

April showers may bring May flowers... but not without some help from the rosarian. Here are some springtime items that may help you get started...

COMPOST IN SPRING?? No better time than right now to make garden cleanup pay big dividends all season long. The green stuff that piles up now makes the whole process go. Green residue in a backyard compost pile supplies the enzymes that do the real work breaking down all forms of organic matter. Green stuff makes the pile heat up. There are other starters available, but grass clippings, weeds, yard trimmings and kitchen waste are available now. Green manure works, too, but is a problem for most backyards. Organic material can be recycled into good plant food in just a couple of weeks with the right approach. Start with six inches or so of leaves and what-have-you at the bottom of the heap; add several inches of green material, then layer with some more clippings, shavings or straw. Some cottonseed meal or manure can be added next and topped off with soil. Lightly moisten the whole pile. Leave a slight hollow on top so that water won't run off. In about six days turn with a fork, working from the outside edge. Turn about two more times a week apart. If the pile gets too hot, add more water. If it hasn't heated in three or four days, add more green stuff or manure. If there's no heat, it isn't working. The compost produced adds life to soils and blooms to roses. Gets rid of garden wastes, too.

THRIPS WILL SOON ARRIVE in waves, turning the best buds and blooms into bruised blobs if left unchecked. Damage by these rasping, tan insects can be so severe that buds won't open at all. Thrips usually arrive (by the millions) on warm, humid breezes and head straight for the fragrant, light colored roses. Gardens near open fields are particularly susceptible. Thrips feed through a file-like tube, rasping petal edges and sucking up the juices. Tan and very tiny, they are easily seen by peeling back rose petals; there will be lots moving around.

THRIP CONTROL is fairly ,easy with contact/systemic sprays like *Cygon 2E* or *Orthene*. Hit 'em to get 'em. That means to spray where thrips are attacking. Spray only the bud and bloom areas of the plant; get good coverage of tight buds as well as open blooms. Both *Cygon* and *Orthene* are effective, for about a week. During periods of heavy infestation, mist buds and blooms weekly. Spot control "special blooms" with a fresh mix in a Windex-type sprayer. *Orthene* label warnings advise not to use *Orthene* more than two times without a break, but the misting advised here has never given the Rambler any damaged or disfigured foliage. If damage is noted, switch off to something else. With consistent control, even Royal Highness can come out unblemished.

THE FRAGRANT FORMULA, repeated here by popular demand, is an artificial manure that makes most anything grow. It's for the rosarian who doesn't have a farm friend for the real thing. The Fragrant Formula is just as good (and probably better because it releases more nutrients) and can be produced on any city lot. You'll enjoy all the benefits without the cow. Here's the formula:

Three yards of compost materials or leaves

100 pounds of cottonseed hulls (or something coarse)

100 pounds of cottonseed meal

100 pounds of rough cut alfalfa or pellets

50 pounds of bone meal

50 pounds of fish meal or blood meal

The local feed store will have all the ingredients except the leaves. Use any area suitable for composting; pile the leaves and coarse materials about two feet deep. Add ingredients a little at a time and turn with a garden fork. Moisten LIGHTLY; turn with a fork twice a week for two weeks. Cover with plastic if in a real hurry. When working, the pile will leak an ammonia odor. Don't get the pile too wet. Cottonseed meal turns to a slime that smells dead and crawls along the ground like a fog. If an odor does occur, add more coarse materials and turn more frequently. APPLY FRAGRANT FORMULA about a shovelful per established plant (maybe even two shovelfuls). As a slow, release organic, it isn't likely to burn. If you are a manure gourmet, you may want to add other trace materials such as seaweed, rock phosphate or decomposed granite. If the soil is on the acid side, skip the cottonseed meal and substitute fresh horse-stall manure or blood meal and wood shavings. Make up another batch in late summer, and you'll have fine roses all season.

SOME SIMPLE TRICKS. Staking rosebushes (even very large ones) can be easy with reinforcing bar (or electrical conduit) and some old garden hose. Cut one-fourth or three-eighths inch and rebar into lengths two feet long with a hacksaw. Check out the bush to see where it needs support so that it does not rock in the ground. Carefully drive the support bar into the ground AT AN ANGLE to bind and engage the canes and bud union. Cut a length of old plastic or rubber hose and slip over the bar to act as a pad or cushion. In most cases, further ties or binding won't be needed. Longer lengths will support taller canes, but be sure to pad with hose before using a soft tie.

GROOMING is another easy trick that pays off in better roses. Every time a bloom is cut, consider the effect on the shape of the plant and production of more blooms. Clean up the twiggy stuff in the middle of the plant every time blooms are cut, and enjoy more roses over the season. One meticulous rosarian the Rambler knows has a five-gallon can at the end of each rose bed to take spent blooms and clippings anytime he's out in the garden. Result: the rose garden is ready for visitors anytime... and isn't that what this is all about??

A flurry of workshops and meetings in the last few weeks have encouraged an exchange of ideas on roses that you just can't get anywhere else. Here are a few of the subjects that you might like to try or pass along…

SPIDER MITES… the bane of the rose grower. More and more growers seem to be going to water washing… that high pressure water treatment for undersides of leaves. The *Water Wand* (by K&E) is a popular tool. Some homemade rigs work just as well (maybe even better), but the wand is inexpensive and convenient. Common routine is to begin washing on a weekly basis as soon as the weather turns warm, particularly miniatures or roses in hot, reflective locations. As in fungus disease control, begin BEFORE evidence of damage. If infestation catches up (and it can very quickly), wash two or three times a week. The plants will enjoy the extra water and, unless the garden is very large, doesn't take much time. If a miticide .is absolutely necessary, wash first, then apply the miticide. *Vendex* seems to be used by most serious rosarians followed by *Plictran*. *Vendex* availability may be a problem as *Ortho* has suspended marketing of *Orthomite* (ingredient: *Vendex*), except through their agricultural division. There should be a clarification on this product soon. In the meantime, get out the *Water Wand* and make the roses feel good.

BUG ZAPPER… the electric grid with bug-attracting black lights is appearing in more and more rose gardens. It attracts all sorts of flying insects, electrocuting and neatly depositing them in a tray or on the ground. It is particularly effective against the moth that lays the eggs for corn ear worms. Makes the garden a good deal more pleasant without all the mosquitoes and gnats. Most users remove the outside screen so that larger insects can pass through; also, hang the bug grid about eight or nine feet high for safety as well as effectiveness. Most models will attract and protect an area of 100 feet or more. There's some difference of opinion as to location; either on the perimeter of the garden or in the middle. Perimeter folks say it keeps the bugs away from the roses; center advocates say the pests are in the roses anyway. The initial investment is a little high (watch for a Sears *Bugwhacker* on sale), but it is not too bad if you have a power source near the rose garden. It might be the best gift you could give your garden (and yourself) this season.

TO MULCH OR NOT TO MULCH… a delicate question. Growers in hot areas swear by good, thick mulch to hold moisture and lower soil temperatures. Cool climate rosarians say there's no need and that the mulch harbors insects and disease. There's probably some support for both cases. However, if in doubt, mulch. A good mulch of compost, leaves, manure or what-have-you constantly restores the humus in the rose bed and supports the micro-organisms that make soil processes happen. Mulch is a way to feed, cool, smother weeds and conserve moisture at the same time. Apply mulch after the soil warms up; if everything is working right, two or three inches of good organic material will disappear in a single season. That just has to do some good. That's not to say that roses won't grow in sand or soil with some organic content, but growing is a lot easier when nature does her thing.

SOIL TESTS… are they really necessary?? Rosarians don't HAVE to do anything, but a routine soil test helps. Soil tests are available inexpensively and quickly through most state agricultural colleges; county agents have collection packages and instructions. Some private testers do an outstanding job, too, and there are several rose specialists who advertise regularly in these pages. When in doubt, get a soil test, taking samples from several places in the rose bed (where the roots are, not on top) mixing and sending off a representative sample advising the lab that you want to grow first-class roses. When the results come back, remember that modifications need to be made GRADUALLY; otherwise the cure is worse than the ailment. Many good growers test beds annually and then use some common rose sense with the results; that's what makes roses grow.

CALCINED CLAY… an overlooked product that can help rose growers. These tiny pellets support soil processes by taking in air and water and releasing plant-support essentials as needed. Calcined clay can be described as an exploded clay pebble, opening up thousands of microscopic caverns, something like a tiny version of a sponge. It's inert, won't break down, and goes about the business of retaining and releasing nutrients year after year without change. Widely used in potting mixes, calcined clay makes many container applications practical. Kitty Litter is another name, but that's the expensive way to buy it. Marketed under a number of different names, calcined clay is available in 50-pound bags from turf and greenhouse supply firms. Oil-Dri Corp. is probably the biggest manufacturer-distributor and sells under the name *Terragreen*. It's great to incorporate in a new bed or containers, use as a top dressing for pots, or mix in the top two or three inches of a rose bed to hold moisture and provide aeration. It's good for rooting cuttings, too, as it drains well but keeps moisture levels constant. Try some.

ROSE CONDITIONING... as simple as taking a container of warm water to the rose garden when cutting. Plunge the stems into warm water immediately. Allow to stand in a cool, dark place until water cools. The result: roses with moisture and substance. For an extra lift, try cutting the stems under water to inhibit air block. A good many winning exhibitors do it (arrangers, too) so there must be some substance to it. Worth a try anyway.

JUL. 1982

THOUGHT FOR THE MONTH: Advice for Consulting Rosarians:
Stand up to be seen. Speak up to be heard. Shut up to be appreciated.

The best rose growing seems to be done around the coffee urn at rose society meetings, probably because the folks participating aren't afraid to ask. The Rambler jotted down a couple of topics worth sharing from the last meeting... let's call them Favorite Cures.

SICK ROSE?? Slow to start? Try a get well dose of fish emulsion fertilizer in water, using enough to soak the root zone. About an ounce a gallon is about right; treat the sick one about every two weeks. In most cases, roses perk right up and begin to grow again. The easiest application is to make up a garbage can full of prescription and dip it out with a sprinkling can. There are always some roses (and other plants, too) that need a treatment. There's no objectionable smell either as is the case with fish meal. Can't burn, gets right to the root zone, makes the whole soil process work. Another great use, soak in a newly-planted potted rose with fish and water. Really helps transplant shock. After plants are going well again, shift back to a more conventional food.

LIGHT GREEN LEAVES, slow growth. Maybe a supplement of Magnesium Sulfate (*Epsom Salts*) will bring the green and growth back. Broadcast about two ounces per medium size plant; water in well. It is instantly soluble. Common practice in alkaline soils (or when using alkaline water) is to use *Epsom Salts* once in the spring and again in the fall. But it is also effective following very heavy leaching rains. If the green doesn't come back in a hurry, check the Ph of the bed and other feeding practices. Roses are supposed to have green leaves, when we do most of the right things. Check nitrogen, too. It's often depleted before growers realize what has happened.

SPREADER STICKER. Not much need for spreader-sticker as a spray additive because most of the newer formulations have a spreader agent included. More may contribute to leaf burn from the spray mix. But a good, safe water improver is plain white vinegar, particularly in hard, alkaline water. Add about one tablespoon of vinegar per gallon of water BEFORE adding insecticide or fungicide. You'll probably notice that the resulting spray will spread across the leaves more readily and won't puddle. Vinegar as an additive is common practice in the arid Southwest. You may want to try it, too.

SMALL ROSE GARDEN. Want to keep it simple? Ortho's new product, *ORTHENEX*, is a good choice for a small garden. One liquid product will do it all. It's a combination of *Funginex* (for disease control), *Orthene* (insect control) and *Kelthane* (spider mite control). Although in most gardens there's not much real need for insecticide at every spraying, *Orthenex* fills a real market need. Every ten days or so will keep most gardens in pretty good shape, disease and bug wise. However, if the garden has more than 10 or 15 plants, switch to *Funginex* (used alone) for blackspot and mildew and *Orthene* for insect control (particularly thrips) as needed. The spray for specifics approach is not only cheaper but also better for foliage and roses in the long run. But for small gardens with minimum work, the combination is OK. The best intentions (to spray) have never controlled blackspot or killed insects; perhaps if the job is easier, more roses will get the attention they deserve.

DISEASE CONTROL. What's the best? Whatever is working for you. But the practice gaining in popularity all the time is *FUNGINEX*, used faithfully every seven to ten days. Used regularly, *Triforine* (the active ingredient in *Funginex*) will do a good job. Spray the foliage until dripping; spray REGULARLY. For a little extra residual, add one-half tablespoon of *Manzate* per gallon to the regular *Funginex* mixture. During black spot weather, the leaves will stay cleaner and may hold control for an extra few days in the event a spray schedule is skipped. In dry, hot weather the combination has been effective for two weeks. But don't try to stretch it much past two weeks. The mix is safe and easy to use. The ingredients appear to be compatible.

MINIATURES IN HOT WEATHER? Miniature roses can be safely planted even during the hottest weather if given a chance to harden off a bit. A good practice is to pot up the small plants in four or five inch plastic pots for two or three weeks before moving into the miniature beds. Keep the newly-potted plants in a protected location; follow a REGULAR watering routine. If the pots dry out, the whole advantage is lost. The result is excellent initial growth without transplant shock and a well-developed root system able to cope and compete in a rose bed. Some varieties take longer to fill out than others, but when growth is well established, carefully slip from the pot and plant. The mini will never know that it has been moved. What makes it work? The good soil mix and warmer soil temperature in the pot encourages better root development and therefore better top growth. You'll be surprised how well the potting technique works, even in mid-summer.

WATER ON THE LEAVES? Why not?? If the disease spray program is working, the rose leaves will appreciate the water. Under certain conditions (like an outbreak of blackspot) avoid water on the leaves. But if the garden is being sprayed regularly with a reliable fungicide, don't worry about water. In fact, make it a regular practice to wash off the leaves with lots of water just before spraying, particularly if rainfall has been sparse. It washes off excess spray residue, cleans the leaves for better spray coverage and cools off the plant. Almost as good as a shower for a rosarian after a hot day. Roses always appreciate extra water; this is just another way to accomplish two things at the same time.

What were we talking about two or three years ago... what sage advice was being passed along to Rambler readers struggling through hot August weather? Let's look back and see just how effective (and long-lasting) that advice really was...

WORM CASTINGS... Castings HAVE turned out to be that extra ingredient that many rose growers were looking for. Perhaps castings don't qualify as the perfect plant food (as claimed), but it does seem that castings are useful and perform well in a number of rose situations. More and more serious gardeners and rosarians are using castings from small as well as regional suppliers. Castings are highly nutritious, relatively soluble and, most important, are in a form available to plants. As worms ingest organic matter, they excrete castings rich in nitrates, phosphates, potash and calcium. In short, it's a natural plant food.

MINIATURE ROSES seem to thrive on castings, used as a top dressing or in the soil mix for beds or pots. About a half-inch of castings scratched into a mini bed with other organic material produces excellent results with healthy, glossy foliage and good blooms. Visiting with a number of users, no one reported evidence of overfeeding such as oversized blooms, vegetative centers or lush foliage with no blooms. For potted miniatures, most users mixed about 1/3 castings by volume with the usual planting medium, omitting other fertilizers. Some reported that sick potted roses were restored by top treatment with castings or replacement of some of the mix with castings.

CASTINGS SUPPLIERS are often Mom and Pop backyard operations, but the worms and roses don't know the difference. Castings are generally inexpensive and can be used rather generously. Or you can get at least some of the benefits of castings by incorporating plenty of organic matter in rose beds and introducing a few worms. In just a short time, you'll have lots of worms and a healthier soil condition. Incidentally, a high organic worm area is a great place to borrow some soil for special potting mix. Refill the area with raw organics, a bit of soil, moisten, and the whole process starts all over again.

POT UP SOME SPARES for replacements. It's a practice growing in popularity. It's a way to landscape rose beds without a gap and maintain blends of colors. Rosarians had been wary of holding roses in pots and seldom allowed for some spares in the spring like the pros. With the right soil mix, roses can be held over and enjoyed with just a minimum amount of extra care. Replacements can be made late in the season with very little transplant shock if carefully done. And users say that their spares are in much better condition than leftovers at the local nursery. It's a trick you may want to try next spring, deliberately potting up some roses for just such a contingency.

SPIDER MITE CONTROL... we still hear pros and cons for various methods at every rose society meeting. This enemy that comes with hot, dry weather also brings out the hottest comments from rosarians. Some still swear by water, others swear at it. Many still believe in an arsenal of miticides, others let nature take its course. However, for some reason, roses still survive in spite of all this.

VENDEX is far and away the most popular miticide right now. Hard to come by in many parts of the country, it is still growing in popularity. Most use *Vendex* (or *Orthomite*) at 1 teaspoon per gallon, no spreader-sticker, applied to the undersides of the leaves. The product has long residual action and should be applied no more often than 28 days (and only then if REALLY necessary.)

WATER WASHING still has its advocates, too. Probably more advocates than ever. They feel that miticides are nearly as harmful to leaves as mites. Use a water wand if you are fortunate enough to have one, or use a garden hose nozzle adjusted to a fine, hard mist. Wash the plants from the bottom up. Washing breaks up the webs, knocks off the eggs and drowns the hatched mites in the process. Water-wash advocates repeat two or three times a week during mite conditions to get control. If a miticide is really necessary, apply immediately after the second washing. And the Rambler has heard several variations of the Tom Estridge mite story that originally appeared in the South Carolina Rose Society newsletter. It seems that Tom advised, "In the event you are too old to play with a water hose on a hot day, turn it into a fun day for the children or grandchildren. They'll have water allover everything in no time at all. The roses, rosarian and kids will all love it."

GROW LEAVES, THEN ROSES. Still good advice. And more and more rosarians practice good leaf culture and wind up with bushels of roses. It's sometimes hard to tell if more damage is done by spraying or by fungus diseases. In HOT weather, the name of the game is LEAVES. Do everything possible to maintain a good leaf system. And when you do spray, soak the rose beds first and spray during the cooler hours. Roses needing water are already under stress; spray materials just compound the problem. Even plain water on leaves can cause sunburned, coarse leaves that are unattractive and somewhat unproductive. To repeat what every good rosarian knows, well maintained plants with healthy leaves just can't help but produce roses. Whether leaves are lost because of mites, blackspot, mildew, spray burn or dehydration, the results are the same: no roses.

Rose growing can be as easy or as tough as we want to make it... but most rose problems have rather simple solutions when we think them through. Here's a collection of fresh thoughts (or spent blooms if you're an old-timer).

DORMANCY for roses seems to escape us, either the plants are going full bore or have just been frozen back. Rosarians CAN ease into dormancy with a little extra thought. We know -that release of most fertilizers occurs over a period of about 60 days. We also know when hard, killing frost usually occurs. Just shut off the food at the right time and the danger of freeze damage and die back is greatly reduced. Roses are woody plants and respond to the seasons. Don't fight them. Stop feeding at the right time; in the latter stages of the blooming season leave some blooms on to form seed hips which signal the plant that the reproductive cycle is complete. Another slow-down practice is to hold back water (not to stress but reduce the amount) to encourage dormancy.

A HEALTHY ROSE can tolerate a good deal more cold than a weakened one. To say it another way, winterkill should often be called summerkill. The most elaborate winter protection can't make up for poor summer care. As the season winds down, keep up the fungicide spray program; bushes weakened with blackspot and mildew don't have the reserve to take on a cold, dry winter. Keep all the leaves possible; let nature prepare the plant for winter. Defoliated plants don't survive. Good fungicides are available, but don't do any good unless applied. The Rambler's favorite for fall is a combination of *Funginex* (one tablespoon per gallon) and *Phaltan* (1/2 tablespoon per gallon). Keeps mildew and blackspot under control with residual of about ten days. For really severe mildew, double up on frequency or alternate with *Benlate* at three to four day intervals. Plain baking soda (one tablespoon per gallon) helps, probably due to the washing action.

NEW ROSE BEDS NEXT YEAR?? Start now while things are still growing to select a location with good drainage (or where beds can be built up), ample sunshine, away from tree roots and so on. The intended site looks a good deal different when all the leaves are gone and grass brown. To get rid of the grass and weeds for a proposed bed, use the herbicide *ROUNDUP* (or Ortho's *KLEENUP*) on the unwanted plants while still green. Kills the tops and the roots when actively growing. Useless when dormant or nearly dormant. Soil can be worked (even planted) within ten days after application. It's an easy way to get a good, clean start.

FAVORITE WINTER PROTECTION?? Whatever you use, try to make it natural if you can. Pile up leaves and other insulating materials for application at the right time. Not much use to buy what you can get free. Anyway, start a stockpile for the months ahead.

GOOD SPRAY MIXTURES are important, but not many rosarians know how to blend wettable powders (WP) and oil-based insecticides (EC) into compatible mixtures. Warm water is the answer. Use a large glass mixing container to see what's going on. Measure wettable powders into the container first; then slowly add warm water, swirling the mixture into a medium-thick paste. Add some more water to a thin consistency. Swirling seems to work best without foaming or suds. For very alkaline water, add one tablespoon of vinegar per gallon. Ingredients with aromatic distillates (EC's) should be added last, swirling gently. The spray mixture is now ready to be diluted and used without straining, even in sprayers with fine nozzles.

GOOD GARDEN SENSE says to wear gloves and handle spray mixtures with care; the danger of using a glass container is very small. If one of the spray materials precipitates out (cloudy, flaky, buttermilk-like), safely dispose of the whole batch and try to identify the product that caused the problem. An example: old, out-of-date *Cygon* will cause *Benlate* to precipitate out immediately. The result is a clogged sprayer and a mad rosarian.

SPRAY MATERIALS have a limited shelf life; most are safe for two or three seasons. But heat and cold can seriously effect these materials, substantially changing the manufacturer's recommendations. It's important to know just how old spray materials are, but not many rose folks bother to date packages or repackage wettable powders in containers that can be sealed. Quart jars with tight lids are good for this and a label can be taped to the outside.

NOTE YOUR USUAL MIXTURE

proportions on the glass jar with a grease pencil so that you won't have to figure them out again. This simple step can head off leaf burn because a spray concentration was too strong. It's easy to forget. And a must for every spray shelf is a small medicine glass used exclusively for measuring spray materials. They're marked for ounces, tablespoons and teaspoons. Most garden shops have them for about 25 cents. Get a couple and use them wisely.

CLEAN LEAVES make happy rosebushes and happier rosarians. Don't be afraid to wash down the bushes if the garden hasn't had its fair share of rain. Excess spray residue is not only unattractive but hampers the leaf process. A good washing just before spraying does the most good. Spray materials cover better, and if the weather is very hot, burn less. Materials are less likely to puddle, and that sets up that brown, crisp spot on the leaf.

FALL VEGETABLES GOING?? If the vegetable garden is about gone, use the spot to start the fall compost or winter protection pile. It's an investment that pays big dividends.

MEANWHILE, enjoy a bountiful crop of fine, fall roses and let nature do her thing.

OCT. 1982

THOUGHT FOR THE MONTH: Rosarians must wonder how pesticides could harm the environment considering how little damage they do to bugs.

If it sometimes seems that you are growing more roses but enjoying them less, perhaps a "rethink" is in order on varieties and where to use them. It's the right time of year for this pleasant task, as rose order time is at hand. Here are a couple of ideas that the RAMBLER has picked up along the way...

ROSE PLANTINGS UNATTRACTIVE?? Tired of looking at leggy canes? Maybe a front row of dense floribundas would help, or a planting of a vigorous miniature (like RED FLUSH) would make the planting green and/or colorful from soil to sky. Use a green (and also blooming) drape in scale with the taller varieties. The roses in front don't have to be the same variety, but select varieties with similar growth habits. A great new miniature HEARTLAND, is ideal for borders. Blooms, grows and holds its own with big roses. Warm, coral color blends well with pinks.

ROSE SPACING is also important. Some think that wide spacing produces better show blooms, but close planting gives a better rosebed effect. It's the reason that park plantings seem so attractive; the viewer enjoys lots of plant and bloom. Just a plant or two of the same variety on wide spacing may have a very different look. Beds with lots of rose plants also seem to look greener and healthier, maybe because the plants shade one another. At any rate, an attractive mass of roses will stop a visitor every time.

HOW ABOUT FRAGRANCE? Are the fragrant roses where you can get to them? Or maybe buried in the back row somewhere? Try a planting of fragrant roses, planted close together, in a garden spot frequently visited. Or maybe by the back door or garage door, anyplace that suggests a pause. Another good spot is near a garden gate. A great rose for this use is SWEET SURRENDER, the '83 AARS pink HT just loaded with fragrance. A few plants by the gate will stop any visitor. Some other favorites are FRAGRANT CLOUD and PERFUME DELIGHT. Sometimes unnoticed for this quality, SUNSPRITE, a fine yellow floribunda, is very fragrant. Combine four or five plants with warm sunshine on the edge of the patio, and the whole area is perfumed.

ATTRACT ATTENTION to a garden feature with strong colors, something like the miniature CHATTEM CENTENNIAL. Bright orange, good foliage and easy to grow. Goes well with dark or bronzed pots, birdbaths, containers, what-have-you. Another bright performer is CHIPPER; it will become as large and bushy as you permit. Lots of fun to grow. To liven up a dark, green area, plant a few RISE 'N SHINE. This yellow miniature outperforms everything. If it has a fault, it's that it grows too well; but this can be controlled with regular grooming... it bounces back with plenty of blooms in no time at all. And about every second year, dig it up and break into three or four new plants that will match the original in half a season.

ATTRACTIVE LEAVES are useful, too, in screening situations. GRANADA is ideal for the end of a rose bed; the holly-like leaves are always attractive, and there's a good bloom bonus as well. Kept reasonably groomed, Granada fills in with thick foliage and colorful bloom displays. Another rose worth growing for foliage is CHERISH, a very dense floribunda capped with singles and clusters of HT-form, hot-pink blooms. Cherish seems to grow and bloom all the time, even matching the catalog pictures.

MASSES OF FLORIBUNDAS should be high on the priority list for new plantings. Great for color, growth and landscape accent. Five or ten plants of the same variety make a landscape feature; less formal areas can have different varieties although growth habits should be similar. Best new floribunda in years for low planting is SUN FLARE, an '83 AARS winner. It is compact, always green, blooms freely... has all of the attributes of its parent SUNSPRITE but with better growth habit. You have to see an entrance planting of SUN FLARE to believe just how beautiful it can be.

A GOOD SOIL BACKGROUND helps show off roses, too. Miniatures in particular. Wood chips and ground pine bark do a good job as a mulch, and the warm, brown color sets off the miniature plants and blooms. Very neat and attractive. Perhaps the most attractive (and good for the Minis, too) is a deep ground covering of pine bark chunks (two to three inches) filled in under and between the miniature plants about three inches deep. Bark chunks are very long lasting, permit food, air and water to move freely and keep the soil cool and moist. To replant, just pull the bark back, plant and recover. No new look at all. Chunks are ideal for very hot climates; soil stays cool and moist even in 100 degree weather. Fish meal, alfalfa meal, even manures can be broadcast generously and washed in. In contact with the soil, these organics go right to work to produce the finest minis you'll ever see.

LIKE MINIS BUT TIRED OF STOOPING?? It may be easier to raise the miniatures than lower the grower. Just build an oversize planter box with landscape timbers set vertically. Treated with decay retarding salts (wolmanizing), the timbers last a long time, are easy to handle and are relatively inexpensive. Landscape boxes 18 inches to 24 inches high are very attractive when located properly. To build a landscape timber box use just one timber as the inside frame, nail to the flat side with long spikes like gutter nails. Pre-drill the outside timber so that the nail will go through... the treated timber is very dense. The raised planter is also very useful on slopes, something like terracing. Foundations of split-level houses can also use this type planter. And for top-of-the-line growing, add a drip system for watering. Miniatures thrive in good drainage and air circulation. A mini landscaper may be just the project for you to build this fall.

If experience is the name we give to our mistakes, the Rambler gained a heap of experience over the last month or two. All the trouble began in mid-August… but we're getting ahead of the story. The Rambler's daughter announced to the family about mid-summer that a garden wedding would be *just perfect,* particularly in the springtime. Since springtime was a long way off, no particular garden plans were launched except for some day-dreaming on background colors and locations. Shortly after, this rose garden event-of-the-season was moved up to mid-October… setting up a crash program to groom the roses (big ones and little ones) for maximum fall blooms. Since this is routine on the hot humid Gulf Coast, grooming began on August 15 to continue through August 23. Then disaster struck the garden, a NEW date was set for September 18… imagine a rose garden wedding without roses. What to do???

SOME ROSES REPEAT in Houston in about 28 days, although many-petaled varieties need 35 days or more. Some of the floribundas take even longer. Although there is nearly always some bloom from new breaks and growth, a heavy flush of bloom results from grooming per schedule. But it seemed worth a try to accelerate bloom by more food in a liquid form. The usual fall grooming routine calls for two ounces of 12-24-12 dissolved in a gallon of water per plant. Water thoroughly first, then feed. Repeat the same formula in about two weeks. Top off with a high phosphorous like *Carl Pool Instant* (8-56-10) about a week before full flush of bloom (hopefully rose show time). The wedding acceleration formula: a week after the regular feeding, apply two ounces of high nitrogen (15-5-10) with trace elements, plus one teaspoon of *Epsom Salts* (Magnesium Sulfate) plus a dash of Iron Chelates (per plant, dissolved in a gallon of water).

TOO MUCH FERTILIZER BURNS, as the Rambler found out the hard way. About four days after application, the first traces of leaf burn showed up on mature as well as recently produced leaves. Daily temperatures ranged from daytime highs of 95 degrees and nighttime lows of 78 degrees… and no rain. Hot and dry every day. At the end of the first week, lower leaves began to turn yellow and drop off (had previously been leafed all the way to the bud union). Brown and yellow leaves turned up here and there all over the plants. Bright, reddish-green new growth spread over the tops of the bushes; yellow leaves spread up from the bottom. And all this happened with enough water to feed a small swamp. Apparently the combination of too much food and hot weather shocked the bushes. Another Rambler garden groomed and fed in the normal way came on with good growth and no burn… and by mid-September had just as many blooms (and many more leaves).

WHAT HAPPENED on September 18?? The garden wedding came off on schedule in a setting of a few rose blooms, lush green growth on top, and canes with no leaves on the bottom. Fortunately some of the landscape beds of floribundas were not affected as badly and put on a good display. The lawn was a fertilizer advertiser's dream as a result of all the food and water.

OVERFED MINIATURES turn yellow, too. Even a light broadcast feeding of high nitrogen in place of Fish Emulsion and Carl Pool Instant knocked off leaves in less than a week. Later growth has been fantastic, if you like miniature blooms on low floribunda growth. The moral: roses big and small like a LITTLE food, slowly released all the time. A good organic soil mix, lots of water and half-strength feedings at regular intervals still work best.

TOO MUCH TRIMMING works against the grower, too. Plants need leaves to produce roses. Cutting to a five-leaflet is gospel to most rose folks. It is supposed to make a new bud develop faster, encourage plant vigor and generally give more blooms per season. But such grooming (and trimming of light growth) isn't ALWAYS in the best interest of the bush. Some good rose observers note that simply cutting off a spent bloom results in just as many breaks that come on as fast or faster than canes trimmed to a lower five-leaflet. Cut to a high leaf axil, the bush puts out new growth and leaves without hesitation. It's particularly noticeable in mass plantings, as varieties have growth differences. Light trimming of mass plantings produces more leaves throughout the season and considerably less winterkill. It follows that healthy, vigorous plants with more leaves (the food producers) are in better condition to take on whatever nature has to offer. You might want to make a note of some leafy plants in your own garden and see if there's a relationship between plant size this year and a start next spring. Of course, if you are an avid exhibitor you'll want to direct all of the strength of the plant to a few canes and blooms. But in the long run, there's a price to pay.

VINEGAR TREATS ALKALINE WATER in spray mixtures, but it's easy to use too much. Alkaline water in the 7.5 to 8.0 pH range needs only about one tablespoon of white vinegar per gallon for optimum results. More can cause browning of the leaf edge or occasional spotting. Add vinegar to alkaline water BEFORE adding spray materials. Sprays so treated seem to have a better wetting action and longer residual.

ROSES NEED A TONIC?? It's the Rambler's conclusion after years of trying one miracle after another that organics still work better and more consistently. Fish meal and blood meal encourage beautiful leaves that support blooms. Manures and alfalfa meal build strong plants. A tonic of fish emulsion in water makes big roses and miniatures happy. Some good, aged cow tea makes the sick well and the well even better. Feed the processes that make nutrients available. Then you'll be ready for a garden wedding almost any time (in season)!

The Rambler once noted that "growing roses is the art of getting used to what you didn't expect"… and that's still the case with the Rambler's overfed rose garden. As painfully reported in these columns in November, the September garden wedding turned out to be the non-rose event of the season… and all from too much fertilizer. Here's an update on the garden now (late October) when Gulf Coast gardens should be at peak bloom…

LONG, WEAK STEMS with lush, overgrown leaves top rosebushes with virtually no green growth on the lower canes. Blooms are sparse and small. Some of the new growth is blind with no sign of bud at all. The overall effect is spindly growth on top of long, thorny sticks. Complicating the problem is powdery mildew on the new lush growth. What's the solution: Water and lots of it. Rose beds with the best drainage and most water are beginning to respond… that is, more normal growth and development is appearing. The beds are now getting about four or five inches of water per week in an attempt to flush out the excess.

MINIATURES HAVE REBOUNDED better than the big roses. Yellow leaves in the center have dropped and are gradually being replaced with new growth. However, new top growth is completely out of proportion. RISE 'N SHINE is now nearly three feet tall, CHIPPER about the same (and laced with mildew). Even ROSMARIN is a robust two feet high and the same wide. Most mini blooms have disappointing vegetative centers or are grossly oversized for the variety.

FERTILIZING MORAL: Roses big and small like a LITTLE food, slowly released all the time. A good, organic soil mix, lots of water and low-strength feedings at regular intervals produce the most roses consistently. And keep this in mind when building a new rose bed… let the soil mix (not magic formulas) support good growth nature's way.

SUNSHINE makes roses grow and bloom… there's no substitute or cheating on the amount required. Marginal sunshine produces marginal roses. I made an interesting observation recently when reworking a long rose bed that ranged from full sun to filtered shade in a distance of about 50 feet. All one variety, the bushes ran from puny (With dieback) to vigorous. Bushes in the sun had good root systems, heavy canes and lots of leaves. Virtually no roots had developed on the shaded plants. Bloom production for the past three seasons had followed the same pattern. The point is that sunshine affects all aspects of plant growth and production. Don't waste time, money and plants in the shade. Switch off to shade-loving plants and enjoy gardening even more… with plenty of roses in the sun, of course.

ROSE BED DEPTH must be considered, too. It's possible to grow good roses in relatively shallow beds, and it's often done in beds raised above garden grade. It's routine on the wet Gulf Coast to ignore the heavy gumbo at grade and simply bring in a good soil mix and build a bed edging of some kind, winding up with a planting medium about a foot deep. It drains well, grows some good roses and is relatively easy to care for… until a long period of heat and drought. Then it is almost impossible to maintain moisture and growth. After digging up a number of existing rose plants for reworking or replanting over the years, the Rambler is convinced that deeper beds grow better roses. Raised beds are great, hut dig into the grade soil or gumbo at least a good shovel depth (deeper if you can) and work in some of the good planting medium; then add and mix until the desired depth is reached. Digging just a few old plants from deep-mix beds will make a believer of any rosarian. Or, to put it another way, pull up shallow-grown plants and compare the root systems. There's no comparison. It's worth the extra effort to put that $10 rosebush in a $10 hole… you'll get $100 worth in roses.

WINTER PROTECTION is a season-long exercise. In most parts of the country, roses have been put to bed and mostly forgotten. Check your protection again this month and add as necessary. *American Rose* September issue had a great series on winter protection; get out that issue and read it again. Whatever method makes you (and your roses) comfortable… do it. Insulating materials settle, so add some leaves that fell late. If wind is a factor, run another roll of rabbit wire around the rose bed to hold materials in place. Or, the Rambler thought that the trash bags with leaves was a great idea. This may not make an interesting scene for the front garden but is a practical way to hold protection in place in less public areas. And keep an eye on what's happening in the rose beds on a regular basis; it's much better than a big surprise next spring.

LIGHT SOIL MIX for roses… get it if you can. All kinds of soils will grow roses, but a light, friable mix laced with organic materials makes roses thrive. Light mix takes more water more regularly but pays off in blooms. Plants dug from light soils have masses of roots with less tendency to come to the surface. And it doesn't seem to make much difference if the rootstock is *Multiflora* or *Dr. Huey*. If some new or reworked beds are on your rose calendar for '83, think light. Add some sharp sand. Calcined clay works, too. Coarse organic matter helps. Soil, air and water work together to convert nutrients to a form available to roses; open up the soil for roots and everything works better.

And don't forget to enjoy roses more in '83. HAPPY ROSE YEAR!

JAN. 1983 — *No column printed this month.*

FEB.
1983

THOUGHT FOR THE MONTH: *An authority (on roses?) is a person who can tell you more about something than you really want to know.*

"Don't make your rose garden too big if your wife tires easily."

THIS BIT OF WISDOM still applies, particularly at this time of year when rose nuts are already thinking about trophies and certificates sure to be won at the spring rose shows. It's easy to dream about winners now... catalog promises and splashes of color are easy to believe. Thinking, planning and just plain looking at the world through rose colored glasses once in a while helps remind us that roses are a hobby and ought to be easy and fun.

ROSES ARE MORE FUN if you try something different once in a while. Instead of getting all of those new exciting selections this year, how about expanding and replacing with some of the old favorites that have brought pleasure to rosarians year after year. Most of the hype heard around the rose society centers on the new exhibition varieties, and that's logical because of the great influence of exhibitors. But the Rambler suspects that there are a good many growers out there who would like to enjoy some of the old-timers without feeling guilty. Maybe some of these great roses will fit your scheme this year...

A ROSE GARDEN hardly seems complete without *Dainty Bess,* delicate and fragile but vigorous in its own way. And stop to enjoy the fragrance of *The Doctor,* rich and warm with beautiful stamens at full-blown state. A tremendous rose. Another fragrance-maker is *Chrysler Imperial*, not much of a challenge on the trophy table now, but still full of color, fragrance and loads of blooms. *Avon* is a fragrant beauty, too. It likes warm weather and sunshine to really produce. Even the most insensitive nose can pick up what *Avon* offers. And how about a corner in the garden where *Crimson Glory* can spread and ramble and fill the area with blooms and fragrance. Great in a rose bouquet or low bowl, *Crimson Glory* continues to reward the grower smart enough to put in a couple of plants and leave alone.

MOUNDS OF ROSES are produced season-in and season-out by *Duet,* a great pink that is exquisite when cut and arranged in a silver bowl. Good garden color, stems, foliage, repeats quickly. A fun rose that's not seen much anymore. And the Rambler still likes *Tiffany,* reliable and beautiful in

any kind of weather. We used to have three *Tiffany* tree roses in front of our dining room window, and they were breathtaking. Bush or tree, *Tiffany* belongs. *Charlotte Armstrong* belongs in every garden, too. Somewhere in the parentage of most of the *new* roses we grow, *Charlotte Armstrong* still has qualities that most growers don't appreciate. Free-flowering, colorful, undemanding, this rose simply asks to be left alone to build up some good wood and then produces bushels of roses year after year.

BIG, LUSH ROSES appeal to many growers. And what could be bigger or prettier than *South Seas* or *Hawaii??* Both have some faults, but those huge blooms in healthy foliage are outstanding in the garden. When fully open, *Hawaii* is one of the prettiest roses you'll ever see. *Confidence* comes on in much the same way. Plenty of leaves, big blooms, not reluctant to bloom. And *Medallion,* probably confused somewhere along the way by a camellia. All worthwhile... all fun to grow.

VISITORS ENJOY all kinds of roses, and you should, too. Remember how much you enjoyed *Lemon Spice* when it was first introduced?? It may be hard to find now, but the search is worth the effort. *Apricot Nectar* grows much the same way... sprawling and uncontrollable, but full of blooms and fragrance. There are good ways to use *The Fairy,* too. Try planting on a wall or a bank, even a disreputable fence. In no time at all, *The Fairy* will soften and cover the scene with blankets of blooms. If you can find it, *The Fairy* on a tree standard is a real treat. It is particularly good when used with miniatures as a landscaping feature, probably easier to care for (spray) as a tree also.

CERTAIN ROSES BELONG TOGETHER. Like a planting of *Europeana* with *Iceberg* or *Summer Snow* in front. Plant these close together, get a massed effect. Particularly good along a driveway or foundation. *Europeana* and *Summer Snow* are even attractive when not in bloom. *Europeana* has very dark, red-green foliage that's more attractive than many landscape shrubs; *Summer Snow* is lighter green that looks more like a vine. And the Rambler's all-time favorite for a: mass of pink and foliage and well-mannered growth, *Rose Parade,* just has to be grown to be fully enjoyed. *Rose Parade* is hard to find now, but shouldn't be. It blends with almost anything.

TREE ROSES?? Great for mild climates, worth the effort in the colder areas. Just be realistic about the special protection that may be needed. For a real traffic-stopper, accent the landscape with two or three *Ole* tree roses. They can light up a landscape like no other rose. Not worth cutting, they bloom to be admired with the glossy, holly-like foliage. In a formal planting, try *Ole* trees with the miniature *Green Ice* as a white carpet. Very attractive.

GOT THE IDEA?? Build a rose collection as well as a rose garden. Some of the smaller nurseries can furnish these plants; or you may have to propagate some from cuttings… there's bound to be a grower-collector in your area who has been quietly enjoying these roses for years. Maybe you should be enjoying some of them, too.

If asked what part of the rose society program they like best, most members would probably have *refreshments time* high on the list... because that's the time the most interesting rose questions are answered. Wouldn't it be great to share some of this practical know-how with everyone workshop style?? Anyway, here's a garden collection of topics the Rambler was hit with over coffee just the other night...

DOING ANYTHING NEW THIS YEAR?? Not really, just trying to do things the old way... but a little better. Like less-formal miniature rose plantings with rocks, changes of elevation, weathered wood, maybe a garden accent or sculpture. Miniature roses are very attractive with other perennial materials, even small evergreens if kept in scale. Instead of a rock garden, how about a miniature garden with rocks?? Maybe a bonsai tree. An interesting stump, or a bird on the ground. Kept in scale, garden accessories are much easier to use with miniature roses than with big ones. It's easier to change your mind later, too. One of the most attractive mini gardens the Rambler has ever seen had roses, rocks, bulbs, annuals, fragrance plants and a shape that seemed to go from here to there with no apparent reason. It was an attention-getter year-round. Just hope that the Rambler's back and rocks give out at about the same time.

STILL LIKE ALFALFA FOR ROSES?? You bet. Every new rose bed, planting or rework has alfalfa (meal or pellets). For a new rose bed, add about 50 pounds for 100 square feet. A replacement rose here and there... add a handful to the soil in the hole. After pruning, broadcast about two cups per plant and scratch in a bit. You've never seen an unhealthy rabbit, have you?? Which is a reminder that alfalfa pellets are rabbit food, sold at a feed store. Your plants will literally hop out of the ground... seriously, alfalfa is a great conditioner-stimulator. Try some.

PLANTING IS A JOB. Is there an easy way? Planting new roses is a hands-and-knees business and a lot easier than bending over. Get a short shovel and get down to where the work is. If the bed is properly built, it's easy to scoop out a hole, rebuild a cone to support the roots and bush; then let water and soil do the rest. Cover the roots lightly and begin to run water slowly in the hole; add some soil that was placed aside. More water, more soil. A good rosarian is a muddy one; there's no need to tamp or pack. Hill up with some excess soil and mulch (bring in a little extra rather than scrape from the rose bed) to protect canes and conserve moisture. Keep moist with an overhead sprinkler... nothing to it.

ROOT PRUNING?? Generally. The Rambler lightly trims the ends of most of the roots and cuts out broken roots. Root tips are most prone to drying out; trimming exposes healthy tissue for new root hairs to develop. In my experience, trimming results in a healthier root system. Others disagree. If it works for you, keep it up. And if roots are excessively long for the planting area, shorten them up a bit. You're planting roses, not making an excavation.

WATER IS THE KEY IN PLANTING. Soak bare root bushes in water overnight before planting; add one of the magic *rooting elixirs* if it makes you feel better, but it really is not necessary. And when pruning and trimming up for planting, ALWAYS drop the trimmed plants into a garbage can of water and keep there until actual planting. As a last planting step, fish the bush out of the water and put it directly into the prepared hole. Don't scatter the bushes out in the bed waiting for you to get to them. Move from water to soil and the whole process works better.

CONTAINER-GROWN ROSES are high on the Rambler's list this year. The new mini-floras and large growing miniatures are ideal for containers that can be moved around and enjoyed. If something is not blooming, move up something that is. Containers can be redwood, cedar, clay pots, small barrels... whatever strikes your fancy and fits the landscape scheme. The soil mix needs to have good drainage as well as moisture-retaining qualities. This means addition of calcined clay (kitty litter) with its millions of pores to hold air, water and nutrients. A good mix is about 1/3 garden soil, 1/3 humus material sharpened with a little sand (builders' sand) and 1/3 calcined clay granules. It's sold under various names, but most feed stores, landscape supply firms or other outlets that cater to greenhouses, golf courses or large-scale plant propagators will have suitable granules in 50-pound sacks or by the ton. Calcined clay is what made growing tree roses in containers possible. It's good for propagating cuttings yourself, too. Try a few sacks, and it will become part of your regular garden routine.

FAST ROSE BEDS ARE NO PROBLEM. It's better to prepare beds in advance and allow the ingredients to mellow, but with organics, a first-rate rose bed in two weeks is easy. Build up the rose area, don't worry too much about what's below. Bring in some light soil first, a couple of inches, till it in well with existing soil. Then add organic matter and sand (something gritty) so that the final mix is about 1/3 soil, 1/3 sand and 1/3 organic stuff. Mix well with a roto-tiller or fork. Then add alfalfa pellets, rock phosphate or superphosphate, an inch or so of horse manure to get the whole mixture going and stir up again. Water down to settle. In a day or two, mix again and water. About the second weekend, you're ready to plant. No problem with bare root or transplanted roses. Natural ingredients blend and work for the rosarian who is in a hurry. But a caution, be ready to jump back out of the way because the roses are going to GROW!

APR.
1983

THOUGHT FOR THE MONTH: *With some rosarians, it's hard to tell if they're contributing to the solution or adding to the problem.*

ROSARIANS ARE FAMILIAR with the old put-down that goes "when all else fails, read the directions," but the Rambler wonders if the directions are as clear as they ought to be. Had a good example just recently when a "follow the directions" rosarian phoned to comment that it seemed a bit much to use alfalfa pellets, fish meal, fish emulsion, manure and *Osmocote* to get roses started in the spring (all of which had been recommended by the Rambler from time to time). After some explanation, the idea came across that these were alternatives to be considered, something like choosing between Tylenol and Anacin. But I think the grower still had a headache. You might want to get "fast, fast, fast relief" by following some of these directions...

COW TEA... As good for sick roses as chicken soup for sick rosarians. Back in BC (Before Chemicals), good gardeners always had a barrel working behind the garage. There's not much direct nutrient value, but the boost given soil micro-organisms makes everything work better. Rainwater works best, keep a couple of plastic garbage cans steeping all the time. Potato or onion sacks make good tea bags; fill with cow chips and tie with a long piece of rope or wire. Steep for about 10 days, slosh around once in a while. Use about 2 gallons of tea per sickly bush for super results. Great for roses in "sick bay," too. That is, those bushes in pots or cans that need restoration before returning to the rose bed. Cow tea twice a week works wonders.

OR TRY FISH EMULSION... instead of cow tea. Easy to mix in barrel or can. Works the same way. Gets the soil processes going in a hurry. Again, rainwater or well water works best; dilute according to directions on the bottle for large roses. Cut strength to 1/3 for use on miniatures. Greenest, happiest roses you'll ever see.

ANOTHER CLARIFICATION... The Rambler commonly recommends use of fungicides and insecticides at "full strength." This doesn't mean application as it comes out of the bottle or box without dilution... it means at the dilution rate specified on the label. A half-strength recommendation means following the label and reducing to a solution half as strong as labeled. Will try to be more specific in the future... and

you should, too.

SPRAY ALTERNATIVES... Good rose gospel says that a fungicide cleanup spray should be applied immediately after pruning, not waiting until leaves appear. The idea is to begin fungus control early and clean up over-wintering insects. In some cold climates, dormant sprays (oil, sulfur, etc.) are popular. But the Rambler recommends a safe approach for all climates, use of a combination fungicide-insecticide at LABEL SPECIFIED STRENGTH, thoroughly wetting the canes, bud union and mulch area. A good combination is *Manzate-Spectracide*, adding a little dishwashing detergent for better coverage. Or *Phaltan-Isotox* is good. Or *Funginex-Orthene* will clean up any bed of newly-pruned or planted roses (also available in combination as *Orthenex*). Use just ONE of these combinations, whatever you happen to have on hand. One is just as good as another. The same goes for a continuing fungus control program. When mildew conditions are right, the Rambler likes a combination of *Funginex* and *Phaltan* (*Funginex* at label dilution, *Phaltan* at 1/2 strength). Seems to give a longer residual. When blackspot is prevalent, use *Funginex* and *Manzate* (*Funginex* at label dilution, *Manzate* at 1/2 strength). Definitely a longer residual on the blackspot-prone Gulf Coast. During the hottest part of the summer, use *Funginex* by itself. Use just ONE of the combinations as required by the conditions.

OSMOCOTE??? Should it be used in addition to conventional surface feeding?? In most cases, probably not. *Osmocote* (or *Precise* or any other controlled release fertilizer) is used for convenience, a one-shot application that takes most gardens through the season. It doesn't make much sense to pay for controlled release convenience and then come right back with 12-24-14 or some other favorite food every six weeks or so. The only supplement that's needed with *Osmocote* is a source of trace elements if the soil is not well enough endowed with these important growth supporters. Most of the time, soils rich in organic matter combined with controlled release foods will support all the roses you'll ever need.

ANOTHER RECOMMENDATION... And this one's specific. You ought to get a copy of Beverly Dobson's *COMBINED ROSE LIST*, 1983. At $3.50 a copy, it lists Roses in Commerce and Cultivation, Rose Registrations since *Modern Roses 8* and hard-to-find roses and where to find them. Bev has done a great job, and you can count on her information. Easy to read, too. Before the rose season gets underway, you exhibitors and judges in particular ought to fire off a check to Beverly R. Dobson, 215 Harriman Road, Irvington, NY, 10533.

ODDS 'N ENDS... Cross-section cuts of old nylon hosiery make great rose ties, particularly for climbers or to tie heavy canes to stabilizing stakes. Has good stretch and won't cut the bark ... A SHADY ROSE SPOT?? Try planting micro-minis or miniatures bred for growing under lights. They seem to tolerate less sunshine and in fact perform better. Some plants of *Tiny Flame* in the Rambler's garden struggled until moved to an area with less than a half-day of filtered sun... A DOSE OF SALTS helps roses in the spring, Epsom Salts (magnesium Sulfate), that is. An ounce or two of *Epsom salts* per established plant in early spring seems to encourage basal breaks and green growth. Just broadcast over root area and water in. One of the best spring tonics you'll every try.

Some months ago, the Rambler offered this bit of wisdom for roses and rosarians: Whatever isn't growing wears out. And if you're not growing in your rose hobby, try out some of these *seedlings* thoughts this season...

MINIATURES IN POTS... decorative pots, that is. Lots of possibilities for blooms and landscaping. And with the new varieties coming on, any rosarian can make a patio, deck, side yard or walkway come to life. Although they are somewhat expensive, minis budded on short standards are very productive and beautiful, setting of planter pots. You're missing some real rose pleasure if you don't have miniatures in containers one way or another. Plus, they are easy to prepare and care for.

SOIL MIX IS THE KEY for roses in pots. Blend sandy loam for drainage, organic matter and calcined clay for moisture supply and enough volume to let plants develop. Feed with an organic support like Fish Emulsion to get the whole process started, and you're on your way. There are other variations, too. Some like to use *Osmocote* in the mix; others prefer inorganic liquid feeding with *Carl Pool Instant* or *Schultz*. Just get on a regular schedule and stay with it. Pay some attention, and your minis will tell you what they need.

PROBLEM WITH WATERING? If you can't water (or get someone else to) every-other-day or so, rig up a trickle water system with an emitter terminating in each large container. There are a number of inexpensive kits on the market, and easy to put together. Containers of various sizes? Each emitter can be regulated for just the right amount. For the real rose pro, add a siphon feeding system to the network. Anyway, you get the idea. The prospects are unlimited.

CONTAINER PLANTS come naturally when it's easy to make up a new batch. Keep a pile of soil mix handy (maybe next to the compost pile.) Whenever there's a need, you're ready to go. It's just as easy to mix up a big pile as a small one, and you'll find all kinds of good uses for the material.

GOOD EDGING MATERIAL. Try landscape timbers (wolmanized) cut in one-foot lengths and set on end. If the soil is reasonably soft, trench the perimeter edge a few inches and tap the cut timbers in place. Tamp the sides for a stable, decorative edging. The timbers can be stained, allowed to weather or even softened with plantings of spreading annuals (like alyssum) if the visual effect is too heavy. Curves, insets or straight runs are easy to build. Vary the length of the blocks (and reusable too), short lengths can be cut with an ordinary crosscut, tree-trimmer saw (and a little muscle power) and a new bed in place in no time at all.

INTO BUDDING ROSES? Practice with miniatures with understock of appropriate length and create your own mini-trees. Or they might be called miniature rose mushrooms, a good, stout understock cane with a blooming head of miniature roses. It's frequently seen in Florida; they bud miniatures on *Fortuniana* understock and get the productive plants a foot or so off the ground. Easy to spray and very colorful. With just a little skill and some patience (in short supply with most rosarians), you can beat the high price of tree-standard miniatures and grow the varieties that YOU want to grow, not just what the nurserymen want to sell. In the long run, you'll buy more miniature varieties than ever, so you are not really depriving the grower of his livelihood, just keep them in your own garden.

FUNGICIDE SPRAY PROGRAMS. A spray program is really not a program unless it is planned and regular. The best fungicide on the market can't do the job unless applied to the leaves. Keep a calendar, note material and day. If there's a failure along the way, the problem is easy to identify. Weekly application means just that: every week. *Funginex* will do the job under even severe conditions if applied weekly. But don't try to stretch the routine. When blackspot/mildew conditions are right, the protective spray must be on the leaves. Otherwise, it's an uphill battle all the way. A good way to ruin an otherwise-good season.

SOME ROSE SHOW TIPS. It's hard to keep an addicted exhibitor away from the show, but even more difficult to induce that novice grower to get on the show tables. Maybe some fun classes would help. The Open Bloom classes are a good example. Nearly every grower can have some good open blooms. Maybe some better trophies or better show position might encourage more participants. The public always enjoys the open blooms; we should, too. How about a Fragrance Class: Not to be judged on the basis of form, etc., but on fragrance. Have a cleanup regular judging team eliminate the really poor roses, then turn loose a team of sight-impaired folks and let their sharpened senses select the most fragrant. Stretch the fragrant roses out the full length of the table where visitors can get to them. It will add a whole new dimension to the show. And notice that I didn't suggest that there are sight-impaired judges... recruit the sniffers from a blind-related group.

A GUIDE TO ROSE SHOWS... visitors can't make heads or tails of a show schedule. Give them a simple guide that says hybrid teas compete first by variety and then against other varieties. Judges are looking for form, color, substance, etc. Floribundas compete against other floribundas... challenge classes are for specific requirements in collections, colors or varieties. Visitors to rose shows like roses or they wouldn't be there. Let's not frighten them away with bewildering schedules. Make roses easy and fun, and we won't be able to handle all of the membership applications.

If you're looking for a liberal rose education, you'll get all you bargained for around the rose society refreshments table. There's an answer (or two or three) for everything. How to choose?? Try a laid-back old timer who doesn't insist he's always right... might be just the answer you need. For a starter, here are some (not too laid-back) suggestions to

POWDERY MILDEW... Why and how. Caused by a fungus that thrives on new leaves, stems and buds. It's hard to control once started. Mildew likes dry weather (just the opposite of blackspot) with cool nights and warm days. Heavy dew conditions are ideal when the temperature is about 70 or so. The spores travel on the wind and set up new colonies on susceptible growth when conditions are right. Late spring, early summer and fall are right for the gray, disfiguring disease to appear.

Mildew fungus is dormant when conditions aren't right, but can spring into an epidemic nearly overnight. All it takes is a host plant and a breeze. Some rosarians even keep a sort of Judas-goat plant like Orange Flame, that will show traces of mildew well in advance of other varieties. And every rose grower knows how Christian Dior and mildew go together. Most varieties with lush, green growth are mildew-prone. The best protection is EARLY application of fungicide, well in advance of mildew conditions, redoubling efforts (and perhaps spray schedules) at the first sign of the grayish powder.

CONTROL MILDEW AT THE HOST. Don't let it get a start in late fall on green growth; maintain a good spray schedule. Thoroughly spray ramblers and climbers. Since it is hard to get good coverage on climbers and shrubs, spores carryover and then carry on to roses all over the garden. A fence covered with climbers can be beautiful but is a real problem with disease control. More frequent application, better wetting, better spray pressure and even spraying from a ladder will

FUNGICIDE USED ALONE seems to work better than when mixed with insecticide, and is an essential when using *ACTI-DIONE PM*, an old standby for powdery mildew. And this eradicant doesn't seem to work as well anymore. *Benlate* (*Benomyl*) has been popular the last ten years or

so.

The most recent hope for rosarians has been *Triforine* (*Funginex*), a combination for blackspot, mildew and rust. It's easy to use and gaining in popularity. And, by the way, if you have a large rose garden, buy *Triforine* packaged by *Ortho* (an 18% formulation) in preference to *Funginex* (6% active material). I'm told that the two formulations have different carriers, and I know that the 18% *Triforine* is less expensive in the long run. Use just one teaspoon of *Triforine* per gallon vs one tablespoon of *Funginex*. The shelf price for a quart of *Triforine* may floor you, but it really is cheaper.

SPRAY EVERY WEEK religiously when conditions are right. Concentrate on the new, green growth. The old, tough leaves on the bottom are safe. Or you may want to alternate *Triforine* and *Benomyl*. For really serious infection, the Rambler still goes back to *Acti-Dione PM*, used twice a week in bright sunshine. With hard, alkaline water, add about two teaspoons of white vinegar per gallon as a wetting agent. Otherwise, try to plant resistant varieties in areas with good air circulation (cuts down dew) and hope for the best. Relax a little, too. In really hot, dry weather, mildew will go away all by itself.

NEED A SPRAYER?? Not too expensive?? All most gardens need is a Hudson tank sprayer... there's a model and size for almost every garden. Some gardens even have more than one, using a smaller tank for herbicides or spot thrips control. Other tank (pump up) sprayers seem to be copies of Hudson; but whatever you buy, make sure that the garden shop or feed store carries gasket and repair kits for what you buy. That's about all that ever wears out (maybe the operator). The fiberglass tank model is good if you're a bit careless about washing out after use. For quite a bit more money, you can get a stainless steel model that will never rust.

PUMP UP SPRAYERS of three gallons or so work fine for up to 200 roses or so, dispensing materials evenly and effectively. Easy to fill, easy to wash out. For a large garden, or one with lots of climbers, a *Hudson Suburban* is a good investment, available in electric or gas-engine driven models. But be prepared to take out a loan at the bank. It sprays almost everything around the garden with a quick change of spray heads; it's also easy to fix and keep running.

LAST BUT NOT LEAST, keep a pistol-grip sprayer at hand, like the ones that dispense Mr. Clean. Most hold about a pint and are ideal for *Cygon* or *Orthene* application for thrips. A spray here and a spray there on buds and blooms makes white roses possible again. Cheap and easy… isn't that a good idea for a rose grower anytime??

For a real rose education, get out on a garden tour. Growers are doing things out there you won't believe (some good — some bad). It's all part of the fun of growing roses... like these ideas:

ROSE TRELLIS from electrical conduit. As attractive as wrought iron at a fraction of the cost. U-shaped and located at ends of formal beds about six feet wide, the trellises framed the plantings and supported a fine display of small-flowering climbers (including the Miniature Climber JEANNE LAJOIE). Nearly as easy to handle as wood, conduit can be shaped for a number of uses with a little practice and a good bending tool. A climber on a brick wall??? Offset heavy galvanized wire mesh about four inches using conduit as a sleeve over machine bolts. Drill the brick or mortar first, then epoxy bolts into place. Offset with conduit and secure with large washers and nuts. Not only very attractive but much easier to secure climbing canes.

MINIATURES in informal beds with garden features or other landscape materials are particularly attractive. Formal plantings are fine, but some varieties just seem to fit better with rocks or weathered wood, particularly with a change in elevation. One way or another, get minis up to be seen in another dimension.

HANGING BASKETS, BARRELS AND TUBS... really in this season. Mini-floras and spreading miniatures are very attractive used this way. A tub on or over an old stump, a half-barrel of roses to soften a harsh sidewalk or a hanging basket to set off a trellis or overhang. Fun to do... even in mid-summer.

WHERE TO HANG BASKETS has often been a problem, but the Rambler has stumbled on a solution that you ought to try. Build an A frame hanging basket rack; it can be moved from place to place (like in the sun in the spring, partial shade in the summer) and displays all manners of hanging baskets. Also can be dismantled as needed for storage. It's not the Rambler's design; Jack Walter of *Kimbrew-Walter* came up with the idea to display mini hanging baskets at shows and educational programs. About six feet long and six feet high, three racks are available for baskets and a bench for pot displays. Made of wood, galvanized pipe, machine bolts with wing nuts and cotter pins,

it's a cinch for anyone to build. To make it RE-ALLY easy, the Rambler will send you a detailed plan with materials list if you'll include a self-addressed business envelope. Guaranteed easy. The Rambler and helper built one in less than an hour and a half.

WHEN ROSES WON'T OPEN. Probably thrips, but many growers don't recognize the signs unless the blooms are open and discolored. Thrips can affect heavy-petaled and light-petaled roses, reds, whites and pinks. Heavy infestation can close down a whole garden. Look for bruised, discolored edges on tight buds. If they do open, they will be brown and deformed. Control thrips in the bud form. Mist buds and blooms regularly (at least weekly during heavy infestation), using *Orthene* or *Cygon 2E*. No need to spray the whole bush, concentrate on blooms; that's where the thrips are. The Rambler likes to alternate *Orthene* and *Cygon*; others prefer various combinations. Follow the directions. The Orthene marketed this year has a NEW PERCENTAGE of active ingredient; the directions call for THREE TABLESPOONS per gallon of water, twice as much as last year's formula. Check your supply. *Orthene* in powdered form is a better buy, but is a little more trouble to use. *Cygon* is available at most farm stores and is relatively inexpensive. But none of these materials will work unless applied. Like mildew, once the damage is done, nothing will restore the bloom to its intended beauty.

MULCHES BELONG. The Rambler is more and more convinced that mulches contribute to the wellbeing of roses even in climates where soil insulating and water conservation properties are not important. Soils can get tired; good organic mulches feed soils and keep them productive. Use materials that break down and add nutrients and humus to the soil. Mixtures work best, they stay loose so that water, air and fertilizers can pass through. A mulch doesn't have to be nitrogen robbing. Throw on a little extra nitrogen at the next feeding and the end result is far better than nitrogen fertilizer alone. Some of the best roses the Rambler has ever seen were grown with a four-inch mulch of wood chips just like the tons of chips hauled away by tree trimmers every day. Compost a while if you can, but don't be afraid to combine some rough-cut and shredded material and let it break down in the beds. For some reason, many growers think that organic matter has to be completely composted before using. Not true. Some of the best things happen while the composting process is going on.

USE THE COMPOST. It won't do a bit of good in the bin. The more you use, the more you'll make. Keep two or three bins or piles: going all the time. It's a sure sign of a good grower.

AUG. 1983

THOUGHT FOR THE MONTH: The quickest way to get a rosarian interested in a project is to tell him it's none of his business.

HAPPY ANNIVERSARY RAMBLER! 13 years and 154 RAMBLING columns wiser, we're ready to impose on you good readers another season of rose ideas you won't want to miss… keeping in mind the old saying that "Ideas are much like children; our own are wonderful." Anyway, here are some wonders for the month:

HOT WEATHER brings to mind (and an aching back from a good watering system would sure roses more fun. But how to do it without taking out a loan at the bank. The *Dramm* nozzle irrigation system may be just the answer for many rosarians. It's a cheap and easy way to put water where it will do some good, and can have a system running over a weekend. Since the *Dramm* system is not buried, it's simple to relocate or modify and works equally well in hot or

DRAMM NOZZLE makes it all possible. It's a three-piece nozzle of hard plastic with a tapered thread that screws into a neoprene saddle-washer inserted in rigid plastic pipe. A pin diffuser sprays water in a full circle parallel to the rose bed. Water sprays out, not up. Distribution is even, easily controlled without waste. Saves time, too. A rose bed 40 feet can be soaked in about 20 minutes. Miniatures thrive on a *Dramm* system; the flat, fine spray washes off mites and creates 100% humidity.

USE SCHEDULE 40 PVC PIPE, either 1/2-inch or 5/8ths available at most lumber yards, hardware stores or plumbing shops. PVC pipe cuts easily with a hacksaw; all connections are made with PVC cement. It's very easy to work with, even for a beginner. Lay pipe in the rose bed (or other planting); mark locations for spray heads. Remove and drill holes (15/32nds) at nozzle locations in the pipe with drill press or drill with centering attachment; be careful with alignment (that is, get all the holes in the top of the pipe). Nozzles are usually spaced feet apart or custom fitted to plants. Clean the drilled hole with a pocket knife and insert tapered washer (fits screw in the nozzle. The nozzle is also threaded and tapered; two or three turns by hand will give a tight fit. All the connections can be made without tools, just like a hose connection.

ASSEMBLE the pieces in place with PVC cement (but be fast, the stuff sets very quickly). Stabilize the system with a leg formed by a tee connection and stuck into the A leg on each end and in

the middle is good to an ordinary garden hose with a quick coupler, nearly as convenient as a buried supply line but more flexible and less work. About 45 pounds of house pressure will supply 1/2-inch, 40-foot irrigating line with 15 to 18 nozzles an area from three to four feet in diameter, depending on pressure. Control volume (and spread) at the house tap or install a control valve at the head of the line. Runs longer that 40 feet may require 5/8-inch pipe to deliver enough volume.

MAINTENANCE is easy. If a nozzle has an uneven spray or stops up, pull the deflecting pin, and a thin stream of water shoots straight up and clears most junk out of the line. For a serious obstruction, unscrew the top half of the nozzle and the whole system can be flushed, usually without getting wet. Lift and drain during winter months; take out the nozzles and store. *Dramms* are cheap, too. Nozzle and washer cost about 75 cents. Available from many greenhouse supply companies or by mail order from advertisers in these pages. Our rose mail order friends offer an advantage; they include instructions and diagrams with each order. Install a *Dramm* system in just one bed, and you'll soon convert the whole garden.

ROSE CLIPS FROM HERE AND THERE… Manure mulch is still the greatest; if you have a source, use it. Good cow tea with each watering is a real asset; it makes the whole process work better. Continually enriching the soil, manure/compost/organic matter mixtures attract earthworms, assuring the grower that the roots like the conditions, too… LIQUID FEEDING make things happen fast, getting nutrients into the root zone to be used. Works best when the rose bed is soaked first; then apply about two gallons of mix per plant. Water again lightly. Exhibitors will routinely liquid-feed two and four weeks before a show. What to use?? Depending on availability, try *Carl Pool, Schultz, Peters, Ra-Pid-Gro* or anyone of a number of soluble foods. Add about a tablespoon of fish emulsion per gallon to the mix, and it works even better (something like cow tea in a jug)… WEED PROBLEMS?? Get some *ROUND-UP*, the herbicide that does not stay in the soil. It's available in small quantities now as *KLEENUP*, sold by Ortho. But the best buy is still a gallon of Roundup split up among several rosarians. Most farm/feed stores will have it. Watch spray drift, it works on anything green. Rather corrosive, too. A fiberglass spray tank is a good idea... even better, set aside a small sprayer for herbicides only. Then there's no chance of carryover to good leaves... FINALLY, the American rose market is getting shrub-type roses that bloom and bloom. Confetti, introduced this year by Armstrong is a great example. Easy to grow, vigorous, colorful, happy in a mass or as a single plant, this rose will never make the show table but WILL make anyone who sees it want to share in this fun way to enjoy roses.

SEPT. 1983

THOUGHT FOR THE MONTH:
Always do right. This will gratify some rosarians and astonish the rest.

SOME BITS AND CLIPS FROM HERE AND THERE... hopefully not too many spent blooms but some real prize-winners to make your rose garden more fun...

WANT A DIFFERENT ROSE PRO-GRAM?? Have just the thing for you. Hold a rose social, an informal meeting with the emphasis on fun. Regular meeting place or someone's garden. Houston had one in July: Garden Center building and adjacent rose gardens. Strolled and visited in the gardens for a half-hour or so, fortified with popcorn and lemonade. Consulting Rosarians held forth in all their wisdom. Entertainment inside later. Two singing groups with guitars (all rose growers and members). Then a Rose Password game with prizes... one-word clues, audience in two teams. All rose-related, then a rose sing-a-long, new lyrics for familiar tunes. How about a few stanzas of "Growin' in The Wind" such as "How many trees must a grower cut down, before there is plenty of sun?" Lyrics by Mary Fulgham. If you would like an outline for the evening with game, lyrics and what-have-you, drop the Rambler a note. Will be glad to send along the whole package.

MADE AN ERROR (OR TWO) LAST MONTH, first ones this season (I keep the score). Recommended *ROUNDUP* as a bargain in a gallon quantity as a best buy. Was a VERY expensive buy; suggest you buy the QUART size instead so you won't have to take out a garden loan. Also, the alternative to one-half inch PVC Schedule 40 pipe is three-fourths inch, not five-eighths. Will carry lots more water and is only moderately higher in cost. But both ideas are still very sound. Roundup does a fine job on green materials and breaks down in the soil very quickly. Ideal for clearing out growth in an area this fall for a new rose bed. And seriously, get going on a *Dramm* nozzle watering system for an existing bed or any new beds you are planning. Both you and your roses will like it.

RECOMMENDATIONS. Not lightly given by the Rambler, but both of these are worthwhile. Before ordering roses this fall, get Bev Dobson's *Combined Rose List*, 1983. Lists roses in commerce, new rose registrations and hard-to-find roses. A bargain at $3.50. Send to Bev at 215 Harriman Road, Irvington, NY, 10533... Save a stamp by joining the Rose Hybridizers Associa-tion (RHA) at the same time; Bev is Treasurer. A great quarterly publication that will expand your interest in all phases of roses. Great group, too. Dr. Bob Harvey and Annette Dobbs edit the materials from outstanding pros and serious amateurs from all over the world. Just $5.00 a year. Get an envelope ready right now; you won't regret it.

THE GREAT VINEGAR FLAP... Have been reading authoritative articles picked up by local bulletin writers from here and there that there is no clinical support of the effectiveness of adding small amounts of white vinegar to spray mixtures to reduce alkalinity and increase effectiveness of certain insecticides. Whatever the lab folks say is fine, but a good many serious growers report that about two teaspoons of vinegar per gallon of water (IF the water is alkaline) increases coverage of spray materials without danger of burn. And that's the whole idea when spraying. Get good coverage with good materials in the right concentration. Anyway, for whatever reason, it seems to work, and it's cheap and safe. You might want to give the idea a try. Watch for spray materials to spread out, not bead up on leaves.

TIRED BEDS?? Rose beds and rosarians get tired near the end of a long season. Probably all the rose beds need is a little light cultivation from time to time to let water and air in the soil. Helps move organic matter, too. Mulches and some soils tend to pack from rainfall and sunshine. Break up the crust first. Then open up tight soils with a spading fork. Punch some small holes around the drip line of the bush with a fork, the four-prong kind that's about six inches long. Spade all the way in and work back and forth a few times (easier when soil is damp). Food, water and air can get into the root zone where the work is going on faster. It's particularly good for rock phosphate or superphosphate. Give each bush three or four good jabs; it's a good practice most anytime.

CHECK YOUR *ORTHENE*. You may not be getting the results expected as the concentration of active ingredient has been changed in new supplies. Read the label carefully for recommended application. It's still a good product, you'll just have to use more in the mix. Best buy is probably the wettable powder form of *Orthene*. It goes into the mix easily and leaves no noticeable residue.

COLD WEATHER is coming. And healthy roses tolerate more cold than weakened ones. Winter kill might well be called summer kill. Even good winter protection can't make up for poor summer care. As the season winds down, keep up the fungicide spray program. Roses with sick leaves don't have the reserve to take on a cold, dry winter. Keep all the leaves possible; let nature prepare plants for winter. And don't skimp on water even though the hot part of the season may be over. Roses need lots of water; if the bed is properly built, it's almost impossible to use too much. Deep soak, don't sprinkle. You'll know your beds have enough when water runs out of the beds. Then water again before they dry out completely.

COMPOST TIME is almost here. Don't throw anything away that can be added to the soil later. Pile up some of those leaves, and the Rambler will tell you next month how to make the world's best conditioner/fertilizer without much effort at all.

Reflecting on the rose season now winding down, it seems that nature gave us her best (worst) shot this year with unseasonable lows, record breaking highs and generally unpredictable conditions… but have you noticed that the rose survived in spite of all this, producing loads of blooms like they always do? Which leads the Rambler to believe that it's the rosarian who needs the tender care more than the roses. Anyway, here are some items to help you feel better while planning ahead for next year…

MOUNDS OF LEAVES become a problem for many rosarians this month… a very pleasant problem to have. It's a rich harvest and should be made available for roses with some sort of compost pile even if all the leafy production can't be used. Used for winter protection or composting, leaves return far more to the garden than the small amount of work required to make them effective. Experience the benefits of compost just once, and you'll find space for more leaves next year. If no space at all is available for a compost pile or rick, use a vegetable or flowering annuals area or maybe the spot where the new rose garden is planned.

COMPOSTING IN PLACE is easy. Just turn and dig the soil in the bed area making a wind-row of soil. Anything green helps the process, or add a good source of nitrogen like manure or cottonseed meal. Keep moist and turn lightly now and then while the weather is good. Add some more leaves as the pile goes down. Before hard-freeze time, the partially composted material should be broken down enough to till and mix in place or can be added to other bed areas. The composting season can be stretched a bit by covering trench or pile with black plastic to hold heat. It works even in freezing weather.

LEAVES USED AS WINTER PROTEC-TION also breaks down, but much more slowly. The object in winter protection is to keep the covering light with plenty of air space, in much the same manner as insulating materials. Leaves tend to moderate weather conditions, both hot and cold, and when piled in the beds, will leave behind some good humus material to begin a new season. If a leaf blanket is your winter protection method, don't forget to add more leaves as the blanket settles, something like cornflakes in a box.

Winter protection is simply a matter of preventing the freezing-thawing cycle and drying out of rose canes. Leaves can do the job very well.

A MOUND OF SOIL or compost over the bud union and lower canes plus lots of leaves will keep most roses in good shape with temperature ranges from 20 below to 50 above, even complicated with cold, dry winds and bright sunshine. Wire baskets, rabbit-wire fences, evergreen boughs or even a short snow fence will help keep leaves in place. Some cold climate rosarians even use a combination of cones and leaves for protection. Trim canes and set cones first, then fill in bed space with lots of leaves, making a protective insulation for the cones and maintaining a more even temperature.

NATURAL WINTER PROTECTION WORKS. Really cold climates may require burying in soil so that freeze-thaw and drying are eliminated. But most areas do very well with soil over the bud union and an insulating blanket by nature. Here's a typical comment from a reader in Ohio: "I don't have time or energy to build boxes or to bury roses, so I have always thrown on some dirt from the garden area and piled on leaves as high as they would go. Even get some leaves from the neighbors. It's not very fancy, but my roses always do all right."

RAIN PLAGUES ROSARIANS, TOO almost as much as drought, but that doesn't have to happen. Good drainage yields dramatic results but is commonly overlooked by rosarians who otherwise go to great lengths to make the bed just right. Some gardens are blessed with good drainage, but many are not. If you don't have it, make it.

AGRICULTURAL DRAIN LINE is the way to go in many cases, and fall is a good time to install. Relatively inexpensive, ag drain comes in rolls, corrugated for greater flexibility and can be laid over, under and around garden problems. To make a new bed or rejuvenate an old one, dig a trench the length of the rose bed and about a foot below the normal root level, gradually sloping down to a drain, ditch or even a gravel leaching pit. Use an inch or so of gravel in the bottom of the ditch; lay the line and partially cover with tar paper to keep drain holes open. Then backfill with sand or light garden soil for a couple of inches and top off rose bed with a good, friable soil-sand-humus mixture. You'll enjoy dramatic results the first season. Water, air and soil begin working together as nature intended.

Speaking of working together, you might recruit a helper for the trench project. Which is another way of saying that a rosarian's season is never done. Good Luck!

How's your rose-score-card this season?? More successes than failures?? Now's the time to note what worked and what didn't. Reflecting on the season just ended, here's how some of the Rambler's favorite treatments fared...

CONTAINER GROWN floribundas and miniatures worked fine, and a tree-standard *Oklahoma* developed into a robust plant with loads of blooms in just one season. Floribundas planted three to a half-barrel were much more striking than two plants or two plants with a tree rose. The floribunda *Charisma* was particularly good; three plants filled a half-barrel with good growth and color. Feeding program was Osmocote with monthly light applications of fish emulsion. To encourage new leaves after some storm damage, I applied two ounces of Epsom Salts (magnesium sulfate). All of the containers were heavily mulched with pine bark chunks. Even during the hottest part of the summer, watering every other day kept the plants in good growth.

OAK BARRELS or large clay pots are far superior to plastic containers or even redwood containers as far as moisture retention is concerned. Roses in the oak barrels performed the best of all. Whatever container used should be plenty large to hold enough roots to support top growth. Moisture retention is a factor, but every growing plant has to develop a root to top growth balance.

EXHIBITION MINIATURES can be grown in containers, and except for the watering are as easy to care for as minis grown in beds. Growth is much easier to control under these conditions. Once the roots have filled the container, future size and top growth is up to the grower. It's really interesting to work with some minis in this way. Once the formula is worked out, there are no more vegetative centers or rank growth from too much nitrogen. And it is very colorful to move minis in full bloom around on the patio. Don't be afraid to give them a try.

OSMOCOTE plus supplemental feeding?? Seems like a contradiction to use controlled-release fertilizer for convenience and then supplement on a regular basis, but the practice does produce bigger plants and more blooms Obviously a controlled release material keeps some food available for the plants all the time, and they take advantage

of it. Supplemental feedings with trace elements or a timely stimulant just keep up the good work. Supplements seem to do the most good when dissolved and applied in a liquid form and go to work much faster. It's more work, but the effort is worth it in better blooms and foliage. The Rambler noticed great difference in beds and containers with *Osmocote* PLUS supplements compared to *Osmocote* alone.

PALE LEAVES on container-grown plants respond to a good gypsum flush every now and then. Salts tend to build up in containers, especially with clay soils and alkaline water. The clay particles tend to stick together, upsetting the balance of soil, air and water. In this condition, gypsum opens up the spaces and the good soil processes take over again. Dr. John Gannon wrote an article for the *Annual* some years ago in which he described the action "like pulling the cork out of a bottle." Gypsum, of course, works in alkaline clay rose beds, too. A small handful of gypsum per whiskey half-barrel is just about right. Scale up or down depending on the container size; application can be inexact. Water in well and enjoy results.

WORM CASTINGS... really work. Miniature roses thrive on this natural food, used as a top dressing or in soil mix for beds or pots. About a half-inch of castings broadcast in a mini bed and scratched in with other organic material produced excellent results with health, glossy foliage and top blooms. Saw no evidence of overfeeding such as oversized blooms, vegetative centers or lush foliage without blooms. Potted minis had about one-fourth castings by volume in the potting mix; no other foods added (such as *Osmocote*). It's cheap and it works if you can find a local supply. Check an organic gardening friend for information.

ROSES WITH GALLS frighten many rosarians all out of proportion. Roses have had galls for a long time and will continue to have strange growths, but not necessarily disabling. The Rambler has had huge plants with galls, but they still grew and had roses. Infected and uninfected roses grow side by side. But if the growths bother you too much, pull up the plants and consider it an opportunity to try some new varieties without having to expand to rose beds. Fewer galls are noticed (or are disabling) in sandy, light soils. Bad unions and shanks have fewer galls (or they dry up) when exposed to sunlight. Trim galls, expose to sun and air. Paint on some *Lysol* or *Clorox* if you want, but it doesn't seem to make any difference. The Rambler trimmed and exposed galls of various sizes all season and still had lots of roses. You can do the same. And remember, roses are fun.

The year-end routine for columnists is to review and reflect on the dwindling days, arriving at some carefully qualified conclusions (mostly hindsight) for the benefit of those readers who haven't gotten to their summer magazines yet. It's a fun way to lay some conclusions on the readers without having to take the consequences. Like the Rambler always says, "if it doesn't grow right, you must have done something wrong." Here are some things that DID grow right, but you'll have to wait until spring to find out...

GOOD ROOTS grow in light, friable soil, supported with lots of organic material. In a late-season landscape revamp (we can do that in Houston), even one-year plants dug from a bed sandy enough to plow with your fingers had masses of fine roots going all directions. As any rosarian knows, good roots make good roses. It's amazing to compare root system in heavy, tight rose beds and roots from sandy locations. There are drawbacks in sandy beds, sure but the advantages are way ahead. It takes more water and consistent feeding to make sandy beds produce, but the results are worth it. It's the Rambler's conclusion that the roots spread out looking for water and food. If light mixes are good for rooting cuttings, similar soil combinations ought to grow roots and roses. Get some grit in your next rose bed.

MINIATURE TREE ROSES... really fun to grow. Minis budded on tree standards (about 18 inches) add a new dimension to a rose garden, even one with lots of other miniatures and big roses. Ideally used as accents; perform beautifully in containers, tree minis are on the expensive side, but worth it in special situations. The Rambler has two containers of Beauty Secret that have outperformed the same bush types three to one. Wouldn't trade them for anything. A couple of Sunspray, too. Beautiful.

Confetti... one of the most fun roses around. Makes a colorful hedge, mass, thicket or specimen plant of yellow-cerise-orange blooms hard to believe. It's listed as a red blend floribunda, but that doesn't tell the story. Grows vigorously, handsome foliage all the way to the ground, loads of bright color (fair form) that drops its petals cleanly and stays in bloom all the time. A staggered row of confetti in just one year will make an impenetrable

barrier for kids, dogs, mailmen (maybe even blowing dust). Striking and colorful. A good variety for a rose beginner. Only one drawback: stops traffic in the street.

Simplicity... appropriately named. Another hedge rose (pink) that is very vigorous, hardy and busy. Almost no maintenance, prolific bloom, abundant repeat. Will never make it to the rose show but will make friends of a lot of neighbors. As good as a fence and more colorful. Want to hide something? Plant *Simplicity*. Great rose that hopefully will be the forerunner of similar types with better individual blooms and a wide range of colors. Meantime, enjoy what's available.

Red Flush... the miniature answer to sidewalk edging. A landscaper's rose. Makes a basketball-size mound of green leaves and warm red blooms. Shear it once in a while if it gets too big. Shape like a boxwood or yupon. Has consistently good blooms and few complaints. Particularly good when used in a group.

LIKE YELLOW?? Then Rise 'n Shine is the landscaper (and exhibitor, arranger, ordinary gardener) miniature rose for you. Does all things well. Don't overfeed or it will get out of hand. Probably the most versatile miniature you'll grow.

OTHER GREAT MINIS this season for the Rambler...

Minnie Pearl is the hit of the season just like its namesake. Vigorous, good pink that doesn't fade, super form and seems to like anywhere it is planted. Just a super mini that does well in the shows or on the breakfast table. Buy a couple and really begin to enjoy minis...

Helen Boehm is another good one hybridized by Jack Christensen, widely available now as well as from Armstrong. Light pink with a little cream, usually exhibition. Medium plant that is quite attractive. Beautiful in a silver or pewter container.

Chattem Centennial is a mini orange-red spotlight. Glows with color. Not much at rose shows, but consistently in bloom. Looks great used in front of Marina or Charisma. Overall effect is like an orange mound.

Center Gold... a promotional mini recently released by the American Rose Foundation for commercial sale. This one by Harm Saville is a beauty with deep gold color and top form. You'll see more of this one as it becomes more widely available. The Rambler liked Harm's comment that it occasionally throws a white bloom, but that's like getting two roses on the same plant. Smaller than *Rise 'n Shine*, but really good.

OUT FOR A WHILE... and maybe not in your garden but ought to be. *Brandy*, an apricot blend hybrid tea, gets off to a slow start, but once established puts out great color and substance. Probably as pretty full blown as in exhibition stage. Just be patient, in cool weather this rose really performs. Smells good, too... *Mon Cheri* is another that has been overlooked, possibly because of the exhibitors. Super red blend hybrid tea, color just vibrates. Shading perfect, form less than perfect. But lots of them. Holly foliage like *Granada*. Enjoy a couple this year for sure... *Madras* is another HT to be enjoyed. Pink blend, but bright, outstanding color. Vigorous, good foliage and sometimes short stems. Can hardly wait for springtime to see it again.

DISCLAIMER... If these fun roses don't do for you what they did for the Rambler, you must be doing something wrong (see first paragraph). Happy Ordering!

Howard Walters, 1984.

Rosarians become semi-dormant in January... it's too early for really hard work to begin in the garden but late enough for last year's roses to get better and better. The story about the Queen of the Show winner is told more often when snow is on the ground; it's the only rose that has more form, color, size and character with old age. But if your eyes are weak from catalog visions and you're tired of rose stories, put on some rose colored glasses and ramble along with some of these ideas for more fun with roses in '84...

APPLY COMMON ROSE SENSE REGU-LARLY... It's an ingredient a good many rosarians leave on the shelf in the garage as they apply secret ingredients and miracle cures to rosebushes, somehow beating Mother Nature at her own game. But the game rules haven't changed: good soil, good water, good sunshine and good practices grow roses. Tack that reminder on your garden shelf, and '84 is already off to a good start.

SUNDAY SYNDROME occurs when rosarians become overanxious. If you don't recognize this problem, Sunday Syndrome describes a rose-bush worn out from pruning, grooming, feeding, scratching, watering, spraying and fussing (not necessarily in that order). Most rosebushes are relieved to see the rosarian go back to work on Monday morning. The symptoms commonly appear on Thursday of each week... yellow leaves, burned leaves, limp foliage and so on... only to go through another ordeal on Sunday. Happens in early spring, too. Warm Sunday morning; uncover bushes, throw on fertilizer, water a little, enjoy springtime feeling only to have hard freeze on Tuesday night while rosarian is out bowling. Nature works her wonders gradually; rosarians shouldn't try to improve on the process.

ROSE CATALOGS are great in the winter, but keep an eye on what's happening outside as well. Watch for some clues on the effectiveness of your winter protection system. Does it keep up with changes in the weather?? The best methods handle a broad range of conditions and usually use natural materials. Leaves and soil have been nature's way to protect things since time began. If the insulating materials are running low (settling, blowing away) add some more. Be generous. Just do what comes naturally.

ORDERING NOW?? PLANNING?? What's the best rose source?? The best source is the grower-outlet who is able to deliver a fresh #1 plant, will stand behind it and who wants to keep you as a customer. The source may be mail order or local nursery, California or Texas, bare root or potted. Check with some other rose growers in your area on their sources. Specify delivery dates for your area; don't rely on that order-blank phrase "arrival for spring planting". Look into how roses are shipped and handled: does the local nurseryman know how to hold roses?? What kind of a potting job does his crew do?? If a source has been taking good care of you, let him know. If a problem needs correcting, let him know about that, too.

ROSARIANS MAKE MISTAKES, TOO; it may not be the grower's fault. Hope that you aren't guilty of the most common mistake in handling a new rose... roots drying out in the sun while the rosarian decides on spacing, location, takes a coffee break etc. Soak bare root roses in water overnight, and keep them in water until just before final pruning and planting. Dry roots and dehydrated bushes just won't start. The commercial nurseryman goes to great lengths to deliver a fresh plant. It can all be undone with careless handling.

DEHYDRATED ROSES just don't grow. Don't be taken in by new crop packaged roses at the supermarket, drugstore or street corner peddler, no matter what kind of bargain it appears to be. Supermarkets should sell groceries; nurseries should sell roses. Packaged roses with chopped roots, butchered tops and a handful of wood shavings are seldom bargains... and are worth even less after a few days in a sunny store window. Plant good roses in the first place. It takes a good deal more time and effort to try to grow a poor plant than to grow a healthy plant... and the results can't be compared.

FOR MORE IN '84, work out your rose schedule now, particularly a spray schedule. Fungus control is a matter of prevention. Start a program IMMEDIATELY after pruning, no matter where you live. Drench the canes and bud union (if exposed) the same day plants are pruned. Some areas like oil-sulfur cleanup sprays, but good, safe practice recommends combination of a broad spectrum insecticide with your favorite fungicide

(*Benlate, Manzate, Funginex, Phaltan*). Use at label strength and maybe add a little spreader-sticker to encourage penetration into the cracks and crevices of the older canes and bud union. The object is to control over-wintering spores BEFORE temperature and humidity are right for growth of these organisms. Do NOT wait for new leaves to appear. And don't forget to spray climbers and shrub roses at the same time. An infected host plant can spread spores like wildfire when conditions are right. In about two weeks, use the insecticide-fungicide combination again. Then follow regular fungicide program (week to ten days) throughout growing season, adding insecticide ONLY when really necessary. A clean start will go a long way toward a clean garden all season long.

ENJOY A ROSY '84.

Everyone is a great rose grower in February... there's no critical panel of judges around to find fault(s). Unless you have an energy conserving greenhouse, you won't have to show how good a grower you are for several months. But now is the time for good growing to start...

TIRED ROSE BEDS?? Rework and rebuild around the weather man when plants are dormant, preferably just before the soil warms up. Attempting to doctor up planting locations where roses have been removed just won't accomplish the same thing as overall rejuvenation of the bed. Some sure winners may still be growing in the bed, but the transplant risk doesn't outweigh the advantages of afresh bed. Remember how the roses grew when the beds were new?? Most old rose beds become depleted as organic matter breaks down and the soil becomes tight. Mulch on top doesn't do the same job as organics in the root zone. And the more we feed, the faster beds wear out. Nitrogen breaks down and uses up the materials that bring life to the soil. Rose growth gradually declines; more fertilizer won't reverse the process.

DIG BUSHES T0 BE SAVED with a spading fork; don't prune or otherwise encourage new growth. Bury or cover with soil, sacks or other material that will keep bushes cool and moist while the bed is being reworked. Try to preserve dormancy in every way possible; it's safe to hold roses for two weeks or so if necessary. Rebuilding is just like a new bed: a mixture of about 1/3 loamy soil, 1/3 compost or other organic matter and 1/3 gritty sand is about right for most areas. Add some bone meal, rock phosphate or superphosphate (your choice) and thoroughly work into the future root zone where it will do some good. For 100 square feet of bed, add 50 pounds of alfalfa meal or pellets and 50 pounds of gypsum, especially if you have a clay soil. A reliable soil test may suggest other modifications, particularly if pH is off. But most of the time, just organic matter and soil will make beds productive again.

DON'T ADD SOLUBLE FERTILIZERS if the bed is to be replanted in a short time. It's safer to feed from the top when bushes are established. Deep cultivate the new mix two or three times, wet down after each tilling. In about two weeks, if the weather has been cooperative, the rejuvenated bed is ready to plant. Transplanting dormant roses is just like handling bare root roses. Prune canes according to the usual practice for your climate. Wash off the roots and trim out any dead or broken parts. Trim root ends lightly to encourage callousing and new feeder roots. Also trim out any root galls or gall growths on the shank or bud union. If very large galls girdle the shank or involve many roots, throw them away and start over. It's more work to grow a sick plant than a good one.

COLD WET WEATHER is considered a blessing in this part of the country; we try to get new roses into the ground just before or even during a rainy spell so that bushes will come established with lots of water. Until feeder roots start, bushes have to rely on moisture stored in the roots and canes. Warm weather or dry, cold wind can cause real stress; canes dry out before roots are ready to go to work. It's the reason that canes of new plants (or transplants) should be hilled up with soil to hold moisture and maintain a constant, moderate temperature. Around here, a muddy rosarian is a smart one... letting nature do part of the work.

THE FRAGRANT FORMULA... an *olde tyme* favorite for artificial manure that grows grass on a fence post. This is for the rosarian who doesn't have a farm friend for the real stuff. The Fragrant Formula is just as good (maybe better because it releases more nutrients) and can be produced on any city lot. Enjoy all the benefits without the cow. Here's the formula:

3 ample yards of compost materials or leaves
100 pounds of cottonseed hulls (something coarse)
100 pounds of cottonseed meal
100 pounds rough cut alfalfa meal (or pellets)
50 pounds of bone meal
50 pounds of fish meal

YOUR LOCAL FEED STORE will have all the ingredients except the leaves. Use any area suitable for composting, maybe the corner of an annual bed. Pile the coarse materials about two feet deep. Add other ingredients a little at a time and turn with garden fork or pitchfork. Moisten LIGHTLY; turn with a fork twice a week for two weeks. Cover with plastic if in a hurry, but allow SOME heat to escape. When the pile is working properly a sharp ammonia odor will leak out. A DIFFERENT ODOR will leak out if the pile gets too wet or if there is not enough coarse composting material. Wet cottonseed meal turns into a slim~ that smells dead. If you do have an odor, add more roughage and turn more frequently (wear your oldest shoes as you will have to throw them away).

THE FRAGRANT FORMULA is ready in about thee weeks. Use about two garden shovelfuls per established plant for first feeling in the Spring. Repeat in late Summer with another shovelful. If soil is acid, skip cottonseed meal and substitute horse-stall manure with wood-shavings or other manure source. Organic manure in the Spring makes other fertilizers work better. Organics feed the micro-organisms that do all the work converting nutrients into a form that roses can use. Anyway, you'll have live soil, organisms and: rosebushes. And that's what produces loads of roses.

SAP RISES IN ROSES AND ROSARIANS about the same time… the first warm day. How about controlling yours this season with just a little patience (can't be bought anywhere) and a couple of these guaranteed-to-grow rose ideas that work WITH nature rather than against her…

OLD ROSARIAN TALES are passed on from old-pro rose growers to novices on how to plant roses… and some are tough on both plants and planter. For example, "firmly tamp soil around roots to eliminate air." Now THAT'S foolish. Tamping not only gets rid of the air but also breaks the roots and compacts the soil so that water and air (both essential to soil processes) don't have a chance. The whole idea is to settle the soil to provide a good foundation for the roots. The best planting tool is plenty of water… thorough, deep soaking. The Rambler is a "cone" type planter, supporting the root system with a cone of well-prepared soil. Properly placed on the cone, a bare-root bush will stand by itself. Cover the roots lightly and begin to run water slowly in the hole. Add some more soil, water will fill in the voids. While one bush is soaking, plant the next one. Then come back with more soil, more water etc. A GOOD rosarian is a muddy one; your roses will like it, too.

HILL UP NEW ROSEBUSHES as a last planting step. Use all the soil, mulch or other insulating materials you can get your hands on. Cover the bud union and canes until just the tips are showing. Bring in some mulch materials; don't dig up the just completed rose bed. Hilling not only protects from the cold but keeps canes from drying out. Until roots are well established, canes are very vulnerable to sun and wind. Constant temperature and moisture help roses start. Keep new plantings moist; mulch will gradually settle and wash down in a natural process.

PLASTIC TENTS can help plants really slow to start. Throw a handful of wet sphagnum moss over the bud union, maybe add a little mulch; then form a tent of clear plastic material over the bush and secure at the shank (or cover edges with soil). The result is a moist, warm greenhouse that encourages breaks. Cut some small holes in the plastic when growth has started to gradually lower temperature. Uncover but protect in the same manner as any other tender plant. Same practice works great for tree roses, too. In fact, plastic tents should be routine for tree roses. Moisture has a long way to go up a tree standard; and until the tiny hair roots develop very little of the moisture lost through evaporation is replaced. In short, tree rose canes dry out in a hurry. Keep them moist with wet moss and plastic; same technique as air layering, only easier. At today's prices, can't afford to be careless with trees. Don't forget the "splint stake" either. That light stick furnished by the nursery won't hold much of anything. Use 3/8 inch reinforcing bar or electrical conduit, pad by slipping a piece of old garden hose over the entire length. Place carefully along the tree standard when planting, allowing about 18 inches in the ground. Use electrician's tape or something similar to secure the splint to the standard. Wrap in several places. The result is a good, secure support that will handle almost any wind.

WHY DO WE PRUNE the way we do?? Pruning technique can make a big difference in die-back, healing of cuts and a vigorous spring start. For large, woody canes, use a small keyhole saw instead of the crushing jaws of a lopper. Cuts heal fast, particularly on the bud union. And make it a regular habit to keep the BLADE of the pruning shear DOWN so that the opposing jaw of the shear does not bruise good rose cane. Look at it this way: let the jaw bruise the cane material that is cut off. Use pruners that are large enough and sharp enough to make smooth, clean cuts. If it isn't easy, you're using the wrong tool. And clean up the bud union whenever you can. Use a small pruning saw with fine teeth to trim off old shrubs flush with the bud union so that it can heal over and form a base for new breaks.

BELOW-GROUND BUD UNIONS are handled almost the same way. Trim out the stubs; keep going until you find live wood. A healthy rose WANTS to make new canes if we offer half a chance. To paint or not to paint?? If borers are a problem, seal cuts on large canes. Many growers like *Elmer's Glue*, some like carbolated *Vaseline*. Just stay away from the asphalt materials; if the temperature is right, some die-back may result.

OUT-ON-A-LIMB RECOMMENDA-TION. I may be wrong (occasionally), but the Rambler thinks that it is impractical and a waste of time to attempt to disinfect pruning tools with *Lysol*, alcohol or what-have-you between rosebushes. It's hard to imagine rose pruning under antiseptic conditions. Doesn't have a thing to do with galls, mosaic, cankers or other dread diseases. Thousands of roses pruned by the Rambler over some 25 years have never shown signs of cross infection. A careful rosarian with clean, SHARP tools can do a good job without worry.

NEED SOME GOOD HELP?? Get into the garden of another rosarian or call one of the Consulting Rosarians in your area for a chance to swap rose stories. We often overlook the very best advice because we are too close to it. Not that the CR's are always right (including the Rambler), but they have had the experience to assist in many ways. You'll find that roses are more fun than ever.

APR.
1984

THOUGHT FOR THE MONTH: To cultivate a rose garden, Takes much time and labor.
Some folks live next door to one and cultivate the neighbor.

Roses grow on shared ideas... many of them not particularly scientific but practical and useful in most parts of the country. Maybe you can make good use of some of these observations (adjust seasoning to taste) and keep the chain of fun and roses going.

NATURE'S TONIC. It's the Rambler's conclusion after years of trying one miracle food after another that organics still work better and more consistently. Fish and meal and blood meal encourage beautiful leaves that support blooms. Manures and alfalfa build strong plants. Compost in the rose bed keeps nature in balance. A tonic of fish emulsion in water makes big roses and miniatures happy. Some good, aged cow tea makes the sick well and the well even better. Feed the processes that make nutrients available. You'll have live soil, organisms and rosebushes. And that's what produces loads of roses.

SOLUBLE INORGANIC FERTILIZERS are here to stay, too. Used wisely, these foods provide the extra boost that plants need for top production. Nitrogen is easy to supply; chelated trace elements bring out the best in bloom and color; Just make sure that the working soil is healthy first. Then the best of both worlds works together.

ROSARIANS enjoy a number of fertilizer choices, but the most expensive isn't necessarily the best. Check the percentage of nutrient (by weight) which appears on the label of any fertilizer you buy. A 15-30-15 formula contains 15% Nitrogen, 30% Phosphoric Acid and 15% Potash (the N-P-K ratio). Trace elements will be listed if included in the mix. In many cases, the 12-24-12 or 13-13-13 formulation used on the lawn is the best buy for roses, too. Add chelated trace elements in solution as needed. Obviously, fertilizer choice depends on the size of the garden, convenience, cost, need and availability. Just use a little rose sense with a regular program that makes YOU happy; your roses will be happy, too.

APHID CONTROL receives a lot of attention for some reason, although the solution is really very simple. Safe, reliable Malathion cleans them up quickly without disturbing the rest of nature. Spray the affected areas (host plants, too) about five days apart to catch the new hatch and the unsightly problem is licked. Grandmother used to take care of aphids by throwing the soapy water over the bushes, really cleaning up the leaves. That's probably environmentally unacceptable now (quite a bit of work, too), but it was effective. Not much mildew on the wash water-treated roses either. But it remains a mystery to me why enthusiastic rosarians use broad spectrum-kill everything insecticides for aphids or treat roses with systemic fertilizers. Even a squirt from the garden hose will do a better job.

SPEAKING OF HOSES, have you let the garden hose run slowly in the rose bed lately?? Maybe with just a tomato can over the end so the water won't wash. The result is deep watering that does some good, or a shallow ditch system can connect several bushes. Roses mostly grow on water; deep soaking is best. Any system that gets water to the deep roots makes roses happy. Does yours??

REGULAR FUNGICIDE SPRAY PROGRAMS are recommended at every rose society meeting and with good reason. Control is accomplished through prevention; blackspot damaged leaves cannot be restored. Leaves, buds and blooms twisted with mildew won't become sleek and productive again after spraying. Spray to prevent this damage (or control further spread) and start early. The most common mistake is to wait until infection appears; and by that time, it's too late. It's an uphill battle from then on. Get on a 7-10 day schedule and stay with it. Don't cheat. The fungus spores will catch you every time. The best practice is to begin fungus control the day the roses are pruned, long before leaves appear. Then keep it up. Good fungicides like *Funginex, Phaltan, Benlate* or *Manzate* will do the job if used on the plants, not on the garage shelf. It's a garden chore that pays off in roses. Slack off on some other job, but not on fungus control. In most areas, the fungicide program is the key to good roses.

CONTAINER-GROWN ROSES are meant to be enjoyed by rosarians. If you aren't into roses (minis, Floribundas, tree roses) in containers, you're missing some real pleasure. There's still plenty of time this season, one of the real advantages of containers. No new bed to build, no roots to dig up, no drainage to worry about. Fill the container with a light, organic mix, plant and enjoy.

The best bargain today (and one of the most attractive) is the half whiskey barrel. I don't know what the distillers used to do with their old oak barrels, but general availability now is great for the rosarian. One barrel holds three compact floribundas, or one tree rose, or one tree rose and miniatures, or a calico quilt of miniatures... maybe with a Green Ice cascading over the side. The possibilities are endless. The barrels are large enough to hold plenty of soil mix and moisture, water two or three times a week. These rosy containers can be moved around with a two-wheel hand truck by a rosarian and a helper, or just left in place to brighten up a garden corner, walkway or some other spot that is otherwise impractical to plant. Some really interesting blooming features can be created inexpensively. Try some.

Opportunity never comes... it's here. And that's the way it is in the rose garden right now... still plenty of time to make this the best rose year ever. Maybe some of these budding ideas (or spent blooms) will help.

MIXTURES OF STUFF on the leaves usually mean trouble... when the leaves do turn yellow and drop off the grower can't decide what caused it. The all-in-one approach may work for some, but conservative practice says to spray for specifics. There is no need whatsoever to add insecticide to a fungicide spray program every week. And a good number of growers compound the assault on the leaves with foliar food, spreader stickers and an extra touch of this and that. A week later the attack is repeated (plus all the pollution drop-out) on leaves that have not been washed off. It's a wonder the leaves work at all. No-problem advice: follow a weekly fungicide spray program with *Funginex* or *Benlate*; use the appropriate insecticide by itself only as needed, and wash off the leaves with lots of water every week or so if it doesn't rain. And, for good measure, water-wash UNDER the leaves for spider mites on a regular basis. The extra water can't hurt the bushes and may well eliminate the need for a miticide later on. Which reminds me of the old Gulf Coast rosarian who washed off his roses two or three times a week if it didn't rain, ignoring the conventional advice that blackspot was sure to follow. Old Bill used either *Phaltan* or *Manzate* every week, spot-sprayed insecticide now and then, washed off his rosebushes and cooled off with a cold beer whenever he could and had the cleanest, healthiest roses you have ever seen. No blackspot, no mites; Bill had a happy garden.

ON WATER WANDS... Water really DOES work on spider mites if applied generously and consistently. Just get a strong stream of water underneath the leaves, particularly on low growing, dense plants and miniatures. Start the water before there's evidence of mites — that grey-green, pale look that says mites are just sucking the life out of the leaves. Some good wands are available with either cone or fan-shaped sprays, about three feet long and curved on the end to reach under the leaves, just like the long wand on your sprayer. Buy one (advertised in the magazine) or make one yourself. If water fails (or if you failed to apply

it), the best bet is *Vendex*, a very effective miticide with long residual. Use no more often than every 28 days; one application will usually do the job. A little *Vendex* goes a long way: about two teaspoons per gallon, used alone. Not generally available except through rose specialty suppliers like *Kimbrew Walter*, nursery wholesalers or farm supply stores. The two pound package (about $28) is enough for ten rose growers for several seasons.

WATER FEATURES add so much to a rose garden that it's surprising that more hobbyists don't use them. Use of water doesn't have to be elaborate with pumps, sprays, ponds and statuary. A birdbath in a style and material appropriate for the garden adds interest and attention. Plant miniatures around and under this kind of feature, or bring the feature in front of some full-growing floribundas. Water splash is no problem with regular fungicide use. Or try varying the height of the birdbath basin. Nothing says that it has to be exactly 30 inches off the ground. Or use two basins at different levels. There's a very attractive Memorial Garden for Adele Eaton at the American Rose Center that features a water basin at ground level surrounded by miniatures. Charisma floribundas add depth to the irregular garden shape with tree roses in the background for accent. The overall effect is very pleasing and relaxing. " and well used by the birds. Another way to do the same thing is to place a large natural stone with water basin in a mixed, informal planting of miniatures. Very effective in a sloping bed or as part of a rock' garden planting with roses. The next step, of course, is a basin or pond with a small recirculating pump... the possibilities are endless.

SINCE THE SUBJECT IS WATER, if you can't consistently get water to hanging baskets (miniatures, begonias, ferns, etc.) you really should rig up a trickle water system with an emitter terminating in each large container. Hanging baskets on racks add a whole new dimension to the garden in much the same way as other containers. It's a great way to use certain miniature rose varieties, and the water system makes it easy. There are a number of inexpensive kits on the market that are a cinch to put together. Each emitter can be regulated for just the right amount of water for each size container or type plant. A real rose pro adds a syphon feeding system to the network. If you failed to get the plans for the Rambler's Hanging Basket Rack last year, write for one. Guaranteed easy. Your miniature baskets will appreciate you.

SHOULD HAVE BEEN DISCOVERED SOONER... rose ties from stretch hose, panty hose or any elastic nylon fabric. Cut into strips, it's amazing how much stretch there is. And that's what helps roses. Stretch nylon won't cut into canes or bark and has a certain amount of give. Very useful in training a climber along a fence and lasts almost indefinitely. For a wooden fence, use electrician U staples and slip the tie through. The result is a flexible sling easy to tie, change or relocate. Works better than any wire or wrap the Rambler has ever tried.

HELP!! Some 14 years and 165 Rambling Rosarian columns later, the Rambler is running short on THOUGHTS FOR THE MONTH. If you have some zingers you would like to share, pass them along... they may be used (with appropriate credit) to bolster the Rambler's sagging imagination.

JUN.
1984

*THOUGHT FOR THE MONTH: Whoever said, "It's not the purchase but the
upkeep that gets you," had to be talking about the rose garden.*

Rose garden tours are fun events... a kind of outdoor show and tell for old pros and beginners. Old timers learn how to teach basics again and new growers see first-hand what it is all about. Amusing, too... have you ever noticed that there are more comments about the one sick rose in the garden ("What's the matter with it?") than about the magnificent specimen that's the best you've ever grown?? Anyway, here are a few items that prompted a lot of discussion on tours that the Rambler recently enjoyed...

MULCH... how little or how much? Growers in hot, sunny areas swear by good, thick mulch to hold moisture and lower soil temperature. Cool climate (or shaded) rosarians say there's no need and that the mulch sponsors insects and disease. There's probably some support for both cases. But the consensus is, if in doubt, mulch. A good layer of leaves, compost, manure or what-have-you organic mixtures constantly restores humus in the rose bed and supports the micro-organisms that make soils work. Mulch is a way to feed, cool, smother weeds and conserve moisture... all at the same time. Apply mulch after the soil warms up; if everything is working right, two or three inches of good organic matter will disappear in a single season. That has to be good. That's not to say that roses won't grow and thrive in sand or soil with a lesser organic content; but growth WITH nature is easier.

SUMMER MINIATURES... never too late. You'll often see outstanding miniature rose displays with plants that haven't been in the ground more than a month... all because minis can be planted almost anytime the temperature is over freezing and under boiling. Mini propagators have come up with some good shipping techniques to make it possible to order and get plants in good condition, even in mid-summer. Once received, some careful handling will help ease the shock. A just-rooted mini plant in a two-inch pot needs to be transferred to a five-inch or larger pot in a soil mix that encourages root growth. Something like *Peters Commercial Potting Mix* is ideal. Protect the new mini in a shaded spot for two weeks or so, gradually exposing to more sun and higher temperatures. When new growth has started well, transfer CAREFULLY to the mini bed or planter box. And don't be afraid to trim minis back. The result will be a healthier, bushier plant that will support more blooms. If the planting area is protected or the conditions moderate, skip the larger pot routine but use some light planting mix to help the tiny roots along.

THRIPS... where and how? It's amazing, but many growers don't recognize the problem (or the insect) until buds refuse to open or petals are badly bruised and discolored. Thrips (always plural, usually by the millions) come from the grasses, fields, host plants, from EVERYWHERE during warm Spring weather. They arrive in waves to particularly damage light-colored, fragrant blooms. They do their damage by bruising tender petals as they suck juices from the tissue. Blooms turn brown on the edges; buds sometimes won't open at all. Watch carefully for the first signs. To control thrips, spray where they are: on the buds and blooms. Lightly mist only the tops of the bushes with *Orthene* or *Cygon*. During heavy infestation (or just before a rose show), twice a week may be necessary. When using *Orthene*, check the label for application rate. Older supplies (more active ingredient) call for one to one-half tablespoons per gallon; recent product calls for THREE TABLESPOONS per gallon of water. Wettable powder *Orthene (75 %WP)* is a better buy but is a little more trouble to use. *Cygon* is available at most farm stores and is relatively inexpensive. But none of these materials will work unless applied. Like mildew, once the damage is done, nothing will restore the bloom to its intended beauty.

SPRAY HOST PLANTS, too. Thrips hosts like lilies, amaryllis, gladiolas and other light-colored, fragrant flowers should be sprayed along with roses. But take heart, as summer heats up, thrips usually move on. Until then, specific spray control on buds and blooms is the only answer.

POWDERY MILDEW can spring into an epidemic nearly over night. When conditions are right (warm days, cool nights), spores borne on the breeze set up new colonies on susceptible tender growth. Late Spring, early Summer and Fall are right for the gray, disfiguring disease to appear. The best protection is EARLY application of fungicide, well in advance of mildew conditions, redoubling efforts (and spray schedules) at the first sign of the grayish powder.

CONTROL MILDEW HOSTS. Thoroughly spray ramblers and climbers. Since it is hard to get good spray coverage on climbers and shrubs, spores carry over and infect nearby plants. A fence covered with climbers can be beautiful but a real problem with disease control. More frequent application, better wetting, better spray pressure and even spraying from a ladder will help. Spray religiously every week when conditions are right; concentrate on new, green growth. Old, tough leaves on the bottom are safe. *Funginex* and *Benlate* are popular controls; but for really serious infection, the Rambler goes back to *Acti-Dione PM*, used alone and twice a week in bright sunshine. In hard, alkaline water, use about two teaspoons of white vinegar as a wetting agent.

LEARN TO RELAX... plant mildew resistant varieties in areas with good air circulation and hope for the best. And remember that in really hot, dry weather, mildew will go away all by itself.

July heat separates the rose growers from the rosarians... the time when good habits payoff and hot growers layoff. Maybe these Summer suggestions will payoff in more roses for you.

DISEASE CONTROL... a regular schedule is the key. Several good fungicides are safe and readily available but won't do any good until on the leaves. *FUNGINEX* is gaining in popularity and is very effective when used faithfully every seven to ten days. No residue, no burn. *Triforine* is the active ingredient in *Funginex* and is also available as an 18 % EC... more cost effective for large gardens. For a little extra residual, add 1/2 Tablespoon of *Manzate* (*Maneb*) per gallon to the recommended *Funginex* (or *Triforine*) mixture. During blackspot weather, the leaves will stay cleaner and fungus will be controlled for a few extra days in the event a spray schedule is skipped. In hot, dry weather, the combination has been effective for two weeks, but don't try to stretch it much past two weeks.

FEED IN THE SUMMER... even in very hot growing areas, provided any source of water is available at all. Rosarians have thought for years that roses should rest during very hot weather, but that's really not true. Just use plenty of water and feed light amounts to enjoy blooms and foliage all the time. Blooms may be smaller and foliage less lush, but they're worthwhile just the same. The plants also go into Fall better able to produce a bumper crop of show-stoppers. Miniatures in particular thrive on a regular LIGHT diet. It is much harder to bring miniatures out of a slump than to keep them busy all Summer.

IS YOUR WATER WORKING??? That is, in the root zone delivering nutrients to the bush? Roses need lots of water; deep watering is best. Make sure that the mulch (or soil crust) doesn't shed water rather than provide easy passage. Sprinkling and short showers won't do much good. Slow soaking sets off the food chain that makes roses grow. Break up the mulch or crust from time to time -no deep cultivation that disturbs feeder roots but a loosening that lets water, air and food get to the roots... and that's where the work is being done. Grandmother's old watering method... hose running slowly in a tomato can... still works.

MITES: THE SUMMERTIME

SCOURGE... but not necessarily a disaster. Watch for signs of spider mites (lower leaves losing color; dry, parched look) and act right away. Better yet, make water-washing undersides of leaves a regular routine. A severe outbreak may occur in spite of water treatment, but damage is less severe. Mites like miniatures and dense growing floribundas, particularly plants in hot, dry locations (reflective heat off a brick wall). Undersides of leaves will have salt-pepper look with tiny webbing. Don't worry about seeing mites move; if gritty residue -is there, so are the mites. If a miticide MUST be used, water-wash first; then thoroughly spray undersides of leaves with *Vendex* or *Plictran*, used alone. Both are effective. The insecticide mixtures with *Kelthane* won't provide control very long; new generations of mites are stronger and hungrier than ever. The Rambler still believes that excessive use of insecticides contributes to the mite problem by killing off mite predators. But when mites appear, act fast. Bushes can defoliate in a week.

SPRAYING... an art as well as a science. Rosarians have good equipment available, safe to use and relatively inexpensive. The object of a sprayer is to get materials to specific locations in safe, reliable concentrations. The rosarian operator can make the system work or not work. Pump-up tank sprayers are the best for most growers; a three-gallon size fits an average garden. The Rambler used to think that hose-on sprayers were OK for small gardens, but the cost of materials and unreliable mixtures make hose sprayers a poor choice when a tank sprayer (Hudson has all kinds of models) is so reliable and easy to use. The Rambler has a three-gallon Hudson that has been used on away-from-home gardens (150 bushes each) for five years or so and it is still going strong. A washer/gasket kit each season keeps it in top condition... in service weekly for eight months every year is a lot of use. Maybe a new sprayer should be on your Summer shopping list.

COMMON SENSE PRECAUTIONS... spraying is as safe as the nut that holds the wand. Just use a little common sense. Be careful in handling materials; more accidents probably happen in mixing than in actual spraying. Wear rubber gloves... cheap and easy... and a long sleeve shirt. Protective glasses and clothing obviously limit exposure. Respiratory protection?? A dust or paint mask with disposable pads may be in order, particularly if you are sensitive to certain spray combinations. Avoid spraying when it is windy; direct spray pattern away from you. Most tank sprayers put out a very controllable pattern, there's no need to be caught in spray drift. Power sprayers and turbine type sprayers are much more difficult to control. Another control trick is to replace the short application wand with one about 36 inches long. Check any store selling supplies and parts to exterminators. They will have nozzles of various patterns, valves, tubing and some practical advice on how to make spraying even safer. Simply keep spray equipment in good condition and handle with care. You'll be safe and so will your roses.

THANKS!! Thoughts for the Month have been coming in to the Rambler, but a few more rose-related punch lines would still be appreciated. Will try to share a collection of them with you in the months to come.

This Rambler once quipped "The quickest way to get a rosarian interested in a project is to tell him it's none of his business"... but the quickest way to get a response is to disagree with his favorite rose formula: "Everybody knows that," he claims. Anyway, here are some rose clips that may get you excited, but just remember that more roses grow in spite of us than because of us...

PINCH BASAL BREAKS?? Seems like a strange way to grow rosebushes, but SOMETIMES it helps. Some growers believe that pinching the tip of a basal when it reaches about 18 inches results in more secondary canes at lower leaf axils. Those who practice pinching claim that basals allowed to grow naturally terminate in a candelabra of bloom usually inferior in quality. When this candelabra is cut, the basal may become unproductive and fail to push out low breaks. The cut basal may even deteriorate to the point that it must be removed the following year. At least that's what the pinchers think. Well... maybe. The Rambler has tried pinching and not pinching and hasn't noticed much difference, EXCEPT for those varieties that are very vigorous and put out a tremendous basal cane and a peanut size bud. Color Magic frequently does this; First Prize will also grow like this on occasion. It seems that the better way of handling the fast-growing basal would be to disbud or else take out an early terminal bud and allow two or three side buds (and stems) to develop. Century Two does this quite well. Better yet, pinch one basal and allow another on the same plant to develop normally... it's interesting to find out what happens. If you only have one basal, you're in trouble.

SOIL pH... MISUNDERSTOOD. Some growers give the impression that the pH of the rose bed is a delicate balance on which hangs the life or death of the bush, or at least its ability to produce an adequate bloom. Maybe... but roses tolerate a wide range of acid/alkaline soil conditions and continue to produce roses.

Good, common sense rose practices keep soils in balance... the constant tampering with nature is more likely to get soils into an intolerable condition for roses. What's good practice?? Good drainage with a mixture of soil types: sand, clay, loam... big particles, small particles, flat particles. Add organic matter and the soil will tend to keep itself

in balance. Unless the grower drastically exceeds good sense in application of fertilizers or remedies, periodic addition of organic matter (compost, humus, bark, manures, what-have-you) will keep the soil healthy. In brief, nature will balance itself. There are exceptions, of course. Heavy application of Ammonium Sulfate fertilizer over the years may make a rose bed too acid. Periodic treatment with dolomite lime will take care of it. Heavy soils growers on the Gulf Coast have a rule of thumb formula: for every three pounds of nitrogen (from an acid source), use one pound of dolomite lime. Be careful about POUNDS of nitrogen; a 10-10-10 analysis has 10% available nitrogen by weight. Therefore, 50-pound bag of this analysis actually has five nitrogen. It doesn't take much lime to balance this out. Moral: when tampering with the pH, think nature and proceed slowly and carefully.

TIMED RELEASE FERTILIZERS... The Rambler used to think that timed release fertilizers were just for small gardens, or pots, or for rose growers who were just too lazy to "feed the way they should." Not any more. Timed release can be a boon to the grower and supplement all of the other good practices. There's no need to give up good organics like fishmeal, blood meal, manure and mixtures of all of these to enjoy the slow, steady support of timed release foods. Just use some discretion in rate of application. With timed release, you're sure that the bushes get some food every time water is applied. And that's not bad. Some timed release products respond to temperature, some to water rate. Follow the directions and KNOW what's happening. There are three-four month formulas and seven-eight month formulas. Use the food to fit the season. Miniatures respond particularly well to LIGHT applications of timed release foods. *Carl Pool Timed Release* (available primarily in the Southwest) is a dandy; it has a 13-13-13 analysis with trace elements. An all-in-one food. There are equally good; best known is *Osmocote* (14-14-14) and *Osmocote Sierra Blend* (with iron). Look into availability and suitability for your area; timed release may be the "secret formula" of the guy with the GREAT garden.

MOSAIC... IS IT CATCHING? No, not really. Virus mosaic (yellow-white patterning on leaves) is disfiguring, but certainly not disabling.

Sometimes mosaic shows up on just a cane or two and maybe only once during the season. Cut the affected cane off and the balance of the bush may be clean and healthy for the rest of the season. No one LIKES virus, and the reputable rose suppliers are making real strides in growing and shipping plants free of virus. Virus is transmitted through the root stock, infected stock affects the budded scion. It DOES NOT transmit from bush to bush when cutting blooms; it will not infect other plants in the garden except due to root stock injury. If the bush is unsightly, get rid of it. Think of it as an opportunity to plant something else.

LAST BUT NOT LEAST... enjoy roses, not rose problems. There was an article in Reader's Digest recently that was titled something like "The Good News Is That The Bad News is Wrong." The point is that we hear more about the bad news (or problems) than the good news (great results). Same way with roses. Enjoy them.

If reading the volumes of stuff put out by the rose authorities prompts you to worry about all sorts of new rose problems, you may read on in rosy comfort. The Rambler has only good news this month.

ROSES LIKE FRIENDLY PLANTS... annuals and lilies and some seasonal perennials. I visited a beautiful garden in Colorado this summer; flower beds along a fence enclosing a large back yard, framing a luxuriant lawn. About 200 roses were mixed and matched with low-growing annuals, delphinium, daisies, phlox, alyssum, some ornamentals and an occasional garden feature. The roses were excellent... colorful and dominant... ranging from hybrid teas to miniatures. This reminds us that roses don't have to be used in formal settings; in fact, unless roses are planted in a mass, individual plants or small patches are not particularly attractive in a landscape plan. Maybe your next rose effort should be to develop a mixed bed to enjoy year-round. A flower bed is a little more difficult to maintain, but a very pleasant sight to enjoy.

MULCH... not likely to raise a controversy, but apparently misunderstood. The Rambler believes in mulch as a convenient, cheap way to conserve moisture, reduce weeds, add humus to the soil and attractively frame plants of all types. Ground pine bark, humus, compost, leaves, manures, mixtures of all of these have helped a good many rose growers. However, in recommending three or four inches of mulch for roses to a group in a very dry area, they responded that "the stuff might stay on there for two or three years before breaking down." Is that really bad?? Mulch is supposed to act as an insulator, and when it disappears, add some more. The Rambler never removes mulch from the beds; it gets worked in and moved around and cleaned up a bit from time to time, but NEVER removed. Keeps soil and roses happy.

POWDERY MILDEW... bothersome in the fall with warm days and cool nights: But there's a new systemic fungicide available for ornamentals that works over an extended period. *BAYLETON*, a 25 % wettable powder, provides 30-45 day ornamental disease control. *Bayleton* is absorbed rapidly and works systemically from within the plant. Good coverage and thorough wetting of the foliage is recommended. Long residual action means fewer applications — about every four weeks in most cases. Put out by Mobay Chemical, *Bayleton* is available primarily through nursery specialty products distributors. Rose growers are familiar with Brighton By-Products Co., Po. Box 23, New Brighton, PA 15066. The material is expensive ($75 for 2 pounds), but used in VERY low concentration (2 ounces per 50 gallons). Would be a good idea to split a supply with other growers. *Bayleton* just MAY be the fungicide that makes fall a fun time for rose growers.

WINTER... get ready in the summer. Winter protection for roses really begins in the summer. Healthy, vigorous plants tolerate cold better. Weak, diseased roses just won't make it. Keep roses healthy, then EASE bushes into dormancy with just a little extra care. Dormancy often escapes us; either the plants are going full-bore or have just been frozen back. Rosarians understand that most fertilizers release over a 30-60 day period. We also know when hard, killing frost usually occurs. Just shut off the food at the right time, and the danger of freeze damage and die back is greatly reduced. Roses are woody plants and respond to the seasons. Don't fight nature. Stop feeding at the right time for your climate; in the latter stages of the season leave some blooms on to form seed hips which signal the bush that the reproductive cycle is complete. Another slow-down practice is to hold back water (not to stress but reduce the amount) to encourage dormancy. If your roses need a September shot in the arm, use a quick-acting liquid material like *Ra-Pid-Gro* or *Peters*. Some common rose sense will tell you just how late this can be applied. Most liquids work for about 30 days, depending on rainfall, drainage, soil temperature and composition. If in doubt, don't. Roses will grow anyway.

A FALL PROJECT... clear out grass and weeds for a new rose planting (springtime). The easy way is to kill out unwanted grass with *ROUNDUP* rather than dig and pull. But *Roundup* MUST be applied while the grasses and weeds are growing. Application on dormant grass won't do a bit of good. Follow the directions, wet green matter thoroughly. About a week later, spade up the plot and add some organic material like leaves, manure, clipping, what-have-you. Maybe turn a little more. Winter moisture and frost will go to work for you. By spring, the now-loosened soil is ready to work, probably adding more soil conditioners and light soil for a productive rose bed. It's easier to do now than when the sod is heavy and wet. Try it.

ROSE-RELATED PUNCH LINES... The Rambler got quite a batch of catchy phrases after a summertime plea and will share a collection of the best one of these days. However, here's one that deserves to be shared right now since this turned out to be a good-news Rambling this month... It's from Laura McClelland of Jackson, Mississippi (a great rose gal who really loves roses), who offers, "Doing what you like is freedom... liking what you do is happiness." And THAT just has to apply to rosarians, the greatest folks in the world.

The Rambler has more good news this month... winter will soon be here, allowing roses and rosarians to rest. And to help both rest more comfortably, here are some tips on how to change the weather... at least as far as roses are concerned.

LEAVES ARE THE ANSWER... considered a problem by many, but a most pleasant one for rosarians -falling from the trees, a rich harvest of soil-builder, insulator, fertilizer and natural cover... at no cost. Even if all the leafy production can't be used, take advantage of this gift from nature. Used for winter protection or composting, leaves return far more to the garden than the small amount of effort required to make them effective. Experience the benefits of compost just once, and you'll find space for more leaves next year. If no space at all is available for a compost pile or rick, use a vegetable or flowering annuals bed or maybe a spot where the new rose bed is planned. Nature will work all winter for you.

NO CONSTRUCTION REQUIRED. Composting in place is easy; just turn and dig the soil in a bed area making a wind-row of soil. Pile leaves, clippings, etc. in the trench and add some excess soil on top for dressing. Anything green helps the process, or add a good source of organic nitrogen like manure or cottonseed meal. Keep moist and turn lightly now and then while the weather is good. Before hard-freeze time, the partially composted material should be broken down enough to till or mix in place or can be added to other bed areas. If bad weather comes in early, no problem. By spring the area will have the richest prepared soil available. The season can be stretched a bit by covering the trench or pile with black plastic to hold heat of decomposition and collect heat from the sun.

LEAVES USED AS WINTER PROTECTION also break down, but more slowly. Keep the covering light with plenty of air space in the same manner as insulating materials. Leaves tend to moderate temperatures, both hot and cold. When piled high in the beds, leaves will leave behind some good humus material to begin a new season. If a leaf blanket is your winter protection method, don't forget to add more leaves as the blanket settles, something like cornflakes in a box.

Winter protection is simply a matter of preventing the freezing-thawing cycle and drying out of rose canes. Use nature's insulation... free.

IN MORE SEVERE CLIMATES, a mound of soil or compost over the bud union and lower canes plus lots of leaves will keep most varieties in good shape with temperature ranges from 20 below to 50 above. Copes with cold, dry winds and bright sunshine, too. Wire baskets, rabbit-wire enclosures, evergreen boughs or even short snow fences will keep leaves in place. These pages also described how one cold-climate rosarian filled garbage bags with leaves, placing the bags around the perimeter of the rose bed. Results: a natural insulating barrier that kept leaves in, cold out. By spring, even the leaves in the bags were nearly composted. Some rosarians use a combination of cones and leaves for protection. Trim canes and set cones first; then fill in bed space with leaves as a protective insulation and more even temperature.

REALLY COLD, COLD AREAS may require burying in soil so that freeze-thaw and drying are eliminated. The first time that the Rambler saw the Minnesota Tip method used on tree roses and climbers, the most amazing aspect was the stamina of the rosarian and the roses. All that digging, tipping and covering has to come from a VERY dedicated rosarian. But most areas do very well with soil over the bud union and an blanket by nature. If you don't have enough leaves, get some. You'll make a neighbor with an excess very happy.

EASE ROSES INTO DORMANCY with a little extra care now. Stop feeding at the right time for your climate; the danger of freeze damage and die back is greatly reduced. Leave some blooms on the bushes to form seed hips, signaling that the reproductive cycle is complete. Another slow-down practice is to reduce water to encourage dormancy. Roses are woody plants which respond to the seasons. Work along WITH nature.

MINIATURES are particularly easy to carry through the winter. Many growers virtually bury the plants with a mix of soil, leaves and compost. The small canes hold the insulation in place so that the free-thaw cycle does not occur. Again, mixtures work best; allow some air space. Just be careful not to uncover too early in the spring. Even minis in pots and planters can be protected by storing in a spot out of the wind if there's a shortage of snow. Otherwise, enjoy rose winter by the fireplace with some promising catalogs.

Now that we have adjusted winter weather for roses, how about ordering some good, soaking rains for dry, dry Texas?? We would like a good winter, too.

"A smart rosarian knows what to do with what he knows"… which is another way of saying that most rose problems have simple solutions when we think them through. How has your rose score-card been this season?? Reflecting on the season just ended, here's how some of the Rambler's favorite rose ideas fared

BLACKSPOT CAN BE CLEAN UP… if regular schedule replaces wishful thinking. A very large garden on the Gulf Coast came down with a terminal case of blackspot in late summer. Badly infected old roses furnished a constant supply of spores that were carried on moist, southerly winds. In no time at all, some 700 roses, large and small, were in the process of defoliating. The cause?? Irregular spray schedule and poor fungicide coverage. The goal?? A clean, respectable garden for a District Meeting tour in mid-October. Some fast action was called for. First, the garden was sprayed twice a week with a combination of one teaspoon *Triforine* and one-half tablespoon *Manzate* per gallon of water, wetting leaves and canes thoroughly, top and bottom. Water was softened with one teaspoon white vinegar per gallon and wetted with a few drops of dish washing detergent. Second, the worst of the infected leaves were pulled off and the bushes lightly trimmed. Miniatures were cut back to eight inches or so. Third, a tonic of *Epsom Salts* (Magnesium Sulfate) was broadcast lightly with a handful of *Fertilome* per large bush and watering schedule increased to three times per week. Spray schedule was doubled the second week also using the same combination of *Triforine* and *Manzate*. The bushes responded by the third week and spraying was reduced to weekly, just after watering. In just four weeks the garden already looked respectable and was on the way to recovery. By tour time, most of bushes (even some of the old roses) were coming into bloom… not bad for a simple solution applied with rose sense.

THE RAMBLER LAPSED on one garden project and should have known better. As usual, too many garden projects and not enough time. Beds of floribundas and hybrid teas needed feeding in a hurry in early September (that's when we do it here for good bloom in October). With the clouds and weatherman threatening thunderstorms, it seemed like a good idea to broadcast some *Ferti-*

lome on the already-damp soil before the rains hit. Since some of the beds are deep and quite thick, the *Fertilome* was broadcast over the tops of the bushes for a quick fix. When the rain did not appear on schedule, the bushes were washed down and drenched with the hose… but too late. In just a few days, the lower leaves in particular had a "hash-brown" burned look. Other burned spots appeared like a rash. Obviously, the organic-based fertilizer had stuck to the leaves. Nothing left to do but pull leaves and trim, and turn the rose beds into a swamp with water. After three weeks, the roses are recovering nicely, thank you. But the resident rosarian is still burned over a dumb mistake.

BUT THERE'S GOOD NEWS, TOO… rosarians will soon be enjoying new patio rose introductions that bring a whole new dimension to rose growing. A program at the ARS convention in Pittsburgh in September colorfully illustrated that we are in for a treat. Patio roses might be defined as compact in growth habit, larger in bloom and habit than miniatures but smaller than floribundas. Some grow in pots, others in planters and beds. But they grow and BLOOM. Even AARS for 1985 has a near patio type… the outstanding red dazzler called Showbiz. About 18 inches tall, spreading, glossy foliage all the way to the ground, repeat blooms of brilliant scarlet. The Rambler has three plants in a half whiskey barrel that make a mound of color. AARS calls Showbiz a floribunda, but it certainly is not typical. The hybridizers/propagators say that the new breed of compact roses will be marketed as Sweetheart roses, playing on a nostalgic theme. Whatever they are called, these new roses will bring new color to patios and decks, balconies and town house gardens. Hope that you will enjoy your share. And think about the possibilities for these compact beauties in front of taller-growing floribundas, hybrid teas… or as a background for smaller miniatures. 1985 is going to be a 'great rose year!

TREE ROSES TAKE A GOOD DEAL OF PUNISHMENT… from weather as well as rosarians. Aside from growing in very severe climates (and they survive well there using the Minnesota Tip), tree roses can add new scale and beauty to most gardens with just a little care. First, stake a tree rose to provide a good foundation support.

The thin sticks from the nursery just won't do the job. Use a length of reinforcing rod three-eighths inch in diameter all along the tree standard and driven into the ground about 18 inches. Cut off or drive to be just even with the double bud unions. Slip a length of old plastic garden hose over the entire length of the support rod and cut. Tape the cushioned rod to the standard with friction tape or plastic electrician's tape. It's easiest to fit the rod in place when planting but can be installed on established plants with careful probing to miss major roots. The result is a stable, supported planting of two roses (remember, double-budded) to accent a number of locations. Wind and rain are no problem and often these standard-bedded roses far outperform their bush counterparts.

TREES TOO BIG?? STANDARD SPLIT-TING?? Do a little tree surgery with a drill and bolt, probably a "u" bolt. Secure the split bud union in place with temporary tape. Then drill through BOTH bud unions. Insert the bolt, add some washers and turn nuts on until firm. In less than a season, the whole thing will have grown together again until it is hard to tell that tree surgery was performed. Saves an expensive investment, too. Tree roses belong... use them.

THERE'S MORE GOOD NEWS NEXT MONTH... we'll ramble some more with roses.

Winter is the time when it is too cold to do the job it was too hot to do last summer... but even rosarians deserve a bit of rest. Suggestions this month are mostly easy, nothing really very physical. Sometimes called, "Looking at the world through rose colored glasses"...

LET WINTER DO THE WORK... the freeze/thaw cycle can do much of the work in making a new rose bed. If the ground isn't frozen yet, loosen just a little and pile on-lots of leaves or other organic material. Throw a little soil on top or cover with black plastic. Freezing and thawing over the winter will reduce and blend the organic matter and soil into the loam that most rosarians like. As moisture freezes and expands, tissues break down and even tight soils open up... a sort of blend. Nature has been building this natural way for a long, long time.

GUANO GOOD NEWS... This gourmet organic fertilizer from the islands of Peru really does work. After use for a full season in one garden and emergency late-season applications in other gardens, it's obvious that seabird droppings restore health, vigor and blooms to roses that seemed beyond help. One garden in particular had been nearly defoliated with blackspot; following control of the infection and light trimming, guano brought on lush, green leaves and sensational blooms. In fact, the flush of bloom in mid-October was every bit as good as a spring bloom following dormancy. Although somewhat expensive, you may want to ask Santa Claus for a supply to use on "a few special plants" next season. Ask him for Plantjoy.

HOLIDAY GIFT LIST... What could be better than an ARS membership for a gardening friend?? Plus introduction and membership in the local society, of course. Makes you feel good, too... And every rose grower needs a good rain gauge. Stop guessing how much water was left behind by the thundershower. Get one with graduated markings that can be mounted on a post for an accurate reading. A farm supply store usually has a reliable, practical selection. The fancy ornamental kind may look good but be misleading... Maybe a *bug-zapper*?? An electric grid insect killer is good for roses and rosarians. The insects are attracted by an intense blue light and electrocuted on a grid... mosquitoes, moths, beetles and what-have-you are attracted. It's a good control for the corn ear worm by killing the moth in transit to the developing rose bud. Be sure to hang the zapper 8 feet or higher off the ground. Not only safer and less distracting, but attracts bugs better.

MORE GARDEN GIFTS... A good water wand belongs in every garden. Washes leaves, spider mites, spray accumulations and other gunk bad for roses. There are several wands advertised in these pages and usually are rather inexpensive. Just get one that is long enough to reach well under the bush and direct a high pressure stream of water under and through the leaves.

Most of the wands are made out of brass and accept various standard sprayer nozzles. Others are made up with high pressure PVC pipe. Either will be a boon come hot weather and mites. A useful addition might be some quick couplers to attach wand or watering system to the garden supply hose without having to work the thread coupling. Nelson makes a good brass one (actually they come in pairs, male and female) and *Dramm* makes a twist lock of hard plastic. All of the Rambler's hoses, irrigating nozzles and attachments) are equipped with quick couplers. Makes working with a hose much easier... Good rose name markers are great to have, too. *Harlane* makes one advertised in the ARS magazine regularly. Markers come engraved with names or blank with a marking pen. The Rambler uses blanks and punches out the names with a Dymo-Tape punch. Plastic tapes come in a variety of colors and make inexpensive, attractive and easy-to-read rose markers.

PICKED UP FROM AN EXHIBITOR... Cut roses can last longer when kept in water with two tablespoons of *Listerine* per gallon. Seems to encourage the take-up of water to the bloom. Very practical when refrigerating roses prior to a show. Another good trick: cut the stems UNDER WATER so that air is not taken up in the fine tube system in the stem. Air impedes the take-up process. With just a little practice, the whole operation becomes easy and a matter of habit.

OUT IN FRONT FOR '85... Plan a rose bed for the front yard this time. Use just one variety for a massed color effect, or at least roses with the same growth and bloom habit. Floribundas are ideal for plantings of this type. Rosarians talk about beautification and then keep the beauty to themselves. If you want to sell roses, show the product. Besides, sharing is half the fun of having a rose garden. A real attention-getter is a bed or border of miniature roses to add color to a front planting.

Most casual visitors don't even know what they are. For a small planting, consider the new Sweetheart roses... the sentimental look-alikes that are compact and free-flowering. Described as larger in bloom and habit than miniatures but smaller than floribundas, these sweethearts bloom and bloom. Save some money and space and enjoy some in 1985. They will be available through nursery outlets initially and probably by mail order later on. Really great for the grower with a small space.

Hope that you enjoy a Happy Holiday Season and a Rosy '85.

Rose wisdom abounds during this semi-dormant time... there's not a thing to be proved in the rose garden or on the show table. And have you ever noticed how roses get bigger and better with retelling?? Anyway, here are some bigger and better ramblings you may want to try in '85...

TRADE IN some old roses for new varieties... in cars it's called "trading up." For most of us, new roses mean getting rid of something already in the ground. To justify this expenditure, make a good deal by giving the old, reliable plants to a gardening friend or start a "satellite" garden yourself for a church or school. A retirement center would be a great place for a new garden. You'll get more satisfaction (and probably compliments) than your home garden ever enjoyed. Most rose growers don't wear roses out; they dig them out. Give these bushes a new home and yourself a good excuse for indulging in some new roses like these...

'85 WILL BE A GREAT ROSE YEAR with some varieties sure to please. Showbiz, the brilliant, scarlet-red AARS floribunda is a dandy. Compact, always in bloom, beautiful foliage, ideal for bedding or barrels. Probably not to the exhibitor's liking but a reliable producer of roses all season. Don't get just one; buy three or more. Milestone is another introduction by J&P (their Rose of the Year), that you will want to try. Hybridized by Bill Warriner, Milestone is a winner in every respect, difficult to describe as it ranges from scarlet to coral to pink to red, changing colors as the bloom matures. Something like Color Magic, only better. Very winter hardy, too. This one will please exhibitors as well as garden growers. Get two plants so that you can enter the "bowl of roses" competition for hybrid teas. Chablis is an outstanding hybrid tea for '85 from Armstrong, excellent form, white with a "peachy/creamy" tinge. Color varies with sunshine and temperature. Really fun to grow, show and admire. Exhibitors all want Esmerelda, a striking coral hybrid tea that is available (short supply) from Edmunds or Canada. Stands out on a show table like nothing you have ever seen. Growers say it takes some patience, but it is worth it. Lady is a fine rose from Weeks that has form, color and substance to go all the way. Lady is a medium pink hybrid tea with gorgeous high centered blooms. May need some special care

just before a show, but a real contender. Watch for it at your garden center. Want a really good floribunda?? Grow several plants of Cherish. A former AARS winner by Bill Warriner of J&P, Cherish has a warm coral color, hybrid tea-form blooms, good foliage, occasional sprays, super buds... and blooms all season without complaining. Good for buttonholes or bud vases. Buy three.

BAYLETON is the "in" rose product for '85; it effectively takes away the threat of powdery mildew. Effective for up to 30 days, this mildewcide delivers what is promised. Best of all, *Bayleton* is a curative as well as preventative. Put out by Mobay Chemical, it is the product of the future. Here's what it can do: a miniature rose *Charley* was so covered with mildew it looked like snow had arrived. One application at curative rate cleared it up, and new growth emerged quite clean. In another garden, several bushes of *Granada* were badly infected; same good results. *Chipper* is a notorious mildewer on the Gulf Coast; not a trace of mildew throughout the fall. Other varieties had similarly dramatic results. Some users caution that stems may be shortened a bit with use of Bayleton, but, given a choice, most would rather have mildew-free roses and lots of them. Bayleton is a 25 percent wettable powder that is absorbed rapidly and works systemically from within the plant. Good coverage and thorough wetting of the foliage is recommended. Application rates: preventative 1/4 teaspoon per gallon; curative 1/2 teaspoon per gallon.

The Rambler experienced better coverage when used alone with just a little spreader-sticker (like *Palmolive* dishwashing liquid). After a curative application on infected plants, preventative rate was used two weeks later. Probably the cleanest fall garden ever. A bit on the expensive side to buy, but a little goes a long way. Share an order with a rose grower friend or two. Available from a good many Mobay product distributors, but quite a few rose people have been ordering from Brighton ByProducts Company, PO Box 23, New Brighton, PA 15066, Phone (412) 846-1220. Brighton lists two pounds at $75.40. Incidentally, Brighton carries all sorts of greenhouse and landscape supplies used by rosarians. Would be a good club project to pool orders and take care of a number of rosarians at the same time. One last word on Bayleton: as with any other insecticide or fungicide, it is IMPORTANT before using any product to read and carefully observe directions, cautionary statements and other information appearing on the label. READ THE LABEL BEFORE USE.

STILL LIKE ALFALFA FOR ROSES?? You bet. Every new rose bed, planting or rework should have alfalfa meal (or pellets). For a new rose bed, add about 50 pounds per 100 square feet. For a replacement rose here and there, add a handful to the soil in the hole. No need to overdo it. Just a little is needed. Too much in a soil mix turns sour. This spring, after pruning, broadcast about two cups per plant and scratch in a bit. You've never seen an unhealthy rabbit have you?? Which is a reminder that alfalfa (pellets or meal) is a rabbit food, sold in a feed store. Your feed store is a great place to visit… they have all kinds of things (usually cheaper) that rose growers need. Your plants will literally hop out of the ground… but seriously, alfalfa is a great conditioner-stimulator. Try some this season.

WONDER PRODUCTS FOR '85?? Nothing that has gotten the Rambler very excited. Most of the wonders promised in the sales literature are available with good, sound cultural practices and common rose-sense. Let nature do her thing… and a lot cheaper. Bayleton is a curative as well as preventative. Put out by Mobay Chemical, it is the product of the future.

FEB.
1985

THOUGHT FOR THE MONTH: If you must open a can of worms, a compost pile seems like a handy place. RHA Newsletter, Lou Stoddard

Rose season is on again… time to go to work. For those of us in the milder climates, pruning and planting will soon be underway; the cold-country folks will just have to see roses in the snow a little longer. Roses and nature do things on schedule, and wise rosarians stay in step. Here's what the early rose folks are talking about…

FAST ROSE BEDS ARE NO PROBLEM… even for the determined procrastinator. It's better to prepare rose beds well in advance and allow them to mellow, but with organics, a first rate rose bed in two weeks is easy. The trick is to build up the rose area; don't worry too much about what's below. Built-up beds are a good idea, anyway. Bring in some light soil first a couple of inches, and till in well with the existing soil. Then add organic matter and sand (something gritty) so that the final mix is about 1/3 soil, 1/3 sand and 1/3 organic stuff. Mix well with a roto-tiller or a fork. Then add (for about a 100-square foot bed) 50 pounds of alfalfa meal or pellets, 25 pounds of gypsum, 10 pounds of superphosphate (0-20-0), an inch or so of horse manure to get the whole mixture going and stir up again. Water down to settle. In a day or two, mix again and water. About the second weekend, you're ready to plant. No problem with bare root or transplanted roses. Natural ingredients blend and work for the rosarian who is in a hurry… and those new roses will start in a hurry, too.

THE EASY-PLANTING METHOD. Is there an easy way?? Planting new roses is a hands-and-knees chore, a lot easier than bending over. A good rosarian is one with dirty knees. Get a short shovel and get down to where the work is. If the bed is properly built, it's easy to scoop out a hole, rebuild a cone to support the roots and bush, then let water and soil do the rest. Cover the roots lightly with soil and begin to let water run slowly into the hole; add some soil that was placed aside. More water, more soil. No need to tamp or pack. Hill up with some excess soil or mulch (bring in a little extra rather than scrape from the rose bed) to protect canes and conserve moisture. Keep moist with an overhead sprinkler… nothing to it.

ABOUT HILLING… nothing more than a protective cone of soil or mulch or other insulating material that just lets the tips of new canes stick out. Not just a handful of material, a real cone, a shovelful or two per plant. Hilling primarily conserves moisture in the canes; hilling keeps canes from drying out before the roots have a chance to deliver. Constant temperature, moist conditions, help roses start. Brown-bag covers and plastic tents also work, but hilling is the easy way.

A LITTLE ROOT PRUNING?? A good practice (applied with rose sense) for most bare root roses. The Rambler lightly trims the ends of most of the roots and cuts out broken roots on the theory that root tips are most prone to drying out; trimming results in a healthier root system. Others disagree. It it works for you, keep it up. But if the roots are excessively long for the planting area, shorten them up a bit. You're planting roses, not making an excavation.

PACKAGED ROSES? Mere mention of packaged roses brings on strong response from "rosarians"… mostly negative. Given a choice, most of us prefer a #1 bare root rosebush direct from the grower or carefully handled plants potted by a reliable local nurseryman. But we can't ignore that there are millions of packaged roses sold every year, and SOME of them have been carefully handled, shipped and sold at a fair price. It's a turnoff for new rose hobbyists to be told that "packaged stuff is junk."

Obviously, packaged roses with chopped roots, broken canes and a handful of wood shavings aren't worth taking home and are totally worthless after a few days in a hot store window. A fresh, packaged rose can be trimmed, soaked and planted with the same care as a grower's Jumbo, and can produce as many fine roses. Some roses now come ready to plant, pot and all. If still dormant, good practice suggests that the plant be removed from the pot, trimmed and planted, spreading the roots normally. For more advanced growth, trim the pot off, leaving the planting medium intact so that the roots can expand into the rose bed area.

HERESY?? We are in the business to ENCOURAGE rose growing, and we owe something to the newcomer to show him how to get better results. We need all the rose friends we can get, too. The rosarian or society who finds fault with a nursery supplier who sells packaged roses can't expect a warm welcome when THEY want something. It will pay all of us to learn more about packaged roses, roses in containers, roses on their own roots and roses from regional suppliers. More and more of our roses are going to be supplied this way, and we had better be prepared.

EXPAND YOUR ROSE INTEREST IN '85... subscribe to the excellent specialty publications offered by ARS, edited quarterly by rose hobbyists just like you and me. Bulletins on exhibiting, miniatures and rose arrangements are available from ARS at $5.00 each per year. If you're REALLY into roses, become a member of the Rose Hybridizers Association, a congenial group of serious to not-so-serious growers and hybridizers who put out an OUTSTANDING quarterly publication, edited by Dr. Bob Harvey and Annette Dobbs. You may never germinate a rose seed, but your understanding of roses will be tremendously expanded through RHA. Just $5.00 per year. Send to Larry Peterson, RHA Sec-Treas., 3245 Wheaton Road, Horseheads, NY, 14845. RHA now has 1600 members, all enjoying roses... and isn't that what it is all about??

The best thing about spring is that it always comes when it's most needed... along with floods, rains and sudden cold snaps. But since roses grow in spite of rosarians and the weatherman, here are some tips on how to break dormancy without frostbite or frustration...

LEARN FROM YOUR MISTAKES... Take a good look at how your roses came through the winter, or maybe the suggestion should be WHY they came through the winter. When the time is right (and please don't hurry Mother Nature) pay particular attention to the amount of good wood on some plants and the total loss of wood on others. Was the protection a little better in some cases ?? Less wind, more moisture, looser insulation able to breathe, more gradual dormancy, less disease... all could be factors in survival. You can learn a great deal for future reference if you pay attention.

DON'T HURRY THE WEATHERMAN, particularly in uncovering roses. More plants are probably lost in the springtime when the temperature suddenly drops than during the winter. New growth and swelling canes can't handle low temperatures. It's a good idea to let Nature proceed at her own pace; let whatever winter protection you use stay on a little longer than usual. Pruning and probing gives the bush a signal that it's time to grow. Give some natural signals a chance this season. In the springtime, roses bloom when it's time to bloom, and early uncovering and pruning seldom speeds up the process. You'll be doing yourself and your roses a favor with a little extra patience.

PRUNE WITH A SHOVEL. When spring really arrives, don't waste time on plants that have been unproductive for more than one season, even though you may be reluctant to give up on them. Shovel pruning is the answer, but to make your conscience feel better, offer the plants you don't want at a plant exchange. This takes a little extra spade work and care, but it is a good way to get someone going with roses. The bushes that didn't quite meet your expectations can produce loads of roses for someone else. Most everyone has had the experience of giving away a less-than-successful plant only to have it come back with vigor that amazes the donor.

MOVE 'EM AROUND if you feel like it, too.

If a bush doesn't seem to be doing well in a particular location or if the color is "all wrong", move it somewhere else. Transplanting often seems to give a rosebush a new lease on life. Some growers say that even a good "out-you-go threat" works wonders. Move them while they are dormant; trim up and handle like a bare root plant. There are roses to gain and not much to lose. Wash off the roots and trim out any dead or broken parts; trim root ends lightly to encourage callousing and new feeder roots. Also trim out any root galls or gall growth on the shank or bud union. If very large galls girdle the shank or involve many roots, throw the bushes away and start over. It's more work to grow a sick plant than a good one.

DOCTORING GALLS... some respected growers maintain that disinfecting trimmed galls with *Lysol* or *Clorox* retards reoccurrence, but an equal number disagree. Most growers have galls they don't even know about and have had for a long time. If the gall is on the shank or a bud union, sunshine seems to do the most good. Don't worry too much about the infection; nature and a well-drained soil are probably the best remedies.

HORMONES AND ELIXIRS for new or newly-transplanted bushes ?? There are a number of products on the market that claim to have potent powers to make the roots develop "millions of tiny root hairs" for fast and vigorous growth. Some seem to help, but the Rambler suspects that the rosarian willing to go to that much extra expense and effort had built a pretty good 'rose bed in the first place. Maybe the extra water in planting helped. Who knows for sure?? If you have a favorite added ingredient, use it with plenty of water. Just don't add any fertilizer even though the label says, "Can't burn when used as directed."

LIQUID COMPOST is a great organic starter. It is also called cow tea. Back in BC (Before Chemicals), good gardeners always had a barrel or two steeping behind the garage or fence. It was a good practice and still is. There's not much direct nutrient value to cow tea, but the boost given soil organisms makes everything work better. Keep several plastic garbage cans of tea brewing all the time (rainwater is best). Onion or potato sacks make good tea bags; fill with cow chips and tie with a long piece of wire or rope. Steep for about ten days, sloshing around once in a while. You'll know when it is ready.

FOR ESTABLISHED BUSHES, add some soluble fertilizer to cow tea and apply when danger of frost is past. Hold off until the soil warms up; then use a half-bucket of cow tea laced with something like *Ra-Pid-Gro* or *Peters Instant* and stand back. The bushes are going to grow. Food in an available form brings a fast reaction; be prepared for results.

April is the month when rose fun really begins... keeping in mind that growing roses isn't hard work — unless you would rather be doing something else. To make roses '85 even easier, tryout a couple of these springtime tuneups...

A DOSE OF SALTS helps roses in the spring — Epsom Salts (magnesium Sulfate), that is. Just an ounce or two of Epsom Salts per established plant in early spring seems to encourage new breaks and greener leaves. Just broadcast in the root area and water in. One of the best spring tonics you'll ever try.

WARM ROOTS WORK. Fertilizers applied to cold soils won't do much good until the root zone warms up. The canes, warmed by sunshine, may be waking up, but the roots are waiting for a clear signal that spring has arrived. Take a look at new roses planted in black plastic pots and set out on a warm, reflective surface. In just a week or so, new, tiny roots have spread throughout the pot, and the bush is off to a fast start. Roses in the ground start the same way, when the soil warms up and the roots begin to work. For growers in a hurry, feed in solution (soluble fertilizer in water), soaking the root zone when the soil warms. That's a real tonic.

COLD, WET WEATHER is considered a blessing on the Gulf Coast; rosarians around here try to get new roses into the ground just before or even during a rainy spell so that bushes become established with lots of water. Until the feeder roots start, bushes have to rely on moisture stored in roots and canes. Warm weather or dry, cold wind can cause real stress; canes dry out before roots are ready to go to work. It's the reason that canes of new plants (or transplants) should be hilled up with soil to maintain a constant, moderate temperature and retain moisture. Observation: a good rosarian is a muddy one.

FERTILIZERS WITH SYSTEMIC IN-SECTICIDES... of doubtful value for most rosarians. Controls only aphids at best, and that can be done with the garden hose. Expensive, too. Get on a feeding program with trace elements and control insects AS NEEDED with specific spray applications. It's the Rambler's experience that excessive use of fertilizers with "systemic action" tends to stunt growth, particularly in potted roses. When roses have to be sprayed for fungus control anyway, why punish the root system with systemics.

MANURE GETS BAD PRESS... an undeserved reputation. Horse, cow, sheep, rabbit or whatever, manure is a great organic soil conditioner/micro-organism supporter that makes soils come alive. There are some drawbacks, but most can be controlled. The dehydrated stuff in sacks may have too much salt; just run through a leafy compost routine first and add some gypsum to leach the salt. Trouble with weeds? Compost first and apply generously. What weeds are left over are easy to pull. Or, get some manure from horse stalls, free of weeds or grasses. The results from manure are certainly worth the extra effort. But for the very best manure (without a cow), read on ...

THE FRAGRANT FORMULA... an olde tyme favorite for artificial manure that will grow grass on a fence post and roses on concrete. This is for the rosarian who doesn't have a farm friend (and a pickup truck) for the real stuff. The fragrant formula is just as good (maybe better because it releases more nutrients) and can be produced on a city lot. It's as good a soil amendment, top dressing, basic feeding formula... especially in the spring. Enjoy all the benefits; here's the formula:

3 ample yards of compost materials or leaves
100 pounds cottonseed hulls (or something coarse like
ground pine bark)
100 pounds cottonseed meal
100 pounds rough cut alfalfa meal (or pellets)
50 pounds of bone meal
50 pounds of fish meal

A farm feed store will have all the ingredients, except the leaves. If fish meal is not available, substitute a couple of sacks of manure and maybe add 20 pounds of bloodmeal or beef and bone. There are lots of variations to accomplish the same thing. The feed store is a great place to shop; they carry most of the supplies that rosarians need.

THE DIGESTION PROCESS... Make a pile of the coarse materials about two feet deep, using any area suitable for composting, maybe the corner of an annual flower bed. Add the lighter ingredients (bone meal, etc.) a little at a time and turn with a garden fork or a pitch fork. Mix well. Then moisten LIGHTLY and turn with a fork twice a week for two weeks. Cover with plastic if in a real hurry, but allow some of the heat to escape. When the pile is working properly, a sharp ammonia odor will leak out. A DIFFERENT ODOR will leak out if the pile gets too wet or if there is not enough coarse composting material. Wet cottonseed meal turns into a slime that smells dead. If there is an odor, add more roughage and turn more frequently.

APPLICATION... The formula is ready in about three weeks. Use about two garden shovelfuls per established plant for first feeding in the spring. One shovelful can be repeated in late summer. If soil is acid, skip the cottonseed meal and substitute manure with straw or some other manure source. Organic manures in the spring make other fertilizers work better, feeding the micro-organisms that do all the work converting nutrients in the soil into a form that roses can use. With the Fragrant Formula, you'll have live soil, healthy organisms and lots of roses. Use generously; it really works.

The Rambler's quip that "A rose garden is a thing of beauty and a job forever" remains true, but, here are some tips on how to make the job a little easier...

NATURE'S MIRACLE... It's the Rambler's conclusion after years of trying one miracle breakthrough after another that good old organics still work better and more consistently. Blood meal and fish meal and cottonseed meal encourage beautiful leaves that support even more beautiful blooms. Manures and alfalfa build strong plants. Compost in the rose beds keeps nature in balance. Fish emulsion in water is a tonic that makes big roses as well as miniatures happy. Some good, aged cow tea makes the sick well and the well even better. Feed the processes that make nutrients available. You'll have live soil, organisms and healthy rosebushes.

THE CHEMISTS' CONTRIBUTION... Soluble inorganic fertilizers are here to stay, too. Used with discretion, these foods provide the extra boost that bushes need for top production. Nitrogen is easy to apply (and leached most rapidly). Chelated trace elements bring out the best in bloom and color. If the working soil is healthy, the best of both worlds (organic and inorganic) work together.

ROSES CAN'T READ... A rose doesn't know if there's a rose picture on the fertilizer sack or not; it's the formula inside that counts. The most expensive rose special isn't necessarily the best. Check the percentage of nutrient (by weight) which appears on the label of every fertilizer you buy. A 5-10-5 formula contains 5% nitrogen, 10 % phosphoric acid and 5 % potash (the N-P-K ratio). Trace elements will also be listed if included in the mix, as well as the percentage of sulfur, most commonly found in ammonium phosphate fertilizers. The 12-24-12 and 13-13-13 formulations used on the lawn are often the best buys for roses, too. Add chelated trace elements in solution as needed. Fertilizer choice depends on the size of the garden, cost, convenience, needs and availability. A little rose sense with a regular program will make YOU happy, and your roses will be happy, too.

OFF THE SHELF AND ON THE LEAVES... Regular fungicide spray programs are recommended at every rose society meeting, and with good reason. Disease control is established through prevention; blackspot-damaged leaves cannot be restored. Leaves and buds disfigured by mildew won't become sleek and productive again after spraying. The most common mistake is to wait until infection appears; and by that time, it's too late. It's an uphill battle from then on. Get the safe, effective disease controls off the shelf and on the leaves... the sooner the better..

STAY ON SCHEDULE... Get on a 7-10 day schedule and stay with it. Don't cheat. The fungus spores will catch you every time. The best practice IS to begin fungus disease control the day roses are pruned, long before leaves appear. Good fungicides like *Funginex, Benlate, Manzate* or *Phaltan* will do the job if used on the bushes. Slack off on some other job, but not on fungus control. In most areas, the fungicide program is the key to good roses.

FUNGINEX **WORKS...** if used on schedule. Safe and convenient, it's probably the most popular fungicide ever to hit the market. But it MUST be used on schedule, thoroughly wetting the leaves. To stretch the residual, use *Funginex* at recommended strength and add *Manzate* at 1/2 recommended strength. *Phaltan* at half-strength works, too. *Manzate* tends to be more of an eradicant; *Funginex* may not clean up a bad infection. As a cost-saver, buy *Triforine* (the active ingredient in *Funginex*), which is also marketed by *Ortho* through agricultural supply stores. The Rambler has used *Triforine* for years and has had consistently good results, particularly when combined with *Manzate*.

THE IN-PRODUCT FOR MILDEW... *Bayleton* by Mobay Chemical. Systemic in action, this highly effective wettable powder can be used at preventative or curative rates and only has to be used every three to four weeks. Preventative rate is only 1/4 teaspoon per gallon of water; curative rate is 1/2 teaspoon per gallon. Really works. Begin use as soon as leaves appear; slack off during hot, dry summer months as the conditions aren't right for mildew anyway.

SOURCES... It doesn't do much good to recommend a material if it is not readily available in quantities suitable for a home gardener. Most everything the Rambler suggests can be purchased through an agricultural supplier locally or regionally, like Brighton By-Products, mentioned in this column in January. Another good supplier for rose specialty items is Kimbrew-Walter Roses, Rt. 2, Box 172, Grand Saline, TX 75140. They now have available by mail order four-ounce packages of *Bayleton* ($14.95) and *Triforine EC* one quart ($24.95). *Vendex, Manzate, Benlate*, too; drop a line for a price list of rose-related products.

GOURMET FOOD FOR ROSES... Guano de las Islas, the gourmet organic fertilizer from the islands of Peru. These bird droppings make roses GROW. Discussed in these pages last year, here's an update on cost and effectiveness. Container-grown plants thrived on guano, even during a very hot summer. Large roses in bed performed equally well, but not quite as dramatically. Cost of application was about 75c per large bush per season, purchased in 39-pound pails. Cost will vary depending on the length of the growing season. Cholito, Inc. markets *PLANTJOY* and is a regular advertiser in these pages.

For every rose problem, there's a solution... even if it's learning to live with it. But you'll live lots longer and your roses will be happier if you learn to look and listen to what roses are trying to say... for example:

COARSE, WEATHERED LEAVES are the first signs of spray burn, almost like sunburn on the rosarian. Spray burn occurs in stages, just like sunburn, almost like sunburn on the rosarian. Leaves don't have to turn brown and drop off to have burn. Watch for brown edges on the leaves or yellow-brown spots on the leaves (NOT blackspot) as further evidence. Spots on the leaves may be from droplets on spray material acting like a magnifying glass for bright sunshine. Solution: for better leaf coverage, add one teaspoon of white vinegar to soften each gallon of alkaline water plus a drop or two of ordinary dishwashing detergent. Makes spray materials spread out over the leaf evenly. If droplets form to runoff, tap a large cane on the bush with the spray wand and shake off the excess. This simple trick may save the foliage of a really fine specimen.

KEEP A SPRAY LOG so that if a mistake is made there's a basis to reason out what might have gone wrong. If a new combination of ingredients causes a problem, look back to see just what change was made. If roses could really 14lk, the Rambler suspects that they would ask for one-ingredient spray application rather than everything in the garage plus, a dash or two of something extra. Products from the same manufacturer will usually specify what things are compatible, such as *Funginex* and *Orthene*, as in *Orthenex*, or *Phaltan* and *Isotox*. Many others are compatible but should be used carefully and observed. Some insecticides and fungicides will specifically warn against mixing, and the user proceeds at his own risk. In cool weather under ideal conditions, foliar fertilizers can be added to the spray mix without a problem, and many growers think blooms and leaves are improved. But talk to another grower who added that extra ingredient on a hot day "just to make the leaves glossy" and the story may be quite different.

LOOK AT THE SPRAY MIX... there are several good indicators as to how well the ingredients are getting along. Mixes sometimes curdle, others separate, some form greasy lumps. All the straining in the world won't make these chemicals work together. When they do react, it will be on the leaves. Example: out-of-date *Cygon* will cause most wettable powder fungicides to precipitate out of the solution. Get rid of the mix and start over with a fresh batch. A good trick for any wettable powder is to mix carefully with a swirling action in a glass jar. Start with warm, softened water; then add the wettable powder; then the EC (emulsifiable concentration) with the petroleum distillate base. You'll be able to observe lumps, reactions and general compatibility before putting in the sprayer.

LIMP ROSE FOLIAGE begging for water is not going to be receptive to ANY spray, even in the middle of a hot day. Water plants thoroughly and allow enough time for moisture to reach the leaves BEFORE spraying. Transpiration in the leaves works just like perspiration for rosarians and that moisture has to be replaced. Early morning or late evening spraying is the safest if the leaves are turgid with moisture. If in doubt, when spraying in the evening, hose down the plants first; then spray. Washes off the old spray material, too, plus the pollution fallout. It's not a bad weekly practice for any rosarian.

WATER IS AN INSECTICIDE, TOO... washes off spider mites and aphids without poisoning the whole environment. More and more growers seem to be recommending waterwashing, the high pressure water treatment for the undersides of the leaves. Many wands and rigs are available (advertised in these pages) to conveniently get lots of water to the undersides of the leaves. Any way this can be done is OK. The plants love it. Begin washing on a weekly basis as soon as the weather turns warm, particularly miniatures or roses in hot, reflective locations. As in fungus disease control, begin BEFORE evidence of damage. If infestation catches up (and it can very quickly) wash two or three times a week. If a miticide is absolutely necessary, wash first, then apply the miticide. *Vendex* seems to be the choice of most serious rosarians, followed by *Plictran*. And remember to spray the UNDERSIDES of the leaves where the mites are, not the bud and bloom areas, where the thrips are.

THE *BUG ZAPPER*, ANOTHER CON-

TROL... for all kinds of insects that plague roses and rosarians. The zapper (known by many names) is the electric grid with bug-attracting black lights ... and it is appearing routinely in more and more gardens. It neatly electrocutes all sorts of flying insects, depositing them in a tray on the ground. It is particularly effective against the moth that lays eggs for corn ear worms. And it makes the garden a good deal more pleasant without all the mosquitoes and gnats. Most users select a model with a large diameter grid screen so that larger insects can pass through. Also, hang the zapper about eight or nine feet high for safety as well as effectiveness. Most models will attract and protect an area of one hundred feet or more. There's some difference of opinion on location... either on the perimeter of the garden or in the center. Perimeter folks say it keeps the bugs away from the roses; center folks say the bugs are in the roses anyhow. The initial investment for a zapper is a little high, but watch for a Sears *Bugwhacker* on sale. If you have a power source near the garden, it could be the best gift you could give yourself and your garden this season.

LEARN TO LOOK. See what's happening in the rose garden. Figure out why. Then do something about it. Insect and fungus damage won't get well. Just catch that damage at an early stage, and you're on the way to control.

Good ideas are not a bit particular about who has them... they show up in all kinds of gardens, large and small. For BIG results, try these...

ROSE MARKERS turn a rose patch into a garden. They make the grower look good, too. And they enable the gardener to remember all the names without stumbling. Visitors love them. A good marker going is the Harlane, advertised regularly in these pages. Variety names come pre-printed or you can letter the markers yourself. In pure garden pleasure, they are worth a good deal more than the modest cost... QUICK COUPLERS for hoses and attachments make sense and garden work easier. No more having to couple and uncouple balky connections that refuse to thread. Nelson makes a fine brass model: buy enough male ends for all nozzles, sprinklers, soakers, water wands and what-have-you. *Dramm* (makers of *Dramm* nozzles for plastic sprinkler systems) has a twist-coupler that is a dandy. Couple and uncouple without getting wet even with the water on full force. A real convenience with a watering system... A RELIABLE RAIN GAUGE belongs in every rose garden. Not the fancy ornamental kind but a well-marked, calibrated gauge that knows the difference between 1/4 and 1/2 inch. Know just how much water the summer thundershower delivered. Find a good gauge in a farm supply store -sometimes they are giveaways. Place in an unprotected area for most accurate readings. Your roses will appreciate it ...

TRASH BUCKETS (five-gallon cans) placed in strategic locations in the garden are great for collecting spent blooms, disbudded growth, odd leaves and so forth as the grower tours the garden. Makes a neat, better-groomed garden. Just pull and pinch and drop into the bucket without having to go after the trash can... A RAIN BARREL sounds old-fashioned but gives old-fashioned results. Good water for those "special plants" without chlorine, alkalinity or treatment problems. Use for container plants, pots, barrels and starter beds. Ideal for brewing up cow tea, too. If tea is not on the fertilizing menu, try fish emulsion and rain water. Makes ANYTHING grow.

MINIATURES START FASTER if potted-up before planting in regular beds, particularly in hot weather. Small miniature roses will develop root and top growth faster in a five-inch pot (with good potting soil) and can be gradually hardened off before setting out in direct sun. Just two or three weeks makes a big difference. Keep in a protected location, water regularly, add a touch of no-burn food (like fish emulsion) once a week and enjoy great results. When new growth is well established, carefully slip from pot and plant. The mini will never know it has been moved.

HOW MUCH WATER is enough? Since water is essential to every soil, leaf and growth process, make sure that every rose plant and bed is well supplied. Depending on the leaf area, a rosebush uses three or four gallons of water per day, moving nutrients from the soil to the leaves, feeding, cooling and controlling at the same time. Just like a human blood supply. If in doubt, water some more. Moisture availability depends on the makeup of the soil: heavier soils hold more water: sandy soils dry out faster. Any time of day is OK; deep soak, don't sprinkle. Grandmother's soaking system with the end of the hose in a tomato can still works.

SOIL OUT OF BALANCE? Try a gypsum (calcium sulfate) purge. Particularly good in heavy, alkaline soils, gypsum acts to flush excess salts from the soil and let nature get back into balance. Opens up a tight soil, too, with an ion exchange that separates flat clay particles. One writer described use of gypsum in pots "like pulling the cork out of a barrel." A grower does not have to understand the process to benefit from the results. For rose beds, broadcast about 20-25 pounds per 100 square feet: scratch in lightly and water well. Use lots of water. Results will be noticeable in about two weeks. Then begin to feed lightly with an organic-base fertilizer. Can't hurt, and often helps. Give gypsum a try.

SOILS WORK HARD and need to be fed — the soil organisms, that is. Many growers tend to overlook the fact that the soil micro-organisms make everything happen in the soil. The most carefully formulated foods are of no use to the plant until converted into a useable form by these soil workers. What do the workers like?? Quick foods like nitrogen to burn for energy, but in a moist, humus environment with oxygen. How to get there? Plenty of organic material from whatever source:

leaves, compost, manures, ground bark or mixtures of all of these.

A TESTIMONIAL... the Rambler added two or three inches of horse manure, wood shavings, alfalfa and straw mix to the rose beds with established roses about two weeks after pruning this year. Paid little attention to whether the manure was fresh or composted, and most of it was quite fresh. Some of the piles waiting to be spread steamed on cool mornings... the organisms were working. Applied the mix generously, scratched in lightly and gave the beds all the water they could hold. The result: best growth, basals, leaves and overall growth ever. Weeds?? None so far: These horses were kept in stalls and not allowed to range. In past years, an occasional sprig of oat might come up. A small price for rose production. It works.

A rosarian who never makes a mistake is one who never does anything... and that applies to most growers. Here are some right-ways and some wrong-ways to have fun with roses this summer...

WATER FIRST, then feed. Sounds simple but all of us fall into the trap at one time or another, thinking that we can "do it just this one time". The result is usually yellow leaves and a bush in stress. The culprit is the ammonium compound that supplied the nitrogen; it absorbed water, even to the extent of pulling moisture from the roots. The grower sees the end result, burned leaves. When applying any fertilizer, water first, feed lightly, then water again. Make sure that the roots have PLENTY of water available. Most of plant growth comes from water anyway, why skimp on something so readily available?? And, by the way, the Rambler has noticed some seriously yellow/brown leaves on some miniatures recently fed. Must have been the day the water pressure was down.

GARDEN TOURS... a great way to learn. Notice how sickly the roses are under the trees or in competition with roots. How about the "cooked" looking foliage on bushes planted on the hot side of a brick wall. Or the anemic plants in a poorly drained spot. Sometimes more can be learned from a sick plant than a hearty one. Visit a rose garden every chance you get. It will payoff big dividends in roses.

TIMED RELEASE FERTILIZERS... the Rambler is more and more impressed with the results after visiting gardens using these products of the chemist's art. Not to suggest that organics be forgotten, but the steady, regular supply of nutrients can make a good garden into a great one. The Rambler used to think that timed release fertilizers were just for growers who were too tired to work regularly in the garden. Timed release can supplement good practices and make them even better. Just use some discretion in application; know when to slow plants down. There are some three-month formulas available that can still be used in many parts of the country. Some timed release products respond to temperature, some to water. Use the formula to fit the season and the need. Miniatures respond particularly well to LIGHT applications of timed release foods. Look into the availability of these convenience foods in your area, you and your roses may enjoy the results.

THE JET-ALL... one of the best rose items to come along in years. It's a spider mite killer, plant cooler, easy-on-the back appliance that takes the worry out of hot weather and defoliation by mites. Even if you don't believe that water-washing leaves can control spider mites, washing WILL help when used before spraying with a miticide. The Rambler has gotten the very best control by washing early in the season and, if an outbreak of spider mites does occur, water-wash and then spray with *Vendex.* Water washing definitely helps. The Jet-All has three high pressure jets on the end of a long wand, fan-spraying 160 degrees or more. And all the water goes to the leaves, not on the user. The long, curved handle reaches under the bushes and gets the water to the right place. The Rambler has used one for a year and wouldn't be without it. For about $25.00, it's the best gift you could give your garden if you have mites, and who doesn't?? Available by mail order (and frequently advertised in these pages) from Jet-AI Products, 7731 Long Point, #15, Houston, TX 77055. They will send one right away along with an invoice (they trust rosarians). Or you may just want to ask for their sales folder to take a look. Good folks, good product.

WEED PROBLEMS?? Get some Roundup, the herbicide that does not stay in the soil. It is also available in smaller quantities as *Kleenup* (an Ortho product), a more dilute formulation. But the best buy is still a gallon of *Roundup* shared by several rosarians. Most farm/feed stores have it. Watch spray drift when using *Roundup*, it works on anything green. Rather corrosive, too, use a fiberglass tank. The best idea is to set aside a small sprayer for herbicides only, then there's no chance of a careless mistake. Just spray the offending weeds or grass and in about four days it's dead. Doesn't harm the soil at all. A weedy area' can be replanted in a week. It sure beats having to pull or dig weeds and grass from in and around rose beds.

EXPAND YOUR INTERESTS... join the Rose Hybridizers Association. It's a good group anxious to share the fun and practical know-how of hybridizing. RHA publishes an excellent quarterly bulletin available for just $5.00 per year. Put a check in the mail payable to RHA, Larry Peter-son, 3245 Wheaton Road, Horseheads, NY 14845. Even if you never harvest a seed, you'll benefit from RHA.

SAVE THOSE CLIPPINGS... make mulch. Compost, mix, add leaves and what-have-you. There's a great harvest of green stuff that will make roses happy. Don't waste it. Takes a little extra time, but the rewards are worth the-efforts. You'll be surprised at how fast the good humus material piles up. Just don't pile the grass clipping in the rose beds; they will heat, shed water and rob nitrogen from the soil. Break down before apply-ing (or adding to the soil) and you'll have a real garden friend. The Rambler has several piles of organic material working all the time. It's called letting nature work for you instead of against you.

How many roses have you seen on bushes without leaves?? Very few. Which suggests that rosarians ought to be growing leaves as roses are sure to follow. Anyway. here's a leafy harvest of tips on how to make leaves work for you (and roses)…

KEEP THE LEAVES… they are doing most of the work. Leaves that are cut plucked, burned, eaten up, diseased or poorly fed just can't perform. When the leaves go, the blooms go. So does it make sense to ALWAYS cut those long stems (and leaves) when it isn't necessary?? Bushes that are not yet established are severely set back when too much is cut. Use some discretion with the pruners, save some leaves.

GROOMING rosebushes is an art, not a science, and needs to be practiced throughout the season. Shape and control every time spent blooms are cut, no need to perform major surgery. Cut to the first five-leaflet on some stems, lower on some and higher on some. The resul1 will be a bush with more blooms over a longer period and an overall healthier plant. Common advice is to "open up" the center of the plant for that vase shape, usually cutting out twiggy or unwanted growth. But take it easy with this cleanup routine: if the leaves are healthy and sunshine can get to developing eyes (the next batch of blooms). Why pull or cut leaves producing the food to make those blooms? The same restraint applies to lower leaves: pulling seldom avoids spider mites. The practice just makes it easier for the grower to get under the leaves. When those lower leaves have outlived their usefulness. They will drop off anyway. Roses are more attractive when leafed to the ground, and healthier too.

BLIND SHOOTS TWIGGY GROWTH… To remove or not remove. Try a middle-of-the-road approach. Cut back to a three or five leaflet on some shoots, they will often develop into healthy, bloom-producing canes. Trim out the rosettes of leaves if they bother you. But remember that they are no more prone to disease than other leaves if you are doing a good spraying job. The Rambler's advice, trim some, leave some.

LEAVES SEND SIGNALS… like a dry, burned look when spider mites have moved in. Loss of color, parched, gritty residue on the underside… get out the water wand and wash the under-sides of ALL the leaves thoroughly. Don't wait get busy right away because the mites are busy sucking the very life from the leaves. The Rambler's routine is to water-wash weekly beginning early in the season, and if mites break out, continue with water and supplement with a specific miticide like *Vendex*. Pale, light-colored leaves probably indicate lack of available iron. *Sequestrene* will remedy the problem in a hurry. In cool climates, foliar application is all right. In hot humid areas, soil application in solution is safer. Anemic leaves may also signal lack of nitrogen, perhaps leached from the soil by heavy rains. Easy to correct by granular soil application, or, for faster results, in solution. *ORTHO, Ra-Pid-Gro, Peters, Carl Pool Instant* and many others can do the job in a hurry. But remember that these applications are used up (and leached out) in a hurry, too. There's still no substitute for slow-acting organics and a well prepared rose bed.

FOLIAR FEEDING… does work and-produces outstanding results when used with some discretion. Cool climate growers routinely add foliar food to the spray mix: those of us in hot areas can safely use foliar foods in early spring and late full only. Foliar mixes can coarsen or bum foliage in hot weather. Why take a chance? And the Rambler has always been reluctant to mix insecticides and foliar foods. If conditions are right, use one of the good foliars like *Ra-Pid-Gro* or *Peters* alone.

WET LEAVES… why not?? Occasional overhead watering or washing of the foliage is beneficial to leaf function. With all the junk and pollution in the air, the leaves deserve a good washing from time to time. Removes spray residue, too. For better leaf coverage, wash first then spray. Healthy, happy leaves.

A LEAFY TEST… A municipal garden in Central Texas removed spent blooms by trimming blooms only, no leaves, throughout the season. A check plot of identical varieties was trimmed by more traditional methods with stems and leaves. The lightly trimmed plot outperformed the check in overall bloom, more leaves, healthier plants and better overall display. Plus, the planting with blooms-only removed suffered very little winter damage with no loss. Which says again that winter hardiness follows good growing practices during the growing season. This is not to suggest that serious hobby-growers snap off rose blooms but illustrates that leaves have an important function in the overall performance of the plant.

SLOW LEAVES (AND BUSHES) down in the fall to prepare for winter cold (and sudden freezes). Stop feeding six or eight weeks before frost. Later in the season, don't cut spent blooms, let rose hips develop (colorful and attractive on many varieties). Cutting blooms signals a plant to produce another bloom (and tender, green growth). Left alone, the plant slows down, having completed its seed function. Gradual dormancy can definitely be encouraged by the grower... it's all in the leaves.

LEAVES WEAR OUT... learn to recognize when a leaf has completed its job and when it needs help. Some yellow leaves in the center of the plant are usually of no concern: they have done a job and are being replaced in a natural sequence. It's the sudden, unexplained change that needs some attention.

Indian Summer has arrived for most of us, that "happy and flourishing period occurring toward the end of something"… a period of happy roses, putting out a harvest that's bigger, better and more colorful. But it's not an end, just a pleasant time to enjoy roses… perhaps with a few of these ideas.

COMPOST PILE too old fashioned for you? Just remember that the fancy organic mixes for sale at the nursery are simply commercial applications of nature's own recipe, return everything to the soil. Fall is a great time to start a compost pile, as all the raw materials are available. Mounds of leaves are a pleasant problem to have… good for insulating and composting. If you have a few cinder blocks or even some old lumber, fashion some kind of loose-fitting enclosure so that air and water can feed nature's process. Air and the right balance of moisture are essential. Most good rose gardens have compost piles hidden away somewhere in the yard. Some are fancy affairs; others are piles of clippings, dirt and what-have-you. How about a pile of leaves mixed with a little dirt in the vegetable or annual garden area? Wherever or whatever, the results are the same when compost gets to the garden… better aeration, better root growth, better bushes and therefore better blooms. No garden is too small. With just a little effort, anyone can convert organic material into the best plant foot that nature can produce.

ROSEBUSHES ON THE WAY?? If fall planting is your thing, try starting in oversize plastic pots rather than in prepared beds, particularly smaller bushes that come in from Canada. It's more work to move pots in and out of the garage or garden shed during really cold weather, but the results are worth it. During the warm days of fall, roots have a chance to develop more rapidly as the soil remains warm. Black plastic pots absorb and pass on heat very readily. Protect when it gets cold. It's the same recommendation the Rambler has passed on for sick roses… pot them up in a good, friable mix and work toward roots, not tops. At planting time don't try to shake the root ball out of the pot; the mix and roots may be too loose to handle. Cut the bottom out of the pot, place in the planting location and carefully cut away and discard the sides. No shock and no loss of the roots so carefully developed. Plastic pots are cheap, rose-

bushes are not.

INSULATING WRAP for tree roses might have an application in your area. Several cold-climate growers have reported good success with fiberglass rafter or duct insulation, the pink panther blanket with foil backing. Loosely wrap the standards from bottom to top, foil side out, and tie loosely with cord. Flare out just under the bud unions and work a little of the protection over the bud unions and major canes. The insulation protects from sudden freeze-thaws and drying winds. The method has been quite successful and is certainly easier than burying the entire tree rose. If you're a skeptic, use your usual method on some bushes and the wrap method on some. And pass on your observations next spring.

INSULATING LEAVES on rose beds may not be decorative but do the job. Winter protection is simply a matter of preventing the freezing-thawing cycle and drying out of rose canes. A mound of soil or compost over the bud union and lower canes plus lots of leaves will keep most roses in good shape with temperature ranges to 25 'below, even complicated with cold, dry winds and bright sunshine. Keep leaves in place with wire baskets, rabbit-wire fences, evergreen boughs or even short snow fence. Some cold-climate rosarians use a combination of cones and leaves for protection, the leaves serving as a sort of protective insulation for the cones and maintaining a more even temperature.

A READER'S TESTIMONIAL: I don't have the time or the energy to build boxes or bury roses, so I have always thrown some dirt from the garden area on the bud unions and piled on leaves as high as they would go. Even get some leaves from the neighbors. It's not very fancy, but my roses always do all right.

YOU CAN FOOL MOTHER NATURE… the latest is an anti-transpirant sold as CLOUD COVER, a protective foliage spray that works for deciduous plants and hardwood cuttings by reducing water lost through the leaves (transpiration). The material is an emulsion (water soluble) that can be sprayed on leaves or applied by dipping. It forms a transparent, flexible film that is semi-permeable to water and permits the normal breathing process of the plant to take place. The film is good for two months or so under normal rainfall conditions, forming on leaves and stems to help reduce water loss through the pores of the leaf, lessening the water stress of the plant. When water stress occurs, growth rates are reduced or stopped until the stress is eliminated. This typically happens when plants are propagated, transplanted, moved or stored. Drying winds, high and low temperatures also cause moisture stress.

CLOUD COVER is easy to apply and relatively cheap. Mix one part *Cloud Cover* and 20 parts of water. Spray or dip (for cuttings). Available in quarts or gallons from nursery or greenhouse supply houses. Read through the technical guidelines on each container; you'll be amazed at the number of applications for the home gardener. And, it really does the job. The Rambler potted up some Floribundas in full leaf in early summer… came right through without shock OR yellow leaves. Now THAT'S a testimonial. Check with your local supplier.

With roses, it's what you learn after you know it all that counts… at least that's what the Rambler has learned the hard way. Here are some good/bad experiences that might help you…

CONTAINER-GROWN PLANTS tend to turn pale near the end of the season but will respond to a good gypsum flush. Cold climate rosarians won't see the difference until next season, but the results will be dramatic. Salts tend to build up in containers, especially with clay soils and alkaline water. In other words, the soil doesn't "work." For this condition, gypsum "opens up the spaces" and the good soil processes take over again. One author described the action as being "like pulling the cork out of the bottle." Gypsum, of course, works in alkaline clay rose beds, too. Doesn't disturb the pH and furnishes calcium as well. How much to use? About 20 pounds per 100 square feet of rose bed or a handful per whiskey half-barrel is just about right. Scale up or down depending on container size; application can be inexact. Water in well, and let good things happen all winter.

BURY FOR THE WINTER… new rosebushes, that is. Bushes received in November or December (or newly budded plants) are far better off buried than potted and moved in and out of protection all winter. It's a natural sort of dormancy, much like the Minnesota Tip method of winter protection. Select a garden spot where it's easy to dig (about 18 inches or so), loosen the spoil dirt with plenty of leaves, and the "dormancy vault" is ready to receive bushes. Tie the tops with twine and combine bushes in loose bundles. Line the bottom of the vault with some dirt-leaves mix, heel in the bundles (not quite horizontal) and cover with the mix. Remember to tie a rope on the bundles so that you can find them next spring. Cover the area with lots of leaves. Then wait for spring. It really works.

WARM CLIMATE ROSARIANS also like to get Canadian roses late in the fall but are concerned with new growth likely to be frozen back in January or February. These plants can also be buried for dormancy, but the most common practice is to pot these newcomers and winter protect in a garage or garden house for the cold snaps of short duration. In black plastic pots, roots have a good chance to develop, and the bushes get off to a roaring start the following spring when set out in the beds. It's an old trick of thoughtful rosarians: grow the roots first, then the tops (and blooms). If potting doesn't match the strength of your back, compromise by planting in the beds and mulching almost to the tips of the canes. Don't trim canes at all. Encourage dormancy. If some new growth at the top gets nipped, trim off next spring and there will be plenty of cane left.

POTTING NEW ROSES is a sound practice in areas subject to warm/sharp frost conditions. These roses are not only easier to protect, but the roots have a chance to develop before planting out. Black plastic pots are best; use a light, friable soil mix to make roots want to grow. Resist the temptation to add exotics to the mix; the warm soil in the pot is going to do all the work. Since mail order roses seem to arrive at the whim of the shipper, a potting routine is a good insurance policy. Some growers carry potted roses well into the season to serve as "replacements" or to hold a spare plant for a mass planting of one variety.

TIRED LEAVES usually get that way because of the rosarian, not the bush. A case in point: the Rambler was anxious to get some strong fall growth in a mass planting of Sunsprite and broadcast some 12-24-12 on fairly dry soil (and during a period of heat and no rain). Obviously the subsoil was dry also. The Rambler watered routinely after application and twice a week thereafter, but many of the lower leaves lost color with a burned look. The new growth progressed nicely, but the overall beauty of the bushes suffered. Moral: SOAK beds first, then feed (lightly), then soak again. When in doubt, WATER.

RUBIGAN EC, a locally systemic fungicide for the prevention and therapeutic control of powdery mildew on roses, may be the latest (and expensive) IN product for rosarians. Introduced with considerable fanfare at the ARS Chicago meeting in September, the Elanco product has considerable promise. *Rubigan* is absorbed into the foliage and is not easily washed off by rain or overhead irrigation. There's no residue accumulation; the material is very active and concentrated. It's absorbed quickly and not susceptible to wash-off; once dry, the protection begins. Joseph Klima, ARS President Emeritus, has tested *Rubigan* for several years and reports good control for four weeks or more in his mildew-prone San Francisco area. Joe reports application rate at two teaspoons per five gallons of water. But, it is somewhat expensive: $78 per one pint can from Kimbrew Walter Rose Growers (Grand Saline, TX) and somewhat higher from Brighton By-Products (New Brighton, PA). Since it is late in the season for most growers, the Rambler will report trials along the Gulf Coast during October and November in an early '86 issue.

But just remember, NO material will work until taken off the shelf and applied to the leaves. A systematic program does the job.

The year-end routine for columnists is to review and reflect on the dwindling days, arriving at some carefully qualified conclusions (hindsight) for the benefit of those readers who haven't read the summer magazines yet. Looking over '85, it seems that roses and rosarians haven't really changed much...

CONTROVERSY... Does *Bayleton* (mildew control) retard growth, shorten stems?? Could any product retard growth to the extent reported in some rose circles without killing the bush?? Will someone PLEASE stand up and give anxious rosarians a *Bayleton* endorsement? We have a big investment in the stuff on our shelves. The Rambler still likes it for big roses and LOVES it for miniatures. But, on the other hand, the Rambler thinks that *Rubigan* (the newest systemic mildew control) is also great. As of this writing in late October, *Rubigan* is providing excellent control during perfect conditions for severe mildew infection... even on varieties like Granada, First Prize, Peach Beauty, Charlie, Chipper, and Over The Rainbow. Smells bad, but seems to be doing the job with just two applications since September 1. This Eli Lilly product was used at 2 teaspoons per 5 gallons in combination with *Triforine* (1 teaspoon per gallon) and *Avant* foliar. Excellent leaf coverage, no leaf damage even during a period of very hot weather. The Rambler plans one more application to carry through November (we have a long growing season here). The disadvantage? Another substantial investment on the shelf at $70 per pint. And have you noticed the cartoon that shows a rosarian busy in the garden while the wife remarks, "Those roses eat better than we do." Will give you a season-end report in an early issue.

SUNSHINE FOR ROSES... How much or how little. Rosarians still insist on making beds and planting roses where nature never intended such activities. The sunny spot in the early spring may be shade by mid-summer. Save your back and bank account severe strain by looking ahead. Sunshine makes roses grow and bloom... there's no substitute or cheating on the amount required. Marginal sunshine produces marginal roses. If in doubt, don't. Use a shade-tolerant annual in that location for a season instead. The Rambler still has trouble with a long rose bed that ranges from full

sun to filtered shade in a distance of about 50 feet (the garden owner INSISTS on roses regardless of cost and care). All one variety, the bushes run from puny (with dieback) to vigorous. Bushes in the sun have good root systems, heavy canes, and lots of leaves. Virtually no roots have developed (but plenty of galls have) on the shaded plants. Season after season the same results. Completely replant with #1 bushes every spring. Good first bloom', then a gradual decline. The point is that sunshine affects all aspects of plant growth and production; don't waste time, money, and plants in the shade. Switch off to shade-loving plants (or cut down the trees) and enjoy gardening even more... with plenty of roses in the sun, of course.

SWEETHEART ROSES... Are the new Sweetheart roses here to stay (with the same name)? Will all of the hybridizers, nurserymen, registration authorities; garden centers, and the ROSE BUYERS finally agree that this is a new classification? Let's go with something and get these fine new roses into the gardens and on the show tables. Sweethearts (or whatever) are great roses for patios, small gardens, balconies, containers, and what-have-you. Larger in bloom and habit than miniatures but smaller than floribundas, these Sweethearts bloom and bloom. Save some money and space and enjoy a new dimension in roses in '86. Available through nursery outlets initially, and in limited numbers by mail order. Whether they are called Sweethearts, Maxi-Minis, Mini-Floras, or Patios these roses are really great for the grower with a small space. Buy some. WANT A BARGAIN?? For a major landscape project, consider buying 1 1/2 grade plants at wholesale or at substantially reduced prices (compared to #1's). In most cases, 1 1/2's will catch up with #1's by the end of the first season. Plant the smaller bushes a little closer together (close spacing looks better anyway) and enjoy a good many roses that you might not otherwise be able to afford.

It's a good way to plant a driveway or grow a blooming screen. Why are park plantings so eye-catching? Many bushes, close spacing, one variety. You can do the same thing in your public viewing area. The Rambler wouldn't take anything for the free-form bed of 30 Sunsprite in the front garden; or for the 10 Don Juan climbers along a neighbor's driveway fence. You can enjoy the same thing on a budget. Grade 1 1/2 plants come in bundles of 10, and your local nursery supplier can often get what you need (ordered early). You may have to consider substitutes, but the savings are often worth the trouble. Another suggestion: order some bundles of 10 and split with other rose folks. These smaller plants will turn out to be real bargains; and, like it or not, all of us are likely to be buying smaller plants in the future and maturing them in our home gardens.

WHAT ELSE IS NEW?? Lots of roses; every type, color, size, and form 1986 promises to be a banner rose year. How about buying a few extra patios, sweethearts, floribundas, or miniatures for potting and gifts to gardening friends?? Or a gift membership in ARS (new members get a free bush of the '86 AARS winner Broadway. Or a ride to the local rose society meeting. 1986 will be a banner rose year when we share roses… and maybe just a little help to get them going.

JAN.
1986

THOUGHT FOR THE MONTH: A rose expert is the guy who will know tomorrow why the things he predicted yesterday didn't happen today.

As our 1986 rose year breaks dormancy, rose fever spreads from south to north... which proves again that we can't outgrow roses as a hobby. There's always something new with roses or something that needs repeating. Hope that your 1986 is a rosy one and that you'll continue to share the world's greatest hobby.

RUBIGAN REPORT... Not particularly scientific, but the Rambler thinks that it really works on powdery mildew. As reported in earlier columns, *Rubigan* application at 2 teaspoons per 5 gallons began September 1, repeated October 10. Final application was made November 16 (remember, the Gulf Coast enjoys a very long growing season). Powdery mildew conditions were ideal during most of the period (ideal for mildew). However, even the most mildew-prone varieties (like Granada, Chipper, Medallion) are free of mildew or mildew damage as of late November in three different gardens. Also, no evidence of leaf or bloom damage, even when applied during a period of hot weather in mid-October. Easy to use and apparently quite effective, you may want to include *Rubigan* in your '86 rose plans. Probably available through nursery/greenhouse supply firms regionally or definitely by mail order from Kimbrew Walter Roses in Grand Saline, TX or Brighton By-Products in New Brighton, PA.

SAP RISES in roses and rosarians at about the same time... the first warm day. But this season, how about some common rose sense?? Nature and roses perform best gradually; crash spring programs usually crash with the first cold snap. It's similar to the Sunday Syndrome that occurs in the summertime. Sunday Syndrome is a rose affliction induced by the rosarian; roses worn out by pruning, grooming, pulling, feeding, pinching, scratching, watering, and fussing (not necessarily in that order). In the spring it takes the form of uncovering, digging, probing, feeding, cutting, and drenching with gunk before the soil is warm enough to support growth. Let spring and rose work come on gradually, you'll get better results.

DORMANT SPRAYS are overdone and over-rated in the Rambler's opinion, often causing more cane and new leaf damage than good. The lime-sulfur-oil concoctions are hard to use (particularly when it's cold and roses are really dormant) and do not offer the safe and effective control of overwintering diseases and insects that specific fungicides and insecticides do. These controls are already on the rosarian's shelf. For more roses in '86, start a PREVENTATIVE program immediately after pruning, no matter where you live. For southern growers, that means early February. Drench the canes and bud union (if exposed) the same day plants are pruned. Safe practice recommends a combination of a broad spectrum insecticide with your favorite fungicide (*Funginex, Phaltan, Benlate*). Use at label strength and maybe add a little spreadersticker to encourage penetration into the cracks and crevices of the older canes and the bud union. Be particularly careful in coverage of climbers, ramblers, and shrub roses. Infected host plants can spread spores like wildfire when conditions are right. The object is to control over-wintering spores BEFORE temperature and humidity are right for the growth of these organisms. Do Nor wait for new leaves to appear. About two weeks after the pruning application, use the insecticide-fungicide combination again. Then follow the regular fungicide program (every week to ten days) throughout the growing season, adding insecticide ONLY when really necessary. A clean start will go a long way toward a clean garden all season long.

ROSES START better when planted the right way, too. If there's a key to planting, it's water. Thorough, deep soaking for all steps of the planting process. The Rambler is a cone-style planter, supporting the root system of the rose with a cone of well-prepared soil. Cover the roots lightly and begin to run water slowly into the hole. Add some more soil mix, water will fill in the voids. Don't stomp on the roots to tamp the soll in place. Let water do the work. It makes a real rosarian cringe to see a 200-pound enthusiast breaking and displacing rose roots with size 12 boots.

HILL UP NEWLY PLANTED ROSES as the last step. Use all the soil, mulch, or other insulating material available. This not only protects from the cold, but keeps canes from drying out. Until roots are well established, canes are very vulnerable to sun and wind. Constant temperatures and moist conditions help roses start. It's the same principle with plastic tents over plants slow to start. Throw a handful of wet sphagnum moss over the bud union, form a tent of clear plastic material (like the plastic roses are shipped in) over the new bush and secure at the shank or cover edges of the plastic with soil. When bushes have started, gradually cut holes in the plastic to lower temperature. Remove in a few weeks, depending on the weather.

PRUNING? Not as difficult or exotic as many rosarians would have you believe. Assuming that there are some canes left to prune, there are some techniques that can make some difference in healing of cuts and a vigorous spring start. For large, woody canes, use a small keyhole saw rather than the crushing jaws of a lopper. Cuts will heal faster, particularly on the bud union. And make it a regular habit to keep the BLADE of the pruning shear DOWN, so that the opposing jaw of the shear does not bruise good rose cane. To say it another way, let the jaw bruise the cane material that is cut off. Use pruners that are large enough and sharp enough to make cuts smooth and clean. If the cut isn't smooth and easy, you're using the wrong tool.

FEB.
1986

THOUGHT FOR THE MONTH: Smart rosarians learn from the mistakes of others.
We don't have time to make them all ourselves.

The Winter of '85 may never melt, but it's time to break dormancy in many parts of the country and take advantage of whatever spring has to offer... like rain, floods, and sudden cold snaps. It's a good thing that roses and rosarians are remarkably resilient. Roses grow in spite of rosarians and the weather man.

DON'T BE IN A HURRY for springtime to come, particularly in uncovering roses. More plants are probably lost in the springtime when the temperature suddenly drops than during the dead of winter. It's a good idea to let Mother Nature proceed at her own pace; let whatever winter protection you use stay on a little longer than usual. Pruning and probing gives the plant a signal that it is time to grow. In the spring, roses bloom when it is time to bloom, and early uncovering and pruning seldom speeds up the process. You'll be doing yourself and your roses a favor with a little extra springtime patience.

TAKE A GOOD LOOK at how your roses came through a tough winter, or perhaps why they came through. Pay particular attention to the amount of good wood left on some plants and the total loss on others. Was the protection a little better in some cases? Less wind, more moisture, insulation, able to breathe, more gradual dormancy... all could be factors in survival. You can learn a great deal for future reference if you pay attention. If experience is the name we give to our mistakes, let's learn from them too.

FIND NEW HOMES, move 'em around, if you feel like it. If a bush doesn't seem to be doing well in a particular location or if the color is all wrong, move it somewhere else. Transplanting sometimes seems to give a rosebush a new lease on life. Move 'em while they're dormant; trim up and handle like a bare root plant. There are roses to gain and not much to lose. Prune canes according to the usual practice for your climate. Wash off the roots and trim out any dead or broken parts. Trim off root ends lightly to encourage callousing and new feeder roots. Also trim out any root galls or gall growths on the shank or bud union. If large galls girdle the shank or involve many roots, throw the bush away .and start over. It's more work to grow a sick bush than a good one.

RX FOR GALLS?? Some respected growers maintain that disinfecting trimmed galls with *Lysol* or *Clorox* retards reoccurrence, but an equal number disagree. Most growers have galls they don't even know about, and have had for a long time. If the gall is on the shank or the bud union, sunshine seems to do the most good. The Rambler suggests that you don't worry too much about infection; nature and a well-drained soil are probably the best remedies.

HORMONES AND ROOT STIMULANTS for new or newly transplanted bushes?? There are a number of products on the market that claim to be hormones and catalysts to make soils work and roots develop "millions of tiny root hairs" for "fabulous" plant growth. Some seem to help, but the Rambler suspects that the grower willing to go to that extra effort and expense probably had built a pretty good rose bed in the first place. Maybe the extra water in planting helped. Who knows for sure?? If you have a favorite product, use it... but with plenty of water. Just don't add any fertilizer, even though the label says "can't burn when used as directed."

LIQUID COMPOST is a great organic starter. It's also called "cow tea". Back in BC (Before Chemicals), good gardeners always had a barrel or two steeping behind the garage or fence. It was a good practice then, and it still is. There's not much direct nutrient value to cow tea, but the boost given soil organisms makes everything work better. Add some soluble fertilizer for ESTABLISHED bushes when danger of frost is past and the soil warms up a little. Food in an available form brings a fast reaction. Just use a half-bucket of cow tea laced with something like *Ra-Pid-Gro, Peters* or *Carl Pool* and stand back. Those bushes are going to grow. Keep several plastic garbage cans of tea brewing all the time (rainwater is best). Onion or potato sacks make good tea bags; fill with cow chips and tie with a long piece of rope or wire. Steep for about ten days, sloshing around once in a while. You'll know when it's ready.

TREE ROSE SPLINTS... a must for tree roses if they get any size at all. The time for splinting is when planting or when trees are dormant, in case the roots are disturbed. At the time of planting, carefully place a length of three-eights inch reinforcing bar or conduit pipe next to the tree standard so that it does not interfere with the roots. Carefully drive the splint into the ground a foot or so, depending on the stability of the coil. Top of the splint should be just about even with the bud unions. Then slip a length of old garden hose over the bar or pipe to ground level. This acts as a cushion or pad so that the bar does not chafe. Then tape the covered bar securely to the tree standard with plastic electrician's tape or friction tape. Tape in three or four places, just like a broken arm. The result is a stable, secure tree able to survive most winds. Bud unions can still split from the standard, but even this can be helped with bandage-tie figure eights linking canes from both bud unions. It really works. ALFALFA MEAL OR PELLETS… still a great addition for an old or new rosebed. Work in about 50 lbs. of alfalfa per 100 square feet of new rosebed. For existing beds, use a cup or so per large plant, scratch in lightly before spring growth begins. For those of us who are not soil scientists, alfalfa supplies an alcohol-chain hormone that makes growth processes work better… better breaks, better leaves, more color, and an overall healthier plant. How many rabbits have you seen that weren't lively??

DOING ANYTHING NEW THIS YEAR?... the part of the rose society program that members like best... questions and answers during refreshments time. These coffee workshops share practical know-how, not necessarily new but great for more enjoyment of roses. Here's a sampler of new responses from a recent session. "

PRUNING MINIATURES... think small. Start with small pruning shears like the *Corona Mini-Shear No. 6*. Cut back all canes and growth to about six or eight inches (or whatever is alive), depending on the growth habit and vigor of the plant. Cut out all of the really old, woody canes. Don't be afraid to cut. Miniatures are on their own roots and hard pruning is a must for quality blooms and well-shaped plants. New growth keeps miniatures young and blooming. Some growers even take the easy way out, using the hedge shear method of pruning, essentially the method that commercial propagators use. However, the serious miniature hobbyist will usually get down on the knees to selectively groom and prune to the best eyes on the most productive canes. Not much different than trimming a floribunda. But if you like your minis BIG, trim lightly and don't worry. Minis will grow anyway.

DIG AND DIVIDE miniatures just like chrysanthemums. Radical?? Not at all. Most vigorous miniatures thrive on dividing every two or three years, depending on the climate of course. The centers of most minis get very woody after a few seasons and production drops off (since blooms are on newer growth). The dig-and-divide routine is very simple; just before the plants break dormancy, dig and shake the soil off the roots. With a small pruning saw or shears, divide the plant into two or three pieces of roots and younger canes. Trim out and discard the woody stuff. Trim the tops to the best eyes. Most minis will divide naturally, much like the mums referred to above. Replant immediately just like a new plant. By the end of the season, the new plant will be almost as large as the original mother plant, and with more bloom. Try it on some vigorous varieties... you'll be amazed.

OLD ROSE BEDS NEVER DIE... but they may fade away. There's still time to do something about it this season if your roses are still dormant. Even though a few old reliables may still be growing in an old bed, it may be better management to rebuild the bed before it finally gives up. Rose beds get old when organic matter is depleted. Additions of mulch on top won't do the same job as bacteria-supporting organics in the root zone. Some rose beds last longer than others; heavy feedings of nitrogen are a factor in using up materials that bring life to the soil. Soil organisms thrive in a medium of organic matter, air, and water. As materials are broken down, soils become tighter and less able to support root systems. Rose production gradually declines, and more fertilizer won't reverse the process.

REBUILD BEDS when roses are dormant, preferably just before breaking in early spring. Carefully dig keeper bushes with a spading fork, don't prune or otherwise encourage new growth. Bury or cover bushes with soil, sacks, straw, or any other material that will keep plants cool and moist while the bed is being rebuilt. Roses can be safely held this way for a week or more if necessary. Rebuild the bed in much the same way as a new one: a final mixture (by volume) of 1/3 organic matter (peat moss, compost, manure, etc.), 1/3 loamy soil, and 1/3 sandy, light material. Local conditions may call for other additives, such as gypsum for loosening clays, or an acidifier for alkaline soils. Turn the whole mix with a fork or tiller. Wet down the whole area and turn again the next day. Two or three times is usually enough. Allow the bed to settle (wetting helps) before replanting (same way as bare-root roses). Old and new roses will enjoy the new home.

TREE ROSES WORTHWHILE?? Tree roses in tubs, planters, and barrels have a place in most gardens, even in severe climates. While a tree rose represents a pretty good investment, it's worth every dollar in beauty. Use tree roses as garden and patio accents during the summer and move into a garage or garden shed in winter. In very cold areas, trees can be pulled from planters (they form a big ball of roots) and buried with the Minnesota tip method. For a really sensational accent, plant some miniature roses around the base of the tree rose. Mix or match colors, the effect is great... and they get along very well together.

PLANTER SECRET?? If there's a secret for planters, it's a soil mix with good drainage, air in the root zone, and ability to retain moisture. Reliable and easy to prepare is a mix of 1/3 garden soil, 1/3 Canadian peat moss, and 1/3 calcined clay granules (kitty litter). Use the granular kind without additives. Greenhouse, nursery, and landscape supply houses have it; calcined clay is widely used by professionals. The clay granules are extremely porous, something like a microscopic honeycomb: Each granule takes in moisture for slow release to feeder roots without souring, packing, or breaking down. Some growers like to add some sharp sand for even better porosity. Makes a great general purpose potting mix, too. Just pick out a spot in the corner of the yard on some paving bricks or boards; make a big pile of ingredients, mix and sift and mix again.· Moisten and stir some more. Mix/moisten lightly in about a week and be ready to enjoy roses in containers.

Why do rosarians refer to "growing secrets" when we can't wait to tell them to someone else?? There's really not much that's new about growing roses, so here are some not-so-secret rose routines that should work for you...

A GOOD SPRING TONIC... feed the processes that make nutrients available. Organics still work better and more consistently than the breakthrough products that come in jugs and bags. The chemist's contribution of carefully balanced, soluble inorganics is here to stay, too, but these laboratory miracles work best in conjunction with good organic practices. Manures and alfalfa build strong plants. Blood meal and fish meal (or cottonseed meal) encourage beautiful leaves that in turn support even more beautiful blooms. Compost (make your own) in the rose beds keeps nature in balance. Like chicken soup, cow tea or fish emulsion in water makes the sick well and the well even better. Feeding the processes results in live soil, active organisms and healthy rosebushes.

THAT EXTRA BOOST comes from the chemist's bag. Used with discretion, these foods supplement nature with something extra for top rose production. Nitrogen is easy to apply (and is leached most rapidly). Chelated trace elements bring out the best in bloom and color. Convenient and effective. But if the working soil is healthy, the best of both worlds (organic and inorganic) work together.

DO ROSES LIKE ORGANICS?? Absolutely. Here's an example. The Rambler dug some bushes that had been in for three or four years; root growth was tremendous in a light, organic soil. The root pattern was also consistent... great masses of fine hair roots had grown around cores of fish meal or Fragrant Formula, the artificial manure the Rambler mixes up. When initially planted, three cores of soil about one foot deep had been lifted about 18 inches from each rose shank and filled with a cup of fish meal or Formula and then covered. The developing roots invariably found the fish meal and set up a feeding station. When dug, the root systems looked like a tripod, balanced and sturdy. Apparently the Indians with the fish knew what they were doing all the time. If fish meal is hard to come by in your area, make friends with a fisherman or substitute chicken, horse, or rabbit manure.

ANOTHER FISH STORY. A rambler family member not noted for his growing expertise decided to try some roses at a newly-constructed home (formerly an alfalfa field) near Boulder, Colorado. With the Rambler's help, some 50 bushes got into the decomposed granite-sandy soil... all in a row to be irrigated by a trench. Water disappeared as if connected to a drainpipe, but reached the last bush at the end of a long day (or overnight). Good well water. After the first burst of bloom, it was suggested that some manure might increase the fertility of the gravel. Another food source came from the nearby lake: buckets and buckets of bluegills and perch caught by willing grandchildren. Shallow furrows (dug with a pick) were filled with fish and covered (volume unknown). Fresh cow manure (this was in the country) was heaped on the bushes, a grain shovelful at a time. Start the well water running and forget it. Result: no burn and growth to five feet by full, no small task in that short growing season. Great roses nature's way.

WORTH REPEATING... Get the fungicide off the shelf and on the leaves. Disease control is established through prevention; blackspot-damaged leaves cannot be restored; leaves and buds disfigured by mildew won't become sleek and productive again after spraying. The most common mistake is to wait until infection appears; by that time, it's too late. It's an uphill battle for the rest of the season. Get on a 7-10 day schedule and stay with it. Don't cheat... the fungus spores will catch you every time. Good fungicides like _Funginex, Benlate, Manzate,_ or _Phaltan_ will do the job if used on the bushes. As a cost saver, buy _Triforine_ (the active ingredient in _Funginex_), which is also marketed by _Ortho_ through agricultural supply stores. _Triforene_ is an 18% active ingredient vs 6% for _Funginex._ Safe and convenient, _Triforine_ is probably the most popular fungicide ever to reach the market... used on schedule.

OTHER RAMBLINGS... FINGERNAIL PRUNING is the removal of small guard buds from new growth so that strength can be directed to the principal shoot. Many varieties will break three eyes; when growth pattern is established (no more frost), flick off the unwanted growth with a fingernail... ALFALFA (meal or pellets) is a good

organic tonic in the spring. About one cup per
established bush, scratch in lightly... GYPSUM
lightens heavy alkaline soils and provides calcium. Flushes salts, too. Half a cup per plant in
the spring... WHITE VINEGAR added to alkaline
spray water makes insecticides work better and
leaf coverage more even. Add one tablespoon per
gallon of water BEFORE introducing fungicides
or insecticides. No other sprayer-sticker usually
needed... DOSE OF SALTS (Epsom salts) greens
up foliage and encourages new breaks. The magnesium supplied is essential for leaf processes; an
ounce or two per bush can't hurt and may bring
out new life... AND that makes life more fun for
the rosarian.

The best thing about spring is that it always comes when it's most needed... so here's a spring tonic of rose ideas that may help the season along...

POWDERY MILDEW can spring into an epidemic almost overnight. When conditions are right (warm days and cool nights), spores borne on the breeze set up new colonies on susceptible tender growth. Late spring and early summer are right for the disfiguring disease to appear. The BEST protection is early application of fungicide well in advance of mildew conditions, redoubling efforts (and spray schedules) at the first sign of the grayish powder. Good controls are available: *Funginex, Benlate, Phaltan, Acti-Dione PM, Bayleton*, and *Rubigan*, just to name a few, but won't do any good at all until applied on the leaves.

MILDEW HOSTS are commonly overlooked. Thoroughly spray ramblers and climbers. Since it is hard to get good spray coverage on climbers and shrubs, spores carry over and infect nearby bushes. A fence covered with climbers can be beautiful, but a real problem with disease control. More frequent application, better wetting, better spray pressure, and even spraying from a ladder will help. Spray religiously every week when conditions are right (except for the long residuals like *Bayleton* and *Rubigan*); concentrate on new, green growth. Old, tough leaves on the bottom are safe. And, learn to relax. In really hot, dry weather mildew will go away all by itself.

A NEW LOOK?? It's too late for most of us for major landscape changes this season, but some substantial enhancements are still possible. How about some miniature roses planted underneath the tree standards?? Mix or match colors. Since the minis like less food, punch holes around the root perimeter of the tree rose and pour in some timed-release fertilizer to keep the trees performing vigorously. The roots will reach out and find the food every time. A very colorful combination.

MINIS FOR ANNUALS... Try a grouping of garden beauty miniatures in place of the usual annual plantings, at least in a few spots. For bloom production and landscape attractiveness, miniatures are very competitive. And, these little gems don't have to be replaced every year. Use two or three plants of the same variety together for more striking color; consider growth habits when mixing varieties. There's nothing wrong with using just one or two plants of a variety, but the size of the bed should be a consideration to create the calico effect. Miniatures in the foreground of a rose bed also give a whole new look. They tend to cover up the not-so-attractive canes of the big roses and fill in the gaps. They'll get along well together.

FINISH OUT A ROSE PLANTING with some selected sweetheart-patio-maxi-mini roses (call them whatever you like). Like adding a frame to a good picture, or an accent to a colorful view. Available in pots, they can be planted almost any time. Larger growing and more prolific than most miniatures, they give lots of color with the same care given the bigger roses. Something died?? Fill in with a couple of sweethearts. Patio dull?? Add some containers filled with these fast-growing roses. You'll be glad you did.

BEDS NEED EDGING?? Major construction may be out this time of year, but several methods are easy to handle. Treated timbers are now available to make gentle curves, cut in 8, 12, and IS-inch lengths and joined with galvanized wire, much like a snow fence. These short timbers are cut lengthwise also; use the flat side (wire stapled) on the inside. Make a shallow ditch in the shape needed, tamp the edging in place and backfill. Easy. Another late-season method is to lay a soldier course of bricks — bricks set vertically in a mortar base. Good for straight lines, curves, or even circles. Dig a shallow trench wide enough to accommodate the bricks, fill with soft mortar or concrete-mortar mix, then press bricks into the mix. Align each brick carefully and allow to set before backfilling. Use a half-inch spacer board between each brick when setting. The result is good drainage and an attractive edge without being a skilled bricklayer.

STAKING ROSEBUSHES (even very large ones) can be easy with reinforcing bar or electrical conduit and some old garden hose. Cut one-quarter or three-eighths-inch bar into lengths two feet long with a hacksaw (or the guy at the lumber yard may do it with his shears for a little something extra). Check out the bush to see where it needs support so that it does not rock in the ground. Carefully drive the support bar into the ground AT AN ANGLE to bind and engage the canes and the bud union. Cut a length of old plastic or rubber hose and slip over the bar to act as a pad or cushion. Works on tall stakes, too.

OTHER RAMBLINGS... Grooming is an every-bloom-cut trick that pays off in better roses. Every time a bloom is cut, consider the effect on the shape of the plant's future bloom production. Clean up the twiggy stuff in the center of the plant every time blooms are cut, too... CHUNK BARK makes a great mulch for miniatures. Pine, redwood, or whatever, two or three inches of chunk mulch conserves moisture, curbs weeds, makes an attractive background and permits fertilizer and water to percolate through. Lasts season after season... ROSE TIES from nylon stretch hose work better than most plastics, ropes, cords, or what have you. Cut in strips, panty hose will stretch, won't cut, will tie easily to fences or stakes, and last at least a season. To tie a climber to a wooden fence, use electrician's staples tacked to the fence and slip the nylon ties easily through the loop... GARDEN TOURS... greatest rose classroom anywhere. Visit gardens and learn.

JUN. 1986

THOUGHT FOR THE MONTH: LOOKING AHEAD My time for showing roses Is soon coming to a close; I can't see to groom my entries, Nor identify the rose. But the future still looks rosy, So I will not hold a grudge. If my eyesight fails completely I can always be a judge. John McFarland, Norman, OK

Rose ideas are much like children... our own are wonderful. But these garden offspring suggestions have been sufficiently punished to talk about in polite company... better yet, get out in the garden and get the job done.

MULCH... how little or how much? Growers in hot, sunny areas swear by good, thick mulch to hold moisture and lower soil temperatures. Organic gardeners live by the rule that mulches restore soils and keep the whole process alive. Cool climate rosarians think there's no need and that mulch sponsors disease and insects. It's true that roses can be grown successfully with no mulch at all, provided there's enough organic material in the soil. But growing WITH nature is easier. Restore the humus with a good layer of leaves, compost, manure or what-have-you mixtures supporting the microorganisms that make soils work.

Mulches feed, cool, smother weeds, and conserve moisture... all at the same time, and at very low cost. Advice: get mulch on after the soil warms up; if everything is working right, two or three inches of good organic matter will disappear in a single season.

THRIPS... where and how. It's amazing, but many growers don't see the problem (or the insect) until buds refuse to open or petals are badly bruised and discolored. Thrips (always plural, usually by the millions) come from grasses, fields, from EVERYWHERE during warm, spring weather. They arrive in waves to ruin light-colored, fragrant blooms. They do their damage by bruising tender petals as they suck juices from the tissue. Blooms turn brown on the edges, buds won't open at all. Watch carefully for the first signs. To control thrips, spray where they are: on the buds and blooms. Spray the bloom areas only with *Orthene* or *Cygan*; two or three times a week may be necessary during heavy infestation. Don't worry about the leaves; the thrips are on the blooms. The Rambler's best control has been *Orthene 75S* (soluble powder) at one teaspoon per gallon. The soluble is more cost-effective than the EC (liquid) material and seems to give better control with no discoloration of the blooms. Don't mix with other materials (foliar foods, fungicides, spreader-stickers); this is a thrips operation only. However, in highly alkaline water, add about a tablespoon of white vinegar per gallon. Just seems to make it work better. Most important: don't put off "until the weekend." By that time, it's too late.

MILDEW... At this writing the mildew season has run its course on the Gulf Coast and the Rambler is happy to report that *Rubigan* again came through as a good control. Conditions were ideal for powdery mildew this year: cool, dry nights, warm days and plenty of lush, new growth. *Rubigan EC* (Blanco) was used at two teaspoons per five gallons every 21 days, sometimes sprayed alone, sometimes used in combination with *Funginex* (or *Triforine*). Spreads on the leaves very well, no sign at all of leaf damage. Of course, *Triforine* (one teaspoon per gallon) application was continued on a weekly basis. Result: no mildew, no blackspot, clean garden... even on mildew-prone varieties like Granada and Chipper. *Rubigan* is available by mail order from specialty suppliers like Kimbrew-Walter or Brighton By-Products.

SEND MITES INTO ORBIT... Water is an insecticide, too; washes off spider mites with no risk to environment or plants. Water washing, the high pressure water treatment for the undersides of the leaves, is easy with any of the wands or similar rigs advertised in these pages. The plants love it. Begin washing on a weekly basis as soon as the weather turns warm, particularly miniatures or roses in hot, reflective locations. As in fungus disease control, begin BEFORE evidence of damage. If 'infestation catches up (and it can very quickly), wash more frequently. Or, if a specific miticide is necessary, wash first, then apply the miticide. *Vendex* is the choice of most serious rosarians at one and a half teaspoons per gallon, used alone. As with other insecticides, the Rambler likes vinegar to neutralize alkaline water. *Plictran* is another good miticide. Follow the directions and remember to spray the UNDERSIDES of the leaves where the mites are, not the bud and bloom areas where the thrips are.

ODDS 'N' ENDS... SAVE the leaves, nature's

food factories by cutting shorter stems whenever possible. No need to waste this resource by cutting unnecessarily. It goes without saying that leaves lost to blackspot weaken the bushes also... WASH the leaves from time to time. The junk from the air and spray residues just has to affect the productive capabilities of the leaves, contribute to bum and coarsening, and is just plain unsightly. During dry periods, water overhead or wash by hand with one of the "water breaker" wands. Gives roses an extra drink and pleasant for the rosarian as well... LIQUID FEEDING (not foliar) is made easy using the siphon technique attached to the garden hose. Calculate the amount of fertilizer required per gallon of water, make up the concentrate and let the hose do the work. Some applicators (like Ortho's) are already calibrated others may take a little trial and error testing. It sure beats having to haul buckets of liquid mix around the garden. Since the cheaper devices are somewhat inaccurate, make any mistake on the WEAK side, the rose will appreciate the extra water.

Now's the time to do it right, or you'll need the time to do it over... especially with summertime rose chores. Have you ever seen a patient spider mite?? Or thrips that would hold off "til the weekend??" Here are some thoughts to get going on right now.

MITICIDES take a lot of abuse... the user claims "it's not working." But it is usually the rosarian who is not working hard enough to get good coverage. A good rule of thumb is to use twice the volume of spray material when applying a miticide as compared to routine fungicide applications. Use a long wand, spray the UNDERSIDES of the leaves until dripping. Another assist is to make sure that the spray material spreads and sticks to the leaves... *Funginex* or *Triforine* in combination with *Vendex* gives great coverage (along with a tablespoon of white vinegar per gallon to soften the water). And don't expect one-day service from your miticide. The real test is control of newly-hatched eggs in three or four days. If the job's been done right, there's no need to do it over (until next month).

HOT WEATHER spraying can be tricky, but not if a little rose sense is applied along with the spray. There's not much sense in spraying to save the leaves if the spray does the job instead of the blackspot or the spider mites. Water roses thoroughly BEFORE spraying and allow enough time for the roots to move the moisture to the leaves. Dry, limp leaves will burn; turgid leaves tolerate spray material better. A good practice is to deep water in the evening and spray early in the morning. Some prefer to water in the morning and spray in the evening; but the leaves will have less substance, having lost some of the moisture due to transpiration during the day. Avoid the middle of the day if possible; even plain water can burn and coarsen leaves in intense heat. You'll recognize spray burn when leaf edges turn brown or speckled, then yellow and drop off. The damaged leaves will hang on for a while and then drop off, pushed off by a new crop ready to go to work. A waste of good leaves.

SPIDER MITE LEAVES look different. Leaves affected by spiders gradually lose green color, have a parched, dry look and sometimes turn gray-brown. A bush can defoliate in just a few days during hot weather. Mites suck the moisture out of leaves, an effect something like drying and ageing of leaves in the fall. If mites are suspected, check the undersides of the leaves carefully and look for gritty gray and white specks, similar to a mix of salt and pepper. Webbing mayor may not be present. ANY evidence of mites is a crisis... get to work right away. DON'T WAIT. Wash/spray as you prefer, but hurry.

QUARANTINE new rosebushes for mites, particularly miniatures. Before introducing new minis to a clean garden, wash the leaves a time or two and keep the plants separated. A good trick is to use a teaspoon of liquid Ivory in a bucket of water and dunk the tops, sloshing the leaves around. Allow a week for any eggs to hatch and dunk again. Plant out a few days later, fairly confident that a new strain of mites won't be mating with your favorites to make SUPERMITES.

A SUMMERTIME REFRESHER... ALFALFA TEA, for roses, of course. Neater and cleaner than cow tea, alfalfa releases tricontanol, an alcohol compound that does wonders for roses. Not a food in itself, but makes the whole process work better. Alfalfa pellets broadcast on the soil have to be scratched in lightly or will form a crust that sheds water. That's easy in the springtime when adding mulch and pruning, but much harder when plants are bushy and leafed out. By the bucket or watering can, use two cups alfalfa pellets per two and a half gallons of water. Steep for two to three days. Use about a half-gallon of tea per miniature or a gallon per large rose that needs a tonic. Growth and bloom will increase dramatically, particularly with minis, Marion Klima of San Francisco reports. Barrel or bucket, make some tea this summer.

WATER MAKES IT HAPPEN. But how much is enough? Since water is essential to every soil, leaf, and growth process, make sure that every rose plant and bed is well supplied. Depending on the leaf area, a rosebush uses three or four gallons of water per day; moving nutrients from the soil to the leaves feeding, cooling, and providing most of the substance of the plant... all at the same time. Just like the human blood supply. If in doubt, water some more. Moisture availability depends on the makeup of the soil; heavier soils hold more water, sandy soils dry out much faster. Deep soak, don't sprinkle. The Rambler is growing the best roses in years (a subjective opinion) and the ONLY change in routine is water and more water. All the water the beds can hold and then some more. The lawn grows four inches a week -in a poor week. But the roses are producing leaves and blooms in a profusion that is remarkable. Why didn't we think of that sooner?

ODDS 'N ENDS... CHUNK PINE BARK makes a great mulch, particularly for minis. Keeps soil cool and free of weeds, water, and nutrients pass right through. Cheap and decorative... MAKING TEA?? A small sump pump will move that special mix from the barrel to the roses and save the rosarian's back. Adaptable for garden hoses and inexpensive; some pond and fountain pumps can do the job, too... TOENAIL TRIMMERS for roses?? Veterinarian trimmers for dogs and cats have TWO cutting blades that make as clean a slice as you'll ever see for cutting rose blooms, big roses or minis... The Rambler will be reporting on them next month, but admits that the "doggie clips" are already a part of his exhibitor's box.

AUG. 1986

THOUGHT FOR THE MONTH: Have you heard about the rosarian who entered the Garden of Eden and ordered fertilizers right away??

If you think you're too old for growing pains, add some more roses... But here are some painless tips on how to get the most out of what you've got...

SMALL ROSE GARDEN -KEEP IT SIMPLE. That's where Ortho's *Orthenex* comes in, a one-shot combination for the grower with a few roses. It's a liquid mix of *Funginex* (disease control), *Orthene* (insect control), and *Kelthane* (spider mite control). Although in most gardens there's not much real need for insecticide at every spraying, *Orthenex* fills a real market need. Every ten days or so will keep most gardens in pretty good shape, disease and bug-wise. However, if the garden has more than ten or 15 bushes, switch to *Funginex* (used alone) for blackspot and mildew and *Orthene* for insect control (particularly thrips) as needed. The "spray for specifics" is not only cheaper but also better for foliage and roses in the long run. But for small gardens with minimum work, the combination is OK. The best intentions (to spray) have never controlled blackspot or killed insects. Maybe if the job is made easier, more roses will get the attention they deserve.

KEEP 'EM AWAY... Japanese beetles, that is. Researchers report that beetle traps in the rose garden (a favorite control of many rosarians) attract MORE beetles that do MORE damage than plantings with no controls. But there's one bright spot: rosarians who can get their neighbors to put out traps for them have lower beetle populations and less damage. That's what is called a GOOD neighbor. Will take lots of rose blooms over the season to repay this favor. Meantime, stick with *Diazinon* granules in the beds in the spring and *Sevin* spray on the blooms during the beetle season.

MINIATURES IN HOT WEATHER?? Ever wondered why newly-planted miniatures lost their leaves and just sat there for a month? A simple case of summer shock. But minis can be safely planted even during the hottest weather if given a chance to harden off a bit. Pot up small plants in 5-inch plastic pots for two or three weeks before moving into the miniature beds. Keep the newly-potted plants in a protected spot, follow a REGULAR watering routine with just a much of food in solution. All is lost if the pots dry out.

Some varieties take longer to fill out than others, but when growth is well-established, carefully slip from the pot and plant... the mini will never know it has been moved. What makes it work? The good soil mix and warmer soil temperature in the pot encourages better root development and therefore better growth. Isolation of new minis helps hold down new spider mite population, too.

"JUST THE BLOOM, PLEASE." If roses could talk, that might be the request. By cutting just the spent bloom (without stem and leaves), we're saving the productivity capability of the rosebush... at least that's the reasoning forwarded by Dr. Eldon Lyle, Plant Pathologist, former ARS President and world-class rosarian. Leaves make roses; therefore keep all the leaves possible. Lyle observes that the stem dies back and new buds push out from axils capable of supporting good blooms, not just the uppermost five-leaflet rosarians usually trim to. He believes that more good low breaks occur on the canes also. Lyle's private garden is a forest of rose leaves (and blooms), fully leafed to the bud union. The Rambler is a creature of habit and STILL cuts down on some stems, but the spent-bloom-only tactic seems to work. The bush suffers enough at rose show time, arrangements time, garden visitors time... anytime we want those long-stemmed beauties.

DOGGIE CLIPS... just right for spent blooms. Last month the Rambler promised a report on toenail clippers for dogs and cats, but used on roses instead. Well, they really do work. These veterinarian trimmers have two cutting blades that make a clean slice. In and out of the pocket; light and sharp. Great for exhibitors to recut stems underwater. Ever tried to get a *Felco* in the top of a vase?? The trimmers are a project of the MOUND-BUILDERS ROSE SOCIETY of Newark, Ohio, who suggest that societies get together and order in lots of ten at $6.25 each. Contact Moundbuilders at Box 767, Hebron, OH 43025.

ODDS 'N' ENDS... Seems that alfalfa tea bags can be reused. Marian Klima says that 2 cups of alfalfa pellets in a large sprinkling can will make several batches of tea. Just add more water. Pour the liquor on potted minis until it runs out; otherwise about a half-gallon of refresher per bed mini every two weeks... DWARF FLORIBUNDA is a description that Royal National Rose Society personage Dick Balfour came up with to describe the "patio, maxi-mini, mini-flor, sweetheart" roses now gaining in popularity. Anyway, you ought to be growing some... RALPH MOORE, Mister Miniature of the World, came up with another good quote at the Seattle Convention: "There's a lot of beauty out there if we don't wear blinders." He was referring to the proliferation of types, shapes, colors, and habits of roses available and under test... EXPAND YOUR HOBBY, join the Rose Hybridizers Association for just $5.00 per year; quarterly 22-page newsletters are full of information and inspiration for rosarians. Make check payable to RHA and mail to Larry Peterson, 3245 Wheaton Road, Horseheads, NY 14845. Amazing what these folks are doing.

September marks the Rambler's 16th anniversary... 192 RAMBLINGS wiser (??) and still left with a few rose cuttings to share. After all, there's nothing to writing a rose column: Just sit down at the typewriter and open up a vein...

WINTERIZE in the summer and enjoy good fall roses, plus live bushes next spring. Healthy, vigorous plants tolerate cold better. Weak, diseased roses just won't make it. Keep roses healthy, then EASE bushes into dormancy with just a little extra care. Dormancy often escapes us; yet, we KNOW when hard, killing frosts usually occur. We also know that most dry fertilizers release over a 30 -60 day period. There's a slow-down period that's good for roses and rosarians. Just shut off the food at the right time and the danger of freeze damage and dieback is greatly reduced. Roses are woody plants and respond to the seasons. Don't fight nature, work with her. In the latter stages of the season, leave some blooms on to form seed hips which signal the bush that the reproductive cycle is complete. Continue to water; dry roses are under stress. But if your roses need a September shot in the arm, use a quick-acting liquid material like *Ra-Pid-Gro, Peters*, or *Schultz*. Some common rose sense will tell you just how late this can be applied. Most liquids work for about 30 days, depending on rainfall, drainage, soil temperature, and composition. If in doubt, don't. The roses will grow anyway.

BUG ZAPPER... makes life in the rose garden pleasant again, reducing the populations of mosquitoes, moths, and flying insects of many kinds. Helps control corn ear worms, too, by electrocuting the gray-white moth that lays the eggs on rosebuds. These electric grid lanterns are attractive, safe and can cover a half-acre or so. Hang from a post or tree near the rose garden; 7 or 8 feet off the ground is about right. Sears usually has a sale on zappers in the fall; invest in one and get it up right away. You'll be glad you did.

JAPANESE BEETLES... a disheartening pest. Picked, sprayed or trapped, they still cause a lot of damage during short periods of the season. The Rambler has no beetle experience (although we have BILLIONS of mites here on the Gulf Coast) but passes on this suggestion by John MacIndoe in the Arlington, VA Rose Review:

"Leave the fading blooms on the bushes instead of being so prompt in removing them. We find that the beetles seem to be drawn to the dying bloom and eat there until there is nothing left before going after new blooms; we have tried this and are pleased with the results."

GYPSUM... a good fall RX for pots. The clay particles of alkaline soils tend to pack during the season, particularly when using alkaline water (most city water is loaded with alkaline salts). This stops up pot drainage and retards growth. Just a tablespoon or so of gypsum per pot (roses, geraniums, etc.,) and water in, is like pulling the plug. Good source of calcium, too. Cheap, easy, effective.

MORE ON ALFALFA TEA... a good growth stimulator, particularly for miniatures. If 2 cups of alfalfa pellets is good for a 2 1/2-gallon watering can, then 12 cups is about right for a 30-gallon garbage can. Pellets will last for two or three fillings; steep just a couple of days. Some users complain of the smell while steeping. Advice: (1) Put on the lid. (2) Consider smell as incentive to get tea on the bushes. A half-gallon of tea refresher per mini, a gallon per large rose, really works.

HOW DO ROSE ROSES BURN?? It's simple: from too much fertilizer and not enough water. But why does it happen? Roots are made up of cells whose activity is supported by water, just like human skin or tissue. Burn occurs when water is removed or displaced from the cells.

Most chemical fertilizers use ammonium nitrate or ammonium sulfate as a source of nitrogen, synthesizing the same compounds found in manures. These ammonium compounds are HYGROSCOPIC, that is, have the ability to take up water. If the ammonium compounds (organic or inorganic fertilizers) are too concentrated, moisture is absorbed from the soil, and even the roots, thereby destroying the moisture support system for the cells. Depleted root cells can't supply nutrients (in solution) to the leaves. Leaves turn yellow, drop off.

Nature likes to keep things in balance. Concentrated solutions want to add water and will perform this trick through osmosis, pulling moisture through cell walls. The solution to the whole burning problem is to use appropriate fertilizer amounts only, and always with plenty of water. That's the reason for the recommendation: water first, feed, water again. And, if in doubt, water again. Result: no burn.

ODDS 'N' ENDS... A bucket at the end of the rose row is a great receptacle for spent blooms, yellow leaves, disbudded stuff gathered up in a short visit tot he garden. Saves steps to get the trash barrel and keeps the garden neat... ROSE STEMS cut under water really DO last longer. Air partially stops up water-carrying cells in the stem; recut under water after hardening off. A good use for the doggie toenail clips noted in these columns recently... TOUCH OF CLASS is the class of the 1986 AARS roses. Very vigorous, super form, eye-catching color. Good for exhibitors and garden growers. Get a couple of these for sure for 1987. The Rambler can hardly wait for the new season to start.

It seems that Mother Nature gave us her best (worst) shot again this year with record-breaking highs, unseasonable lows and generally unpredictable conditions… but have you noticed that the roses made it in spite of all this, producing loads of blooms like they always do. If only rosarians could be as durable. Anyway, here are some Rambler observations on the season, something to make you feel good while planning for next year.

MULCH did the trick in the hot Southwest (and even hotter Southeast) this year, stretching a short water supply and reducing soil temperatures. Comparison of well-mulched and hardly any cover gardens on the Gulf Coast this season illustrated sharp contrasts in bloom production, plant vigor and general attractiveness. The Rambler gave both gardens exactly the same… fertilizer, water, spray schedule and so forth. One garden had a light application of compost in the early spring; the other had a 3-inch mixture of compost, leaves, ground bark and stable cleanings, replenished during the season as necessary. The non mulched garden began to go downhill about the middle of the second bloom cycle (we cycle here about every 30-35 days). By mid-July the bushes showed real stress and didn't pick up until mid-September. It's obvious that the mulched bushes are going to be superior in every way in October. Take this into consideration in YOUR planning for next year.

SHORT ON SUNSHINE?? Be ready to work harder for fewer blooms, weaker bushes. The Rambler went all out to make a shaded rose garden perform this year, having struggled and tried everything you can think of in previous seasons. The conditions are so bad in this garden that roses are grown like annuals and replanted each year. The owner insists on keeping the trees and doesn't mind replacement cost. But hope springs eternal, and encouraged by some limited tree-trimming, a new start was made. Beds were built up even higher with a specially-prepared soil mix. The sprinkler system was tuned and timed, no cost was spared in trying to make this a superior garden. Bare-root #1 bushes (130) were planted the third week of February, carefully mounded and tended. About 30 miniatures were set out at the same time. First blooms appeared right on schedule in mid-April, lots of leaves, good low breaks and all the classic signs

of vigor. By the second bloom in May, production was already slowing. Dieback started in June and continued all summer. Fertilizer in solution, foliar foods, mulches, cultivation and careful grooming could not reverse the process. At this writing (September), six bushes are dead, the balance weak and thin. We're in for total replacement again next year. Only the miniatures performed reasonably well, and they are tall and weak-stemmed. Advice: a shaded rose garden is a lesson in frustration.

DRIP SYSTEM for container-grown plants -a real breakthrough for many rosarians. Observed two drip installations this year for large pots, planters and hanging baskets and was pleasantly surprised at the results. In spite of very hot weather, no attention at all during the week and complete reliance on the automatic system, the roses, hibiscus and other semi tropicals thrived. The system was easy to fabricate, inexpensive and made a neat installation. After a little tuning for flow rate, no more problems. Obviously a great solution for growers who cannot attend plants on a regular basis.

RUBIGAN EC… still the Rambler's choice for powdery mildew control, especially during severe mildew conditions. Locally systemic, control is good for 14-21 days (although *Triforine* is also used weekly). For you rosarians with long growing seasons, there's still time to enjoy some clean blooms this full. Apply at 2 teaspoons per 5 gallons until leaves glisten, particularly new, tender growth. Really works.

TRIFORINE proved itself again this year; reliable, safe and consistently effective. The Gulf Coast is blackspot heaven. Weekly use of *Triforine* (1 teaspoon per gallon) kept gardens clean of disease, with a little help from *Rubigan* in spring and fall. Reminder: *Triforine* is a better buy than *Funginex*, and has a good shelf life. Use it.

SPRAY BURN… Some users report that a combination of *Funginex* and *Vendex* (the miticide) caused some spray bum and leaf drop. The Rambler used the combination successfully without damage, but application rates and conditions vary widely. It's always a good idea to try out a new combination or product on a few bushes and then watch for a few days. If it is going to bum, you'll know in four to five days. The reason that

Funginex and *Vendex* were combined was to take advantage of the wetting qualities of *Funginex*. However, when in doubt, don't.

GLISTEN... that's the latest "in" word for spray application. It used to be that leaves should be sprayed until dripping. That's apparently too much.

The run-off puddles, beads or otherwise stay on the leaf, a potential source for bum or leaf damage. Fungicide/pesticide suppliers now say "glisten," which is easy for the pro with good equipment but somewhat more difficult for the backyard rosarian. However, there's a lesson to be learned here: drenching is wasteful and unnecessary and may lead to leaf problems. Have you glistened your roses today?

Nov. 1986

THOUGHT FOR THE MONTH:
Rosarians know that each day comes bearing its gifts. Untie the ribbons.

With winter at hand, let's take stock of our modest rose successes and plan ahead — visit the non-fiction section of your local library and check out some rose catalogs. Or you may wish to ponder these rose truths instead of digging up that new rose bed…

DON'T DIG — LET WINTER DO IT… the freezing/thawing cycle can do much of the work in making a new rose bed. If the ground isn't frozen yet where you are, loosen just a little and pile on lots of leaves and other organic material. Throw a little soil on top or cover with black plastic. As moisture freezes and expands, tissues break down in much the same way as decomposition during the summer. The winter action reduces and blends the organic matter and soil into the loam that most rosarians like. Nature has been building this natural way for a long, long time.

SOUTHERN ROSARIANS need to get compost piles going to cash in on the harvest of leaves and garden green wastes. Composting doesn't have to be fancy. A pile, a row, a bin, or a rack will do equally well. The secret is moisture and air and a source of nitrogen to feed the organisms doing the work. Whatever is easy, do it. Speed up the process most by turning frequently with a pitchfork. It's amazing how quickly leaves and what-have-you break down. No smell. No cost. Better than anything that comes in a bottle or bag for roses.

SAVE THE LEAVES… advice by the Rambler earlier this year to encourage leaf and bloom production. Rather than cut spent blooms to a long-stemmed five-leaflet, just a minimum trim was made. Result?? Tremendous bushes, lots of blooms but fewer show-quality specimens. Although roses just naturally grow tall during the long Gulf Coast growing season, Color Magic bushes 10 feet high are a bit much. Granada went way over 8 feet; Pristine, Olympiad and Century Two are 7 feet or better and still growing. All had been pruned to 2 feet in February. Obviously, "save the leaves" is a trade-off for more blooms but less pleasing landscape effect. Will try a compromise clip next season.

FINALLY A SHRUB… and it's a dandy. Bonica '82 (Meidomonac), the 1987 AARS winner, of course. Growers in all parts of the country should enjoy this one. The Rambler is anxious to see if the seed hips turn as orange-red as promised during what we smugly call our "winter" season. But this carefree grower has plenty of other landscape attributes going for it. Great in a mass planting; just leave it alone and enjoy blooms and more blooms. Only one problem: the name. Who can remember how to spell the show name Meidomonac? Just enjoy this fine garden rose.

PLANT CLOSER… or cover up the rose "knees." Most rosebushes are not particularly attractive as specimen plants, and when strung out in a rose bed fail to have the impact they should. We see canes with foliage and blooms on· top. What makes park plantings so effective? Masses of roses planted close together for bloom and foliage. The backyard gardener can't duplicate many of these applications but can stagger roses in rows and screen the foreground with bushy, low-growing varieties. The garden effect is much more pleasing. The sweetheart, patio, mini-flora, maxi-mini, whatever-you-call-them roses are ideal for this. Many miniatures do well here, too. Varieties like Red Flush, Winsome, Kathy, Rise 'n Shine, Cheers and Green Ice. You get the idea. Frame the beauty of rose beds by pulling them together.

FRAGRANT ROSES… meant to be enjoyed but often scattered in the back row. Concentrate some fragrant varieties near the back step, the patio, along the fence on the way to the garage where they can be savored every day. Three or four bushes of Sunsprite on the corner of the patio can do amazing things on a warm day. Crimson Glory should be grown for the fragrance alone… close up where you can get to it.

ATTENTION GETTERS… the open bloom class at the rose shows. Ever notice how the public crowds around these displays? They RELATE to roses like these. Hope that you are giving them a prominent place in your shows. And the English Boxes. Our show visitors feel confident they can grow roses like these, and that's what we want. Brandy snifter classes are popular in this part of the country; even a small show will have two or three dozen entries. A modest investment in snifters by the show committee pays big dividends with beginners and visitors. Great for miniatures, too; smaller size, of course. Last, but not least, a fragrant class. Judge for reasonable cultural condition but concentrate on the fragrance. Make the blooms easy to get to; single rows or tiers. Or fill a round table. There will be a crowd around all day.

COUNT YOUR BLESSINGS... and thank the products people for the incredible assortment of fungicides, insecticides and fertilizers that are so convenient and easy to use. Liquids like *Funginex* (*Triforine*), *Orthenex* and *Orthene*. *Miticides* like *Mandex* and *Pentac*. Mildew protection with *Rubigan*. *Mavrik Aquaflow* as a broad spectrum insecticide. How did we ever make it with the old powders and potions? With just a little rose sense (and a regular schedule) roses are easier to grow than ever. Hope that you feel the same way.

If experience is like manure — only good when spread around — here's a whole pile that's easy to apply, fully composted, ready for use.

LESSON IN FRUSTRATION... not enough sun, reported earlier by the Rambler. This shaded garden continues to go down hill, but at a faster rate. Nearly one-third of the bushes are dead or near-dead, the remainder struggling... if the Gulf Coast had a hard winter they would all be dead by spring. Roses MUST have sun; all the tricks and springtime enthusiasm won't make up for lack of sunshine energy. In planning for '87, look to the sun... that's where the roses are.

WEAKENED PLANTS... get even weaker as nature attempts to eliminate them. Ever notice how a weak plant attracts more blackspot, mildew, mites and assorted problems than a vigorous bush, even in the same bed? Healthy roses apparently do have some sort of immune system, an ability to fight back. The Rambler has noted time after time that bushes weakened early in the season by mites are more prone to blackspot infection. And as blackspot further reduces the food-making capacity of the leaves, the bush struggles and gets even weaker. Lesson: practice preventive rose care, something like preventive medicine. Be healthy, stay healthy.

COMPACTION... keep your big feet out of the rose bed. This short lesson was brought out quite vividly in a program by Dr. Carl Whitcomb, ARS fall convention in Oklahoma City. Field trials and landscape examples clearly showed that shrubs, trees and grasses in compacted soils performed poorly compared to aerated, friable soils. In one dramatic example, a hardwood tree planted on a fence line had good, balanced growth on the pasture side and poor, stunted growth on the roadway side, a dirt track frequented by farm vehicles. Landscape plantings fared much the same way. Lesson: loosen up the soil to permit air, water, and nutrients to work together. Add humus to keep the air spaces open and hold moisture. Then stay OFF the soil as much as possible. "Uncle Charlie" Dawson says it better than the Rambler; "For years I have wished that every rose grower would have a sign at the entrance to the garden saying PLEASE KEEP YOUR BIG, FRIENDLY FEET OUT OF MY ROSE BEDS — STAY ON THE WALKS.

THANK YOU."

ROSE BED PREP... still time in most parts of the country to get that "perfect mix" down and ready to mellow over the winter months. Works much better that way. You may have your own formula, but most growers agree that a mix of about 1/3 soil, 1/3 gritty sand, and 1/3 organic matter is about right. Some like more organics and less soil, but that depends on drainage, depth of the bed, water and length of the growing season. If the Rambler were to build a new bed this month (heaven forbid), it would go something like this: spade (or till) lawn-level soil to about 12 inches, adding 25 pounds of gypsum and 10 pounds of Superphosphate (0-20-0) per 100 square feet. Add about 4 inches of organic matter (compost, manure, ground bark, whatever) and mix again. Then build up bed another 8 to 10 inches with the 1/3-1/3-1/3 soil mix and lightly blend with base mix. Use whatever edging method fits your landscape scheme. Let the new bed mellow; turn a time or two if the ground isn't frozen. In the spring, work in some alfalfa pellets, rock phosphate, compost and perlite in the immediate planting areas, making up a sort of special planting mix. New or transplanted roses will take right off. This over-the-winter preparation makes springtime even more pleasant.

TO POT OR NOT TO POT... warm climate rosarians like to get Canadian roses in the late fall, but are concerned that new growth will be frozen back in January and February if planted out. There are three choices: plant, pot, or bury. Burying for dormancy is the easiest, and commonly practiced by northern growers. Potting is more work, but it seems to payoff. Pot up the newcomers in a light, friable soil and winter protect in a garage or garden house for cold snaps of short duration. In black plastic pots, roots have a chance to develop and the bushes get off to a roaring start in the spring when set out in the beds. Idea: grow roots first, then the tops. Caution: pots dry out, have to be moved. No long winter vacation permitted. If potting doesn't match the strength of your back, take a middle road by planting in the beds and mulching to the tips of the canes. If some new growth at the top gets nipped, trim off next spring and there will be plenty of cane left.

SOURCES... The Rambler gets letters every time *Triforene, Rubigan, Vendex* and so on are mentioned asking, "Where do I get it?" Response: find a farm or nursery supply store in your area, or, use a mail order supplier. The Rambler recommends two good ones: Kimbrew-Walter Roses and Brighton ByProducts. Kimbrew-Walter handles specialty rose products; Brighton has a full line of nursery-landscaping supplies. The addresses are: Kimbrew-Walter Roses, Route 2, Box 172, Grand Saline, TX 75140; phone: 214-829-2968. Brighton By-Products Co., P.D. Box 23, New Brighton, PA 15066; phone: 412-846-1220. In case you're wondering, are the WALTER (Jack & Dorothy) and WALTERS (Howard & Millie) families related? No, but we call them our northern cousins (no S on the name)… great folks and rose family we're proud to claim.

Looking ahead is a popular theme for columnists as a new year begins… items that can be disclaimed if they don't work out or showcased as new and innovative if they should happen to come about as claimed. Thought you might like to hear about what the Rambler plans to do for more fun with roses in '87.

REWORK THE MINIATURES… Open up the miniature beds for more space and sun (and hopefully better blooms) as many of the bushes are too large and crowded. Those small plants have grown into monsters and just aren't as productive as they should be. Minis can be very attractive in the landscape if we give them a chance. And transplant so that roses with similar growth habits go together. A rangy Jean Kenneally just doesn't go with a compact Lavender Lace. A mix of Colors is okay as long as the bushes are about the same size. Some terracing or arrangement from front to back of the bed is in order, too. Most minis don't mind transplanting, particularly when dormant. And be careful not to plant too deep. Mulches and covers have a way of piling up.

DIG AND DIVIDE… Many of the Rambler's minis have gotten too large, with woody centers. It's easy to dig and split up the mother plant, trimming out the unproductive woody stuff. Leave some good roots and young growth with each new plant. By the end of the season it will be nearly as large as the mother. With the long (ten-month) growing season on the Gulf Coast, many minis need to be divided every two or three years, usually about mid-February when dormant. Use a saw, shears, or just pull apart like a chrysanthemum. Gives them a new lease on life.

GIVE SOME AWAY… there are some varieties that just need new gardens. It's easy to collect and collect and then put up with so-so performance, particularly with minis. Recycle these to someone else's garden; will make both of you happy. Grow the roses that you really enjoy, not just put up with.

SOME MINI ONE-LINERS… Plant several bushes of the same variety in a clump for maximum effect; helps in growth habit appearance also… Prune a little harder this season and see if the results aren't better. Minis bloom on that new, low growth… Grow some garden varieties for interest in the landscape; Red Flush is a good example, plus all the good new sweetheart roses now being introduced… Which brings to mind minis in containers. There will be many more around the Rambler's garden this season… And hanging baskets on the fence add interest; Sweet Chariot is a good one for this use, as fragrant as the name implies.

FRAGRANT ROSES are coming back into the Rambler's garden… Crimson Glory and Mirandy have been away too long. Adding a couple of Mister Lincoln, too. Will give Oklahoma another chance as well. Gardens need roses for "floaters," too -roses for floating in bowls or brandy snifters like Paul Neyron, Hawaii, Chrysler Imperial and Lady Elgin. Our favorite floater is Color Magic, but we like Double Delight, also. There are some minis that also look great in a small snifter — Magic Carrousel, Over The Rainbow, Red Beauty and Simplex.

ROSES T0 BE ADDED… Need several more plants of much Touch of Class, the real class of the '86 winners. Good for show, cutting, color, growth. As mentioned in earlier columns, Bonica (the 1987 AARS shrub) has a lot going for it. Plan to put out several more to screen a storage area. And, the hips really DO turn red and hang on. It is going to be very attractive during the off season. Another shrub that has many uses is Dream Cloud, a massed screen of pink throughout the season. Handsome foliage, petals drop cleanly, huge sprays, no disease; needed a little shaping up with the hedge shears just once during the season. Now THAT'S a trouble-free rose. In another planting, the Rambler is adding more Carefree Beauty, Griffith Buck's carefree pink shrub. In spite of plant competition, infrequent watering, and general neglect, this rose throws small sprays and lots of canes from April 1 to January 1 (in our climate). Buck's Prairie and Dancer series of winter-hardy roses should be planted more often. They are rewarding, considering the little care they require.

TIMED RELEASE FERTILIZERS fit into more Rambler plans in '87, particularly in the miniature beds and in containers. Properly applied, timed-release fertilizers like *Osmocote* offer a steady, balanced diet that rosarians might otherwise neglect. Other foods and supplements (organic and inorganic) will be used, too, but it makes sense to have some food available all the time. And have you noticed that *Osmocote* (a registered trademark of Sierra Chemical Co.) is becoming a generic description? It takes a successful, widely used product to do that. Add appropriate amounts to container and planting mixes, broadcast in existing beds, use in all kinds of container growing.

START SMALL — GROW BIG with some roselings, tissue culture roses that are fun to watch grow up. These own-root roses will be in our future gardens; perhaps we need a little practice as parents first. Other own-root roses are coming into the market as well; smaller than the budded plants we are used to, but offering real benefits in winter hardiness and freedom from suckers. Before long, these smaller roses will be priced right, encouraging rosarians to mature them in their own gardens. There are great things ahead for roses (and rosarians) in '87. Enjoy a rosy one.

FEB. 1987

THOUGHT FOR THE MONTH: Spraying roses is like telling your wife you love her. It has a short residual and has to be repeated regularly. "Pop" Warner, Orange, Texas

Having ordered only ten more rosebushes than the garden will hold, it's time to get busy on the perennial problem of overcrowding... dig up some more lawn. But maybe just a little rebuilding or expansion per these suggestions may take care of those new members of your rose family...

ROSE BEDS GET TIRED after five years or so of Queen of the Show production, usually when organic matter is depleted. And some of the old reliable rosebushes may show signs of old age, perhaps prematurely. Rebuilding is a good solution for both problems and a lot less work than making a whole new bed. Every grower has experienced the super growth and production from new rose beds; makes even a beginner feel like a winner. Then performance gradually begins to slip. Some rose beds last longer than others; high nitrogen applications (typical exhibitor formulas) use up organic materials that bring life to the soil. Soil organisms thrive in a medium of organic matter, air and water. As organics are broken down, soils become tighter and less able to support root systems. More fertilizer won't reverse the decline, but rebuilding will.

DORMANT ROSES can be dug and set aside for up to a week or so while rebuilding an existing bed. A good time is just before breaking in early spring. Dig carefully with a spading fork; don't worry about taking a ball of soil. Check over the roots for galls and to see just how much of the root system is alive. Trim out or discard depending on the severity. Remember that it takes just as much (or more) work to care for a weak plant as a healthy one. Bury or cover the bushes with soil, sacks, mulch, straw, or any other material that will keep plants cool and moist while bed is being rebuilt. Old-timers refer to this as "heeling in" (or perhaps the right expression is "healing in"), but you get the idea.

REBUILD by bringing the old area up to new specifications: a final mixture (by volume) of 1/3 organic matter (peat moss, compost, manure, etc.), 1/3 loamy soil, and 1/3 sandy, light material. Other additives may be called for, such as gypsum for loosening clays or an acidifier for alkaline soils. Turn the whole mix with a tiller or fork; wet down and turn again the next day. If the mix is too heavy, add some more organics. Allow the bed to settle (wetting helps) before replanting the sleeping bushes the same way as bare-root roses. Prune back the same time as other rose plantings. Result: good growth and roses with a new lease on life.

A FRIENDLY GARDEN... now's the time to build one. A rose garden for friends you don't even know yet. Choice locations are available at your church, retirement center, nursing home, neighborhood park, school... unlimited possibilities. Just a small rose planting that you can care for comfortably offers huge rewards in self-satisfaction and beauty. Recruit some help for construction and first planting, but be prepared to commit YOUR time and care for the season. Good things come about gradually; helpers are slow to volunteer. Think of a friendly garden as a chance to get more rose experience, an extension of your own garden, a place to grow some excess roses or roses you always wanted to try but couldn't find room for. The Rambler has had "friendly" gardens for may years now and wouldn't take anything for the experience. A friendly garden always gives back fur more than you put in.

PRUNING TIME is almost here. And a new pruning saw for rosarians IS here: a folding job that's about five inches long, narrow blade, extra fine teeth that cut clean and close... the best rose tool since the *Felco* pruner. The Rambler really likes this one. The *Harlane* Company sells them at just $10 each (regular advertisers in these pages). They are the same folks who make the Garden Guide name stakes for roses, still the best and most attractive rose markers anywhere. You owe yourself a new rose tool after a long winter.

ODDS 'N ENDS... How about a rosebush exchange (friendly rose needs new home) at your local rose society pruning/planting meeting? Really warms things up. Some groups like to swap, others offer as door prizes, sell chances or give to new members. The donation makes it easier for the giver to justify new roses. And how many of us have seen that orphan rose really perform in a new garden? Must be some sort of gardening law... ROSE RAFFLES are fairly ordinary, but how many give away a truckload of horse manure as the Grand Prize? Houston picks up several hundred dollars at every holiday party this way and gives away a heap of rose-related gifts as well. As long as the ponies at the polo grounds keep producing, it's a real rose winner -for everyone... FIND A FEED STORE to make rose growing more fun. Garden shops are all right, and nurseries carry lots of things that rosarians need, but it's hard to beat a good feed store. They'll have all sorts of organics and fertilizers and sacks of stuff like alfalfa pellets, cottonseed meal, fish meal, bone meal, and rock phosphate to warm the heart — not to mention the roots. Might even pick up a "gimmie cap" that says "FRED'S FEEDS," the mark of a real dirt gardener.

The best part of a typical rose society program is the "coffeetime workshop" at the end of the meeting. Now THERE'S where the really great rose wisdom comes out. Here's a sampler of timely topics from recent sessions…

SPRINGTIME STARTER… A dose of salts, Epsom salts (magnesium sulfate), that is. Just two or three ounces of *Epsom Salts* (not really a salt) per established bush just after pruning will get bushes off to a fast start. Encourages new breaks and green leaves. Broadcast or dissolve in a gallon of water; the solution works faster. Magnesium levels in a typical soil are not up to the demands of the bush during spring growth.

ALFALFA TEA also gives established bushes as well as newly-planted roses a boost. Brew up a mix of about 10 cups of alfalfa pellets per 30-gallon garbage can; steep for two or three days, pour on a gallon for big bushes, half-gallon for minis. A good growth stimulator. Pellets will last two or three fillings. If the smell bothers the neighbors, keep the lid on. But the roses love it.

HORMONES AND ELIXIRS?? A popular fad for new and newly-transplanted bushes. There are a number of products which claim to have potent powers to grow "millions of tiny root hairs" for fast growth. But the RAMBLER suspects that the extra water from application did the most good. Roots re-establish in a good soil mix. But if you have a secret ingredient, use it with plenty of water. Just don't add any fertilizer, even though the label says "can't burn when used as directed."

BANDING PHOSPHATE MAKES SENSE. More and more agricultural authorities and rosarians are recommending banding phosphate rather than mixed in the soil when planting. A rosarian usually mixes a handful of phosphate or bone meal in the planting soil cone. Studies show that less material placed as a band (or handful in the case of roses) directly under the plant produces better results. The mix method is somewhat inefficient because the phosphate reacts in the soil to form non-available phosphorous compounds. What makes it work? To keep phosphate alive, active and available to the plant, fertilizer particles must somehow be protected and the soil kept in a suitable pH range (about 5.8 to 7.5). One way is to keep the fertilizer particles together. Laid down in

a close-knit mass, the particles sacrifice some of the outer members, but the core remains somewhat protected and intact. This is the reason that a handful of superphosphate (or rock phosphate) two or three inches below the roots of a newly-planted rose seems to do so much good.

TO PINCH OR NOT TO PINCH? A tough question for rosarians anxious to see a bloom of a new variety. And a very painful problem when new basals shoot up. But first things first.

Grow bushes with leaves, then add roses. Keep new rosebushes vegetative until they are well established. Pinch out the buds or go down to the first five-leaflet. Encourage bud eyes in the middle of the cane, that's where the biggest and best buds are. Pinch the tips so that the cane and leaf structures can develop. Bud eyes on roses are apically dominant, that is, the top bud wants to break. But let the strength go to lower, stronger buds.

NEW BASALS should not be allowed to flower (well, maybe just once in a while). Depending on the vigor of the variety, when the basal hits 20 inches or so or begins to form a bloom bud, pinch back to a five-leaflet or a good blunt bud eye. The top eye will tend to be pointed, the husky ones are blunt. About the term "pinch;" pinching is a greenhouse/nursery term. It may be done with the fingernails but most often with a sharp knife (rosarians use shears). A practiced grower with a sharp knife can go through a lot of bushes in a hurry and leave clean cuts.

MOUNDING new or transplanted roses is a practice somewhat misunderstood. While protection from sudden freezes is a consideration, the main idea is to conserve moisture in the canes until the roots have had enough time to become established. The practice is good for warm or cold climates. New growth will break from stored nutrients (in solution). But this moisture must be replenished to support and sustain growth. Hot sun, cold winds, low humidity pull moisture from the canes. Protect these canes with mulch, soil, hay or mixtures of all of these, mounding almost to the tips of the canes. Some growers use grocery bags to hold the protection. Bring in some extra insulating material; don't pull it all up from the beds. Use plenty of water on the mound as well as in the bed to support the roots. Don't be anxious to remove;

two or three weeks is about right, then gradually wash away with the hose. You'll find all kinds of good breaks and growth that have been protected. If in doubt (or in a cold climate), leave on a little longer. This dehydration process is the reason that tree standards are difficult to start. The moisture has a long way to go. More damage is done to those expensive tree roses in the sales nursery by indifferent watering and protection than in all the rest of the harvesting, shipping process. Stay away from the dehydrated stock (bush or standard) unless you like to live dangerously. They may LOOK dormant, but they may also be dried out.

WATER makes roses grow. All the rest of the routine is useless unless there's plenty of water available. Have you WATERED your roses lately?

A smart rosarian knows what to do with what he knows… and now's the time to put it into practice. *Funginex* on the shelf has never been known to curtail mildew. And a coiled-up watering hose doesn't encourage much new growth. Now that we understand schedules, here are some items to include in April.

FISH MEAL is the stuff for rosarians who want to ENJOY roses, not just work at it. If you can find some at your local feed store (widely used as poultry feed), get 50 pounds or so and apply in "cones" around established roses. Use a bulb digger or similar tool and lift about three cones of soil 6 inches deep and 18 inches away from the shank of the rose. Pour a total of 1 to 2 cups of fish meal in the holes; re-cover with soil and listen for the roots being called to the dinner table. The result will be greener leaves, better growth and overall better bloom. Use in early spring and again in late summer. Years from now when those bushes are dug, masses of hairy feeder roots will have found the fish meal, supporting the bush in grand style. Broadcast feedings of other fertilizers may continue, but a feeding miss once in a while won't make as much difference.

PREVENTION is the name of the game in disease control. If ANYTHING is scheduled in the rose garden, the fungicide spray program should be. Start early; stay on schedule. The most common mistake is to wait until the infection appears; by that time it's too late. It's an uphill battle from then on. Blackspot leaves cannot be restored. Leaves, buds and blooms twisted with mildew won't become sleek and productive again after spraying. The best practice is to begin fungus control the day roses are pruned, long before leaves appear. Then get on a seven-to-ten day schedule and stay with it. Good fungicides like *Funginex, Benlate, Phaltan* and *Manzate* will do the job if used on the plants, not on the shelf. Slack off on some other job but not fungus control.

RUBIGAN EC promises to be the powdery mildew control rosarians have been looking for, especially during severe mildew conditions. Locally systemic, control is good for 14 -21 days (although *Triforine 'Funginex'* is used weekly). The Rambler has used *Rubigan* and *Funginex* in combination with NO sign of leaf damage and no residue. Would be a good idea for rosarians in severe mildew areas to begin *Rubigan* treatment two weeks BEFORE mildew conditions (cool nights, warm days) are right. Although expensive at $78 a pint, application at 2 teaspoons per 5 gallons makes a pint go a long way. Split a buy with other rose folks. Then spray until leaves glisten, particularly new, tender growth. Do a particularly thorough job on ramblers and climbers to cut down the spores for reinfection.

A MISCONCEPTION… Many rosarians think that mildew spores grow on rose tissue damp from dew. They don't. Mildew spreads on DRY leaf and plant tissue in periods of low humidity. Early morning dew on leaves comes from temperature differential (the same combination that promotes mildew) but does not contribute to the problem. Blackspot grows on WET leaves… not much of a problem in dry climates like Albuquerque or Denver. But a good fungus control program is still the answer.

MAVRIK AQUAFLOW insecticide may also be on your spray program this year. This broad spectrum contact insecticide is particularly effective on cucumber beetles, a pest that seems to defy other insecticides. *Mavrik* is also good on thrips, bud worms, some beetles and even spider mites. Use at rates ranging from 2/3 to 1 2/3 teaspoons per 5 gallons; low rate for thrips and beetles, higher rate for spider mites. Use alone for best results; tends to separate in solvents and oils. *Mavrik* is a Zoecon Corporation product and sells for about $20 for 8 ounces. Mail order suppliers like Brighton and Kimbrew-Walter have it.

THE FRAGRANT FORMULA… official signal that the rose season has begun. It's an olde tyme favorite for artificial manure that will grow grass on a fence post and roses on concrete. This is for the rosarian who doesn't have a farm friend (and a pickup truck) for the real thing. The fragrant formula is just as good (maybe even better because it releases more nutrients) and can be produced on a city lot. It's good as a soil amendment, top dressing, basic feeding formula… especially in the spring. Enjoy all the benefits; here's the formula.

3 ample yards of compost materials or leaves

100 pounds of cottonseed hulls (or something coarse like

ground pine bark)

100 pounds of cottonseed meal

100 pounds of alfalfa meal (or alfalfa pellets)

50 pounds of bone meal

50 pounds of fish meal

A farm store will have all the ingredients, except the leaves. If fish meal is not available, substitute a couple of sacks of manure and add maybe 20 pounds of bloodmeal or beef and bone. There are many variations possible. Make a pile of coarse materials about two feet deep, using any area suitable for composting. Add lighter ingredients and turn with a pitchfork or garden fork. Mix well. Then LIGHTLY moisten and turn twice a week for two weeks. When the pile is working right, a sharp ammonia odor will leak out. A different (DEAD) odor will leak if the pile is too wet or if there is not enough coarse composting material. The formula is ready in two to three weeks; apply two garden shovelfuls per bush in the spring. Use again late summer. Be generous; you're feeding the microorganisms that do all the work converting nutrients in the soil into a form that roses can use. ENJOY!

A studied rose perspective is important with rose shows close at hand... if your roses should happen to wind up on the trophy table, try to hide your astonishment. But it's okay to be amazed with the results of these exhibitor's tips...

WELL-GROWN ROSES win ribbons; all the grooming, storage, travel and selection tricks in the world can't make a mediocre rose into a winner. Exhibiting skills enhance a rose, but the beauty has to be there in the first place... and that begins in the garden. Extra effort here pays off on show day.

WATER is the most important "show additive," believe it or not. Nothing moves through the bush without water; no lush leaves, long stems, substance in the blooms. Every essential to growth (except sunshine) has to go into solution. Good growers SOAK the rose beds and then go back with some more the next day. Some watering by hand is in order, too. Many exhibition gardens have "soak basins" around bushes, filling the basin to the brim with water every evening. Regardless of how it is done, EXTRA water pays off in better blooms. When water runs out of the bed, that's enough. Then repeat.

BLOOD MEAL is a favorite exhibitor's additive here on the Gulf Coast. With warm soil temperatures and lots of water, it goes to work faster. It is in most of the spring starter formulas (about a cup per bush) and again with a half-cup two weeks before a rose show. Result: rich, green leaves and lots of color in the blooms. Remember that blood meal is high in nitrogen when combining with regular feeding formulas. Some growers prefer fish meal, but it takes a little longer to work. Fish meal is a GREAT choice for miniatures; two ounces (a shot glass) per month promotes super growth and bloom without vegetative centers.

SOLUBLE FERTILIZERS applied every two weeks (or even weekly) prior to rose shows are popular with many growers. Look for a high available phosphoric acid formula with trace elements (like *Superbloom, Peters, Carl Pool Instant, MiracleGro*) and follow the directions. A typical formula is *Carl Pool* (8-55-7) with magnesium, copper, iron, manganese, and zinc. *Peters* has a number of good formulas. The important ingredient is solubility to get to the roots right away.

About a tablespoon per gallon per bush is about right for most of these products, but READ the directions. And ALWAYS reduce to one-third of recommended amounts for miniatures. If weekly applications are in your rose work schedule, cut the amounts accordingly. A favorite around here is called the *SUPER-WHAMMO* (by Suzie Spydermite from Corpus Christi), a water soluble mix used every other week from time of pruning until rose show. It features a high phosphate combined with fish emulsion, magnesium and *Sequestrene*. But soluble applications are an inexact science; try one thing at a time and see how it works. There's an advertising slogan for a fertilizer that says it all: "Plants need minerals, not miracles."

PROTECT THE BLOOMS that have taken so much effort to produce. Thrips love fragrant, light-colored blooms just like the judges. The most reliable and widely used protection seems to be *Orthene,* somewhat systemic with good residual. Just spray the bud and bloom areas; there are not thrips on the lower leaves. Some growers spot-spray show blooms and buds with a Windex-type sprayer every other day. Use a fresh batch each spraying, leaves no residue. The Rambler prefers *Orthene Soluble Powder* (75%) for effectiveness and economy over the 9.4% Emulsifiable Concentration. Use *Orthene SP* at a scant teaspoon per gallon. Much better. Buffer alkaline water with one tablespoon of white vinegar per gallon for better residual.

CUCUMBER BEETLES can eat up show blooms in a hurry. Try *Mavrik Aquaflow* as a control. Described in Ramblings last month, testimonials to its effectiveness have arrived in a steady stream. Also good on thrips, bud worms and even spider mites. No residue, a boon for exhibitors. Use at rates from *213* to pH teaspoons per 5 gallons; there's an excellent applications booklet wrapped with each 8-ounce bottle. Use alone, buffer the water. Use as required at five-to ten-day intervals.

UNDERSTAND THE SHOW SCHEDULE. Read and read again. Ask questions. Concentrate on those sections where your blooms have the best chance. If your three bushes of *Mister Lincoln* consistently produce fine blooms, try the three-stages of bloom collection, the open bloom section or the fragrant class. If you are a floribunda grower, look for FL collections or combinations where good sprays are important. Plan ahead, and keep in mind the strengths of your roses. Know WHAT and WHERE you will enter before leaving the house for the show. You'll have a much better chance.

GIVEAWAYS... The Houston Rose Society has come up with a series of folders on various aspects of growing roses... folders we use to promote membership, inform and introduce roses to gardeners at .rose shows, garden centers, outside programs and for visitors. This information helps us maintain a membership of 1300 -1500 every year. The folders cover Rose Suggestions for Houston, Fundamentals of Pruning, Planting, Growing, and Enjoying Miniature Roses and a Membership Information/Application. We'll share all five with you if you'll send a self addressed stamped envelope (legal-size) or even just a 22-cent stamp to the Rambler at the address above. You're free to copy, adapt, quote, or otherwise use these folders for the benefit of roses. We think they are great... hope you will, too. Just what you need for YOUR rose show.

Good ideas are not a bit particular about who has them... so how about keeping your ears (and mind) open to some of these suggestions as well as those you pick up around the coffee/cookies session at the rose society meeting...

I LIKE 'EM ALL... the schedules and special twists, the secret formulas (which they are anxious to pass along), the "whammo" show feeds, the impossible-to-get varieties, and the plastic surgery that transforms also-rans into show queens. But most of all the Rambler likes the routines and foods that produce good roses week in and week out and leave enough time to enjoy the roses. Organics work fine; pelletized (or timed-release) fertilizers make life easier; occasional foliar feeding is like icing on the cake; a basic spray schedule keeps leaves clean and working... and water does most of the work. Whatever YOU are comfortable with... keep it up. Try a variation once in a while but don't be swayed by the fantastic grower stories; his special routines (and roses) may not fit your garden at all.

FISH MEAL ROUTINE... The Rambler's favorite has produced basal breaks, canes, leaves and blooms that exceed even this writer's superlative. Hard to get for a while, fish meal has brought new life to the old and productivity to the new. If you can get some at your local feed store, PLEASE do so. Broadcast on the mulch or bury in the soil, about one cup per large bush, less for minis. Smells a little the first couple of days, but roses really respond. And try some alfalfa pellets (or meal); a cup per bush in the spring or anytime the leaves look a little light. Alfalfa tea or broadcast; it works. Miniatures especially like a drink of alfalfa tea. A monthly tea routine for pots and plants can't hurt a thing. Roses are the best thing to happen to alfalfa growers since rabbits and reproduce just as fast.

EPA IS AT IT AGAIN... Some of our favorite rose nostrums are on the way out. Most serious is *Acti-Dione PM*, the powdery mildew eradicant/ preventative. It is not going to be re-registered so what's on the shelf is all there's going to be. And even some of that is being recalled. That's even more reason to get on a *Rubigan* routine, the locally systemic mildewcide that WILL do the job if you stay on schedule. This ARS issue describes the mildew process; the July ARS magazine will

have the test reports on *Rubigan* from the National Committee on Product Evaluation, Dr. Tommy Cairns, Chairman. But the Rambler says, "Don't wait for the report. If you are faced with mildew conditions, add *Rubigan* to your spray routine IMMEDIATELY."

KELTHANE is also going to be dropped because of its DDT content; not really much of a loss since it didn't do much good on spider mites anyway (at least vigorous ones). You'll soon see a new formula for *Isotox*, again because of *Kelthane*. And the pipeline for *Orthenex* is not filled for the same reason. ALL of these products will continue to be available as Ortho is making a great effort to reformulate. As long as rosarians have *Funginex* (*Triforene*) and *Orthene*, we can get along fine. Reminder: unless your garden is VERY small, *Orthenex* is NOT a good buy. Use *Funginex* with an occasional addition of *Orthene* and save considerable money. And if you are a big *Orthene EC* user, consider a switch to *Orthene 75% SP* (soluble powder). Much less costly and the Rambler thinks that it works better. Use two teaspoons of *Orthene SP* per gallon for good thrips control, probably spraying buds and blooms twice a week;

MAVRIK is the real comer in insecticides. Good for beetles, thrips, spider mites and a wide range of insects. No residue, no leaf damage. Compatible with *Funginex*. *Mavrik Aquaflow* (it's a liquid) is used at two teaspoons per five gallons of water, but buffer the water to near-neutral (7.0) for greater effectiveness. It's a non-restricted material based on its high level of human safety. Look for this Zoecon product at a "growers store" or mail order from one of the distributors. The small garden centers won't have it, but agricultural supply and nursery support outlets will. Cost: about $23 for eight ounces.

ANTI-TRANSPIRANTS for powdery mildew control. The Rambler has used anti-transpirants for transplant shock and cold protection but has no experience with mildew applications. Sold as *Cloud Cover*, *Wilt-Pruf*, *Vapor Guard* and *Thermo-Chem*, the products coat the leaves and inhibit moisture transpiration. Apparently, the coating inhibits mildew spore penetration as well. However, the Rambler thinks that normal leaf processes are better unless a really abnormal situation (like transplant) exists. And how is new growth protected without repeated applications? We need a good test program before taking off in this direction. Nature has been moving moisture through leaves for a long time.

ODDS 'N ENDS... Rosarians with blind wood often go into a blind rage, but a little judicious pinching back takes care of it. If a well-developed stem is blind, pinch back to a five-leaflet and see if the immature bud develops. Short, blind rosette growth can be pinched out entirely if you have the back and patience to do it... And don't be in a hurry to cut back frost-damaged growth. The rosebush will tell you when and where to cut back by sending out new growth. There's little to be gained and much to lose by trimming back too soon... A little grass in the rose bed is not all bad; the Rambler calls it "Green Mulch," a healthy crop of chickweed that seems to spring up overnight. Visitors on a recent garden tour marveled at the ingenuity in using the green mulch (applied very carefully) followed by a more conventional bark mulch which will tend to smother remaining starts. Aren't garden tours GREAT as a learning experience? Hope your society gets into the gardens often.

If you have wondered how pesticides could harm the environment considering how little damage they do to bugs, maybe you're just going at it the wrong way. Here are some approaches/applications that may help...

WATER is nature's miticide, applied copiously to the undersides of the leaves. A strong, fine spray washes the varmints off, breaking up the webbing in the process. In most gardens, a good washing with a water wand (or similar device) twice a week will give good control. Water makes the bushes feel good, too something like a good shower after a hot day in the garden. If this doesn't work, try *Mavrik Aquaflow* at 2 teaspoons per 5 gallons of water (buffered to near neutral [7.0] for greater effectiveness). *Mavrik* can be safely used every seven to ten days if necessary, but the Rambler suggests *Vendex* (21-28 days residual) after an application of *Mavrik*. Then go back to *Mavrik* again (if really necessary) or regain natural control with lots of water.

LOOK FOR MITES... spider mite leaves LOOK different, gradually losing green color and taking on a dry, parched look. Mites suck the moisture right out of the leaves, an effect something like drying and aging of leaves in the fall. Check the UNDERSIDES of the leaves for gritty gray and white specks, a sort of salt-and-pepper look. Then get to work right away; wash/spray as you prefer, but HURRY.

STUNTING of rosebushes usually provokes a rosarian response with more fertilizer and great anxiety. But what should really be done is a soil test for pH as most rose soils become too acid as a result of heavy nitrogen, acid-forming fertilizers. Ideally, roses like a 6.5 to 7.0 pH range but will tolerate wide variations. The pH of soil affects plant growth in several important ways: (1) it has a distinct effect on availability of important nutrients; (2) it has an effect on soil microorganisms; (3) it has a direct effect on root cells to absorb both nutrients and water and on the solubility of toxic substances. In short, pH controls growth.

A SOIL TEST puts you in control again. The County Extension Service offers boxes and instructions for inexpensive samples to the area agricultural college. The Ags will specify pH and offer recommendations for lime and/or acid-form-

ing applications to bring pH to levels for roses. Be sure to specify ROSES as the crop. Another way is to buy an inexpensive soil tester kit (uses litmus paper) and make your own test. The Rambler isn't comfortable with NPK readings of these kits, but it's hard to go wrong on a pH test. Use some common rose sense; take samples from several areas in the rose bed (not where you have just fertilized) and blend for an average sample. Get down into the areas where the roots are. Then use the same rose sense in correcting any imbalance; give whatever you are using some time to work.

MANY TOP GROWERS keep pH in balance by using dolomite limestone (agricultural lime) in amounts equal to nitrogen applications. For example: a 40-pound bag of ammonium sulfate (12-24-12) contains 4.8 pounds of nitrogen (and same amount of sulfur). Routinely add 4.8 pounds of agricultural lime to the same area. It takes the agricultural lime a little longer to work but will show good long-term results if used regularly. Dolomite lime contains both magnesium carbonate and calcium carbonate; magnesium and calcium are vital to plant growth. Just broadcast over the entire soil area, scratch in a bit and water well. But make a soil test, then adjust and keep in balance for roses with regular applications. The basics are quite simple, and the results astonishing.

AIR in the soil is important, also. Nutrients become available to plants when air, water and nutrients are present. Compact soils don't work. Mechanically open up the soil with a fork, cultivation or tine technique. Use organics and particle materials like perlite and vermiculite generously. Raised beds breathe better, but any bed construction that allows good drainage will also drain air through the soil crumbs. Keep your feet OUT of the rose bed, especially if the soil is moist. Use stepping stones, boardwalks or narrow beds to care for (and enjoy) the roses. The soil, roots and roses will appreciate you.

MAKE MULCH... Save those clippings and cleanings from the lawn and flower beds. Gather, mix, add leaves and what-have-you and then compost. It's a green harvest that makes the roses happy. You'll be surprised at how fast green humus material piles up. Just don't pile the grass clippings in the rose bed; they will heat, shed water and eventually rob nitrogen from the soil. You'll have a real garden friend by breaking down these materials before adding or applying to the soil. Let nature work for you instead of against you.

ODDS N' ENDS... If you don't have a water wand, get one or make one. Any kind of device to reach under and wash down rose leaves... A water breaker is another fine rose tool to apply a soft flow of water in a concentrated stream. Makes sense to give roses a hand watering on occasion; gives the rosarian a chance to look over and get acquainted with the roses (and maybe see some areas where the bushes need help)... Post your spray and feeding schedule on a handy calendar hung in the garage or tool shed. What day did you spray and with what? When did you last feed? How much rain fell last Sunday?... *Super-Whammo* noted by the Rambler in May is NOT a commercial product just a name given a home-brew mix for rabid exhibitors... A type gremlin missed a line in this column last month — commenting on green mulch (weeds), the Rambler recommends *Roundup,* applied VERY carefully, followed up with conventional bark mulch. This month the Rambler reports that the chickweed in the rose beds is gone, replaced by Bermuda grass creeping in from the sides. But the roses are happy.

If experience is yesterday's answer to today's problems, let's go back to the good old days. Maybe we skipped some basics as we hurried to try the latest things. If your results have been less than sensational, read on...

SPIDER MITES... caught up with the Rambler in just ten days (overstayed rose vacation at the Charlotte ARS meeting). A dense planting of floribundas against a brick wall (facing south) and miniatures along a wooden fence were clean one week and moving with mites the next. Control had been good with water wand and two applications of *Mavrik*. Some traces of mites but apparently all dead and under control. The foliage was beautiful, growth robust. BUT, there had been more applications of *Orthene* than usual to control aphids and thrips after a warm winter. "Welcome Home" included mites five feet off the ground in *Sonia, Cherish,* and *Pristine*. Most of the leaves were already gone off *First Edition*. Some of the minis looked like mid-winter. Battle plan: wash first with lots of water, then *Mavrik* underneath the leaves, followed by *Vendex* three days later. Resume the water wand in three weeks and as of this writing (late June), leaves are green again (the old stuff dropped oft) and new growth and blooms are healthy and productive. Mistake: trying to stretch the spray schedule, especially in hot weather. But we live and learn (again).

SPRAYING is an art as well as a science. Obviously the materials have to be right, but the application is all important. The name of the game is COVERAGE. A "once over lightly" won't do the job, in spite of the systemic claims. Here's a good way to make sure of leaf coverage: wash the leaves first, get rid of the residue and dirt and insects in the process. Then spray underneath, overhead and sideways until the leaves glisten with material. Depending on the sprayer, this is not too difficult if the spray water has been buffered or neutralized (7.0) so that it tends to spread across the leaves. White vinegar does this very well, about 1 tablespoon per gallon for most alkaline water. Try a little less or a little more and see what it does on the leaves. Be very cautious about adding other spreader-stickers, as most materials already have them built in. If spray material beads up on the leaves or puddles at the tips, adjust the additives/techniques accord-

ingly. Makes good rose sense.

SPRAYER to use?? Lots of good ones on the market; buy the best one you can afford, sized appropriately for the job. A 2 ^{1}/2 gallon pump-up is not a good choice for 300 roses, and a $300 power outfit is overkill for 30 bushes. Hudson makes some fine sprayers for small to medium gardens; plastic tanks, lightweight, adjustable nozzles, good wands. Their half-gallon *Bugwiser* is great for thrips control but would be lots of work for many roses. There are other good pump-ups, too; just make sure that repair kits are available for the annual work over. The *Atomist* is the sprayer of choice for many rosarians... lightweight, electrically driven, puts out a very fine wet-wind-fog that gets the job done in a hurry with little spray material. There are some disadvantages: needs no electrical outlet and long, grounded cord, hard to control in wind, needs careful application to really wet leaves. At wet setting in the hands of a careful applicator, *Atomist* can keep gardens clean.

THE NEWEST SPRAY RIGS use sealed, rechargeable wet batteries to power 12-volt motors and centrifugal pumps at about 60 pounds pressure. Mounted on two-wheel carts, 5-gallon capacity, long hose and wand... these rigs are simple and effective. GreenLeaf is a regular advertiser in these pages and has a good rose following. The Rambler uses *SpotShot,* now distributed nationally by Garden Way. Trouble free and does a consistently good job. Going into the fourth season, the Rambler's *SpotShot* has sprayed 1000 plus bushes a week for 40 weeks a year without a breakdown or a clog. The battery rigs are in the $300 price range but worth every penny of it if you want to enjoy a large rose garden(s). Check out some growers in your area before making any major sprayer decision. It's one of the most important you'll make in the rose garden.

COMBINATIONS OF SPRAY MATERIALS concern many rosarians, and others mix up everything on the shelf and seem to get by with it. The Rambler wonders if the "mixers" report their mistakes as accurately as their successes. At any rate, a thoughtful review of the excellent "Agro-Chemicals" article in the May '87 issue by Dr. Thomas Cairns is in order. You may rig up the sprayer with an entirely different outlook.

ODDS N' ENDS... To improve the effectiveness of your pressure sprayer (and ease your back) change out the short applicator wand for a longer one, preferably one with a swivel end to direct spray up and under the leaves. A 36-inch wand reaches all the way back and under, and keeps the spray even further away from the rosarian. Pest control suppliers have these kinds of parts and a broad selection of nozzles... Concerned about the salts in bagged manure?? Easy to leach out by composting with a pile of leaves; sprinkle about 10 pounds of agricultural gypsum for every 100 pounds of feedlot manure. Wet, mix, and turn a couple of times over two weeks and it's ready to use. Salts will flush out, so use enough water to do the job. Makes a fine soil conditioner... *Maneb* is now available in a liquid formulation (rather than a wettable powder) in many parts of the country. Disperses in water better and has less tendency to settle out. Rosarians in blackspot-prone regions routinely add *Maneb* at one-half strength *(V2* tablespoon per gallon) to *Funginex* (1 tablespoon per gallon) for longer residual or to get rid of infection. Look for it; very convenient... And that's important to all of us who want to enjoy roses more... and work less.

If you have put off rose chores until they are no longer necessary, here are some quick cures to reap a September harvest of roses... there's still plenty of time to save the season.

LIQUID FEED... that is, feed roses appropriate formulas in solution, Nor with pelletized fertilizers broadcast over the rose beds. Food in solution goes to work right away and also goes away without disrupting the fall dormancy slowdown. A little like a shot in the arm rather than a long-term diet. If the roses and rose beds are reasonably receptive, a gallon or two of liquid mix will show results in just three or four days. Apply now, then repeat in about ten days, at least in the more temperate zones of the country. Warmer areas can keep up the treatment until mid-October. Use a formula high in available phosphoric acid with trace elements (like *Superbloom, Miracle-Gro, Carl Pool Instant, Peters)* and force all the water the rose beds can take. The Rambler still likes *Ra-Pid-Gro;* makes lots of leaves, stems and roses. And that's what we're trying to grow.

APPLICATION by bucket gets mighty heavy, even with the trash barrel located near the rose beds. To save your back, you might want to try a syphon system with the garden hose, working from a concentrated solution. Several lawn feeders use this method. The Rambler likes a mix accurately diluted and pumps from the barrel with a small "Little Giant" fountain or pool pump. The pump is mounted on a board that hangs outside the barrel, even though the pump is submersible. Guesstimate the flow rate and go from bush to bush. All it takes is a barrel, fairly long grounded electrical cord and a small pump. Makes your back and roses very happy. Don't forget to run some clear water through the pump when the job is finished; fertilizers eat up pumps in a hurry. Even works with alfalfa tea... just don't stir up the sediment.

GROOM VS PRUNE in the fall. The Rambler cringes every time a well-meaning rosarian advises "fall pruning for best bloom." This suggests heavy trimming, and that's not the idea at all. Roses in the fall appreciate grooming, the light trimming up of unproductive wood and blind growth that isn't going anywhere. It's just a more thorough job of cutting spent blooms with an eye for the next bloom cycle. Call it a sort of fall house-

cleaning. Don't have a field day on leaves; the bush needs them to produce food. When bushes have to recover from defoliation, bloom production is delayed that much longer. Leaf loss, whether caused from disease, insects, drought, or trimming shears, results in fewer roses and weaker bushes for winter survival. The name of the game is "Grow leaves, then Roses."

SPRAY SCHEDULES are important. Don't wait for disease problems to appear; get ahead with a preventive program. New leaves and old growth need this protection. This is especially important in powdery mildew control. Mildew strikes new, lush growth when climatic conditions are right (cool nights, warm days). Sounds like fall, doesn't it? *Rubigan* is effective when started two weeks or so before conditions are right for mildew. This gives the systemic material a chance to protect and inhibit before mildew spores are spreading all over the garden. The Rambler uses *Rubigan* at 2 teaspoons per 5 gallons of water every two weeks, beginning about September 15th. The ramblers and climbers get special attention and good coverage. On the Gulf Coast this continues through about mid-November. It's great to have a clean fall garden.

WANT NEW FALL COLOR? How about some miniature roses set out as soon as possible? Minis don't mind cooler weather; they still put out growth and color in a hurry. Cold weather doesn't bother them either; just some soil and leaves about frost time will see them through until spring. By that time the little bushes will have become well established and ready to take off. It's amazing just how hardy miniatures are. Just don't force lush new growth before winter sets in. Let them slow down naturally, and they will take care of themselves.

ODDS 'N ENDS... BUILDING/REWORKING rose beds this fall? Keep in mind that organics offer the best of both worlds. Leaves, humus, bark, compost or whatever will loosen up tight soil and tighten up loose soil. Sounds like a contradiction, but it really isn't. Organics work anywhere, so use them generously. Don't waste any of those life-giving leaves this fall... A WHITE VINEGAR solution run through the sprayer after use cleans up deposits and residues. About two tablespoons in a half gallon of water will do the job... WASH OFF MILDEW with ordinary baking soda. This treatment won't kill the spores, but it does clean them off quickly and without damage to the leaves. Use about 2 teaspoons of baking soda per gallon of water (use alone) and spray generously. Again, don't expect to control mildew with this treatment. You are only washing off the external evidence of spore growth and preparing the leaves for application of a good mildewcide (like *Rubigan*)... SAUCERS AND TRAYS under roses in pots hold water, and that seems like a good idea — but really isn't. Roses in containers (big ones or little ones) like good drainage; water from the top delivers nutrients and air throughout the planting medium. Standing in water acts like a stopper; the whole process slows down. Retain moisture (and air) in the planting mix with lots or organics. Let the soil work naturally.

SEPTEMBER is the Rambler's 17th Anniversary... 204 RAMBLINGS wiser (??) and still left with some rose stuff to share. Hope you enjoy roses as much as I do.

Fall is arriving on schedule, much to the relief of tired rose growers. But there are just a few more chores to be done before winter takes over... all easy ones (depending on who is doing the work).

LEAVES WILL DO THE WORK... except for a little gathering-up. Falling from the trees -a mixed harvest of soil builder, insulator, fertilizer and natural cover... at no cost. Take advantage of this gift from nature, even if all of the leafy harvest can't be used. Used for composting or winter protection, leaves return far more to the garden than the small amount of effort required to make them effective. Experience the benefits of compost just once, and you'll find space for more leaves next year. If there's no out-of-the-way space available for a compost heap, use a vegetable or flowering annuals bed or maybe a spot where the new rose bed is planned. Nature will work all winter for you.

COMPOST IN PLACE... just turn and dig the soil in a bed area making a wind-row of soil. Pile leaves, clippings, etc., in the trench and add some excess soil on top for dressing. Something green helps the process, or add organic nitrogen (and microorganisms) with manure or blood meal. Keep moist and turn lightly now and then while the weather is good. It will probably settle enough to be able to add more leaves. Before hard freeze time the partially composted material should be broken down enough to till or mix in place or can be added to other bed areas. If bad weather comes early, no problem. By spring the area will have the richest prepared soil available anywhere. Composting time can be accelerated a bit by covering the trench or pile with black plastic to hold the heat of decomposition and collect heat from the sun.

INSULATING LEAVES also break down, but more slowly. Keep the covering light with lots of air space in the same manner as insulating materials. Leaves moderate temperatures, both hot and cold. Winter protection is simply a matter of preventing the freeze-thaw cycle and drying out of rose canes. If a leaf blanket is your protection method, don't forget to add more leaves as the blanket settles, something like cornflakes in a box. Keep leaves in place with wire baskets, rabbit-wire fences, evergreen boughs or even a short snow fence. Some cold climate rosarians use a combina-

tion of cones and leaves, the leaves acting as a sort of protective insulation for the cones and maintaining a more even temperature.

MORE SEVERE CLIMATES require soil and leaves; a mound of soil over the bud union and lower canes plus lots of leaves on top... this will keep most varieties in good shape with temperature ranges from 20 below to 50 above. Copes with dry, cold winds and sunshine, too. REALLY, REALLY COLD areas may require burying in soil, popularly know as the "Minnesota Tip" method. It's a lot of work, but it DOES WORK.

MINIATURES LIKE LEAVES, too. Pile on leaves, add a bit of soil to help hold in place, and they will sleep safely until spring -in most cases, more safely than the big roses. There's something about being on their own roots that makes them more hardy, something most growers do not appreciate. Even minis in pots can be protected with leaves in a spot out of the wind; just don't forget to add water now and then if there is insufficient snow cover.

FERTILIZE UNDER THE MULCH?? Many cold-climate rosarians do, calculating that the soil process goes on all winter long for a better spring start. If you want to try it, put down a layer of leaves, broadcast a cupful of pelletized fertilizer per large bush, then add some more leaves. In the spring the lower layer will be broken down to a rich humus, often threaded with white feeder roots. As a trial, winter feed one bed and skip another. Compare results next spring.

FALL is a good time to apply dolomite lime, too, if your feeding routine calls for periodic raising of the pH. Lime takes time to break down and get into the root zone; let the job take all winter. A gypsum flush in the fall might also be in order. Alkaline clay soils get tighter and tighter; gypsum opens them up and flushes out excess salts. Doesn't disturb the pH and furnishes calcium and magnesium as well. How much to use? About 20 pounds per 100 square feet of rose bed or a handful per large container.

OTHER FALL TREATMENTS... Put up a *BUG-ZAPPER* light to control hungry corn earworms. The electric grid takes care of the gray moth that lays the eggs... SPRAY roses in October with *Rubigan* to control and eradicate powdery mildew. It's the best thing to come along in years; just 2 teaspoons per 5 gallons every 10 days or so. Can be safely used with *Triforine (Funginex)*. Roses weakened with mildew are going to have a hard winter. And there's no need for it. Get some from your favorite mail order supplier; about $80 per pint, split with a rose friend for an applied cost of less than 35 cents per gallon.

NEW *PRODUCTS... Avid,* the SUPER new miticide is now available in 8-ounce containers for around $40; at ~ teaspoon per gallon application rate this is also less than 35 cents per gallon... *Maneb liquid Fungicide* is often used in combination with *Triforine* in hard-to-control blackspot areas. The liquid seems to mix and stay in suspension better than the wettable powder form... *Benlate* fungicide is now available as a dispersible granule, labeled 50DF (dry flowable). Much easier to use. Check your mail order supplier (or greenhouse supplier) for these items.

The best way to succeed with roses is to act on the advice we give to others... but we somehow seem to run out of time. If that's the case, here are some FAST suggestions...

ANTI-DESICCANT SPRAYS may help in the winter protection process, retaining moisture in the canes that might otherwise be lost with cold, drying winds. Products like *Wilt-Pruf* and *Cloud Cover* are available in most parts of the country, easy to handle and apply. When the bushes go dormant and drop their leaves, trim up to suit your winterizing situation and thoroughly spray the canes before applying any covering materials (or cones or boxes or combinations of these materials). Apply liberally, get good coverage. This trick is particularly good for climbers and ramblers exposed to sun and wind on a fence. More canes are probably lost to drying out than to actual cold; this winter blanket can make a difference.

WHEN TO WINTERIZE... Thanksgiving weekend seems to be the favorite of most rosarians. Better to get the job done right rather than just a few hours ahead of the cold front. The whole idea is to insulate... to maintain constant temperature and avoid a freeze-thaw situation. Combinations of loose materials seem to do this best, held in place with fences, boughs, cones or what have you. Your roses will appreciate these "thermal blankets."

PRODUCT NOTES... no problem with shelf life of *Rubigan;* that $78 investment will carry over from season to season just don't let it freeze in the garage. Better yet, ask Santa Claus for some and split with another rosarian. For rosarians who still enjoy leaves on roses this month, continue *Rubigan* routine for powdery mildew right up to dormancy... *Danitol,* Ortho's new insecticide still has not made its debut. But it's worth waiting for. Compatible with the Ortho product line, safe and effective, *Danitol* promises to be the "one insecticide" answer to most rose garden pests. Keep an eye open for this in early '88... *Bravo* is an overlooked fungicide that many large users prefer. Combined with *Benlate* for powdery mildew protection, it can keep a rose garden free of blackspot at very low cost.

FRIENDLY GARDENS (a rose garden on someone else's property) have been discussed in these columns from time to time. Takes roses to the people and so on. Get friendly right away and line up some small rose garden sites for next season. Organize suppliers, workers (as chief you get to do most of the work) and schedules as a "Rose Is The National Flower" project. If you have been really friendly (and supportive) with your local rose supplier, he will probably be willing to order Grade 1 1/2 roses in bundles of 10 for you, saving a bundle in cost. He can late-order from his supplier and everyone comes out ahead. By the end of the first season, you won't be able to identify a 1 1/2 from a Grade 1 bush. Your rose public(s) will love you.

FRUSTRATION is still the best word to describe growing roses with too little sun. You may recall the Rambler's brief a year ago: roses steadily going downhill all season requiring replacement each year. This is a Friendly Garden, the property owner just HAS to have roses. The '87 season started with great promise: beds were reworked with coarse perlite and horse manure for better drainage, pH was perfect. Planting medium was loose enough to work without a shovel. Roses (100+ HTs and FLs plus 50 forced minis) were planted March 1. Everything was in bloom at Easter, good leaves and excellent blooms. Began liquid fertilizing schedule, second crop in May also good but not as prolific. Then, in spite of everything, the bushes got progressively weaker and weaker. The minis responded best with heavy shearing, but the big roses died back, refused to break and produced long, spindly stems. As of this writing, most of the big roses ought to be pulled up. Another replanting for next year. MORAL: Don't waste time (and money) with roses in marginal sun.

WATER TRIALS... The Rambler assists with two other friendly gardens at a retirement center; about 125 roses in each with ideal sun and soil conditions. Bushes, planting, feeding, spraying and pruning are nearly identical. But there's ONE difference; one bed is wider by about 2 feet, but spacing of the bushes is the same. Water is retained in the wide beds much more readily; there's more surface to accept water. The narrower beds drain faster and run off more. The roses with access to more water are half-again more bushy, produce at least one-third more roses and maintain a gorgeous display all summer. Water has to be the difference. Think this over as you plan new beds (expansions) for next season.

ODDS 'N ENDS... RESTORE organics each year in rose and flower beds. Applied from the top, trenched in or worked in, organics prevent tired soils. You may be able to put off complete reworking several additional years by annual natural boosts... MEIDILAND (say May-D-Land) all-terrain roses are going to be available in many parts of the U.S. next season. Described as a "whole new family of hybrid flowering shrubs," these roses are hardy, low maintenance and vigorous. *Meidomonac* is a member of the family, with white, scarlet and coral cousins. You'll love *Ferdy,* pink and thick and reminiscent of *The Fairy.* Conard-Pyle outlets will have them, or mail order through Wayside Gardens. Great for landscape; really handsome shrubs with roses all over. Watch for the promotional materials at your local nurseries, then buy right away because these are going to be POPULAR.

Having already ordered ten more roses than the garden will hold, there's no need to fool around with New Year's resolutions about limiting the garden. Just let it all hang out and get ready to enjoy a great rose year... made easier by these timely tips.

GIVE ROSES for the holidays — rose plants, of course. Gift certificates are great, but here's a way to give away and get yourself. Watch for blooming minis in your floral shop, six-inch mounds of decorative blooms that are as colorful as ANY holiday plant. The are low-light tolerant, long-lasting and will live indoors for a long time. 'Red Minimo' (developed by J&P) is just right for the season; the 'Minijet' and 'Sunblaze' series are also good. Take a pot of these blooming roses to your party hostess, helpful neighbor, whatever. Then offer to give a hand at planting outdoors when the time comes. You'll find there are FOUR plants in the six-inch pot, and each one will grow into a vigorous and attractive bush about the size of a basketball. Keep one for yourself as a "planting fee." Give away several colors and types to expand your collection; and don't be surprised if the lucky recipients think they are garden mums... your chance to show off your expertise.

HYBRID SHRUB ROSES belong on your "want" list, too. Use them for massed landscape color, hedges, ground covers, screens for difficult locations. The pros will have first call on these, but they will be available at retail, too. On their own roots, these flowering shrubs will cost less than budded plants. Check them out if you are planning some major landscape changes.

TIRED ROSE BUSHES? If the ground's not frozen, December is a good time to dig and discard the bushes that aren't quite making it. Or at least to check them out. The Rambler dug a bed of about 50 Sunsprite and Leprechaun last month to find out why the bushes didn't respond. The bushes had been in some eight years, in full flower about eight months of the growing season. But this year all of the stimulants and remedies could not make the leaves green and the sprays healthy. The reason was obvious after the first couple of bushes: galls, huge growths on roots, shanks and bud unions. The plants had settled over the years and mulch gradually covered up the evidence. And many of the ma-

jor roots had turned brown and died. Otherwise, the soil was in good shape, friable and organic, pH about 6.5. But if some major amendments HAD been needed, November would have been a good time to get the job done. After a good dressing with compost, turning with a fork and light raking, the bed was ready for a winter crop of pansies. Your climate might not support color until rose planting time, but the mellowing process (assisted by freezing and thawing) would have the reclaimed bed in good shape for spring planting. The same idea applies to individual plants; work over the planting area ahead of time.

DECEMBER is also a good time to apply agricultural lime (if needed), provided that the soil area is workable. Since lime is relatively insoluble, top application is not particularly effective. To adjust pH (raise) with lime, remember that the process is a REACTIVE one; the lime must be physically mixed in the soil to work. This is what happens: lime, in the presence of Hydrogen ions (the indicator for pH) reacts with those ions to form water. By reducing the ions the pH goes up. And it is a fairly slow process. If a rose bed needing lime can't be tilled or spaded or turned, stick a spading fork into the soil near the root areas and rock back and forth. Then sprinkle the lime into the holes. Lightly scratch the soil back. Then let water and nature do its thing. Don't worry about raising the soil above 7.0 (neutral) as the process only works when there is an excess of H ions. However, it's wasteful to overdo lime as it continues to convert hydrogen potential from acid-forming fertilizer until it is used up. A good rule of thumb in areas with potentially low pH is to add a pound of agricultural lime (calcium carbonate) or dolomite lime (magnesium carbonate and calcium carbonate) for every pound of nitrogen. Example: 5-10-5 ammonium sulfate, 50-pound bag, contains 2.5 pounds of nitrogen. Use 2.5 pounds of lime for the same area.

BEFORE ADJUSTING PH, get a reliable soil test. Take soil from the areas where the roots are. Get a recommendation from the tester on how to reach and maintain a pH of 6.5 or thereabouts. Unless you have more confidence than the Rambler, don't rely OR the probe testers which measure conductivity. There are too many variables to throw off the reading (and throw off the soil if you begin to adjust). Several litmus paper kits are available, easy to use and cheap. Many rosarians use the *PlantCheck System*, quite reliable and yet simple. The pH of the soil is very important to good plant growth; pay some attention and you'll enjoy more roses.

ODDS 'N ENDS... BIG PLANTER POTS would look good under your Christmas tree, and even better full of miniatures or sweetheart roses next spring. Rose growing in pots is so controllable that you'll wonder why you didn't think of it sooner... particularly with inexpensive drip watering systems available. Install a system, add a timer, and you can take off on vacation without worry (well, almost)... BUY a good rain gauge for a favorite gardener; don't guess at how much water that thundershower left behind. Your plants will know, but you won't... LET THEM GROW is good advice for floribundas. By nature, FL's want to put out many lighter canes, which in turn produce leaves which in turn produce blooms. Except when the rosarian cuts them down. Try a LIGHT hand with pruners on FL's this spring; just trim them up a bit (assuming winter left some wood to work with). When the bushes get as big and as full as you like, trim lightly, just like a haircut. ..THE RAMBLER hopes you enjoy some rosy surprises over the holidays with a warm fire to remind you of spring.

If experience is the name we give to our mistakes, the Rambler has experience(s) to share. See if you can avoid some of the Rambler's pratfalls in '88...

OVERFED MINIATURES turn yellow, drop leaves and then throw vegetative centers as a last insult. It's SO easy to be careless in a miniature feeding program. An extra tablespoon per gallon of the stuff that "produces dark green foliage and abundant bloom" may have just the opposite effect. Follow the dilution instructions for minis and then cut it some more. Better too little than too much. And consider the fact that volume as well as concentration affects these smaller roses.

TOO LITTLE TOO LATE with mulch cover means weeds, grasses and all sorts of undesirables in the rose beds. Then comes the tedious task of pulling, spraying and sweating. It all can be avoided with a THICK mulch; weeds just can't get a foothold. Even works with nutgrass. Covering causes new nut growth nearer the soil surface, making it easier to dig and pull. The Rambler promises no less than three or four inches of mulch on all rose beds from pruning time on.

SPRAY BURN continues to be a periodic problem with *Orthene* on miniatures. And it seems to make no difference using 75% Soluble Powder or the 6% EC form. Application at recommended concentration for thrips on big roses is very effective and safe, but not on minis (at least most of the time). Misting the tops of minis with half-strength *Orthene* seems to work better, but this is sometimes hard to do in a mixed garden. Another observation: *Mavrik Aquaflow* handles thrips and beetles with NO sign of leaf or bloom damage, minis or large roses.

STRETCHING the fungicide spray program just does not work. The grower feels comfortable and complacent looking at the clean foliage, but suddenly the spores catch up with a vengeance. Remember that it takes about two weeks for infection to show visible leaf damage. If a preventative spray program had been followed on a seven to ten day basis, the whole problem could have been avoided. Also, if an outbreak occurs, increase the frequency of the spray program, not the concentration. It's coverage that counts.

DENSE MINIATURES planted next to a brick wall (south exposure) are sure to get spider mites no matter what the grower does. It happened to *Red Flush* this season (one of the Rambler's landscape favorites), and the battle lasted all summer. Water, *Vendex*, *Mavrik* and even *Avid* brought only temporary relief. (Not all at the same time, of course). Mites love hot, protected breeding grounds. Solution: spread out and open up for better spray coverage (away from the wall). Also noticed for the first time: spider mites on the seven-foot level of *Color Magic* and *Touch of Class*. No signs of mites on the lower leaves or bushes around this planting. Will keep a sharper eye on the upper leaves this season.

ROOT INTERFERENCE cannot be ignored, nor can a grower feed the problem away. When tree and shrub roots invade a rose bed, more food just means more roots, and the roses won't get their fair share. Extra food postpones the inevitable (barrier systems, moving the bed or cutting the trees) but won't handle the problem. Foliar feeding helps also, but rose growth is still retarded by tree roots sucking up most of the available moisture. Face it; trees and roses don't mix well.

NOSTALGIA AND SYMPATHY have no place in the rose garden. If a bush doesn't put out, pull out. Poor producers take as much (or more) time to feed, spray and coax into bloom as vigorous roses. If there's no clear diagnosis and all treatments have failed, get rid of it. You'll enjoy the really good roses that much more, and there's always next year for an old favorite.

FIGHT the temptation to squeeze an extra bush into the bed. What seems like enough space in early spring will be overgrown like a jungle in July. Established plants overcome newcomers in the bed, depriving them of light, water and food. Competition is terrific. Give each bush a fair shake. It's one of the reasons that all new plantings do better. If you MUST have a new bush in a tight, established bed, try potting first and forcing the root system along so that it can compete. By the time the potted rose is ready, the hole may have closed up... just as well. But at least the newcomer will have a better chance.

WATER PARTED ROSES every day during hot weather or suffer devastating results. All it takes is a hot, dry weekend without water for roses in two to three gallon pots to go into deep shock and drop their leaves. The larger the container, the longer the interval. If potted roses have to be carried over for later planting, consider a larger container in the first place. Most nursery pots were not intended to support roses indefinitely.

BUT THERE'S GOOD NEWS ALSO. Alfalfa pellets, alfalfa tea and fish meal are still doing the job for the Rambler and for many, many rosarians around the country. Have never observed or heard of adverse results with these easy-to-use organics. Will be giving you more specific 'how-to' advice in the months to come, as well as some alternatives if you can't find fish meal or whatever in your area. Also, the Rambler is absolutely sold on the effectiveness of *Rubigan* on powdery mildew. Buy and share a pint with a rose friend; applied cost per gallon is only about 35 cents.

MORE GOOD NEWS — the '88 rose season is just around the corner. Enjoy it.

If you think you're too old for growing pains, try a few more roses in '88. But to help you break dormancy gradually, here are a few tips to make this the best rose year ever…

NEED A ROSE BED FAST? No problem. Although it's better to prepare rose beds well in advance and allow them to mellow and settle, a fast rose bed rich in organics is easy to build in two weeks or less. The trick is to build up the rose planting area; don't worry too much about what's below. Built-up beds are a good idea anyway. Clear away the area to be planted, and bring in some light soil first — a couple of inches or so. No need to buy the expensive 'garden mix;' what you're going to make is better than anything that comes off a truck. Till this soil in well with the existing soil; then add organic matter and sand (something gritty) so that the final mix by volume is about one third soil, one-third sand, and one-third organic material. Mix well with a roto-tiller or a fork. Then add (for about a 100-square-foot bed) 50 pounds of alfalfa meal or pellets, 25 pounds of gypsum, 10 pounds of superphosphate (0-20-0), and a couple of inches of horse manure to get the whole process going. Till again, water down to settle. In a day or two, mix again, and water. After about the second weekend, you're ready to plant. No problem with either bare-root or potted roses. Natural ingredients blend and work for the rosarian who is in a hurry… but still last a long, long time.

ADDITIVES FOR THE NEW BED… If manure is in short supply, substitute (or supplement) with fish meal. Sheep, cow or chicken manure can be substituted for horse manure; just keep in mind the relative nitrogen availability. The manures are the activators in the process, feeding the microorganisms associated with the organic materials. Horse stall combinations of manure, wood shavings and alfalfa hay are just right. The lab man in the white coat couldn't come up with a better growing medium for microorganisms. Worried that manures will be too hot? No cause for alarm. Mixed in the soil and reasonably moist, these warm soil processes just FORCE growth of feeder roots. Last summer the Rambler mixed light bank sand and horse manure, DIRECT from stalls, half and half. Watered bed once, turned lightly, planted container roses one week later… all in mid-July.

The heat from the mix came right through gloves. With plenty of water, the new bushes took right off, didn't drop a leaf and produced a bumper crop of blooms in September. Lesson: manures don't have to be composted if mixed in the soil.

GET ON SCHEDULE… a spray schedule, the day roses are pruned. Fungus control is a matter of prevention. Start a program IMMEDIATELY after pruning, no matter where you live. Drench the canes and bud union (if exposed) right away. Spores live over on green materials, not dead tissue. Some areas like oil-sulfur "clean-up" sprays, but good, safe practice recommends a broad spectrum insecticide combined with your favorite fungicide *(Funginex, Benlate, Phaltan, Maneb)*. Use at label strength and add a little extra spreader-sticker to encourage penetration into the cracks and crevices of the older canes and bud union. The object is to control over-wintering spores BEFORE temperature and humidity are right for growth of these organisms. Spray climbers and shrub roses particularly well; an infected host plant can spread spores like wildfire when conditions are right. In about two weeks, use the insecticide/fungicide combination again. Then follow regular fungicide program (week to 10 days) throughout the growing season, adding insecticide ONLY when really necessary. A clean start goes a long way toward a clean garden all season long.

DON'T HURRY SPRINGTIME… For many readers that's a long way off, but there are many temptations to uncover roses too soon. More bushes are probably lost to "springtime winterkill" than sub-zero temperatures in January. Let nature proceed at her own pace. Let whatever winter protection you use stay on a little longer than may seem necessary. Pruning and probing give bushes the signal that it is time to grow. In the spring, roses bloom when it's time to bloom; early uncovering seldom speeds up the process. You'll be doing yourself and your roses a favor with a little extra springtime patience.

LEARN FROM YOUR ROSES. Take a good look at how and WHY your roses survived a tough winter. Pay particular attention to the amount of good wood left on some plants and a total loss on others. Was the protection a little better in some cases? Less wind, more moisture, insulation able to breathe, more gradual dormancy… all could be factors in survival. You can learn a great deal for future reference if you learn to observe. And then put this new understanding to work.

ODDS N' ENDS… You deserve a new pruning saw after a long winter. Best one out is a folding job that's about five inches long, narrow blade, extra fine teeth that cut clean and close. The Harlane Company (advertisers in these pages) sells them for just $10 each… the best thing since the *Felco* pruner… speaking of *Felco,* these pruning shears just have to be the best anywhere. Available in various models: right-handed, left-handed, rotating handle, and two-handed shears. Repair parts always available; a good pair should last a lifetime (if your pruning partner doesn't make off with them). Harlane and Kimbrew-Walter have them mail order, as do many of the nursery folks. One of the best investments you'll ever make… QUESTION: How do you explain the success of the brown-thumb guy down the block who buys a package rose, sticks it in the middle of the lawn, systematically ignores it… but the rose grows and blooms ahead of your pampered beauties? Guess that proves that roses can't read… or something.

Rosarians who itch for success should start scratching... in the garden. It's the first warm day that brings on this rash of activity... how about controlling yours with just a little patience (can't be bought anywhere) and a couple of these guaranteed-to-grow rose ideas that aren't much work.

A DOSE OF SALTS is a good spring tonic, Epsom salts, that is. Magnesium sulfate seems to make the other chemical/soil processes work better, producing greener leaves, more breaks and an overall healthier rosebush. Use about an ounce per established bush at pruning time and again after the second bloom. Broadcast and water in; Epsom salts are instantly soluble. Buy at the drug store or the feed store; you'll be impressed with the results.

THINK SMALL when pruning miniature roses. And remember they're on their own *roots*. New, low breaks are going to produce the best blooms. For most varieties, cut back all canes and growth to about 6-8 inches, depending on the growth habit and vigor of the plant. In some climates this growth reduction comes with the territory, and that's not all bad. Cut out the really old, woody canes, open up the center and shape up the bush. Some growers even take the easy way out, using hedge shears or equivalent. This is essentially the method that commercial propagators use to force bushing and new growth. However, the serious hobbyist will get down on hands and knees and selectively groom and prune to the best eyes on the healthiest canes. But if you like your minis BIG, trim lightly and don't worry. Minis will grow anyway.

CLIMBERS are another problem. It takes more space and time than allowed here to cover all of the variations for all of the types and all the climates. However, there's one thing that ALL climbers have in common: APICAL DOMINANCE. That's a big-sounding phrase that means roses want to bloom on the top of a bloom lateral. The bud on the TOP is going to bloom first; dormant buds lower on the bloom lateral may force out and bloom, and they may not. That's the reason that *CL Queen Elizabeth* may throw canes 12 feet long and have one lone bloom on the end UNLESS the cane is trained laterally along a fence or other support so that dormant buds are on top of the cane. Sun-shine will force out the dormant bud at the leaf axil (where the leaf joins the cane), producing a bloom lateral that reaches for the sun. Repeat blooming climbers can have spent blooms cut from these laterals in the same way as hybrid teas, provided you can get to them. The practice multiplies bloom throughout the season. Anyway, the whole idea is to stretch out climbing canes to produce more bloom laterals that produce more roses.

MINIATURES WOODY?? Dig and divide just like a chrysanthemum. It sounds radical, but it really isn't. Many vigorous miniatures thrive on dividing every three years or so, depending on the climate, of course. The centers of many minis get very woody after a few seasons, and production drops off (since blooms are on newer growth). The dig-and-divide routine is very simple; just before the plants break dormancy, dig carefully with a fork and shake the soil off the *roots*. With a small pruning saw or shears, divide the bush into two or three pieces of *roots* and younger canes. Trim out and discard the woody stuff. Trim tops to best eyes. Most minis will divide naturally, much like the mums referenced above. Replant immediately just like a new plant. By the end of the new season, the "new" plant will be almost as large as the original mother plant and with more bloom.

HILL UP those new rosebushes if you are planting now, even if danger of frost is past. Cover until just the tips of the canes show; use soil, mulch or whatever insulating material you can find. The idea is to keep moisture in the canes until new *roots* develop to deliver moisture and nutrients to cells and canes. The delivery chain has to work for the plant to grow. Uncover gradually over a period of several weeks. This warm, moist micro-climate is a must for tree roses; their moisture delivery chain is even longer. Use a plastic tent secured around the head of a tree rose; supply the moisture with a large handful of wet sphagnum moss on the bud union. When growth is clearly started, usually in about two weeks, cut some small holes to reduce the temperature. Remove entirely in another week. It works even with very dried out stock.

ODD 'N ENDS... COLD STRESS hits roses in pots and planters first, mostly as a result of drying out. Dry soil and dry canes are candidates for winter kill, which ought to be called "dry kill." Keep the water going... WD 40 is a good treatment for pruning shears, dissolves the build-up on the blades with just a little encouragement. Crocus cloth (a very fine abrasive) works fine. A small pocket whetstone touches up blades quickly... GRAPE CLIPPERS prune smaller miniatures very well. Corona makes a good model with long, tapered blades. They are used to reach in and cut grape stems. *Felco #7* is a good all-around pruner for miniatures; cuts even woody canes and has good leverage for use by the ladies. The thing that the Rambler likes about *Felco* is the replaceable blade, available for all sizes. *Felco costs* a little more, but it's world class... A HANDFUL OF BONE MEAL or superphosphate at the bottom of the rose planting hole Gust under the cone) works better than scattering through the planting mix. Keeps phosphate available to the bush longer, located just where the *roots* can reach it. Called "banding," it's just the old practice of bone meal under the tulip bulbs.

Since now's the time to do it right rather than taking time later to do it over, here are some time and effort savers for springtime…

SPRING TONIC FOR ROSES… feed the processes that make nutrients available. Organics still work better and more consistently than the "scientific" products that come in jugs and bags. The chemist's contribution of carefully balanced soluble in organics is here to stay, too, but even these laboratory miracles work best in conjunction with good organic practices. Manures and alfalfa build strong plants. Fish meal and blood meal (or cottonseed meal) encourage beautiful leaves that in turn support beautiful blooms. Compost (make your own) in the rose beds helps keep nature in balance. Humus is important because of its high buffer capacity which does not allow soil to become either acid or alkaline in spite of chemicals which might change the pH dramatically. Organic tonics like cow tea, alfalfa tea or fish emulsion work just like chicken soup for rosarians… they make the sick well and the well even better. Feeding the processes results in live soil, active organisms and healthy rosebushes.

WARM ROOTS, THEN FEED… Fertilizers applied to cold soils won't do much good until the root zone warms up. The canes, warmed by sunshine, may be waking up, but the roots are waiting for a clear signal that spring has arrived. To illustrate the point, take a look at new roses planted in black plastic pots and set out on warm reflective surfaces. In just a week or two, tiny new roots have spread throughout the pot, and the bush is off to a fast start. Roses in the ground start in the same way: when the soil warms up and the roots begin to work. For rosarians in a hurry, apply readily available fertilizers in solution (bypass some of the conversion process), soaking the root zone when the soil warms. That's a real tonic.

OFF THE SHELF, ON THE LEAVES… That's the best fungicide formula. Disease control is established through prevention; blackspot leaves cannot be restored; leaves and buds disfigured with mildew won't become sleek and productive again after spraying. The most common mistake is to wait until infection appears; by that time it's too late. It's an uphill battle for the rest of the season. Get on a 7-10 day schedule and stay with

it. Don't cheat… the fungus spores will catch you every time. *Funginex* (Triforine) is probably the most popular fungicide ever to reach the market; safe and effective… used on schedule. *Rubigan* is the answer for severe powdery mildew areas… applied BEFORE the damage is evident. Check out the testimonials for *Rubigan* in these pages over the last few months; then buy some, share with a rose friend and begin spraying. It's low cost insurance for a clean garden, even though the initial purchase seems expensive.

TRIFORINE AND RA-PID-GRO… Here's a tip for miniature growers in particular. For really outstanding foliage (plus blooms), a combination spray of *Triforine* and *Ra-Pid-Gro* seems to give results all out of proportion to the products used separately. Use the application rates recommended for each, do not add an insecticide. Used weekly during periods of high growth (and moderate daytime temperatures), the miniatures will respond beautifully. There's something about the combination that WORKS.

pH TESTING… Rosarians always seem to be looking for a cheap, reliable system to check soil pH. Whatman LabSales has testing strips that do the job. The 5.2 to 6.8 range strips most commonly needed by rosarians cost just $10 for 200 strips. Order from Whatman LabSales, P.O. Box 1329, Hillsboro, OR 97124. Or call 1-800-942-8626. Ask for catalog no. 2628R990. Each paper strip has its own printed color comparison chart. Other pH range strips are available also.

TO USE INDICATOR STRIPS… take a soil sample from 8 -10 inches deep in the root zone. Put about a half cup in a glass container and add enough water (same water as used on the roses) to cover the soil sample. Stir and allow to settle. Immerse the test strip up to the arrow. The central color strip is the guide. Match it to the numbered stripe as closely as possible; the number at the color match is the approximate pH of the sample. Whatman claims accuracies of 0.2 to 0.3 pH units. Good practice suggests tests in many parts of the garden as pH range is so variable.

ODDS 'N ENDS… GYPSUM (calcium sulfate) is incapable of neutralizing soil acidity even though the "sulfate" compound name suggests it. Gypsum works in the soil to improve permeability, leaches salts, supplies calcium. Gypsum will do lots of good things for roses but won't change pH... *MIKADO* is the '88 winner described as "dramatic." And it really is. Great for garden display. *AMBER QUEEN* is very long lasting and has good fragrance, too. It has been winning awards for a number of years but is a newcomer to U.S. growers. Very attractive displays... WHISKEY HALF-BARRELS will help rosarians brew up some potent miniatures and Floribundas. Try three or four minis in a barrel this season and get ready for masses of blooms. A mini tree with three low growing minis underneath is really striking. Almost any kind of rose with a spreading growth habit can find a good home in a barrel. Use a soil mix with some extra organic matter to hold the moisture, feed regularly with solubles. Be ready to enjoy lots of blooms... CALCINED CLAY (also known as kitty litter or floor sweep) is a good soil additive to hold moisture. Has thousands of tiny reservoirs for air and water. Lasts forever, too... LET NATURE work for you in '88.

Rosarians who know all the answers haven't asked all the questions, so here are some questions WITH answers to help get you going…

WHAT IF there's some good, fairly fresh horse manure available; should it be spread right away, composted for a year or so, or turned down?? The best answer is to keep the manure source a secret (so that you can have it all for yourself). Then get it out on the rose beds, in the rose beds, mixed in the compost pile, and used wherever organic matter and bacterial action are needed. There is NO need to compost horse manure/shavings/alfalfa hay/straw mixtures before using on roses. Just stir in the soil and use plenty of water. The results will be amazing. Much of the beneficial activity is lost by waiting for the well-rotted stage. Let the action rejuvenate the rose beds rather than be leached away. The Rambler's roses think it's a special treat to get an inch or two of horse manure mulch just a week out of the horse. Yours will, too. Just use a little rose sense.

INSECTICIDE every week a poor practice? For most rosarians, yes. There's no need for this overkill, and it's easy to make a mistake. Combine an insecticide with a fungicide when there is an observable insect problem. If it's not there, don't kill it. Fungus spores are ALWAYS THERE; control them. Excessive insecticide brings on spider mites by killing off the beneficial insects. The mites also built up a resistance to repeated applications of the same material. Suggestion for springtime: get along without insecticides as long as possible, then use SPECIFIC materials for SPECIFIC problems. Most gardens can go a whole season with just two or three general insecticide applications by letting nature work properly.

WHAT ABOUT THRIPS? These tiny, tan insects bruise rose petals by a rasping action to suck juices. In severe infestations, buds can't open because the damage is so great. It's easy to spot thrips: check a light-colored, fragrant bloom for bruised edges. Then unfurl some petals and you'll see tiny tan specks moving around. Control is fairly easy by misting bud and bloom areas with *Orthene,* but it must be done fairly often, probably two or three times a week during peak bloom. Don't spray the leaves and the whole bush, just the buds and blooms. Many rosarians have a small half-gallon sprayer used just for *Orthene* misting of the bloom areas. For a small garden, a *Windex* pump sprayer will do. But make a fresh mixture each time and get into the blooms. Contact is important. *Orthene* 75 % *SP* works best in the Rambler's experience, but the 9.4% *EC* is also good. *Mavrik* also does a good job. Thrips tend to come and go in the springtime; be patient and they will head off for some fragrant field grasses and blooms (if you're lucky).

FERTILIZER SOLUBILITY IMPORTANT? Just watch rose response to fertilizers (especially those with trace elements) in solution and the question is answered. In just a few days, leaves can change color, new growth appears and blooms take on a richer look. Why? The solutions got to the root zone immediately and were picked up by the root system. But ALSO note that the effect doesn't last very long. The food flushes right out in well drained rose beds. That's the reason for ALSO using granular fertilizers that release more slowly, timed-release fertilizers, and organic sources (like blood meal and fish meal) in combination. Look for a total application of slow and fast foods. Find a good combination that fits your rose expense and energy level. What does the Rambler use? A granular fertilizer with trace elements, fish meal, alfalfa pellets, horse manure mulch and occasional "instant" foods in solution, usually just before rose shows. Need a little more iron -add *Sequestrene*. More breaks and leaves — add Epsom salts. And always use LOTS of water. Roses can't help but grow.

WATER WAND OR WATER BREAKER? A water wand directs a strong stream of water (usually in a cone or fan shape) underneath rose leaves to wash off spider mites. Fine droplets at high pressure (something like the dishwasher) really clean them off. Regular washing controls mites in many gardens, particularly if insecticides are used sparingly. Other benefits: cleans spray residue and pollution dropout, cools bushes and adds water. On the other hand, a water breaker (on a long handle) directs a smooth flow of water to basins, beds, individual plants, pots and planters. This special hand application is an extra touch for roses in beds; while the water is soaking in, the rosarian can get better acquainted with the bushes to know what they are doing, seeing things that can't be observed by just turning on the hose. Water basins formed by soil around rosebushes hold a gallon or two of water; the effect is all out of proportion to the effort. Roses really like this hand care. No rose garden is complete without a water wand and a water breaker.

ODDS 'N ENDS... *AVID*, best miticide ever, now available in 8-ounce containers and used at 1/4 teaspoon per gallon. Costs about $40 but worth it for severe spider mite problems... GROW LEAVES, then roses is still good advice. Trim sparingly to keep a good crop of leaves all the time. Particularly true for new bushes. Cut short stems (or don't cut any blooms at all) for the first bloom cycle or two... LIGHT SOIL MIXES grow better miniatures. Loose, friable soils with lots of organic matter are more receptive to the fine feeder roots that minis put out. Even a bucket-sized island of light mini-mix in a sea of tired, tight soil will please minis.

To succeed with roses, act on the advice that you give to others… and if you don't have any of your own, try some of these gems…

FRESH SOIL is advocated by a number of leading growers, but fresh really has very little to do with successful rose growing. What's needed is a "live" soil, full of organics, microorganisms, soil particles of various sizes, air and water. To keep a soil alive (even with roses growing in it), lay on the organics and a favorable balance somehow persists. Even in the worst case, rebuild after a few years by adding manures, compost, leaves and what-have-you; mix and turn and replant. Save yourself and the roses all this aggravation by adding humus to the top regularly.

FISH MEAL is still the best all-around fertilizer, activator and conditioner for rosarians who want to enjoy roses, not just work at it. Locate a friendly feed store out in the country (widely used as a poultry feed), transport to the rose garden without pilling (fish smell in the trunk never leaves) and apply in cones around the bushes. Use a bulb digger and lift about three cones of soil 6 inches deep and 18 inches away from the shank of the bush. Pour in a total of 1 to 2 cups of fish meal, cover with soil and watch the rosebushes perk up. Another way is to broadcast meal on top of the mulch, scratch a little and pour on the water. Smells just a little but usually gone in three days or so. Worried about dogs? The Rambler has had more than his share of dogs in the rose beds (and on the rosebushes) with no appreciable problem. The Rambler's rose garden guard cat could care less.

HOW DO ROSE ROOTS BURN? It's simple: from too much fertilizer and not enough water. But why does it happen? Roots are made up of cells whose activity is supported by water, just like human skin or tissue. Burn occurs when water is removed or displaced from the cells. Most chemical fertilizers use ammonium sulfate or ammonium nitrate as nitrogen sources, synthesizing the same elements found in nature. These ammonium compounds are HYGROSCOPIC, that is, have the ability to take up water. If the ammonium compounds (fertilizers) in the soil are too concentrated, moisture is absorbed from the soil and even the roots, thereby destroying the moisture support system for the cells.

NATURE likes to keep things in balance. Concentrated solutions want to add water and will perform this trick through osmosis, pulling moisture through cell walls. The solution to the whole burning problem is to use appropriate fertilizer amounts and ALWAYS with plenty of water. That's the reason for the recommendation: water first, feed, water again. And, if in doubt, water again. Result: no burn.

LEAVES DROOP, ROSES WILT for the same reason — loss of water from the cells in excess of replacement. This is often seen in new rosebushes: lush leaves, hot days, and developing roots inadequate for the job of moving moisture up through the bush. Transpiration by the leaves exceeds supply. Like a hot rosarian, wet down the leaves, and make sure there's plenty of water in the intake zone.

WHY DEEP SOAK WITH WATER? Water disperses throughout the soil medium, attaching to each soil particle and partially filling the air spaces. This process needs to reach the roots; light watering is held tightly by the surface layers. To get food to the rose roots (it has to be in solution), water first and coat the soil particles. Food in solution (like liquid application) follows, dispersing through the soil. Follow up with MORE water, driving the solution to the root zone. In the process, air is pulled along to support the microorganisms. Simple, isn't it?

SERIOUS ROSE BUSINESS… skimming a rose publication recently, the Rambler picked up a phrase to act immediately if the rosarian experiences "giddiness, mental confusion or feelings of euphoria." The Rambler thought the writer had found a Queen of Show and was reacting typically. But it was really an admonition to be aware of the effects of toxic exposure… through inhalation, dermal absorption, or ingestion. Theme of the article: treat pesticides, fungicides and herbicides with respect. Handle carefully, wear protective clothing. Be aware of potential toxicity: READ THE LABEL. Anyone who has ever experienced a careless spill of an aromatic material like *Orthene* or *Cygon* on one unprotected arm and smelling it in a matter of minutes on the OTHER arm knows just how quickly the human body picks up these materials. Protect it.

ALFALFA TEA... a summer pickup. Steep 10 or 12 cups of alfalfa pellets in 30 gallons of water in a garbage can for about three days, stirring occasionally. Dip off the liquor and apply one gallon per established bush (after watering). About a half-gallon for a mini. Smells a little but worth it. For a smaller batch (and less smell) use 2 cups in a typical 10-quart sprinkling can. Pour off and then add more water; can usually get two or three refills on the same pellets. Great for all kinds of roses; it's an enzyme pickup that has to be seen to be believed.

ODDS 'N ENDS... BE PATIENT, the pH indicator strips from Whatman LabSales are in temporary short supply (see the description in the April Rambler column). These good suppliers hope to catch up with demand soon. Must be a lot of sick rose beds out there... KEEP A CALENDAR for the rose garden. Make a note every time the roses are fed (and what), detail the spray program. Record rainfall. You'll know a lot more about what's happening in your rose garden... BUY A LONGER WAND for the rose garden sprayer, preferably one with a swivel tip to keep the spray material away from the applicator. A 42-inch wand is about right; find one at the local pest control supply store. Most all the parts are interchangeable. While your at it, consider a higher quality control valve, the most likely thing to go wrong on a sprayer. Nothing much worse than spray material leaking down your gloves, leg and into your shoe. Get a GOOD rig.

When your work speaks for itself, don't interrupt... but you might want to explain how it happened. And that's what the Rambler will try to do this month...

THRIPS have been a real scourge this season in most parts of the country. Maybe there's a new roach-like strain that resists the best controls we can muster. But be assured that thrips CAN be controlled if we use materials presently available to us properly and often enough. For relatively thrip-free blooms, a twice a week schedule with *Orthene* 75% *SP* is going to be required. Spray for good coverage on the buds and blooms, starting as soon as sepals begin to come down. The avid exhibitor will probably hand spray every day or every other day. The extra effort is worth it to save those light colored, fragrant blooms. These buds took a lot of time and work to get to this stage; don't give up now.

SPIDER MITES have also rebounded (or bred and re-bred) in staggering numbers this year. Just when growers thought that *Vendex* had the mite situation in hand, they got out of hand. The Rambler still thinks that *Vendex* has a place in mite control, but rosarians should recognize its limitations. *Vendex* controls mites when populations are low, starting early in the season. Applied every 21 days, it has some ovacide properties that work rather well. But as a knock-down control for really heavy infestation, it lacks punch. *Avid* is the answer when mites get out of control. It cleans them up in a hurry and can be used weekly if necessary. A wiser course is *Avid* two weeks in a row, then *Vendex,* which is good for about three weeks. At that point the grower may decide on water-wanding for a while. Conclusion: for low populations, use water or *Vendex;* for high populations, use *Avid*.

AVID has several outstanding qualities. Used at just 1/4 teaspoon per gallon, it is relatively inexpensive (although 8 ounces cost $44). *Avid* leaves no residue, penetrates leaf tissue where a reservoir of active ingredient is formed, is easy on beneficial insects, is non-phytotoxic to roses at recommended rates and is safe in the environment. The Rambler has observed good action by *Avid* on thrips as well as safe combination with *Triforine* — an overall fungicide-insecticide shot. However, pay attention to this statement from the *Avid* Technical Bulletin:

"Test *Avid,* and compatibility with other products, in small areas before general application." The Rambler is usually not comfortable with "everything in one mixture" sprays, but *Triforine* and *Avid* seem to get along fine.

THE CASE FOR WATER on spider mites needs to be made as well. Frank and Gertrude Hirsh of Clearwater, Florida, offer a testimonial that has to be seen to be believed. They have one of the most outstanding gardens in the South (where mites spend the winter and the summer), are national-level exhibitors, produce thousands of show quality roses of all types consistently... and control mites ENTIRELY with water. And they have been doing this for 17 years. Frank and Gertrude relate their experience in the April, 1988, issue of *Tampa Talks Roses* newsletter edited by Willis Evans. At first they tried a water wand and faithfully hosed the bushes weekly while continuing to spray weekly with insecticide mixed with fungicide. The mites continued to thrive. Then they switched to water wanding every week and VERY LIMITED use of insecticides. When insecticides are used, they use a small pistol-grip sprayer and spray lightly just the buds, blooms and top few inches of new growth, as they reasoned that's the only part of the bush aphids, thrips and bud worms attack. Recommendation: Hose the bushes with a good water wand every week, the day before spraying with fungicides, and only spray lightly over the tops of the bushes with insecticides when insects are present. The Rambler hopes that readers attending the Tampa National Convention this fall get to visit the Hirshes and the garden; you'll love them both.

CUCUMBER BEETLES need *MAVRIK,* a flowable insecticide that really works. Most users report application ONLY in the bud and bloom areas with good control. The material is safe for roses and rosarians, leaves no residue, low concentration (scant 2 teaspoons per 5 gallons), and is available from serious garden suppliers.

WHAT'S BROWN AND ORGANIC AND GOOD ALL OVER? Can't let a month go by without recommending FISH EMULSION as the fertilizer-tonic-soil activator-remedy that's good for most everything that grows. A tablespoon per gallon of water really works wonders. Good for pots, hanging baskets, miniatures, big roses, small roses and sick roses. Visited the garden of a rosarian who consistently uses fish emulsion in a foliar application with great results. He enjoys good leaf color, lots of growth, plenty of bloom. He is able to avoid the bloom with his spray application method so there's no discoloration. Anyway, try some yourself. The Rambler wouldn't even THINK about starting a miniature or potting a rose (or anything else that blooms) without a fish emulsion solution.

ODDS 'N ENDS... SHRUB ROSES are attracting more attention all the time. The new Meidiland (say May-d-land) selection being introduced by Conard Pyle is certainly worth growing. Exhibitors may not favor these shrubs, but anyone who wants an attractive, maintenance-free shrub with lots of blooms will enjoy them. *Meidomonac* ('Bonica') is typical of these new roses, now available in a number of colors and growth habits... *MANALFA* is a new pelletized product combining manure and alfalfa, produced by Shattuck Farms in Oklahoma. Now only marketed regionally, you can expect to see this combination picked up in other parts of the country. Analysis is 1-1-1 with .4 % iron. Easy to handle, fairly cheap, a good conditioner as well as a food. Can be used in a soil mix, broadcast or scratched into the soil. Watch for more on this... *DRAMM* NOZZLES, the inexpensive do-it-yourself water system emitter, now comes as a two-piece unit: a nozzle base and a diffuser pin. It's more rugged and diffuses the water out in a circle, not up in the air. Really works.

When the glass is at ninety, a man is a fool
Who directs not his efforts to try to keep cool.

With this is mind, here are some cool rose ideas guaranteed to please roses and rosarians...

NEW MINIATURES get heat stroke, too, after emerging from shade-cloth propagation houses. Suffering from shipping stress or stand-by time at a nursery, new minis deserve some special care before setting out in a bed in full sun. Try a two-step approach to help minis adjust in mid-summer. First, re-pot in a larger container, using a light soil-less or near soil-less mix. This gives greater water-holding capacity and new medium for root expansion. Then place in a partially shaded area, gradually moving to full sunlight. The minis will hardly know they have been transplanted and will take right off. After a few weeks, carefully transfer to the rose bed. Result: no shock, no yellow leaves, no growth suspension. The Rambler likes to use a weak fish emulsion starter on a weekly basis while the minis are in pots, stretched to once every other week in the beds until they are competitive in size.

HANGING BASKET MINIS are fun, too. Summer is a good time to start a couple. Two or three small plants to a 10 or 12-inch basket will fill out to a beautiful display in no time at all. The Rambler likes *Peters Potting Mix,* a soil-less blend that is light and easy to use (fairly cheap, too). A little extra peat moss helps hold moisture, but this may not be a problem in some areas. Try varieties like *Green Ice, Spring Song, Orange Honey* or *Sweet Chariot.* A reminder, baskets need water every day or every other day in hot weather. When fine, hairy roots dry out, minis go into terminal shock. But baskets are worth the extra effort when properly displayed.

TRACE ELEMENTS are getting more attention these days from wise rosarians. Just a little does a lot of good. Dr. Herb Owen came up with an appropriate summary of the importance of trace nutrients with this observation: "Liebig, a German plant physiologist of the 1800's, formulated the Law of the Minimum, which states, 'The growth of plants is limited by the plant nutrient present in the smallest relative amount.' In other words, if boron is deficient, all the nitrogen in the world won't offset this deficiency. For healthy roses, one needs a sufficient amount of ALL the required elements or nutrients." Herb, a long-time friend and teacher, knows what he is talking about. You may want to try a pinch of micro-nutrients this season to see what happens. Several soluble formulations are available, or you may want to go the organic route with seaweed concoctions or fish emulsion. To really CONFIRM results, treat one bed, skip the next one while keeping all other feeding and watering routines the same. Most rosarians make a mistake by making a number of changes at the same time; they never know WHAT made the difference.

PLASTIC BAG ROOTING is a summertime activity for out of-the-sun rosarians that takes advantage of warmth and sunshine. Miniature cuttings are particularly easy to start; light wood of larger roses takes off as well. Every rosarian has all the equipment necessary: foam coffee cups, clear plastic newspaper bags, light potting mix, *RooTone,* plant ties, tree with low branches and rose favorites you would like to propagate. Here's the routine: take a cutting about 5 inches long with four leaflets and a spent bloom. Pinch out the bloom, pull off two lower leaflets and leave two upper leaflets, pinching to two small leaves each. Trim cutting on a diagonal at lowest leaf axil. Poke three or four holes in bottom of foam cup with pencil, fill cup with soil-less mix *(Peters,* maybe) that has been moistened. Make insertion hole in rooting medium with a pencil. Dip moist cutting stem in *RooTone* and insert in cup, firm with fingers. Two leaflet axils will be below surface, two small leaflets will be above medium level. Water well until excess drains from the bottom of cup. Carefully slip the cup into the plastic bag until it rests on the bottom. Twist the top of the bag, allowing room for the leaves and secure with a length of plant tie. Hang from a low tree branch... and just be patient for about three weeks.

SUNSHINE is the rooting key; the top leaflets produce food, new roots take up moisture... all in a warm, humid environment. Moisture condenses on the plastic and drips back to the pot. Meanwhile, the anxious rosarian gets to watch the rooting progress. The bag-in-the-tree method MUST have filtered sunlight for fungus control as well as growth. Don't open the bag unless there appears to be a lack of moisture. New leaflets will appear in two to three weeks; roots are apparent in about four. Gradually adapt the new rooted cutting to normal temperatures and humidity. Then it can be re-potted or planted in a bed with a little special care. So, if you see a rosarian with a tree full of plastic bags, ask for some of the crop. He'll be glad to share his 80% success rate.

ODDS 'N ENDS... Hand watering makes roses happy. Slowly fill soil basin at base of plant, get friendly (and familiar) with bush at the same time... Epsom salts (magnesium sulfate) three or four times a year helps keep leaves green, bushes growing, especially if bed drainage is good. An ounce or so per bush broadcast on the soil and watered in is easy and productive... FOLIAR FEEDING FANS like the combination of *Triforine* and *Ra-Pid-Gro Forti-5,* especially for minis. Just watch the temperature and concentration. It really works (micro-nutrients?).

Rose ideas that work are those you put to work... so get busy on some of these now that fall rose weather has finally arrived...

HAPPY ANNIVERSARY RAMBLER! September is the 18th anniversary for the Rambler, some 216 ramblings wiser and still willing to go out on the limb... because that's where the roses are. Hope that you are willing to try these suggestions from time to time; they're garden tested.

WHAT DOES HE KNOW? The Rambler at least knows enough not to drop an idea on you loyal readers without a thorough garden test, or you'll let me know in a hurry that it's no good. But there's the disclaimer, "You must have done it wrong." Obviously, there are regional and climactic differences, but most of the ideas set out here work in any rose garden.

THE RAMBLER GROWS ROSES in gardens as varied as the readership; a total of five different gardens in Houston, plus some smaller plantings here and there. One garden is built up about 18 inches, double row planting (125 bushes). It gets plenty of sun, good air circulation, super drainage... and has the biggest bushes. Another has full sun, concrete walkways, built up about 6 inches; it has a problem getting enough water, even though it has a *Dramm* system. The garden was designed for the enjoyment of a retirement community and has Floribundas, hybrid teas and miniatures, about 150 floriferous bushes in all. The Rambler's downfall is a "sponsored" garden, in heavy to medium shade, poor air circulation; and the owner wants to cut lots of good blooms. About 150 bushes are replaced each season. Weak light means weak leaves and even weaker bushes. Otherwise, growing conditions are ideal.

HOME GARDEN for the Rambler has 100 or so Floribundas; a collection of shrubs, climbers and roses in containers; about 150 hybrid teas and 350-plus miniatures of all sizes, shapes, and habits (this is MILLIE's specialty). Several of the rose areas don't get enough sun although everything grows pretty well. But there's an obvious difference in the growth and bloom of the front beds in good sun and the filtered-light roses in the back garden. Added up, there are about 1000 roses in the various gardens that require some care and spraying each week. One of these days the Rambler will

share some of the tricks on how to cover this many roses and still work at a PAYING job. Moral of the story: you have to grow roses to learn about roses.

FALL IS MILDEW TIME... get busy with the *Rubigan* treatment. Begin spraying BEFORE the first evidence of mildew spores; that means as soon as the nights begin to get a little cooler and the days are bright and warm. Good coverage with *Rubigan* at 2 teaspoons per 5 gallons every two weeks will do the job. It is also compatible with *Triforine*. Routine: every week with *Triforine*, every other week add *Rubigan*. Make sure that NEW growth gets good coverage.

CUCUMBER BEETLES also like full weather and fat blooms. Fight them with *Mavrik*, a flowable insecticide that's safe and easy to use. Spray the bloom and bud areas as necessary at 2 teaspoons per 5 gallons. *Mavrik* won't discolor blooms, is safe on the leaves and leaves no residue. Can be used AFTER beetles appear, and then two or three applications will be sufficient. Doubles as a thrips fighter as well.

AVID miticide is still the product of choice if hot weather and mites persist. Water-wash undersides of leaves first, then spray undersides with *Avid* at 1/4 teaspoon per gallon. Repeat again in five to seven days. Then most growers switch back to water-washing, but keep a good eye on lower leaves for early signs of new mite populations. Timing is most important. Begin control before mites get out of hand. Initial purchase is expensive, but cost per gallon applied is quite low, due to the very low application rate.

WHERE TO GET THESE GOOD THINGS? Greenhouse and nursery suppliers carry most of the products that rosarians use but sometimes won't sell retail or in small quantities. Try a combined purchase through your rose society and identify the feed store outlets that carry the good organic stuff (like fish meal). If this doesn't work, the Rambler suggests mail order through Kimbrew-Walter Roses, Route 2, Grand Saline, TX 75140. KW has a good products list, right prices and ships UPS promptly (they will even respond to a phone call: area 214-829-2968.) Other mail order sources are Brighton Byproducts (PA) and CASCO (GA).

MANY READERS ASK for sources of fish

meal, often found in feed stores with alfalfa pellets, specialty fertilizers and Epsom salts. But if you just CAN'T find a source, Southwest Fertilizer in Houston will ship fish meal in 50 lb. lots via UPS. Fish meal price varies but ordinarily is about $20 for 50 lbs. I suppose it depends on whether the fish are biting or netting or something. Anyway, Southwest will box it up and ship, adding the UPS charges. Their address is 5828 Bissonnet, Houston, TX 77081; or you can call (713)-666-1744; ask for Randy Martin, a very knowledgeable young man who knows how to take care of rosarians.

ODDS 'N ENDS... Use liquid fertilizers and stimulants now for faster results and no carryover into cold weather. You should be enjoying some of the best roses of the year right now... KEEP THE LEAVES, there isn't enough time to grow a new crop before frost. And how many roses have you seen on bushes without leaves? DRAMM NOZZLES are the Rambler's choice for rose hobbyist watering systems. Plan new beds or convert old beds with this system in mind. *Dramm Nozzles* are available from Kimbrew-Walter... And now it's time to get busy with the sprayer.

If experience is what you get when you were expecting something else, the Rambler has been getting more than his share of "learning experiences" lately. But sharing with you good readers makes it all worthwhile. Rambler pain, your gain.

CLEAN THE SPRAYER... clean, flush, purge or otherwise wash out spray solutions with wettable powders from your sprayer, even if the sprayer has no pressure at all. *Maneb* clings to tubing and sprayer parts like cholesterol to veins and then flakes off at the most critical times. Don't let the material stand in the tank or tubing. Flush and then flush again with the best means available. If your tubes DO get a buildup, flush with a weak vinegar solution, followed by an ammonia solution... both found in the kitchen cabinet.

SPRAYER TIPS don't like clearing with a pin or fine wire. The soft brass of most spray nozzles is easily damaged, resulting in a spray pattern you don't expect. Put an old toothbrush in your sprayer kit and brush away the plaque.

MINIATURES IN POTS under hanging baskets get a double dose of everything, including fertilizer. A good reason for them to get yellow leaves. Think about it: fertilizer in solution runs right through the basket, re-fertilizing the mini pots below. An obvious solution is to feed only the top and let the runoff take care of the bottom. Works with minis used as foreground plantings with hybrid teas, too. Let the runoff from HT feedings take care of the minis; even then the minis may get too much.

RUBIGAN **REMINDER...** Don't expect *Rubigan* to work a miracle on powdery mildew when treatment is started late. This material is systemic and works to prevent new infection. It kills and controls mildew spores as well but makes no claim as an absolute eradicant. Give *Rubigan* time to work. If infection is severe, use *Rubigan* in combination with *Triforine* one week, *Triforine* alone the following week. The every-other-week routine will soon clean up the most stubborn mildew. Even water can help. Wash off spores with water before they can wind-glide to green, dry leaves and set up new colonies. Many rosarians don't appreciate the fact that powdery mildew grows on DRY plant material, not on wet leaves. Blackspot must have a wet surface to multiply. Both like high humidity situations (when the dew point drops during transition from cool nights to warm days) but prefer different leaf environments.

MAKE YOUR OWN ROSE LAB... Have you ever wondered EXACTLY what happens, or makes something happen, or what WOULD happen with a certain rose treatment? It's easy to learn a good deal about rose response by growing some test roses in controlled conditions, as in pots or large containers. Whatever happens, the grower put it there. Trying some new soil combinations? Very easy. Which one drains best, which retains moisture better, which encourages better roots? Pale leaves? Is it nitrogen deficiency? Try some nitrogen sources... chemical, organic, soluble, timed-release. What made green leaves come back. What's the difference in nitrogen and iron deficiency? Does extra iron make the nitrogen source work better? Do Epsom salts (magnesium sulfate) make leaves green, encourage new growth and basal breaks? Watching roses in controlled conditions will make you a better observer under garden conditions. It's amazing how quickly rose problems can be solved once we learn how to identify them properly... and associate the correct solution. Get some pots, barrels, containers, or whatever, and start your own lab, the sooner the better.

FERTILIZE UNDER WINTER MULCH?? This practice was discussed in these columns last year and readers were asked to report good, bad or no opinion. To bring the new readers up to date: many growers feed under the mulch when putting roses to bed for the winter, figuring that soil processes go on all winter. The practice is to put down a layer of leaves, broadcast a cupful of pelletized fertilizer (13-13-13) per large bush, than add some more leaves. In the spring, the lower layer is broken down into a rich humus, sometimes threaded with white feeder roots (or maybe mycelium). Does the fertilizer encourage unwanted growth? Do bushes start faster (or too fast) in the spring? The consensus is that a light feeding over a layer of mulch in the fall DOES help break down the organic material and sets up the soil for better activity in the spring. The Rambler suspects that the organic matter feeding the soil actually makes the benefit happen. Organics make the soil more alive, more able to process the nutrients available when the soil warms up. The process is like composting in place to enrich the soil below. One precaution: don't disturb the lower decomposing layer any more than necessary in the event feeder roots have reached for the compost. Otherwise, the Rambler has had NO reports that bushes put on untimely new growth, either in the fall or in the spring. It seems that growth is a function of temperature more than availability of fertilizer. Most of the reporters say they plan to continue the practice. No one thought that winter fertilizer contributed to winter kill. You may want to give this practice a try yourself. So that you will REALLY know how it works, winter feed one bed, skip another in a similar situation. Compare results next spring.

ODDS 'N ENDS... Use leaves this fall to make compost, winter protect and generally complete nature's cycle. Tons of benefits in a few pounds of leaves. Leaves have been nature's insulation and restoration process since time began. Gardeners really haven't improved on the system. Why not go with it? BURY LATE FALL ROSE-BUSH ARRIVALS under a blanket of leaves (what else?) and soil. The roses will like it so much they may never want to come out. But tie a rope on the bushes anyway to help you find them when spring comes... NO LEAVES OF YOUR OWN? Some friends and neighbors will be glad to help you out. Happy raking!

We all admire the wisdom of those who come to us for advice, proving again that you good readers are the smartest rosarians around. Show off your expertise with some of these rosy gems over coffee this winter...

LET WINTER DO THE DIGGING... The freezing/thawing cycle can do much of the work in making a new rose bed. If the ground isn't frozen where you are, loosen just a little with a spading fork and pile on lots of leaves and other organic material. Shovel a little soil on top. As moisture freezes and expands, tissues break down in much the same way as decomposition in the summer. The winter action reduces and blends the organic matter and soil into the "loam" that most rosarians like. Nature has been building good soil this way for a long, long time.

NEED A GYPSUM FLUSH? Container-grown plants tend to turn pale near the end of the season but will respond to a good gypsum flush. Cold-climate rosarians won't see the difference until next spring, but the results will be dramatic. Salts tend to build up in containers, especially with clay soils and alkaline water. The clay particles tend to stick together, upsetting the balance of soil, air, and water. We say the soil is "tight." For this condition, gypsum opens up the pores and the good soil processes take over again. The effect is like pulling the cork out of the bottle. Gypsum works in clay rose beds, too. Doesn't disturb the pH and furnishes calcium as well. About 20 pounds per 100 square feet of rose bed or a handful per 5-gallon container is about right. Scale down or up depending on container size; application can be inexact. Water in well and let good things happen all winter.

CHAPSTICK FOR ROSES? Anti-dessicant sprays may not fit this description but WILL help in the winter protection process, retaining moisture in canes that might otherwise be lost with cold, drying winds. *Wilt-Pruf* and *Cloud Cover* are available in most parts of the country, easy to handle and apply. When bushes go dormant and drop their leaves, trim up to suit your winterizing situation and thoroughly spray the canes before applying any covering materials (or cones or boxes or combination of these materials). Remember that canes are round and the backside has to be covered

also. Apply liberally, get good coverage. The trick is particularly good for climbers and ramblers exposed to sun and wind on a fence. Rose canes are primarily lost through dehydration, not cold. This winter protection can make a difference.

pH ADJUSTMENT — A GOOD WINTER CHORE... Winter is a good time to apply agricultural lime (if needed) provided that the soil is workable. Top application is not particularly effective since lime is relatively insoluble. In adjusting pH (raise) with lime, remember that the process is a REACTIVE one. Lime mixed in the soil is going to work faster and better than when applied on top. Here's what happens: lime in the presence of hydrogen ions (the indicator for pH) reacts with those ions to form water. By reducing the hydrogen ions, the pH goes up. It's a fairly slow process, even when mixed in the soil. If a rose bed needing lime can't be tilled or spaded, stick a spading fork into the soil near the root areas and rock back and forth. Then sprinkle the lime into the holes. Lightly scratch the soil back. Then let water and chemistry do its thing. Don't worry about raising the soil above 7.0 (neutral) as the process only works when there is an excess of hydrogen ions. Lime continues to convert hydrogen potential from acid-producing fertilizer until used up.

STAY IN BALANCE... A good rule of thumb in areas with potentially low pH is to add a pound of agricultural lime (calcium carbonate) or dolomite lime (magnesium carbonate and calcium carbonate) for every pound of nitrogen. Example: 5-10-5 ammonium sulfate, 50-pound bag, contains 2.5 pounds of nitrogen. Use 2.5 pounds of lime for the same area. But BEFORE ADJUSTING pH, make a reliable soil test. Take soil from areas where the roots are. You'll want to determine how to reach and maintain a pH of 6.5 or thereabouts. The county agent does soil tests (generally with a very small charge) or you may want to do it yourself (see below). The pH of soil is very important to good plant growth; pay some attention and you'll enjoy more roses.

DO IT YOURSELF... Make your own soil test; it's easier than you think. Whatman LabSales has come up with a cheap, reliable method for checking soil pH with indicator strips that are easy to read. The 5.2 to 6.8 range strips most commonly needed by rosarians cost just $10.25 for 200 strips. Each paper strip has its own printed color comparison chart. Use once and discard.

TO USE INDICATOR STRIPS, take a soil sample for 8-10 inches deep in the root zone. Put about a half-cup in a glass container and add enough water (same water as used on the roses) to cover the soil sample. Stir and allow to settle. Immerse the test strip up to the arrow. The central color block is the indicator. Match it to the numbered stripe. The number at the color match stripe is the approximate pH of the sample. Whatman claims accuracy of 0.2 to 0.3 pH units. Since the test is so easy and so cheap, good practice suggests tests in many parts of the garden as pH range is so variable. Note the instruction to use the SAME WATER as used in the garden, not distilled. Using the same water duplicates action in the rose bed. Want some indicator strips? Order from Whatman LabSales, P.O. Box 1329, Hillsboro, OR 97124. Or call 1-800-942-8626. Ask for catalog No. 2628R990 (5.2 to 6.8 range). It's one of the best garden investments you'll every make.

The best way to grow good roses is to act on the advice we give to others... preferably with some enthusiasm. Here's a recap of the advice the Rambler offered in '88... hope you tried at least some of it...

RUBIGAN was the "in" product for powdery mildew in '88 and was highly successful for growers who started the program BEFORE mildew conditions were right. Much of the discussion centered on the cost (about $80 a pint), but at the recommended application rate (2 teaspoons per 5 gallons), the real cost per applied gallon ran about 35 cents... a cheap price for really clean foliage. Smart rosarians were careful to get extra good coverage on mildew-prone hosts like ramblers and old roses. Systemic in action, *Rubigan* was safe to use every 14 days and worked well in a weekly program alternating a *Rubigan/Trijorine* combination and *Triforine* alone.

THRIPS populations declined with more widespread use of *Orthene 75% SP*, a cost effective alternative to *Orthene EC* (better residual, too). Rosarians sprayed bud and bloom areas PLUS rose beds to break up the reproduction cycle. For the first time, many sprayed other thrips hosts (gladiolus, lilies, other fragrant flowers) as well as the planting beds. Dealers stocked (or ordered) the 75 % soluble powder formulation; *Orthene EC* sold by the Ortho home garden division, *Orthene 75%* marketed by Ortho's agricultural group. Good savings with the SP version.

MAVRIK AQUAFLOW proved to be the answer for cucumber beetles as reported by many growers. Used at 2 teaspoons per 5 gallons, *Mavrik* was effective for up to 14 days once the populations had been reduced. Exhibitors sprayed buds and blooms as well as the rose bed area in much the same manner as *Orthene*. Some used the spray bottle technique on developing buds for the week prior to a show for added protection, just like *Orthene*. Growers reported no residue and no apparent bloom damage. Another benefit: it's listed for thrips also.

AVID, the translaminar miticide has changed our thinking on mite control. Mites have built up resistance to previous controls; so far that hasn't happened with *Avid*. Most serious observers have used Avid for two applications, followed by *Vendex*, encouraging control BEFORE populations get out of hand. Expensive initially, *Avid* applied at 1/4 teaspoon per gallon results in a cheap, reliable control. Users report greater effectiveness when applied alone, a good practice for most spray materials. Makes sense to direct the spray to the undersides of the leaves also.

INDICATOR STRIPS for soil pH testing have caught on with rosarians. The Whatman Lab-Sales indicators are easy to use and read, cheap and consistent. Check out the details in the November '88 Rambler column. Many rosarians have been amazed at their soil pH after making the test. With appropriate amendments to reach an acceptable pH range, roses have begun to grow and bloom again. Even some of the old-pro rosarians have not been able to believe the difference pH makes. Here's what really happened: they didn't know what pH they had.

BENLATE 50% DF has been a more popular fungicide this year compared to the wettable powder form previously sold. Still with a familiar blue and white label, the DF (Dry Flowable) version comes in a box and goes into solution instantly, just a swirl or two. Rosarians remember how difficult it was to get the talc-like powder into the spray mix. The new DF has the same effectiveness (same price, too) but easier to use.

MICRO-NUTRIENTS have attracted more attention, applied as a supplement to a feeding program or included with the basic fertilizer. If there's a rosarian consensus, it seems to be that supplements in a controlled feeding program work best, although that approach is more work. The Rambler doesn't care as long as the micro-nutrients are consistently available.

ALFALFA TEA and/or ALFALFA PELLETS are definitely in vogue for most rosarians. Tea has been useful as the fast supplement to bring new growth and green to leaves; alfalfa pellets add a boost to the soil processes. Most alfalfa advocates use a cup or so of pellets per bush in the spring, some alfalfa tea a time or two during the summer and another cup of pellets about September 1. It's good, it's organic, it's cheap. It can be overdone. Just use some rose sense.

CONTROLLED RELEASE FERTILIZERS are now better understood and more widely used for convenience as well as part of a sound feeding program. The fertilizer makers have responded with more formulations and have added iron and trace elements. Formerly the province of the pro nurseryman, timed or controlled release fertilizers are now affordable and available to the hobbyist.

SOMETHING NEW... landscaping film impregnated with pre- and post-emergence herbicides for weed control in rose beds. Sounds too good to be true, but Phillips Petroleum is reported to have a film material ready to market soon. Water and air pass through the impregnated plastic readily. To install, just pull back the mulch, lay the film, and cover again. Good for three to four years in most garden situations. The plastic strips come 30 inches wide in 10-foot rolls. Retail cost about $5. Testers say it even works on nutgrass and oxalis. Has applications in many perennial and woody plant situations. How's THAT for a way to enjoy roses with less work?

Hope that you and yours enjoy a Happy, Rosy New Year.

If you're taking roses too seriously, now's the time to break the habit with some Rose Resolutions for '89... gathered here from the diaries of rosarians similarly afflicted. Roses are hardly any fun unless there are some rules to break, so try your willpower out on these...

THIS ROSARIAN RESOLUTELY RESOLVES TO:

• Order only ten more roses than the garden will hold.

• Save money by ordering three of everything.

• Dig up no more than 10% of lawn area per year for roses.

• Restrict reading of rose catalogs to one hour per week.

• Buy only two miracle rose cures for "testing."

• Tell Queen of the Show story only when asked.

• Let weatherman handle rainfall without help.

• Accept bugs as part of nature's balance.

• Allow limited cutting of roses for the house.

• Come in from garden for supper on time.

•Encourage rose growth without swearing.

• Wear clean shirt for Sunday rose garden work.

• Use some common rose sense.

RESOLUTIONS out of the way, the Rambler plans some additional rose adjustments in '89, hoping to get more and better blooms with less work. This may be wishful thinking, but here are some practices the Rambler feels confident will payoff...

PLANT FEWER, CARE BETTER. More isn't necessarily better when it comes to rosebushes. Concentrate on roses you can reasonably care for. Get rid of the marginal bushes and beds; set up a feeding, spraying and grooming program you know you can keep. Go for the best, not the most. You and your roses will be happier.

WATER MORE, and then water again. Water is absolutely essential for good roses and one of the easiest fundamentals to overlook. It's easy to spot a rose bed that has had all the water it can hold on a regular basis. Growth and bloom are spectacular compared to a similar planting with

less water. If beds/plantings are well drained, it's almost impossible to use too much. Rule of thumb: water until it runs out of the bed, then do it again at the first sign of dryness.

REWORK TIRED BEDS... don't put off what should be done this season. Most rose beds are depleted in five or six years; roses will continue to grow, but not the way they should. Top amendments may postpone the inevitable, but it is less work in the long run to rebuild when it's time. Dig existing bushes when dormant, bury or otherwise hold dormancy while reworking.

Till in ample additions of manure, compost, peat moss, leaves, perlite, sand or whatever to new bed condition. Recipes may vary; just be sure to add plenty of organics. Let the bed settle. If replanting previous bushes, don't prune until regular pruning time. Another word to the wise: don't mix old and new bushes. Keep old bushes in one area, new bushes in another.

FISH EMULSION should be included in every rose starter kit. It works better than any root stimulator the Rambler has ever tried. Make it a regular routine to water in new bushes with an ounce of fish emulsion per gallon of water. Repeat the application in two weeks. The roots and results are amazing.

TIMED-RELEASE FERTILIZERS can be a big assist when planting potted roses with well-developed root systems. The idea is to get new roots to reach well beyond the ball. In the bottom of the planting hole, put about an ounce of *Osmocote* or similar timed-release and mix a little. Cover with a few inches of fill mix. Place the intact root ball in the hole and add some fill mix. Add two more ounces of timed-release around the perimeter of this fill, keeping the pellets away from the roots. Backfill some more with fill soil to about three inches of bed level. Finish off the job with fill soil laced with another ounce of timed-release. Flood with lots of water, then hill up to protect canes. This ONLY works if potted rose has intact roots and rosarian uses lots of water. Then the results are great.

SPRAY TIMING is as important as the spray itself. For powdery mildew, add *Rubigan* to the *Funginex (Trijorene)* spray routine BEFORE infection appears. During mildew-prone conditions, this means when well-developed leaves appear in the spring and when evening temperatures begin to drop in the fall. Use *Funginex* one week, *Funginex/Rubigan* mix the following week, alternating this routine during mildew season. Don't forget the ramblers on the fence. For spider mites, use a water wand underneath the leaves weekly as soon as the leaves appear. Hold mite populations down. In the meantime, keep a close eye on the leaves. At the first sign of active mites, use *Avid,* two applications a week apart. Then go back to water. *Mandex* has a longer residual but lacks the knockdown power of *Avid.* Go for control as early in the game as possible. Mites are ALWAYS out there in garden warm spots; just keep the populations from exploding.

 AND A ROSY NEW YEAR to all of you.

Since you can't build a rose bed by turning it over in your mind, turn over a new leaf (and some soil) early this year with some of the Rambler's earthy suggestions. If some of this digging is a little too early for your rose climate, enjoy catalog reading just a little longer... but remember that the '89 rose season is almost here.

ROSES APPRECIATE a friendly, well-prepared rose bed and respond accordingly. What's a friendly bed? One that's loose and friable and full of organics to encourage roots to spread out and take up nutrients. This in turn supports vigorous growth. Nothing much happens on top if the foundation isn't right. It's just another way of saying, "don't plant a $10 rose in a $1 hole."

THE OLD RELIABLE FORMULA calls for about 1/3 soil, 1/3 sand, 1/3 organics of some kind. And Old Reliable works no matter where you live. Don't worry too much about the proportions, but if in doubt add some more organics. Organics should be at least partially broken down; let animal manures go through a composting heat if possible, but it's not essential. Compost, manures, ground bark, leaves and combinations of all these materials work to keep the bed friendly for roots and microorganisms. Many growers like sphagnum peat, the more fibrous the better. Others like brown peat moss. Just keep in mind that mixtures last longer. For a really long-lasting soil conditioner (so that soil, air and water can work), use coarse *Perlite* generously. The rose bed will stay alive for years to come.

GOURMET ROSE BED BUILDERS season their beds with fish meal, alfalfa meal (or pellets), some gypsum and some bone meal. For a 100-square foot rose bed, add 15 pounds of fish meal, 20 pounds of alfalfa, 20 pounds of gypsum, and 15 pounds of bone meal. Mix the whole thing up, let it settle a week or so, and it's ready for roses. Old Reliable works for built-up beds, beds in place, old bed and new beds.

TIRED SOIL is the Rambler's description of a problem many rosarians experience... a gradual decline in vigor and production that defies all of the fertilizers and elixirs the rosarian can apply. The roses were great when first planted in a new bed; even replacements and transplants did well... for the first four or five years, maybe less. The grower thought "weak bushes" and replaced more and more WITHOUT replacing the organic materials to keep the soil alive. These new bushes didn't fare much better than the old ones. The grower suspected that something was terribly wrong and invented all sorts of "scientific" explanations, ranging from toxic substances to nematodes. It's a shame that more time and effort had not been given to keeping the soil alive and working. The rose bed was tired.

SOIL DOES NOT WEAR OUT, but its life sources need to be rejuvenated from time to time. Rebuild and restore old beds to "like new" condition without starting all over. Just use organics and similar conditioners to get back to the 1/3-organics formula. Restoring a complete bed is best, but even a small area will help. Don't bother to haul out the tired soil, just dig in the organics, even if it amounts to little more than a couple of shovelfuls of manure per planting hole. The more complete the bed restoration the better... the Rambler believes that most rose beds deserve restoration every five years or so, especially if the grower has been on a fast track with lots of inorganic fertilizers. Try a restoration yourself this season.

THE FRAGRANT FORMULA is a favorite of the Rambler... the rose season isn't officially on until mixing up a batch. The Fragrant Formula is a descriptive term for artificial manure, guaranteed to grow grass on fence posts and roses in rocks. This is for the rosarian who doesn't have a farm friend (and a pickup truck) for the real stuff. FF is just as good (maybe better because it releases more nutrients) and can be produced on a city lot. It's a good soil amendment, top dressing, basic feed formula... especially in the spring. Enjoy all the benefits; here's the formula:

> 3 ample yards of partial compost or leaves
> 100 pounds of coarse organic stuff (bark)
> 100 pounds of cottonseed meal
> 50 pounds of bone meal
> 50 pounds of fish meal

A farm store will have all of the ingredients, except the leaves. If fish meal is not available, substitute a couple of sacks of manure and maybe add 20 pounds of blood meal or beef and bone. There are lots of variations that will accomplish the same thing.

THE DIGESTION PROCESS... Make a pile of the coarse materials in any area suitable for composting, maybe an old flower bed. Add the lighter ingredients a little at a time and turn with a fork. Mix well. Then moisten LIGHTLY and turn with a fork twice a week for two weeks. If the pile is working properly, a sharp ammonia odor will escape. A DIFFERENT (dead) odor will leak if the mix is too wet or if there is not enough coarse material. The FF is ready in about three weeks. Use about two garden shovelfuls per established bush for the first feeding in the spring. One shovelful can be repeated in the summer. If the soil is acid, skip the cottonseed meal and substitute compost. These organics in the spring will make other fertilizers work better, feeding the microorganisms that do all the work converting nutrients in the soil into forms that roses can use. With the Fragrant Formula you'll have live soil, healthy organisms and lots of roses. Use generously. It really works.

The first day of spring is one thing; the first spring day is another… but it may already be past time to spring into action with some of these guaranteed-to-please seasonal ideas…

DARE TO BE DIFFERENT… How about some round rose beds this year? There's still time to build one or two if you get right at it. Size depends on the types of roses to be used, but a bed six or seven feet in diameter can be very attractive. Don't make the circle TOO big or maintenance becomes a problem. For a deep bed, set some stepping stones in an inner circle and loosen up the planting. Roses thrive in a round bed with good light and circulation all around. All one variety can be very striking, but don't be afraid to try a calico effect PROVIDED that the growth habits of the varieties are similar. Spreading varieties blend best, another reason to have more floribundas in the garden.

SHAPES tend to soften the hard lines of fences, houses, garages. Come away from the fence with a series of round shapes instead of a straight bed. Equally attractive on the side of a house as well. The Rambler has often admired a layout in Houston that alternates a long rectangular bed with a round bed, then another rectangle and so on along the length of a fence. On a smaller scale, try a round bed with miniatures with a tree mini in the middle or a taller standard with a smaller-flowered floribunda. Guaranteed to stop any visitor in his tracks.

ARCHES AND ARBORS can be beautiful, too, for a rosarian with stamina and time to winter protect. It's work to cut those spent blooms, train the canes and spray out of reach. But worth it. Consider a combination of *Pele* (white) and *Don Juan* (deep velvety red). You'll wonder why the idea hadn't come before.

WHAT'S THE CLASS OF '89? The Rambler thinks that *Class Act* is the classiest in a long time for landscape use. Here's a white floribunda that's well-mannered, has attractive foliage, clean white blooms that hang on and a bush that never seems to look ungroomed. Imagine a combination of *Showbiz* and *Class Act*. For lots of color and landscape punch, plant a few *New Beginning,* an '89 ARS miniature winner by Harm Saville. This little rose will make believers of many rosarians

who thought that minis didn't belong in a REAL rose garden. *Debut,* the '89 ARS mini, is attractive also with blending color and form. These minis will be available as dormant, field-grown plants as well as pot-propagated. Backyard gardeners will find these roses fast-growing and nearly impossible to kill. Introduce a friend (and yourself) to some.

DON'T HURRY MOTHER NATURE, particularly in uncovering roses. It's a good idea to let nature proceed at her own pace; let whatever winter protection you use stay on a little longer than the first warm day suggests. Roses are killed in the springtime when the temperature suddenly drops. New growth and swelling canes can't handle low temperatures. Pruning and probing give the bush a signal that it's time to grow. In the springtime, roses bloom when it's time to bloom, and earlier uncovering and pruning seldom speeds up the process. You'll be doing yourself and your roses a favor with a little extra springtime patience.

RX FOR GALLS… Some doctoring urgency is bound to come up when pruning this spring. Many respected growers maintain that disinfecting trimmed crown galls with *Lysol* or *Clorox* retards reoccurrence, but an equal number disagree. Most growers have galls they don't even know about and have had for a long time. If the gall is on the shank or the bud union, sunshine seems to do as much good as anything. Just trim off the offending tissue and let sun and air get to it. Don't worry too much about the infection; nature and a well-drained soil are probably the best remedies. If it's too bad, dig it out and try something new.

TO PINCH OR NOT TO PINCH? That's a tough question for rosarians anxious to see a bloom of a new variety. And a painful decision when new basals shoot up. But first things first. Grow bushes with leaves, then add roses. Keep new rosebushes vegetative until they are well established. Pinch out the buds (just like disbudding) or go down to the first good leaflets. Encourage bud eyes in the middle of the cane; that's where the biggest and best buds are. Pinch the tips so that the cane and leaf structures can develop. Bud eyes on roses are apically dominant, that is, the top bud wants to break. But let the strength go to lower, stronger buds. New basals should not be allowed to flower (well, maybe just once in a while). Depending on the vigor of a variety, when the basal hits 18 inches or so or begins to form a bloom bud, pinch back to a five-leaflet or a good blunt bud eye. The top eye will tend to be pointed, the husky ones are blunt.

ODDS 'N ENDS... Back in BC (Before Chemicals), good gardeners always had a barrel or two of liquid compost brewing behind the garage or fence. Some called it cow tea, some called it smelly. But it called plants out of the doldrums like no other elixir. Fish emulsion is a fast fix now, or brew up some alfalfa tea. When the soil warms up, pour on a half-bucket of mix and stand back... FOR ESTABLISHED BUSHES, add some soluble fertilizer to the tea and use when all danger of frost is past (whenever that is). Food in an available form brings a fast reaction; be prepared for results... DON'T FORGET THE SALTS... the Epsom salts, that is. Two ounces per big bush in the spring brings up the magnesium level quickly with new growth just behind. HAPPY SPRING!!

A lot of rose growing advice is spoiled by someone who knows what he is talking about… the Rambler will leave which is which to you good readers. Anyway, here are some surefire suggestions for your decision…

HILL UP THOSE NEW ROSES until the roots have a chance to catch up with the tops. Hilling up adds frost protection, too, but the primary purpose is to keep canes from drying out. The Rambler ALWAYS hills up a new bush, potted or bare-root. New canes have stored food and moisture that pushes out into new growth and leaves. Meanwhile, the roots are called on to replace that substance the ONLY way it can be replaced. New roots have to form in a hurry to keep up. To reduce the load on the delivery system, conserve the moisture in the canes. Use mulch, soil, leaves or combinations of organic materials to hill up eight inches or so. Don't scoop it up from the beds. Gradually uncover in two or three weeks, leaving material in place in the beds as a summer mulch. Use some care when uncovering; it's easy to break off new basals and low breaks. A slow stream of water from the hose now and then displaces the hill… and the rose likes the extra water, too.

A FISH EMULSION SOLUTION is the best rose starter the Rambler knows. Think of fish emulsion being to soil as lighter fluid is to charcoal-it gets everything going. An ounce or two of fish emulsion per gallon of water applied generously to just planted roses gets the soil organisms working and supplies water in a safe, non-burning way. This can't be said for all of the root stimulators. About the time the hilled-up mulch has been gently washed away, apply fish emulsion in solution again. Roses treated with it withstand stress, produce better new growth and consistently stay ahead of roses not similarly treated. Miniature roses love it too; just use about half as much.

SPRAY LEAVES BEFORE THEY COME OUT… this may sound like a tricky application, but it works. Disease spores have overwintered on green cane tissue, just waiting to multiply like wildfire when moisture and temperature conditions are right. Control the spores on the canes, thereby protecting the leaves. The same approach is useful for control of insects, unseen by the rosarian in the cracks and crevices of older canes. Start a preventative program SOONEST. Use a combination of *Funginex (Trijorine)* and *Orthene* for example, thoroughly wetting the canes and emerging buds. Use some spray on the rose bed as well. And then keep up a weekly program with your choice of fungicide, adding insecticide ONLY when really necessary. *Funginex* is the choice of most rosarians, although *Benlate* and *Maneb* are widely used as well. And don't forget about powdery mildew… it won't forget your garden. Add *Rubigan* to the *Funginex* mixture every other week throughout the mildew season. It is a great CONTROL material and must be used BEFORE mildew infection gets started. *Rubigan* is safe and effective at a ratio of two teaspoons per five gallons of spray mixture. Expensive initially (about $75 a pint), the applied-to-the-leaves cost is just 35¢ a gallon. Buy some and split with a rosarian friend or two. A pint should last two gardens two years.

THERE WILL BE MUCH ADO ABOUT MITES when the weather gets hot, but the rosarian doesn't have to get hot also. Spider mites CAN be controlled, even under the most difficult conditions. Choose your weapons: water wash the undersides of the leaves (it really DOES work); or start early with *Vendex* every 28 days; or use *Plictran* at one teaspoon per gallon every 10 days or so; or move up to the miticide of the *90's… Avid*. This relatively new miticide has everything going for it-quick kill, safety for leaves, no resistance buildup, systemic and can be used every 10 days (even in greenhouse applications). It's also claimed to be TRANSLAMINAR, i.e. able to penetrate the top of the leaf and provide control on the bottom of the leaf (where the mites are). Here's the Rambler's routine: Water wash weekly early in the season. Then when it gets hot or at the FIRST SIGN of mites, spray undersides of leaves with *Avid,* two applications with seven-day interval. Then go back to water or *Vendex*… If new outbreak of mites occurs, switch to *Plictran* but this is unlikely. Just don't use *Avid* every time as this increases the odds for resistance buildup. Use *Avid* BY ITSELF at 1/4 teaspoon per gallon of water. Buffer water first with one tablespoon of white vinegar per gallon. And don't forget to spray mite host plants as well: violets, pansies, monkey grass, etc. There's no need to be mite-defoliated this season with *Avid* around. Cost is about $42 for eight ounces, but that goes a long way at 1/4 teaspoon per gallon.

ROOTS NEED OXYGEN, and your rose roots may be starving if you have been stomping around in the beds this spring. Friable soil admits air and water-roots need both. Keep soils loose with organic materials; use a four-time fork to loosen soil and admit air around the perimeter of a bush. Organics drop in to build a honeycomb effect. "Uncle Charlie" Dawson, greenhouse rose professional and long-time contributor to this magazine even erected a sign in his outside rose garden: "Enjoy the roses but keep your big feet out of the beds." For servicing access, use stepping stones, decking or make the planting narrow enough for access in the first place. The whole soil process works better with good movement/drainage of air and water.

IF IT'S WORKING, DON'T QUIT. Rosarians are drenched with advice like a summer shower, which then goes away. It's the good, steady rains (and common sense practices) that grow roses. Consider the overall season, and if your roses are doing all right, stay with it. Roses grow more than one way and in spite of rosarians. Compare your results with others, and if you need some improvements, make them gradually. You and your roses will enjoy the season more.

The best thing about spring is that it always comes when it's most needed. Out in the rose garden, all kinds of good things are happening right now. During this warm good fortune, it's worthwhile to think through the reasons WHY the roses are doing well… ways to make sure that good things continue. Here are some solid rose practices that the Rambler knows will work… and that you should find out for yourself.

WATER, not fertilizer, is what makes roses grow. The best plant food in the world won't do a bit of good until it is in solution and in the root zone of the plant. Pelletized fertilizers are great IF there is a regular, ample supply of water to dissolve the material and carry the nutrients to the roots. For a faster start, get food into solution and soak the roots. Old-timers also know that deep soaking BEFORE using any food (dry or liquid) also speeds up the process. For a real shock, try dissolving your favorite dry rose food in water. It may be less soluble than you think.

ROSES TOLERATE COLD AND STRESS much better when well watered. The Rambler noted during the late cold snaps that the really SOAKED roses had less cold burn, fewer blind shoots and responded more quickly than roses on the dry side. These are simple facts, easy to observe, that ought to tell us something about future practices.

FUNGICIDES ON THE LEAVES WORK, fungicides in the garage don't. Take your choice: *Triforine, Benlate, Maneb*… all will work when applied consistently and effectively. Most fungicides get a bad reputation, because they aren't used, not because they are ineffective. Use the fungicide that best suits your needs. *Triforine* (marketed by Ortho in a 6.5% formulation as *Funginex)* is probably best for most gardens. It's easy to use, safe for roses and rosarians (and the ONLY fungicide endorsed by the American Rose Society.) Use on a weekly basis, just like the directions say. In the springtime (and fall), when powdery mildew conditions are right, add two teaspoons of *Rubigan* per five gallons of solution, alternating every other week. This is a good mildew control and ought to be in your spray program. Remember that *Rubigan* is a PREVENTATIVE primarily; get the material applied early and regularly.

ALFALFA PELLETS (of meal) have really caught on with rosarians. Broadcast in the rose bed and scratched in lightly, nothing but good things can happen. Most alfalfa feeds are about 17% protein; the balance is fiber and fat. Alfalfa releases a growth hormone called Tricantanol, and it really works. Use just a cup or so per established bush. A farm feed supply store will have alfalfa in pellet or meal form for rabbits and horses… and most farm stores have other good organic stuff for rose growers. Just think of alfalfa pellets as being a much more convenient fertilizer source than keeping a horse. The end product is the same.

THE DROUGHT LAST SUMMER makes this advice on watering systems and water conservation worth repeating again and again. Control water delivery. You'll save water, water bills and roses at the same time. As a starter, backyard rosarians ought to look into the *Dramm* nozzle irrigation system. It's a cheap, easy way to put water where it can do some good. Easy to build-most anyone can have a system running over a weekend. The *Dramm* nozzle makes it all possible. It's a one-piece nozzle of hard plastic, with a tapered thread that screws into a "saddle washer" inserted into rigid plastic pipe. A pin diffuser waters in a full circle, parallel to the rose bed. Water sprays out, not up. Distribution is even, easily controlled. A rose bed 40 feet long and 5 feet wide can be thoroughly watered in about 20 minutes via an ordinary house tap. The flat, fine spray is ideal for miniatures, too. Washes off mites before they have a chance to start.

USE SCHEDULE 40 PVC PIPE, either 1/2 inch or *3/4* inch. The larger carries more water, if your neighborhood has enough water pressure. Connections, elbows, tees and adapters are available in most lumberyards, hardware stores or handyman shops PVC pipe is cut with a hacksaw; all connections are made with PVC cement. It's easy to work with, even for a beginner. Lay the pipe system on the surface of the rose bed; connect to a water hose with a quick-coupler. About 45 pounds of house pressure will supply a 1/2-inch, 40-footline with 15 to 18 nozzles. Each nozzle will spray an area from 3-4 feet in diameter, depending on pressure. Control volume (and spread) at the house tap or install a ball valve at the head of the line.

DRAMM **NOZZLES** are inserted in the pipe (drilled out *15/32-inch)* with a tapered neoprene washer. Line up straight; space about 3 feet apart. All the connections can be made with hand tools, just like a hose connection. Stabilize the pipe system with "sleepers", legs formed by tee connections and inserted into the rose bed. Maintenance is easy. If nozzle stops up, just pull the pin, and the water pressure will ordinarily clear the obstruction. Or, the nozzle can be flushed out by unscrewing and blowing out.

CHEAP, TOO. Nozzle and washer cost about 75¢ each. They are available from greenhouse supply companies (big Users of *Dramm* equipment) or mail ordered from several sources. Kimbrew-Walter Roses, Route 2, Box 172, Grand Saline, TX 75140, lists *Dramm* nozzles in their products price list. They offer installation drawings and instructions as well. If you install a *Dramm* system in just one bed, you'll soon convert the whole garden. For a demonstration, just stop by the Rambler's garden.

Rose ideas are much like children... our own are wonderful. You may want to try out some of these on your own family (rose) tree...

TIMED RELEASE fertilizers deserve another look by large and small garden rosarians. Cost considerations and availability limited timed release to small gardens, with the extra cost charged off to convenience. But more favorable cost/result comparisons and availability of all sorts of mixes have recently made these products of the chemist's art affordable and worthwhile for even large gardens. The Rambler compared overall performance of gardens with timed release and without timed release last year and conclusively found that the gardens with a steady diet, plus trace minerals, produced more and better roses. All other feeding and cultural practices were the same; the timed release gardens had two applications of 13-13-13 with trace minerals (April and September) in addition. Cost was about 50¢ per bush per season. In another planting, only timed release with trace was used on a rich, organic rose bed, but at a rate half again greater than when used with other foods. This timed-only bed also produced well and with much less effort. This leads the Rambler to believe that timed release rose foods ought to be in more rose feeding programs. It stands to reason that a steady diet of everything that roses need will do some good, even though the grower also uses fish meal, alfalfa pellets, ammonium nitrate and some other organic-based rose specialty foods (when on sale).

MINIATURES like timed release with trace also, provided that the grower doesn't use too much. Use at one-fourth to one third the rate recommended for big roses and take into consideration the area to be fertilized, as well. Leaves are greener, bloom color richer and overall growth in better scale than on minis without the routine that gives them just a tiny bit of food every time water is applied. The Rambler's favorite timed release is *Carl Pool 13-13-13 with Trace Elements*. It responds to water without much regard to soil temperature, not a problem on the Gulf Coast. *Osmocote* and others have similar formulations for three to four month applications and up to six month applications. Check around with area Consulting Rosarians and experienced nursery growers/suppliers who actually grow nursery materials for recommendations and application rates. Just make sure to get the formulation with trace elements, and your roses will respond.

ALLELOPATHY is getting quite a play in rose bulletins from here and there, alleging that there's a serious new problem for rosarians to worry about. For us unscientific rosarians, ALLELOPATHY is "suppression of the growth of one plant species by another due to the release of toxic substances." In other words, roses planted in spots where roses have been won't grow well. To put your mind at ease, however, roses don't do it to roses. And that's from the best authorities the Rambler can find. There may be a variety of reasons why roses don't do well when planted in an old spot, including lack of organics, out of range pH, poor drainage, lack of sun and just plain tired soil. But it is not allelopathy. There may be phytophora, a fungus that causes root rot in many plants, especially in wet areas. But phytophora is treatable with chemicals *(Subdue)* or situation-improved with mixing of organic materials to encourage microbial activity. At any rate, look for tired soil first and don't worry about roses resenting replacement with other roses.

COARSE, WEATHERED LEAVES are the first signs of spray burn, almost like sunburn on a rosarian. And we are susceptible to both when really hot weather hits tender leaves and tender skin. Spray bum occurs in stages, just like sunburn. Leaves don't have to turn brown and drop off to have bum. Look for coarsening of the leaf surfaces, brown edges on leaves or yellow-brown spots on the leaves (not blackspot) as evidence of bum. Spots on the leaves may be from droplets of spray material acting like a magnifying glass in bright sunshine. Solution: For better leaf coverage, add a tablespoon of white vinegar per gallon of spray mixture; it neutralizes alkaline water and makes spray materials spread out over the leaves more evenly. If droplets form to runoff, tap a large cane on the bush with the spray wand and shake off the excess. A good sprayer will put out a fine mist that makes rose leaves "glisten", and that's just right. It saves spray materials, too.

WILTING worries many rosarians, but the cause(s) can usually be understood. When a rose is under stress to move moisture from the roots through the canes and stems to the leaves and blooms and just cannot keep up, the stems and leaves wilt. Hot weather induces the stress; the transpiration needs of the bush just can't be met. Too many leaves and not enough roots means wilt in hot weather, common with bushes just getting established. Or soggy soil with too much water inhibits pickup by the roots. Poorly aerated soil does the same thing. Not enough organics in the soil to hold moisture, surface-only watering and impenetrable mulches contribute also. Very dry soil obviously can't support leaves and is a sure way to lose minis, with their tiny feeder roots. Look for the causes and then go to work. Moisture may be there but just can't be delivered.

SUMMERTIME ODDS 'N ENDS... AVID is the miticide of choice now, as reported by rosarians from all over the country last season. The WATER WAND is still popular, too... *Orthene 75% SP* is working well on thrips, particularly for growers who spray the rose bed surface also. Spot control by misting the buds and blooms only is a good adjunct to overall coverage. Use at two teaspoons per gallon of water, neutralized with about one tablespoon of white vinegar... *Rubigan* really does check powdery mildew when used early enough in a preventive program... CLEAN LEAVES are also good for roses in hot weather. Wash them down occasionally in the morning to get rid of the spray residue. The Rambler doesn't even worry about washing down in the evening, provided that the fungicide spray program is on schedule... ALFALFA TEA is as refreshing to roses as iced tea is to rosarians. Makes them turn green and grow (not good for rosarians). Steep up a batch soon.

JUL. 1989   *No column printed this month.*

Since experience is like manure... it's only good when spread around... the Rambler is spreading from a new location this month. The Rambling Rosarian (and wife, Millie, too) has been transferred to Greenville, South Carolina. We're leaving behind ALL of our roses and a home representing 10 years of hard work. But we're looking forward to building a NEW rose garden in Greenville as soon as we get organized. The Rambler has already found a rose garden in Greenville that needs some tender care. Remember that advice about starting a "friendly garden?" You can be sure that the Rambler won't get out of practice.

THESE COLUMNS will share the building of the new garden with all of its failures and successes, just like every other grower experiences. There will be some new things to learn after 35 years on the Gulf Coast, but there are a number of really good rose growers in the area to help. Might even be able to share some tips with them. We're anxious to get on with the project and share roses again with you. If you have questions, suggestions or comments, just drop a line to the Post Office Box above, and your letter will find its way to the Rambler's desk and typewriter... and interest.

THE RAMBLER'S MAILBAG has had some interesting inquiries lately that deserve to be shared. A common question concerns availability of a certain product, *Carl Pool 13-1313 Timed Release* material, often noted in these columns. *Carl Pool,* like many other limited-application products, is distributed regionally. The best solution is to locate a regional equivalent rather than to try to import the real thing. It's what the product DOES that's important, not the brand. And someone is always inquiring about sources of hard-to-find or expensive products to "split" with others. This is a very friendly and supportive thing to do, but it is also against labeling laws and potentially dangerous. Labeling is an important consideration of the FDA folks and rightfully so. If you DO split an order, make sure that it is an equivalent, safe container and carefully labeled with the WARNINGS. The Rambler's advice: If in doubt, don't.

SOURCE REFERENCES make the Rambler a little uncomfortable as I don't want to give the impression that this is the ONLY source. There are usually a number of supplier/sources serving the nursery trade. You just have to develop them and share the information with others. But here is my favorite source of rose specialties: Kimbrew-Walter Roses, Route 2, Box 172, Grand Saline, TX 75140. They have *Rubigan, Triforine, Mavrik, Vendex, Plictran, Sequestrene* and all sorts of other things for rosarians. They are really good folks, active rose society supporters and live roses 24 hours a day (and are not related to the Rambler). They will even take your order by phone (214) 8292986 and trust you to pay for it. Get acquainted with their rose service soon.

LOSS OF EFFECTIVENESS is often cited by rosarians who use this as a reason to increase the strength of a spray material. This is the worst thing to do. If blackspot seems to be getting ahead of the *Triforene* routine, first check the routine and then increase the frequency. Or add a supplemental fungicide like *Maneb* at half-strength. Nothing has really changed in the *Triforene,* but application may have slipped. Insecticides (and miticides, in particular) often do lose their effectiveness as the predators build up resistance. It's always a good idea to switch off materials from time to time to delay this process.

ORTHENE 75% SP is a product of choice for thrips- more effective and much cheaper than *Orthene* 9.4% *EC*. About 2 teaspoons per gallon (water) of *Orthene* 75% *SP* does a good job on thrips. Many growers think that it is a good idea to spray the bed area with *Orthene,* as well, to break up the reproduction cycle-something like *Diazinon* with midge. The Rambler has not been able to conclusively confirm this ground spray effectiveness, but it does seem to help. However, the more spray material used, the more spray material that will HAVE to be used in the future.

WHITE VINEGAR as a spray buffer has been widely misunderstood. Most insecticides work better and last longer in a slightly acid solution. Most water used in spray mixtures is alkaline. The objective of the vinegar is to at least neutralize the water and, at the same time, act as a spreader... coating leaves evenly rather than in droplets. For most water, 1 to 2 tablespoons of white vinegar per gallon will increase effectiveness. Partially fill the spray container with water, then add vinegar, then add any soluble or wettable powder. Swirl to blend. Then add emulsifiable concentrations (the EC on the label) and swirl again. Finish filling with water to the required volume and agitate from time to time, if the sprayer does not have a return feature. To discover how vinegar works for yourself (and decide just how much to use) add vinegar to water without any other chemicals and see how it spreads on the leaves. Of course, if you should happen to have highly mineralized or acid water, there's no need for vinegar. What you need is a better water source.

ODDS 'N' ENDS... Why do FERTILIZERS IN SOLUTION seem to give out? It's because of the constant leaching through irrigation and rainfall. It's hard to maintain a constant level. The best bet is to use liquid foods in more dilute solutions more frequently. This keeps more of the nutrients present and available... ORGANICS stabilize nutrient availability from all sources, catching on and holding plant-available foods. When a plant's diet gets too thin, add some organic matter, as well as some organic food sources. Nature has a way of staying in balance... if we help a little.

I'm not sure if roses bring out the best in people or just the best people, as Carolina rosarians have given these displaced Texans a very warm reception (along with some tough rose questions). Greenville is going to be a great place to live and to grow roses (besides making enough money to indulge in roses as a hobby). We're into "friendly gardens" and regional rose activities already.

"HOME SUITABLE FOR ROSES" is an unusual requirement for local realtors who want to show properties described as "heavily wooded" or "secluded", which really means lost in the woods. But there's bound to be a sunny solution somewhere with just a few trees to make the landscape interesting. The red clay of the Piedmont is something else, too. It supports woody plants and trees in spectacular fashion, but turns away shovels and water like baked brick. It's going to take huge volumes of leaves and sawdust and wood chips and manure to build beds for happy roses. Regional rosarians who have mastered the trick are growing some outstanding roses. It's interesting to note that most of the gardens have built-up rose beds, not so much for drainage but to be able to get air and water into the growing medium. Own-root roses are popular here, too. Established bushes have 10 to 12 canes, all larger than your thumb, supporting long, heavy stem laterals. Fall bloom should be spectacular.

SEPTEMBER ROSES should be among the best of the season, even if some of the rose chores may have been skipped during the summer. The trick is to make some nutrients available to the bush without upsetting the dormancy program in late fall. Liquid fertilizers provide appropriate formulas in solution right away unlike pelletized fertilizers broadcast over the rose beds. Food in solution goes to work immediately without interrupting the fall dormancy slowdown, a little like a shot in the arm rather than a long-term diet. If the roses and rose beds are reasonably receptive, a gallon or two of liquid mix will show results in a week. Apply now, then repeat in about 10 days, at least in the more temperate zones of the country. Warmer areas can slay with the program until mid-October. Use a soluble formula with trace elements... *Miracle-Gro, Ra-Pid-Gro, Forti-5, Carl Pool Instant, Peters* and others will do a great job. And

the Rambler thinks that an extra ounce or two of magnesium sulfate (Epsom salts) helps, too. Some alfalfa tea also encourages a spurt of growth.

GROOM ROSES FOR FALL, NOT PRUNE. The Rambler cringes every time a well-meaning rosarian advises "fall pruning for best bloom". This suggests heavy trimming, and that's not the idea at all. Roses in the fall appreciate grooming, the light trimming up of unproductive wood and blind growth that's not going anywhere. It's just a more thorough job of cutting spent blooms with an eye for the next bloom cycle. Grooming is not a "field day" on leaves; the bush needs leaves to produce food. When bushes have to recover from defoliation, bloom production is delayed that much longer. Leaf loss, whether caused by disease, insects, neglect or trimming shears, results in fewer roses and weaker bushes for winter survival. The name of the game is: "Grow leaves, then roses."

POWDERY MILDEW CONTROL begins now. Don't wait for disease problems to appear. Mildew strikes new, lush growth when climatic conditions are right (cool nights, warm days). That means the fall season. *Rubigan* is effective when started two weeks or so before mildew conditions are right. This gives the systemic material a chance to protect and inhibit before mildew spores are spreading all over the garden. The Rambler uses *Rubigan* every other week at 2 teaspoons per 5 gallons of spray solution, added to the *Triforine* fungicide sprayed weekly. *Rubigan* and *Triforine* are compatible, and together will do a good job on mildew. Be sure to give ramblers and climbers special attention and good coverage. They can be deadly sources of spores and infection for the whole rose garden. Keep up the routine until first frost.

ALFALFA PELLETS are still widely misunderstood. Alfalfa pellets, the small ones for rabbits, are simply alfalfa meal with a little binder. Pellets contain no more salt than meal, break down with the first application of water and are easy to apply. Pellets can be broadcast, added to mulches, used to make "tea" and incorporated in soil mixes. Scratch in pellets that are broadcast soil contact hastens the nutrient release/breakdown process. It keeps down any odor, too. Alfalfa tea smells more, but it goes to work much faster. Tea is ideal for pots and planters, minis and first-year bushes. Get acquainted with your friendly feed store man for a bag or two. It's cheap, stores easily and makes roses respond nature's way.

GYPSUM is a good fall Rx for pots and planters or even beds on the alkaline side that have become packed and tight during the season. Clay particles attract under alkaline conditions, particularly when using alkaline water (most city water is loaded with alkaline salts). This stops up pot drainage and retards growth. Just a tablespoon or so of gypsum per pot (roses, geraniums, chrysanthemums, etc.) watered in is just like pulling a plug. Gypsum is a good source of calcium, too. It can't bum, and it leaches the excess salts. You'll find it cheap, easy and effective.

CUCUMBER BEETLES also like fall weather and fat blooms. Fight them with *Mavrik,* a flowable insecticide that's safe and easy to use. Spray the bud and bloom areas at 2 teaspoons per 5 gallons of water, buffered with a couple of tablespoons of white vinegar. *Mavrik* won't discolor blooms, is safe on the leaves and leaves no residue. It can be used AFTER beetles appear, and then two or three applications will be sufficient. Doubles as a thrips fighter, as well.

SLOW DOWN FOR FALL and smell the roses. Now's the time to enjoy what nature has provided... with a little help from the rosarian.

Oct.
1989

THOUGHT FOR THE MONTH: The way to avoid mistakes is to gain experience. The way to gain experience is to make mistakes.

A rosarian who never makes a mistake is one who never does anything… but, fortunately, you good readers are willing to share your successes and failures. We'll pass along some of these this month.

RUBIGAN, a systemic mildewcide, really is a miracle control, but miracles won't happen unless the material gets on the leaves BEFORE severe infection. *Rubigan* works from within the leaf tissue (systemic), controlling and killing mildew spores. It makes no claim to be an absolute eradicant. Give it time to work. Use *Rubigan* in combination with *Triforine* one week, *Triforine* alone the following week. The every-other-week routine will soon clean up the most stubborn infection, PROVIDED that the grower sticks to the schedule. Readers are amazed that water helps control powdery mildew as well, washing off spores before they can windglide to new, dry leaves to set up new colonies. They have new appreciation for the fact that powdery mildew grows on DRY plant material, not on wet leaves. Blackspot needs a wet surface to multiply. Both mildew and blackspot like high humidity situations (when the dew point drops with cool nights and warm days), but prefer different leaf environments.

YELLOW LEAVES are the subject of most inquires to the Rambler. However, most growers can diagnose their own problems with a step-by-step elimination of possible causes. Yellow leaves (the clear yellow kind) are caused by: too much water (not enough oxygen in the soil), too little water (bush sheds leaves to cope), too much fertilizer (roots bum and can't deliver enough water) and not enough nitrogen for the leaf processes. There are a few other causes that are easily identified, including leaf bum (the leaves will be brown and coarse) and plain old "tired leaves," leaves which have lost their usefulness and are dropped naturally. Try the elimination process and reduce rose anxiety considerably.

SAVING THE LEAVES is always a good routine but sometimes misunderstood in practice. New bushes need leaves to grow and mature; when cutting blooms, take the shortest stem possible, just down to the first set of leaves or so. Long stems will come later. Use the same practice for bushes which have lost leaves for one reason or another. For established, vigorous bushes, trim blooms at the first five leaf junction to encourage new stem growth and another bloom. Remember, that the NEW stem will be sized in proportion to the supporting cane. This grooming process keeps the bush sized the way the grower prefers and supports the blooming/growth process. In a mass planting for lots of leaves and color, cut blooms to the first immature leaves. New buds will break at the leaf axils below and send up more growth. There's a trade off, of course. The blooms will be smaller and stems shorter, but there will be more of them.

STUBBORN BLACKSPOT? Readers consistently endorse alternating materials and increasing spray frequency to gain control. *Triforine* at 1teaspoon per gallon combined with *Maneb* at 1/2 tablespoon per gallon sprayed twice a week will clean up blackspot with four applications. Then go back to *Triforine* or *Funginex* or *Benlate* on a weekly basis. Remember that *Maneb* may be sold under different labels: *Manzate, Dithane M-45* or may be the active ingredient in a combination spray material. What's important is that it works. Why not just use *Maneb* all the time? It leaves quite a residue on the leaves and can bum when the weather is hot or the grower makes a little application mistake. It's hard to get into the spray solution also, except for the flowable (aqueous) formulations.

FEED UNDER WINTER MULCH? Many readers reported great spring results following an early-winter broadcast of 1 cup of 13-13-13 fertilizer over a layer of leaves and covered with another layer of leaves. This is done when putting roses to bed for the winter. In the spring, the lower layer of leaves is reduced to a rich compost, setting up the soil for better microbial activity as the soil warms up. Call the process composting in place. Just don't disturb the lower layer any more than necessary in the spring as feeder roots may have found their way to these natural nutrients.

READERS RECOMMEND, and the Rambler concurs, that the *Garden Handy* nitrile-coated gloves advertised in these pages are just right for rosarians. These gloves are flexible, impenetrable by rose thorns, waterproof and endure season after season. They have sizes for ladies, too. For rosarians who have planted roses in a muddy mess, *Garden Handy* gloves have been lifesavers. Also, there is almost universal recommendation for the *Felco* pruner, widely sold by mail order and in upscale garden stores. *Felcos* cost more but are certainly worth it. The Rambler has had a pair for years and years and has changed out the blades only once.

SAVE THOSE TREE LEAVES and let them work for you... easy on the rosarian except for a little gathering. Enjoy this mixed-harvest of soil-builder, insulator, fertilizer and natural cover... all at no cost. Used for composting or winter protection, leaves return far more to the garden than the small amount of effort expended. If there's no out-of-the-way place to compost, use a vegetable or flowering annuals bed or the area where a new rose bed is planned. Nature will work all winter for you.

ODDS 'N ENDS... Don't forget HOUSTON ROSETIME '89, the late October ARS convention and rose show in Houston. We promise an agenda of back to rose basics with tours and topics by ordinary rose growers. See the August issue for registration information... TYPE GREMLINS crept into the August column: the correct telephone number for Kimbrew-Walter Roses (mail order suppliers of all sorts of good rose stuff) is (214) 8292968... THE RAMBLER AND MILLIE are enjoying South Carolina roses and rosarians more and more. No rose garden yet, but soon.

For every rose problem there's a solution... even if it's learning to live with it. But living with roses may be a little easier with some of these suggestions learned the hard way:

DON'T DIG — LET WINTER DO IT... the freezing/thawing cycle can do much of the work in making a new rose bed. If the ground isn't frozen yet where you are, loosen just a little and pile on lots of leaves and other organic material. Throw some soil on top or cover with black plastic. As moisture freezes and expands, tissues break down much the same as in composting during the summer. The winter action reduces and blends the organic matter and soil into the "loam" that most rosarians like. Nature has been building soils this way for a long, long time.

TIME TO WINTERIZE... Thanksgiving weekend seems to be the favorite of most rosarians. It's better to get the job done right rather than just a few hours ahead of the cold front. The whole idea is to insulate-to maintain constant temperature and avoid a freeze/thaw situation. Combinations of loose materials seem to do this job best, held in place with fences, boughs, cones or what have you. Roses appreciate these "thermal blankets".

ANTI-DESSICANT SPRAYS may help in the winter protection process, retaining moisture in the canes that might otherwise be lost to cold, drying winds. Products like *Wilt-Pruf* and *Cloud Cover* are available in most parts of the country and are easy to handle and apply. When bushes go dormant and drop their leaves, trim up to suit your winterizing situation and thoroughly spray the canes before applying any covering materials (or cones or boxes or combinations of these). Remember that canes are round and the backside has to be covered, too. Apply liberally, get good coverage. This trick is particularly good for climbers and ramblers exposed to wind and sun on a fence. More canes are probably lost to drying out than to actual cold; this winter blanket can make a difference.

FRIENDLY GARDENS (gardens on someone else's property) have been discussed in these columns from time to time. It takes roses to other people and so on. The time to get friendly is right now so that rose bed preparation won't interfere with your own efforts later on. Line up a site (or sites) for next season, organize suppliers and a helper (but as chief you get to do most of the work) and schedule the undertaking as a "Rose is the National Flower" project. If you have been friendly (and supportive) with your local rose supplier, he will probably be willing to order some Grade 1 1/2 roses in bundles of 10 for you. He can usually late order these from his supplier and everyone comes out ahead. By the end of the first season, you won't be able to tell the difference between these smaller plants and Grade 1 bushes. Your rose public will love you.

BURY FOR WINTER... new rosebushes, that is. Roses received in late November or December (or newly budded plants) are far better off buried than potted and moved in and out of protection all winter. It's a natural sort of dormancy, much like the "Minnesota Tip" method of winter protection. Select a garden spot where it is easy to dig (about 18 inches or so), loosen the spoil dirt with plenty of leaves and the "dormancy vault" is ready to receive bushes. Line the bottom of the vault with some dirt/leaves mix. Tie the tops of the bushes with twine and combine bushes in loose bundles. Heel in the bundles (not quite horizontal) and cover with the mix. Remember to tie a rope on the bundles so that you can find them next spring. Cover the area with lots of leaves. Then wait for spring. It really works.

WARM CLIMATE ROSARIANS also like to get Canadian roses late in the fall but are concerned with new growth likely to be frozen back in January or February. These bushes can also be buried for dormancy, but the most common practice is to pot these newcomers and winter protect in a garage or garden house for cold snaps of short duration. Roots have a good chance to develop in black plastic pots and get off to a roaring start in the spring when set out in the beds. It's an old trick of thoughtful rosarians: grow the roots first, then the tops (and blooms). If potting is not on your exercise agenda, compromise by planting in the beds and mulching almost to the tips of the canes. Don't trim the canes at all. Encourage dormancy. If new growth at the top gets nipped, trim off next spring and there will be plenty of cane left.

DON'T FORGET THE WATER... Roses need water in winter, too. It's part of the antifreeze process of woody plants. Mulch and leaves help conserve moisture, but check underneath from time to time to see what's needed. Roses that dry out, die out.

THE RAMBLER PROMISED YOU A ROSE GARDEN... and is now getting underway in Greenville. The house is new construction on a gently sloping lot with some young trees and some sunshine. The site was heavily wooded to begin with. The back garden area extends out to a golf course screened with ornamental trees-a great spot for some old roses. The builder saved most of the woodsy topsoil (a red soil/clay mix) and did a good job of finish grading. We are starting from scratch-no landscaping by the contractor. All building debris was cleaned up BEFORE grading was done-no surprises with bricks and mortar under future rose beds. The site has been seeded with winter grass to control washing; it was up within a week. We are watching runoff and drainage carefully before building any beds. Some tentative locations have been staked but not disturbed, although a few "test holes" have been dug to see how the water drains. Future beds will be built up, but this gives an indication of how much work needs to be done below lawn grade. Drainage got a real test as Hurricane Hugo swept through with lots of water, but we will watch and fill and rake for another month yet. Coming next month: Adventures with landscape timbers.

If your garden is giving you new problems before you've solved the old ones, don't worry. They will soon be old problems, too. Here are a couple of approaches to wind up a good rose year...

PRACTICAL pH... December is a good time to get into balance, pH balance, that is. A long growing season with liberal applications of inorganics can dramatically drop soil pH level below 6.0 — a level that begins to tie up nutrients and trace elements, even though they are in the soil and supposedly available. Roses literally starve to death when pH drops below 5.0, even with liberal fertilizer applications. The solution for low pH is dolomite lime, but the process is slow. Now is the time to apply lime (if needed), provided that the soil area is workable. Since lime is relatively insoluble, top application is not particularly effective. To adjust pH (raise) with lime, remember that the process is a REACTIVE one; the lime should be physically mixed in the soil for best results. This is what happens: lime, in the presence of Hydrogen ions (the indicator for pH) reacts with those ions to form water. By reducing the H ions, the pH goes up. And, it is a fairly slow process.

TILLING, SPADING AND TURNING lime into an existing rose bed isn't very practical, but some careful probing with a spading fork will work. Stick a spading fork into the soil near the root areas and rock back and forth. Then sprinkle dolomite lime into the holes and lightly scratch the soil back. Let water and nature do their thing. Don't worry about raising the soil above 7.0 (neutral) as the process only works when there is an excess of H ions. However, it is wasteful to overdo lime as it continues to convert hydrogen potential from acid-forming fertilizers and acidifiers until it is used up. The rule of thumb for raising pH one point (1.0) is approximately 5 pounds of dolomitic limestone per 100 square feet of sandy soils up to 10 pounds per 100 square feet for heavier clay soils.

BALANCE REGULARLY... Since acid-forming fertilizers are added regularly, a good practice is regular use of lime to maintain a pH balance of 6.5 to 6.7. In rosebeds with low pH, add up to a pound of dolomite lime (a combination of calcium carbonate and magnesium carbonate) for every pound of nitrogen. Example: 5-10-5 ammonium sulfate, 50 pound bag, contains 2.5 pounds of nitrogen. Use 2.5 pounds of lime for the same area. Used regularly, it tends to keep the pH in a range suitable for roses.

DETERMINING pH is easier than you think. Whatman LabSales and other labs have come up with pH indicator strips that are cheap, reliable and easy to read. The 5.2 to 6.8 range strips most commonly needed by rosarians cost just $15 for 200 strips. Each paper strip has its own color comparison indicator. The routine is easy: mix a half-cup of soil from the root zone with one cup of distilled water. Stir the soil and water vigorously for 30 seconds and let settle. Then immerse the indicator strip into the water for 5 seconds, taking care not to disturb the soil layer. Compare the color of the center pad on the indicator strip with the colored squares above and below. The number of the matching square is the soil pH. Take a number of samples, rather than mixing soils from various areas for an average. You may be surprised how pH conditions can vary in different parts of the garden.

INDICATOR STRIPS are available from Whatman LabSales, 5285 N.E. Elam Young Pkwy., Suite A-400, Hillsboro, OR 97124, or you can call (503) 648-0762. Request Comparison Strips #2628Y990 for pH range 5.2 to 6.8. It's one of the best garden investments you'll ever make.

HUMUS HELPS pH, TOO... Humus is the well-decomposed organic matter that comes from peat, compost, leaf mold and rotted animal manures. This humus is important to plants as it has a high buffer capacity over a wide range of pH values. That is, humus does not allow the soil to become overly acid or overly alkaline in spite of chemicals (fertilizers) that normally induce such change. Humus and organics tend to stabilize the soil structure, hold water, permit air for soil processes along with a high base exchange capacity. In short: humus helps keep soils and nature in balance.

GYPSUM is another wintertime soil amendment that needs some time to go to work, particularly in alkaline, clay soils. Gypsum (calcium sulfate) helps drainage and curbs salts buildup. It is also a good source of calcium, a secondary element for roses. Whenever soil can be worked, broadcast about 25 pounds per 100 square feet of rose bed and work in lightly with a spading fork, taking care not to disturb the roots. Gypsum works best when in contact with the soil, although it is reasonably soluble. For new beds with clay, use about 50 pounds per 100 square feet.

I PROMISED YOU A ROSE GARDEN and adventures with landscape timbers last month. But rains and moving activities have shut down new rose bed construction. Does that sound familiar? The weatherman and work schedule promise better conditions soon. At this writing (mid-October) there's still plenty of time left. In the meantime, a daily check of drainage test holes is making a profile of what to expect in the future... built-up beds or not.

ODDS 'N' ENDS... Looking for a holiday gift? Buy yourself or your live-in rosarian the best sprayer you can afford. Nothing takes the work out of rose growing like a really good sprayer... Or how about a rose gift certificate? Many nurseries have these available, and you get in on the fun of the selection process. A good kneeling pad is also a boon to a rose pruner, miniature grower (or weeder). It keeps your knees dry and more comfortable.

Many garden shops have them now, as well as the discount outlets. It makes you look like a real pro. The pads are made of inch-thick plastic foam covered with heavy vinyl. Get one for the wife for sure.

Having already ordered only ten more roses than the garden will hold, the Rambler's rose catalog reading has been restricted to one hour per week. But you good readers are under no such constraint, so enjoy yourselves before the really hard work begins.

YOU AND YOUR ROSES will be happier if you plant fewer and care better. More isn't necessarily better when it comes to rosebushes; concentrate on the bushes you can really care for. Get rid of the marginal bushes and beds-set up a rose program that you can live with. Trade in some old roses for new ones... in cars it's called "trading up." For most of us, new roses mean getting rid of something already in the ground. To justify this expenditure, make a "good deal" by giving the old, reliable bushes to a gardening friend or start a "friendly" garden in your area.

TIRED SOIL? Old rose beds can be restored in much the same way as building new beds but with much less work. If your roses have slowed down in a bed that has been in production for five years or so, it's time to rebuild. The secret is to make the soil alive again with organics to support the micro-organisms. Soil doesn't wear out, but it loses some of its support capabilities. Begin restoration when frost is out of the ground... just before pruning. Lift out the roses to be saved from an old bed and heel them in. Then turn in all of the organic matter that the existing bed will hold, at least 1/4 by volume. Keep adding until the restored bed is light and friable.

GOOD ORGANICS include manures, compost, ground bark mixtures, partially composted leaves, alfalfa pellets and so on. Peat moss works fine, too, if you have the patience and back to mix it. Mixtures of all of the above are best. The bed will be raised considerably, but that's all right. The bed will settle some but will still retain its loose texture so important for air and water. Water a time or two; stir a little. The restored bed will be ready in about a week. Then move the transplants back, or put in new roses. Another tip: don't mix old bushes and new bare-root roses if you can help it. Plant the old roses in one area, the new ones in another. You'll get a much better growth pattern with less competition.

DORMANT DIG AND DIVIDE... Minia-ture roses can be dug and divided when dormant... a practical activity for many varieties at pruning time. Vigorous minis get very woody centers after a few years, and new growth is forced to the outside. It's easy to lift up a large bush with a spading fork, shake and carefully remove the excess soil. Then break up or cut up the mass of roots and small canes into smaller bushes, carefully pruning out the dead, woody material. Minis break up much like chrysanthemums.

The smaller plants will equal the size of the mother plant in about one season. Also, they will be much more vigorous and productive. Prune when replanting, of course. Then hill up a bit with mulch, water well and watch some strong new plants emerge.

SOIL SCIENCE... Soils are made up of mineral particles, among other things.. These particles vary in size from gravel and rocks to sand to silt to clay in a decreasing size gradient. Clay particles are very small; therefore, the cohesive force between them in water is so strong that it tends to prevent their settling out. In a soil, these clay particles are important in holding elements so that the rose roots can absorb them. The surfaces of these minute clay particles carry a negative charge, much like a magnet, and they attract positively charged particles to them. The positively charged particles that are attracted are ions of potassium, calcium, magnesium, et al. When on the particles, these ions can be absorbed by the roots.

THE ROLE OF HUMUS... Partially decomposed organic matter is called humus. Humus acts like a glue to bind clay particles into granules or crumbs. This causes the soil to be quite porous, and water and air enter quite readily. Combined clay and humus act together to hold· water, giving the soil a high water-holding capacity. It also allows excellent gas exchange so that the roots have a sufficient supply of oxygen so necessary for mineral absorption. In brief, the humus derived from organic matter helps build a "table" where rose roots can absorb water and minerals needed by the plant. In addition to binding together the day particles into granules, the humus also has a tremendous ability to hold positively charged ions, up to three or four times better than clay. It is this holding capability that slows leaching from the rose bed. Organic matter (humus) is really the key to good rose growing. It helps hold and make available water and minerals, it increases porosity of the soil, releases needed nutrients and makes other nutrients available. Need any more reasons to have up to 25% organic matter in your rose bed? Just check out the loads of roses enjoyed by growers who have understood this wonder of nature all along.

I PROMISED YOU A ROSE GARDEN... but it is slow in developing. The Carolina red clay is not at all cooperative. Solution for new rosebeds: Work about 50 pounds of gypsum per 100 square feet into the top six inches of existing soil along with about four inches of organics. Till again and again. Then start to build up the bed with soil mix brought in or prepared elsewhere. Till each new addition so that there are no layers. Easy way out: Don't fight the heavy stuff, build on top of it. More next month.

ODDS 'N' ENDS... Check out winter protection from time to time, add some more as necessary. Watch what's happening in the garden... SPRAY MATERIALS go bad when they freeze or get close to freezing. Box up and keep from cold and heat... CLEAN up your sprayer if you haven't already. Run a weak vinegar solution through the system to pick up residue, rinse thoroughly, store carefully. Put off installation of a new washer kit until springtime... And a ROSY NEW YEAR to all of you.

If you want to leave footprints, you'd better wear work shoes. And work is what Ramblings is all about this month… suggestions for some great WORK programs that should be kicked off soon.

ROSE BED CONSTRUCTION is a matter of taste, terrain, budget, landscape theme and a dozen other considerations… often overlooked while concentrating on the composition of the rose beds, the actual media that helps roses grow. Planned and constructed together, edging materials (or even lack of materials) and soil media produce better roses.

MATERIALS to distinguish and identify rose plantings are limited only by the imagination of the builder. Remember gardeners (?) who used to plant shrubs in the middle of automobile tires? A short list of hobbyist-handy materials includes concrete curbing, treated lumber, landscape timbers, railroad ties, bricks, concrete blocks, steel edging, plastic edging, rocks, live materials and even the old-fashioned way… nothing at all. We'll discuss a few of the pros and cons of some of these materials.

LANDSCAPE TIMBERS and/or TREATED LUMBER are high on the rose bed popularity list right now. Most growers can handle the construction, wood is fairly cheap and available, lasts a long time, doesn't bother roses and has almost unlimited flexibility. Landscape timbers can be formed into all kinds of shapes with just a little Skilsaw or chainsaw skill. Treated wood takes on a soft patina in a year or so or can even take on a penetrating stain. Erection up to three timbers high is fairly easy by anchoring the bottom timber with reinforcing bar driven into the ground through drilled holes followed by drilling pilot holes in the timbers and nailing. Timbers cut into 8-inch to 10-inch lengths and tamped into the soil also make a sturdy and decorative edge. Another good trick: add a treated wood "foot" around the bed to run the lawn mower wheel on. Saves lots of trimming.

RAILROAD TIES are separating many rose beds from lawns, walks, slopes and whatever, but they have to be used carefully. Weathered ties are not only heavy but have a very heavy look. Consider the scale and proportion before taking off on a railroad tie construction project. Ties used for terraces or erosion control are usually more pleasing visually. It takes a very dense planting of roses and plenty of space to justify the weight and size of ties. Used ties are OK if used properly… and make sure that the creosote has weathered and leached.

CONCRETE CURBING makes a very attractive edge (put in some drainage holes), but it is beyond the capability of most gardeners to frame and pour. There is a continuous-pour curbing machine now that lays down concrete like toothpaste, making curves and changing elevation with ease. Home improvement contractors in major areas are promoting this technique, and it's beautiful-not too expensive either. Color can be added to the concrete, and you can make your own design. About all it takes is stripping the sod, tamping and easy changes of direction. Rambler thinks that we will see a lot more of this in the future.

CONCRETE BLOCKS and CINDER BLOCKS (the kind with holes) are fairly easy for most hobbyists to use. Hands-and knees laying (follow a string) is slow but sure, no footing is required, no mortar (unless you really want to be fancy); and you can always change your mind. Blocks are available in widths from an oversize 4 inches to 8 inches. They can be stained to rid them of the "hard" concrete look. A Rambler favorite is latex redwood stain (penetrating) liberally diluted with water. Slap on generously with a heavy brush, the stain pigment will soak in. If the patina is not dark enough, go over the blocks again. The result is a porous, natural look. For an added trim, fill the open block spaces with good soil and plant with portulaca, alyssum or similar bedding plant. Pansies are nice for spring, too. Be sure to avoid violets… they will continuously supply spider mites by the millions.

BRICKS make great edging and can be laid formally or informally, depending on the skill of the gardener. For a formal treatment, be sure to pour a footing, or the bricks will eventually sag, sink and crack. An informal method uses bricks in a "soldier course" — bricks placed on edge and tamped into a soft concrete footing. Allow drainage space between each brick, do not use additional mortar. Use a 1/2-inch board as a spacer between bricks (or maybe a little less.) The soil and mulch will hold very satisfactorily, and the edge takes on a weathered look in a short time. A soldier course can follow contours, edge along a walk, keep soil from washing… all sorts of good applications.

A NATURAL LOOK is appropriate for many rose plantings, even with beds built up 10 inches to 12 inches. Just contour the edges off gradually and use plenty of thick mulch. To keep the grass out or as a very low edging, use steel edging like Ryerson. It fits very naturally as compared to the aluminum, plastic and fiberglass materials. The Rambler likes the natural look, but it doesn't fit everywhere and is more of a maintenance problem. Whatever YOU like, plan the constructed look while planning and preparing the soil. Your roses will be happier and prettier.

I PROMISED YOU A ROSE GARDEN. If not this season, maybe next. It seems that the Carolina clay the Rambler has been working with is alive. It can undergo a complete transformation in just a few days. The friable mix one day is heavy and hard just a few days after a rain. However, more organic material (various sizes) and gritty sand are making a difference. The Rambler is now up to 80 pounds of gypsum per 100 square feet of bed. This may do the trick, but it will bear watching. More later.

If you're calling roses by another name you're probably pruning or planting... or both. Here are some tips to make rose chores lighter and springtime more welcome.

HANDS-AND-KNEES PLANTING is the easy way for bad rose backs-much less strain than bending over. A good rosarian is one with dirty knees. Get a short shovel and get down to where the work is. If the rose bed is properly built, it's easy to scoop out a hole, rebuild a cone to support the roots and bush, then let water and soil do the rest. Cover the roots lightly with soil and begin to run water slowly into the hole; add some of the soil mix that was set aside. More water, more soil. No need to tamp or pack. Hill up with some excess soil or mulch (bring in a little extra rather than scrape from the top of the bed) to protect canes and conserve moisture. You can keep it moist with an overhead sprinkler... nothing to it.

BUILD A HILL... Hilling up roses is nothing more than building a protective cone of soil or mulch or other insulating material that lets just the tips of new canes stick out. I don't mean just a handful of material but a real cone-a shovelful or two per bush. Hilling primarily conserves moisture in the canes, but it gives cold protection, too. New root hairs must form to deliver moisture to the canes; hilling keeps canes from drying out before the roots have a chance to deliver. Constant temperature and moisture help roses start the natural way.

PRUNE THE ROOTS? It's a good practice (applied with some rose sense) for most bare-root roses. The Rambler lightly trims the ends of most of the roots and cuts out broken roots on the observation that root tips are prone to drying out; trimming exposes healthy tissue for new root hairs to develop, resulting in a healthier root system. Also, if the roots are way too long for the planting area, shorten them up a bit. You're planting roses, not making an excavation.

PHOSPHATE "BANDING" works better. Wise rosarians and ag authorities agree that "banding" phosphate rather than mixing makes phosphate more available to roses. Rosarians have been mixing a handful of phosphate or bone meal in the planting soil cone for years, but studies show that less material placed in a band (or handful in the case of roses) directly under the plant produces better results. The mix method is somewhat inefficient because the phosphate reacts in the soil to form non-available phosphorous compounds. What makes it work? To keep phosphate "alive," active and available, the particles must somehow be protected and the soil kept in a suitable pH range (about 5.8 to 7.5). One way is to keep the pellets together. Laid down in a close knit mass, the pellets sacrifice some of the outer members, but the core remains somewhat protected and intact. A handful placed 2 or 3 inches below the roots of a newly-planted bush remains available longer. The technique is not much different than bone meal under bulbs... and they certainly bloom.

ACTIVATORS AND HORMONES? Popular additives for new and newly-planted bushes. There are a number of products claiming powers to produce "millions of tiny root hairs" for fast growth. But the Rambler believes that the extra water and well conditioned soil did most of the good. If you can't resist the "secret ingredient," just use it with lots of water.

COW TEA, ALFALFA TEA AND FISH EMULSION solutions still work the best with new roses, including miniatures. These mixtures feed the soil supporting the organisms which convert nutrients into forms available to plants-a long chain but a simple one. Food value is built in as well, but the primary boost comes from activating the soil organisms. It can't bum; tiny hair roots love it. If you haven't brewed up one of the Rambler's teas, your roses have missed a natural treat. Just add a big sackful of manure or about 12 cups of alfalfa pellets to a barrel of water and let steep for a few days, stirring once in a while. Bailout a gallon or so per bush for a healthy boost. Fish emulsion (about a cup in 5 gallons of water) does about the same thing and is somewhat easier. Aging in a barrel with a handful or two of alfalfa pellets makes it even better.

CLEANUP SPRAYS... somewhat misunderstood. The object is to control over-wintering spores and insects before temperature and humidity are right for new-season outbreaks. This means starting a program immediately after pruning. Thoroughly wet canes and bud union (if exposed) with a fungicide/insecticide mixture like *Fungin-*

ex/Orthene or *Maneb/Diazinon* or *Benlate/Mala-thion*... whatever you commonly use for disease/insect control. Use at label strength. Spray climbers and shrub roses particularly well; an infected host plant can spread spores like wildfire when conditions are right. Repeat cleanup in about two weeks, then follow a weekly fungicide program.

I PROMISED YOU A ROSE GARDEN... and it's finally taking shape thanks to a modified commercial potting mix for the built-up beds. The commercial mix has very little actual "soil" but plenty of organics like ground, composted pine bark, peat moss plus a compost of who-knows-what. The mix also has about 20% *Perlite* by volume and some sharp sand. The modifications (Rambler's recipe) include fish meal, alfalfa meal, lime and bone meal. The final mixture is quite loose, drains well and feels very light. It seems to be ideal for the informal miniature planting areas (no edging) and for the deeper built-up beds with landscape timbers. A couple of slow rains and time for settling should tell the tale. We'll be testing the gypsum-treated subsoil before planting.

ODDS 'N ENDS... Rosarians deserve some new tools in the spring. Start off with a new pruning saw... best one out is a folding job that's about 5 inches long, with a narrow blade, extra fine teeth that cut clean and close. The *Harlane* Company (advertisers in these pages) sells them for just $10 each... best thing since the *Felco* Pruner. And a good *Felco* is anther thing you should have, available in various models, with repair parts always available. A good pair should last a long, long time.

When offering suggestions,
Keep them soft and sweet.
You never know from day to day
Which words you'll have to eat.

THESE WORDS OF WISDOM, gained from long experience, haven't inhibited the Rambler; so here's a springtime round of inspired suggestions for your rose benefit...

DISTILLED WATER is the thing to use when testing for pH with the Whatman LabSales Indicator Strips, according to my scientific researchers (per LabSales instructions, too). The Rambler had advised use of the same water used on the rose beds and, in most cases, this had given satisfactory results. However, rose friend Larry Johnson, a retired Houston M.D., and Dr. John Dickman of Columbus, Ohio, report that results with distilled water are more consistent with reports from professional labs. Dr. Johnson says, "I tried the indicator strips three different ways: I used (1) distilled water, (2) well water from my own well used on the roses and (3) Houston city water. Results were very similar with the distilled water and the well water which, of course, is untreated with any chemicals. I got altered and conflicting readings when I used Houston city water, and I suspect there may be chemicals and additives which alter the pH readings on the strips. I believe these tests are accurate with distilled water or untreated well water, but the chemicals added to city water may completely distort the pH reading."

CONFIRMING LAB TESTS support the distilled water recommendation and report a high degree of accuracy. Dr. John Dickman, research chemist and former Beginner's Column writer for this magazine, adds, "The indicator strips are easy to use, accurate when used correctly and can really surprise the grower on his pH situation. I couldn't believe how far the pH in my rose beds had dropped." For more discussion on pH testing and indicator strips, check the December, 1989, Rosarian Ramblings.

HERE'S A ROOTING SYSTEM that may appeal to growers with limited space and support facilities. John Bender of Charlotte, NC prepared a small rooting bed in a filtered light corner using sharp sand, perlite and ground peat; it was about 10 inches deep and well-drained. Then he rigged a mister nozzle and control to a garden hose... very simple. Then cuttings (two to three eyes below surface and two leaflets above) are inserted in #7 *Jiffy* pots after treatment with rooting hormone. *Jiffy* pots are set in the rooting bed, about 3 inches deep, and the rooting area is kept moist by adjusting the mister activator valve. No covering is used. In warm weather, cuttings root in 14 to 21 days with about a 75% success rate. Roots come out of the *Jiffy* pots and can be checked by gently pulling away some rooting mix. When rooted, transfer each to a small pot with a light rooting/potting mix and harden off in filtered sunlight. In six weeks or so, the vigorously growing own-root roses are transferred to a propagation bed (out of the pots) for more growth. To avoid competition, only roses in various stages of propagation are in this bed, which also gets special feeding attention with fish emulsion and similar, frequent, diluted solutions. John's system really works; you may want to adapt it for your situation.

ROSES IN CONTAINERS. Here's an interesting potting method used by George and Kathy Noble of Austin, Texas. The Nobles had a tree-root and drainage problem. Solution: build a treated wood deck and grow roses in 15-gallon black plastic containers — about 40 of them. Since container drainage is so important, George lined the sides of the sturdy plastic planters with Inca Drain, a plastic material commonly used for drainage and air circulation on foundation walls. Inca Drain is a flexible sheath material, with weep holes, backed with a honeycomb-like matrix about 1/4-inch thick. Air and water flow freely through it. Line the container sides with the honeycomb side to the pot. Then use a light planting mix with lots of organics, perlite and sharp sand. The result is a very well-drained container that encourages root development. George also has an interesting "bush anchor" for containers that the Rambler will discuss in future issues.

SPRING TONIC FOR ROSES is a treatment that feeds the processes which make nutrients available. That means organics, which work better and more consistently in start-up than the products from the chemist's lab. In organics are a boon to rosarians, too, but they work best in conjunction with good organic practices. Manures and alfalfa build strong plants. Fish meal and blood meal encourage beautiful leaves that will support blooms. Compost humus keeps nature in balance. Organic tonics like cow tea, alfalfa tea or fish emulsion work just like chicken soup for rosarians… they make the sick well and the well even better. On your rose beds they promote live soil, active organisms and healthy rosebushes.

I PROMISED YOU A ROSE GARDEN… still moving ahead slowly but surely in the red Carolina clays. The light mix is draining well, while retaining good moisture content. Clay does contribute something besides a tired back. Gypsum, at 80 pounds per 100 square feet, has been effective. Applications in the lawn area (with no fertilizer yet) have also made a dramatic difference. Hope to report on first plantings next month, if the rains, cold, rose society activities and the necessity of making a living don't interfere too much. Sound familiar? Oh, well, we wouldn't enjoy it any other way.

Nothing so needs reforming as someone else's habits... to something like our own. If you're in the market for some new garden habits, here are some that are easy to take or break:

PROGRAMMED ROSES is a computer-age term suggesting that the variables for growing roses can be predicted and planned, and appropriate action taken... just by using the right program. Rose garden example: Tender, green leaves are susceptible to powdery mildew in the spring (cool nights, warm days). *Rubigan*, an effective systemic fungicide, is a better preventative than an eradicant. Initiate a program of protection before mildew signs appear. There are also similar programs which will achieve a wide range of rose goals, provided that the grower thoughtfully considers variables, options and goals. Build programs now to schedule response. A blackspot-free garden begins with a weekly spray schedule using *Funginex* (*Triforine*) or perhaps *Daconil*, backed up with a *Funginex/Maneb* combination if the garden gets "off" schedule. *Triforine/Rubigan* is a good program when both blackspot and powdery mildew are likely to occur. Got the idea? Now if we could just get a programmed robot to get the spray on the leaves.

CONTAINER ROSES were discussed last month with a mention of a bush-anchoring device dreamed up by George Noble. Fabricated of Schedule 40 rigid PVC pipe (3/4 inch), the support for the rose shank looks like a two-legged tree stand. Start with a "T" coupling and extend two legs to fit the container. Couple a 90° elbow to the third outlet of the "T" and add a pipe support just long enough to match up like a splint with the rose shank. Place a mat of Inca Drain over the two supporting legs and cover with soil to stabilize the support. When planting, bind the splint with nylon hosiery for a little give. With just this little extra stability, the full-grown bush is unlikely to tip in the very light soil. It's a simple device, but it works.

IF YOU DON'T HAVE A HORSE, make some Fragrant Formula (FF), a descriptive term for artificial manure guaranteed to grow roses in rocks. This is just as good as horse manure (maybe better, since it releases more nutrients) and can be produced on a city lot. It's a good soil amendment,

top dressing or basic feeding formula... especially in the spring. Enjoy the benefits without a horse. Here's the formula:

    3 ample yards of partial compost or leaves
    100 pounds of coarse-ground bark or mulch
    100 pounds of cottonseed meal
    100 pounds of alfalfa meal (or pellets)
    50 pounds of bone meal
    50 pounds of fishmeal

A farm store will have all of the ingredients except the leaves. If fishmeal is hard to find, substitute a couple of sacks of manure and maybe add 20 pounds of bloodmeal or beef and bone. Variation won't hurt a thing.

DIGESTION PROCESS... Make a pile of the coarse materials in any area suitable for composting, perhaps behind the garage. Add lighter stuff a little at a time and turn with a fork. Mix well. Then moisten lightly and turn with a fork twice a week for two weeks. When the pile is working, a sharp ammonia odor will leak. A different (dead) odor will leak if the mix is too wet or if there is not enough coarse material. The FF is ready in less than three weeks. Use about two garden shovelfuls per established bush for the first feeding. Repeat with one shovel later in the summer if the bushes slow down. These organics make other fertilizers work better, feeding the soil's micro-organisms which convert nutrients into forms roses can use. With the Fragrant Formula, you'll have live soil, healthy organisms and lots of roses. Use generously. It really works.

ALFALFA FREAKS were delighted last month with the scholarly discussion of enzymes by Dr. Bill Nettles in the Bits 0' Bulletins section of this magazine. Dr. Nettles pointed out that enzyme production is as simple as alfalfa tea. The tea introduces enzymes into the soil, increasing the rate of breakdown reaction and making food more readily available. He also explains why it smells (bacterial action) and how this benefits roses. Re-read the reasons for alfalfa tea and then get out and enjoy some with your roses... on your roses, that is.

ROSE ROOTS NEED OXYGEN — a growing fundamental worth repeating. Your rose roots may be starving if you have been stomping around in the beds this spring. Friable soil admits air and water. Roots need both. Keep soils loose with organic materials to give a honeycomb effect. The late "Uncle Charley" Dawson, greenhouse rose professional and long-time columnist in these pages, even erected a sign outside his rose garden which said, "Enjoy the roses but keep your big feet out of the beds." For servicing access, use stepping stones or decking, or make the planting narrow enough to begin with.

I PROMISED YOU A ROSE GARDEN... New roses arrived early, and beds developed late, resulting in roses in containers. However, they are busy making good root systems. Now there's no hurry to get them in the ground. A watering system is next on the project agenda-something flexible (can be changed around), cheap and trouble-free. I will explore some alternatives with you next month.

ODDS 'N ENDS... Roses in containers do form roots faster in wanner, better aerated soil. Except for the extra planting, handling and regular watering, it is not a bad way to start... rose garden tools are fun and useful. How about a holster for the pruning shears to avoid poking a hole in your pocket? A bulb planting tool is also useful for fishmeal and bone meal application. Also every garden needs a scratcher, a three-tine cultivator with long or short handle to keep the mulch loose and nutrients percolating. A good rosarian just can't have too many tools — a happy rosarian, anyway.

Good ideas are not a bit particular about who has them, so here are a few from the Rambler to help you enjoy more June roses...

FIND A HORSE... or a horse friend, for some manure. What if it's fresh? No problem. Should it be spread right away, composted for a year or so, or turned down? The best answer for these concerns is to keep the manure source a secret (so that you can have it all for yourself). Then get the manure (fresh or old) out on the rose beds, in the rose beds, mixed in the compost pile or used wherever organic materials and bacterial action are needed. There is no need to compost horse manure/shavings/alfalfa hay/straw mixtures before using on roses. Just till in the soil a bit and use plenty of water. The results will be amazing. Much of the beneficial activity is lost by waiting for the "well rotted" stage. Let the action rejuvenate the rose beds rather than be leached away. The Rambler's roses think that it is a special treat to get an inch or two of horse manure mulch just a week out of the horse. Yours will, too. Just use a little rose sense.

THRIPS CONTROL is important in June as the tiny insects seem to come in waves on moist breezes from field grasses and annual flowers. Severe infestation will bruise buds to the extent they refuse to open; good roses with brown edges are not worth cutting. The tiny, tan insects rasp petal edges, sucking the juices from the petals. In between rasping binges, they reside in petal spaces, making them hard to reach with spray material. Unfurl a light-colored bloom and it's easy to spot dozens scurrying around.

EVIDENCE SUGGESTS that thrips control should include good spray coverage of the entire plant as well as the rose bed area, contrary to earlier practice of spraying bud and bloom areas only. Bud and bloom spot coverage is good (as in preparing for a rose show) when used as a supplement to overall coverage. The most popular control is *Orthene* 75% SP (Soluble Powder). Use at two teaspoons per gallon of water, neutralized with about one tablespoon of white vinegar per gallon if you have alkaline water. *Orthene* will not discolor blooms and has a fairly good residual, with weekly spraying recommended during thrips season. Of course any spray material (including plain water) can damage delicate colors when applied in sunshine on a hot day. Spray early or spray late for best results. Drop *Orthene* from spray schedule when thrips season is over.

DOWNY MILDEW is a seldom-discussed subject among rosarians as most growers don't know how to identify the problem. Fortunately, it doesn't occur widely, but areas with cool, damp conditions are susceptible. The Bay Area of California might be considered a perfect home for downy mildew... if it ever rains again. The first thing that growers notice is a sudden defoliation of either miniature or large roses. Affected plants have purplish to dark brown leaf spots of varying sizes. The spots can also appear on stems and peduncles. Whereas, powdery mildew spores appear on both leaf surfaces, the spores of downy mildew are produced only on the lower leaf surfaces, making the problem more difficult to spot in the early stages. But, left unchecked, the affected leaves will fall off, and then the rosarian will know there's a problem.

CONTROL of downy mildew is not too difficult with the multipurpose fungicide *Daconil* 2787, which Ortho sells as *Vegetable Disease Control*. This product has been around for a long time and is effective on blackspot, as well, but not on powdery mildew. The flowable formulation by Security called *Fungi-Gard* is *Daconil* 2787, as reported by the ARS New Products Evaluation Committee in the April issue. *Ortho's Vegetable Disease Control* is used at two teaspoons per gallon of water every seven days for two consecutive sprayings, then every third spraying to disrupt the cycle of the downy mildew fungus. Do not combine it with insecticides. The Rambler has had no experience with *Fungi-Gard* and downy mildew, but I feel confident that used according to label directions, it will be just as effective as the Ortho formulation.

GARDEN HYGIENE is important in control of downy mildew as the spores are viable for over a month and can be found on infected leaves, stems, flowers and sepals. It also overwinters as dormant mycelia. If infection occurs, a good cleanup and spray program should have the problem under control within two to three weeks. The rosarian won't want to look at the purplish-red leaves, anyway.

I PROMISED YOU A ROSE GARDEN, but it is slow in developing. The Rambler hasn't made much progress since the last report, but the miniatures seen to like the somewhat heavier soil of the Carolinas and the roses in pots are doing okay. The watering system project has stalled (it's a good thing it rains a lot here), but I will pass along developments next month.

ODDS 'N ENDS... The Rambler recommends some publications for rosarians who want to expand their interest, especially Bev Dobson's *Combined Rose List 1990,* which sells for $15 or her bimonthly *Rose Letter* for $12. Write to Bev Dobson, 215 Harriman Road, Irvington, NY 10533...The Rose Hybridizers Association has a great quarterly newsletter (20 or so pages every time) for just $7. Just out is a new R.H.A. prepared booklet, *Rose Hybridizing For Beginners,* for $5. Write to Barbara Maas, Editor, 550 North 117th Street, Wauwatosa, WI 53226... The best all around growing guide for roses is Ortho'*s All About Roses,* which sells in most garden *centers. All About Roses* is endorsed by ARS, very well written and illustrated and belongs in every library. And don't forget your ARS district newsletters; most are available by subscription — great sources of cultural and activities information that's timely. Any District Officer or ARS Judge in your area will be able to give subscription information.

If you think that you're too old for growing pains, try more roses… or for a rosier, easier summer, try some of these Rambler suggestions…

ROSES LIKE TO STAY COOL in the summertime, just like rosarians. Nature's air conditioner is mulch, an insulating blanket that saves water, controls weeds and adds to the richness of the soil at the same time. Just a few inches of loose organic mulch dramatically reduces soil temperature and moisture evaporation. Most "home mix" mulches are combinations of wood chips, ground bark, leaves, straw or what have you. By the bag, truckload or compost pile, mulches really work. Skeptics say that these organics "leach" nitrogen from the soil, but all it takes is an extra handful of any cheap nitrogen source to release soil building humus. What if it doesn't break down right away? No problem. Leave it in place, incorporate in winter protection and just add to it from time to time. Old wive's tales hold that mulches harbor insects and blackspot spores. Not true. Insects live in soil and mulch, and blackspot spores spread by splashing from green tissue. Ask your roses; they'll recommend mulch.

WHERE DID THE BLOOMS GO? In many parts of the country rose midge is the culprit this time of year. Blackened tips where a tiny bud should emerge is the evidence left behind. Blind growth will result, no blooms. The best control is granular *Diazinon* broadcast in and around the rose beds much like fertilizer, usually following the first bloom cycle. This gets the soil-borne insect at the source. *Diazinon* liquid sprayed on the bushes and on the ground also helps. But midge season is short, so just two applications should do the trick.

JAPANESE BEETLES like to vacation in rose gardens in July, but it's possible to limit their fun. Beetle traps are a first line of defense, placed away from the rose beds, preferably in a neighbor's yard. If there aren't too many, pick off the iridescent scavengers morning and night and kill them in a jar of soapy water or *Clorox*… this practice is not for the squeamish rosarian. *Cygon* or *Sevin* dust or *Sevin* spray will kill them, too, but by that time they have ruined the blooms anyway. Many rosarians find that they can lure the creatures away from new blooms by leaving the spent blooms on light-colored roses. The beetles work on these first and make better targets for spraying or picking. *Milky Spore* is a good control and lasts for years and years, but it is impractical as most of the neighborhood has to be treated. It's a hard sell to convince the neighbors that a "spore disease" is going to be good for quality of life.

SPIDER MITES AND HOT WEATHER go together, the hotter the better. And it all happens with a terrible swiftness. One day the bushes look healthy and green; in just two or three days the leaves lose color and appear dried out. The tiny specs on the undersides of the leaves have literally sucked the life juices out of the leaves while propagating at an astounding rate. Fast action is the key. Check the undersides of leaves regularly, particularly on miniatures and dense-growing varieties. Anything planted next to the foundation or along a concrete walk is susceptible and suspect. Try washing undersides of leaves with water first. If the infestation has been caught early this may do the trick. A fine, strong water spray two or three times a week works. It's easy and fun, especially if you can get the kids to do it (water goes all over the place). If a miticide is required, the most readily-available product is *Vendex*, used alone at 1 1/2 teaspoons per gallon at 21-day intervals. Avid, the newest and most promising miticide, is restricted to commercial growers only, i.e., not available to the home gardener through local sources. Rosarians had hoped that Avid would be registered for home use.* But the Rambler knows that water and restrained use of pesticides on beneficial insects can support a mite-free garden. Frank and Gertrude Hirsch of Clearwater, FL have been doing this for years, and their garden is outstanding.

Editorial Note: Avid was made available to the ARS Product Evaluation Committee for testing purposes. Mr. Walters and many others on the committee have written glowingly about it, as it had been anticipated that it would be approved for home use. However, our most recent conversation with a representative of the Merck Chemical Company indicated that they were not pursuing registration for home use.

ROSE BED REBUILDING AHEAD?? Put off the job for several more years with just a spading fork, some organic material and a little effort.

Soils become depleted and tight over the years, resisting air, water and nutrients. Deliver soil conditioners and nutrients to the root of the problem by working a spading fork around the perimeter of the bushes to about two feet. Rock the fork back and forth, leave the holes. Then add a surface dressing of about two inches of compost, manure or some other organic mix to build the soil. The dressing falls into the holes and goes to work. Same trick can be used for fish meal, gypsum, timed-release fertilizers or lime. It works from the inside out — makes sense.

KEEP YOUR EYES OPEN for the new "English Roses" by David Austin, who has created repeat-flowering, disease-resistant shrub roses for the smaller gardens of today. If that sounds like a commercial, it is. These roses are new, but they're old, having mixed parentage which is bewildering and personalities all their won. In short supply right now, availability will improve as gardeners become aware of their qualities. Growth habits of the English roses are more mannerly than their sprawling ancestors. This reminds the Rambler of an observation by Ralph Moore, Father of the Modern Miniature. "There's a world of beauty out there if we don't wear blinders." Ralph is still infusing new life into miniatures using teas and hybrid perpetuals. His latest catalog (Sequoia Nursery) is full of parents and progeny, all grown on their own roots-a must for anyone serious about rose collecting today.

The best thing about rose growing is that if you put it off long enough, it won't be necessary. So, don't put off these summertime chores, or you'll be sorry.

MITICIDES take considerable rosarian abuse... the user claims it's "not working." However, it is usually the rosarian who is not working hard enough to get adequate coverage. A good approach is to use more volume of spray material when spraying a miticide as compared to a routine fungicide. Note the word is "volume," not concentration of spray ingredient. Use a long wand, spray the undersides of leaves until they are dripping. Another assist is to make sure that the spray material spreads and sticks to the leaves. Addition of 1 tablespoon of white vinegar per gallon or a few drops of a spreader sticker helps. Also, don't expect one-day service from your miticide. The real test is control of newly hatched eggs in three to four days. Give your favorite miticide a chance; then repeat if necessary, following the directions.

SUMMERTIME spraying can be tricky, but not if a little rose sense is applied along with the spray. There's not much sense in spraying to save the leaves if the spray does a job on them instead of spider mites or blackspot. Water the roses thoroughly before spraying and allow enough time for the roots to move the moisture to the leaves. Dry, limp leaves burn; turgid leaves tolerate spray materials better. A good practice is to water in the evening, spray in the morning. Roses watered in the morning and sprayed in the evening have lost some substance due to transpiration during the day. Avoid the middle of the day if possible; even plain water can bum and coarsen leaves in intense heat. You'll recognize spray burn when leaves coarsen, take on a sunburned look (like a rosarian's skin), turning brown on the edges or speckled. The damaged leaves will hang on for a while and then drop off, pushed off by a new crop ready to go to work. This is a waste of good leaves.

SPIDER MITE LEAVES LOOK DIFFERENT. Leaves affected by spiders gradually lose green color, have a parched, dry look and sometimes turn gray/brown. A bush can defoliate in just a few days. Mites suck the moisture out of leaves-an effect something like drying and aging in the fall. If mites are suspected, check the undersides of leaves carefully and look for gritty gray and white specks, similar to a mix of salt and pepper. Webbing may or may not be present. Any evidence of mites is a crisis... get to work right away. Don't wait. Wash/spray as you prefer, but hurry.

QUARANTINE new rosebushes for mites, particularly miniatures. Before introducing new minis in a clean garden, wash the leaves several times and keep the plants separated. Some growers use a weak solution of Safer's Insecticidal Soap or some Ivory Liquid in a bucket of water, dunking the tops and sloshing the leaves around. Allow about a week for eggs to hatch and dunk again. Plant out a few days later, fairly confident that a new strain of mites won't be mating with your favorites to make super mites.

COMPOST PILE SLOW? If you are in a low-humidity area, lack of moisture slows the process. To keep moisture available for the decomposition process, treat in the same manner as potting soil... add some calcined clay (cat box litter). This picks up the moisture and gradually releases it to support the process. The clay won't break down; it's cheap and works well with the finished compost. Buy it in big bags and use a shovelful or so per cubic yard of leaves, etc. You'll like the results.

A HANGING BASKET RACK ought to be in your summertime plans. Rose bed construction is over, and a very attractive rack can be made in a single afternoon in the shade of a tree. Ideal for baskets with miniatures, other plant materials plus benches for pots and flats. Made in an "A" frame shape, you'll find all sorts of applications. The Rambler has an easy-to-follow construction plan and a materials list that he'll share with you. Write to the Rambler at the P.O. Box above and enclose a self-addressed, stamped business envelope. The plans will be on the way in a hurry. If you have a rose question or comment, include it as well. Perhaps you have a THOUGHT FOR THE MONTH? The Rambler is running very short of thoughts appropriate for rosarians. I would appreciate your help and look forward to hearing from you.

ODDS 'N ENDS... More attention is being given soil-borne infections and rosarian exposure-and what rosarian doesn't have a collection of nicks and scratches? The Rambler suggests *Garden*

Handy nitrile-coated gloves. They are waterproof and virtually impenetrable by rose thorns, which makes rose growing easy on the hands. They have sizes for all sizes of rosarians. Rose markers by *Harlane* deserve a mention also. Nothing is worse than visiting a garden and not being able to identify the roses (short of no roses at all to look at). Both *Garden Handy* and *Harlane* are regular advertisers in these pages.

I promised you a rose garden, but the Rambler's garden is at a stand still except for 60 miniatures thriving in Carolina clay, sand and horse manure. They like it. The Rambler will like it even better when the big roses get into the beds.

Slow down for fall and smell the roses. Now's the time to enjoy what nature has provided with a little help from the rosarian.

POWDERY MILDEW will soon be dusting those choice fall blooms and lush green foliage with white unless a consistent fungicide spray program is started now. Prevention/control is the key as spores will erupt with cool nights and warm days. Systemics are effective when started two weeks or so before conditions for mildew are right. The Rambler uses *Rubigan* every other week at two teaspoons per five gallons of spray solution, added to the *Triforine* fungicide sprayed weekly. *Rubigan* and *Triforine* are compatible, and do a good job on mildew when mixed. *Rubigan* is expensive, but so are rosebushes.

Washing leaves with water before spraying encourages coverage, an absolute must when using any fungicide. If powdery mildew infection is severe (perhaps the rosarian is off schedule), increase the spray frequency, NOT the concentration. It's wise to maintain the program until frost.

NEED A FALL TONIC? Try a half-cup of alfalfa pellets or meal per bush plus an ounce or two of Epsom salts. Leaves are healthier, greener — supporting bigger and more colorful roses. Alfalfa does not induce soft growth like nitrogen, but it makes nutrients available in a natural process without upsetting the dormancy program in late fall. If fertilization is needed for fall shows, use soluble formulas of *Miracle-Gro, Ra-Pid-Gro*, Peters and others with trace elements. These go to work immediately. Two applications should do in most parts of the country.

SOIL POLYMERS are the most talked-about new rose product since systemic fungicides. They promise great benefits when used properly. Polymer granules or crystals absorb many times their weight in water (and nutrients in solution), releasing them to the roots as required. These nutrient reservoirs stabilize the soil processes, particularly in sandy soils and container mixtures. The advantages are obvious: reduced water requirements, reduced fertilizer-which is retained rather than leached away-increased soil aeration and reduced plant stress from lack of moisture. Also, polymers last up to five years according to most manufacturers. This is a soil amendment that roses and rosar-

ians will enjoy.

Rosarians will have to learn how to use these water wonders. Mixed into the soil in the hydrated (wet) form or as dry granules, the volume of polymers can be overdone, creating a gelatin-like, wet mass. Just follow the directions. Dry mixing works best for the Rambler, but many users soak the granules and then add them to the soil mix. Allow for expansion in the dry mix routine, saturating the soil mix with water before planting. Water normally for a week or so, then reduce by about one-half. Don't forget which beds, containers, baskets and pots have polymers. They won't appreciate too much water. The Rambler has observed a great reduction in transplant shock of miniatures, begonias and other succulent plants when root balls are dipped in a sticky polymer gel before planting. Digging later shows masses of roots attached to the granules. It works the same way on bare root roses. Though moderately expensive when purchased in 25 pound bags from a nursery supplier, polymers payoff in convenience and dollar savings over the years. Check out your regional pro-supplier before your next soil mix project and enjoy the wonders of modem soil science.

KEEP THE LEAVES. Fall rose care suggests a light grooming of unproductive growth, not pruning. There's just not enough time to grow a new crop of canes and leaves before growth slows for winter. Bushes need leaves to produce food; nature gives the signal when to switch from bloom production to winter survival. Rosarians with overactive shears send the wrong message, resulting in fewer roses and weaker bushes.

SOME FALL PROJECTS. Don't winter protect too soon. Let the ground cool off and soil processes slow before adding insulating mulch/soil/protection. Otherwise the bush may respond as though it is still growing time only to be hit with as sudden temperature drop.

Fall sales are something to watch for; containers, sprayers, bug lights and all sorts of garden items go on sale before the snow flies.

Whiskey Barrels (really half-barrels) make great containers for miniatures and usually sell for $8 to $10 each in the fall. They'll last for 5 years or so and add a new dimension to your garden. Three or four minis or a couple of small floribundas in a barrel make a real show.

ODDS 'N ENDS... *Floralife*, the cut-flower preservative, should be on every rosarians shelf. It definitely prolongs the vase life of roses, is cheap and easy to use. The home-made mixture with citrus-based soda also helps, but *Floralife* combines all of the basics sugar, acidity, bactericide, etc., to support blooms. It's available, neatly packaged, from any nursery supplier. The pros have been using this for years, and they don't increase their costs without good reason.

Carefree Wonder™, an ARS winner for 1991 is going to be a real winner for rosarians who want an everblooming landscape rose that shuns care. It's not for the show table, but the pink reverse blooms on a mannerly bush make quite a show in hot or cold climates.

The danger label on *Funginex* (*Triforine*) warns of irreversible eye damage by the inert ingredients. Handle the concentrate with great care, using gloves, goggles, common sense. It's a widely-used, effective fungicide that deserves respect.

The trouble with good advice is that it usually interferes with our plans. But if you plan on having some good fall roses as well as some live roses next spring, you may want to review these bits of advice and revise accordingly:

SLOW DOWN for fall. Your roses will appreciate a chance to get ready for winter. There really is a natural process that all perennial plants go through as hours of sunlight shorten and temperatures drop-provided that rosarians don't send out conflicting signals. Roses want to mature, make rose hips, store nutrients in the roots and canes. Trimming and feeding tells the plant it's time to grow. Slow-down time varies, but it's a good rule of thumb to stop feeding nitrogen six to eight weeks before the first anticipated heavy frost. This gives roses and woody shrubs time to manufacture the natural antifreeze that protects each cell-fluids with reduced capability of expanding when frozen. A neat trick performed by Mother Nature if we don't interfere.

PLANTING IN THE FALL. This is a "maybe," depending on regional weather. Temperate area rosarians often plant in the fall hoping to establish the roots for a faster start in the spring. However, these bushes must be carefully winter protected to save all the canes possible. On the Gulf Coast, the Rambler would plant Canadian roses in November, lightly trim only, and hill up with soil and mulch with just the tips of the canes showing. This discouraged new top growth and freeze damage later. The idea was to keep the fall-planted bushes as dormant as possible. Cold climate rosarians are better off, in the Rambler's opinion, to bury fall bushes for retrieval and planting in the spring. The protected pot routine is a lot of work and too many bad things can happen with roses in a garage or shed. The Rambler still likes spring planting whenever possible. This allows the grower to take on the winter risk.

ROSES NEED WATER in the fall, too. Plant processes just don't happen without water. Transpiration still occurs during warm and cool periods; replace the moisture lost from the leaves. Spray burn happens even in cool weather, reducing the capability of the leaves to produce food. Water, leaves and common rose sense prepare roses for winter.

POWDERY MILDEW persists in October, so the rosarian must stay with a spray program as well. The Rambler likes *Rubigan* and *Triforine* in combination, adding *Rubigan* to *Triforine* every other week. Many readers are surprised that water helps control powdery mildew as well, washing off spores before they can wind-drift to new, dry leaves to set up new colonies. Growers who use water on the foliage appreciate the fact that powdery mildew grows on dry plant material, not on wet leaves. Blackspot needs a wet surface to multiply. Both blackspot and mildew like it when the dew point drops with cool nights and warm days, but they prefer different leaf environments.

CORN EAR WORMS will drill small holes in many choice rose blooms this fall if the rosarian isn't alert (even if he is alert). *Mavrik* is the insecticide of choice. Spray the bud and bloom as well as the bed areas. A careful check of developing buds for tiny, cream-colored eggs laid in the seams of the sepals is another line of attack. Squash the eggs before they hatch. Many growers have great success with *BUG ZAPPERS*, fluorescent bug lights with electric grids. These control the moths that lay the eggs on the sepals, and they get rid of hordes of mosquitoes that bother rosarians. Hang a zapper about 8 feet off the ground, away from the rose bed. It helps protect a wide area, depending on the size of the tubes. If there is electric power near the rose bed, a zapper is one of the best investments you'll make in roses.

QUESTIONS FROM YOU GOOD READERS: Does heavy dew on the leaves reduce the effectiveness of spray materials? Not at all; in fact a moist surface offers better leaf coverage. Many growers routinely wash off the leaves before spraying to get the same effect.

Is the **Minnesota Tip** winter protection method still used? Absolutely, by rosarians with strong backs or young helpers. The tip method actually buries a rosebush in a trench after securing the canes. Loosen the roots when the soil is moist and tip into place. A "must" for tree roses in Minnesota.

Do miniature roses in containers get rootbound? Well-grown minis will often get rootbound in two seasons or so, reducing their new growth capability. They can be re-potted, even divided, with great effectiveness. However, there is no need to re-pot until the bushes show definite signs of decline.

ODDS 'N ENDS... Clean up your sprayer before winter. Give it a thorough flush with a weak vinegar-and-water solution followed by an ammonia solution. Old residues will be carried away before setting up and causing trouble later. It's a good idea to take the sprayer apart to check the screens, gaskets and what-have-you. A springtime gasket kit may be in order.

Rose hips belong on roses in the fall-leave them alone. Many varieties are very colorful at this stage of maturity. Even some leaves change color-all a very natural process.

Condition the soil now so that winter rains/snow/freezing/thawing can work. Compost, partially decomposed leaves, old manures and ground bark are appropriate right now. You'll see a difference in the spring.

ENJOY a great fall rose harvest.

A wiser rosarian than the Rambler once said that common sense is genius in working clothes. Here are some common sense ideas that will work for you if given a chance:

A WINTERTIME SNACK for roses may be in order. The "snack" is a feeding of pelletized fertilizer under and in the mulch cover when putting the roses to bed for the winter. To bring new readers up to date, the Rambler has been reporting on this practice for four straight years and has received no irate letters from disappointed growers.

The theory: Soil processes continue through winter. Especially in organic materials used to mulch and protect. Method: put down a layer of leaves, broadcast a scant cupful of pelletized fertilizer (13-13-13) and then put down more leaves.

By spring, the lower layer will have broken down to a rich humus, sometimes threaded with white feeder roots (or maybe mycelium). Readers report that the practice does not encourage unwanted growth and does get bushes off to a faster spring start. The light feeding helps break down the organic material and sets up the soil for better activity as it warms up. The Rambler suspects that the fertilizer feeds the organisms that break down the organics that feed the soil. The process is something like composting in place to enrich the soil below. When spring comes, don't disturb the lower decomposing layer any more than necessary to avoid disturbing any feeder roots that may have reached for the compost.

BECOME A SOIL SCIENTIST. To know if winter feeding really works, feed one bed and skip another in a similar location. Compare the results. Most try-it-and-see reporters say they plan to continue the practice, You'll be surprised at just how much activity there is in the garden when you thought everything was frozen solid.

NOVEMBER IS pH ADJUSTMENT MONTH. It's time to test pH and let lime do its thing (if necessary) over the winter months. Lime works slowly, and that's good, to reach an appropriate balance. Test the pH in a number of rose bed locations right away and begin the treatment. For easy testing, use the *Whatman* pH strips often described in these columns. Call toll-free 1-800-WHATMAN to order — a good investment of time and money. One rosarian recommends cutting the test strips lengthwise to get two strips out of one (really cheap). Find out what need to be done with the soil before bad weather arrives.

NEMATODES have been a nemesis for many sandy-soil rosarians, but Dr. Eldon Lyle, retired pathologist for the Texas Rose Research Foundation, reports that ground pine bark has a remarkable deterrent — even curative — effect.

Dr. Lyle ran trials on a number of field-grown *Mister Lincoln* plants that had more nematodes than roots, He replanted in containers with a half-and-half mix of perlite and ground pine bark. By the end of the first season, healthy new roots nearly filled the containers with very little evidence of active nematodes. The roses thrived. The next year brought the same results. The third year the bushes were planted in beds with a high pine bark content. Now after five years, the roses are still doing well with no evidence of nematodes. Dr. Lyle is not sure if something in the pine bark works on the nematodes or whether the bark supports some other organism that controls the nematodes-but it works. The experience may have an application in your planting.

POWDERY MILDEW is still a problem in some sections of the country, and rosarians are always trying to come up with a new control twist. The latest fad is baking soda, tried by growers and discarded many years ago. The method is to spray infected plants with a solution of 1 tablespoon of baking soda per gallon of water. This washes the mildew evidence away but does not kill the spores. Plain water will do the same thing. It doesn't really hurt anything (clean leaves), but it doesn't do much good either. Stick to *Rubigan* on a scheduled basis or the newest control, *Systhane,* which will be available in '91.

AN ATOMIST IN YOUR CHRISTMAS STOCKING? If there is an *Atomist* electric sprayer in your future, make sure that it is the 1026A model. This one has a new seal and coupling that does not leak, and the model is really easy to use.

Another bit of advice: don't change the spray solution concentration because of the fine fogging capability of the machine. Use the same concentration as with a tank sprayer. *Atomist* will make the same volume of material go farther but does not reduce the solution requirement. How does it cover the undersides of leaves in all that wind? The leaves flutter. Use the wet setting and move along quickly. The Rambler's stocking had a new *Spot-Shot* sprayer in it last year. This battery-operated tank sprayer on wheel does an outstanding job. Just remember that a sprayer is only as good as the rosarian who uses it.

I PROMISED YOU A ROSE GARDEN. The Rambler and Millie Rambler are beginning to show miniature roses this fall. The minis have thrived in a very light mix of Carolina clay, sharp sand, horse manure and perlite-heavy on the perlite. This is almost the same mix as in the whiskey barrels. All the plantings are doing very well, and the limited beds prepared for big roses (never planted) supported a bonus crop of impatiens, salvia and begonias. The soil feels really good. Growth of the minis in the light Carolina mix exceeds a heavier Houston bed by three to one. Minis in 2-inch pots in March now average 18 to 24 inches high very full and loaded with blooms. Even *Starina*, a disappointment in Houston, is a ball of color 18 inches in diameter. As the song goes, "Nothing could be finer..."

DEC. 1990

THOUGHT FOR THE MONTH: OPTIMIST: A rosarian who saves catalog pictures to compare them with the flowers next spring. Ralph Moore

Reading rose books lets rosarians worry about all sorts of new things. But these Rambler recommendations are guaranteed to reduce stress-at least until springtime.

FREQUENCY IS THE ANSWER, NOT CONCENTRATION. The Rambler faced a severe powdery mildew problem earlier this fall, having enjoyed Indian Summer a little too much while neglecting the spray program. One bed of minis looked like an early snow had hit. *Rubigan* is ordinarily regarded as a preventative rather than an eradicant. On this occasion, this excellent systemic product was called on to do both-and in a hurry. The frequency of *Rubigan* in combination with *Triforine* was stepped up to every five days, replacing a 14-day schedule. Concentration was 2 teaspoons per 5 gallons for *Rubigan*, and 1 teaspoon per gallon for *Triforine*. Results were very dramatic. No new mildew appeared after the second spraying. In three weeks all new growth was absolutely clean. At this writing (October), the spray schedule has been reduced to weekly, and the bushes are clean and thriving.

SOIL POLYMERS promise much, and mostly deliver. Although the Rambler's experience covers only one season, it is clear that polymers (granules that take up and then slowly release water and nutrients) are a boon for container-grown roses. Water requirements for containers are greatly reduced, and the plants are not stressed, even during periods of hot weather. Rosarians have to learn how to use these water wonders (see LEARNING CURVE in the September Rambler), but the results are worth the effort and expense, at least for container-grown roses.

The clay soils of the Carolinas combined with lots of organic matter do not seem to benefit from polymers, but a light, sandy bed definitely does. Used in combination with organics, the rose beds that used to suffer from water stress keep up with heavier soil mixes. I suggest you use some on a trial basis in '91.

OWN-ROOT ROSES are gaining in popularity around the country — at least where they are readily available. The Rambler is impressed with the number of canes and increase in low breaks that own-root roses produce. Production the first full season is impressive, too. To get these rooted roses off to a faster start, plant in a 2- to 3-gallon black plastic pot first, using a light soil or soil free mix. Then use a soluble fertilizer weekly (maybe with a touch of alfalfa and fish emulsion). The pots will be full of roots, and the bushes thriving in no time.

You'll know it's time to plant in the beds when roots come out of the bottom holes. But all is lost if the transplanting is not done carefully.

Prepare the planting hole, and then try the pot in it for depth. Cut out the bottom of the pot and carefully place the almost-pot in the hole. Back fill a little. Then cut the sides of the pot in two places and remove the pieces. Back fill and soak. The young bush will never know that it's been transplanted. You may want to keep up the special liquid feeding routine for a few more weeks to encourage well-being in the new home.

COMPOSTING. This is the season, and there are plenty of leaves and garden materials for an area vacated by some annuals following the frost. The process doesn't have to be fancy; just get some organic matter in touch with micro-organisms in the presence of moisture, and nature will do the rest. Speed up the project by chopping the leaves first and mixing rather than layering the soil and green material. It's easy to chop and shred leaves with a rotary lawn mower. Rake up the leaves in a sort of windrow, not too deep. Then run a rotary mower with side discharge up and down the sides of the pile, chopping and placing at the same time. Your neighbors will think that you are a practicing field-farmer. Make a loose pile with dirt or manure plus some green stuff and lightly moisten as the pile grows. A pound or two of a high-nitrogen fertilizer helps, too. For really cold weather, cover with black plastic, but lift the plastic and turn the pile (for aeration) every two weeks. By spring you'll have the world's best soil conditioner.

STILL POPULAR OR REDISCOVERED IN 1990 are a number of rose garden products that should be in your '91 plans. *Rubigan* is still the "in" treatment for powdery mildew, possibly replaced by *Systhane* in '91 (if available). *Orthene 75% SP* is still the best for thrips; *Mavrik Aquaflow* is regarded as the most versatile of all insecticides (plus the best for cucumber beetles). Avid is the choice for spider mites for those growers who have access; otherwise Vendex is the standby. Benlate is making a comeback for blackspot and powdery mildew in the DF (Dry Flowable) form. Daconil 2787 (the active ingredient in Fungi-Gard) has been rediscovered as a solid performer on blackspot and on downy mildew. Triforine (Funginex) is still the blackspot/powdery mildew/rust choice of most rosarians. Diazinon spray and granules provide the best relief for midge. Add the regular use of alfalfa pellets (or alfalfa tea), some fish emulsion, manure from time to time and lots of organic matter and your roses are bound to grow.

I PROMISED YOU A ROSE GARDEN. The Rambler's new mini garden looks like a blooming jungle. The minis are planted too close for the growth potential in the Carolinas. The next bed will have them planted 2 feet apart. FISH MEAL and BONE MEAL attract the neighborhood dog. But Orthene sprayed in the bed and mulch area seems to keep the dog at bay until the attraction disperses. More on fall/winter planting next month.

| NOTE | *Beginning in 1991, the* **American Rose Annual** *replaced the December issue of* **American Rose**. *From this point forward, no columns were printed in December.* |

We all admire the wisdom of those who come to us for advice, and here's a sampling questions to the Rambler by letter, card and call-and maybe some of the right answers.

MANURE in the winter? Absolutely. Animal manures and other organics are primarily soil-builders rather than fertilizers. They won't cause too-early spring growth, but they set the stage for soil organisms to go to work converting nutrients when the soil warms up. The Rambler's favorite is horse manure, liberally applied any time.

ARE SOIL POLYMERS worth the cost? It all depends on your soil and water situation. Sandy soil, hot weather and scarce water combine to make polymers worth their weight in gold-if those are your conditions. Short of time to water container-grown roses? Polymers are the answer.

But if you have fairly heavy soil, ample organics mixed in and water availability, polymers are an expensive (and largely unnecessary) luxury. Use soil polymers only in soils that need extra water-holding capability. And then use them according to directions. Soils soggy from too many polymers drown roses just like soils with poor drainage.

DOES EARLY PRUNING RESULT IN EARLIER BLOOMS? The Rambler assumes that there is some good wood for this rosarian to prune. Early pruning (trying to out-guess the weather) more often results in frozen new growth than in earlier blooms. This is bad for the bush and for the rosarian who has to re-prune to a lower bud.

Roses bloom in the spring as a result of soil and air temperature, not following a pruning calendar routine. Some new growth may appear in the top of the bush during a warm spell, but the low emerging bud eyes will produce the new bloom canes so coveted by rosarians. When a rosebush is pruned, it gets a signal that it's time to grow again, and it does its best to produce new, strong growth.

Time spring pruning so that the bush only has to make the effort one time. Hedge the bet just a little by pruning high so that there is some wood left to re-prune if a freeze comes. You cold-climate rosarians with no wood left in the spring can also follow the same basic routine. Don't uncover and encourage too soon. Let spring really arrive.

WHAT NEW VARIETIES SHOULD I PLANT? That's an impossible question. If you plan to exhibit check out recent lists of show winners. Want lots of roses? Go for garden varieties. For landscaping, shop for floribundas. For accents and small beds, nothing beats miniatures. Even they come in a wide variety of styles, shapes, colors and growth habits.

Grow the varieties that fit you-the roses that make you happy. The best way to know roses is to visit other gardens and talk with other rosarians in your area. Then you are more likely to make good long-term choices.

WHAT'S YOUR FAVORITE ROSE? The one I saw last. But there's a long list of old favorites that the Rambler just can't do without: roses like *Mister Lincoln, Century Two, First Prize, Granada, Pristine* and *Double Delight*. Then there are floribundas like *Europeana, Cherish, lceberg* and *Sweet Vivien*. Our garden has to have a couple of *Don Juan* climbers. And our miniature beds will always have *Red Beauty, Rainbow's End, Minnie Pearl, Millie Walters* and *Rise 'n' Shine*. Got the idea? Rose selection is a very personal matter.

ARE ROSES ON THEIR OWN ROOTS BETTER? It depends. Some own-root roses are better performers than when budded; others are not. Roses on their own roots are gaining in popularity and availability in many parts of the country. Suckers are a thing of the past.

Well-adapted own-root varieties usually produce more canes and have less winter damage. They also seem to live and thrive longer. Of course, there a drawback. Own-root roses take somewhat longer to get to rose production size. Even a well-grown, own-root bush is not going to make it to the trophy table (or your dinner table) very often the first season. But once established, watch out. The Rambler predicts that hobbyists will be growing and enjoying more and more own-root roses in the future.

HOW DO YOU PRUNE REALLY BIG BUSHES? This grower lives in a climate that encourages main rose canes that are 1 inch plus in diameter and 6 feet long, topped with more canes and lots of roses. Unless you want to enjoy roses from a stepladder, these will have to be pruned back to a manageable size. Once roses have been allowed to carry over old wood this size, it's difficult to prune lower and get the old canes to break dormant buds (they just aren't there) or to produce new basals.

However, the Rambler has had success pruning half the cane or more to an encouraging node, carefully trimming stubs and bark from the bud union, hilling up about a foot with mulch to keep the bark soft and moist, and then force-feeding with Epsom salts and a heavy jolt of urea for available nitrogen.

Use the tonics when the soil is warm and force plenty of water. Follow up again with a liquid nitrogen application in about two weeks. There's a good chance that the bush will put out some new breaks that will begin to replace the old wood. It's worth a try anyway.

I PROMISED YOU A ROSE GARDEN. I'm still promising. This year in the Carolinas is just bound to be a good year for roses and the Rambler. Hope you have a good New Rose Year as well.

Faith will never die as long as there are rose catalogs. And do you think that winter will ever let up this season? If you're a believer, it's time to break dormancy — at least for our fortunate warm-zone rosarians.

Try some of these guaranteed-to-work suggestions:

GROUND PINE BARK is much maligned by the uninformed, but glowingly praised by those who have enjoyed the benefits of this cheap, readily available soil improver. Short of compost, leaves or peat moss? Try working about 25 percent fine-ground pine bark (by volume) into the soil — even more if the soil is particularly hard. The newly-worked area becomes friable almost overnight.

Concerned about acidity? Work in about 10 pounds of lime per 100 square feet, plus 5 pounds of 10-10-10 fertilizer to support the decomposition process. Pine bark lasts for a long time and encourages root growth that has to be experienced to be believed. One national writer points out that it seems to reduce rots and diseases. Perhaps it contains some anti-fungal properties or creates an environment that is adverse to disease organisms. Ordinary gardeners think that its physical character encourages healthy roots. Whatever, it works.

PINE BARK in the soil is also a nutrient reservoir, retaining a large quantity of nutrients derived from fertilizers. The process is adsorption: the ability to hold nutrients on the surface rather than within. (Absorption, on the other hand, takes nutrients in to the point of saturation. This is the process that takes place with soil polymers.)

Pine bark becomes only surface-saturated with nutrient solutions. It then distributes the nutrients over a very large surface area. This has a dilution effect, and soils are less likely to be overfertilized. Like a good reservoir, it releases what plants need over a long period of time, as it decomposes. Try pine bark in a whole bed or a planting hole. You (and your roses) will like it.

PHOSPHATE UNDER A PLANTING CONE seems to do more good than when mixed in the bed or added to the planting cone soil. Most rosarians have routinely added a handful of superphosphate or bone meal to the soil cone just before planting, believing that proximity was a virtue. But less material placed in a handful under the cone tends to be more available to the roots for a longer period of time.

Phosphate pellets react in the soil to form unavailable phosphorous compounds. To keep phosphate "alive" and available to the plant, lay it down in a close-knit mass. Some outer particles are tied up in the soil, but the core remains somewhat protected and intact, releasing nutrients gradually. A "band" or mass of phosphate or bone meal works well with bulbs, roses or any plant requiring available phosphate.

REBUILDING BEDS? SAVE THE ROSES. Dormant roses can be dug and set aside for a week or two while rebuilding an existing bed, giving both a new lease on life. Dig carefully with a spading fork; don't worry about taking a ball of soil. Check the roots for galls and to see how much of the root system is alive. Trim out or discard, depending on the severity. Don't bother with a weak bush; it takes much more work than a healthy one.

Set the bushes aside and bury or cover with soil, sacks, mulch, straw or any other material that will keep the bushes cool and moist. Old-timers refer to this as "heeling in," but my father (a practical, dirt-and-manure gardener) always maintained that shrubs were "healed in" and thus protected until they could be planted. It makes no difference; it works.

FRAGRANT ROSES should be in more gardens. That's what our visitors expect. Form and color and substance may be great, but fragrance stops us every time. H. Scott Hansen of Glendale, Arizona, has quite a nose for roses and shares it with the readers of The West Valley Rose, the Glendale newsletter. As a starter, Scott suggests (and the Rambler heartily endorses) roses that have won the ARS James Alexander Gamble Fragrance Medal. Since the first award in 1961, only nine roses have been so recognized: Crimson Glory, Tiffany, Chrysler Imperial, Sutter's Gold, Granada, Fragrant Cloud, Papa Meilland, Sunsprite and Double Delight. Scott also references an excellent article on the nature of fragrance and various rose fragrances in the 1962 American Rose Annual by Neville F. Miller-a very definitive study.

The Rambler will share a couple of pages of Scott's excellent discussion if you drop me a note with a self-addressed, stamped envelope. Then get some of these fragrant roses in your garden this season.

IF IT'S WORKING, STAY WITH IT. Rosarians are drenched with advice like a summer shower, but then it goes away. It's the good, steady rains (and common-sense rose practices) that grow roses. As you begin the rose season, compare your results with others, and if you need to make some improvements, make them gradually. You and your roses will enjoy the season more.

Roses are like golf... you keep thinking that you'll do better next time. The next time is here, so try some of these practical practices to help your rose score...

HILL-UP, BAG UP those new rosebushes if you're planning now so that the roots will have a chance to catch up with the tops. Hilling up adds frost protection, too, but the primary purpose is to keep the canes from drying out. The Rambler ALWAYS hills up a new bush, potted or bare-root. New canes have stored food and moisture that pushes out into new growth and leaves. Meanwhile, the roots are called on to replace the substance, the ONLY way it can be replaced. New roots have to form in a hurry to keep up. To reduce the load on the delivery system, conserve the moisture in the canes. Use mulch, soil, leaves or mixtures of these to hill-up 10 inches or so. Some growers like paper bags or newspaper bands to help hold the material in place. Gradually, uncover the canes in 2 or 3 weeks, leaving the material in place as a summer mulch. Be careful when uncovering; it's easy to break off new basals and low breaks. A slow stream of water from the hose now and then GRADUALLY displaces the hill... and the roses like the extra water, too.

A MOIST-MICRO-CLIMATE is a must for starting tree roses, or for starting new bushes that may have dried out in shipment. Use a plastic tent secured around the head of a tree rose, supplying moisture with a large handful of wet sphahnum moss on the bud unions. When growth is clearly started in two weeks, cut some small holes in the bag to reduce temperature. Remove entirely in another week. Plastic bags are ideal for reluctant bush roses, too. Hill-up with good, moist material. Then form a tent and hold down the edges with mulch and soil, much like a hot cap for tomatoes. The practice has saved many a valuable bush.

PRUNING CLIMBERS is always a topic of conversation over coffee at rose society meetings this time of year. It takes more time and space (and maybe illustration) than allowed here to cover all of the variations for all of the types and all of the climates. However, there's one thing that ALL climbers have in common: APICAL DOMINANCE. That's a big sounding phrase that means roses want to bloom on the top of a rose lateral. The bud on the TOP is going to bloom first; dormant buds lower on the lateral may force out and bloom or they may not. That's the reason that Climbing Queen Elizabeth may throw canes 12 feet long and have only one bloom on the end, UNLESS the cane is trained laterally along a fence or other support so that some dormant buds are on the top of the cane. Sunshine will force the dormant bud at the leaf axil (where the leaf joins the cane), producing a bloom lateral that reaches for the sun. Repeat blooming climbers can have spent blooms cut from the laterals in the same manner as hybrid teas, provided you can get to them. The practice multiplies bloom throughout. The Rambler used to have a fence-full of Don Juan in Houston that produced bushels of good, fragrant blooms three or four times a season. Anyway, the whole idea is to stretch out climbing canes to produce more bloom laterals that produce more blooms.

MARCH IS THE TIME FOR A DOSE OF SALTS... *Epsom Salts* (Magnesium Sulfate), that is. An ounce or two of Epsom salts per bush broadcast right after pruning encourages new breaks and growth. You'll get more growth, greener leaves and an overall healthier bush. This application should be followed with a readily-available source of nitrogen (probably a nitrate form) dissolved in water. This nitrogen shot-in-the-arm is in addition to the regular springtime formula. Just follow the application directions for the nitrogen source. It's better to use smaller amounts more often than a heavy application. Many growers follow the first bloom with *Epsom Salts*/Nitrogen again, with a re-application in late August for rosarians enjoying a long growing season. A two-pound box of Epsom salts from the drugstore will treat 30-40 rosebushes one time.

IF YOU DON'T HAVE A HORSE, you may want to make up some FRAGRANT FORMULA, the Rambler's descriptive term for artificial manure guaranteed to grow roses in rocks. It's a soil amendment, fertilizer, mulch, top dressing all in one. Ingredients include leaves, ground bark and mulch, cottonseed meal, alfalfa meal, bone meal and fish meal. For the recipe (and all the rose rewards), send a self-addressed, stamped envelope to the Rambler, who will send along the step-by-step instructions (with variations) and throw in a sheet on alfalfa applications, how to make tea and how to balance this enzyme support with feeding programs. You'll want to be the first on your block to make manure and tea... and the first with the best roses this season.

I PROMISED YOU A ROSE GARDEN... The Rambler is potting new roses for the almost-completed rose beds, preferring to transplant later rather than fight the cold and mud right now. There's another advantage: these potted bushes will have root systems off and growing by the time really warm weather arrives. Reason? Soil in black plastic pots warms up faster, encourages growth. Will describe *Osmocote* transplant technique next month.

If you must open up a can of worms, the compost pile seems a likely place. So here's a pageful of rosy recommendations that should do about the same thing in your rose garden... but you'll have to get them into your garden (just like the worms) to make them work.

A NON-TRADITIONAL PLANTING TECHNIQUE... Traditional wisdom says "Never use fertilizer with a newly planted rose." But there are some exceptions... like the use of a timed-release fertilizer when planting a well-developed potted rose. Many nursery-supplied roses have been confined in pots for two months or more, developing a fairly good system of new roots. The gardener wants to encourage these roots to expand into the planting bed as soon as possible. Lure the roots with some strategically-placed, timed-release food... a sort of carrot in front of the horse. And this can be done very safely if applied with some rose sense.

CONCENTRATION is the key. Dig the hole to the appropriate depth and try the potted rose in it (still in the pot). Then mix an ounce of something like *Osmocote* with some soil in the bottom of the hole, about an inch or so under the root level. Carefully slit the plastic pot with a sharp knife and cut out the bottom. Gently position the root ball in the hole (there should be all sorts of white feeder roots on the outside). Backfill with an inch or so of bedding mix and add another ounce of *Osmocote* on top of this band, broadcasting away from the roots and all around the ball. Add some more soil, two inches or so this time, and repeat the slow-release application. Finish backfilling with bedding mix and just a touch of *Osmocote* and flood with lots of water. Hill up slightly and keep moist. The rose will never know it has been transplanted. But use NO MORE than 3-4 ounces of *Osmocote* per well-started bush. You'll see good top growth throughout the early season knowing that the roots are growing also.

IS FERTILIZER SOLUBILITY IMPORTANT? Just watch roses respond to fertilizers (especially those with trace elements) in solution and the question is answered. In just a few days, leaves can change color, new growth appears and blooms take on a richer look. Why? The solutions went to the root zone immediately and were picked up by the root system. But ALSO note that the effect doesn't last very long. The solution formula flushes right out in well-drained rose beds. That's the reason for ALSO using granular fertilizers that release more slowly, timed release fertilizers and organic sources (like blood meal and fish meal) in combination. Plan a total application of fast foods and slow foods that fits your rose expense and energy level. What does the Rambler use? A granular fertilizer with trace elements, fish meal, alfalfa pellets, horse manure and occasional "instant desserts" in solution, usually just before rose shows or when a quick response is needed. Need a little more iron? Add *Sequestrene*. More leaves and breaks? Add Epsom Salts. And always use LOTS of water. Rose can't help but grow.

FRIABILITY IS IMPORTANT, TOO. Roots need air, water and foods replenishment on a regular basis... and may be starving if you have been stomping around in the rosebeds too much this spring. Friable soil makes the whole process work. Keep soils loose with organic materials, applied on top of and incorporated into the soil. When the rosebed gets too tight, use a four-tine fork to loosen soil and admit air around the perimeter of the bush. Broadcast a top layer of some sort of organic material like compost or fine-ground pine bark. These organics will drop into the tine holes with a sort of honeycomb affect. Many rosarians also broadcast gypsum (Calcium Sulfate) around the perimeter, about a cup per bush. Gypsum definitely helps open up the soil and leaches salts at the same time. In spite of its "Sulfate" designation, gypsum does NOT alter the pH of the soil.

"UNCLE CHARLEY" DAWSON, greenhouse rose professional and longtime contributor to this magazine (plus rosarians everywhere) even erected a sign in his outside rose garden: "Enjoy the roses but keep your big feet out of the beds." Incidentally, Uncle Charley was the first professional to abandon the practice of stomping and tamping new rosebushes in greenhouse benches. At the time the practice was to pack soil tightly around the roots. His "innovative" approach resulted in faster early growth, reduced loss and longer bench life for rose plants. If your "big feet" have been in the rose beds too much, loosen up and then devise some sort of servicing access. Use stepping stones to distribute the weight, lay some decking on top of loose mulch, or make the planting narrow enough for access in the first place. The whole soil process works better with good movement/drainage of air and water.

NEED MORE ADVICE? Just get out into the rose garden and enjoy the world's greatest hobby.

Rosarians believe in luck — the harder they work the luckier they get. And here are some tips on how to improve your luck with May flowers...

WELL-GROWN ROSES win ribbons; all the grooming, storage, travel and selection tricks in the world can't make a mediocre rose into a winner. Exhibiting skills enhance a rose, but the beauty has to be there in the first place... and that begins in the garden.

THE MOST IMPORTANT SHOW ADDITIVE, believe it or not, is water. Nothing moves through the bush without water; no lush leaves, long stems, substance in the blooms. Every essential to growth (except sunshine) has to go into solution. Good growers SOAK the rose beds and then go back with some more the next day. Some watering by hand is in order, too. Many exhibitors put soak basins around bushes, filling the basins to the brim every evening. Regardless of how it is done, EXTRA water pays off in better blooms. When water runs out of the beds, that's enough. Then repeat.

BLOOD MEAL is a favorite booster of exhibitors. Warm soil and lots of water makes it go to work fast. It is in most of the spring starter formulas (about a half a cup per bush) with a similar amount about two weeks before a rose show. Result: rich, green leaves and lots of color in the blooms. Remember that blood meal is high in nitrogen when combining with regular feeding formulas. Fish meal works about the same way, but takes a little longer. Fish meal is THE CHOICE for miniatures; about two ounces (shot glass) per month promotes super growth and bloom without vegetative centers.

BLOOM BOOSTERS usually have a high available Phosphoric Acid formula with trace elements, applied in solution every two weeks (or even weekly) prior to rose shows. Common formulas are 10-50-10, or 9-17-5 or 9-58-8. The important element is solubility to get to the roots right away. About a tablespoon per gallon per bush is about right, but READ the directions. If weekly applications are in your show plans, cut the amounts accordingly. And ALWAYS reduce to 1/4 of recommended amounts for miniatures, maybe less.

SUPER WHAMMO water soluble mixes need to be used with care. Suzie Spydermite, a legendary exhibitor in Corpus Christi, Texas, regularly used a super solution every other week from pruning time to show time, consisting of a high phosphate combined with fish emulsion, magnesium, and *Sequestrene*. But it's an inexact science, try one thing at a time and see how it works. There's an advertising slogan for a fertilizer that says it all: "Plants need minerals, not miracles."

PROTECT THE BLOOMS that have taken so much effort to produce. Thrips love fragrant, light colored blooms just like the judges. *Orthene 75% SP* is the favorite control, systemic and safe for the most tender blooms. The Rambler prefers the Soluble Powder form for effectiveness and economy over the 9.4% EC (Emulsifiable Concentration). Use *Orthene SP* at 2 teaspoons per gallon of water, get good coverage of buds and blooms and hit the bed area as well.

WHAT IS SPRING WITHOUT MILDEW, powdery mildew, that is. *Rubigan* is the best control, added to the *Funginex* (*Triforine*) program every other week before the onset of mildew season (cool nights, warm days). Drop *Rubigan* from the program in hot weather and pick up again in the fall. All it takes is 2 teaspoons per 5 gallons of water. And what a difference it will make in clean, glossy foliage.

DISBUDDING is a daily routine for rosarians who want the biggest and best blooms, forcing the strength of the bush to one bloom per stem rather than several. Pinch out the excess side buds on HTs for size and exhibition and on GFs (unless you want a spray). The sooner unwanted side growth is pinched out, the less noticeable the scar. On Floribundas, pinch out the terminal (center) bud on a spray as early as possible so that the other florets will develop and bloom at the same time. The terminal bud usually blooms and fades before the rest of the spray has matured.

CHELATED IRON brings out the green in foliage and richness in blooms. How does it work? Chelating iron forms a metallic protective ring so the trace element will not be locked up in the soil by a chemical reaction. The word "chelate" comes from the Greek for claw or pincer, holding material tightly. The chelated form is then available in solution and available to the roots. A common source for rosarians is *Sequestrene 330FE*, a trade name coined from the word "sequester" meaning to "set apart or hold in solution." Check your fertilizer source to see if it has "chelated" trace elements. The good ones do.

MORE on the Rambler's Carolina garden next month.

In growing roses, after all is said and done, there's more said than done. But here are some easy tips to say and do...

HORSE MANURE HAS A BAD NAME... why else would timid growers insist on disguising this wondrous product by composting and aging it? Well-rotted? Why? Most of the good comes from the bacteria cultured on the organic matter. Let the bacteria work on and in your rose bed for best results. As long as manure has organic matter, air and water for a complete process, it will not burn. If the first day or two has a little odor, you know that you got your manure's worth.

HOW DO FERTILIZERS BURN? It's simple, too much high nitrogen fertilizer and not enough water. But why does it happen? Roots are made up of cells whose activity is supported by water, just like human skin and tissue. Burn occurs when water is removed or displaced from the cells. Most fertilizers use ammonium sulfate or ammonium nitrate as a nitrogen source, synthesizing the element found in nature. These compounds are HYGROSCOPIC in nature, that is, have the tendency to take up water. If the compounds (fertilizers) in the soil are too concentrated, moisture is absorbed from the soil, and even the roots, thereby destroying the moisture support system for the cells.

NATURE SEEKS BALANCE; concentrated solutions want to add water and will perform this trick through osmosis — pulling moisture through cell walls. The solution to burn is to apply appropriate fertilizer amounts and ALWAYS with plenty of water. That's the reason for the advice: water first, feed, water again. If in doubt, water again.

HOW DOES AIR MOVE IN THE SOIL? Water disperses throughout the soil medium, attaching to soil particles and partially filling air spaces. In this form it becomes available to the roots, carrying along nutrients in the process. Deep soak to start the process, coating the soil particles. Nutrients in solution follow the soaking, dispersing throughout the soil. Water actually DRIVES the solution to the root zone, pulling along air to support the bacteria busily converting nutrients into forms available to plants. Simple, isn't it?

SPIDER MITES WILL SOON BE IN A REPRODUCTIVE FRENZY, brought on by hot, dry weather. Rosarians can hold the mating to a minimum with a water wand, washing underneath the leaves with a strong, fine water spray. In many cases this works, if you have a small garden and time to wash twice a week. The next step is a miticide like *Vendex* or a broad spectrum insecticide like *Mavrik*. *Vendex* can control mites when populations are low, starting early in the season, about every 21 days. Use carefully and not in combination as it's easy to burn the leaves. *Mavrik* has a quick knock-down but needs to be alternated with other controls as mites develop resistance rather rapidly.

OTHER SPECIFIC MITICIDES have not been released for roses but are available regionally without an applicator's permit. There's even a sex attractant additive for miticides and insecticides called *STIRRUP M*, luring the mites to the control (and I assume to the leaves as well). But good coverage will do the trick, the secret of all spraying. Where to get these exotic products? Send along a SASE to the Rambler and I'll pass on a list of mail order supplies and a sheet of RAMBLING ROSARIAN SPRAY FORMULATIONS.

I PROMISED YOU A ROSE GARDEN... and the Rambler finally has one in the Carolina clay. Notice how the Rambler appears to have aged in the recent photo nearby? Credit the clay, or maybe the 40-some years the Rambler has been at it.

CAROLINA RED CLAY GAVE IN to leaves, and lots of them. The Rambler is growing in what appears to be a compost pile, but what is really a clever natural concoction of clay soil, sharp sand, perlite, fine-ground pine bark and lots and lots of leaves. The rose beds are so spongy that the footprints spring back. Holds moisture extremely well, but also drains. The activator is horse manure and cottonseed meal. The leaves were partially composted and steaming when forked from the pile. The same leaf pile mounded the newly planted bushes and replenishes four inches of bed mulch. Great stuff. Just like nature does it in the forest.

SUMMERTIME RESULTS next month.

In the summertime, roses like lots of water... mostly in the form of sweat. But for other water sources and systems, check out some of these cool, damp suggestions for better roses and less work in the hottest of weather.

DO-IT-YOURSELF watering systems can be rewarding to roses and rosarians... the grower becomes part of the process, adding flexibility and ingenuity that the commercial setups can't provide. Goal: get water to roses as effectively as possible with least possible effort, conserving this most valuable resource. The system that the Rambler likes is the *Dramm Nozzle*, having installed and revised and reworked more of these efficient water deliverers in more rose and flower beds than he cares to remember. Besides, *Dramms* are cheap, readily available, made up with simple hand tools and flexible enough to change around anytime your rose plans change.

THE *DRAMM NOZZLE* is a two-piece nozzle of hard plastic with a tapered, threaded connection. A pin diffuser sprays the water out, not up. Just pull the pin out to clear a water line and adjust the height of the pin for the amount of water to be delivered. The nozzles are installed in Schedule 40 (rigid) PVC pipe, available in most lumberyards and hardware stores. Most systems use 1/2 -inch pipe, 3/4-inch has greater deliverability if enough water pressure is available. Each nozzle puts out a flat spray about 3 feet in diameter. Water delivered to the system at about 40 pounds through a 5/8-inch garden hose will support a water line of about 45 feet with 15 nozzles or so. More pressure, larger delivery line, larger pipe will support even longer runs and more nozzles. The pipe with *Dramm* nozzles can be attached permanently to a water source or connected (use a quick-connect) to a garden hose.

TO INSTALL, layout the pipe in the rose bed and mark where the nozzles should be. All sorts of configurations are possible, just like Tinker Toys. The hardware store has every sort of connector, "T", cap, angle and reducer needed. The pipe can be fed from the end, the middle or in-between. The pipe cuts easily with a hacksaw and all connections made with PVC solvent cement. Drill holes (7/16-inch) in the pipe, keep the holes aligned. A drill press helps, but a simple centering device on

a hand drill works just about as well. Clear out the shavings and place the saddle washer (comes with the nozzle assembly) in the hole. Screw in the nozzle; the tapered thread makes the seal tighter and tighter as it is screwed down. The assembled pipe can be laid on the top of the bed, elevated on blocks, stabilized with anchor "legs" or positioned in a number of ways. Best of all, it can be changed any time to suit. For a really "finished look", the pipe can be painted with any thinned latex paint and become inconspicuous. If these instructions aren't enough, the Rambler has an illustrated assembly sheet he will be glad to send along.

SOAKER SYSTEMS are appropriate for many growers, weeping droplets of water through porous rubber hose, usually made from recycled tires. Most of these systems are easy to install and adapt as they can be laid on top of the bed, under the mulch or buried in any configuration the planting requires. Some of the more popular systems are *LEAKY PIPE, HYDRO-GRO* and *MOISTURE MASTER*, although the Rambler is sure there are other regional providers just as worthy of consideration. The weeping systems conserve water, delivering at or near the roots. There is little or no evaporation, runoff or washing.

WHEN TO USE A SOAKER... The planting bed should be porous and well drained. Heavy, tight soil will be saturated in the hose area, dry in other parts of the bed. And the grower can't be sure what's happening when the porous hose is buried. Buried systems usually run the hose on both sides of the rose-root system, not just down the middle of the bed. For a trial, the Rambler suggests the *MOISTURE MASTER*, which comes with a hose connection, ready to go. Other systems come with connectors, drain cocks and a box-full of attachments to custom-build.

ALL THE SYSTEMS can use proportioners (or siphons) for liquid fertilizer application accurately and easily. Electronic water timers can also be installed (just screwed on) at the water source to turn the water system on and off on a regular schedule. These timers runoff small alkaline batteries and do not need an electrical power course. Just set the timer and go off on vacation. These systems and attachments can be as elaborate or as simple as your needs dictate. Best of all, roses get the water they need.

GIVEAWAYS... The Rambler still has some copies of giveaways previously discussed. They include: Fragrant Formula, Alfalfa Tea, Spray Formulations, Mail Order Sources, Hanging Basket Rack, Fragrant Roses... and this month *Dramm Nozzle* Plans. Drop a note with a SASE if any of these interest you.

SUMMERTIME RESULTS in the Rambler's garden were promised last month. Report: The compost pile, leaves, clay, pine bark and what-have-you mix is supporting some of the best newly-planted roses the Rambler has ever had. The bed holds moisture but drains well, nutrients are obviously available, roots are spreading throughout the mix (VERY carefully inspected). A few mice have moved in, but they are easy to control. We'll see what happens when the really HOT weather comes on and tell you next month.

The time to relax is when you don't have time for it... but the Rambler's tips this month are so relaxing that you can put them off until the weather gets cooler.

WATERING SYSTEMS for rose beds make rosarians really relaxed. Several types were discussed in this column last month except for the ultimate hands-off system... the drip irrigator. Programmed by computer, the emitters will faithfully perform with little help by the resident rosarian. But there's a price to pay for this convenience. Delivery lines have to be carefully laid from the control source for uninterrupted service. Once in place in the area to be watered, the system has great flexibility. Initial cost is also a little higher, but forgotten when the grower can go off for a week and not worry about the roses.

WATER CONSERVATION will be a major issue in future gardens, as the folks in California will testify. Drips are the most miserly of all the systems and let growers cope with the tightest restrictions. The Rambler has always lived in an area with lots of cheap water and has had little experience with a major drip installation. But a drip system is now being strung like spaghetti for hanging baskets and potted roses. Details on how the thing works in future issues.

WATER WAND OR WATER BREAKER? A water wand directs a strong stream of water (usually in a cone or fan shape) underneath rose leaves to wash off spider mites. Fine droplets at high pressure really clean them off. Regular washing controls mites in many gardens, particularly if insecticides are used sparingly. Other benefits: cleans spray residue and pollution fallout, cools bushes and adds water. On the other hand, a water breaker (on a long handle) directs a smooth flow of water to beds, basins, pots, planters and individual plants. This hand application is an extra touch for roses in beds; while the water soaks in, the rosarian can get better acquainted with the roses to know what's going on with the bush, seeing things that aren't obvious when turning on the hose. Roses really like this hand care. No rose garden is complete without BOTH a water wand and a water breaker.

OWN-ROOT ROSES... The Rambler takes back whatever unkind (and uniformed) remarks about own-root roses that might have been made in the past. Roses growing on their own roots DO have a place in ANY rose garden without having to wait years for decent-sized plants and blooms. It's amazing how quickly rooted roses catch up with budded bushes. The Rambler has an own-root bush of Uncle Joe, taken from a cutting last September, planted next to a budded, bare-root bush that went into the bed in May. Both bushes are doing well, but the own-root has more bloom-supporting canes (four husky ones), foliage and blooms than the budded version. Same experience with two bushes of Touch of Class.

CULTURAL CONDITIONS obviously control how quickly a cutting can make a good bush. Protected conditions in cold weather speed up the process. The most important factor is a good potting mix in which the roots can develop. The Rambler begins with a 4-inch pot, then graduates to a 1-gallon and then to a 2-gallon before transplanting into the bed. The warm soil and controlled, regular feeding helps cuttings develop in a hurry. Adapt a system to suit your climate and enjoy some great roses that you "grew yourself."

I PROMISED YOU A ROSE GARDEN and have finally delivered. Not a really LARGE garden yet, but growing. Millie has about 150 miniatures in two large beds, some deck containers and four whiskey barrels. Soil mix is approximately the same for the containers and the beds, with polymers added to two barrels. The mix is very light with lots of compost, Perlite, ground pine bark and partially decomposed leaves. A typical 4-inch pot miniature develops into a mature plant in about 60 days here.

THE RAMBLER has 75 hybrid teas in a formal, built-up bed, 60 Floribundas and spreading types in beds around the deck and some late additions in 4-gallon containers. Both plantings will expand considerably next season. The very light, almost-compost planting mix has just enough red clay to hold moisture. These roses are on a twice-a-week watering schedule. July has been very hot and dry, but no sign of wilt or leaf stress. Everything is mulched with 5 to 6 inches of composted leaves. The mix stays cool, moist and loose all the time. Bushes are anchored with 1/4-inch reinforcing bar cut into 15-inch lengths and inserted at an angle across the bud union and through the canes.

A short length of old plastic hose is slipped over the bar to prevent chafing. No ties are used. In just a year or so the bar/bud union/bush will become one unit that's there to stay.

More on the leaf mulch in future episodes. Even the Carolina license plates say "Nothing Could Be Finer."

SEPTEMBER marks the 21st Anniversary of the Rambler, making some 250 columns' worth of wisdom and wonder on how roses manage to grow in spite of rosarians. Just for the fun of it, these Ramblings recap the column from September, 1981... and find that things haven't changed much.

HARVEST MONTH for rosarians was declared for September with rose buckets overflowing. Except for the first spring bloom, fall roses can be the best of all... and the best time for a check list of what happened and why it happened for plans and practices that will payoff NEXT season.

LEAVES AND OTHER COMPOSTING MATERIALS will be plentiful for most growers in the next month or so. It's a rich harvest that the smart growers will use and the uninformed will stuff into trash bags. Leaves should be made available for roses with some sort of composting, even if all of the leafy production can't be used. Experience the benefits of compost just once and you'll find space for more leaves next year. Rake aside a BIG pile of leaves for winter insulation, make new soil with the rest.

COMPOSTING IN PLACE is easy. Just turn and dig the soil in a bed area, making a wind-row of soil. Pile leaves, clippings, etc., in the depressed trench and add some excess soil as a top dressing... plus a nitrogen/microorganism source like manure or cottonseed meal to make the process work faster. Keep moist and turn lightly now and then. Add some more leaves as the mound goes down. Before hard-freeze time, the composted material will be broken down enough to till and mix in place or to add to other bed areas. Let the freeze-thaw cycle complete the job over the winter. Nature works the same way, season after season.

TIRED ROSE BEDS... sound familiar? Soils pack near the end of a long season and need some freshening up to help water and air move through the soil. The catalyst is organic material, propping open the soil to keep it alive. Cultivate compost on crust to mechanically mix some of the humus product with the top soil. No need to penetrate too deep, an inch or so really helps.

TIGHT SOILS respond to a spading fork also. Punch some small holes around the drip line of a bush with a fork, the four-prong kind that's about six inches long. Spade in all the way and rock back and forth. Fertilizers, air and water get into the root zone faster. Give each bush three or four good jobs anytime.

TRANSPIRATION is the reason for this opening up routine. "Tight" soil does not have the same transpiration (water movement) capability as light, well aerated soils. Think of soil as a sponge with air space, vast particle surface and organisms capable of making nutrients available to roots. Calcined clay (kitty litter) was an example cited in 1981; crumbs of clay with millions of pore spaces. What does it do? Calcined clay absorbs and holds air, water and nutrients for slow release to roots. And that's what roses still like.

COARSE PERLITE is a great soil conditioner, too, and a useful additive in potting mixes, particularly for miniatures on their own roots. Use the spading fork trick noted above for tight soils and rake or pour Perlite into the holes left by the prongs. Last a long, long time. A timely note: The Rambler recently had to return some old rose beds (built in 1979) to lawn area. (The Rambler's former garden in Houston.) Perlite and calcined clay were STILL evident in the mix. That's after more than 10 years of cultivating, rebuilding, adding organics, fertilizing and 50 inches or more of rainfall a year, plus a staggering water bill.

THE RAMBLER'S CAROLINA ROSE GARDEN benefits from this experience. Hope that your garden benefits as well. More tips for fall next month. Happy Harvest!!

Clever men make quips, and clever columnists repeat them... and they also repeat some of the more clever advice — because it works. Here are some thought-provokers that have been tested by time...

MIRACLE CONTROLS work when the miracle gets on the leaves, as in the case of RUB/CAN, the systemic mildewcide (powdery) that needs to be used BEFORE severe infection. RUB/CAN works from within the leaf tissue (systemic), controlling and killing powdery mildew spores. But it's an absolute eradicant only when pushed to the limits of frequency and concentration. Use *Rubigan* in combination with *Triforine* one week, *Triforine* alone the following week. The every-other-week routine will control mildew provided that the rosarian starts as soon as evening temperatures drop. And many rosarians are surprised that water helps control powdery mildew as well, washing off spores before they can wind-glide to new, dry leaves to set up new colonies. Powdery mildew grows on DRY leaf material, not on wet leaves. Blackspot needs a wet surface to multiply. Both blackspot and mildew like high humidity situations (when the dew point drops with cool nights and warm days), but prefer different leaf environments.

WINTER FEEDING? It's a practice worth considering. A better description might be "composting in place". Growers in severe as well as milder climates put down a layer of leaves in the rose bed, broadcast a cupful of pelletized fertilizer (13-13-13) per 10 square feet, then add some more leaves. By spring, the lower layer of leaves is broken down into a rich humus threaded with white mycelium. The fertilizer works on the leaves, not the soil, breaking down the organic material and setting up the soil for better activity in the spring. Don't disturb the lower layer any more than necessary at pruning time in the event that feeder roots have reached for the compost. Advocates of winter feeding report no untimely new growth either in the fall or the spring when roses are put to bed with this "nightcap."

FOOL MOTHER NATURE with anti-transpirant applications for freeze-prone climbers or shrubs in exposed locations. Here's how it works: Water loss (transpiration) is substantially reduced by spraying canes and remaining leaves at the onset of dormancy with *Cloud Cover, Wilt-Pruf*, et al. These products form a transparent flexible film which is semi-permeable to water and permits the normal breathing process to take place. But the film retains the natural anti-freeze in the canes and tissues. Major winter damage occurs from drying out (desiccation), usually more severe than pure cold. Anti-transpirants are relatively easy to apply with ordinary spray equipment, taking extra care for good coverage. And be sure to clean the sprayer thoroughly... it coats sprayer parts as well as canes. The technique is a natural for climbers on fences or walls, canes that can't be protected in any other convenient way. Apply upon dormancy, repeat later in the winter if weather is unusually mild. You'll be pleased with the results.

INSULATING WRAP for tree roses is a cheap insurance for live bushes in the spring. Fiberglass rafter or duct insulation, the "pink panther" blanket with foil backing, works well. Loosely wrap the standards from bottom to top, foil side out, and tie with cord. Flare out just under the bud unions and bundle wrap the major canes. The insulation protects from sudden freeze-thaws and drying winds, and is certainly easier than burying the entire tree rose.

INSULATING LEAVES on rose beds works well, too. Begin with a mound of soil or compost over the bud union and lower canes, then add lots of leaves in a loose blanket. This will keep most roses in good shape with temperatures to 20 below, stressed with cold, dry winds and bright sunshine. Keep leaves in place with wire baskets, rabbit-wire fences, evergreen boughs or even short snow fence. Some very cold climate rosarians use a combination of rose cones (foam) and leaves for protection, the leaves serving as a protective insulation for the cones while maintaining more even temperature and moisture.

READER'S TESTIMONIAL: "I don't have time or energy to build boxes or bury roses, so I have always thrown some dirt from the garden area on the bud unions and piled on leaves as high as they would go. Even get some leaves from the neighbors. It's not very fancy, but my roses always do all right."

Hope that you enjoy an all-right fall.

If occasional failure is the price of improvement, some of us may be paying too much. If you would like to reduce your high cost of roses, try some of these suggestions...

SLEEP UNDER THE SNOW... new rosebushes, that is. Roses received in November are far better off buried than potted and moved in and out of protection all winter. Burying is a natural sort of dormancy, much like the "Minnesota Tip" method of winter protection. Select a well drained garden spot where it is easy to dig (about 18 inches or so), loosen the removed soil with plenty of leaves and the "dormancy vault" is ready to receive bushes. Line the bottom of the vault with soil/leaves mix. Tie the tops of the bushes and loosely bundle. Heel in the bundles (not quite horizontal) and cover with the mix. Tie a rope on the bundles so that you can find them next spring. Cover the area with leaves, wait for spring. It really works.

FROST CONSCIOUS ROSARIANS in warmer climates like to get Canadian roses in the fall but worry about January/February freezes. These bushes can also be buried for dormancy, but the most common practice is to pot these newcomers and winter protect in a garage or garden house for cold snaps of short duration. Potted roses develop good root systems and get off to a roaring start when set out in the beds. Thoughtful rosarians know: Grow the roots first, then the tops (and blooms). If potting is not on your exercise agenda, compromise by planting in prepared beds and mulching to the very tips of the canes. Don't trim the canes at all. Encourage dormancy. If new growth at the top gets nipped, trim off next spring and there will be plenty of cane left.

NEED A GYPSUM FLUSH? Roses in built-up beds and in containers tend to turn pale near the end of the season, but will respond to a good gypsum flush. Cold-climate rosarians won't see the difference until next spring, but the results will be dramatic. Salts tend to build up over a season, especially with clay soils and alkaline water. The clay particles tend to stick together; we say the soil is "tight." For this condition, gypsum "opens up the pores" and the good soil processes take over again. The effect is like "pulling the cork out of the bottle." Works fine in clay rose beds, too. Doesn't disturb the pH and furnishes calcium. About 20 pounds per 100 square feet of rose bed or a handful per 5-gallon container is about right. Application can be inexact. Water in well and let good things happen all winter.

NOVEMBER IS pH ADJUSTMENT MONTH. It's time to check the pH and let lime do its thing (if necessary) over the winter months. Lime works slowly, and that's good, to reach an appropriate pH level (slightly acid, 6.5-6.8). Test pH in a number of locations right away and begin treatment. For easy testing, use the *Whatman* pH strips often described in these columns. Call toll-free: 1-800-WHATMAN. Ask for a box of strips in the 5.2-6.8 range. Very easy to use, complete instructions with each 200-strip box (about $20). *Whatman* strips are a really good investment in time and money.

MAKING ADJUSTMENTS... Winter is a good time to apply agricultural lime (if needed) provided that the soil area is workable. Top application is not effective since lime is relatively insoluble. The process is a REACTIVE one, that is in the presence of soil. Lime in the presence of Hydrogen ions (the indicator for pH) reacts with those ions to form water. By reducing the hydrogen ions, the pH goes up. It's a fairly slow process. If a rose bed needing lime can't be tilled or spaded, use a spading fork to open up holes to receive the lime. Lightly scratch soil back. Let water and chemistry do its thing. To STAY in balance, a good rule of thumb is to add a pound of agricultural lime (calcium carbonate) or dolomite lime (calcium carbonate and magnesium carbonate) for every pound of nitrogen. Example: 5-10-5 ammonium sulfate, 50 pound bag, contains 2.5 pounds of nitrogen. Use 2.5 pounds of lime for the same area. And always TEST before adjusting.

I PROMISED YOU A ROSE GARDEN... The Rambler and Millie Rambler are exhibiting again with modest success, both exhibition roses and miniatures. Two new rose beds are underway for planting in February. Still using a little day, lots of composted leaves. Will tell you about them in January.

HAVE A HAPPY, ROSY NEW YEAR.

Rosy Resolutions are in order for '92, a break from taking roses too seriously. Here are some gems gathered from the diaries of rosarians who believe that roses are more fun if there are some rules to break…

ROSE RESOLUTIONS:

• Order only ten more roses than the garden will hold.

• Save money by ordering three of everything.

• Restricted reading of rose catalogs.

• Accept bugs as part of nature's balance.

• Encourage rose growth without swearing.

• Tell Queen of the Show story only when asked.

• Dig up no more than 10% of lawn area.

• Buy only two "miracle" rose potions for "testing."

• Let weatherman handle rainfall without help.

• Come in from garden for supper on time.

• Wear clean shirt for Sunday rose work.

• Use some common rose sense.

ROSARIANS ASK… some of the darndest questions, like "How big should I let my rosebushes get?" In many parts of the country, the weatherman decides this, but a grower has considerable control over growth and shape. Rule of thumb: fewer canes produce bigger stems and blooms, more canes produce more blooms, usually smaller. You do have a choice.

SPRAY START?? As soon as the bush is pruned in the spring, the SAME day. This routine controls fungus spores and overwintering insects. The keyword is CONTROL. These rose problems are just waiting for the right combination of temperature and humidity. Get ahead of the game and stay on schedule.

ALFALFA PELLETS NOW?? Why not? Alfalfa is a soil conditioner that makes nutrients more available when the soil warms up. Caution: pellets on top of the snow may feed more rabbits than soil. After this wintry entire, our furry friends have appetites for green canes. Precaution: scratch into soil or mulch. Another winter trick is to lay down 3 or 4 inches of alfalfa hay mulch in the rose beds. The hay breaks down over the winter and blends well with soil and organic material. Your feed store friend probably has a bale or two of moldy hay for sale cheap.

WHEN TO DIG AND DIVIDE?? Miniature roses can be dug and divided when dormant, a practical activity for many varieties at pruning time. Works on own-root roses, too. Vigorous minis get woody centers after a few years and new growth is forced to the outside. It's easy to lift up a large bush with a spading fork and shake off the soil. Then break up or cut up the mass of roots and small canes into smaller bushes, carefully pruning out the dead, woody material. Minis break up much like chrysanthemums. The smaller plants will equal the size of the mother in about a season, greatly exceeding previous production. Plant in rebuilt soil, hill-up with mulch and watch strong, new plants emerge. The Rambler supplied half of the Houston Rose Society with plants of *Rise 'n' Shine,* starting with just five bushes.

PRUNE EARLY?? Not a good risk. Assuming that there is wood to prune, there is little to be gained by jumping the season. This usually results in frozen new growth rather than earlier blooms, setting back the rose and rosarian. Roses come into bloom in the spring as a result of sunshine, soil and air temperature rather than a pruning calendar. The routine is good for cold-climate rosarians with no wood left in the spring. Don't uncover and encourage too soon. Let spring really arrive.

I PROMISED YOU A ROSE GARDEN… Two new rose beds (8 x 16 feet) are now mellowing with winter rains. The beds are built up with landscape timbers 2 or 3 high to accommodate a slope. The soil mix is 1/4 red clay, some leftover garden soil, mortar sand from the new house next door, 4 big bags of Perlite per bed, some alfalfa and cottonseed meal and LOTS of partially composted leaves (about 2/3 by volume). A wonderful mix that roses love. Easy to work, plant, water and maintain. Just like nature intended.

CAN'T WAIT UNTIL SPRING. How about you??

All things come to he whose name is on a mailing list… these Ramblings among them. Can spring be far behind the rose catalogs? If these rosy tips are a bit too early for your climate, enjoy catalog reading a little longer… but real rose work begins soon.

ROSE BEDS BEHIND SCHEDULE? Don't worry. Your new rosebushes don't have to know that you enjoyed fall too much. A fast rose bed rich in organics is easy to build in two weeks or less. Just build up the rose bed and don't worry too much about what's below; a major excavation is not necessary. Clear away the area to be planted and bring in some light soil first, a couple of inches or so. No need to buy an expensive "garden mix." What you're going to mix is better than anything that comes off a truck. Till this soil in with the existing soil as deep as you can.

OLD RELIABLE FORMULA comes next, resulting in a final mix (by volume) of 1/3 soil, 1/3 organic matter and 1/3 gritty sand. Mix well with a tiller or a fork. Then add (for about 100 square feet of rose bed) about 50 pounds of alfalfa meal or pellets, 25 pounds of gypsum, 10 pounds of superphosphate (0-20-0) and a couple of inches of horse manure to get the whole process going. Till again and water down to settle. Mix again in a week, water. Plant the following week, bare-root or potted roses. Won't burn, roots take right off.

HORSE MANURE SUBSTITUTE? Use partially composted leaves and other organics (ground bark, coarse peat) laced with cottonseed meal (about 25 pounds per 100 square feet). Decomposition begins immediately, resulting in a manure-like material. Just use PLENTY of leaves, moisten and turn often. Resulting bed will be full of earthworms, too.

GET READY TO SPRAY. On schedule. Too many rosarians so admire the emerging leaves that they forget the fungus spores are emerging also. Spores overwinter on green tissue and the bud union crevices. Spray the day bushes are pruned with a combination fungicide/insecticide.

Maintain control EARLY and stay on schedule. It's too late when blackspot appears or new leaves and buds are deformed and covered with powdery mildew. The Rambler is an enthusiastic fan of *Rubigan* for powdery mildew, added to *Tri-forine* every other week when mildew conditions are right (cool nights, warm days).

DOWNY MILDEW control also begins early. Alternate *Triforine* and *Daconil* weekly during cool, damp weather. If downy mildew has been a problem in the garden previously, increase the frequency of *Daconil* (*Fungi-Gard* or other formulation of *Daconil 2787*) and spray carefully for good coverage. Make sure that canes and leaves (especially undersides) are evenly moistened; a spreader-sticker may help. Beads of spray on the leaves won't do the job.

SPRINGTIME PATIENCE PAYS OFF. Spring may be a long way off for some readers, but there are many temptations to uncover roses too soon. It's called "sap rising in roses and rosarians." More roses are probably lost to "springtime winterkill" than sub-zero temperatures in January. Let nature proceed at her own pace. Let whatever rose protection you use stay on a little longer than may seem necessary. Pruning and probing gives roses the signal that it's time to grow. In the spring, roses bloom when it's time to bloom; early pruning seldom speeds up the process. You'll be doing your roses and yourself a favor with a little patience.

LOOK AHEAD WHEN PRUNING. Allow for a late freeze and loss of top growth. Be able to re-prune to a lower dormant bud whenever possible. Cold climate rosarians who prune to the bud union think ahead with a generous covering of insulating materials like leaves and straw. Insulating materials want to maintain an even temperature, including warmth that encourages new growth. Use generously and then let the material compost in place in the beds.

I PROMISED YOU A ROSE GARDEN… The Rambler's newly-constructed rose beds (one month old) already have lots of worms. A mild winter, generous rainfall, lots of organics, cottonseed meal starter and aeration with coarse Perlite have made the beds alive and working. Will tell you about planting in this loose mix next month.

MAR.
1992

THOUGHT FOR THE MONTH:
I was gratified to be able to answer the rose question promptly. I said I didn't know.

Growing roses isn't hard work… unless you would rather be doing something else. So these fun tips should be no work at all for you enthusiastic rosarians.

BAD ROSE-BACKS like hands-and-knees planting, much less strain than bending over. A dirty-knees rosarian is a good rosarian. The trick is to find a small shovel with a short handle, something like the old army foxhole tool. If the soil has been well prepared, it's easy to scoop out a hole, rebuild a cone to support the roots and bush, then let water and soil do the rest. Properly placed, the roots and shank will be stable without holding. Cover the roots lightly with soil and begin to run water slowly into the hole, add more soil, than more water. No need to tamp or pack. Hill up with some EXTRA soil and mulch; keep moist with an overhead sprinkler.

COVER UP WORK. Hill up newly planted roses with a loose, protective cone of mulch or other insulating material until just the tips of the canes stick out. Not just a little material, a real mound, a couple of BIG shovelfuls per bush. Moisture conservation in the canes is important, not sunshine. Protection from cold, too. Moisture in the canes is supported by new root hairs; hilling keeps canes from drying out until the roots have a chance to deliver.

ABOUT CLEANUP SPRAY for newly-pruned bushes. It is misunderstood and controversial. The objective is to get ahead of spores and overwintering insects without damaging the cane tissue. Rosarians in the really dormant, cold regions like oil and sulfur or lime/soil/sulfur combinations, but they MUST be applied when canes are still dormant. And they make a terrible mess on the side of the house or fence. The Rambler likes to use the same controls in cold or warm weather; a fungicide/insecticide combination with a little extra spreader-sticker for good coverage, used at label strength. Spray climbers and shrub roses particularly well; infected bushes can spread spores like wildfire when conditions are right.

SPRINGTIME ADDITIVES/INDUCERS/ HORMONES are always popular at the springtime nursery shop, but less popular in the rose garden. If the bed has been well-prepared and kept alive with regular additions of organics, miracle cures aren't required. The Rambler likes a cup of gypsum per bush in early spring, a cup of alfalfa meal or pellets, a small handful of *Epsom Salts* and a good source of nitrogen, preferably organic like fish meal, cottonseed meal or blood meal. Get all of this stuff in contact with the soil and let nature and the micro-organisms go to work.

NEW BUSHES LIKE A FISH DIET, low fat and high in protein and minerals just like rosarians. Fish emulsion is the easy way. Water in bare root bushes with 2 tablespoons of fish emulsion per gallon of water. Repeat in about two weeks. Roots will develop quickly without burning. This works with miniatures, too.

WANT BASAL BREAKS? A one-two punch with *Epsom salts* (Magnesium Sulfate) and readily available source of Nitrogen brings results at pruning time as well as after the initial bloom cycle. Magnesium, so essential to the rose tissue process, leaches readily, as does Nitrogen. Kick off the process with up to a half-cup of *Epsom salts,* followed by an every-other week application of a soluble 20-20-20 like *Peters* or *Ra-Pid-Gro*. New basals require lots of energy. Get that energy into the root zone for results.

ODDS 'N ENDS… The Rambler is impressed with the porous pipe irrigation setups made from recycled tires. The water really "oozes" from the pores… and is easy to install.

POT UP SOME SPARES this spring for some ready replacements. Need a rose(s) in late spring, you're ready with a bush that's far ahead of those left in the nursery…

RE-POT NEW MINIS, too, so that they can take off in new plantings. A month or so in a larger, warm pot with special treatment gives minis a good start.

I PROMISED YOU A ROSE GARDEN… and new planting is underway in the very loose, organic beds. This season new bare root bushes are staked when planting to stabilize and support the first season. Use old nylon hosiery or *Plastic-Ty* with long treated wood stakes or reinforcing bar covered with hose. ENJOY the springtime.

Nothing seems impossible to the rosarian who doesn't have to do it himself. But these tips are so easy that even the impossible becomes routine.

THE BEST FERTILIZER… WATER. Absolutely essential for feeding program… and the most overlooked. Nutrients are not available to the plant until in solution and in the root zone. That calls for lots of water and good drainage to get rid of the excess. Water picks up nutrients from granular fertilizers like a drip coffee maker and carries solutions to where the work is being done by the micro-organisms. Water deeply, and then water again. You'll like the results.

ROOT PRUNING? It's a good practice (applied with some rose sense) for most bare-root rosebushes. The Rambler lightly trims the ends of most of the roots and cuts out broken roots. Trimming exposes healthy tissue for new root hairs to develop, resulting in a stronger system. And if the roots are too long for the planting area, shorten them up a bit. You're planting roses, not making an excavation.

PINCH NEW BUDS? It's a tough decision for rosarians anxious to see the bloom of a new variety. But first things first. Grow bushes with good canes and leaves, then add roses. Reduce flowering until the bushes are well established. On at least some of the new, strong stems, pinch out the buds Gust like disbudding) or go down to the first good leaflets. Encourage bud eyes lower on the stem. That's where the biggest and best buds are. Bud eyes on roses are apically dominant, that is, the top bud wants to break. But let the strength go to lower, stronger buds which will in turn develop strong stems and new buds for more blooms.

NEW BASALS… are candidates for pinching, too… a very painful process for rosarians. Depending on the vigor of a variety, when the basal hits 18 inches or so and begins to form a bloom bud, pinch back to a five-leaflet or a good, blunt bud eye. Lower buds will break, multiplying the canes available for roses. The Rambler has the willpower to pinch about half of the really strong basals, and the resulting growth is nearly always better.

YOU DESERVE A BREAK TODAY. Give yourself (or ask your gardening partner for) a Mantis tiller/cultivator. The Rambler got one for Valentine's Day and garden soil has been flying ever since. Takes the work out of new rose bed construction… cultivates, aerates, edges and generally makes a large garden really fun. Weighs about 20 pounds with sharp tines that dig and mix and chop with amazing speed. Tills to about 12 inches (even in red clay) and will dig a hole for planting in no time at all. The Rambler saw the Mantis demonstrated at a nursery open house a year ago and dismissed it as "not husky enough." A very poor conclusion. The Mantis tiller/cultivator is advertised regularly in these pages; costs about $350 with attachments. Take a really good look at this garden wonder. A Rambler Note: This isn't a Mantis-sponsored promo. After borrowing a Mantis from a friend, the Rambler became a full-price buyer and a happier rosarian.

SPIDER MITES CAN BE CONTROLLED… and it's time to start as the weather warms up. Choose your weapons: water wash, hold back the broad-spectrum insecticides or, as an ultimate solution, use AVID, the translaminar miticide that has made rose growing in hot climates possible again. For many rosarians, water washing the undersides of the leaves weekly basis works rather well, usually combined with less-liberal use of insecticides. Natural predators can handle mite populations if given some support. However, if mite populations get out of hand, go for Avid.

THE RAMBLER'S ROUTINE FOR MITES: Wash undersides of leaves early in the season, but at the first sign of mites (gray-green lower leaves, dry looking with salt and pepper residue on the undersides) spray with Avid at 1/4 teaspoon per gallon, with good coverage under the leaves. Buffer water with 1 tablespoon of white vinegar per gallon; do not mix with other materials for greater effectiveness. Two sprayings at 6-day intervals usually cleans up the mites. Then stay alert for a new outbreak. And don't forget to spray mite host plants also: violets, pansies, monkey grass etc. It's safe, effective and mites do not seem to build up resistance. If there's a "magic bullet" for mites, it's Avid.

The quickest way to get a rosarian interested in a project is to tell him it's none of his business. But these rose tips are too good not to share.

A TAN WAVE OF THRIPS will arrive in most gardens in May and June, borne on moist breezes from field grasses and annual flowers. Severe infestation will bruise buds to the extent that they refuse to open; otherwise, good roses with brown edges are not worth cutting. The tiny, tan insects rasp petal edges, sucking the juices from the petals. Between rasping binges, they reside in petal spaces, making them hard to reach with spray material. Unfurl a light-colored bloom and it's easy to spot dozens scurrying around.

THRIPS CONTROL IS CONTROVERSIAL: Some rosarians maintain good spray coverage of the entire plant as well as the bed area is necessary. Others think careful spraying of bud and bloom areas only provides good control without killing off the beneficial insects (who like spider mites). The Rambler is a bud and bloom man with *Orthene®* 75% SP (Soluble Powder) used at two teaspoons per gallon of water buffered with about one tablespoon of white vinegar. Use weekly during thrips season, spot coverage more often just before rose shows. Drop *Orthene®* from the spray program as soon as thrips subside. Other good thrips killers without bloom discoloration: *Mavrik, Avid* or *Cygon 2E.*

ROSES GRAY? Powdery mildew has moved in to disfigure new buds and leaves and curtail growth. Powdery mildew is common during periods of cool nights and warm days. With the demise of *Acti-Dione PM*, the rosarian's favorite control is *Rubigan*, used at two teaspoons per five gallons. Start spraying BEFORE mildew conditions are right, or a twice-a-week schedule will be necessary, and even that routine may not clean up the bushes until hot weather arrives and mildew disappears naturally. The Rambler likes to alternate *Triforine* alone one week and *Triforine* with *Rubigan* the next week. Get particularly good coverage on the tender new growth at the top of the bush.

PURPLISH, DARK BROWN LEAF SPOTS? Downy mildew is the culprit, sweeping through rose gardens in cool, damp weather. Left unchecked, downy mildew will defoliate bushes in a matter of days. It's hard to spot initially; spore masses take hold on the undersides of leaves, although stems and peduncles can be infected also. Control with *Daconil 2787* (11 percent formulation) at two tablespoons per gallon every seven days for three sprayings. Garden hygiene is important also as spores are viable for over a month and can be found on infected leaves, stems, flowers and sepals. It also overwinters as dormant mycilia. *Daconil* is also effective for control of blackspot and can be combined with *Rubigan* if powdery mildew is likely.

ROSE ROOTS LIKE FISH... meal or otherwise. The Rambler transplanted a few (and gave away a few) roses this spring after one year's growth. The bushes had grown well all last season but just didn't fit the rosebed (and more new roses had arrived than the beds would hold). What's unusual? Tremendous root growth for young plants; great masses of fine hair roots had grown around cores of fish meal and fragrant formula buried 18 inches or more from the shank. When planted last March, three core foot deep had been lifted with a bulb planter and filled with a cup of fish meal. The roots "found" the fish meal and set up a feeding station, extraordinary root systems, balanced sturdy like a tripod.

ANOTHER FISH STORY worth telling. A Rambler family member not noted for gardening wisdom decided to try some roses in a former alfalfa field in Colorado. With the Rambler's help, some 50 roses were planted in a decomposed granite, silty soil that had two passes of the tractor. Trench irrigated from a ditch, water disappeared as if connected to a drain pipe. A 200-foot row took all night to irrigate. After the first burst of bloom, the Rambler suggested manure as a fertility booster. Another source, fish from a nearby lake, buckets and buckets of bluegills and perch caught by willing grandchildren. Shallow furrows (dug with a pick) were filled with fish (volume unknown) and covered with soil. Then fresh cow manure (this was in the country) was heaped on, a BIG grain shovelful at a time. Start the water down the trench and forget it. Result: no burn and roses to five feet by fall, no small task in a short growing season. Years later, these roses are still growing... nature's way. There must be something to be learned here.

With roses, it's what you learn after you know it all that counts. Add these June Specials to your rose knowledge.

DOWNY MILDEW, discussed in this column last month, continues to be a frightening problem for many rosarians. Otherwise healthy bushes can defoliate in a matter of days. But relief is on the way.

When ambient temperatures hit 80 degrees, the infection will stop, but it will likely over-season as dormant mycelium or fungal strands in rose cane tissue. Another relief that doesn't depend on weather is a metalaxyl-based fungicide by Ciba Geigy called *PACE*. Ridomil-Bravo has a similar basis. Pace is labeled as "a fungicide with systemic and contact properties which controls downy mildew in turf grasses and St. Augustine grass."

Pace is NOT labeled for roses, but the Texas Plant Disease Diagnostic Laboratory requested crisis exemption for the use of Pace on roses from the Department of Agriculture. This fungicide DOES work, and is available from agricultural suppliers without a permit. You may wish to discuss its use with your supplier.

SPRINT IS ANOTHER new name for rosarians, but applies to a familiar and popular product: *Sequestrene 300*. This is the chelated iron material that's included in most exhibitors' formulas when a readily-available iron source is needed. Same material, same two-pound package, now called Sprint.

COARSE, WEATHERED LEAVES are the first signs of spray burn, occurring in stages like sunburn on rosarians. Leaves don't have to turn brown and drop off to have bum. Watch for brown edges on the leaves, or yellow-brown spots on the leaves (not blackspot) as further evidence. Spots on the leaves may be from droplets of spray materials acting like a magnifying glass in bright sunlight.

Solution: For better leaf coverage, add one Tablespoon of white vinegar per gallon of alkaline water, plus a drop or two of dishwashing detergent. These are "surfactants" that help spray materials spread over leaves evenly. If droplets form, tap a cane on the bush with the spray wand and shake off the excess. This simple trick has saved the foliage of many fine specimens.

TIME FOR TEA. A June-time pick-up, even if alfalfa meal or pellets have been used in the spring. Steep 10-12 cups of alfalfa pellets in 30 gallons of water, using a garbage can with a tight lid (you'll find out why). Stir the liquor occasionally for about three days. When it smells, it's ready.

Dip off the liquid and use one gallon per established bush (after watering), about half that much for a mini. Container plants love this tea. For a smaller batch (and less smell), use two cups in a 10-quart sprinkling can.

When the liquid is dipped off, add more water and steep again for two batches from the same pellets. Great for all kinds of roses. This enzyme pick-up has to be seen to be believed.

MIDGE SEASON is almost here in many parts of the country. This tiny critter feasts on tiny developing buds, only the smallest and tenderest will do. Before the rosarian knows there's a bud, it's gone and the stem looks like blind growth. Midge is a soil-emerging insect and has to be controlled at the soil/mulch level. Use *Diazinon* granules broadcast in the beds and immediate area. Also spray with *Diazinon* during the relatively short period that midge are active.

ODDS 'N ENDS: MIRACLE-GRO has a new garden and lawn feeder that's a dandy. It has an aspirator syphon action that doesn't clog and delivers liquid-soluble foods to bushes quickly and easily. Just hook it up to the hose, add the solubles and deliver a measured amount. Neat.

GET A LONG WAND for your sprayer, about 36 inches, to reach into and under rosebushes. While you're at it, buy a GOOD control valve that doesn't leak. Visit your local exterminator do-it-yourself store. You'll find all sorts of good stuff for spraying.

ENJOY a June filled with roses and rose friends.

Spraying roses is like telling your wife you love her... it has a short residual and needs to be repeated regularly. So that you can spend more time with your spouse and less time spraying, here are some summertime suggestions.

SCHEDULE SPRAYING and then stick to it. This is probably as important as the material itself. Fungus spores don't take holidays... insects follow the rules of nature. Just figure out what to do, and then do it. Even the old wives' tale "never wet the leaves" can be ignored if the garden is on a regular schedule.

COVERAGE is next on the priority list, and the most commonly overlooked. Your spray material has to get on (and hang on) the parts to be protected leaves, stems, peduncles, buds, blooms, etc. Spray (and cover) what needs it: Under lower leaves for spider mites; blooms and buds for thrips; tender, lush growth for mildew (including the peduncle), and so forth.

Coverage takes some time, care and observation. All that's necessary is application of the right material in the right place to the glistening stage. Spray does not have to be applied to runoff, which is wasteful and suggests that the sticking qualities are not quite right.

SURFACTANTS help coverage, and there are some good ones on the market. However, ALL commonly used fungicides and insecticides have built-in surfactants. More stuff may just get in the way. The Rambler thinks that "buffering" the water with one tablespoon of cheap, white vinegar per gallon helps get wettable and soluble powders into the mixture, shifting alkaline city water to a neutral or slightly acid pH. It's like Lemon Fresh Joy, which acts like an acid wetting agent.

MIXOLOGY is an art, not a science. You may have to resort to some trial and error with your water. The Rambler puts about a gallon of water in the spray canister (a six-gallon see-through plastic), adds the vinegar, a couple of drops of dishwashing liquid and sloshes gently. Then add the wettable or soluble powers and SWIRL, not agitate. Agitation makes suds. Then add EC (emulsifiable concentration) liquids and swirl again. Take a good look to make sure the mix is smooth and blended. Then fill with water and swirl again. You're ready to spray. The Rambler has used *Maneb* and *Sevin* and *Phal-*

tan this way for years and has never resorted to straining or suffered with a stopped-up sprayer.

COMPATIBILITY is an issue that often comes up. Most materials are compatible, that is they won't curdle or react when mixed. The broader question is, "Do they work as well together as they would separately?" Some combinations seem to contribute to spray burn, or don't appear to work. When in doubt (and if you have the time), use products separately.

The Rambler has safely (and effectively) used *Triforine, Rubigan* and *Orthene SP* together. *Mavrik* and *Triforine* seem to get along all right. Malathion 50 percent EC works with everything. But Avid, the translaminar miticide, definitely works better when used alone with buffered and wetted water. Besides, it goes underneath the leaves in the lower part of the bush, not over the entire plant.

SPRAYER? Buy the best one your budget and garden can afford. Consider the time spent in the garden as a form of expense. Make the job easier and you're more likely to do it regularly. Rosarians don't give a second thought to adding 20 bushes at $10 each, but pale at the idea of a $200 sprayer.

Match the sprayer to the task. The Rambler likes the rechargeable, battery-powered sprayers with tanks on wheels. There are some good ones available. Others swear by the electric blower types. Just buy good, well-built equipment that works. Check around your society and go for a test spraying before you buy. You'll be glad that you did.

CLEAN-UP? Vinegar again. A weak vinegar solution run through a sprayer picks up wettable powders before they can create a buildup. Ammonia solutions clean lines and nozzles, too. And use LOTS of clear water to flush the sprayer when you've finished. The sprayer and parts will last a long time with a little care.

I PROMISED YOU A ROSE GARDEN... summer time chapter next month... all about water, heat and how to cope.

These August Ramblings mark 22 years of chatting with you good folks each month, sharing ideas and experiences to enjoy roses more. You've been loyal, responsive readers... the Rambler appreciates the opportunity to be with you on these pages.

HOW DID THIS ALL BEGIN? Where did the Rambler come from? Does he know what he is talking about? Sometimes. You can draw your own conclusions from this thumbnail sketch.

THE RAMBLER comes from a gardening family in Colorado whose passion was dahlias (and some roses) plus several city lots of annuals and perennials of all kinds. We lived and breathed flowers, and even had a home-made greenhouse warmed by a pot-bellied coal stove. The Walters family could sweep the dahlia and annuals competition routinely. Dad was a superintendent of parks for 40 years. Mother could turn a bucket of flowers into an exhibition. We knew every garden in Colorado. It was a great life.

THEN MILLIE RAMBLER arrived on the scene and landscaping started in a small GI house in Boulder, CO, trying to cope with adobe, rocks and the mess left by the builders. Dad supplied truckloads of plant materials. And the roses thrived as we learned how to winter protect from bright sun and cold, dry winds. We began to appreciate nature's materials. Millie grew up on a ranch near Boulder. We hauled tons of manure and alfalfa hay.

WE RAN OUT OF ROOM to grow things, so we took on a new house and an acre of ground in the country. More roses, more shrubs. Experienced water conservation the hard way. Appreciated built-up rose beds. Then came a move to Houston, Texas, and a totally different climate. Roses became serious in 1955.

HAD TO LEARN GROWING all over again. Supportive Dad shipped 10 bundles of roses (10 each) as a "starter." Somehow survived the first couple of seasons and then discovered the Houston Rose Society. Changed the landscaping and rebuilt the beds about every other year after that. Gained PLENTY of experience and began editing the *Houston ROSE-ETTE* in the early '60s. One thing led to another and Houston hosted an ARS National Convention in 1969, the first of three in which the Rambler would be involved.

BY THIS TIME the Rambler had some 600 roses to look after, and Millie was rapidly expanding her miniature collection. We had show gardens, sponsored gardens, friendly gardens. Lacking something to do, I decided that the emerging gardens at the American Rose Center needed some help, too. What a great way to learn and share.

ROSARIAN RAMBLINGS first appeared in September 1970, and the BIG news was the FDA approval of *Benlate* for use in home gardens, called a "deliverance for the rose faithful." A long list of products and practices followed over the years.

MOST READ IN THESE COLUMNS have been the "Quote of the Month" quips. Readers favorites include: "Don't make the rose garden too big if your wife tires easily"... "Faith will never die as long as there are rose catalogs"... "Experience is like manure, it's only good when spread around"... "Roses are supposed to have yellow leaves; they just turn green sometimes."

BIGGER GARDEN, ANOTHER HOUSE in 1979, just in time to host guests of "Houston Rosetime '79," an ARS convention. Roses in the landscape became more important, miniatures essential. Maintenance routines had to be good in order to keep up. Had opportunities to work with other gardens as well.

"I PROMISED YOU AROSE GARDEN" phase of the Rambler is familiar to more recent readers. The Rambler and Millie transferred to Greenville, SC in 1989 and started all over again in red clay. We've been sharing the trials and triumphs in building new beds, coping with trees, adjusting to a new climate and trying to establish new sources for all the stuff that rosarians need.

Fortunately there are great rosarians in the Carolina and Colonial Districts, and we became part of the rose family.

Now if we can just adjust to the Japanese beetles, the only unfriendly around. In the coming months, the Rambler will try to fill you in on how 400 roses, assorted pests and disease, a busy rose schedule and a full-time job get along.

THANKS for sharing your rose hobby with the Rambler.

In the event that you have put off rose chores until they are no longer necessary, here are some quick cures to reap a September harvest of roses... there's still plenty of time to save the rose season.

FORTIFIED TEA... (alfalfa tea) is a great fall potion that doesn't interfere with normal fall processes. Alfalfa tea releases a growth hormone that makes everything work better. Just add 10 to 12 cups of alfalfa meal or pellets to a 32gallon plastic garbage can (with a lid), add water, stir and steep for four or five days, stirring occasionally. You may also "fortify" with 2 cups of Epsom Salts, 1/2 cup of *Sequestrene* (chelated iron, now called "Sprint 330") or your favorite trace elements elixir. The tea will start to smell in about three days. Keep the lid ON. Use about a gallon of mix on large bushes, 1/3 that much on miniatures. And keep the water going. One load of meal will brew up two barrelsful, but add more fortifiers. You'll see greener growth, and stronger stems within a week.

FALL IS MILDEW TIME... get busy with the *Rubigan* treatment. Begin spraying BEFORE the first evidence of mildew spores. That means as soon as nights begin to get cooler and days are bright and warm. Good coverage with *Rubigan* every two weeks at 2 teaspoons per 5 gallons will do the job. It's also compatible with *Triforine* or *Daconil*. Routine: every week with *Triforine*, every other week add *Rubigan*. *Systhane* (Nova) is also a good powdery mildew preventive.

CUCUMBER BEETLES also like fall weather and fat blooms. Fight them with *Mavrik*, a flowable insecticide that's safe and easy to use. Spray the bud and bloom areas as necessary at 2 teaspoons per 5 gallons. *Mavrik* won't discolor blooms, is safe on the leaves with no residue. Can be used AFTER beetles appear, and then two or three applications will do the job. Doubles as a thrips fighter as well.

AVID **MITICIDE** is still the product of choice if hot weather and mites persist. Waterwash undersides of leaves first, then spray undersides with *Avid* at 1/4 teaspoon per gallon. Repeat in five days. Some growers switch off to *Mavrik* now and then if conditions are right for mites. The Rambler has switched position on *Stirrup-M*, the sex attractant for mites. Used with either Avid or *Mavrik*, *Stirrup-M* DOES seem to increase the effectiveness of the miticide. Another note: Avid is again available in 8-ounce packages (about $55). It's a high initial cost, but the cost per gallon applied is quite low, due to the very low application rate.

FALL FEEDING? It's wise to slack off on nitrogen applications in the fall so that the bushes can go into a normal dormancy... begin making a sort of natural antifreeze. But growers CAN use some liquid applications that stop working in three or four weeks. It's possible to have good fall blooms with lots of color and still be prepared for winter.

TREATED TIMBERS BAD?? The organics folks have expressed some concern about the use of treated lumber or landscape timbers by hobbyists, particularly for vegetable gardens. The Rambler has used landscape timbers (treated against decay) for many years and has NEVER observed any adverse effects on growth or inhibition of natural soil processes or worms. This includes miniatures. If some new fall beds are in your plans, landscape timbers continue to be an inexpensive and versatile edging material.

ODDS 'N ENDS... POLYMER WATER CRYSTALS really do work to retain moisture in rose bed and container mixtures. Somewhat expensive for regular bed use, polymers might be used in the immediate root area, such as dipping the roots of bare-root roses in a tapioca-like slurry of polymer crystals when planting. The Rambler considers polymers a MUST for containers and hanging baskets. Will help you get through very hot weather... *FLEX-TY* is a convenient tie material that's easier to use than strips of pantyhose. Comes in 1/2-inch wide rolls, cheap...

JAPANESE BEETLE TRAPS do work, the Rambler caught a bumper crop this season (alas, not all of them). It's amazing to see swarms of beetles fly to the yellow vanes and the attractant and then fall into the bags. Good riddance.

THE RAMBLER has some giveaways again, from formulas to sources. Send an SASE (business size) and the Rambler will fill it up with good rose stuff.

Experience is what you get when you were expecting something else... like success. Here are some '92 experiences of the Rambler that may help YOU grow better roses.

POWDERY MILDEW got out of hand in two of the Rambler's gardens in mid-summer during a cool spell... for a couple of reasons. First, mildew wasn't expected during that period so no supportive fungicide was added to *Triforine*. Second, the affected bushes had been mulched with a heavy application of sewage sludge (very high in nitrogen and quick acting). This resulted in LOTS of lush new growth. The combination was deadly. One day there was NO mildew, three days later the tops were white.

RECOVERY TACTICS... Alternately added *Rubigan* or *Systhane* (Nova) to *Triforine* and shortened the spray schedule to every five days. In 20 days the problem was licked, although the badly infected leaves were still deformed. All new growth has been clean and healthy (also not so lush).

REGARDING SLUDGE... Greenville has a recycling effort to reduce the load on the landfill. It is combining sludge with partially composted leaves for use as a mulch on acid-loving woody plants. The Rambler used about three inches of the material on the Greenville Rose Society sponsored rose garden in the park (and even heavier on my azaleas at home). Great for azaleas, not so great for roses. Leaves alone would have been better for roses. Please keep in mind that this was NOT a carefully processed sludge product like *Milorganite*, which is widely used on roses in many areas. *Milorganite* is still one of the best soil conditioners around; the Greenville product conditioned the soil, but had some adverse side effects.

BLACKSPOT, TOO... An outbreak of blackspot turned up in some other park beds, primarily on a bed of 20 own-root roses, mixed varieties. Nearby beds with some blackspot susceptible varieties were nearly clean, but these were budded bushes that had gotten off to a very vigorous start. All other conditions (planting, feeding, spraying, etc.) were the same. The own-roots were much smaller and would need nearly a season to catch up. These weaker, smaller bushes could not seem to handle the infection. Many rosarians have observed that weak bushes get sick, strong bushes are more resistant. This may be the case here. Footnote: All of the bushes are healthy again by spraying twice a week with a combination of *Triforine* and *Maneb* or *Triforine* and *Daconil*. Situation cleared up in three weeks.

SUN, SOIL, SPRAY... the three "S" formula for good roses. The Rambler cheated on one "S," sun, and paid the price. Earlier this year the Rambler described two new beds with the perfect mixture of red clay, organics, sand and what have you. Each holds 40 bushes. Spray and feeding programs are identical. After an even start, one bed began to slow down, the bed with about two hours less sun per day. Today the more shaded bed has significantly less growth, 25 percent fewer blooms and weak stems. This means that some trees are going to have to go this winter if we are going to grow really good roses.

THE RAMBLER'S NEW ROSE BEDS are doing quite well, except for the more shaded one. The clay/organic/soil/sand mix has supported strong, continuous growth without having to make mid-season corrections. The mix holds water well, is alive with worms and stuff (the robins are scratching in there all the time), encourages expansive roots and is very easy to work (no packing). Composted leaves have been used as a mulch (about six inches). The leaves have broken down rapidly. The Rambler is going to use leaves AND shredded pine bark next season to keep the coverage more consistent, and throw on some horse manure when available.

A GOOD ROSE YEAR is winding down and the bushes will soon begin to slow down in the Carolinas. Wherever you are, your bushes should be doing the same thing-responding to the season. A healthy bush with some organic insulation can handle the best and worst of winter (except for the VERY WORST). We'll get ready for next year, beginning next month.

Winter is the time when it's too cold to do the job that was too hot for summer. But these

ROSE ANTIFREEZE?? That's exactly what happens in rose tissue when roses go dormant naturally, triggered by shorter days and colder nights. It's a gradual process, approaching full dormancy after two or three spells of freezing/ heavy frost. Understanding this helps a rosarian set a program to work with nature and its vibrations.

PROTECTION?? Recommended for all but the mildest climates. A sudden drop to 20 degrees, holding for a day or two, is devastating to roses that are not dormant. If this is likely to happen, minimal protection is a couple of shovelfuls of soil over the bud union plus a good layer of leaves or some other sort of insulating material, applied BEFORE the cold snap. This relatively easy task can save 10 to 12 inches of good cane. Take the soil from outside the rosebed and mound up.

Remove any excess next year. That's why soil/mulch is so good… it breaks down over a period of time and does not need to be removed.

COLD-CLIMATE ROSARIANS have to add more insulating materials, just like adding blankets. The Rambler likes soils and leaves, lots of them, kept in place with wire fencing or collars of some sort. Just remember that good insulation has air space that breathes. The idea is to moderate temperature changes so that canes do not go through freeze/thaw cycles. And roses still need water during cold weather. Lacking a good snow cover, get out the hose when weather permits.

ANTI-DESICCANT SPRAYS may help in the winter protection process, retaining moisture in the canes that might otherwise be lost with cold, drying winds. Products like *CLOUD COVER* and Wilt-Prof are readily available, easy to apply. When bushes go dormant and drop their leaves, trim up to suit your winterizing situation and thoroughly spray the canes before applying any covering materials. This trick is especially good for climbers and ramblers exposed to wind and sun. More canes are probably lost to drying out than actual cold; this liquid blanket can make a difference.

ROSE PRODUCT SOURCES. The Rambler gets almost as much mail about where to find rose products as how to use them. A sources search is a good wintertime chore. As a serious rosarian, you are often looking far beyond the scope of a typical garden shop. Get acquainted with a feed store/ farm store in your locality. You'll find all sorts of things like organic meals and supplements, fertilizer formulas to stretch your imagination, sprays and tools to make the job easier for a country place or an oversize rose garden. If the proprietor wears a rose cap that says "Bill's Feeds," he has to carry or be able to find almost anything a serious gardener needs.

AGRICULTURAL SUPPLY houses are also good sources. And many of them sell retail if you take the time to get acquainted. That's where you'll find things like *Rubigan, Cygon, Avid, Milban, Triforine* and other fungicides/insecticides used on crops and in greenhouses. Products that the Rambler suggests do not require an applicator's permit, just common sense. And don't overlook the rose specialty suppliers' advertising in these pages: good folks like *Kimbrew-Walter* and *Reece*. The classifieds are a gold mine of information.

A WINTER NOTE FOR ROSE STUFF. Sprayers and tools need winterizing too. Give them a good cleaning before storage. A good purge of weak vinegar or household ammonia solution will pick up the wettable powders and residues left in hoses and valves. *WD-40* is a friend, too. Store spray materials where they will not freeze. Seal tightly. Don't expose to excessive light AND keep away from curious children. With just a little extra effort you'll be ready for next season.

ENJOY a Happy Holiday Season and a Rosy '93.

The Rambler's rose budget for '93 is already shattered, having saved money by ordering three of everything. If the garden will just hold all of this rosy surplus, there will be ample opportunities for the Rambler to offer really GOOD advice during the New Year.

MISTAKES TO BE FIXED... Occasionally failing to follow my own wise counsel, a stretched-interval spray program wound up with some late-season powdery mildew on roses that should never mildew. Don't even be tempted to "go another week" before spraying. Get on a schedule and stay with it.

DENSE ROSES IN FRONT OF A WALL result in a regular mite incubator. The last time this happened was with *Red Flush* and the mite generals sent out raiding parties into the garden all season. This time *Playgirl* became infested, almost overnight. Solution: spread out and open up for better spray coverage (away from the wall). You'll save a lot of trouble later in the season.

ROOT INTERFERENCE cannot be ignored, nor can a grower feed the problem away. When roots from trees and shrubs invade a rosebed, more food just means more roots, and the roses won't get their fair share. Extra food postpones the inevitable (barrier systems, moving the bed or cutting the trees) but won't cure the problem. Foliar feeding helps also, but rose growth is still retarded by tree roots sucking up the moisture. Face it: trees and roses don't mix well.

FIGHT THE TEMPTATION to squeeze an extra rosebush into the bed. What seems like enough space in the spring will be overgrown like a jungle in July. Established plants overcome newcomers in the bed, depriving them of light, water and food. It's tough competition, survival of the fittest. Give each bush a fair shake. It's one of the reasons that all-new plantings do better. If you MUST have a new bush in a tight, established bed, try potting first and force the root system along so that it can compete. By the time the potted rose is ready, the hole may have closed up... just as well. It's an opportunity to grow another rose in a container.

BE PREPARED TO WATER container-grown roses every other day during hot weather or suffer devastating results. Even with the new poly-mers, all it takes is a hot, dry weekend without water for roses in 3-gallon or smaller pots to go into deep shock and drop their leaves. Hanging baskets can be wiped out.

The larger the container, the longer the interval. If potted roses have to be carried over for an extended period, consider a larger container in the first place. Most nursery pots are not intended to support roses indefinitely. If you are going to grow roses in containers, invest in a simple, do-it-yourself drip system and run an emitter to each container.

The Rambler has two short drip systems for "spares," and, when the occasion arises, hooks up to a hose supply line controlled with a timer. The hanging basket rack couldn't make it through the summer without the drip emitters. Try it this year.

READ AND FOLLOW LABEL DIRECTIONS... That's the theme that you're going to hear month after month this year. Every home-garden insecticide and fungicide you buy has a label that must be approved by USDA. Follow it for your own good.

TIMED RELEASE FERTILIZERS are high on the Rambler's approval list for '93. Not as the ONLY or even the primary source of nutrients for roses, but as the steady, reliable, on-call nitrogen supply. In replicated situations, beds lightly fed with timed-release fertilizers (*Osmocote* et al.) produced more and better roses more consistently than beds without timed-release fertilizers. Otherwise the beds had exactly the same treatment with granulars, liquids, organics, tonics... whatever. Product of choice: a timed-release with trace. Keeps what roses need on the dinner platter all the time.

I PROMISED YOU A ROSE GARDEN... The Rambler has some neat, new rose stuff coming up in '93 to be shared with you loyal readers. Watch for: a rose bed moved after one year; "thinned out" rosebeds; more clay, less sand.

Here's wishing you a Rosy '93.

When catalogs come, can spring be far behind? More reliable than the weatherman, catalogs break dormancy for a New Rose Year… along with some tips from the Rambler.

A SHORT STAY. Some 40 roses in a bed constructed just last season had to be moved in a landscape-improvement (?) program in January… and also to get more sun. It's amazing how many fine roots developed in just one year. But remember that the Rambler uses a VERY light, friable soil mix high in organics. Dug with a spading fork, the roots clung to soil particles, perlite and bits of pine bark to form a loose root ball. Replanted bare-root in a similar mix, these roses will never know they have been moved. In a final step, the canes were mounded with soil and mulch and the new bed filled with leaves… ready for spring.

I also took the opportunity to thin out some nearly-new bushes. Roses planted too close just don't have a chance to branch out and produce. By mid-season, the vacant spaces will be filled with rose canes again, and the whole bed will be easier to care for.

MORE CLAY THIS SEASON? Yes. Very light mixes are great, but require more water. The Rambler's newest built-up-bed mixes have about 25 percent Carolina red clay by volume, well tilled with ground pine bark, compost, manure, sharp sand, perlite, leaves and gypsum with fish meal, alfalfa meal and blood meal activator. There's probably some garden soil in there, too. A similar bed last season turned out to be a winner.

MILLS MAGIC ROSE MIX. The Rambler has never claimed that the organic feeding formulas (and artificial manure variations) recommended in these columns were magic (well, almost), but there is a *Mills Magic Rose Mix* available to rosarians throughout the country that faithfully follows the Rambler's formula. Introduced in this issue. *Mills Magic* makes an organic-based program convenient and easy… and without the smell. Somehow the fish meal has been deodorized, and that's probably a plus. It has all the good stuff a Rosarian could ask for: bone, alfalfa, cottonseed, blood and fish meals combined with activated sludge. And an organic activator to speed up the process. In the Rambler's words, "The soil comes alive." Used side by side with the Rambler's formulas last season, *Magic Rose Mix* performed equally well. Give some a try this season. As an ARS sponsor product, some introductory promotions will be available through local rose societies and by direct shipment. With a plus: no smell.

CLIMBERS are cussed and discussed by rosarians this time of year, generally complaining about a lack of bloom and what to do about it. Variety selection and training of the canes are the most important considerations, and the most overlooked. True climbers are bred for vigorous growth and lots of bloom. Climbing sports of Hybrid Teas (like *First Prize*) are not in the same class. These sports will put on a fair flush in the spring (if the canes are trained horizontally), followed with an occasional flower. If not trained, canes get 10 feet long with one bloom on top.

Training climbing canes to a horizontal support is a gradual process. Bloom laterals will emerge at each leaf axil, reaching for the sun. Each bloom lateral can be cut and enjoyed (or spent bloom removed) just like a Hybrid Tea. Some Climbers cascade naturally, blooming all along the cane. A Rambler favorite is *Don Juan*, a rich, velvet red with great fragrance. For a traffic stopper, cover a fence or support with *Altissimo*: blood red, seven-petals with gold stamens. Or *Handel* with clusters of pink and cream. *Blaze* is probably the most popular climber in America, and now there is a *Yellow Blaze*. You'll never forget *Dortmund,* beautiful for blooms, foliage and hips… a year-round standout.

TIPS WORTH CONSIDERING:

RODENT PROBLEMS? Do you have rodent problems in winterized rosebeds? Sprinkle the insulating blanket of leaves with *Diazinon* granules (or *Dursban*) and mice will move on to more hospitable quarters. Not too late this season.

YOU DESERVE A BREAK THIS SEASON. Get a Mantis tiller-cultivator. Best tool ever for working up a rosebed. Lightweight, it digs and chops and cultivates with ease. If you see one work, you'll HAVE to get one. Advertised in these pages, write for the promo folder… better yet, buy one.

MAR. 1993

THOUGHT FOR THE MONTH:
Things looking down? Try looking up.

The only things we never lose are those we give away, so use and pass on some of these springtime tips.

RX FOR GALLS... Some surgical urgency is bound to come up when pruning this spring. Many respected growers maintain that disinfecting trimmed crown galls with *Lysol* or *Clorox* retards re-occurrence, but an equal number disagree. And there are some "pharmacy lab" treatments labeled for roses, too. Most rosarians have galls they don't even know about, and have had for a long time. It's the Rambler's observation that if the gall is on the shank or bud union, sunshine seems to do as much good as anything. Just trim off the offending tissue and let sun and air get to it. Don't worry too much about the infection; nature and a well drained soil are probably the best remedies. If it's too bad, dig it out and try something new.

EVERYONE WANTS BASALS BREAKS... They're available with help. A one-two punch with *Epsom salts* (magnesium sulfate) and a readily available source of nitrogen brings results at pruning time as well as after the initial bloom cycle. Magnesium, so essential in the rose tissue process, leaches readily, as does nitrogen. Kick off the process with up to a half-cup of Epsom salts, followed by every-other-week applications of a soluble 20-20-20 like *Peters* or *Ra-Pid-Gro*. New basals need LOTS of energy. Get that energy into the root zone in a nitrate form for results. And don't forget... LOTS of water.

WATER, not fertilizer is what makes roses grow. The best plant food in the world won't do a bit of good until it is in solution and in the root zone of the plant. Pelletized fertilizers are great IF there is a regular, ample supply of water to dissolve the material and carry the nutrients to the roots. Old-timers also know that deep soaking BEFORE using any food (dry or liquid) speeds up the process. For a rude awakening, try dissolving your favorite dry rose food in water. It may be less soluble than you think.

ROSES TOLERATE COLD AND STRESS much better when well-watered. The Rambler noted during late cold snaps that the really SOAKED bushes had less cold burn, fewer blind shoots and responded more quickly than roses on the moist side. These are simple facts, easy to observe, that ought to tell us something about practices.

TO PINCH OR NOT TO PINCH? A tough question for rosarians anxious to see a bloom of a new variety. And a painful decision when new basals and low breaks shoot up. But first things first. Grow bushes with leaves, then add roses. Keep new rosebushes vegetative until they are well established. Pinch out the buds (just like disbudding) or go down to the first good leaflets. Encourage bud eyes in the middle of the canes, that's where the biggest and best buds are. Bud eyes on roses are apically dominant, that is, the top bud wants to break first. But let the strength go to lower, stronger buds. You'll wind up with more canes and stronger canes, producing lots of good roses later on.

ODDS 'N ENDS... For those of you with spray system equipment on your power or pump-up sprayer, try a Tee-Jet 8004 nozzle. It makes a fan spray 80° wide with a very fine droplet. Check out an exterminator supply place. They have all kinds of good parts for sprayers...

AND FIND A FEED STORE, the real thing that smells like alfalfa and pasture... and has a couple of cats napping on the feed sacks. This is the place to get alfalfa meal and all of the other good things that roses like... My feed store also sells rabbits, deserving of a five-star organic gardener rating.

APR.
1993

THOUGHT FOR THE MONTH:
Learn to listen. Rose opportunity sometimes knocks very gently..

"Be not the first by whom the new is tried; nor yet the last to lay the old aside…" good advice any season, so here's some old and some new to work on…

BUILD A HILL… Many of you should be hilling up those new roses, both bare-root and potted. Hilling up roses is nothing more than a protective cone of soil or mulch or other insulating material that just lets the tips of new canes stick out. Not just a handful, a real cone, a shovelful or two per bush. Hilling primarily conserves moisture in the canes, but gives cold protection, too. New root hairs must form to deliver moisture to the canes; hilling keeps canes from drying out until the roots have a chance to deliver.

THINK FRIABILITY… Soil that lets air, water and nutrients percolate through and through. Roots need air, water and food replenishment on a regular basis… and may be starving if you have been stomping around the rosebeds this spring. Friable soil makes the whole process work. Keep soils loose with organic materials, applied on top and incorporated into the soil. When a rosebud gets too tight, use a four-tine fork to loosen and admit air around the perimeter of the bush. Broadcast a top layer of compost or fine-ground pine bark, which will drop into the tine holes with a sort of honeycomb effect. Many rosarians also broadcast gypsum (Calcium Sulfate) around the perimeter, about a cup per bush. Gypsum definitely helps open up the soil and leaches salts at the same time. Despite its "Sulfate" designation, gypsum does NOT alter the pH of the soil.

NON-TRADITIONAL FEEDING… Traditional wisdom says "Never use fertilizer with a newly-planted rose." But there are some exceptions, like the use of a timed-release fertilizer when planting a well-developed potted rose. Many nursery-supplied roses have been confined in pots for two months or more, developing a fairly good system of new roots. The Rosarian wants to encourage these roots to expand into the planting bed as soon as possible. Lure the roots with a carrot-in-front-of-the-horse trick.

SET A NUTRIENT TABLE… around the roots. Dig the hole and try the pot in it for size. Then mix about an ounce of *Osmocote* with some soil in the bottom of the hole. Slip or slit the rose out of the pot and position the roots (you'll see all sorts of white feeder roots). Then backfill with some bedding mix (two inches or so), then a band of *Osmocote*, then more bedding soil, then *Osmocote*. Finish with bedding mix, hill up and flood with water. But use NO MORE than three to four ounces of timed-release per bush. You'll see good top growth throughout the early growing season, proof that the roots are growing also.

ORGANICS ARE BEST IN SPRING… and work all season. Since organics feed and condition soil, it makes sense to get them going as early as possible. The Rambler likes fish meal, alfalfa meal and gypsum in the spring, just as the soil warms up, about one cup each per large bush, less for minis. Or some bloom meal/cottonseed meal. Maybe some fragrant formula (artificial manure), or the real thing, right out of the horse. Horse stalls with wood shavings, straw and alfalfa are gold mines of nutrients and conditioners. Use liberally and watch the changes in the soil… and the roses.

DOWNY MILDEW… the fungus disease evidenced by purplish blotches on leaves and canes during cool, damp weather can be controlled early-on by some adjustments to the spray program. Like blackspot, it's easier to control than it is to eradicate. Beginning with the first spring spraying, add one tablespoon of *Dithane M-45* (*Manzate 200*) per gallon the usual *Funginex/Triforine*. The next week, use *Daconil*, conveniently packaged as *Fungi-Gard*, two tablespoons per gallon. Alternate until temperatures routinely hit 80 degrees or so, when the spores don't multiply. Perhaps your garden won't become infected, but this bland routine can't hurt a thing. Much easier than having to respond to defoliated bushes with Pace or one of the metalaxyl combinations like Subdue. You won't have blackspot, either.

MAY 1993

THOUGHT FOR THE MONTH: *If a Rosarian were to enter the Garden of Eden...*
he would probably order fertilizers right away.

Growing good roses should be as easy as falling off a diet... suggest that you be tempted with these morsels of rose advice.

WEEKLY INSECTICIDE?? This is a poor practice in most gardens, as it winds up killing off the beneficial insects that help control spider mites. You should combine an insecticide with a fungicide only when there is a SPECIFIC problem, then us a SPECIFIC control where and when needed. Fungus spores are always there; that's the reason for the weekly spray routine.

WATER... the most important growth additive, is often the most ignored. Water is more than rain showers; water is the deep-down soaking that makes nutrient solutions supporting lush leaves, long stems and substance in the blooms. Every essential to growth has to go into solution. Good growing SOAK the rosebeds, and then go back with some more the next day. Regardless of how it is applied, EXTRA water pays off in better blooms. When water runs out of the beds, that's enough. Then repeat.

FEEDING FORMULA?? This is a personal choice, depending on the money and effort the grower wants expend. For a casual grower, an organic start in the spring with a half-cup of balanced fertilizer with trace elements every six weeks will produce lots of good blooms. The "dedicated" grower will use a more exotic mix of organics in the spring plus palletized plus every-other-week solutions of 20-20-20 with trace elements. And just before a rose show or special event, blood meal and all sorts of unusual mixes will contribute to prize winners. What's the best? It's up to you. The Rambler has seen some great gardens with well-prepared soil that relied on *Sierra* timed-release (18-6-12 with trace) with one shot that lasted all season. And LOTS of water. Whatever your approach, set a plan and observe the results. There's always next year.

ROSES IN CONTAINERS... These can be lots of fun, and can give you blooms where you want them. They are also less work than many growers think. The Rambler has six half-barrels with Miniatures that are a striking landscape feature. And some large clay pots with Minis like *Snow Bride* and *June Laver* that prefer a root-bound condition. Some tricks: use a soil less mix, add a little calcined clay (Kitty Litter) or soil polymers to hold additional moisture, feed with organic starter like fish emulsion, alternating with a *Miracle-Gro* or *Ra-Pid-Gro* in solution. Mulch heavily, water regularly and enjoy. To slow rotting of the barrels, perch on bricks to allow air circulation.

WATER WAND? Or is it a water breaker? There's a difference. A water wand directs a strong stream of water (usually in a broad cone or fan shape) underneath rose leaves to wash off spider mites. Fine droplets of water really clean them off. Regular washing controls mites in many gardens, particularly if insecticides are used sparingly. Other benefits: cleans spray residue and pollution dropout, cools bushes and adds water. On the other hand, a water breaker (on a long handle) directs a smooth flow of water to basins, beds, pots and planters. This hand application is a n extra touch for roses in beds; while the water is soaking in, the resident Rosarian can get better acquainted with the bushes to know what they are doing, seeing things that can't be observed by just turning on the hose.

WATER BASINS... formed by soil around rosebushes hold a gallon or two of water; the effect is all out of proportion to the effort. Roses like this hand care. No rose garden is complete without BOTH a water wand and a water breaker.

RAMBLER NOTE... the Rambler is installing a complete water system this month. Will tell you about the watery results next month.

Topics for June follow "What is old but works well... what is new and worth a try," subjects that the Rambler discussed at the mid-May ARS National Convention in Columbia, South Carolina. Here's a sampling...

STILL WORKING... *Daconil 2787, Manzate 200* and all their variations do a job on blackspot when used regularly... and have for a long time. And particularly good when used in combination with *Funginex (Triforine)*, which we think of as a new product but has really been around since 1979. The Rambler like *Triforine* one week, *Triforine/Daconil* the following week, or *Triforine/Manzate*. Use both materials at label recommendations. Alternating fungicides heads off resistant strains and seems to prevent downy mildew (check the April '93 Ramblings for details). The good news is that *Daconil* is now available in a WD (water dispersible) formulation that goes into solution immediately and leaves less residue.

A NEW SHORTCUT for downy mildew control is *PACE*, a combination of *Subdue* and *Manzate*. Apply as a foliar spray when downy mildew conditions are present (cool, damp weather). Late in the season to worry about now, but it also will clean up a lingering infection when used three times at five-day intervals (one tablespoon per gallon). If the garden has been infected, begin spray program BEFORE the conditions are right for a new outbreak... either one of the *Triforine* combinations or PACE.

OLD WITH NEW NAME... *Benlate*, the much maligned fungicide for blackspot and powdery mildew, plus some other benefits as a soil treatment. It's now available as *Cleary's 3336*, a water-blend, flowable product. Still good when used in combination with Triforine.

NEWEST FOR POWDERY MILDEW is *Systhane*, available in many areas as *Nova, Eagle* or *Rally* in a 40 WP formulation. May be safely used at 14-day intervals as a control and eradicant. However, the BEST approach seems to be *Rubigan* EC at two teaspoons per five gallons with *Triforine* in an alternating program: *Triforine* one week, *Triforine/Rubigan* the next week. Think of *Systhane* as a "back-up" fungicide if mildew appears to be getting out of control. It's important to get SOMETHING on the new growth each week, as that's where the infection is going to break out.

ADVANCED DESCRIBES *AVID*, the translaminar miticide that positively checks spider mites, and to which the mites seem to build up no resistance. It's systemic and actually passes through the leaf (translaminar). Use at one-fourth teaspoon per gallon, apply to UNDERSIDES of leaves. Get good coverage. To enhance the properties of *Avid*, add *Stirrup-M*, a sex attractant that gets the mites in contact with the spray material. It really works. The OLD mite control (still works) is the water wand that directs a fine, forceful spray of water underneath the leaves, knocking off the mites and interrupting the breeding cycle. Use the water method first, then the Avid as necessary.

GOOD SPRAY PROGRAMS recognize that water is really not all that wet. When making up a spray solution, start with about a gallon of water, add white vinegar at one tablespoon per gallon to "buffer" the solution, i.e., change water pH to slightly acid. Add a few drops of ordinary dishwashing liquid as a spreader-sticker, then swirl. Next add any EC (solvent-based materials, swirl again, and last, add WP (wettable powders). You'll wind up with a blended spray mix that spreads out on the leaves without beading.

WATER IS OLD AND NEW... and roses need lots of it. If the bed is well-drained, it's hard to use too much. The best growth-inducer for roses is water, not fertilizer. The Rambler is enjoying watery proof this spring with a new automatic system. Rosebeds on the system are substantially ahead of those not similarly soaked, by perhaps as much as one-third. All other conditions are equal. Now THAT'S the way to grow roses... and proved in just six weeks. More on the proliferation of foliage next month.

**JUL.
1993**

THOUGHT FOR THE MONTH: *When offering suggestions, Keep them soft and sweet.*
You never know, from day to day, Which words you'll have to eat.

Rose ideas are much like children… our own are wonderful. And they need to be passed around for the unique joy of discovery and adventure. You may want to venture with some of these…

THE NEEM TREE is probably an endangered species by now with all of the glowing reports of mysterious properties to repel insects and cure disease. The Rambler recommends that you carefully re-read the fine articles on neem oil by Herb Persons and Tommy Cairns in the June *American Rose*. Sounds too good to be true… but it DOES work in an integrated pest management program. It's the Rambler's experience that it doesn't take care of EVERYTHING, but has a place in a thoughtfully prepared spray program.

JAPANESE BEETLES were the primary neem oil target for the Rambler, having suffered through weeks of infestation in the 1992 season that stripped tender leaves and blooms like locusts in the old famine movies… they ate very well in the Rambler's rose garden. This season, the Rambler sprayed twice at five-day intervals just as the beetles were beginning to come in, using the *Margosan-O* botanical insecticide concentrate by Grace Sierra. *Margosan-O* was mixed with buffered water at one tablespoon per gallon, plus one teaspoon of *Triforine*. Coverage was excellent; the leaves took on a bright sheen. And the beetles SEEMED to be repelled by the material. One bed was left unsprayed as a check and it had a moderate beetle problem for about 10 days.

BEETLE POPULATIONS were reduced all over the garden, compared to neighboring properties. The Rambler's garden backs up to a golf course, apparently the maternity center for the beetles. There was also less evidence of thrips, but the light colors still had damage. I noted no leaf damage at all. And my nose couldn't pick up any odor.

COMPARED NOTES with Herb Persons who has had three seasons of experience with neem oil, and he convinced me that addition of a polymer like *Vaporguard* or *Cloud Cover* enhanced the effectiveness. In fact, his formula for success has been one tablespoon of *Margosan-O*, half teaspoon of *Triforine*, two tablespoons of *Vaporguard* and one tablespoon of *Liquid Seaweed* per gallon of water. Spray for good coverage but not until dripping. Start BEFORE the Japanese beetle season, spray twice at five day intervals, then lay off for a week. Says that he has good protection and excellent leaf growth. So the Rambler tried the same thing last week (the beetles were still in the neighborhood) and was amazed at the spray coverage. Have had some very hot days since then with NO sign of leaf burn or coarseness. AND, virtually no beetles.

TRY SOME now if you are about to have a beetle invasion. And if you are REALLY brave, skip one bed to see for yourself what a difference it can make. You'll be pleasantly surprised. The downside: *Margosan-O* is about $50 for a quart size, but is available from most major greenhouse/nursery suppliers.

MORE ABOUT WATER. The Rambler's new automatic water system continues to support dramatic growth, applying about three inches of water per week to the rosebeds. The system comes on every other day at 5 a.m., spraying into the beds from the side with good-sized drops, not a mist. Except for the Minis, the blooms are four to five feet off the ground and seldom get wet, but the foliage is well-washed. So far, no sign of blackspot as the spray program of *Triforine/Manzate* alternating with *Triforine/Daconil* weekly keeps spores under control. Also, no powdery mildew this year, attributed to *Triforine/Rubigan* early in the season with an occasional clean sweep with *Systhane*. And I'm reminded of a comment by Dr. Eldon Lyle of the Texas Rose Research Foundation some years ago observing that roses with wet leaves are not good hosts for powdery mildew spores. Dr. Lyle had one large rosebed which he watered with a soaker hose with fine pin holes which sprayed up to three or four feet. Leaves were cool, foliage lush, bloom prolific… and no mildew. Give the idea some thought. But most of all, give those roses LOTS of water… the best growth-inducer ever.

My idea of an agreeable person is someone who agrees with me… and I know that you'll agree that this is solid rose advice worth following.

HEAT STROKE hits rosarians and new Miniatures, too… bound to suffer after emerging from shade-cloth propagation houses. Suffering from shipping stress or stand-by time at a nursery, new Minis deserve some special care before being set out in a bed in full sun. First, re-pot in a gallon container, using a light mix or soilless mix. This gives greater water-holding capacity and a new medium for root expansion. Place them in a partially shaded area, gradually moving to full sunlight. After a few weeks, carefully transfer your new Minis to the new rosebed. Result: no shock, no yellow leaves, no growth suspension. The Rambler likes to use a weak fish emulsion fertilizer on a weekly basis while the Minis are in pots, stretched to once every other week in the beds until they are competitive in size.

PLASTIC-BAG ROOTING is simple and easy in the summertime. Miniature cuttings are particularly easy to start; light wood of large roses takes off as well. Every Rosarian has all the equipment necessary: form coffee cups, clear plastic newspaper bags, a tree with low branches and rose favorites you would like to propagate.

Take a cutting about five inches long with four leaflets and a spent bloom. Pinch out the bloom, pull off the two lower leaflets and leave the two upper leaflets, pinching to two small leaves each. Trim the cutting on an angle at the lowest leaf axil. Poke three or four small holes in the bottom of the cut with the tip of a pencil. Fill with a soilless mix that has been thoroughly wetted. Make an insertion hole in the rooting medium with a pencil. Dip your moist cutting stem in *RooTone* and insert in cup, firm with fingers. Two leaflet axils will be below surface, two small leaflets above. Water well until excel drains from the bottom of cup. Carefully slip the cup into the plastic bag until it rests on the bottom. Twist the top of the bag allowing room for the leaves and secure with a length of plant tie. Hang all this from a low tree branch… and just be patient about three weeks.

Sunshine is the rooting key; the top leaflets produce food, new roots take up moisture… all in a warm, humid environment. Moisture condenses on the plastic and drips back to the pot. Meanwhile the anxious Rosarian gets to watch the rooting progress. The bag-in-the-tree method MUST have filtered sunlight for fungus control as well as growth. Don't open the bag unless there appears to be a lack of moisture. New leaflets will appear in about two weeks, roots in about four. Gradually adapt the newly-rooted cutting to normal temperature and humidity, then re-pot. If you see a Rosarian with a treeful of plastic bags, ask for some of the crop. He'll be glad to share his 80 percent.

MULCH AND SUMMER just naturally go together. In hot, dry weather, conserve what moisture is in the soil with an insulating cover of mulch. Keep it loose but in place so that water and air can percolate to the soil. Mixtures of materials are best: ground bark, leaves, compost, pine needles… pieces of all sizes and shapes so that the mulch does not pack. An extra benefit: adds organic matter to the soil, supports organisms. Throw on a little extra nitrogen to make up for the loss in the decomposition process. It WORKS.

ODDS 'N ENDS… ALFALFA TEA is good about every six weeks, less frequently if using meal or pellets broadcast in the beds. The Rambler likes tea fortified with some trace elements and some *Sequestrene* (iron)… AVID is still the choice for spider mites. DO NOT mix it with other spray materials, except *Stirrup-M*, the mite sex-attractant… The Rambler has some recipes and formulas available again… and some sources. If you want some good rose stuff, drop a note to the P.O. Box above with a SASE. Might even find time to answer a question or two (or share your rose wisdom). It's always good to hear from you.

SEPT.
1993

THOUGHT FOR THE MONTH:
A man of words. And not of deeds. Is like a garden. Full of weeds.

If you and your garden have suffered from "hot weather hiatus," there's still time to reap a September harvest of roses… here are some quick-cures.

FAST FOOD… appropriate formulas in solution rather than palletized fertilizers broadcast over rosebeds. A tonic in solution goes to work right away and also goes away without disrupting fall dormancy. It is like a shot in the arm. If roses and rosebeds are reasonably receptive, a gallon or so of liquid mix will show results in less than a week. Apply in early September, repeat in about 10 days, at least in the more temperate zones of the country. Use a formula high in phosphoric acid with trace elements (like *Miracle-Gro, Peters, Superbloom*) and force all the water the beds can take. The Rambler also like *Ra-Pid-Gro*…it makes lots of leaves and that's what makes roses.

THIS ALSO REPLENISHES THE nitrogen that has been lost (leached) with heavy rainfall. All this will get you a jump-start in place of the slow charge of nutrients that have to be first dissolved on the surface and find their way to the root zone.

TIRED BACKS… won't enjoy lugging and pouring buckets of tonic, even with the trash barrel located near the rosebeds. You may want to try a siphon system with the garden hose, working from a concentrated solution. Several lawn feeders use this method. The Rambler likes a mix accurately diluted in a trash barrel, sometimes adding some "secret ingredients." Pump from the barrel with a "Little Giant" fountain or pool pump. Mount the pump on a board that hangs outside the barrel, even though the pump is submersible. I guesstimate the flow and go from bush to bush.

All it takes is a barrel, a fairly long, grounded electrical cord and a small pump. And run some clear water through the pump when finished; fertilizers eat up pumps in a hurry. This method even works with alfalfa tea, just don't stir up the sediment.

FALL GROOMING… The Rambler cringes every time a well-meaning Rosarian suggests "fall pruning for best bloom." This suggests heavy trimming, and that's not the idea at all. In the fall, roses appreciate grooming — a light trimming of unproductive wood and blind growth that isn't going anywhere. It's just a more thorough job of cutting spent blooms with an eye for the next bloom cycle. Call it a sort of "fall housecleaning."

KEEP THE LEAVES… The bush needs them to produce energy for bloom. When roses have to recover from defoliation, bloom production is delayed that much longer. Leaf loss, whether from disease, insects, shock or trimming shears results in fewer roses and weaker bushes for winter survival. The name of the game is "grow leaves, then roses."

SPRAY ON SCHEDULE… in the fall. Don't wait for disease problems to appear, especially important in powdery mildew control. Mildew strikes new, lush growth when climatic conditions are right (cool nights, warm days). Sounds like fall doesn't it? *Rubigan* is effective when started two weeks or so before conditions are right. Or you may prefer *Systhane*. This gives the systemic material a chance to protect and inhibit before mildew spores are spreading all over the garden. The Rambler has safely combined *Rubigan/Triforine* or *Systhane/Triforine* for total fungus disease control. You'll have a clean fall garden.

ODDS 'N ENDS… WATER really makes roses grow. The Rambler's new automatic water system has clearly given the roses a boost this season. And NO blackspot, even though the foliage is wetted at least three times a week. The blooms seldom get wet since the water sprays in from the sides of the beds. Remember: good fungicide coverage on a weekly basis…

OWN-ROOT roses continue to impress the Rambler. Small, rooted plants have caught up with the budded bushes in just one season (set out at the same time)…

SEAWEED FOLIAR feeding is looking good, now that the weather has cooled off. This may be the "magic bullet" of the future for roses. More on this next month.

If experience is the name we give our mistakes, the Rambler gained plenty of experience this season. Here are some of the "experiences:"

HIGH NITROGEN in late summer is not the way to catch up on a missed feeding program... at least if you want good fall blooms. I got lots of foliage, tremendous bushes and small blooms. What worked in the spring to get plants going did not have a good bloom effect in the fall. A bloom tonic in solution would have been a much better solution.

IMPATIENCE does not pay. At the beginning of the season the Rambler threatened to dig out the Austin roses and some other shrub types because they "hardly grew, had a handful of blooms" the first season. Gave away several, kept the rest. This season they are sensational... growing out of bounds, repeat blooming throughout the hot, dry summer. Wish that I had the giveaway bushes back.

STIRRUP M (sex attractant for mites) added to *Avid* really adds to the miticide's effectiveness. I had doubts about the pheromone additive, but careful comparisons showed that *Stirrup M* and *Avid* worked better. And either approach worked better when NOT MIXED with other insecticides or fungicides. Get the spray water slightly acid (with vinegar), add a spreader-sticker and get good coverage underneath the leaves. Two applications 10 days apart will take out the most persistent mites.

MARGOSAN-O, the botanical repellent insecticide works best in Japanese beetle control when started two to three weeks before the noxious pests appear. Makes sense since the neem material is systemic. Beds sprayed early had FAR less damage, confined to fragrant blooms or foliage on some particularly attractive bushes. Beetles seem to LOVE the leaves and blooms of *Fragrant Memory* and also *Crystalline*. Adding an anti-transparent to *Margosan* worked OK initially, but then the Rambler must have made a mistake during a period of hot weather. Leaves on certain varieties like *Granada* and *Peach Beauty* developed a broad band of yellow on the leaves until they looked variegated. The leaves still haven't recovered, but at least they haven't dropped off. Other bushes sprayed at the same time WITHOUT anti-transparent had no leaf discoloration. In '94 it's *Margosan-O* and *Trifo-rine*, nothing else.

THICK MULCH proved itself again after the Rambler decided to skip the mulch on some high-organic, well-built beds. The mulched beds (pine bark, manure, leaves, etc.) had virtually no weeds, took less water, were attractive and more productive. Just the opposite on the no-mulch. Had a major hands-and-knees weed-digging chore at least every two weeks. This was in a park garden the Rambler maintains. Seems like any smart Rosarian would figure out how to perform less manual labor in the hot sun.

ORGANICS supported roses more consistently throughout a very hot season than any of the other combinations that the Rambler tried. Mixtures like *Mills Magic Rose Mix*, the *Fragrant Formula* and all sorts of variations of organics did a better job... supplemented with some palletized and liquid applications. Miniature beds exploded with the *Mills Mix*; good foliage, excellent blooms, consistent. And NO vegetative centers. Some container-grown roses fed exclusively with liquids didn't fare nearly as well. We NEED all types of fertilizers/approaches. Just don't lose sight of some fine results that come naturally.

DOWNY MILDEW can be controlled with *Triforine/Daconil* and *Triforine/Manzate* applications, alternating every other week during cool, damp weather. Perhaps the fungus spectrum is affected. But in most gardens, it works. Start early, stay with the program. Frequency of application also seems to be a key. If Pace is not available in '94, try what we already have on the shelf.

WATER... Still the best fertilizer, tonic, bush-grower of them all. A hot, hot summer in the Carolinas proved it again to this rosarian.

Faith will never die as long as there are rose catalogs; but winter reading comes right after these rose chores:

WINTER ADJUSTMENTS... Winter is a good time to apply agricultural lime (if needed) provided the soil is workable. Top application is not particularly effective since lime is relatively insoluble. Also, the process is a reactive one, that is in the presence of soil. Lime in the presence of hydrogen ions (the indicator for pH) reacts with those ions to form water. By reducing the hydrogen ions, the pH goes up. It's a fairly slow process.

DOING THE JOB... If a rosebed needing lime can't be tilled or spaded, use a spading fork to open up holes to receive the lime. Lightly scratch the soil back. To stay in balance, a good rule of thumb is to add one pound of lime (calcium carbonate) or dolomite lime (calcium carbonate and magnesium carbonate) for every pound of nitrogen. For example: 5-10-5 ammonium sulfate, 50 pound bag, contains 2.5 pounds of nitrogen. Use 2.5 pounds of lime for the same area. And always test before adjusting.

READY FOR FROSTY... Thanksgiving weekend seems to be the time that most rosarians favor for winter protection. It's better to get the job done right than rush out a few hours ahead of a cold front. The whole idea is to insulate ... to maintain constant temperature and avoid a freeze/ thaw situation. Combinations of loose materials seem to do this the best. These combinations should be held in place with fences, boughs, cones or what-have-you. Roses appreciate these thermal blankets. When organics are used (leaves, manure, compost), there's an extra benefit in the spring as they add organic humus to the soil. And much it's lighter than hauling soil in and out.

WINTER WORKS TOO... Winter will do the digging for you with a freezing/thawing cycle that takes a lot of the work out of making a new rosebed. If the ground isn't frozen where you are, loosen a bit with a spading fork and pile on lots of leaves and organic materials. Shovel a little soil on top. As moisture freezes and expands, tissues break down in the same way as decomposition in the summer. The winter action reduces and blends the organic matter and soil into the "loam" that most rosarians like. Nature has been building soil this way for a long, long time.

ANTI-DESICCANTS? A good idea as a sort of "Chap Stick" for roses, particularly climbers exposed to sun and cold wind. Anti-desiccants like *Cloud Dover* and *Wilt-Pruf* retain moisture in the canes that might otherwise be lost. When bushes go dormant and lose their leaves, trim up to suit your winterizing situation and thoroughly spray the canes before applying any other insulating materials (like sacks). Remember that canes are round and the backside has to be covered also. Apply liberally, get good coverage. Rose canes are primarily lost through dehydration, not cold. Rose "Chap Stick" helps.

TECHNICAL STUFF... A Rosarian friend passed this along recently. "I don't have to understand the process of digestion to enjoy dinner." And that goes for many of the things we do for and with roses. Workable understanding comes from observation. Pay close attention to your roses throughout the season; they're sending signals all the time.

ODDS 'N ENDS... Clean a sprayer thoroughly after using an anti-desiccant; the stuff really gums up sprayers. The Rambler likes a household ammonia solution. Weak vinegar solution also cleans sediment from spray hoses and valves. Particularly good for wettable powders that gum up and coat internal parts in the presence of aromatic oils (the carrier in EC solutions)... **Floribundas** ought to be on your shopping list for '94. Most rosarians fail to plant for mass effect. Many good Floribunda varieties will provide riots of color and foliage month after month with minimum trimming care. The Rambler likes Floribunda's planted two bushes deep, or at least staggered... **A decorative low fence** (rail or slats) makes a great background for Miniatures, maybe with a Mini-Climber on the fence itself, something like the *Klima* Climber. Minis are beautiful in a "framed" setting making an impression all out of proportion to their size. We'll visit again in January. Enjoy a rosy New Year.

Robert Whitaker presents the Gold Honor Medal to Howard Walters in 1994, while Sean McCann looks on.

Having already broken some Rose Resolutions for 1994... Order only ten more roses than the garden will hold... Save money by ordering three of everything... Dig up no more than 10% of lawn area per year for roses... the Rambler encourages you to KEEP these worthy recommendations in your garden...

DIG AND DIVIDE... Miniatures get too big in a hurry, resulting in woody centers that discourage new, productive growth. It's easy to dig and split up the "mother" plant, trimming out the unproductive stuff. Leave some good roots and young growth with each "new" plant. By the end of the season it will be nearly as large as the mother. Rosarians blessed with long growing seasons can go through this routine every two or three years. Dig while still dormant; use a saw, shears or just pull apart like a chrysanthemum. Gives Minis a new lease on life.

GIVE SOME AWAY... There are some varieties that just need new gardens. It's easy to collect roses and put up with so-so performance. Recycle them to someone else's garden; will make both of you happy. Grow roses that you really enjoy, not just put up with.

FIGHT... the temptation to squeeze an extra rosebush into an established bed. What seems like enough room in early spring will be overgrown like a jungle in July. Established plants overcome newcomers in a bed, depriving them of light, water and food. The competition is terrific. Give each bush a fair shake. It's one of the reasons that all-new plantings do better. If you MUST have a new bush in a tight bed, try potting first and forcing the root system along so that it can compete. By the time the potted rose is ready, the hole may have closed up... just as well. Then you can try container growing.

THINK HUMUS in 1994, most any kind will do. Humus is simply partially decomposed organic matter that acts like a glue to bind clay and silty particles into granules or crumbs. This causes the soil to become quite porous and water and air to enter readily. Combined clay and humus act together to hold water, giving the soil a better water-holding capacity. It also allows excellent gas exchange so that the soil has a sufficient oxygen capacity to support the micro-organisms converting nutrients into forms available to plants.

IN BRIEF, humus derived from organic matter builds a "table" from which rose roots can absorb water and nutrients. This crumb-making capability also holds nutrients, up to three to four times more than clay or silty soils, which slows leaching from the rosebed. Organic matter (humus) is really the key to good rose growing. It helps hold and make available water and nutrients, increases porosity of the soil and supports the "living soil" process. Need any more reasons to have up to 25% organic matter in your rosebed? Just check out the loads of roses enjoyed by growers who have understood this wonder of nature all along.

OLD RELIABLE... Try the Rambler's formula for new beds or rejuvenation of old ones. Simple. Just 1/3 soil, 1/3 sand and 1/3 organics. Don't worry too much about the proportions. Till, mix, turn, dig or cultivate this mix a couple of times, let settle and you're ready to plant. If in doubt, add more organics.

GOURMET ROSARIANS season their beds with fish meal, alfalfa meal (or pellets), some gypsum and some bone meal. For a 100 square foot rosebed, add about 15 pounds of fish meal, 20 pounds of alfalfa, 20 pounds of gypsum and 15 pounds of bone meal. Till or mix well, water and let settle. Weather permitting, till again and you're ready to plant.

TOXIC CONCERNS about planting roses where roses have been before?? Need new soil? The Rambler says "not to worry." There's a big word for it, ALLELOPATHY, the suppression of growth of one plant species by another due to the release of toxic substances. The Rambler has NEVER observed this in roses after planting and replanting for years and years. If there is a growth slow-down, it's from "tired soil" that just needs some organic matter to make it alive again. Hauling soils and mixes in and out just does not make sense in most cases. Just give the soil a shot in the humus area. Think POSITIVE for a short winter, long spring.

Rosarians know that you have to do a job to really learn how. Here are some great jobs to try with your "learner's permit…"

ROSEBED CONSTRUCTION… worth a new look at all of the materials and methods available to hobbyist rosarians. While beds are a matter of taste, budget, terrain, landscape theme and many other considerations, well planned beds produce better roses.

A SHORT LIST of materials for bed construction is not so short. Hobby-handy materials include concrete curbing, treated lumber, landscape timers, railroad ties, bricks, concrete blocks, steel edging, plastic edging, live materials and even the old-fashioned way… nothing at all. The Rambler even remembers gardeners who planted shrubs in the middle of automobile tires.

THE NATURAL LOOK is popular with the Rambler, but also likes the softness and patina of wood. Beds can be built up 10 inches to 12 inches above the lawn level and made attractive by contouring the edges off gradually with plenty of thick mulch. Stabilize the edge (and to keep the grass out) with steel edging like *Ryerson*. Another trick is a thick-growing edge like *Lariope*. A natural look is more of a maintenance problem, but has lots of applications.

LANDSCAPE TIMBERS AND/OR TREATED LUMBER are easy to use, readily available and cheap. Timbers also last a long time, have almost unlimited flexibility and can be formed into all kinds of shapes with just a little chainsaw skill. The Rambler builds up two timbers high, anchoring the bottom timber with reinforcing bar driven into the ground through drilled holes. Then nail the top timber with long spikes after drilling pilot holes. That structure WON'T move. Timbers cut into 8 to 10 inch lengths and tamped into the soil also make a decorative edge. In one bed the Rambler uses timbers laid horizontally, broken up with short lengths on edge to form curves and turn corners. For a really finished effect, add a treated "foot" around the bed to runt he lawnmower wheel on.

CINDER BLOCKS WITH HOLES are also easy for most hobbyists to use. Hands-and-knees laying (follow a string) is slow but sure, no footing required, no mortar (you can always change your mind). Available in a variety of sizes. Can also be stained to get rid of the "concrete look." Latex stain liberally diluted with water can be brushed on generously, leaving behind a soft, pigment patina. For an added trim, fill the open block spaces with good soil and plant with portulaca, alyssum or similar bedding plant. Pansies are nice for spring, too. But avoid violets… they support spider mites by the millions.

BRICKS make a great edging and can be laid formally or informally, depending on the skill of the gardener. For a formal brick wall, be sure to pour a footing or the bricks will eventually sag, sink and crack. An informal treatment uses bricks in a "soldier course," that is bricks laid on edge and tamped into a soft concrete footing. Allow drainage space between each brick, no additional mortar necessary. Use a half-inch board as a spacer between bricks when laying. The soil and mulch will hold very well and the edge takes on a weathered look in a short time. A soldier course can follow contours, edge along a walk, keep soil from washing… all sorts of good applications.

CONTINUOUS POUR CURBING is for the high-budget grower. There's a continuous pour curbing machine now that lays down cement like toothpaste, marking curves and adjustments with ease. Home improvement contractors in major areas are promoting this technique, and it's beautiful. Color can be added to the concrete and you can make your own designs. About all it takes is stripping the sod, tamping and easy changes of direction. The Rambler thinks that we will see more of this in the future, and hopes that Easy-Rent outfits catch on to this and make the machine available to weekend garden athletes.

CHECK THE LUMBERYARDS for some of the new pre-cut treated lumber pieces that go together like a puzzle. It's amazing the shapes and looks that can be created. I'm still impressed with the snail-shape, elevated mini bed put up by Bill Soltis (on the Norfolk, VA, tour). Great!

CHECK the tools. Get to work. Time to break dormancy,

The "Coffeetime Workshop" is the best part of a typical rose meeting… THERE'S where the really great rose wisdom comes out. Here's a "sampler" of timely topics from recent sessions…

DORMANT SPRAYS, CLEANUP SPRAYS… widely misunderstood. The objective is to control over-wintering spores and insects before temperature and humidity are right for new-season outbreaks. Dormant spray seems to be declining in popularity, primarily because available fungicides and insecticides are so effective and easy to apply. If you are a lime-sulfur fan, stay with it, but a cleanup spray right after pruning works best. Thoroughly wet canes and bud union (if exposed) with a fungicides/insecticide mixture like *Funginex/Orthene* or *Maneb/Diazinon*… whatever you normally use for control. Use at label strength… and do an extra-good job on climbers and ramblers. An infected host plant can spread spores like wildfire.

FISH EMULSION is the rose starter of choice. Think of fish emulsion to soil as lighter fluid is to charcoal: It gets everything going. An ounce or two of fish emulsion per gallon of water applied generously to just-planted roses gets the soil organisms working and supplies water in a safe, won't-burn way. This can't be said for all of the "stimulators." About the time the hilled-up mulch has been washed away, apply the solution again. Miniatures like it, too… half as much.

BUFFER SPRAY AGENT… a really innovative new product called *Indicate 5.* A misleading name, *Indicate 5* performs five basic functions for more effective spray application: it acidifies the spray solution, buffers (sets acidic limit), makes water wetter, compatible with various spray combinations, and reduces drift of spray material. In short, it works the same way as the vinegar/spreader treatment for spray water that the Rambler has advocated for years.

THE SECRET is a color indicator for the right pH and water hardness factor. When the spray water is slightly pink with addition of *Indicate 5*, the pH and hardness levels are just right. For Greenville water, the Rambler uses ½ teaspoon per gallon. Spray solutions of *Triforine/Daconil* plus *Rubigan* spread well; and it is well known that insecticides are considerably more effective in a slightly acid solution. The Rambler definitely thinks that *Avid* (miticide) works better when applied in an *Indicate 5* solution. *Indicate 5* has limited availability; the Rambler orders from Kimbrew-Walter Roses, (903) 829-2968. They are good folks with a great products list of stuff important to rosarians. Cost of *Indicate 5*: about $30 per quart, a real bargain. Give some a try this season.

HILL UP, BAG UP those newly-planted rosebushes so that the roots have a chance to catch up with the tops. Hilling up adds frost protection, too, but the primary purpose is to keep the canes from drying out. The Rambler ALWAYS hills up a new bush, potted or bare-root. New canes have stored food and moisture that pushes out into new growth and leaves. Meanwhile, the roots are called on to replace that substance, the ONLY way it can be replaced. New roots have to form in a hurry to keep up. To reduce the load on the delivery system, conserve the moisture in the canes. Use mulch, soil, leaves or mixtures to hill up 10 inches or so. Some growers like paper bags or newspaper collars to hold the material in place. Gradually uncover in 2 or 3 weeks, leaving the material in place as a summer mulch. Use a slow stream of water from the hose to gradually displace the hill… and the bush likes the extra water.

A MOIST MICRO-CLIMATE is a must for starting tree roses. Use a plastic tent secured around the head of a tree rose, supplying the moisture with a large handful of moist sphagnum moss on the bud unions. When growth is clearly started in 2 weeks, cut some small holes in the bag to reduce temperature. Take off entirely in another week.

IF IT'S WORKING, DON'T QUIT. Roses grow more than one way and in spite of rosarians. Consider your overall results, and if your roses are doing all right, stay with it. You and your roses will enjoy the season more.

Opportunity never comes... it's here. Your chance to grow the best roses ever in '94. Here are some tips to help you along...

FISH MEAL is the stuff for rosarians who want to ENJOY roses, not just work at it. If you can find some at your local feed store (widely used as poultry feed), get 50 pounds or so and apply as "cones" around established bushes. Use a bulb digger or similar tool and lift three cones of soil six inches deep and 18 inches away from the shank. Pour one to two cups of fish meal into the he holes; cover with soil and listen to the roots being called to the dinner table. The result will be greener leaves, better growth and overall better bloom. Use in early spring and again in late summer. Years from now when these bushes are dug, you'll see that masses of hairy feeder roots have "found" the fish meal, supporting the bush in great style. A convenient alternate is Mills Magic Rose Mix, advertised in these pages.

WARM ROOTS ARE HUNGRY. Fertilizers applied to cold soils won't do much good until the root zone warms up, explaining why some rosarians think the feeding program isn't working. The canes, warmed by sunshine, may be waking up, but the roots are waiting for a clear signal that spring has arrived. To illustrate: check new roses in black plastic pots set out on a warm, reflective surface. In just a week or two, tiny new roots have spread throughout the pot and the rose is off to a fast start. For rosarians in a hurry, apply readily available foods (like fortified alfalfa tea) in solution, soaking the root zone when the soil warms up.

BREAK TRADITION. Traditional wisdom says "never use fertilizer with a newly-planted rose." But there are some exceptions... like the use of a timed-release fertilizer when planting a well-developed potted rose. Many nursery-supplied roses have been confined in pots for two months or more, developing a fairly good system of new roots. The Rosarian wants to encourage these roots to expand into the rosebed as soon as possible. Lure the roots with some strategically-placed, timed-release food... a kind of carrot in front of the horse, done safely if used with some rose sense.

THE KEY IS CONCENTRATION. Dig the hole to the appropriate depth and check the fit (rose in the pot). Then mix an ounce of *Osmocote* with some soil it he bottom of the hole, about an inch or so under the root level. Carefully slit the plastic pot with a sharp knife and cut out the bottom. Position the root ball in the hole (there should be all sorts of white feeder roots on the outside). Backfill with a couple of inches of bedding mix and add another ounce of *Osmocote* on top of this band, all around the ball and away from the roots. Add some more soil (several inches) and repeat the *Osmocote* process. Finish backfilling with bedding mix and flood with water. Hill up slightly and keep moist. Use NO MORE than three to four ounces of *Osmocote* per well-started bush. You'll see good top growth throughout the season and know that the roots are growing also.

PREVENTION is the name of the game in disease control. If ANYTHING is scheduled in the rose garden, the fungicide spray program should be. Start early, stay on schedule. It is a mistake to wait until infection appears; by then it's too late. Blackspot leaves cannot be restored, leaves and buds twisted with powdery mildew won't become sleek and productive after spraying. Begin spraying the day roses are pruned and weekly thereafter. *Triforine*, *Manzate* or *Daconil*... all are effective... when USED.

CHECK DOWNY MILDEW... that purplish-brown leaf spot that can sweep through rose gardens in cool, damp weather. And in short order the leaves fall off. But rosarians can head off the infection by alternating a spray mix of *Triforine-Manzate* one week, *Triforine-Daconil* the next. Use BOTH fungicides at label strength, wet leaves and canes thoroughly. The specific fungicide of choice is Pace applied every 10 days, but really not necessary with the alternating program. Also, downy disappears when temperatures hit 80 degrees. An alternating program is like a change-up baseball pitch... catches the spores unaware.

Good ideas are not a bit particular about who has them… you may want to pick up and claim some of these. All guaranteed to perform.

FRESH HORSE MANURE… Should it be spread right away, composted a year or so, or reported to the EPA?? The best answer is to keep the manure source a secret so that you can have it all for yourself. Then get it out on the rosebeds, in the rosebeds, mixed in the compost pile and used wherever organic matter and bacterial action are needed. There is NO need to compost horse manure/shavings/alfalfa hay/straw mixtures before using on roses. Just scratch in a bit and use plenty of water. The results will be amazing.

SOME OF THE GOOD STUFF is lost by waiting for the "well rotted" stage. Let the microbial action rejuvenate the rosebeds rather than be leached away. The Rambler's roses think it's a special treat to get an inch or two of horse manure mulch just a week out of the horse. Yours will, too.

RAMBLER ERROR is the only explanation for the statement in the March column "*Indicate 5* costs about $30 a quart." Actually this great new buffer spray agent costs about $10 a quart, $30 per gallon. Spray effectiveness is improved by *Indicate 5* as it acidifies, indicates pH, buffers, wets, spreads, penetrates, aids compatibility and reduces volatility. It takes about 2 teaspoons of *Indicate 5* per gallon of water to reach the optimum pH level. Use more or less depending on the hardness of the water. Add the material slowly to the water which will change from milky white to orange to pink. Pink indicates a pH of 5.0. Let stand a few minutes to make sure that the reaction is complete (solution stays pink). Once you have figured out how much your water needs, buffer your spray solutions regularly and enjoy an enhanced spray program.

ROSE SHOW BUFFS converse in a strange chemical language this time of year, describing their SUPER WHAMMO water soluble mixes that produce trophy table winners. There are lots of special blends that do good things for roses, but just remember that this is an inexact science; try one thing at a time and see how it works. I'm reminded of an advertising slogan for a fertilizer that says it all: "Plants need minerals, not miracles."

THRIPS TIME… Thrips love those fragrant, light-colored blooms just like the judges. *Orthene 75% SP* (soluble powder) is the Rambler's favorite control, systemic and safe for the most tender blooms. Use *Orthene SP* at 2 teaspoons per gallon of water (buffered), get good coverage of buds and blooms and hit the beds as well.

SPRING AND POWDERY MILDEW just go together. But there's hope for clean foliage and blooms with early and regular application of *Rubigan EC* at 2 teaspoons per 5 gallons in an alternating program: *Triforine* one week, *Triforine* with *Rubigan* the next week. *Systhane* is the newest powdery mildew control, available in many areas as *Nova*, *Eagle* or *Rally* in a 40 WP formulation. May be used safely at 14-day intervals as a control and as an eradicate. Think of *Systhane* as being a "back-up" fungicide if mildew seems to be getting out of control. It is important to get SOME KIND OF PROTECTION on the new leaves each week as that's where the infection is going to break out. This follows the Rambler's "alternating fungicides" school of thought… keep the spores guessing.

WATER WASH… still a good first-step control of spider mites. Use a water wand that directs a fine, forceful spray of water underneath the leaves, knocking off the mites and interrupting the breeding cycle. Try water first (and often) before bringing out the miticide. *Avid* is by far the best chemical control and when used in a careful program can keep a rose garden free of mites during the hottest weather.

ODDS 'N ENDS… GROW LEAVES, then roses. Focus on good plant and leaf growth and you'll get roses… TRIM NEW BUSHES sparingly; cut short stems (or don't cut any blooms at all) during the first bloom cycle… WRITE FOR THE RAMBLER'S 1994 Spray Formulations. Just send a SASE to request or ask a question. Rose letters are fun… AND REMEMBER to have fun in your rose garden this season.

Rosarians build gardens to relax; but there's never time for it. Maybe these Ramblings will add some hours for relaxation.

FERTILIZER BURN. How does this happen? It's simple: too much nitrogen and not enough water. But why does it happen? Roots are made up of cells whose activity is supported by water, just like human skin and tissue. Burn occurs when water is removed or displaced from the cells. Most fertilizers use ammonium sulfate or ammonium nitrate as a nitrogen source, synthesizing the element found in nature. These compounds are HYGROSCOPIC in nature, that is, have the tendency to take up water. If the compounds (fertilizers) in the soil are too concentrated, moisture is absorbed from the soil, and even the roots, thereby destroying or otherwise interfering with the moisture support system for the cells.

NATURE LIKES BALANCE. Concentrated solutions want to add water and will perform this trick through osmosis, pulling moisture through the cells walls. The solution to burn is to apply appropriate fertilizer amounts and ALWAYS with plenty of water. That's the reason for the advice: water first, feed, water again. If in doubt, water some more.

SPIDER MITES will be in a reproductive frenzy in June, brought on by hot, dry weather. Keep the mating to a minimum with a water wand, washing underneath the leaves with a fine water spray. In many cases this works if you have a small garden and can wash twice a week. The next step is a miticide. *Avid* is the product of choice as it has great knock-down capability. It cleans up bushes in a hurry and can be used weekly if necessary. Used at ¼ teaspoon per gallon, *Avid* is relatively inexpensive on a per-gallon basis. It leaves no residue, penetrates leaf tissue for a reservoir of active ingredient, is easy on beneficial insects and won't burn when used at recommended rates. It is also compatible with *Triforine* and knocks thrips right off light-colored blooms.

SEX ATTRACTANT for mites (as if they needed one) is a pheromone material called *STIR-RUP M*, luring mites to the miticide (and, I assume, to the leaves as well). But good coverage will do the trick, the secret of all spraying. *Avid* is best USED ALONE, applied underneath the lower leaves. Another help for *Avid* is the new buffer, spreader-sticker *INDICATE-5*. The material lowers the pH for longer residual and acts as an effective spreader. With *Indicate-5*, there's no need to spray to runoff. Spray until the leaves "glisten," and the miticide will go to work.

JAPANESE BEETLES. The Rambler dreads late June, as that's when beetles have an international convention in our Greenville garden, chewing up everything in sight and smell. Last season the Rambler tried *Margosan-O* weekly for two or three weeks BEFORE the beetles are expected to arrive. *Margosan-O* is a botanical insecticide concentrate and is systemic. Build-up in the leaves seems to repel beetles. For those who prefer the "knock-out" approach, *Sevin* is still the material of choice. You'll save some of the blooms, but the beetles will get some. A trade-off. *Sevin* leaves some residue on the leaves, can burn, and also kills off the beneficials. A natural control method: pick them off. You'll spend plenty of time in your rose garden with this technique.

PERSISTENT BLACKSPOT?? Add either *Manzate 200* or *Daconil 2787* to the routine *Triforine* spray. Full strength of both compounds if safe for foliage, but the Rambler finds that *Manzate* and *Daconil* at ½ concentration is just as effective. Have you tried the dry flowable *Manzate* or the water-dispersible granule *Daconil* yet? Both forms are marvelous advances over the old materials.

FINALLY, RELAX A LITTLE. Roses have been growing for a long time in spite of rosarians.

If you have always done it that way, it's probably wrong. You may want to check on these summer practices just to see if you're on the right track.

SPRAY COVERAGE is perhaps more important than the spray material, although the materials get most of the blame. Thrips are in the buds and blooms, direct coverage there. On the other hand, spider mites are hiding underneath the leaves at the bottom of the bush. Fungus diseases affect ALL of the leaves, apply materials until the leaves "glisten." The Rambler is a great believer in "buffered" spray solution, water that has been treated to a slightly acid pH. Most insecticides and fungicides have a spreader-sticker built-in, but just a few drops of dishwashing liquid per gallon of spray solution helps spread the materials over the leaves.

AVID, the superior acaricide (gets mites), requires good coverage even though the product is described as "translaminar." This means that it penetrates leaf tissue and deposits a reservoir of active ingredient inside. It also resists wash-off by rain or irrigation. The Rambler likes *Avid* used BY ITSELF in a solution buffered with *INDICATE-5*, Spider mite troubles are a thing of the past with this routine.

WATCH THE CONCENTRATION of active ingredient in spray materials as there are many different formulations. Example: *FUNGINEX* is a 6% formulation of *TRIFORINE*, which is sold in a 18% form. It takes 1 tablespoon of *Funginex* or 1 teaspoon of *Triforine* to do the same thing. *MANZATE* 200DF is a 75% formulation, used at 1 tablespoon per gallon. Other *Maneb* formulations may have different percentages of active ingredient. *Daconil* 2787 is another case in point. The preferred product today is *Daconil* 2787WDG, 90% active ingredient, requiring just 1 teaspoon per gallon. Wettable powder and emulsifiable forms require different application rates. The Rambler likes the WDG form of *Daconil* and the DF form of *Manzate* as the granules are water dispersible (they go into solution readily).

JAPANESE BEETLES will be out in force in many parts of the country in July (be thankful if they haven't found you yet). The Rambler's mailbag shows *Sevin* as the most popular control, followed by picking, profanity and *MARGOSAN-0*, the botanical insecticide concentrate (used at 1 tablespoon per gallon). "Control" is a relative term. The Rambler will have achieved control if there are some roses and most of the foliage left after the invasion.

THE MAILBAG always has questions related to too much fertilizer... what to do. Simply dilute the concentration and leach the excess with LOTS of water. Nature will get back to balance in spite of rosarians.

FREQUENCY OF APPLICATION is also an issue. Some growers think that MORE of a fungicide will eradicate blackspot faster. Not true. For persistent blackspot, switch fungicides (*Triforine, Manzate, Daconil*) from time to time and increase the FREQUENCY to every 4 to 5 days rather than 7 days. The idea is prevention, protecting new leaves from infection. Blackspot is always there, ready to grow on new leaves. When the growth of spores is controlled, we say that the disease is "eradicated." Maintain protection on the leaves and the problem is "gone."

WATER SYSTEMS are of great interest when the weather gets hot. Goal: get water to roses as effectively as possible with the least possible effort while conserving this most valuable resource. The system that the Rambler still likes the best is the *DRAMM* NOZZLE, have installed and revised and reworked more of these efficient water-delivers in more rose and flower beds than he cares to remember. Cheap, easy to build and flexible. If you would like to have the plans and instructions for a *DRAMM* setup, drop a note to the Rambler. You can decide for yourself if it fits your situation. Otherwise, fall back on a soaker system of porous hose that weeps water, delivering water at or near the roots without waste.

SUMMERTIME TONIC: How about some alfalfa tea, fortified with a touch of Epsom salts and some trace elements? More refreshing than lemonade for rosarians. If you want a recipe, drop a note. The greenest leaves your bushes will ever enjoy.

Ever notice that garden visitors always spot the sick rose first? Go right by the "once in a season" bloom. Must be some kind of "Rose Law." To minimize the embarrassment, either dig up the offender or try some of these rose tips...

MULCH... nothing does quite the same job in the rose garden. Choices include compost, leaves, pine needles, ground bark, tree trimmings and mixtures of all of these. Mulches function to cool the soil, conserve water, keep down weeds and add humus to the soil, completing nature's cycle. The Rambler had a hands-and-knees example of the value of mulch this season. One group of beds had ample (four inches) of shredded bark mulch with virtually no weeds. In the "Environmental Partnership" rose garden in the park, the soil was rich and full of humus... but no mulch, and choked with weeds. Had a new crop every three weeks. Solution: mounded the beds with bark, no more weeds.

RISKY BUSINESS... change of rose routine. The park garden has a circular bed of some 30 Miniature roses with a tree standard of *The Fairy* in the middle. Pruned carefully stem by stem in the spring, enjoyed a colossal spring bloom. Ran out of time when cutting spent blooms on the big roses (and pulling weeds), so the Rambler decided to "shear" the Miniature bushes, by this time 18 inches in all directions and covered with old blooms. Against Millie Rambler's advice and judgment, just grabbed a handful of Mini and sheared it off with the clippers, leaving a general round effect. In three weeks the sheared plants were covered with new shapely growth and full of blooms. In fact, the Rambler thinks that the bushes looked the best ever.

FEEDING MINIS... The Rambler has fed Minis, in all gardens this season with *Mills Magic Rose Mix*, a combo of fish meal, cottonseed meal, alfalfa meal and a few magic ingredients. All of these Miniature beauties are doing great. No vegetative centers from too much nitrogen, great leaves, blooms in proportion. No grower could ask for more. The organics are doing the job; if *Mills Mix* is hard to come by, get the raw materials from a good feed store and make your own magic.

CHIPS... not cow chips for tea but chunks from the tree chipper. The Rambler had two hard-wood trees and a large pine taken down and run through the chipper, making a huge pile in the yard. Had to build a new, large rosebed to use all of this good stuff. Tilled up some fairly hard clay near the golf course with some humus and leaves, activated with alfalfa and cottonseed meal and let settle for two weeks. Planted Shrub roses, HTs, Floribundas, Climbers and Miniatures, about 40 in all. Mulched with five inches of wood chips. The roses have thrived the past two seasons. I can walk in the beds without compacting, water and fertilizer percolate through, no weeds and the soil is alive with worms. Some ordinary lawn fertilizer has been broadcast on the chips to make up for the loss of nitrogen through decomposition. The roses have been fed a normal diet of *Osmocote*, organic meals and some fast-acting solubles. About two inches of chips have "disappeared" into the soil as compost. Great bed, looks good, continues to be productive... the *Graham Thomas* Shrubs are 8 feet high and wide. Use YOUR chips wisely.

DO WHAT FEELS GOOD... There's a minor flap appearing in various rose publications debating the merit (even necessity) of adding white vinegar to spray solutions as a "buffer." Some good authorities say, "Don't bother, it's already built in." And a new product, *INDICATE 5*, which buffers, wets, spreads and penetrates is rapidly gaining endorsement among rosarians who like its convenience and effectiveness. Everybody may be right. There is more than ONE way to grow and spray roses. If buffering with vinegar has been working for you, keep it up; the Rambler plans to. I get good leaf coverage, insecticide-fungicide effectiveness... and no adverse effects. Plus, the Rambler REALLY likes Indicate 5 with Avid. Advice to rosarians everywhere (a highly independent bunch): Do whatever makes you feel good.

Until September and the Rambler's 23rd Anniversary of these pages... have a Rosy Summer.

"Rose growing is the kind of hard work that an intelligent man wouldn't do for a living." That was the Thought For The Month when the Rambler began these columns 24 years ago. But since we enjoy rose work so much, let's get on with some tips worth trying…

QUESTIONS NEEDING ANSWERS hits the Rambler's desk like an incoming tide each month… and sometimes the tide is slow to go out. Here are some selected common queries that you may have been afraid to ask:

ALL ORGANICS? Don't you use "chemical" foods? Of course. Supplements should be part of every feeding program. Organics set the table for roses to enjoy a feast of nutrients, thoughtfully applied by the grower. When the process is working right, fewer and fewer "additives" are needed. *Osmocote* (Sierra 17-6-10 with Minors) is a Rambler staple ration …

FAVORITE ROSES? Probably Floribundas. Great for landscaping and colorful displays, good leaves, too. Next come Miniatures which also add to the landscape. Lots of applications from containers to "bare spots." Most spectacular: a bed of 20 *Playboys* in the front lawn and a long bed of mixed-variety Miniatures, landscape rocks and miscellaneous annuals in front of a fence. A couple of bushes of *Playgirl* effectively screen a gas meter and two air conditioning units in the Rambler's garden today.

WHAT ARE YOU BUILDING NOW? Just completed a low, split-rail fence next to the driveway, planted with three vigorous bushes of *Klima Climber* and four bushes of *Cal Poly*. Trained the *Klimas* horizontally to encourage bloom, rewarded with loads of deep yellow blossoms that are too pretty to cut. *Cal Poly* is nearly the same color for a very friendly neighbor fence.

SPRAY SCHEDULE? Absolutely. Every week, rain or shine. Ignore the weather, start early and forget about blackspot. Favorite mix: Triforine and Manzate 200 one week, Triforine alone the next week, substituting Daconil 2787 now and then for Manzate during cool weather. Result: no Downey Mildew either.

A GOOD SPRAYER. The Rambler likes Spot Shot, a good, sturdy piece of semi-pro equipment that consistently does a thorough job. Develops about 65 pounds of pressure, centrifugal, battery-powered pump. I recommend a 30-inch wand and fine-droplet, fan-pattern spray nozzle. A 15-foot hose lets the applicator move around the garden in a hurry. The Rambler can spray 400-plus bushes in less than an hour from startup to cleanup.

ANY SECRETS? Bed preparation, rich and organic, in the sun. Compromise in either area hurts results. A good planting medium grows good roses… all the miracle products on the market can't make roses grow if the nutrients are not available to the plant.

BEST ADVICE: Grow leaves and blooms are sure to follow. Seems too simple to be effective. But it is absolutely true. Bushes with sparse leaves, whether due to disease, bugs or nutrition just do not put out roses.

ANY BREAKTHROUGHS? The Rambler's big breakthrough came with the discovery of fish meal and alfalfa meal. All other progress has grown from this sound foundation. These organics are duplicated elsewhere in nature, but don't have quite the same effect. Horse manure is great, flavored with fish meal makes it even better. Alfalfa (for the growth hormone) brings a special kind of reaction… even faster when applied as tea. Another dramatic breakthrough was *Triforine*, systemic and safe for bushes and rosarians. Important.

DO NOT HAVE SPIDER MITES? Everybody has mites from time to time, but they can be controlled with water or with water and Avid. Stay alert, water wash, get busy with Avid at the first sign of activity. And curtail use of insecticides that kill off the predators. Nature has a balance that we tend to destroy.

HOW MANY ROSES? Just enough to make life worthwhile, about 450, evenly divided between big roses (all types) and Miniatures. Millie works the Minis. The Rambler works a little of everything plus another 150 in an "Environmental Partnership" garden, which means that Millie and I get to do the work.

ENOUGH, ODDS 'N ENDS for now, keep your letters coming. My, how time flies when you're having fun.

People who think they can run the earth should start with a small garden… that's where EVERYTHING happens. To avoid a few surprises, adopt a few of these resolutions…

MAGIC BULLETS… The sure cure for everything in one shot. Not likely in the real world. Nature has a certain sort of rhythm and gets really annoyed when rosarians upset things. Think twice about that concoction of spray materials that has something for everything. Usually the leaves suffer more than the insects and diseases. Many products can be safely combined, like *Triforine* and *Orthene*, as in *Orthenex*. And *Triforine* and *Manzate* are compatible fungicides. *Rubigan* can be added for every broader fungus disease protection, but then the list gets shorter and shorter. Understand what the spray program is supposed to accomplish, then deal specifically with that problem. Your roses will be happier.

AVID in particular works better when used alone, or with *Stirrup-M* (the sex attractant)… This miticide needs to get underneath the leaves in the lower part of the plant. No reason at all to hit these areas with fungicide that interferes with the miticide action. One thing at a time works better.

FALL STUFF… we'll soon have a bumper crop of materials that nature has been growing all year, storing up all sorts of nutrients for us. Leaves, of course. Hope that you are not wasting them. Leaves are the basic ingredient of the Rambler's FRAGRANT FORMULA, the artificial manure that does not have to pass through a horse. The Rambler will reprint the Fragrant Formula next spring so that you observant and nature-conscious gardeners can be the first on your block to make your own manure. Advance information: Besides the leaves, the formula requires alfalfa meal, cottonseed meal, fish meal when available, gypsum and some Epsom salts. Pile up some leaves now and be ready.

ALFALFA… Is there a difference in alfalfa pellets and alfalfa meal?? No, and that is easy to verify by readying the contents and analysis label on each bag put out through a feed outlet. Pellets have a bit of binder added, which releases as soon as the pellet becomes damp. Pellets are easier to use and broadcast, and usually cost about the same as meal. Pellets make great tea for roses.

COMPOSTING in place with leaves is an easy fall clean-up chore. The summer vegetable garden is a likely spot. Chop the leaves a bit first with a lawnmower; run the mower up and down the row of leaves left by a side-discharge mower. Or use a rear-bagger and dump them on the open ground. Rows or piles two feet deep are about right. There will be bits and pieces of green material in the leaves which act as a starter. Or, to speed up the process, sift in some cottonseed meal or another quick-release nitrogen source. Turn once in a while with a pitchfork and let moisture and nature do their thing.

GOOD BED PREPARATION for almost any growing thing can begin with leaves on soil. Just dump the leaves and amendments on the ground to be improved (about 6 or 8 inches deep) and turn over or till lightly. No need for a deep excavation. We're going to let nature do most of the work. Over the winter with freeze and thaw, or, in warmer climates, decomposition, the soil loosens up and begins to become alive. Even frozen soil is working. Gypsum helps this soil process, and some kind of organic starter contributes. The Rambler has a piece of ground working under leaves all the time.

SOME GROWERS break down leaves in plastic bags, adding just a bit of fertilizer and water to a bagful of leaves and securing the top. The Rambler's leaves must be extra vigorous as they usually eat their way out of the bags by spring, but I have seen it work well for others. A rich compost comes out of the bags in the spring. Speaking of eating up containers, fish meal stored in a plastic garbage can will eat tiny pinholes through the sides in just a few months, even though the sides in just a few months, even though the grower swears that the can was tightly sealed. Fish meal works best on the ground, not in a can.

Hope you are enjoying a final rose harvest. Talk with you next month.

Winter is the time when it's too cold to do the job that was too hot to do last summer. But here are some by-the-fire suggestions with a few "nice day" chores...

SPRAY MATERIALS LOSING EFEC-TIVENESS?? Unlikely... the Rosarian was probably the ineffective element. Case in point: A national-level competitor in South Carolina asked for some help, reporting a dramatic decline in the effectiveness of *Triforine* (and *Triforine/Manzate* in combination). Had blackspot all over. Howev-er, when carefully reviewing the spray schedule, it seems that the reviewing the spray schedule, it seems that the Rosarian had "skipped" a few sprayings along the way. Solution: Increase the frequency to twice a week for four applications and then drop back to weekly. By fall the garden was lush with absolutely clean foliage... without changing spray materials.

SEVIN **DID IT.** The Rambler finally chal-lenged Japanese Beetles with Liquid *Sevin* in one part of the garden this summer with dramatic re-sults. No beetle damage to blooms and leaves, but spider mites nearly wiped out the bushes just a few weeks later. A classic example of destroying the natural predators. The mites took over the amazing swiftness. On the other hand, an area sprayed with *Margosan-O* had some beetle damage but NO out-break of spider mites. There certainly is a lesson to be learned here. Old-timers know that excessive use of *Orthene* for thrips can bring on the same results. We have much to learn about Integrated Pest Management.

WINTERIZE?? Anti-desiccant sprays may help in the winter protection process, particularly with climbers and ramblers. Anti-desiccant sprays like *Wilt-Pruf* and *Cloud Cover* retain moisture in the canes that is otherwise lost with cold, drying winds. These materials are readily available and easy to use. When bushes go dormant and drop their leaves, trip up to suit your situation and thor-oughly spray the canes before wrapping or cov-ering (cones, baskets, boxes, etc.). Remember that canes are round and the backside has to be covered, too. Apply liberally, get good coverage. More canes are lost to drying out than actual cold; this liquid blanket can make a difference.

ADJUST pH... Winter is a good time to apply agriculture lime (if needed) provided that the soil area is workable. Top application is not as effec-tive since lime is relatively insoluble. The process is a REACTIVE one in contact with soil crumbs. Lime in the presence of Hydrogen ions (the indi-cator for pH) reacts with those ions to form water. By reducing the hydrogen ions, the pH goes up. It's a fairly slow process. If a rosebed needling lime can't be tilled or spaded, use a spading fork to open up holes to take the lime. Lightly scratch soil back, let water and chemistry work. To STAY in balance (about 6.5), a good rule to thumb is to add a pound of agricultural lime (calcium carbonate) or dolomite lime (calcium carbonate and magne-sium carbonate) for every pound of nitrogen. Ex-ample: 5-10-5 ammonium sulfate, 50 pound bag, contains 2.5 pounds of nitrogen. Use 2.5 pounds of lime for the same area. And always TEST before adjusting.

BURY FOR THE WINTER... new rose-bushes, that is. Roses received in late November or December (or newly budded plants) are far better off buried than potted and moved in and out of pro-tection all winter. It's a natural sort of dormancy, much like the "Minnesota Tip" method of winter protection. Select a garden spot where it is easy to dig 18 inches or so and set aside the spoil dirt. Then loosen the spoil dirt with lots of leaves. Line the dormancy vault with some leaves and it's ready to receive bushes. Tie the tops of the bushes with twine, and then tie in bundles. Heel in the bundles in the vault (not quite horizontal) and cover with the mix. Remember to tie a rope on the bundles so that you can find them next spring. Cover the area with lots of leaves. Then wait for spring. It really works.

GROOMING CONTROVERSY... The Rambler is required to report that the Miniatures that he groomed by shearing are performing no better than the ones carefully trimmed by Millie Rambler... maybe hers had a FEW more exhibi-tion blooms. But, to be fair, shearing was a lot less work.

Talk to you NEXT YEAR !! Have a happy one.

ROSE CATALOGS cause backaches, according to the Surgeon General. But this rosarian will take a prescription for roses anytime. Here's an Rx that will make you feel good, too...

HARD, TIGHT SOIL has got to go in '95. Too many growers are fighting off the consequences of hard-pan beds instead of working with the soil. A rose is absolutely dependent on the soil to deliver nutrients so that the leaves and sun can do their thing. Friable soil that breathes, takes in water and drains will support the tiny organisms that convert nutrients into forms available to plants. And building a live soil is that difficult.

SOIL IS MADE OF PARTICLES, the more sizes the better. Think of soil as a matrix of big pieces, little pieces, all sizes and shapes with plenty of space for air and water. With the right balance of organic material, the soil is alive as nature intended. Heavy clay soils need gritty sand, Perlite and lots of textured organics like ground bark, fibrous peat, manures, leaves, stems and partially composted stuff. These particles "prop open" the flat clay particles and form "crumbs" that attract nutrients and organisms. Roots move right through friable soils, expanding capability.

GRITTY SOILS can also be helped with organics... and some clay. Both hold the moisture so that roots can feed on the crumbs. Cuttings will root in pure sand, but long-term growth is supported by the live ingredients in organics. Build soil, then grow roses.

WHAT TO DO NOW?? Get some soil openers ON the ground to be improved, even if it cannot be worked right now. Gypsum broadcast at 25 pounds per 100 square feet will open up clay or alkaline soils. Dress the ground with leaves, mulch, compost, bark and coarse stuff of all kinds. Work in whenever the ground permits. The best course is to rebuild a bed entirely, but soil can also be improved with the roses in place. If you haven't experienced gypsum, now's the time. Won't change the pH, can't burn anything. Opens up the tightest soil. Try gypsum on a container that won't drain. About 1/3 cup for a 12-15 inch container, broadcast on top. The result is like pulling a cork out of a bottle.

MORE SUNSHINE is on the Rambler's list of things to do in '95. Rosebeds with roses three-deep are tough to care for and retard the roses in the middle, even with 36-inch spacing. Several beds will be reworked this spring to plant two-deep with sun and air on both sides. One planting calls for a single row. You may want to "go for the sun" this season, too.

HAD A GREAT HOLIDAY GIFT... a dump truck load of horse manure from a riding stable (stalls). Was steaming and fragrant on delivery... all it needed was a red ribbon on top. The rosebeds are now tucked away for winter, under a cozy blanket of manure... about five inches deep. What a spring we are going to have.

THE RAMBLER'S OFFER OF INFO on watering systems drew a tremendous response. And that prompted a new look at available systems that are easy to build, relatively inexpensive and flexible for a variety of situations. So... combined with the rosebed rebuilding project for '95 will be installation and trials of four different systems that appear to be suitable for roses. The Rambler is not the world's greatest (or most patient) craftsman, so this should be a real test.

THE OLD RELIABLE *DRAMM* nozzle system installed in rigid schedule 40 pipe will go in one bed. The nozzles will be spaced 36-inches apart. The line feed comes from a 5/8-inch garden hose, 45 pound pressure. The next bed will have a *Dramm Stix* system with nozzles mounted on rigid wires, fed with spaghetti tubing inserted into flexible black poly tubing. Appears to ideal for curved beds and miniatures.

A *DRIPWORKS* system will go into another bed. *DripWorks* also uses spaghetti tubing with an insert barb into flexible poly pipe. An adjustable emitter is mounted on a plastic stake. Also appears to adapt to irregular plantings. The Rambler has seen one of these in action and is most impressed. Last but not least, one bed will likely have *Leaky Pipe*, or *Moisture Master*, or whatever other brand name goes with the porous hose made from recycled automobile tires. The Rambler has some of this now, and it works, but may work even better with different placement.

ANYWAY, THIS IS THE YEAR for friable soil and easy watering. Check these columns monthly for how the projects are going. And I promise to tell the truth... like a Queen of Show story.

If your garden is giving you new problems before you've solved the old ones, don't worry. They will soon be old problems, too. Here are some old/new things to work on in '95.

DIRTY-KNEES ROSARIAN. Roses and rosarians like hands-and-knees planting, much easier on bad backs and roses than bending over. Check out the army surplus store and get a short-handled shovel, like the old foxhole tool. If the soil has been well prepared, it's easy to scoop out a hole, rebuild a cone to support the roots and bush, then let water and soil do the rest. Properly placed, the roots and shank will be stable without holding. Cover the roots lightly with soil and begin to let water run slowly into the hole; add more soil, then more water. No need to tamp or pack. In short, mud them in.

COVER UP YOUR WORK. Hill up newly planted roses with loose, protective cones of mulch or other insulating material until just the tips of the canes stick out. Not just a little material, a real mound… a couple of BIG shovelfuls per bush. Moisture conservation in the canes is important, not sunshine. Moisture in the canes is supported by new root hairs; hilling keeps canes from drying out until the roots have a chance to deliver.

GET READY TO SPRAY. On schedule, at pruning time. A good many rosarians like to admire emerging leaves and forget that fungus spores are emerging, too. Spores overwinter on green tissue and insects are hiding out in bud union crevices. It's too late when blackspot appears.

CLEANUP SPRAY for newly pruned bushes is misunderstood and controversial. The objective is to get ahead of spores and overwintering insects without damaging the cane tissue. Rosarians in the really dormant, cold regions like oil and sulfur or lime/oil/sulfur combinations make a terrible mess on the side of the house or a fence. The Rambler likes to use the SAME controls in cold or warm weather; a fungicide/insecticide combination with a little extra spreader-sticker, used at label strength. There is NO NEED to increase the concentration. Spray climbers and shrub roses particularly well; infected bushes can spread spores like wildfire when conditions are right.

HORMONES/ADDITIVES/INDUCERS are always popular at the springtime nursery shop. But less popular in the real-world rose garden. If the bed has been well prepared and kept alive with regular additions of organics, miracle cures aren't required. The Rambler likes a cup or so of gypsum per bush in early spring, a cup of alfalfa pellets or meal, a small handful of Epsom salts and a good source of nitrogen, preferably organic, like fish meal, cottonseed meal or blood meal. Get all this stuff into contact with the soil and let nature and the micro-organisms go to work.

FISH FOR NEW ROSES. New rosebushes like a fish diet, low fat and high in protein and minerals, just like rosarians. Fish emulsion is the easy way. Water in bareroot rosebushes with about 2 tablespoons of fish emulsion per gallon of water. Repeat in about two weeks. Roots will develop quickly without burning. Miniature roses love it, too.

WANT BASAL BREAKS? A one-two punch with Epsom salts (magnesium sulfate) and a readily available source of nitrogen brings results at pruning time as well as after the initial bloom cycle. Magnesium, so essential to the rose tissue process, leaches readily from the soil, as does nitrogen. Kick off the process with about 1/3 cup of Epsom salts, followed by an every-other-week application of a soluble 20-20-20 like *Peters* or *Ra-Pid-Gro* for three applications. New basals require lots of energy. Get that energy into the root zone for results. This kick-in-the-roots treatment should be used ONLY on established bushes and NEVER on miniatures.

DOWNY MILDEW control also begins early. Alternate *Triforine* and *Daconil* weekly during cool, damp weather. Add *Manzate* to the *Triforine* every-other spraying. If downy has been a problem previously, increase the frequency of *Daconil* and spray carefully for good coverage. Make sure that canes and leaves (especially undersides) are evenly moistened; a spreader-sticker may help. Beads of spray on the leaves won't do the job.

AND REMEMBER, sap should begin to rise in roses and rosarians at the same time.

Thought of the month: Buying cheap roses to save money is like stopping the clock to save time.

GARDENERS will be interested to know that the government says its the soil that's over worked. Have they checked bad backs in early spring?? Check off these early-season tips for less work and more fun.

IT'S NOT TOO LATE for a new rosebed in most parts of the country. Conventional advice says that beds need to "mellow" for a while, but a sharp grower can go from bare lawn to roses in place in two weeks. The trick is to blend the equal thirds of soil, sand and organics without hot chemicals. A small tiller helps, but a spading fork and cultivator can also do the job. Mix and mix and mix again. The Rambler still likes to add gypsum, a source of phosphate, dolomite lime and Perlite to the mix, distributing throughout the bed. To activate the bed and get the processes going, use cottonseed meal or fish meal (about 25 pounds per 100 square feet) and work in well. The micro-organisms will take right off. Fresh manures do much the same thing, but the bagged stuff is more convenient. Water and let settle a day or so between tillings. Plant and stand back. The roses are going to grow.

TREE ROSES ought to be enjoyed in more parts of the country, even in areas where they have to be buried for the winter. Some rosarians are hesitant, saying the trees are "hard to start." Just give the emerging buds and small canes the same kind of "humidifying" that bush roses enjoy. Add a couple of handfuls of very wet sphagnum moss to the bud unions and small canes, much like "air layering." Work some moss throughout the canes and then loosely secure a plastic bag over the whole head, creating a miniature greenhouse. This keeps the canes from drying out until the new roots have a chance to deliver moisture up the long tree standard. Cut some small air holes in about two weeks. Gradually uncover, depending on the weather.

ANOTHER TRICK. When planting a tree rose, provide some stout support for the limber standard. Use a reinforcing bar or an electrical conduit, driving into the ground 12-15 inches with the top just above the bud unions. Slip a piece of old plastic or rubber hose over the bar to avoid chafing the bark. Wrap-tie the support to the standard in about three places with electrician's tape. Just like taping a splint.

AN ATTRACTIVE USE for tree roses is a landscape focal point that can use two or more of the same variety. Underplant these tree roses with some low growing Miniatures, creating a multi-color carpet underneath. Very effective as a defining edge of a patio or to lead your eye to another part of the garden.

SHRUBS LACK BLOOMS?? Maybe there aren't enough long canes to signal the bush that growth has been attained and its time to bloom. Shrubs like to have long, draping canes, which will bloom at every leaf axil, much like a Climber. An example: the Austin rose Graham Thomas has stingy bloom until the canes are 8 or 9 feet long and spreading to the ground, much like a thorny spirea. Lady Rose does the same thing. You'll like Meidomonac (Bonica) more if allowed to spread out; producing bloom clusters all along the canes.

NURSERY FOR MINIS. Many rosarians find its a good idea to pot up small Miniature plants (straight out of the nursery) rather than directly into the planting bed. Well-rooted Miniatures will grow well in either case, but will start off better and produce more bush and bloom when started in a pot. Create a miniature nursery environment with 1 gallon pots, special protection if needed and a regular liquid feeding program. The Rambler's favorite -fish emulsion, of course. The soil mix warms up in the black plastic pots and they develop rapidly. About 6-8weeks of this baby plant care and the Miniature is ready for the real world.

COLORFUL BORDERS are easy with Miniature roses, as long as the varieties are in scale for the application. As an edging, you won't want to mix Green Ice (very low) with Luis Desamero (very tall). But most Miniatures can be sheared to stay in bounds and will respond with lots of blooms. Perhaps not the most likely to produce show-stoppers, but colorful and vigorous. The Rambler used to have a planting of Rise 'n Shine kept trimmed to 18 inches or so that made a beautiful low hedge, almost like turning on a light.

SPRING TREAT. Try a trio of Minis in a half barrel. Or a patio tree in the barrel with Green Ice as a draping ground cover. Puts roses in a whole new perspective.

THE FIRST DAY of spring is one thing… the first spring day is another. If your seasons are confused, relieve rose tension with some of these tips… between snow showers, rain and frost:

A DOSE OF SALTS (*Epsom Salts*, that is) is commonly used on roses at pruning time to encourage basal breaks and new leaf production… and that's a good practice. But even BETTER basal encouragement is Epsom Salts with an available source of nitrogen at the end of the first bloom cycle when the bush has leaves working to produce food. The Rambler likes a nitrate source in solution (doesn't have to be converted for the bush to take up) followed by Magnesium Sulfate… just a few days apart. Nitrogen and Magnesium Sulfate both leach rapidly, and both should be present in the root zone for the greatest effect. There are several good soluble fertilizers available, look for the Nitrate form in the analysis. Follow the directions and add about a quarter-cup of Epsom Salts per large bush. And flood with PLENTY OF WATER for the next two weeks.

GYPSUM is sometimes maligned as not having all of the soil-loosening qualities attributed to it. But for most growers, it is a cheap and easy amendment that can assist and not hurt. Calcium Sulfate reduces high sodium levels in sodic soils… associated with a high water table and poor drainage. It definitely opens up alkaline clay soils. However, it the soil to be treated has poor structure and texture, gypsum may not help much. Some sand, organics AND gypsum worked into the tight soil will do the most good. Just the salt-leaching qualities of gypsum is enough justification for the Rambler, who uses a cupful or so per bush spring and fall and ALWAYS tills into a new bed at 20 pounds per 100 square feet.

NITROGEN DEPLETION in the soil with liberal use of organics concerns some rosarians… a carbon-nitrogen ratio that takes up nitrogen. The Rambler has NEVER worried about organics breaking down in the soil… that was the intent … to feed and support the micro-organisms. Just add some additional nitrogen to make up for any loss. The leaves will tell the grower it nitrogen is low. But almost ANY feeding program in the home garden provides plenty of nitrogen to support the soil process AND make lots of green leaves. A good, steady, balanced diet works on roses and rosarians.

FISH MEAL is still a favorite with the Rambler, bringing almost everything to the rose dinner table. Besides the trace elements, fish meal has sulfur that encourages root development and soil activity. The only drawback to fish meal is lack of availability in some areas. Rosarians MUST make friends at the area feed store. Probably not stocked, but most REAL feed stores can order in 100 pounds or so in about a week. *MILLS MAGIC MIX* is a very convenient source, and it has some other goodies as well, particularly the deodorizer and activator. Many rose societies are now bringing in substantial supplies, passing along a good product at a good price. Mills REALLY DOES make roses grow. Minis love it. And the same group has come up with an even more convenient soluble product called EASY FEED, a 20-10-16 formulation with a soluble fish basis. Check out the recent ads in these pages.

DISINFECT bare-root roses before planting?? Not a bad routine to head off introduction of downy mildew in the garden, particularly with the increased spread of this disease. Many rosarians disinfected before downy, believing that root and crown galls could be retarded. The routine is simple: add one cup of chlorine bleach to a five-gallon bucket of water, dip the whole bush, roots and all, for about a half minute. Then wash off and plant.

PINCH BASALS?? Same old dilemma, painful to rosarians. Depending on the vigor of the plant (and your resolve), when the basal hits 18 inches or so and begins to form a bloom bud, pinch back to a five-leaflet or a good, blunt bud eye. Lower bud eyes will break, multiplying the canes available for roses. The Rambler has the willpower to pinch about half of the really strong basals, and the resulting growth is nearly always better.

ENJOY a great spring rose crop, whenever that is.

FOR EVERY PROBLEM there's a solution … even if it's learning to live with it. Here's how to make learning more fun…

DIBBLE… That's a new word for the Rambler, describing a tool or process that makes holes in the ground. The application here is to "dibble" *Osmocote* or any timed-release fertilizer in or near the root zone. It's a safe tactic as *Osmocote* releases nutrients as a function of temperature. Some "dibble holes" on the perimeter, stocked with nutrients like timed-release or fish meal, serve as feeding stations that roots love. Many growers dibble a bit of timed-release under the planting cone of a bare root bush or near the bottom soil layers of a container-grown. Same function: nearby snack for hungry roses.

FEED THE SOIL… then roses. Noted again this season that newly-pruned roses started much better and put on more good leaves and canes when the first feeding is an industrial strength shot of fish meal, cottonseed meal and alfalfa meal. Roses started with pelletized foods or liquid mixtures did not have the same starting vigor or staying power as those with organics. The organics feed the soil organisms as the soil warms up, setting the table for fertilizers in solution. Mix one 50 pound bag each of fish, cottonseed and alfalfa meal in a large wheelbarrow and broadcast about 1 ½2 cups of mix per large bush and scratch in lightly. Water and water some more. In about 10-14 days, start pelletized or liquid food of choice. Easy… and a great start.

BAKING SODA FOR ROSES ?? Perhaps the time has come. Many growers have been trying various combinations of baking soda and light oil to control powdery mildew, with varying results. This "Canola" mix appears to be the most widely used and most effective, PROVIDED that it is discontinued when the weather gets hot (in the 80's). Per one gallon of spray mix, use 1Tablespoon of white vinegar, 1Tablespoon of Canola Oil, 1Tablespoon of Safer's Insecticidal Soap, and 1 1/2 Tablespoons of household baking soda, in that order. Spray for good coverage of new growth on a 7-10 day basis. Baking soda leaves a white residue; discontinue before show season. This will GET RID of powdery mildew if started early and used regularly. But watch HOT weather, bright sunshine. The leaves will burn.

BLACKSPOT is still with us and will erupt whenever conditions are right and rosarians relax. Try this alternate preventive spray program… something like a change-up baseball pitch to catch the spores unaware. Use *Triforine* at 1teaspoon per gallon on a weekly basis; add *Manzate 200* at 1/2 Tablespoon per gallon one week and a scant teaspoon of *Daconil 2787* WDG (90%) the next week. *Daconil* BURNS in hot weather, discontinue when it begins to get hot. Start early, stay with it. If infection does catch on, increase frequency, not concentration.

INDICATE 5… A great water additive to make spray solutions work better. Buffers, acidifies, conditions… makes water wetter. About 1 teaspoon per gallon of water is all it takes. Check these pages for Indicate 5 sources… mail order.

ROSE CLIPS… CLEAN UP rose pruners with a light spray of *WD-40* and a pot cleaning pad. Takes off the sap and stain and polishes up the surfaces. Oven cleaner spray also works but is a bit harder on the users hands. Clean pruners work better… **SPRAYERS** need to be cleaned, too. A weak solution of white vinegar in water run through the system picks up spray residues and clears nozzles. Flush well with clear water. Household ammonia solutions also pick up and move all kinds of junk in spray lines and nozzles…

NEW GROWTH STARTED at the end of the cane and then died?? Probably not serious, the cane just could not support the growth and when stressed it shriveled up and died. Pruned canes have stored-Up nutrients, and when they are not replaced, the emerging growth stops. No mystery here… **LET ME TELL YOU** one more time about hardwood tree chips used as mulch. Two seasons ago the Rambler mulched with 4-5 inches of hardwood chips from a trimming outfit. This spring all traces were gone… and the soil alive. Reworked the bed, added compost, planted minis, put on more chips. Makes an attractive bed, easy to walk on, holds moisture. Try it.

WILL CHAT with you again in June. Have a great Spring…

FOR A LIBERAL ROSE EDUCATION, take part in your local or regional rose garden tour… seeing is believing… and pay attention. You may see some of these suggestions in action…

RESPOND… An action word that's descriptive of the foliar micro-supplement called RESPONSE. The Rambler has been generally skeptical of foliars that promise miracles, but this RESPONSE material really brings out the best in leaves. A liquid concentrate of Red Australian Kelp, about a half teaspoon added per gallon of spray mixture is safe and effective. Leaves are more lush, have better color and are typical of the best of the variety. No "fake" look here. In VERY hot climates, spray early in the morning and watch carefully. If traces of sunburn appear, discontinue until temperatures moderate. BUT, this is only a micro-nutrients supplement, not intended as a major food source. See if you can spot some leaves on tour that have been "supplemented."

COMPOST PILES are fun and friendly to the environment, recycling all of the stuff that has been poured or scattered on the lawn and garden to make it grow. The Rambler has been adding gypsum and dolomite lime to a compost pile of weeds, lawn clippings, dirt, leaves and what have you (except kitchen scraps) and notes that the windrow pile breaks down faster, makes mellow soil additive and is easy to work. For a row or pile of stuff about two cubic yards, mix in about 25# of lime and an equal amount of gypsum (half-bags). You'll be surprised at the great compost soil additive that comes out.

SPOT A REAL GARDENER wearing a farm supply store cap while on tour. The Rambler has a new one this season —"Family Farm and Home Supply", the place to get fish meal, cottonseed meal, alfalfa meal and all sorts of good things for the garden. The owner-loader-advisor of the operation even gave the Rambler 2 bales of moldy alfalfa last trip in exchange for a couple of rooted cuttings. Good trade all around. Seriously, get to know a farm supply.

COLD FRAMES even have a place in the summertime, and you'll spot some new versions in "advanced gardeners'" yards. They're good for starting seeds in the spring and rooting cuttings during summer and fall. The exotic cold frames are treated lumber boxes with *Lexan* windows, which open and close with solar-powered vent openers. The opener works by thermal expansion of liquid in a cylinder arm… opens up when it's warm and closes when it's cool. Creates a mini greenhouse environment… and cheap. Located in light shade, rose cuttings take right off in a soilless rooting mix. Add a mister and control if you're really high tech. The Rambler remembers the same ability to start and root MANY years ago with a homemade box, old windows and a stick to hold them open. Warmth and humidity came from a 12-inch layer of fresh horse manure and straw in the bottom of the frame. Just like the soil heating cables today (a hot bed).

JAPANESE BEETLES mayor may not plague your garden (or garden tour), but if your area is beetle-prone, start two weeks before the infestation with *MARGOSAN-O*, the botanical insecticide concentrate naturally derived from neem seeds. It's environmentally sound and fits pest management programs. Use 1 Tablespoon per gallon of buffered water (like with Indicate 5) and spray both leaf surfaces to runoff. Seems to work best when used alone, but some growers report good results in combination with *Triforine*. Thrips populations will drop also. Can be safely used weekly while beetles are present.

MAKE SOME TEA… Alfalfa tea. Just brew up a 32 gallon barrelful with 10-12 cups of alfalfa meal or pellets (rabbits), let stand for 4-5 days, stirring occasionally. Dip out about a gallon of tea per bush, with a water chaser. Fortified tea calls for some *Epsom Salts*, chelated iron and perhaps some solubles with trace elements. Anyway, the leaves will green right up, put on new growth… and then more roses. Minis like lesser amounts, but will green up also.

GIVEAWAYS… The Rambler has giveaway formulas for Tea, Fragrant Formula and Sprays. Just send a SASE (business size) for a quick turn around… and maybe a question or two. See address above.

ENJOY A ROSY TOUR.

Nothing seems impossible to the rosarian who doesn't have to do it himself... but this month is a do-it-yourself water systems short course... all possible.

THE WATER AWARD of the month goes to *DripWorks*, the "We make it simple" source of irrigation products. Loyal readers may recall that the Rambler promised to field test four irrigation systems in new rosebeds in '95: *DripWorks* emitters, *Dramm Stix, Dramm Nozzles* (rigid pipe) and Moisture Master, the porous hose made from recycled automobile tires. The BEST report is that ALL of the systems worked well, were relatively inexpensive, delivered water to roses in sufficient quantity and were adaptable to many common garden situations. BUT, the flexibility and ease of installation of *DripWorks'* adjustable flow emitters won the praise of the Rambler... wanting to spend more time with roses and less time in construction.

ADJUSTABLE FLOW EMITTERS are on 5 inch plastic stakes, fed with 1/4-inch spaghetti tubing plugged into 1/2-inch polyvinyl tubing with transfer barbs. The poly tubing connects to a hose end or faucet. Turn it on and each emitter (adjustable) delivers 4-5 gallons of water per hour over a 12-inch radius. Thin streams of water come out in an octagonal pattern, spreading and soaking. No waste, very little evaporation. The watering are can be increased or decreased by turning the top of the emitter. The spaghetti tubing allows placement of the emitter stake well away from the supply tubing, just where the grower wants it.

BOUGHT A KIT called Glorious Gardens Rose Kit out of the *DripWorks* catalog for $49.95, installed it for 18 roses along a fence in just 45 minutes. Use a garden hose QuickCoupler for water supply. To order a catalog with ALL kinds of great garden stuff call 1-800-522-3747.

DRAMM STIX works in a similar manner to *DripWorks*, fed through spaghetti tubing inserted into polyvinyl flexible pipe. The *Dramm* nozzle puts out an umbrella-like spray up to an 18-inch radius, delivering varying amounts of water. The wire "Stix" on which the nozzles are mounted come in lengths from 10 to 30 inches long. Just push the Stix in the ground where water is needed. Each Stix comes with 24 or more inches of tub-ing. *Dramm* does not use a barb to connect the spaghetti tubing. It takes an 11/64-inch drill bit to make a hole in the tubing. Insert the tubing in the hole. Friction holds it in place, even at high water pressure. The *Dramm* delivery is particularly good for Miniatures, directing a fine water spray under the foliage (drown the spider mites). *Dramm Stix* sets up just as quickly as Glorious Gardens. IF you use transfer barbs instead of drilling... not every rosarian has an 11/64-inch drill bit and the urge to run power for a drill out to the rosebed. A really GOOD system, suitable for many rose growers. Information sheets on *Dramm* are available by calling (414) 684-0227. Or write to them at P.O. Box 1960, Manitowoc, WI 54221.

DRAMM NOZZLES used in rigid Schedule 40 PVC pipe should not be overlooked for neat, professional installations. The system accepts fertilizer injection systems, timers and what have-you for reliable delivery. The Rambler has used *Dramm* nozzles for many years with great results. However, the rigid PVC pipe does not adapt well to curved installations, requires more time to lay-out and build, and the holes for the nozzles must be carefully drilled. In a formal straight bed, you can build it and forget it for years and years. Incidentally, Kimbrew Walter Roses, Rt. 2, Box 172, Grand Saline, TX 75140 handles both of the Dramm watering devices.

MEANTIME, MOISTURE MASTER keeps on oozing away with slow water delivery that is as flexible as a garden hose. Just snake the porous hole in, around and through the rosebeds or plants, hook up to a garden hose and let it run for an hour or so... depending on water pressure and the size of the delivery hose. The Rambler's 125-foot line weaves in and out of a large bed of Miniatures, a couple of Shrub Roses and a Climber about 45 plants in all. It takes about 3 hours to soak the bed with 50 pounds of water pressure. It is installed on TOP of the mulch, pinned in place with stiff wire. On top it is easy to see what is happening and watch the spread of the water. Easy to work, patch, couple. GOOD!

ANYWAY, get lots of water on the roses; that's really what makes them grow.

A GARDEN is a thing of beauty and a job forever... whatever happened to "those lazy, crazy days of summer?" Here are some summer tips to think about in the shade...

JAPANESE BEETLES struck the Rambler's rosebeds on schedule in June in spite of several defensive strategies. Beetle traps in the neighbor's yard bagged a good many, but thousands feasted on the roses. *Margosan-O* sprayed weekly (with *Triforine*) deterred some of the infestation but little kill was observed. The beds sprayed with this Neem product also showed some spray burn... coarsening of leaves and yellow edges on the tender varieties like Peach Beauty, Bride's Dream and Double Delight.

SEVIN LIQUID (21.3%) effectively killed the beetles but had to be reapplied every 4-5 days. Many top leaves were skeletonized and the blooms well chewed. The routine apparently has to be followed every 34 days for good control. *Sevin* also killed off the beneficial insects as the beetles were followed by spider mites. The beds sprayed with *Margosan-O* have not shown any evidence of mites. In a tradeoff, the Rambler prefers to keep the beneficials and use less toxic materials as "control" is a relative term. Control is achieved if there are some roses and most of the foliage left after the invasion.

SOME NEW PRODUCTS have had tryouts in the Rambler's garden this summer. *SurfKing Plus* is a new spreader-activator available now in quantities suitable for hobbyists. It is similar to Indicate-5 as it has buffering agents to lower the pH of spray solutions. *Surf-King* does not have a color indicator, but the pH is easily tested. In Greenville water, 1/2 teaspoon of *Surf-King* per gallon helps spray mixtures spread and stick to leaves with no apparent side effects. Costs a little less than Indicate-5, available from Kimbrew-Walter by mail order or from many nursery/greenhouse suppliers. For real peace of mind, the Rambler likes to see the pink color of Indicate-5 and know that the pH is right. Another product new to most rosarians is Response, a foliar secondary nutrient supplement noted in these columns in June. Availability was omitted... you can order from AG/RESPONSE-OHIO, 200 Industrial Parkway, Chagrin Falls, OH 44022. Good stuff for leaves.

SPRAYING is a summer chore most of us don't look forward to. However, with the right equipment, the job is easier. Most important is a good control (trigger) mechanism, a long wand, and a nozzle that produces fine droplets. These mechanics can be added to any sprayer, pump-up, electric or air pressure.

SPRAY SYSTEMS puts out a good control gun that looks like a paint spray gun. Hoses, wands and parts fit this control for a wide variety of applications. Get a 3D-inch wand curved on the end to get under leaves and reach into bushes. The Tee-Jet 8004 nozzle fits a Spray Systems wand and puts out a flat, fan-shaped spray that covers 24-30 inches of rosebush at a pass. Check out an exterminator supply store or a spray equipment dealer. A good source is RGL Sales, advertisers in these pages, distributors of Spot Shot sprayers. They have a complete parts list and will ship by UPS.

SPIDER MITES and hot, dry weather mean trouble. Reproduction increases with temperature for a major infestation in just a couple of days. Cool off the mating mites with a water wand, washing underneath the leaves with a fine water spray. This washing process has to be repeated every 4-5 days and is okay for small gardens. Miticide of choice for larger gardens is Avid, a translaminar (penetrates leaves) product with great knockdown capability and good residual. And mites do not build up a resistance to Avid. Used at 1/4 teaspoon per gallon, it is relatively inexpensive and can be used weekly if necessary. Add *Stirrup M*, a pheromone sex attractant, to Avid for even better results. Just a couple of drops of the pheromone per gallon is all that's needed. Buffers spray solution with Indicate 5, do not add other materials. Spray until leaves "glisten;" get good coverage underneath the lower leaves. In most gardens, two or three sprayings will do the job.

SUMMERTIME MUSTS... Water and lots of it. Soak, drip, hose end, overhead... whatever. Even wash down the leaves from time to time, your roses will enjoy the bath.

EXPERIENCE IS LIKE MANURE... it's only good when spread around. These SILVER ANNIVERSARY Ramblings mark 25 years of chatting with you good rose folks each month, sharing ideas and experiences to enjoy roses more. You've been loyal, responsive readers... the Rambler appreciates the opportunity to be with you in these pages.

HOW DID THIS ALL BEGIN? Where did the Rambler come from? Does he know what he is talking about? Sometimes. You can draw your own conclusions from this thumbnail sketch.

THE RAMBLER comes from a gardening family in Colorado whose passion was dahlias (and some roses) plus several city lots of annuals and perennials of all kinds. All of the Walters' family lived and breathed flowers, and even had a home-made greenhouse warmed by a pot-bellied coal stove. The family could sweep the dahlia and annuals competitions routinely. Dad was a Superintendent of Parks for 40 years. Mother could turn a bucket of flowers into an exhibition. We sold plants and cut flowers (so that we could buy more). We knew every garden in Colorado... it was a great life.

MILLIE RAMBLER arrived on the scene at college and landscaping started on a small GI house in Boulder, CO, trying to cope with adobe, rocks and the mess left by the builders. Dad supplied truckloads of plant materials. Roses thrived as we learned how to winter-protect from bright sun and cold, dry winds. We used nature's materials, hauling tons of manure and alfalfa hay from Millie's former ranch home near Boulder.

NEED MORE ROOM to grow things, so we took on a new house and an acre of ground in the country. More roses, more shrubs. Learned water conservation the hard way. Developed a terrific landscape. Then came a move to Houston, TX, and a totally different climate. Roses became serious in 1955.

HAD TO LEARN GROWING all over again. Supportive Dad shipped 10 bundles of roses (10 each) as a "starter." Somehow survived the first couple of season and then discovered the Houston Rose Society. Changed the landscaping and rebuilt the rosebeds every-other-year after that. Gained PLENTY of experience and begin editing

the *Houston ROSE-ETTE* in the early 1960s. One thing led to another and Houston hosted an ARS National Convention in 1969, the first of three in which the Rambler would be involved. Opportunities came along as District Director and eventually President of ARS.

BY THIS TIME the Rambler had some 600 roses to look after and Millie was rapidly expanding her miniature collection. We worked with every kind of garden imaginable. Lacking something to do, decided that the emerging gardens at the American Rose Center needed some help, too. What a great way to learn.

ROSARIAN RAMBLINGS first appeared in September 1970, when the BIG NEWS was the FDA approval of *Benlate* for home gardens. It was hailed as a "deliverance for the rose faithful." Since then, many thoughts, products and practices have been garden-used and shared by the Rambler.

THOUGHT FOR THE MONTH QUIPS have been the most-read wisdom in these columns... and probably best-remembered. Just a reminder that roses are supposed to be fun.

ANOTHER HOUSE, BIGGER GARDEN in 1979, just in time to host guests of "Houston Rosetime '79," an ARS convention. Landscape roses became more important, miniatures essential. Maintenance routines had to be good in order to keep up. All was right in the garden.

"I PROMISED YOU A ROSE GARDEN" phrase of the Rambler is familiar to more recent readers. The Rambler and Millie (an enthusiastic (?) participant) transferred to Greenville, SC, in 1989 and started all over again in red clay. We've been sharing the trials of building new beds, coping with trees, adjusting to a new climate and establishing sources for all the stuff that rosarians need. Fortunately, there are great rosarians in the Carolina and Colonial Districts and we became part of a new rose family. We learned a lot... fast.

THERE'S MORE TO COME. All about rose gardens, assorted pests and diseases and tricks and trials in the months and years to come. Stay tuned.

THANKS for sharing your rose hobby with the Rambler.

Rose ideas that work are those you put to work… so here's a '95 report on some things the Rambler learned.

BARK MULCH on the rosebeds performed exactly as planned, keeping weeds down, moisture up and soil processes working. And not an exotic mulch at all… just hardwood/pine chips right off the tree trimmer's truck. The City of Greenville dumped a huge load of chips at the park garden the Rambler maintains, about twice as much as needed. But it was easier to load it on the buds than haul the excess away so each bed got at least 6 inches of chips, sometimes more. Laid the drip water system on top, then fed with about a cup of 13-13-13 pelletized fertilizer with trace by broadcasting evenly all over the bed. Result: great roses all season, no weeds and an attractive woodsy patina overall. No additional fertilizer since early May, the bushes don't need it. Hail a passing trimmings truck for a rich reward.

POWDERY MILDEW got out of hand in a friend's garden, who begged the Rambler to put the roses out of their misery (it was really the grower who was miserable). So, sprayer in hand, the pair set off to do battle. But first, the bushes were trimmed severely, cutting off the worst of the powdery-gray, twisted growth. Then the whole garden was hosed down before starting a routine of *Triforine/Rubigan*, followed 5 days later with *Triforine/Systhane*. Kept up the alternating 5-day schedule for three weeks and the garden was clean. Dropped back to weekly *Triforine* after that, garden stayed clean. Stepping up the frequency and good coverage made the difference. Mildew-stricken gardens don't have to be written off until hot weather.

INDICATE-5, the buffer spray agent with pH indicator, is definitely on the Rambler's approved list as the best and most convenient spray adjuvant yet. Performance of spray materials is definitely improved, and the wetting and spreading properties are easily observed. Makes a tremendous difference when using *Avid* for spider mites. And the results with fungicides are no less dramatic. With *Indicate-5*, it's possible to spray leaves until they just "glisten" and get good results with no drip or burn. Easy to use, just add to spray water until pink color holds, then add fungicides, insecticides, etc. which go into solution/suspension readily, stay mixed. Definitely a factor in good spray results, also inexpensive. Get some.

TIMED RELEASE FERTILIZERS (*Osmocote* et al.) should be on your rose dinner plate next season. Steady, patient feeding all season long makes a difference, regardless of other feeding practices. *Osmocote* (the Rambler likes 17-6-10 plus Minors) supplements a feeding program rather than replacing. Rate of release depends on soil temperature, delivering nutrients when roses are hungry. Reduces the summer "doldrums" of roses that tend to go out of bloom. Use about 4 ounces per large bush in late spring when soil warms up. Make some holes around the root line of the bush with a spreading fork and sprinkle the pellets into these serving lines. The roots reach right out and enjoy just a little at a time. Purchased in quantity, *Osmocote* is not expensive, considering the small amount used. Good for miniatures, too, but in much smaller portions. Get some.

SAVE THE FALL HARVEST… leaves, of course. We will soon have a bumper crop of materials that nature has been growing all year, storing up all sorts of nutrients for us. Don't waste them. Leaves are the basis of nature's recycling effort that keeps soils alive and working. Composting in place with leaves is an easy fall chore; the summer vegetable garden is a likely spot. Chop the leaves a bit first with a lawnmower, at least some of them. Then row out the leaves on the ground about 2 feet deep. Bits and pieces of green material will act as starters, sift on some soil to make the process work even better. Cottonseed meal or alfalfa meal will also speed things up. Turn once in a while with a pitchfork and let moisture and nature do their thing. By spring you should have a rich compost ready for the rosebeds.

SOME BROWN, SOME GREEN keeps the pile hot and clean. Don't worry about nitrogen-carbon ratios, just pile up a mixture of leaves and yard stuff, moisten and turn so that air is readily available. Materials of various sizes break down faster and don't pack. Hint: the Rambler always adds some *Perlite* to keep the mix light and open. This lighthearted approach works just like the forest floor.

The best way to succeed with roses is to act on the advice that you give to others. Here's some advice that the Rambler needs to follow more carefully in the future...

SUNSHINE NEEDED... Marginal sun conditions just don't work with roses. Husky, healthy miniature roses moved to a partially shaded area steadily declined all season and suffered more mildew, insect damage and general sickness than roses in the sun. The same varieties moved from sun to sun didn't miss a beat. The grower can be fooled for the first month or so, but in the end the lack of good sunshine dooms the roses.

MANURE ENDORSEMENT... ARS, as reported in the September issue, may not endorse horse manure, but roses do. And that's good enough for the Rambler and thousands of rosarians who find a good source for horse manure and use it liberally. What to look for: horses kept in stalls and maintained corrals, not ranged to crop off the weeds. The few weed seeds that do pass through the horse are easily pulled, a reasonable trade-off for the soil benefits.

WEAN OFF INSECTICIDES... It can be done. Try spot applications for control of thrips and let nature's predators get back into balance. No general insecticide was applied in one planting area this season; a water wand was used for spider mites and blooms and buds were "misted" every other day during peak bloom season with a *Triforine/Soluble Orthene* mixture. Had clean blooms without damage and overall healthy plants. Helped the Rambler get better acquainted with those special blooms, too. For a quart of mix in a spray bottle, use 1/2 teaspoon of *Triforine* and 1/2 teaspoon of *Orthene SP*. Make a fresh batch each time.

WATER WORKS... As a part of the "irrigation trials" this year the Rambler observed just how much difference *plenty* of water makes in the growth and production of roses. All of the trial beds had essentially the same soil mixture; clay, sand and organic matter. All were fertilized the same. Roses deep-watered three times a week grew substantially better than roses watered twice a week. Each raised bed was soaked on schedule until water ran out. Showers and light rains were ignored. All of the roses grew well, but the three-times-a-week roses were one-fourth bigger, had *many* more blooms and leaves that stayed productive all season. Water did the job.

THE CHEATING SCHEDULE... Rosarians often think that a fungicide spray schedule is not important... they'll just keep an eye on developments. This routine fails because the fungus spores are working unseen, and by the time the evidence appears, the infection is well developed. We're comfortable the first week off schedule, "Roses look pretty good. Can probably go a little longer." But about the end of the second week, the sky seems to rain black spots on the leaves. "Must have been some old materials," the rosarian responds. Stretching the schedule is the problem, not the materials. Know the fungicide spray schedule that *your* area requires, and *follow* it. The rosarian who stays on schedule doesn't even have to worry about watering overhead; spore production is controlled and the leaves live happily ever-after.

SOIL pH CHANGES... Over a period of several years it is easy to observe that ample use of organic conditioners and fertilizers maintains a steady pH that's good for roses. Rosebeds with more liberal applications of chemical fertilizers need more frequent adjustment. There's a scientific explanation for it, but the soil crumbs with organics attached stay in balance. And these crumbs accommodate chemical fertilizers as well, provided that application is not overdone. Which is just another way of saying that nature works well when supported.

EXPAND YOUR INTERESTS... Try out some hybridizing in your own garden if you really want to learn more about roses. You'll be the keenest observer in the neighborhood. A great way to start (and you can still be a "breeder" this season) is to join the Rose Hybridizers Association. RHA is a group of some 500 enthusiastic rosarians who would like to create their own roses. RHA publishes a fine quarterly bulletin, 20 or more pages filled with all kinds of hybridizing experiences, edited by Barbara Maas. Just $8 a year, mail to Larry Peterson, RHA Sec-Treasurer, 3245 Wheaton Road, Horseheads, NY 14845. For a crash course, order *Rose Hybridizing for Beginners* by RHA, $5. There are some hips on roses right now... get a booklet... ripen the hips... launch a new rose... maybe.

CHECK YOU AGAIN in '96… have a Happy One!!

The Rambler's rose catalog reading has been restricted to two hours per week due to severe space limitations in my garden. But there's always a way to get around limits ... plant in containers. Get your orders in early and the Rambler will tell you what to do with them next month.

TRADE IN some old roses for new varieties … in cars it's called "trading up." For most of us, new roses mean getting rid of something already in the ground. To ease your rose conscience, justify these "important" roses by giving the old, reliable plants to a gardening friend or start a "friendly" garden at a church or school. A retirement center is also a great place for a new garden. Be prepared to assist/support the new venture and you'll get as much satisfaction as in your own garden. Most rose growers don't wear roses out, they dig them out.

PRUNING PRACTICES... always a controversial subject. Some growers whack off the tops with heavy duty hedge shears or chain saw (depends on how much cane you have and where you live) and get lots of bloom with little or no dieback. In fact, The Royal National Rose Society (UK) did some trials a few years ago and reported that in their mass plantings, roses that were sheared had more blooms and bloom-producing canes than bushes conventionally pruned. The Rambler can't bring himself to do this (and Millie Rambler won't let him), but has practiced on miniatures with great success.

PRUNING REALLY BIG BUSHES takes muscle and resolve. The Rambler lives in a climate that encourages main rose canes one-inch plus in diameter and six feet long, topped with more canes. Unless you want to enjoy roses from a stepladder, these canes have to be cut back to a manageable size. Once roses have been allowed to carryover OLD WOOD this size, it's tough to prune lower and get the old canes to break dormant buds (they just aren't there), or to produce new basals. Many growers have good success pruning half a cane or more to an encouraging node and trimming stubs and bark from the bud union. Then force-feed after pruning with Epsom salts and a heavy jolt of Urea for available nitrogen. Use the tonics when the soil is warm and force plenty of water. Repeat in two weeks. The old-timer may take a new lease on life.

SOIL SCIENCE 101... Soils are made up of mineral particles, among other things. These particles vary in size from gravel and rock to sand to silt to clay in decreasing size gradient. Clay is so small, for example, that it resists settling out in water because the force or friction between the clay particle and the water is greater than the pull of gravity. In soil, these clay particles are important in holding elements so that rose roots can take them up in solution. The surfaces of these minute clay particles carry a negative charge, much like a magnet, and attract positively charged particles to them. The positively charged particles that are attracted are ions of potassium, calcium, magnesium et, al. When on the particles, these ions can be picked up by the roots.

THE ROSE OF HUMUS... Partially decomposed organic matter is called humus, which acts like a glue to bind clay and soil to be quite porous and water and air enter quite readily. The crumbs also hold water, supporting the water needs of the plant, and allow gas exchange so that the roots have a sufficient supply of oxygen to maintain living microorganisms. In brief, the humus derived from organic matter helps build a table where rose roots can feed. Humus also has a tremendous ability to hold positively-charged ions, up to three to four times better than clay. It is this "holding" capability that slows leaching from the rosebed, maintaining a steady nutrient supply. Need any more good reasons for organics in your rosebed? More coming next month.

AND A ROSY '96 to you faithful rosarians.

The Rambler is full of "how(s)" this month so let's get off to a fast start...

VALENTINE GIFT... an institution at the Rambler's house. A dump truck load of horse manure from the stalls of a riding stable... steaming and fragrant on delivery. All it needs is a red ribbon on top. Heaped liberally on the rose beds as winter begins to break, this horsey conditioner, springtime starter will support LOTS of red roses.

DOWNY MILDEW... conditions soon will be right for downy mildew spores to erupt — cool, damp weather. Not all parts of the country are affected, but infection is deadly where it strikes. Watch for purplish-red blotches on leaves and canes. Untreated, the bushes can defoliate in a few days. To check downy, spray the canes after pruning with a combination of *Volck Oil* and Lime and Sulfur. Apply twice 4-5 days apart and hit the soil and mulch as well. As leaves begin to appear, alternate *Daconil* and *Manzate* on a weekly basis until it begins to get hot. You'll be glad that you took a PREVENTIVE approach.

HYBRIDIZER ALERT! The Rose Hybridizers Association is really not lost... maybe by the post office. The CORRECT address for RHA is Larry Peterson, RHA Sec.-Treasurer, 21 S. Wheaton Road, Horseheads, NY 14845. Great quarterly newsletter for $8; booklet *Rose Hybridizing For Beginners* just $5. Start now.

pH FOR ROSES... "Probably the most underestimated factor in growing roses," quoting Dennis Bridges, a professional grower and world-class exhibitor. And the Rambler agrees. We all know that the application of agricultural lime is indicated in many instances, and growers routinely apply lime to maintain a pH of 6.5 -6.8. It's a slow process that is hard to keep up with. The reason is that the process is a REACTIVE one. Lime in solution must come into contact with soil crumbs. Lime in the presence of Hydrogen ions (the indicator for pH) reacts with those ions to form water. By reducing the Hydrogen ions, the pH goes up. The best way to keep an appropriate pH range is to adjust the pH of the rose or rose planting hole when it is being built. Then maintain by adding lime through tilling, spading or opening up holes with a spading fork. It takes about one pound of dolomite lime (calcium carbonate and magnesium carbonate) for every pound of nitrogen applied during the season. Example: 5-105 ammonium sulfate, 50 pound bag, contains 2.5 pounds of nitrogen. Use 2.5 pounds of lime in the same area.

TEST FOR pH... there are several good testing methods available for the home gardener that are easy and accurate. The Rambler has talked about *WHATMAN* test strips from time to time... a litmus paper approach. A NEW direct-read meter is now available that is affordable and accurate. It is a hand-held pH Meter that is lightweight and fits in your pocket. Sold by Cole-Parmer Instrument Company, the Rambler recommends Model H-590000 pH Tester 1, which sells for about $50. It uses a microprocessor powered with three 1.4 volt batteries, highly accurate from 1.0 to 15.0, keypad operation. You can order one from Cole-Parmer by calling their 800 number... 800-323-4340 and pay with your credit card. Cole-Parmer is an international scientific instrument company, headquartered in Niles, IL. They ship promptly, directions are included. ANYONE can use this meter... all it takes is soil, distilled water and a clean container. Way to go!

SANITATION vs. MULCH IN PLACE... Not really a conflict, both approaches have merit. Diseased leaves and canes need to be kept out of the rose beds as much as possible. One cleanup technique is to spray *Volck Oil* et al to smother the organisms. On the other hand, it is not necessary to pull back and throwaway the mulch in the spring in an effort to "clean up." This partially decomposed material builds the soil in a very natural way. Fertilizers can be broadcast on top, nutrients filter through like water through coffee grounds, slowly and evenly. Before discarding that mulch, consider WHY it needs to go.

Let's plant roses next month...

Reading rose books makes rosarians worry about all sorts of new things… now's a good time to stop worrying and start digging (unless you're still under snow).

A DIRTY-KNEES ROSARIAN is a good rosarian… and won't wind up with a bad rose-back. Hands-and-knees planting offers less strain and better results. The trick is to find a small shovel with a short handle, something like the old army foxhole tool. If the soil has been well prepared, it's easy to scoop out a hole, rebuild a cone to support the roots and bush, then let water and soil do the rest. Properly placed, the roots and shank will be stable without holding. Cover the roots lightly with soil and begin to let water run slowly into the hole, add more soil, more water. No need to tamp or pack. Keep your big boots out of the rose bed. Hill up with some EXTRA soil/mulch and keep moist.

WHY COVER? Retaining moisture in the canes is more important than sunshine. Hill up a newly planted rose (bare root or potted) with a loose, protective cone until just the tips of the canes stick out. Not just a little material, a real mound, a couple of BIG shovelsful per bush. Moisture in the canes is supported by new root hairs; hilling keeps canes from drying out until the roots have a chance to deliver.

BACK IN B. C. (BEFORE CHEMICALS), good gardeners always had a barrel or two of liquid compost brewing behind the garage. Some called it cow tea, some called it smelly. But it called plants out of the doldrums like no other elixir. Fish emulsion is a fast-fix now, or you can brew up some alfalfa tea or cow tea. Great for newly-planted roses or as a wake-up call for a late sleeper. When the soil warms up, pour on a half-bucket of mix and stand back… those roses are going to grow. These mixtures feed the soil which supports the organisms converting nutrients into forms available to plants. Some food value is built in, but the primary boost comes from activating the soil organisms. Can't burn; tiny hair roots love it. The Rambler ALWAYS gives new bare-root and miniature roses a dilute treat of fish emulsion in water when planting. It really works.

FIND A FEED STORE to make rose growing more fun. Garden shops are all right, and nurseries carry lots of things that rosarians need, but it's hard to beat a good feed store. They will have all sorts of organics and fertilizers and sacks of stuff like alfalfa pellets, cottonseed meal, fish meal and bone meal and rock phosphate to warm the heart … not to mention the roots. Find the real thing, like a place that has a couple of cats sleeping on the feed sacks and smells of alfalfa and pasture. My feed store also sells (or gives away) rabbits, deserving a five-star organic rating. While you're there, pick up a "gimmie cap" that says "FRED'S FEEDS," the mark of a real dirt gardener.

RX FOR GALLS… Some doctoring urgency is bound to come up when you are pruning your bushes this spring. Many respected growers maintain that disinfecting trimmed galls with *Lysol* or *Clorox* retards recurrence, but an equal number of growers disagree. Most growers have galls they don't even know about, and have had for a long time. If the gall is on the shank or bud union, sunshine seems to do as much good as anything. Just trim off the offending tissue and let sun and air get to it. Don't worry too much about the infection; nature and a well-drained soil are probably the best controls. If it's really bad, dig it out and try something new. Restore, renew, replace the planting mix… your choice.

GIVEAWAYS… The Rambler has a new supply of information sheets expanding on practices noted in these columns… inspirational titles like ALFALFA TEA AND SIMILAR DEFRAGRANT FORMULA (HOW TO MAKE ARTIFICIAL MANURE) and the 1996 SPRAY FORMULATIONS for fungicides/insecticides commonly used in the rose garden. Just send a self-addressed, stamped business size envelope to the Rambler at the P.O. Box shown above. I promise quick turnaround and will even respond to a question or two. Let me know what YOU want to know about. Be ready for SPRINGTIME.

An ounce of prevention is worth a pound of cure... especially with roses. This month we're going to discuss some Integrated Plant Management (IPM) considerations that can make rose growing more fun and rewarding.

IPM relates to the factors which contribute to damage by disease or insects... rather than a narrow focus on the problem itself. Three MAJOR factors are always present: HOST (plant), PATHOGEN (or insect) and ENVIRONMENT (growing conditions). These components are further influenced by TIME. Let's take a look at some examples.

HOST... Some roses are more disease resistant than others. Some may be mildew-prone, others blackspot easily. If these diseases are common to your area, select roses that are resistant or be prepared to take stronger measures against disease. The same idea applies to insects. Some roses seem to attract spider mites, particularly dense-growing miniatures with small leaves. Thrip inflict more damage on light-colored blooms than on darker and less fragrant flowers. Unless the grower wants to live with some damage or go into an aggressive thrip control program, select varieties that are more tolerant.

PATHOGEN... The fungus disease (or insect) can also be controlled with a variety of means. Alternating spray materials is an example. A surface-protective material like *Maneb* or *Daconil* controls spore growth and inhibits leaf penetration. *Triforine*, on the other hand, has some systemic action that also works from the inside out. Fungus spores build up resistance over a period of time. Alternating fungicides helps avoid this. Something like the "changeup pitch" in baseball... catches the spores off guard. Applies to powdery mildew spores as well. Washing leaves reduces spore count, follow up with a specific mildewcide. Insects build up resistant strains even more readily; alternate with spray materials specific for the insect. Management may also include water-washing undersides of leaves to reduce spider mite populations.

ENVIRONMENT... This is an easy one to observe. Roses in full sun have less trouble with fungus diseases than roses in partial or occasional shade. Sun and good air circulation inhibit powdery mildew. Damp climates support blackspot, dry climates are more likely to have powdery mildew. Rosarians can change some things in the environment, some can't be changed. Example: The shrub rose Bonica®, disease resistant, can be covered with blackspot when planted in a semi-shaded spot. The Rambler has a bed of Bonica® in full sun, and one in partial shade. Growing conditions are otherwise the same (water, spray schedule etc.). Sun condition, no disease. Shade condition, 30 percent infected requiring extra spraying to control. And how about miniatures planted next to a foundation? A perfect breeding ground for spider mites in reflected heat. Or planting otherwise-resistant roses near ramblers or hard-to spray roses that become infected and spread spores throughout the garden. An example of a "bad apple" in an otherwise good barrel.

TIME... Time impacts all of the IPM factors. A timely spray schedule for fungus protection is absolutely essential. Given time, spores will reproduce. Understand the time that it takes in your growing environment for evidence of disease to show up. Control the spores BEFORE they emerge. Time of year also comes into play with powdery mildew. When nights are cool and days are warm, powdery mildew goes to work. Weeks of warm, humid weather bring out blackspot; dry spells slow down the process. Understanding time lets you react appropriately. Hot, dry weather brings on spider mites, which can reproduce in 3-5 days. Water-wash more frequently then. Periods of damp, cool weather set up downy mildew. Hot weather stops spore growth. In short, the time factor is important to host, pathogen and environment.

WHAT TO DO... Consider ALL of the parts of the plant management equation. Ignore one factor and you'll have to work harder to overcome the results elsewhere. That's the whole theme of INTEGRATED. Consider and work with all of the parts of the puzzle that produce roses that satisfy us. And some extra thought takes a lot of work out of it was well.

IPM isn't just easy... it's a necessity.

MAY 1996

THOUGHT FOR THE MONTH: Let nature and the rosebush alone as much as you can... both are more experienced than you are.

Growing good roses should be as easy as falling off a diet... and just as much fun. Here are some tips for better May flowers from April showers (or snows).

ONE-TWO PUNCH FOR BASALS... The one two punch for more basal and low breaks leads with a readily available source of nitrogen followed with a chase of Epsom salts applied just after the initial bloom cycle. The bush is at its most vigorous at that time. Epsom salts (Magnesium Sulfate) works best when AVAILABLE nitrogen is present (a nitrate form is preferable).

Use a soluble 20-20-20 the first week, 1/3 cup of Epsom salts the second week, with successive applications of 20-20-20 weeks three and four. Since the 20-20-20 is being applied more frequently than usual, cut the recommended concentration in half. New basals require lots of energy in the root zone for results. Use ONLY on established bushes and NEVER on miniatures.

INDICATE-5... Makes wetter spray water. Actually it is a buffer spray agent that acidifies, indicates pH, wets, spreads, aids compatibility and reduces volatility. It takes about 2 teaspoons per gallon of water to reach the optimum pH level, use more or less depending on the hardness of the water. Add the material slowly to the water, which will change from milky white to orange to pink. Pink indicates a pH of 5.0. Let stand a few minutes to make sure that the reaction is complete. Once you have figured out how much Indicate-5 your water needs, buffer your spray solutions regularly and enjoy an enhanced spray program.

IMMUNEX — **A NEW PRODUCT** is on the way. Soon to be widely available, *Immunex* is a home garden version of the popular fungicide BANNER, used professionally on turf and field crops for many years. Quite good for prevention of powdery mildew, and reasonably effective against blackspot. It is a water-based material, mixes readily, used at 1Tablespoon per gallon for powdery mildew or 2 Tablespoons per gallon for blackspot. Should be applied weekly to PREVENT infection. Has some systemic qualities also. *Immunex* will NOT eradicate severe blackspot, but is a good, new, alternative fungicide for general use. Distributed by Spectrum, the folks who bring us *Spectracide*, available at all major garden retailers. A special bonus, initial purchasers will be sent the new ARS publication *Growing Beautiful Roses* with proof of purchase. The promotion piece is tagged on each pint bottle (sells for about $10 retail). The 24-page booklet really is a bonus as an introductory text on roses... and GOOD because it was written by Dr. Tommy Cairns. *Spectracide* funded the initial printing to be used as a stimulus to join the American Rose Society. Give *Immunex* a try and benefit from the Guide, too.

pH INFORMATION UPGRADE... In February the Rambler described the hand-held, digital pH meter sold by Cole-Parmer Instrument Company but failed to give new buyer-users enough information to make the testing process comfortable. Cole-Parmer deals primarily with scientific applications, not dirt. Their detailed information (if you ask for it when ordering) is enough to frighten a backyard user away. BUT, it is really not hard to use. Test EQUAL PARTS BY VOLUME of soil and water. Stir and let settle for 3-5 minutes. Insert the probe. Get a direct reading. It's also wise to get a pH Tester Calibration Kit for about $16. Additional pH Buffer Tablets (pH 7) are also available. If you want to give this device a try, call the applications section of Cole-Parmer at (800) 323-4340. You are interested in pH Tester AZ-59000-00, pH Tester 1. And if you just want to chat about pH testing in general, call the Rambler at (864) 292-8388. Remember that the Rambler is on Eastern time and his head gets powdery mildew after 11 p.m.

SCHEDULE, SCHEDULE, SCHEDULE. That's what controls fungus diseases. Start on schedule (before signs appear), stay on schedule weekly throughout the season when conditions support fungus. Prevention is so much easier than eradication. Alternating fungicides (on schedule) also helps. Surface type or systemic, the materials have to be sprayed to do any good. Your choice: *Maneb, Daconil, Funginex* and *Immunex* are all labeled for fungus disease on roses and will work. *Cleary's 3336* also works. A special NOTE: *Funginex* is NOT going off the market, so don't rush out and buy a supply. It should be around for a long time.

THE RAMBLER, TOO. Will chat with you next month.

JUN.
1996

THOUGHT FOR THE MONTH:
Give a rose to a friend. It will make both of you feel good.

ALL you need to grow fine, vigorous grass is a well watered rose bed. For fine, vigorous roses, try some of these tips…

LET THE AIR IN… that's essential to the soil processes. How does air move in the soil anyway? Water pulls it along. Water disperses throughout the soil medium, attaching to soil particles and partially filling air spaces. In this form water becomes available to the roots, carrying along nutrients in the process (having been processed by the microorganisms into forms that roots can take up). Deep soaking starts the process, coating the soil particles. As water is taken up, air fills the nutrient solutions to the root zone, pulling along air to support the bacteria. Simple, isn't it? It's the reason that soils should be well-aerated or "friable"… so that water, air and soil can work together.

DOSE OF SALTS… Epsom Salts. The May Rambler discussed the interaction of available magnesium sulfate for the encouragement of basal breaks. The Rambler closed with "Use only on established plants and NEVER on miniatures." Salts CAN be used on miniatures (an ounce or so depending on the size) but NOT in combination with a heavy dose of Nitrogen. Go easy on all fertilizers for miniatures or wind up with vegetative growth instead of blooms. Miniature appetites are not that big. Think of them as "baby" roses that do not need as much food as grown-ups.

A SEVERE WINTER upset the schedules of many rosarians (and rose shows) as canes froze back. Plus some promise of growth for some time, only to give up at the first sign of stress. Relax. Trim back, even to the bud union, and let the bush renew itself. Nature has remarkable recuperative powers. Cold-climate growers have been doing this for years, and they still enjoy some great roses Gust later than many of us).

ALPHABET ACRONYMS… Check yourself out on these identifiers that will make spraying easier (and better). Most growers know that the letters EC (as in *Orthene 9.4% EC*) means Emulsifiable Concentration, a solvent carrying the active ingredient. Another is SP, which indicates a Soluble Powder (as in *Orthene 75% SP*). The active material is soluble, goes right into the solution. *Manzate 200DF* labels the compound as Dry Flowable, specially treated to go into water sus-

pension easily, MUCH better than the chalk-like, greasy stuff that used to settle to the bottom of the spray tank. *Daconil* now comes as a WDG, Water Dispersible Granule. Goes right into the spray mix with no difficulty. The Security people have a formulation of Daconil called *Fungi-Gard*, a very convenient FLOWABLE mix they call Aqua Blend. All of which means that these formulations are easier to use than the WP, Wettable Powders, that often refused to disperse, even requiring straining into the sprayer. The next time you buy, look for SP, DF, WDF or flowable formulation of your favorite products.

HOW MUCH IS ENOUGH? On the subject of sprays, how much is enough on the leaves? Most advice calls for "good coverage", whatever that is. A definition might include even application of the spray material to a "glistening" stage, not to runoff. When a leaf glistens the material has spread over the leaf without gaps or droplets, a sort of even coating. Spreader-stickers and spray buffers help in the process, making water somewhat wetter and able to spread and adhere to the leaf, something like dish washing detergents buffer water without leaving spots on glassware. The rosarians job is to get the spray material on the leaves (over or under depending on the need) in tiny droplets that will spread. Effectiveness depends on the spray mix, pressure and nozzle setting. Careful observation for glistening leads to a setup that saves materials and does the intended job. The Rambler is a strong advocate of *Indicate-5* as a spray treatment that helps sprays work better. See the May '96 Rambler for some of the attributes.

JAPANESE BEETLE TIME… almost here in the Southeast. The Rambler still likes *Margosan-O* to repel and provide some control. But start spraying BEFORE they emerge. Environmentally sound, *Margosan-O* is a botanical insecticide concentrate derived from Neem seeds. Use at 1 Tablespoon per gallon of buffered solution (with Indicate-5) and wet leaves and blooms. The Rambler combines with *Triforine*, but many growers say to use it alone. Take your choice. If you're in a beetle-prone area, unless you do something, you'll get very well acquainted with your garden as you pick them off.

IT'S SUMMERTIME. Keep watering, enjoy

roses and drop a note to the Rambler from time to time. That's how we BOTH learn.

When the glass is at ninety, a gardener's a fool, Who directs not his efforts to try to keep cool. Anyway, here are some cool suggestions for July...

COOL DOWN SPIDER MITES... Spider mites and hot, dry weather mean trouble. Reproduction increases with temperature for major infestation in just a few days. First line of defense is to cool off the mating mites with a water wand, washing underneath the leaves with a forceful water spray. This washing process has to be repeated every four to five days and is OK for small gardens ... even large gardens if you have the time.

MITICIDE OF CHOICE for larger gardens is *AVID*, a translaminar (penetrates leaves) product with great knockdown capability and good residual. And there is a low tendency for mites to build up resistance to Avid. Used at 1/4 teaspoon per gallon, it is relatively inexpensive and nonphytotoxic (won't burn leaves or damage blooms). Add *STIRRUP M*, a pheromone sex attractant, for even better results. Just a couple of drops per gallon of spray.

The Rambler's routine is to water-wash the undersides of the leaves first, buffer spray solution with *INDICATE-5* or *SURF-KING,* add 1/4 teaspoon of *Avid* and three drops of *Stirrup M* and spray up through the bush to get good coverage underneath the leaves to a "glistening" stage. Repeat in 4-5 days to get newly-hatched mites. This approach sharply reduces the mite population and may have to be repeated only 2-3 times during the season. Spray other mite hosts as well; keep a sharp eye out for any new outbreak.

MIDSUMMER is a good time for organics, releasing nutrients and building soil without boosting excessive growth. Broadcast a cup or so of alfalfa meal or pellets per established bush about now and continue with lots of water. Manures, compost, fish meal and mixtures of all of the above maintain green leaves which in turn produce blooms. Miniatures like the same treatment, just in smaller quantities. The Rambler likes *Mills EasyFeed* for container minis, using about a Tablespoon of the material for a 2-3 gallon container. Just sprinkle *EasyFeed* mixture (sort of a moist coffee grounds consistency) on top of the soil and let water pick up the food and deliver to the roots.

Gives a slow release and steady diet. Works the same way as when dissolved in water, but does not have to be repeated as often. Minis really love it.

AN ORGANIC STORY... Many rosarians report that Klima™ (a fine yellow climbing miniature) is slow to start and a reluctant grower. That's too bad because this rose is an excellent one, but it has one weakness ... it loves FISH... fish meal, fish emulsion, *EasyFeed*... any organic with a touch of fish. The Rambler built a special planting area for Klima™ in front of a split rail fence two seasons ago, working 20 pounds of fish meal into an area 18 inches wide and 18 feet long. Also added some compost, cottonseed meal and alfalfa meal. Planted three of the mini climbers, well started in one-gallon pots, one plant per 8-foot fence span. By the end of the season, both rails of the fence were completely covered with multiple canes and in bloom almost continuously. Even Joe and Marion Klima, from the Bay area of California, have not been able to get this kind of growth, and both of them are outstanding rosarians. So, if you want a fine yellow climber, get out the fish meal. Klima™ will respond.

CHECK THIS OFFER. In the May Rambler column, *IMMUNEX* was introduced as a new alternative fungicide for powdery mildew. Readers were encouraged to give it a try and enjoy a BONUS publication called *Growing Beautiful Roses.* Send in the proof of purchase coupon and get the booklet. Somehow the Spectrum people (*Spectracide*) did not get the marketing and distribution people on the same page. Many outlets do not have the coupons. If you have purchased *IMMUNEX* and would like this fine booklet, send your request to the ARS, along WITH a SASE (business size) and a copy will be on the way to you promptly. The Rambler would also like to have a note on how good a job *Immunex* did for you, any comments at all. Will recap the comments received in an early issue.

ANOTHERGIVEAWAY... And worth a lot. A GLOSSARY FOR ROSARIANS has been released by the Bradenton-Sarasota (FL) Rose Society, six well-written pages that define ALL of the words and terms common to rosarians. Initiated by Richard Hedenberg with Russ Bowermaster, it's a fine, easy read reference. The Rambler has printed a bunch and will send you a copy in your SASE. Use the Post Office Box address above and Rambler and Millie Rambler will respond promptly.

   IN THE MEANTIME... stay cool.

ROSE ideas that work are those you put to work… and the tips this month require very little work to be effective.

TONICS FOR SUMMER… One kind for rosarians and another for roses. Foliage often looks pale along about midsummer, and more nitrogen is not the answer. Just apply lots of water and some "tonic tea," a version of the alfalfa tea that the Rambler has long advocated. Use some alfalfa meal or cow chips as a base stock, season with chelated iron like Sprint 330, add *Epsom* salts and some readily soluble balanced food like *Miracle Gro®* or *Carl Pool* with trace elements. For a 32-gallon trash can use 8-10 cups of alfalfa, 1/4 cup of *Sequestrene* 330, 1/2 cup Epsom salts and 1/2 cup of a soluble 20-20-20. Steep and use about one gallon per established bush. Exact proportions are not important… keep the mix weak. You'll see quick results.

ABOUT AVAILABLE IRON… A favorite of rosarians is a chelated form known for years as *Sequestrene 330*, now sold as *Sprint 330*, a product by Ciga-Geigy. It's a micronutrient important to green, healthy leaves. Chelated iron is more available to the plant, something a smart grower looks for on any nutrients list claiming to have trace elements. Used on acid to slightly acid soils, iron goes to work right away.

FIND A FARM STORE… Probably more important than a source for roses. Organic meals and mixes and soil conditioners are available, and most important, affordable from these providers. The Rambler always wears his "gimmie cap" with FAMILY FARM SUPPLY on each visit to this growing emporium. We're soul mates of soil. What he doesn't have, he always will get within a week, and at a reasonable price. It's worth the search.

NITROGEN ROBBER… A really bad rap on copious use of mulches in and on rosebeds. Mulch does NOT "rob" the soil of nitrogen; it uses some nitrogen in a very natural process to break down the organic matter and condition the soil. The organic soil "crumbs" support microorganisms and hold nutrients; the process adds rather than robs. Nitrogen is the most plentiful nutrient as well as the most easily leached from the soil. When nitrogen is used or lost, add some more. This is a cheap, reliable way to keep soils and plants living and growing. Enjoy the benefits of mulch without worrying about using some energy in the process.

MULCH… If there is one miracle product for the rose garden, mulch has to be high on the list. Nothing does quite the same job, regardless of whether you are an "all organic" grower or someone addicted to chemicals. Choices are endless: compost, leaves, pine needles, ground bark, tree trimmings and mixtures of all of these. Mulches function to cool the soil, conserve water, keep down weeds and add humus to the soil, all working with nature. All it takes is a season of pulling weeds in a mulch less garden to make a believer of any grower. It helps with the water bill as well.

HOW DO FERTILIZERS BURN? It's simple: too much available nitrogen and not enough water. But why does it happen? Roots are made up of cells whose activity is supported by water, just like human skin and tissue. Burn occurs when water is removed or displaced from the cells. Most fertilizers use ammonium sulfate or ammonium nitrate as nitrogen sources, synthesizing the element found in nature. These compounds are HYGROSCOPIC and have a tendency to take up water. If the compounds (fertilizers) in the soil are too concentrated, moisture is taken up from the soil and even the roots, thereby destroying the moisture support system for the cells.

NATURE SEEKS BALANCE… Concentrated solutions want to add water and perform this trick through osmosis, pulling moisture through cell walls. Result: dry cells and burn. The solution to fertilizer burn is to apply appropriate fertilizer amounts and ALWAYS with plenty of water. That's the reason for the advice: water first, feed, water again. If in doubt, soak even more.

ENJOY a great rose summer… and lots of water.

GROWING good roses should be as easy as falling off a diet. These suggestions are so easy that you won't mind falling at all.

SENTINEL... A new fungicide for blackspot that promises to make spraying easier... at least less frequent. Near-perfect control is possible with spraying at 28-day intervals. **BEWARE that this product is NOT registered for roses at this time,** but application for shrubs has been made. Serous rosarians in the Golden Triangle of Texas (where blackspot thrives year-round) have been using Sentinel for two seasons with great results, even coming the material with *Systhane* for powdery mildew and Avid for spider mites. The Rambler has a trial going this season comparing *Sentinal* with a *Triforine/Manzate* combination. So far BOTH test plots are absolutely free of blackspot. *Sentinal* is expensive and not package or approved for home use, but at just 1/6 teaspoon per gallon, the final cost is comparable to *Triforine*. Monthly vs. weekly spraying for blackspot will be a real boon to rosarians when (if) approved. More on the Rambler's trials at the end of the season.

HIGH COST OF WATER... and roses are mostly water. Most of the cost of water is in the dispoal of waster water as water districts rush to meet tougher environmental standards. In most localities, disposal (sewer charge) is twice the cost of the water itself. Rosarians with large gardens should look into installing a garden water meter that has now sewer charge. In many cases, a new meter will pay for itself in one season. And you'll be one step closer to a water system or distribution grid to make watering easier.

LUGGING BUCKETS of water with soluble fertilizers, tonics and elixirs is not the Rambler's idea of a good time in the garden... but sometimes necessary. The EASY solution is to us a *Little Giant* submersible pump to pump and meter out the mixes to roses. *Little Giant* is the pump common to small fountains and pons, readily purchased and virtually trouble-free. Works great in a a32-gallon plastic garbage can, limited only by the length of the grounded electrical cord. Can also be mounted outside the container with an intake hose (and strainer) into the mix. Even works with alfalfa tea mixes PROVIDED that the intake does not go into the sediment in the bottom. The sediment can be diluted with water and applied by bucket, or the container refilled for another brewing.

HYPONEX... also makes a variety of syphon to use with a garden hose or some other water delivery system. Syphons are intended to meter out fully soluble fertilizers only. Kept clean, they will deliver just the right dilution... all the rosarian has to do is control the volume.

SEPTEMBER is a good month to take an overall look at the garden and landscape... best done BEFORE the catalogs arrive. Consider some new applications of roses... shrubs, pillars, miniature climbers or some ground covers. Good roses are even better with landscape impact. Consider hybrid teas, floribundas and miniatures used together in a mass planting... the tall ones in the back, medium in the middle and the minis in front. They will get along beautifully if you're careful with the fertilizing. A really GREAT foreground rose the yellow miniature **CalPoly** with strong foliage, color and growth. The possibilities are endless.

TRY SOMETHING NEW... at least to your garden. Not the "New for '96" roses but some recent introductions that are holding up well in gardens just like yours. **St. Patrick™** is the first one that comes to mind. Great color, stems and foliage with just a trace of green. Signature is a winner in every garden. No one seems to have a problem with it. It really is a "Rose of The Year." **Midas Touch™** also lives up to its name, even in cold climates. **Elina**® is also consistently good.

SOMETHING DIFFERENT... A mannerly shrub from Ralph Moore called Sharon's Delight, looks like **Sally Holmes**® but on a much smaller plant. Another fun shrub is **Flutterbye™**, a multi-color yellow, coral, tangerine and pink. You have to see it to believe it... the clusters carry all the colors at the same time.

MINIS that have attracted the Rambler's (and Millie Rambler's) eye included **Tangerine Twist** (my favorite) with color like its name; **Sparks**, a firey red on good foliage; **Sorcerer™** is always free-flowering with bright, medium red blooms; and finally **CalPoly**, the all-around yellow mini that fits anywhere, although Ralph Moore thinks that **Sequoia Gold™** will give it some competition, having recently won "Best Miniature" in

New Zealand trials.

MORE on what, where and how with roses next month.

FALL is the time to enjoy a rose garden harvest, a good payoff for summertime chores. These no sweat tips may help your harvest.

POWDERY MILDEW persists in October, requiring an equally persistent spray program. Rosarians who started in late August are ahead of the game, but there's still time to cut clean roses in most parts of the country. The cleanest gardens have been sprayed with an alternating program of *Triforine/Rubigan* one week and *Triforine* alone the next week. Or use a *Triforine/Systhane* combination. Both *Rubigan* and *Systhane* are used at 1/4 teaspoon per gallon, *Triforine* at 1 teaspoon per gallon. A newcomer (at least to home gardeners) is *Immunex*, a systemic preventive treatment used at 1 tablespoon per gallon. *Immunex* is a derivative of Banner, used extensively by the pros.

WATER helps control powdery mildew as well, washing off spores before there's a chance for wind drift to new growth, establishing new colonies on dry leaves. Growers who hose down the leaves appreciate the fact that powdery mildew grows on DRY plant material, not on wet leaves. Blackspot needs a wet surface and warm temperatures to multiply. Washing first supports better leaf coverage of the fungicide as well. Go over the garden with the hose, then start the spray routine. No routine will restore the damaged leaves and buds, but will protect new growth.

SLOW DOWN in October... good advice for roses and rosarians. Allow roses to go through the natural process as hours of sunlight shorten and temperatures drop. Roses want to mature, make rose hips, store nutrients in the canes and roots. Trimming and feeding tell the plant that it is time to grow. A slowdown period gives roses and woody shrubs time to manufacture the natural antifreeze that protects the cells... fluids with reduced capability of expanding when frozen. A neat trick by Mother Nature when we don't interfere.

FALL INSECTS are minimal... usually, but what is usual in a rose garden? Corn ear worms will drill small holes in choice blooms if the rosarian isn't alert (sometimes IF alert). *MAVRIK* is the insecticide of choice, spraying the bud and bloom area. Another line of attack is squashing the tiny, cream colored eggs laid in the seams of the sepals. Or get the moth that lays the eggs with a BUG ZAPPER, the luminous lamp with electric grids. Fries mosquitoes as well. Hang a zapper about 8 feet off the ground, away from the rose beds. Depending on the size of the tubes, a zapper will protect a wide area. Zappers usually go on sale in the fall. If you have power available, a zapper is one of the best investments you can make.

MILKY SPORE control of Japanese Beetles has new emphasis to growers in the Eastern United States as the material becomes readily available by mail order or from turf supply outlets. *Milky Spore* applied to turf kills the grubs that hatch into beetles. Can be applied in a pattern from March through November, ABSOLUTELY safe for humans, pets, birds, bees and plants. It is a simple spore ONLY affecting beetle grubs. There are a couple of drawbacks. It takes some time for the spores to spread throughout the grub population, and most rosarians are not patient. Even in warm climates, spread takes from one to three years. Also, a broad area has to be treated as the beetles fly in. St. Gabriel Labs, regular advertisers in these pages, packages the spores in quantities suitable for home gardeners. Call 1800-801-0061 for some great promotional information or to order.

OLD HABITS DIE HARD... The Rambler has had an aversion to "dusts" since failing to control anything (insects or diseases) with dusts early in his rose learning. The only way to get good coverage required a liquid application, or so he thought. Until rose friend Baxter Morgan introduced him to the *DUSTIN MIZER*, a low cost dust applicator that is death on Japanese Beetles with 5 percent *Sevin Dust*. The *Mizer* sifts dust into a column of moving air with precise control. Uses VERY LITTLE material, applies quickly, about as fast as you can walk along a row of roses. Dust in the evening when air is calm on DRY foliage. Very lightly. Beetles are dead by morning. Baxter likes twice a week dustings for good control. Using just a touch of *Sevin* doesn't seem to get the beneficial insects and leaves no residue. Could be useful for applying Diatomaceous Earth as well. *Dustin Mizer* is advertised in these pages from time to time, about $35.

COOL AIR is coming on... time to get out in the garden.

If you wait long enough it will be too cold to do rose stuff postponed because it was too hot last summer. These tips are for cool weather rosarians who want to wrap up the season.

FROST ON THE PUMPKIN means time to winter protect appropriately for your climate. Thanksgiving weekend seems to be the time that most rosarians favor for winter protection, getting the job done right rather than rushing out a few hours ahead of a cold front. The whole idea is to insulate... to maintain a fairly constant temperature, avoiding freeze/thaw situations. Combinations of loose materials do this best, held in place with fences, boughs, cones or what have you. Roses like these "thermal blankets." When organics are used, there's an extra benefit in the spring as they add humus to the soil. And much lighter than hauling soil in and out.

REALLY COLD CLIMATES require more soil protection, mounded 6-8 inches over the canes, then covered with leaves. Bring the soil in rather than taking from between the bushes in the beds. Soil/ Mulch combinations are great... they breathe better.

BURY FOR THE WINTER... the ultimate protection and maximum work. Roses received in late fall are far better off buried than potted and moved in and out of protection all winter. It's a natural sort of dormancy, like the "Minnesota Tip" burying method. Select a garden spot where it is easy to dig 18 inches or so and set aside the spoil dirt. Lighten up with some leaves. Line the dormancy vault with leaves and soil. Tie the tops of the bushes with twine, then into bundles. Heel in the bundles in the vault and cover with the mix. Remember to tie a rope on the bundles so that you'll know where to dig next spring. Cover the area with lots of leaves and wait for spring. It works.

WINTER CAN WORK FOR YOU with a freeze/thaw cycle that takes a lot of the work out of building a new rose bed. Loosen the bed area you want to improve with a spading fork and pile on lots of organic materials and leaves. As moisture freezes and expands, tissues break down in the same way as decomposition in the summer. Winter action reduces and blends the organic matter and soil into the "loam" that most rosarians like. Nature has been building soil this way for a long, long time.

WINTER FEEDING is a practice worth considering, although a better description might be "composting in place." Growers in severe as well as milder climates put down a layer of leaves in the rose bed, broadcast a cupful of pelletized fertilizer (13-13-13) per 10 square feet, then add some more leaves. By spring the lower layer of leaves has broken down into a rich humus, .threaded with white mycelium. The fertilizer works on the leaves, not on the soil, breaking down the organic material and setting up the soil for better activity in the spring. Be careful not to disturb the lower layer any more than necessary at pruning time, and you may elect to leave all of the leaves in the bed, broadcasting more fertilizer on top. Advocates of winter feeding report no untimely new growth in either the fall or spring when roses are put to bed with this "nightcap."

HEALTHY BUSHES make it through the winter; weakened ones do not. Keep this in mind when evaluating your cold-weather success. Bushes that have been defoliated with blackspot, retarded by powdery mildew and weakened in poor sunlight won't respond with any winter protection method. Well-grown roses are survivors.

***SENTINEL* UPDATE...** The new 28-day fungicide for blackspot continues to get good reviews, but the jury is still out in some areas. The Rambler will do a roundup of experiences in time for your consideration next spring. Keep in mind that *Sentinel* is NOT registered for roses at this time, although an application has been filed for woody ornamentals. The greatest attribute of *Sentinel* is spraying at three-week to four-week intervals rather than weekly. Leaves no residue, seems to be compatible with other fungicides like *Rubigan* and *Systhane*. But it IS expensive and available from just a few mail-order sources. Stay tuned.

TALK WITH YOU AGAIN in '97... Have a HAPPY ROSY ONE!!

Howard Walters, 1997.

ROSE WISDOM... The month's RAMBLINGS support the worth of both old and new with excerpts gleaned from columns over the last 10 years.

DOES SOIL GET TIRED? Just like the "tired blood" of the *Geritol* ads, soil needs rebuilding from time to time. The tonic for soil is organic matter, and plenty of it. Soils don't wear out, but lose the capability to convert nutrients into forms available to the roots and plants. When this happens there is a general decline in growth that can't be reversed with all of the tonics in chemist's kit. Get some organics and soil-openers like *Perlite* into the soil by the best means possible so that air, water, and soil can work together. This may mean digging the roses when dormant, reworking the bed and replanting or a less strenuous routine of working the "soil builders" into the bed.

MANURE IN THE WINTER? Of course. Animal manures and other organics are primarily soil builders rather than fertilizers. Manures won't cause too-early spring growth, but set the stage for soil organisms to go to work converting nutrients when the soil warms up. The Rambler's favorite is horse manure, liberally applied.

HOLIDAY GIFT... a dump truck load of horse manure from a riding stable (stalls). Steaming and fragrant on delivery... all it needed was a red ribbon on top. Rosebeds are now tucked away under a cozy 5-inch blanket. What a spring we are going to have. A great idea for Valentine's Day, too.

THE RAMBLER'S FAVORITE ROSE... The one I saw last. But there is a long list of favorites that the Rambler has to have, roses like Mister Lincoln, Century Two, Granada, Pristine, and Double Delight. Floribundas like Showbiz, Cherish, Iceberg and Sunsprite. The garden also needs a Don Juan climber. And our miniature beds will always have Red Beauty, Rainbow's End, Minnie Pearl, Millie Walters and Rise 'n' Shine. Got the idea. Roses are a personal matter.

DIG AND DIVIDE... Miniatures in moderate climates rapidly outgrow themselves. Large plants with woody centers are unattractive and unproductive. It's easy to dig and split up the "mother" plant, trimming out the unproductive stuff. Leave some good roots and younger growth with each "new" plant. By the end of the season, the offshoot will be nearly as large as the mother. In some areas, minis can be dug and divided every two years, best when dormant just before soil warms up. Use a saw, shears, or just pull apart like a chrysanthemum. Give minis a whole new lease on life.

NEW YEAR'S RESOLUTION... Save money by ordering three of everything. Good practice for exhibitors so that they will have a good supply of sure winners, but wasteful for the rest of us. Inquire, observe, then order just one of a variety to see how it does in your garden. You can always get some more.

PRUNE EARLY? Not a good risk. Assuming that there is wood to prune, there is little to be gained by jumping the season. Early pruning usually results in frozen new growth rather than earlier blooms, setting back the rose and the rosarian. Roses come into bloom in the spring as a result of sunshine, soil, and air temperature rather than a pruning calendar. The same routine is good for cold-climate rosarians with little or no wood left in the spring. Don't uncover and encourage too soon. Nature knows when it is time to grow.

ROOT INTERFERENCE cannot be ignored, as we tend to do when leafless trees are in the landscape. When roots from trees and shrubs invade a rosebed, more food just means more roots, and the roses won't get their fair share. Extra feeding postpones the inevitable (barrier systems, moving the bed, or cutting the trees) but won't cure the problem. Foliar feeding helps, but rose growth is still retarded by tree roots sucking up the moisture. Face it: trees and roses don't mix well.

FIGHT THE TEMPTATION to squeeze an extra rosebush into the bed. What seems like enough space in the spring will be overgrown like a jungle in July. Establish bushes overwhelm newcomers in the bed, depriving them of light, water and food. It's tough competition-survival of the fittest. It's one of the reasons that all-new plantings do better. If you MUST have a new bush in a tight, established bed, try potting first and force the root system along so that it can compete. By the time the potted rose is ready, the hole may have already closed up... just as well. It's an opportunity to grow another rose in a container.

NEW PRODUCTS AND ROSES are going

to be more available than ever in 1997. The Rambler will help you keep up with what's new... as well as what's old.

OPPORTUNITY... never comes... it's here. Time to get busy for a Rosy '97. Perhaps a few of the Rambler's quips quotes will make it even rosier.

PRUNING... a highly overrated art. Rosarians anguish and agonize over where to cut and how to cut, but most roses will grow in spite of the pruning technique. Practice and observation are the best learning tools, a sort of on-the-job training. Just visualize what you want the bush to look like this season and apply a little rose sense. Get out the dead wood, shape to please, and prune to an outside eye. It's a rejuvenation process that produces a long and productive life cycle. Get out to a pruning demonstration, if you can find one, and then get out into the rose garden when the time is right.

CLIMBERS are cussed and discussed at pruning time, trying to come up with more blooms from an uncooperative bramble of thorns. Variety selection, identification of productive wood, and training of the canes are the most important considerations. True climbers are bred for vigorous growth and lots of bloom. Climbing sports of hybrid teas are not in the same class. These sports can put on in the same class. These sports can put on an impressive flush in the spring, if the canes are trained horizontally, followed by an occasional flowering. Untrained sports throw canes 10 feet long with one bloom on top.

TRAIN CLIMBING CANES to a horizontal support, a gradual process. Bloom laterals will emerge at each leaf axil, reaching for the sun. Each bloom lateral can be cut and enjoyed (or spent bloom removed) just like a hybrid tea. Some climbers cascade naturally, blooming all along the cane. A classic example is Don Juan, a rich, velvet red with great fragrance. Altissimo, Handel, and Dortmund are also good choices. Cane can be trained up and over a trellis or arbor, weaving the canes for a lateral movement. Canes would around a pillar achieve the same result... blooms all over. Get out the dead, shape up, train. Climbing simplicity.

REBUILDING BED?? SAVE THE ROSES. Dormant roses can be dug and set aside for a week or two while rebuilding an existing bed, giving both a new lease on life. Dig carefully with a spading fork; don't worry about taking a ball of soil. Check the root system for galls and to see how much of the root system is alive. Trim out or discard, depending on the severity. Don't bother with a weak bush; it takes more work than a healthy one. Set the bushes aside and bury or cover with soil, sacks, mulch, bark, or any other material that will keep the bushes cool and moist. My dad referred to this as "heeling in," since the bushes were slanted in a trench. But dirt and manure types like the Rambler say that the bushes are "healed in" and thus protected until planting. Whatever you call it, it works.

GROUND PINE BARK is much maligned by the uniformed, but glowingly praised by those who have enjoyed the benefits of this cheap, readily, available soil improver. Short of compost, leaves, peat moss? Try working about 25 percent fine-ground pine bark (by volume) into the soil, even more if the soil is really hard or depleted. The newly-worked soil is really hard to depleted. The newly-worked area becomes friable almost over night. Offset acidity with about 10 pounds of dolomite lime per 100 square feet, plus 5 pounds of 10-10-10 fertilizer to support the decomposition process. Pine bark lasts a long time and encourages root growth that has to be experienced to believe. Why do you think there is so much ground bark in the "soilless" potting mixes? The physical characteristics of ground bark are ideal for rose mixes.

WOODY PARTICLES in the soil are also nutrient reservoirs, retaining available fertilizers in solution. The process is adsorption, the ability to hold nutrients on the surface rather than within. Particles are also the nucleus of soil crumbs, attracting and attaching mineral particles. Bark and soil crumbs are partially saturated, distributing nutrients over a large surface area. Soil organisms thrive under these conditions; humus, air, and water. And, like a good reservoir, bark/crumbs release what plants like over a long period of time. In a rosebed or planting hole, bark works with roses.

EASY-FEEDING TIPS next month. Setting a good table for roses doesn't have to be difficult... and hard on the back.

photo by Jim Hering

In Loving Memory
Millie Walters

July 23, 1926 — January 29, 1997

Millie enjoying a garden tour with Suzie Bridges (left) and Donna Hefner (center).

photo by Margaret Drucker

Millie and Howard Walters.

O sweet the rose that blossometh
on Friendship's tree!
It fills my heart with joy and ecstasy.
I seek the rose's company
because her scent
Recalls the fragrance sweet
of ONE belov'd by me.

*Selections from the Rubaiyat
and Odes of Hafiz
Hafiz, 1300-1388*

photo by Pete Haring

Millie Walters

THE TROUBLE WITH SPRINGTIME is that it usually arrives before we are ready for it. Here are some ways to catch up that are EASY on the rosarian… EASY being a continuing theme in these '97 columns.

"UNCLE CHARLEY" DAWSON Greenhouse rose professional and longtime contributor to this magazine, knew how to make rose growing easy (at least easier) by using some common rose sense. One of his outside rose garden read, "Enjoy the roses, but keep your big feet out of the beds." He knew that packed soil meant more work and fewer roses. Incidentally, Uncle Charley was the first professional to abandon the practice of stomping and tamping new rosebushes in greenhouse benches. His "innovative" approach resulted in faster early growth, reduced loss and longer bench life. If your "big feet" have been in the rosebeds too much, loosen up the soil and then devise some sort of servicing access. Use stepping stones to distribute the weight, lay some decking on top of loose mulch, or make the planting narrow enough for easy access in the first place. The whole process works better with good movement/drainage of air and water.

DOWNY MILDEW The fungus disease evidenced by purplish blotches on leaves and canes during cool, damp weather can be controlled early-on with some adjustments to the regular spray program. Like blackspot, it's easier to control than to eradicate. Beginning with the first spring spraying, add 1 tablespoon of *Manzate 200* per gallon to the usual *Funginex/Triforine*. The next week, use *Daconil*, preferably the WDG (water dispersible granule) type. Alternate until temperatures routinely hit 80 degrees Fahrenheit or so, when the spore don't multiply. Perhaps your garden won't become infected, but this bland routine can't hurt a thing. Much easier than having to respond to defoliated bushes with *Pace* or one of the metalaxyl combinations like *Subdue*. You won't have blackspot either.

DISINFECT BAREROOT ROSES Before planning? A good routine to head off introduction of downy mildew in the garden, particularly with the increased spread of this disease. Many rosarians disinfected before downy, believing that root and crown galls could be retarded. The routine is simple: add 1 cup of chlorine bleach to a 5-gallon bucket of water; dip the while bush, roots and root, for about a minute. Shake off the excess and plant.

YOU DESERVE A BREAK THIS SPRING Give yourself (or ask your gardening partner for) a *Mantis* tiller/cultivator. Millie Rambler saw one a few years ago and garden soil has been flying ever since. Takes the work out of new rosebed construction… cultivates, aerates, edges and generally makes a large garden really fun. Weighs about 20 pounds with sharp tines that dig and mix and chop with amazing speed. Tills to about 12 inches, even in heavy soil, and will dig a hole for planting in no time at all. It's a husky digger in spite of its size. The *Mantis* tiller/cultivator is advertised regularly in these pages; costs about $300 with attachments. Take a really good look at this garden wonder. A RAMBLER NOTE: This isn't a *Mantis*-sponsored promo. The Rambler is a full-price buyer and a happy rosarian.

WARM ROOTS ARE HUNGRY. Fertilizers applied to cold soils won't do much good until the root zone warms up, explaining why some rosarians think the feeding program isn't working. The canes, warmed by sunshine, may be waking up, but the roots are waiting for a clear signal that spring has arrived. To illustrate: check new roses in black plastic pots set out on a warm reflective surface. In just a week or two, tiny new roots have spread throughout the pot and the rose is off to a fast start. For rosarians in a hurry, apply readily available foods (like fortified alfalfa tea, soaking the rootzone when the soil warms up.

GROW ROOTS, THEN ROSES Applies to miniatures in particular. Small newly-rooted miniature plants perform much better if first repotted in a 1-gallon plastic pot and allowed to develop a real root system before planting in a new bed. Use a light, friable mix with some organics like compost, locating the pots in filtered light for a week or so. Feed lightly (weak fish emulsion solution) on a weekly basis and the lightest miniature just jumps out of the pot. Set out when some small roots begin to come out of the bottom of the pot.

TAKE IT EASY And enjoy the roses

MAY 1997

THOUGHT FOR THE MONTH:
Anyone can have dirt. Rosarians have soil.

GROWING ROSES is the art of getting used to what you didn't expect. But you can expect more roses and less work with these Rambler tips.

A HEALTHY DIET FOR ROSES... as variable as climates and rosarians. But all good feeding programs have some common factors. First, feed the soil organisms with organics to get the process going. Second, get a liquid booster of choice for fast initial growth. Third, maintain an available source of nitrogen with pelletized or timed-release fertilizers. Supplement as needed with tonics or "exhibitor secrets" depending on what you want from your roses.

THE RAMBLER RECOMMENDS... ORGANICS: A mix of fish meal, cottonseed meal and alfalfa meal in equal parts, about 1 1/2 cups of mix per bush, scratched in lightly. For convenience, *Mills Magic Mix* has it all. **BOOSTER:** Fortified alfalfa tea, a mix of alfalfa, *Peters 20-20-20*, chelated iron and Epsom salts. **PELLETIZED:** A coated or timed-release 20-10-6 with trace elements. *Osmocote* has a similar formulation that is very easy to use. **WATER:** Lots of it, nothing happens without plenty of water, deeply soaked. With a little help from the sun, the roses are going to grow.

OLD RELIABLES can be counted on to keep a garden fungus free... there's no need to jump to the latest-and-greatest that may or may not have been approved for roses. For blackspot, weekly spraying with *Triforine* will give good results and do a fair job on powdery mildew. A combination punch is better with *Triforine* one week, *Triforine/Manzate* the next week and *Triforine/Daconil* the following week. Then start over. Effective on downy mildew also. For really severe powdery mildew, *Rubigan* or *Systhane* every-other week will give good control. The Rambler has combined *Triforine* and *Rubigan* with no adverse results (and *Triforine/Systhane*) but still believes that these products used separately control better with less danger of leaf burn. Mildew season is relatively short-lived in most parts of the country, so the extra spraying is not an ongoing chore. Healthy, disease-free leaves produce roses... give the leaves a chance to succeed.

A NEW PRODUCT worth giving a try... *Rose Defense* by Green Light. Probably the best in cooler climates. A protectant based on neem oil, *Rose Defense* is touted as a "natural fungicide" that also "smothers" certain pests like mites and aphids. Be careful in hot weather. Consider for cool-weather powdery mildew.

IMMUNEX is gaining some converts. This is the home-garden equivalent of the popular fungicide *Banner*, used professionally on turf and field crops for many years. Quite good for the prevention (even eradication) of powdery mildew. Water based, *Immunex* is used at 1 tablespoon per gallon for powdery mildew, 2 tablespoons per gallon for blackspot. Distributed by Spectrum, *Immunex* is available from most chain garden centers.

BASAL BOOSTER... worth discussing again as the time is just about right in most parts of the country. It's a one-two punch for more basal and low breaks that leads with a readily available source of nitrogen followed with a chaser of Epsom salts just after the initial bloom cycle. The bush is at its most vigorous at that time. Epsom salts (magnesium sulfate) works best when AVAILABLE nitrogen is present (a nitrate form is preferable). Use a soluble 20-20-20- the first week, a large handful of Epsom salts the second week, with successive applications of 20-20-20 weeks three and four. WATCH the dilution of the 20-20-20, use at 1/3 label strength. And always use PLENTY of water. New basals require lots of energy in the root zone for results. Miniatures benefit also but at a MUCH REDUCED strength. *Booster* makes leaves green and bushes grow.

WATER... still the most important fertilizer. Make sure that your system gets plenty into the root zone and not just on the surface. The Rambler still likes the *Drip Works* adjustable flow emitters for ease of installation and effectiveness, meriting The Water Award in 1995. But the Rambler also has some beds well-soaked with *Moisture-Master* porous hose that weaves in and out among the roses, patiently oozing water where it belongs.

RAMBLER GIVEAWAYS... Rambler has some "revised" alfalfa tea, fragrant for spray formulations sheets that you can have with a self-addressed, stamped #10 envelope. Stick in a note with your request, and we'll chat about roses by mail as well.

JUN.
1997

THOUGHT FOR THE MONTH:
My garden was great last week. Sorry you missed it.

WHY ARE THEY CALLED "GROWING SECRETS" when we can't wait to tell them to someone else? These tips are not secrets, but use and pass them on for better roses anyway.

TRY A CHANGE-UP... a baseball expression to catch the batter (fungus) unaware. An alternating program will do just that. Use *Triforine* at 1 teaspoon per gallon on a weekly basis; add *Manzate 200* at 1/2 tablespoon per gallon one week and a scant teaspoon of *Daconil 2787WDG (90%)* the next week. *Daconil* BURNS in hot weather, discontinue when it begins to get really hot. Or use *Triforine* one week, *Immunex* the next week. For really persistent blackspot, increase the spray FREQUENCY, not the concentration.

GOOD LEAF COVERAGE is an absolute in any spray program. Both contact fungicides (*Daconil, Manzate*) and systemic fungicides (*Triforine, Cleary's 3336, Rubigan*) require even coverage that sticks for best results. Coverage is a function of the droplet size (pressure), "wetness" of the spray mix and compatibility of the spray materials. No need to overdo it, just spray until the leaves "glisten." Runoff is not required.

INDICATE-5 is a great water additive to make spray solutions work better... buffers, acidifies, conditions and makes water "wetter." It takes about 2 tablespoons per gallon to reach the optimum pH level, use more or less depending on the hardness of the water. Add the material slowly to the water, which will change from milky white to orange to pink. Pink indicates a pH of 5.0. Once you have figured out how much *Indicate-5* your water needs, buffer your spray solution regularly with the same amount before adding fungicides or insecticides. *Surfking Plus* is another good wetting/buffering agent. It also inhibits foaming, important to users of *Atomist* sprayers.

VINEGAR STILL WORKS, TOO. Before *Indicate-5*, the Rambler regularly buffered spray water with 1 tablespoon of white vinegar per gallon plus a few drops of dish washing liquid. It's amazing how much easier wettable powders go into the spray solution and how evenly the spray spreads across the leaves.

CHOOSE YOUR WEAPON... against Japanese beetles. It's war when it comes to these rose savages. Pick 'em off: OK if you have lots of time and a small garden. Beetle traps: only marginally effective for most rosarians. Milky spore: excellent if you started two years ago and your neighbors joined in. *Margosan-O*: a botanical insecticide derived from the Neem tree that works fairly well if used early enough and persistently. *Liquid Sevin*: knocks beetles down immediately but leaves unsightly residue, discolors blooms and may kill off the beneficial insects. All the weapons have some drawbacks, you choose.

AN OLD BUT "NEW" WEAPON is 10% dust. The Rambler has an aversion to dusts since failing to control anything (insects or disease) with dusts early in his rose learning. Liquid was the only way to go, or so he thought. But then longtime rosarian and rose friend Baxter Morgan introduced him to the *Dustin-Mizer*, a low-cost dust applicator that is death on Japanese Beetles with 10% *Sevin* dust. The *Mizer* sifts dust into a column of moving air with precise control. Uses VERY LITTLE material, applies quickly, about as fast as you can walk along a row of roses. Lays down a fine haze over the top of the bush. Dust in the evening when the air is calm on DRY foliage. Beetles are dead by dark. Use twice a week. Using just a touch of *Sevin* doesn't seem to get the beneficials and leaves little residue. *Mizer* can be used to apply *Diatomaceous Earth* as well. Costs about $35 with the extension tube. Available by mail order from Gardens Alive (812) 537-8650 or from Nitron Industries 1-800-835-0123. Both have all sorts of organic stuff. Fun catalogs.

RELAX A LITTLE. Roses have been growing for a long time in spite of rosarians.

JULY is a tough month for roses and rosarians… both expected springtime to last forever. Here are some cool tips to get through a hot summer.

SPIDER MITES… are the summertime scourge, reproducing at a fantastic rate and literally sucking the life out of rose leaves. Many growers get into trouble by not recognizing the problem early enough. Watch for gray-green leaves losing color near the bottom of the bush. With a practiced eye, you can spot mite infestation from 10 feet away. Check undersides of leaves for salt/pepper look, fine webbing. Then get to work right away.

COOL OFF MATING MITES with a water wand, washing underneath the leaves with a forceful water spray. Needs to be repeated every four to five days to break up reproductive cycle. The miticide of choice for a large garden is *Avid,* a systemic with knockdown capability and good residual. Use at 1/4 teaspoon per gallon, repeat in four to five days to catch a newly-hatched generation. With good coverage, and an occasional washing, mites are licked for a month to six weeks. Rambler routine: water wash first, buffer the spray solution with *Indicate-5* or *Surfking Plus*, add *Avid* and three drops of *Stirrup-M*, and spray up through the bush. Spray other mite hosts as well. *Stirrup-M* is a "sex perfume" for mites, attracting them to the miticide and a timely end.

WARM TEMPERATURES work for the rosarian when trying to use the newly-introduced fungicide *Rose Defense*. This oil product resists emulsifying in water unless it is warmed first and works even better if the spray solution is warm. Another trick: swirl the mixture in a plastic container, don't shake. A one-gallon plastic milk jug (with top) is ideal for blending *Rose Defense* as well as other spray materials.

AIR CONDITION rosebeds with a cooling, water-saving, soil-conditioning mulch this time of year… if you haven't done so already. You'll spend fewer hours in the hot sun pulling weeds and more time enjoying better roses. Lots of choices are cheap and available: ground bark, pine needles, compost, leaves and mixtures of all of these. Use liberally, replace nitrogen used in the decomposition process with a light broadcast of any lawn fertilizer. No need to pull back mulch when feeding roses, broadcast on top or pour though, just like water through coffee grounds. Mulches add to, not rob soil.

MY FARM STORE has a new item, a "gimme cap" that says SOIL MAN, with the name Family Farm Supply in small letters underneath. The proprietor is a jolly guy who stocks, sells and orders all sorts of stuff for soils, every kind of organic meal, mix and conditioner that soils and growers like. If you are a serious grower who wants to have happy soil and better roses at less cost, find your own "soil man" and get to know his products.

SPRAYING is a summertime chore that gets worse as the season swelters on. But with the right equipment, matched to the task, the job is more likely to get done the right way. July is a good time to buy or upgrade, there's a lot of summer ahead.

UPGRADE TO A SYSTEM, such as *Spray Systems,* with interchangeable parts. Start with a good control (looks like a paint spray gun), add a 24- to 30-inch wand and an adjustable or fixed nozzle for your particular application. The Rambler likes a 30-inch wand curved on the end with a *Tee-Jet 8004* nozzle. This combination puts out a flat, fan-shaped spray that covers 24-30 inches of rosebush at a pass. *Tee-Jet* has an assortment of nozzles from adjustable, to cone shape or flat, coarse or fine spray. Check out a spray equipment dealer or exterminator supply store for *Spray Systems* parts. Another good source is RGL Sales, advertisers in these pages, distributors for *Spot Shot* sprayers. RGL has a complete parts list and will ship via UPS.

KEEP ANY SPRAYER CLEAN by running a weak vinegar solution through it, then flushing with clear water. Get rid of old spray (safely). Partially-clogged sprayers are neither effective nor fun to use. Use the vinegar purge every second or third use, flush with water EVERY time. The Rambler has a *Spot Shot* that hasn't failed or clogged in 10 years and a *Hudson* pump-up that is even older than that… just by taking good care of them.

ENJOY SUMMER… and good roses, too.

FOR EVERY ROSE PROBLEM there's a solution… even if it's learning to live with it. Hope that you'll live and learn with these rose tips.

TOO MANY ROSES, TOO LITTLE SPACE… a common problem for those of us who plant "just a few more." You'll live to regret it. An example: the Rambler planted 20 miniatures in a circular bed, part of the park garden the Greenville Rose Society sponsors. The idea was to produce a mass of color in the landscape. The first couple of years the plan worked fine — the bushes were kept pruned and groomed, and the individual varieties had distinction. Then the Rambler began to "shear" the minis rather than prune. Lots of growth and lots of flowers, but the bushes grew together making it almost impossible to cut spent blooms. A real briar patch, and a protected haven for spider mites. Nearly impossible to spray properly. Then, to water "more evenly," a porous hose (*Moisture Master*) was woven between the bushes, creating a high-humidity incubation chamber for blackspot. Between the mites and the blackspot, the minis soon had no leaves at all.

DON'T DESPAIR… help arrived with severe grooming, doubling the frequency of the spray program and sunshine throughout the planting. The turnaround took just three weeks, and the bed looks better than ever, like a calico quilt in a green field. No more mites, blackspot or scratched legs. Lesson learned.

TIME TO SPRINT… get some available iron into the soil to green-up the leaves. Fortified Tea with iron will do the job, but for those growers who prefer a more antiseptic (and less smelly) solution, use a chelated iron in water. A favorite of rosarians is a chelated form known for years as *Sequestrene 330*, now sold as *SPRINT 330*, a product of Ciba-Geigy. Chelated iron is more available to the plant, something a smart grower looks for on any nutrients list claiming to have trace elements. Soil pH can be substantially off and the chelated form will still work. Healthy green leaves, better blooms.

TIMED RELEASE FERTILIZER is not incompatible with a mostly-organic feeding program. A good grower enjoys both. The organics prepare the soil, the timed release fertilizer delivers a steady supply of nitrogen and other nutrients in a well-balanced diet… less work, too. Broadcast on top of the mulch, every time water passes through just a little bit of food is picked up, just like water through coffee grounds. There are some great mixtures available now, with and without trace elements, longer or shorter term. Buy a big bag at your farm supply or nursery supply store for more economy. Store in a dry, convenient location. You'll find all sorts of applications in containers, planting mixes, new plantings and transplants.

FRESH MANURE is still one of the Rambler's favorite soil conditioners/mulches. If there's plenty of water available (and used), there's no danger of burn. The "well-rotted" admonition just doesn't hold true. Rotted is good, but let the decomposition process go on in and on your rosebeds. In combination with shavings, straw, chips or whatever, it's the best treatment your soil can get.

COMPATIBILITY OF SPRAY MATERIALS continues to concern rosarians, and properly so. Do you really need to combine everything into one witch's brew? Doubtful. Most products work better alone, but will still do the job safely when combined. *Orthenex* is a good example: a combination of *Funginex, Orthene* and *Vendex. Triforine* and *Manzate* work well together, and even *Rubigan* can be added to the mix. But the Rambler also notes that *Rubigan* (or *Systhane*) is more effective when used alone in a buffered solution. And *Avid* is much more effective when used alone, or with just a few drops of *Stirrup-M*. It's OK to combine most materials for convenience, but you may be losing something in the process. Proceed cautiously, your roses will appreciate your concern.

WITH ROSES, it's not the hours you put in, it's what you put into the hours. Here are some tips on how to put in fewer work hours and enjoy more fun hours.

CORN EAR WORMS begin drilling small holes in choice buds this time of year, but they can be headed off before the drilling starts. Alert rosarians can squash the tiny, cream-colored eggs laid in the seams of the sepals. Or, destroy the moth that lays the eggs with a bug zapper, the Rambler's name for the luminous lamp, electric grid cage. Small gray moths emerge from the soil to lay the eggs, get them on the way to the buds. Hang the zapper about 8 feet off the ground, away from the rosebeds. Depending on the wattage of the lamp(s), a zapper will protect a wide area. Usually on sale in the fall, a zapper is a good investment to fry flying bugs.

INSECTICIDE of choice for bud worms is *Mavrik*, long lasting and effective. But many rosarians are respiratory-sensitive to this product, even when using a mask. If you elect to spray, read and follow label instructions carefully and you'll be all right.

KEEP THE LEAVES, the best winterizer for roses. Roses that go into fall in a healthy condition are far less likely to suffer in the winter, regardless of winter protection method. Now is not the time to ease up on fungicide protection; stay on a regular program until dormancy sets in.

SOME NEW ROSE JARGON you'll be hearing more frequently uses the phrases "multi-site" and "single-site" fungicides. It's important you know how they work… actually very simple. A "multi-site" fungicide is a surface protectant which does not enter the leaf itself, the active ingredient remains on the surface. Examples are *Manzate 200, Fore, Fungi-Gard, Daconil*, etc. These fungicides attack fungus (inhibit growth) in more than one way. "Single-site" fungicides like *Triforine, Cleary's 3336, Rubigan, Immunex* etc. enter the leaf and act against one site (or function) in the fungus. The locally systemic fungicides do not translocate to new growth, but are effective in treated tissue.

BEST OF BOTH WORLDS is a combination of "multi-site" and "single-site" fungicides, such as *Fungi-Gard* and *Funginex*, or *Fore* and *Cleary's*. One works on the leaf, the other works in the leaf. And, by switching off products from time to time, resistance to the fungal action is avoided. A good consideration when selecting a fungicide spray program.

A PROMISING ADDITION to long-interval fungus control is *Banner-Maxx*, labeled for roses and generally available. Used in a combination program, 14- to 21-day spray intervals are practical for blackspot. *Immunex* is a garden-shop version of *Banner-Maxx*. This product is legal for roses and safe to use. The Rambler is now trying it in combination with *Manzate 200* and so far the results have been good. But powdery mildew season is coming up this month so we'll see how it stands this pressure.

TRIFORINE is going off the market, but *Funginex* version will still be available, according to industry sources. This will cost more, but is still a good single-site choice for smaller gardens.

COMPOST PILES interest the Rambler, always looking for new and better ways to recycle nature's produce. The Rambler accumulated an excess of leaves, green stuff, old turf and miscellaneous clay soil and split the result into two comparison piles. Both piles had a shot of 13-13-13 pelletized fertilizer and some alfalfa meal. Added 80 pounds of gypsum (Calcium Sulfate) to one pile, skipped the other. Each pile had about three yards by volume. The gypsum-treated pile performed substantially better and is ready for use as of this writing. The untreated pile has at least two months to go. Tilling, water and overall mix was the same for both piles. Gypsum made a difference. The product is now being worked into a new bed for miniatures with great results. Try some of your garden roughage this fall.

ENOUGH ODDS 'N ENDS for now. Drop the Rambler a line if you want to chat about roses. No Website for now… I turn off my computer at the office.

ROSY SAYING: "Giving advice is one thing… following it is another." That's the Rambler's dilemma, so we'll chat about some shortcomings this month.

EASY TO FORGET that powdery mildew comes in when nights are cool and days are warm… and that spores are multiplying before we see the gray-powder evidence. Control has to start well ahead of mildew season, preventing and controlling infection. The Rambler forgot this important point in one garden area last spring (not seeing any mildew) and the damage can still be seen in that garden today. Mildew was eventually controlled, but the damage was done. If you haven't already done so, get busy with a systemic product like *Immunex,* a home-garden derivative of *Banner*, a reliable fungicide used by pros for many years. *Banner-Maxx* is a more concentrated form available to serious gardeners. The initial investment in a quart is costly, but more economical in the long run than *Triforine*. Good for blackspot, too, when used properly. Check the Rambler's September column for more detailed information.

TIME TO SLOW DOWN rose growth in October for most parts of the country. Roses need to go through the natural process of getting ready for winter as hours of sunlight shorten and temperatures drop. Roses want to mature, make rose hips and store nutrients in the canes and roots. Rosarians want "just a few more blooms." Trimming and feeding tell the plant that it is time to grow. A slowdown period gives roses and woody shrubs time to manufacture the natural antifreeze that protects the cells… fluids with reduced capability of expanding when frozen. The Rambler's enthusiastic over-application of fertilizer in two beds late last September resulted in severe winter damage and weakened plants as compared to nearby beds that went to sleep naturally. It's still best to work with nature.

MINIATURE ROSES IN CONTAINERS should be on your program next season. Clay pots or heavy, large plastic pots can support rainbows of colors and roses even in very hot climates. And you'll learn a lot about roses in the process because everything you do to container-grown is controlled, immediate and observable. Need to green up the leaves? Just a pinch of chelated iron in solution brings results. Epsom salts encourage leaves; trace elements enhance blooms color; a bloom-blend formula brings on stems and flowers; gypsum promotes drainage and flushes salts. And if the grower makes a mistake, container minis recover more rapidly. The point is that an observant rosarian can learn through experience and translate the activity for roses in conventional beds. The only downside is the daily or every-other-day watering requirement. Tiny hair roots can't be allowed to dry out. A good potting mix that retains water is important, but regular support by the grower is essential. The Rambler has now rigged up a drip water system for the containers and barrels on the patio-like driveway and it works very well. It takes a while to balance the requirements of a barrel vs. 15-inch pot, but drip is reliable and trouble-free when completed.

ALL OF THE RAMBLER'S MINIS grow up in containers before setting out in beds. The object is to develop good root systems as quickly as possible. Soil warms up quickly in 1-gallon black plastic pots, and the roots thrive. Just six or eight weeks in a container has a small mini plant ready to compete in a rosebed or moved up to a larger permanent planter. Pots on a deck or a driveway absorb reflected heat and grow at a near-greenhouse rate. Also it's wise to "quarantine" new minis for spider mites before joining the general population. Saves lots of work later.

EASY ROSEBED CONSTRUCTION next month… with just enough work to keep you warm and limber in late fall gardening. Will chat with you then.

NO ONE can build a rosebed by turning it over in his mind. Now's the time to turn some soil and use the leaves harvested in the paragraphs to follow.

FREEZE/THAW will do much of the work for you this winter, a mechanical as well as a chemical process. Loosen the bed you want to improve with a spading fork and pile on lots of organic materials and leaves. As moisture freezes and expands, tissues break down in the same way as decomposition in the summer. Winter action reduces and blends the organic matter and soil into the "loam" that most rosarians like. A little extra work with the fork speeds the process. Nature has been building soil this way for a long, long time.

WINTER is a good time to adjust the pH of the soil as well with application of agricultural lime (if needed). Top application is not as effective as lime is relatively insoluble. The process is a RE-ACTIVE one in contact with soil crumbs. Lime, in the presence of hydrogen ions (the indicator for pH), reacts with those ions to form water. By reducing the hydrogen ions the pH goes up. It's a fairly slow process.

GET OUT THE SPADING FORK if a rosebed needing iron can't be tilled or spaded. Use the fork to open up holes to take the lime (the Rambler likes pelletized dolomite lime). Lightly scratch soil back, let nature and chemistry work. To STAY in balance (about 6.5) a good rule of thumb is to add a pound of dolomite lime for every pound of nitrogen used during the season. Example: A 5-10-5 ammonium sulfate fertilizer, 50 pound bag, contains 2.5 pounds of nitrogen. Use 2.5 pounds of lime for the same area. And always TEST before adjusting. For NEW beds in heavy clay soils, work in about 25 pounds of lime per 100 square feet of bed. And let it work all winter.

SOME BROWN, SOME GREEN keeps the pile hot and clean. Referring, of course, to composting the harvest of leaves about to descend on us. Nature has been storing up all sorts of nutrients for us all season… a bounty that shouldn't be wasted. Leaves are the basis of nature's recycling effort that keeps soils alive and working. It's a simple process… don't worry about the nitrogen-carbon ratios. Just pile up a mixture of leaves and yard stuff, moisten and turn so that air is readily available. Bits and pieces of green material act as starters, sift on some soil for extra working organisms. Cottonseed meal speeds things up, or add some manure. By spring you'll have rich compost ready to go to work.

WINTER PROTECTION WITH LEAVES is a sort of composting process also. Rosebeds covered with leaves or cages with leaves are small-scale composters. Most of these insulating materials can be worked into the beds next spring, greatly reduced in volume and partially broken down. Other soil amendments like gypsum and *Perlite* can be added at the same time, gradually working all winter.

ORGANIC ENTHUSIASTS with limited space break down leaves in plastic bags, adding a bit of fertilizer to a bagful of leaves and securing the top. The Rambler's leaves must be extra vigorous as they usually eat some holes in the bags by spring, but a heavier mil bag probably solves this. Noting how nature breaks things down, fish meal stored in a plastic trash can will eat tiny pinholes through the sides in just a few months, even with a tight lid. Fish meal needs to be in the ground, not in a can.

LOOKING AHEAD TO 1998, explore some new types of roses for full-garden fun. As Ralph Moore puts it, "There's a world of beauty out there if we don't wear blinders." Join me in '98… have a Happy One.

Howard Walters, 1998.

WARNING: Rose catalogs may cause backaches, according to the Surgeon General. But the Rambler has some prescriptions for rose pain that beat any Rx from the drugstore. Here are some trial samples…

FAIL TO PLAN… plan to fail. As in poor selection of rosebed location. Powdery mildew will be all over roses jammed into a corner with poor air circulation. Or roses on a fence or arbor that are hard to spray. These spots, in turn, become breeding grounds for spores of every description, furnishing fresh and lively infection borne by the breeze. And stay away from locations where leaves stay wet for long periods each morning. Blackspot thrives in these conditions, and even the best spray program has a hard time keeping up.

GET A SPRAY PROGRAM GOING and stay with it, a realistic schedule for your conditions. Stretched-out spray intervals leave too much to chance… and chances are you will be fighting to get the bushes clean again. Think through and plan for alternative fungicides in '98… *Funginex* one week, *Manzate* or *Daconil* the next week. Keep the spores guessing.

DENSE ROSE PLANTINGS in front of a wall or fence are an invitation for spider mites, a sort of warm incubator ready to erupt. The Rambler has made this mistake several times, wanting to achieve a massed color effect with profusely blooming roses like 'Red Flush' or 'Playgirl'. From these safe havens, the Generals of the Mite Armies sent out raiding parties all season. The best defense is to spread out and open up for better spray coverage (away from the wall). You'll save lots of rose leaves and work later in the season.

ROOT INTERFERENCE just can't be ignored, and a grower can't feed the problem away. When roots from trees and shrubs invade a rosebed, more food just means more roots, and the roses won't get their fair share. Extra food and foliar supplements postpone the inevitable (barrier systems, moving the roses or cutting the trees), but won't fix the problem. A rose fact: trees and roses don't mix well. Plan ahead.

LET WINTER WORK… work some gypsum (calcium sulfate) into tight soils. Get some gypsum on the ground now and let it freeze/thaw and water percolation help the action. Gypsum broadcast at 25 pounds per 100 square feet will open up clay and alkaline soils. And work it in mechanically with a spading fork whenever this is practical. It's a good additive for new or rebuilt beds also. Won't change the pH, can't burn, opens up the tightest soil. Container plants benefit as well. About 1/3 cup for a 12- to 15-inch container, broadcast on top. The result is like pulling the cork out of a bottle.

LEARN AS YOU GO… Take a good look at HOW and WHY your roses are coping with winter. Then you'll know how to respond. Pay particular attention to the amount of good wood on some bushes and a total loss on others. Was protection a little better in some cases? Less wind, more moisture, insulation able to breathe, more gradual dormancy… all could be factors in survival. Make it a practice to observe, and then put this new understanding to work. Rosarians just can't shut down for the winter.

GOT MANURE?… even in the winter. This is a good time to broadcast some manure on top of the mulch, letting both of these soil conditioners go to work. Something like composting in place. Premature growth will not result, the process sets up the feeding table for spring. And the Rambler has long followed a practice of a light broadcasting of pelletized fertilizer on top of the mulch in January, letting winter rains and snow carry some nitrogen to where the work is being done on the leaves/humus crumbs et al. This in-place compost is the best ever. The soil microorganisms really go to work in the spring when the soil warms up. AS you may have guessed, the Rambler has never met a product of nature he didn't like.

THINK POSITIVE for a short winter, long spring. Have a Rosy '98.

NO ONE can build a rosebed by turning it over in his mind. Give your rosebeds or plantings some good turns with some of these ideas...

GET A GOOD ROSEBED LOOK this season... there are lots of methods and materials available to hobbyist rosarians. While beds are a matter of taste, budget, terrain, landscape theme and many other considerations, well-planned beds produce better roses.

THERE'S A LONG LIST of materials for rosebed construction. Hobby-handy materials include concrete curbing, concrete blocks, treated lumber, landscape timbers, railroad ties, steel edging, plastic edging... and even the old-fashioned way, nothing at all. Anything to build up the planting area for better drainage and control.

THE MULCHED-NATURAL LOOK is popular with the Rambler, or a combination of mulch and wood. Beds can be build up 10-12 inches above the lawn level and made attractive and practical by contouring the edges off gradually with plenty of thick mulch. Stabilize the edge (and keep the grass out) with steel edging like *Ryerson* or linked plastic sections. Or a defining edge can be made with short sections of landscape timbers set at lawn level, making a grass barrier as well as a foot for the lawnmower wheel. A natural look is a little more of a maintenance problem, but has lots of practical applications that you can do yourself.

LANDSCAPE TIMBERS AND/OR TREATED LUMBER are easy to use, readily available and cheap. Timbers also last a long time, have almost unlimited flexibility and can be formed into all sorts of shapes with just a little chainsaw skill. The Rambler builds up two timbers high, anchoring the bottom timber with reinforcing bar driven into the ground through drilled holes. Then nail the top timber with long spikes after drilling pilot holes. Timbers can also be cut into 8-10 inch lengths and tampered into the soil vertically to make a decorative edge. Or use a combination of horizontal timbers broken up with short lengths on edge to form curves or turn corners. Has a very finished, natural look.

CINDER BLOCKS with holes are also easy for most hobbyists to use. Hands-and-knees laying (follow a string) is slow but sure, no footing required, no mortar. These can also be stained with diluted latex stain, brushed on liberally, leaving behind a soft, pigment patina. For an added trim, fill the open block spaces with good soil and plant portulaca or alyssum. Spring bulbs are nice, too.

BRICKS also make a good edging and can be laid formally or informally, depending on the skill of the gardener. For a formal wall-edge, pour a shallow footing or the bricks will eventually sag, sink and crack. An informal treatment uses bricks in a "soldier course," that is bricks set vertically and tamped into a soft concrete footing. Use a 3/8-inch board between the bricks as a spacer while laying to allow great drainage and air movement. The soil and mulch hold very well, and the edge takes on a weathered look in no time. A soldier course can follow contours, edge along a walk, keep soil from washing... all sorts of good applications.

CONTINUOUS POUR CURBING is for the high-budget grower, but an excellent garden investment. A continuous pour machine lays down cement like toothpaste, forming an edge as well as a foot. Home improvement contractors in major areas are promoting this technique, and it's beautiful. Color can be added to the concrete and you can make your own designs. Maybe the Easy-Rent outfits will catch on to this application and make the machine available to weekend garden athletes.

CHECK UPSCALE NURSERIES for some of the new pre-cut lumber pieces that go together like a puzzle. It's astonishing the shapes and looks that can be created. There's even a snail-shape, elevated mini bed that can be erected by an all-thumbs gardener.

YOU'RE ONLY LIMITED by your imagination. February is a great month to get on your work gloves.

IF YOU are calling roses by another name, you're probably pruning or planting or both. Read on for some tips on how to make rose chores lighter and springtime more welcome.

BAD ROSE BACKS like hands-and-knees planting, much less strain than bending over. A dirty-kneed rosarian is a good rosarian. Find a small shovel with a short handle, something like the old army foxhole tool. If the bed has been well prepared, it's easy to scoop out a hole and rebuild a cone to support the roots and shank. Then backfill and begin to run water slowly into the hole; add more soil, more water. No need to tamp or pack.

COVER UP YOUR WORK. Always hill up a newly planted rose with a protective cone of insulating soil and mulch until just the tips of the canes stick out. Not just a little material, a real mound. Moisture conservation is important, not sunshine. Moisture in the canes is supported by new root hairs; hilling keeps canes from drying out until the roots can deliver. And keep cone and soil very moist as growth begins.

A NONTRADITIONAL PLANTING TECHNIQUE is worth considering. Use on potted roses only, and with a little rose sense. Contrary to traditional wisdom, a timed-release fertilizer can be used when planting a well-developed potted rose. Roses which have been confined to post for a month or so have developed a fairly good system of new roots. The rosarian wants these roots to expand into the planting bed as soon as possible. The roots can be lured with some strategically-placed, time-release rose food like *Osmocote*... a sort of carrot in front of the horse.

CONCENTRATION AND LOCATION ARE IMPORTANT. Dig the hole to the right depth and try the rose (still in the pot) for fit. Then mix one ounce of *Osmocote* with some soil an inch or so below the root level. Carefully slit the plastic pot with a sharp knife and cut out the bottom. Gently position the root ball in the hole (there should be all sorts of white feeder roots on the outside). Backfill with an inch or so of soil and add another ounce of *Osmocote* on top of this band, away from the roots. Add some more soil and repeat the slow-release application. Finish backfilling with bedding mix and flood with lots of water. Hill up slightly and keep moist. The rose will nev-

er know it has been transplanted and will get off to a great start. But use NO MORE than 3-4 ounces of timed-release per well-started bush. The food releases slowly and will not burn. You'll see new top growth throughout the early season, knowing that the roots are growing also.

WANT MORE BASALS? Safely available with a one-two punch using *Epsom Salts* (Magnesium Sulfate) and a readily available source of Nitrate-form nitrogen. Works at pruning time as well as after the initial blooming cycle. Magnesium, so essential in the rose tissue process, leaches readily, as does Nitrogen. Kick off the process with 1/3 cup of *Epsom Salts* per established bush, followed every-other week with applications of a soluble high Nitrate. Two feedings should do it. Get the energy into the root zone with plenty of water for good results.

WATER, not fertilizer, is what makes roses grow. The best plant food won't do a bit of good until it is in solution and in the root zone of the plant. Pelletized fertilizers are great if there is a regular, ample supply of water to dissolve the material and carry the nutrients to the roots. Savvy rosarians also know that deep-soaking before using any rose food (dry or liquid) also speeds up the process.

SPRING SEARCH. FIND A FEED STORE, the real thing that smells like alfalfa and fresh pasture... and has a couple of cats napping on the feed sacks. This is the place to get fish meal and alfalfa meal and all of the other good organic stuff that roses like. The Rambler's feed store also sells rabbits, deserving a five-star organic rating.

IF YOU WANT TO BE QUOTED, say something you shouldn't say. But you can quote the Rambler on these springtime approaches which have been garden-tested.

FISH MEAL is the right stuff for rosarians who want to enjoy roses the natural way. It's the Rambler's favorite springtime starter, feeding the soil that supports the roses. To try a fish diet, locate a friendly feed store, the kind that has sacks full of organic feeds and meals. If the feed store doesn't have any fish meal on hand (they seldom do, it smells after a while), they can order it from their supplier in 50-pound bags. Be careful when transporting to the garden, even a small leak in the bag will leave a residual smell. Then use a bulb digger or similar tool and lift three cones of soil 6 inches deep and a foot or so away from the shank. Pour a scant cup in each hole, cover with soil and listen to the roots being called to the dinner table.

FISH GROWS ROOTS which in turn support greener leaves, better growth and overall better bloom. Use in early spring and again in late summer. Years from now when these fish-fed bushes are dug, you'll see that masses of feeder roots have "found" the fish meal, supporting the bush in great style. The cone method of application contains odor, releases nutrients slowly and is easy to apply. And you can make up your own "root" mix: equal parts of fish meal, alfalfa meal and cottonseed meal. For convenience, *Mills Magic Mix®* does the same thing. Add fish to your diet, NOW.

DIG AND DIVIDE miniature bushes that have grown woody and unproductive… usually getting about three bushes for the price of one. There's still time in most growing areas in April, but the more dormant the better. Simply dig up with the root ball, then gently pull, twist and otherwise break away parts with roots and some good top growth. Some clumps may need some persuasion with pruners. Trim off any old, woody growth and replant like a new bush. Most of these divided portions are as large as the "mother" bushes at the end of the season.

Rx FOR GALLS… Some surgical urgency occurs this time of year during pruning and cleanup; to trim galls or to dig the whole plant. The Rambler subscribes to the surgical school, preferring to trim galls, at least in the early stages. With a very sharp knife, cut away galls on the shank/bud union and then treat with *Lysol* or *Clorox*. Most rosarians have galls they don't even know about and have had for a long time. It's the Rambler's observation that galls on the shank or bud union respond best to cutting and sunshine; let air and sunshine do most of the work. Don't worry too much about the infection (it's not going to spread); nature and a well-drained soil are probably the best remedies. If it's too bad, dig it out and try something new.

SLOW-RELEASE FERTILIZERS keep hungry roses satisfied. And we have a wider selection than ever available to hobby gardeners. Thanks to Scotts (the really big player in fertilizers these days) *Osmocote Timed Release Fertilizer* is available in formulations ideal for rose growers. Called *Osmocote Plus*, formulations include 15-11-13 (three to four months), 16-8-12 (eight to nine months), and 15-9-11 (12-14 months). All have the major trace elements for roses. Timed release fertilizers feed slowly and evenly as a steady diet, not feast or famine. And they can be used in conjunction with organics, the soil feeders. Check availability at a nursery supply company in your area.

ROSE CLIPS… CLEAN UP rose pruners with a light spray of WD-40 and a pot cleaning pad. Takes off sap and stain, makes blades cut cleaner… SPRAYERS need to be cleaned, too. Run a weak white vinegar solution through the system to pick up spray residue. Flush well with clear water. Household ammonia solutions also pick up oily, gummy residues… *Banner Maxx* is probably the fungicide of choice when your *Triforine* supply runs out. Good for 14-21 days, *Banner Maxx* is convenient, safe, effective, registered for roses and as economical as *Triforine*. You'll enjoy (??) spraying every two to three weeks. More time for roses.

ENJOY a very rosy springtime.

ROSARIANS are prone to applying pounds of cure, when just a little prevention will do the job. That's the Integrated Plant Management theme this month... making rose growing more fun and rewarding.

INTEGRATED PLANT MANAGEMENT focuses on the factors which contribute to damage by disease or insects rather than on the problem itself. Think of IPM as a triangle with three major factors always present: HOST (plant), PATHO-GEN (disease or insect) and ENVIRONMENT (growing conditions). These factors are futher influenced by TIME. Let's look at some examples.

HOST... Some roses are more disease-resistant than others. Many are mildew-prone, others blackspot easily. If these diseases are common in your area, select resistant varieties or be prepared to take stronger measures against disease. And some roses are gracious insect hosts also. Spider mites like certain varieties, particularly dense-growing miniatures with tiny leaves. Thrips like light-colored, fragrant blooms; darker blooms attract less and show less damage. Unless the rosarian wants to live with some damage or wage an aggressive war against thrips, select varieties that are more tolerant.

PATHOGEN... The fungus disease or insect needs to be clearly identified and then controlled by a variety of specific means. Alternating spray materials or combining single-site and multi-site fungicides reduces the chance of resistance. A surface-protective material like *Maneb* or *Daconil* inhibits leaf penetration. *Triforine* or *Banner* are systemic and block pathogen reproduction in the leaf. Contact fungicides and systemic fungicides work together very well, focused on the pathogen with less opportunity for resistance. Insects build up resistance, too. As in the case of spider mites. Alternate spray materials specific for the insect or manage with water-washing to reduce spider mite populations. And LESS use of broad-spectrum insecticides spares mite predators which act as a control. Example: less *Orthene* equates to fewer spider mites.

ENVIRONMENT... Around us all the time and easy to observe. Roses in full sun have less trouble with fungus diseases than roses in partial shade or subject to long periods of wet leaves. Sun and good air circulation inhibit powdery mildew. Damp climates promote blackspot; dry climates with cool nights, warm days are more likely to support mildew. Rosarians have some degree of control over the growing environment. Example: Most lawn irrigation systems spray leaves, keep them wet, resulting in blackspot. Even resistant varieties like 'Bonica' can be covered with blackspot when grown in partial shade. Reason: the leaves stay wet longer because of morning dew. Location is important in insect control, too. Miniatures planted next to a foundation are perfect breeding grounds for spider mites. Any location with a warm incubator effect. Or planting otherwise-resistant roses near fungus hosts like ramblers or in an area that is hard to spray.

TIME... Time impacts ALL of the IPM factors. A timely spray schedule is absolutely essential. Given time, spores will reproduce... as will spider mites. Understand the time that it takes in your environment to reproduce spores or insects. Control BEFORE spores emerge, then continue on a timely basis. Weeks of warm, humid weather support blackspot; dry spells slow down the process. Hot, dry weather brings on spider mites, which can reproduce in three to five days. Water-wash more frequently then. The time factor is important to host, pathogen and environment.

CONSIDER ALL OF THE PARTS of the plant management equation. Ignore one factor and you'll have to work harder elsewhere to overcome the results. That's the whole theme of INTEGRATED. Consider and work with all of the parts of the puzzle to produces roses that satisfy you.

IPM isn't just easy... it's a necessity.

HAPPINESS lies in your own back yard... but it is often hidden by the crabgrass. With these rosy tips, your roses will be MUCH taller than the crabgrass.

WATER is the primary ingredient in any rose program, copious amounts applied frequently before any sign of plant stress. Nothing happens in the soil or in the plant without water. Deep soakings, regularly scheduled, keep plants at maximum productivity. It's easy to see the effects on all kinds of plants when rainfall is abundant... as in this spring in the southwest with El Nino. As long as there is adequate drainage, the more water the better. One of the "secrets" of exhibitors is to deep hand-water exhibition varieties every day for two weeks before a show, all in addition to the regular watering program. The winners vow that water beats any of the last-minute exotic fertilizers. Roses are thirsty; serve up the water.

NAGGING QUESTION to the Rambler: "Where do I get that stuff you talk about?" It is a problem for serious rosarians, particularly those growers in larger cities. Developing sources for spray materials, equipment and fertilizers (particularly organic) is as important as variety selection and takes some time and trouble. Network fellow rosarians; search out nontraditional sources like nursery and greenhouse supplies, feed stores, specialty product firms and the classified ads in *American Rose*. Some larger societies even set up their own distribution systems, buying in quantity and passing along good stuff and savings to members. As a start, find a feed store, then find out where growers and greenhouse people are getting their supplies. Larger packages, greater savings. And many suppliers can be induced to sell to "the Rose Society." When you find a supporter, lead other rosarians to him. Both of you will feel good.

THE WAR OF THE BEETLES is a required subject in June... time for a recap of the battle plans for afflicted areas. If Japanese Beetles haven't turned your garden into a ravaged war zone yet, be thankful. Otherwise, pick 'em off, try some traps AWAY from your garden, or leave some spent blooms on the roses and let them eat away. These are non-aggressive approaches. Or try spraying with *Margosan-O* in advance of the attack (Neem concentrate), or *Sevin Liquid* for quick knockdown. *Sevin* leaves an unsightly residue and has to be used three times a week. Spraying only the tops of the bushes may spare some of the beneficial insects (and an onset of spider mites). *Sevin Dust (10%)* is also a good control, used frequently and carefully. The *Dustin-Mizer*, a nifty hand-crank applicator, lays down a fine dust quickly and easily. Check out the *Gardens Alive* or *Nitron* catalogs for this dandy tool and lots of other organic stuff. Good Luck!

SPIDER MITES are already on the make and will erupt in a severe infestation if some alert, preventive steps are not taken. Keep a sharp eye out for gray-green foliage at the bottom of the bushes. Infested leaves quickly lose color and drop off. Get busy at the very FIRST signs. Check undersides of leaves for tiny specks and webs. Wash UNDERNEATH leaves with a strong, fine stream of water, using a water wand (not a water breaker) if you have one. Or devise your own. There are many ingenious ways to fine-spray leaves. If washing with water two-three times a week doesn't do the trick, switch to *Avid,* a specific miticide that has great-knockdown to which mites do not appear to build resistance, unless used repeatedly. Water-wash, spray *Avid*, water-wash again in three-four days. Repeat cycle again in two weeks. That ought to get most gardens through the summer. Good coverage and timely application are important. Get busy.

GROW ROOTS, THEN ROSES is on extended trial by the Rambler this season, comparing bare-root roses planted in containers and grown out for 10-12 weeks before setting in beds with bare-root bushes set directly into prepared beds. Tried on a limited basis last year, it appeared by the end of the season that roses with container-developed root systems outperformed those set in beds. It works fabulously with miniatures, why not big roses? This year 150 roses of the same varieties have been evenly split... 75 in containers and 75 in the beds. We'll see what happens. One good thing has ALREADY happened: container roses moved into shelter before a late cold snap; roses in beds with mulch protection lost 5-6 inches of cane and new growth. Stay tuned.

Enjoy **LOTS** of June roses.

SUMMER RHYME: When the glass is at ninety, a gardener's a fool... Who directs not his efforts to try to stay cool. And here are some cool ideas for summer rosarians.

ROSES LIKE TO STAY COOL in the summertime, just like rosarians. Nature's air conditioner is mulch, an insulating blanket that saves water, controls weeds and adds to the richness of the soil at the same time. Just a few inches of loose organic mulch dramatically reduces soil temperature and moisture evaporation. Most "home-mix" mulches are combinations of wood chips, ground bark, leaves, straw, compost or what heave you. Skeptics say that these organics "leach" nitrogen from the soil, but all it takes is an extra handful of any cheap nitrogen source to release soil-building humus.

CARRY OVER? What if the mulch doesn't break down right away? No problem. Leave it in place, incorporate in winter protection and then add some more next season. Old wives' tales hold that mulches harbor insects and blackspot spores. Only partially true. Insects live in soil and mulch; control with an extra insecticide spray pass. Blackspot spores spread by splashing from green tissue. Ask your roses; they'll want mulch.

WHERE DID THE BLOOMS GO? In many parts of the country rose midge is the culprit this time of year. Blackened tips where a tiny bud should emerge is the evidence left behind. Blind growth will result, no blooms. A good control is granular *Diazinon* broadcast in and around the rosebeds like lawn fertilizer, usually following the first bloom cycles. This gets the soilborne insects at the source. *Diazinon* liquid sprayed on the tops of the bushes and on the ground also helps. But midge season is short, so just two applications should do the trick.

TAKE IT EASY ON INSECTICIDES. Excessive use of *Orthene* (or any other broad-spectrum insecticide) for thrips also kills off the beneficials and rosarians wind up with spider mite infestations that defoliate bushes. When thrips are a real problem, spray just the blooms and buds. For those "special" blooms, mist the buds with a hand-held bottle sprayer, mixing up just a quart of fresh solution each time. There's no need to use an insecticide with each application of fungicide.

Insecticides become addictive — like drugs. Once you're hooked, it's hard to quit. Kick the habit if you can.

SPRAY CONCENTRATION is often an issue. Some growers think that more of a fungicides will clean up blackspot faster. Not true. Same for insecticides. For a persistent problem, increase the frequency of application, or alternate materials. Most blackspot can be safely handled with *Manzate* twice a week, or use a *Funginex/Manzate* combination. Use both at label strength. And it is always a good idea to switch off from time to time with *Funginex, Manzate, Daconil, Cleary's 3336* or *Immunox*. This seems like a real arsenal, but the idea is protection without building up fungus resistance. Insects (particularly spider mites) become resistant, too. Switch rather than fight.

OUT OF *TRIFORINE*? *FUNGINEX* COSTS TOO MUCH? Then you may want to switch to *Banner Maxx* for fungus disease control, particularly if you have a large rose garden. *Banner Maxx* is a very effective control for blackspot and powdery mildew, and, best of all, needs to be applied every two to three weeks rather than weekly. It is a persistent systemic that loses effectiveness very slowly. Used at just 1/3 teaspoon per gallon, most rosarians succeed on a three-week schedule unless fungus conditions are very severe. You must start with a clean garden, then go on a *Banner Maxx* schedule. The initial investment is a bit pricey (over $100 a quart), but a little goes a long way, and it has a long shelf life. If you have a large garden (150 roses or more), *Banner Maxx* is definitely in your future... when your *Triforine* runs out.

SUMMERTIME TONIC: How about some alfalfa tea, fortified with a touch of *Epsom Salts* and trace elements. Refreshing for roses. For a recipe, drop me a note. The greenest leaves your roses will ever enjoy.

IF you occupy a place in the sun, expect a few blisters. Here are some tips for sunny days and fewer blisters in your rose garden...

COMPANION PLANTINGS are in... a point of contention for rose purists. But roses are compatible with other plant materials, increasing opportunities for roses in the landscape. Think "English Garden," colorful and compact plantings of roses, perennials and annuals of varying textures and growth habits. A garden corner is a great place to start; maybe a climber in the back, a floribunda or two, a compact shrub, some day lilies and larger-growing miniatures. How about some bulbs for early season color? The Rambler saw some outstanding examples in Albuquerque a few weeks ago by a gardener-rosarian. Says again that roses make good friends.

BUSH GROWTH and development are important, especially for exhibitors. Healthy, developed bushes produce healthy blooms when you want them. It's common practice for exhibitors to snap off spent blooms during the hot part of the summer rather than cutting to a dormant bud and encouraging new bloom growth. This tends to direct energy to the food-producing leaves resulting in more bush and better roses when cooler weather arrives. It's a little like pinching off buds from newly-planted roses. It takes willpower and patience to do this, but it pays off. The Rambler follows a middle course: snap some and pinch some... but let some blooms develop if you're growing roses in a *hot* zone.

DIVIDED MINIATURES have been discussed in these columns from time to time... the practice of cutting and splitting a large, dormant miniature plant to make three or four new plants ready to take off. Pay attention to the word *dormant*, split only when dormant. You will enjoy the products of your energetic propagation this time of year. The Rambler reworked a bed of 30 large minis that had been in for about four years; cut, sawed and chopped them up to make about 100 good-sized plants. All this was done in February; gave away the surplus. Replanted 20 in the rejuvenated bed, and they are in a full second bloom as this is written in mid-June. Recipients of the freebies are enjoying the same success. Look ahead to next season.

ROSES HAVE TIRED BLOOD? Pale leaves? Restore vigor and color with an iron tonic... with a little *Epsom Salts* on the side. A favorite of rosarians is a chelated form known for years as *Sequestrene 330*, now sold as *Sprint 330*, a product by Ciba-Geigy. It's a micronutrient important to green, healthy leaves. Chelated iron is more available to the plant, something a smart grower looks for on any list of trace elements. Chelated iron delivered to the roots goes to work right away and is not as tied up in the soil chemistry. The word *chelate* comes from the Greek word for claw: chelated iron is held and protected, releasing bits of nutrient... a really neat trick of chemistry. Look for chelated iron on the label. Apply in solution to the soil and enjoy greener leaves. The magnesium in *Epsom Salts* also greens leaves and encourages growth... just an ounce or two in summer works wonders.

SPIDER MITES and dry, hot weather mean a population explosion. Reproduction increases with temperature for a major infestation in just a couple of days. Compound a few more days and no leaves at all. Cool off the mating mites with a water wand, washing underneath the leaves with a fine water spray. This washing process has to be repeated every four to five days during periods of severe mite pressure and is OK for small gardens. The miticide of choice for larger gardens is *Avid*, a translaminar (penetrates leaves) product that has great knockdown capability and good residual, keeping mite populations low. If caught early, most gardens will have mite episodes just two or three times a season.

WASH FIRST, SPRAY SECOND. Use the water wand, then spray *Avid* at 1/4 teaspoon per gallon, repeat in four days. Buffer spray solution with *Indicate-5*, add *Stirrup-M*, a pheromone sex attractant. Just a couple of drops of the pheromone per gallon is all that is needed. Do not combine with other fungicides or insecticides. Spray until leaves "glisten," get good coverage underneath the lower leaves. Repeat the routine as needed and act fast.

WATER... and lots of it... soak, drip, hose end, overhead... whatever. Even wash down the bushes from time to time, your roses will enjoy the summer shower.

SEPT. 1998

THOUGHT FOR THE MONTH:
Some grumble because roses have thorns. I'm thankful that thorns have roses.

SMART ROSARIANS learn from the mistakes of others… you don't have time to make them all yourself. And the Rambler has had plenty of time, this column marking the 28th anniversary of the Rambler in *American Rose*. Even the *thought of the month* has significance, first appearing in September 1970. But enough of the old stuff, here are some observations on growing better roses today.

BLACKSPOT gets our attention this time of year as conditions are just right for the outbreak of disease: warm temperatures, high humidity. Add an irregular spray schedule and the bushes lose their leaves. But it does not have to be this way, there's still time to control the infection, grow some new leaves and enjoy some great roses.

PROTECTIVE vs. REACTIVE SPRAYING… Best results in controlling fungal infections are obtained with a protective/preventive spray program, usually weekly during high stress conditions. If that line of defense has some gaps, go to a reactive program with a combination program of systemic and contact fungicides like *Triforine* and *Manzate* applied at shorter intervals, say twice a week for two to three weeks. Also pull off the infected growth and practice good garden hygiene. You'll be able to go back to a more normal schedule within a month. Increase frequency, not concentration of material.

PROGRAM ROTATION is important to head off disease resistance from continuous use of one systemic material. Program rotation reduces the chance of disease resistance to a given fungicide by introducing a different fungicidal family, i.e. *Triforine, Cleary's 3336, Banner* or *Immunox*. And there are a variety of contact materials, i.e. *Mancozeb, Dithane, Captan, Daconil 2787* or another from the Manzate family. Carefully mixed and matched with systemics, these fungicides are a match for the most virulent spores, provided that you get them on leaves.

COVERAGE IS IMPORTANT, and often overlooked. Use of a spreader-sticker in addition to the built-in surfactant is usually in order. The Rambler still likes *Indicate-5* best, buffering the spray solution and making the water wetter for even leaf coverage. Even has its own pH indicator built in for a slightly acid condition in any water.

Makes spraying easier than ever before.

HIGH STRESS CONDITIONS for blackspot include wet leaves, leaves that remain wet for long periods of time, maybe due to shade or evening overhead watering. The Rambler wondered why blackspot was showing up in some container-grown miniatures while nearby roses on the same routine were clean, then realized the container roses were being watering in the evening with a water breaker on a long wand. Fix: water in the morning before going to work. Another rose section also had some blackspot from an automatic sprinkler system… and no sun until four to five hours later.

SOME *BANNER MAXX* OBSERVATIONS… The Rambler's Environmental Partnership garden in full sun all day every day has stayed free of blackspot when sprayed with *Banner Maxx* at 1/3 teaspoon per gallon every 21 days. A *Manzate*-type contact fungicide was added every-other spraying. During a prolonged rainy period *Manzate 200 DF* was sprayed by itself every two weeks.

SEVERE BLACKSPOT STRESS required *Banner Maxx* every 14 days, again with a contact material every-other spraying. Equally effective was *Triforine* and *Manzate* in combination every week. Also tried *Triforine* one week and *Cleary's 3336* the next week with *Mancozeb* added every other week. This combination did a very good job. The *Mancozeb* was dropped two weeks before showing roses to minimize residue.

OPENING UP THE BUSHES also helped. Trimming out blind and twiggy growth from the center of the bush not only reduced fungus disease and spider mites but also seemed to encourage better low breaks and canes. Routinely cleaning up the center of the bush every time spent blooms were trimmed spread out the chore.

IF YOU MUST MAKE MISTAKES, it will be to your credit to make a new one each time. Here are some repeats by the Rambler (as well as a few positives).

FERTILIZER has to get into solution before it can go to work. Porous soaker hoses do a good job of getting water to rose roots, but don't deliver water through broadcast pelletized fertilizers… especially during period of drought. In really dry weather, do some surface watering as well, either by hand with a water-breaker or by setting the hose. The Rambler noticed a big difference in the growth of a bed with *Dramm* nozzles delivering water on the surface compared to beds with soakers.

SUNSHINE is often taken for granted, but lack of sun means progressive decline in growth. Early spring is misleading; the trees are not in full leaf and the bed THOUGHT to be getting plenty of sun slows down by midsummer. The Rambler tried more fertilizer, but it didn't do much good. The roses just got taller… and weaker. Some aggressive tree roots didn't help either. That rosebed has to be moved next year.

COMPOST PILES need help from time to time, too. Compost bins with old sod, leaves, grass clippings and what-have-you slowed down this year… because the Rambler forgot to add gypsum and cottonseed meal to speed up the process. After the additives and a couple of good turns, the piles began to heat up again.

WATER-WANDS to knock off spider mites DO work, and skipping this step puts a heavier load on the miticides to get control. One bed of big, bushy miniatures close to the water source had a water-wand treatment every week during the early part of the summer… and no mite damage. Other mini beds that required hose-pulling didn't get the water benefit and had mite problems off and on all summer. A good wand is a good investment… if you use it.

FUNGICIDE SPRAY SCHEDULES have to be followed… no cheating. It's easy to skip a week or so and not see any immediate consequences, but the spores are multiplying and sooner or later the black spots will appear. Stretching a schedule means more work to get control later on. And if you do have to play catch-up, increase the frequency rather than the strength of fungicides. Keep a calendar; follow it.

POSITIVE RESULTS always make rosarians feel good, and that's the bottom-line experience again this year… feeding the soil with organics early-on, following up with faster-acting nutrient sources. The Rambler believes in feeding the SOIL (and the millions of soil organisms), then the bushes which in turn produce leaves, followed by roses. Organics worked into the soil at pruning time sets up the rose dinner plate for the entire season. Get to know your feed store man or the friend with horses (kept in stalls) and apply the products liberally in the spring. The feed store stuff (alfalfa meal, fish meal, cottonseed meal) and some roughage provides the same kind of organic manure without having to run it through a horse.

SEAWEED EXTRACT added to alfalfa tea or some other liquid tonic adds a punch to leaves and blooms that has to be seen to be believed. Really dramatic. To become a believer, use some extract on container plants and see results in just a few days. The Rambler likes soil application better than foliar for longer lasting results and less chance of burn.

GROW OUT NEW MINIS in 1-gallon containers with soilless mix for good roots, making these juveniles able to compete in regular plantings later on. Grow roots that will grow bushes. And get these plantings out in good sun in just a few days. Partial shade is a good start, but sunshine gets the job done. Just don't forget to water.

OBSERVE… and then take another look to see what's working and what isn't. Sharp-eyed rosarians grow better roses.

FOR EVERY PROBLEM there's a solution… even if it's learning to live with it. Here are some tips on how to live through the winter… with live roses next spring.

TIME TO INSULATE roses and rosarians. The idea of insulation is to maintain a fairly constant temperature, avoiding freeze/thaw situations. Combinations of loose materials do this best, held in place with fences, boughs, cones or what-have-you. Roses, like rosarians, like "thermal blankets." When organics are used as insulators, there's an extra benefit in the spring as they add humus to the soil. And much lighter than hauling soil in and out.

DEEP COLD requires more soil protection, mounded 6-8 inches over the canes, then covered with leaves. Bring in soil rather than taking from between the bushes in the beds. Soil/mulch combinations are great… they breathe better.

ANTIDESICCANT SPRAYS may also help in the winter protection process, particularly with climbers and ramblers. Antidessicant sprays like *Wilt-Pruf* and *Cloud Cover* retain moisture in the canes that is otherwise lost to cold, dry winds and also provide a bit of fungus protection. When bushes drop their leaves, trim up to suit your situation and thoroughly spray the canes before wrapping or covering. Remember that canes are round and the backside needs some coverage, too. More canes are lost to drying out than actual cold; a liquid blanket can make a difference.

BURY FOR THE WINTER… the ultimate protection but the maximum work. Roses received in late fall are much better off buried than potted and moved in and out of protection all winter. It's a natural sort of dormancy, something like the "Minnesota Tip" burying method. Pick a spot where it's easy to dig 18 inches or so and set aside the spoil dirt. Line the dormancy vault with leaves and soil. Tie the tops of the bushes with twine, then into bundles. Tuck the bushes into the vault and cover the mix. And tie a rope on the bundles so you'll know where to dig next spring. Cover area with leaves and wait for spring. Easy.

FEED/COMPOST IN PLACE. Some growers call it winter feeding. Many rosarians in severe as well as milder climates put down an 8-inch layer of leaves in the rosebed, broadcast a cupful of pelletized fertilizer (10-10-10) per 100 square feet, then add some more leaves. By spring the lower layer of leaves has broken down into a rich humus threaded with white mycelium. The fertilizer works on the leaves, not on the soil, breaking down the organic material and setting up the soil for better activity in the spring. Don't disturb the lower layer any more than necessary at pruning time, and you may elect to leave all of the leaves in the bed, broadcasting more fertilizer on top. Advocates of winter feeding report no untimely growth in either the fall or spring when roses are put to bed with this "nightcap."

SAVE AND USE LEAVES. Most winterizing includes leaves in one form or another. Loose, leafy mixtures work best and don't pack. Uncomposted ground leaves can shed water and are stingy on insulating air space; they work best when worked into the soil. Compost in place over the "garden" area, pile in a windrow, fill up a rick… anything to return nature's nutrients to the soil.

OR JUST SAVE LEAVES over the winter to use as the "bulk" in making up artificial manure next spring. The Rambler will share a time-tested Fragrant Formula at the appropriate time next spring.

CHAT WITH YOU AGAIN in '99… Have a Happy, Rosy One!

ROSE WISDOM is rampant this time of year... there's not a thing to be proved in the garden or on the show table. Which contributes to rose stories that get bigger and better with each retelling. Here's some wisdom that lasts all year...

SAP RISES in roses and rosarians at about the same time... the first warm day... and in some parts of the country it won't be long. But this rose season, how about some common rose sense... a nostrum frequently advised in these columns. Nature and roses perform best gradually; crash spring programs usually crash with the first cold snap. Something like the "Sunday Syndrome" in the summertime. Sunday Syndrome is a rose affliction induced by the resident rosarian: roses worn out by pruning, grooming, pulling, feeding, pinching, scratching, watering and fussing (not necessarily in that order).

SPRING SYNDROME takes the form of uncovering, digging, probing, feeding, cutting and drenching with all sorts of stuff before the soil is warm enough to support growth. Roses are rarely hurt by late pruning; many never recover from "first on the block" cutting. Weather decides when roses are going to bloom in the spring. Rosarians can't jump-start the process. Let nature set the pace.

ROSES APPRECIATE a friendly, well-prepared rosebed and respond accordingly. What's a friendly bed? One that's loose and friable and full of organics to encourage roots to spread out and take up nutrients. This in turn supports vigorous growth. Nothing much happens on top if the foundation isn't right. Prepare a rose mix that YOU would like to grow in.

THE OLD RELIABLE FORMULA is the Rambler's recommendation... call for about one-third soil, one-third sand and one-third organics of some kind. Old Reliable works no matter where you live. Don't worry too much about the proportions, but if in doubt, add some more organics. A good soil has a "friendly" feel; you should be able to work your fingers into the settled bed without a trowel.

ORGANICS should be partially broken down, beginning to form humus; animal manures break down rapidly and condition the soil in the process. Compost, manures, ground bark, leaves and combinations of all of these materials work together to keep the bed friendly for roots and microorganisms. Many growers like sphagnum peat, the more fibrous the better. Others like brown peat moss or fine-ground pine bark. Keep in mind that mixtures last longer with particles of different sizes making up soil crumbs. Coarse *Perlite* is a long-lasting soil conditioner that opens up soil so that air and water can pass freely. If the mix is too loose, add some mellow clay that will hold water. Calcined clay (*Kitty Litter*) is a clay sponge that keeps on working year after year. Get the idea? Friable and friendly.

GOURMET ROSEBED mixtures are seasoned with fish meal, alfalfa meal, some gypsum and some bone meal. And probably some dolomite lime in most parts of the country. For a 100 square-foot rosebed, add 15 pounds of fish meal, 20 pounds of alfalfa meal (or pellets), 20 pounds of gypsum (Calcium Sulfate) and 15 pounds of bone meal. Mix the whole thing up and let it settle for a week or so, and it's ready for roses. Manure or cottonseed meal will activate the process, especially with lots of leaves.

WHEN THE GROUND IS WORKABLE, it's time to build/rebuild rosebeds. And many of the organics can compost in place even before the ground is ready. Then get to work with the spading fork, small tiller, shovel, weak mind and strong back. It's what gardening is all about. Well-prepared beds, planting holes, containers and corners pay big rose dividends for years to come.

THIS IS THE TIME for friendly plantings in '99.

ROSE CATALOGS break dormancy for rosarians, whatever the thermometer says. But if you plan to leave some rose footprints in '99, wear some work shoes... it's that time.

CUSTOM PLANTING... a term made up by the Rambler, describes the one-hole-at-a-time approach to planting roses rather than in a prepared "rosebed." Sometimes it's impractical to build a rosebed or you want some roses scattered around to fit the landscape. No problem, just make sure that a one-hole, custom planting doesn't create a bathtub that holds water. Dig out the are bushel-basket size. Get rid of the old soil, maybe on the compost pile. Loosen the soil in the bottom and on the sides, work in some gypsum and organic stuff. Then fill in with a light, well-prepared mix to a level well above the lawn or planting area for better drainage. Raise the custom planting unless you KNOW that the drainage is good. With a rich, friable planting medium, your rose(s) will live happily ever-after.

HANDS-AND-KNEES rose planting is much easier on bad backs (and on roses) than the bend and twist. Dirty-knees rosarians get better results with less work. Get a short shovel, something like the old foxhole tool. If the soil has been well prepared, it's easy to scoop out a hole, rebuild a cone to support the roots and then let water and soil do the rest. Properly placed, the roots and shank will be stable without holding. Cover the roots lightly with soil and begin to let water run slowly into the hole. Add more soil, then more water. No need to tamp or pack. In short, mud them in. And if mud bothers you, try some vinyl gloves... good for mud or thorns.

COVER UP YOUR WORK. Hill up newly planted roses with loose, protective cones of mulch or other insulating material until just the tips of the canes stick out. Not just a dab, but a real MOUND. Moisture conservation in the canes is important, not sunshine. Moisture in the canes is supported by new root hairs; hilling keeps canes from drying out until the roots have a chance to deliver.

CLEANUP SPRAY for newly pruned bushes is a good idea to get ahead of spores and overwintering insects, but without damaging cane tissue. Rosarians in really-dormant, cold regions like oil and sulfur or lime/oil/sulfur combinations, but they MUST be used when canes are still dormant. Oil plus bright sunshine plus tender growth means burn. The Rambler likes to use the same control in warm or cold weather; a fungicide/insecticide combination at label strength with a little extra spreader-sticker. There is NO NEED to boost the strength. Spray climbers and shrub roses particularly well as carryover spores on green tissue can spread like wildfire when conditions are right.

A LITTLE ROOT PRUNING? A good practice for most bare-root roses. Lightly trim the ends of the roots and cut out broken roots, based on the premise that root tips are most prone to drying out, trimming exposes healthy tissue for new root hairs to develop. The Rambler also likes to dip bare-root roses in bleach solution to head off galls and infection. Make a solution of 1 cup *Clorox* to 5 gallons of water in a tall canister or trash can. Dip the rose, roots and canes, for a half minute or so and then plant as usual. Trim, soak, dip and plant, in that order.

ROSES IN BOXES, ready to plant, confuse many rosarians. Plant in the box or take it out? The box-plant has probably arrived at the nursery fresher and better than the packaged roses and may get better handling than the roses potted on site. The Rambler likes to cut the box away if the plant is still dormant and treat much like a bare-root, spreading the usually short roots out. If a box-rose is beginning to leaf, cut away the box very carefully without disturbing the roots. Well-advanced growth, slice the box, hoping that the roots will quickly find the way out of confinement. Box roses WILL GROW with some extra care.

SPRING STARTERS are on the agenda for March. I'm sure there's something on the menu you'll like.

OPPORTUNITY NEVER COMES… it's here. And now's the time to take advantage of it. Let's look into some rose menus for '99.

ROSES ARE HUNGRY… but also are finicky eaters, so you'll want to have some things on the menu they like. Start with an appetizer, follow with three squares a day (and lots of water) and finish up with dessert. Rosarians like this kind of menu, too.

BEGIN WITH A FISH APPETIZER, fish emulsion, of course, fortified with a bit of urea-type 36-6-0 in solution. Get this mixture into the root zone at pruning time, even if the soil is a bit on the cold side. Fish emulsion or combinations of fish, alfalfa or cow tea feed the soil which supports the organisms converting nutrients into forms available to plants. There's some food value in these mixtures, but the primary boost comes from activating the soil organisms, which will go right after the urea.

WARM ROOTS have appetites. Fertilizers applied to cold soils don't do much good until the root zone warms up, explaining why some rosarians think the feeding program isn't working. The canes, warmed by sunshine, are waking up, but the roots are waiting for a clear signal that spring has arrived. Have you ever noticed how quickly roots grow when newly-planted roses in black plastic pots are set out on a warm, reflective surface? Same thing happens with electric bench blankets in a greenhouse, warming seedlings from the bottom up.

THE NEXT FEEDINGS SHOULD STICK TO THE RIBS (CANES) and support sustained growth. Organics do this very well, releasing slowly with all the right stuff for growth. Timed-release fertilizers also release slowly and evenly and may be a part of your menu. But organic enthusiasts like the Rambler like to mix up a batch of organic stew with a seasoning of 10-10-10 with trace elements, a hundred pounds or so at a time.

FEED STORES sell the staples in this recipe. Mix about 50 pounds of 10-10-10 with trace elements (coated release), 50 pounds each of alfalfa meal and fish meal, 20 pounds each of cottonseed meal and blood meal, 25 pounds of bone meal and 10 pounds of triple superphosphate. Blend these dry ingredients in a couple of big wheelbarrows or in a big pile, but keep it dry as it will begin to work. Analysis will be about 8-8-8; use about 2 heaping cups per bush, about a half-cup for miniatures. Scratch into the soil a bit and flood with lots of water. Repeat this organic feast about mid-August.

ROSE DESSERT follows about two weeks before peak bloom, or perhaps two weeks before a rose show. Typical is a soluble mix of *Peters 20-20-20* and fish emulsion, about 1 tablespoon of each per gallon of water, one gallon per large rose.

SNACKS are also good from time to time. The Rambler likes a tonic of alfalfa tea, cow tea or similar brew laced with an iron chelate like *Sprint* whenever foliage begins to pale or growth slows. Depending on the climate, this may be two or three times a season, delivering a growth hormone as well as iron. *Epsom Salts* (magnesium sulfate) can also be broadcast to encourage basal breaks (small handful per bush), particularly right after the first bloom flush when roses are at their peak of vigor. Just make sure that they have plenty of water to drink during heavy growth. Water is good all the time but absolutely essential when feeding and growing.

CONVENIENCE FOODS… There are some good ones available regionally, like *Mills Magic Mix,* convenient, organic and liked by all kinds of roses. No mixing, no muss, no fuss. Look around your region for *Mills* or a similar source; but remember that you can make up your own mix from scratch, the old fashioned way.

SPRAY PROGRAMS are on the agenda next month, just in time for new leaves.

THE FIRST DAY OF SPRING is one thing; the first spring day is another. Regardless, it's time to spring into action to manage fungal disease in your garden. Here's *Blackspot 101* for your study.

LUSH LEAVES MAKE ROSES, and make great hosts for a variety of pathogens bent on setting up housekeeping. Add free water and specific temperatures for continuous spreading infection. Obviously, this is a maintenance problem.

PROTECTIVE OR REACTIVE... best results come from a protective-preventive spray program; start spraying before the pathogen is most likely to be active. Preventive spraying is regular and cyclical in nature, knowing when to start and when to reapply, depending on the fungicide of choice. Reactive spraying, waiting until the disease is present and then attempting to control, results in irreparable damage and lost foliage. Lost foliage means lost roses.

SYSTEMIC AND CONTACT fungicides are readily available to the hobby grower, and each type has specific approaches. Systemic fungicides are absorbed by the plant into the leaf tissues. In the tissue, systemics are protected from the elements and effective within the sprayed tissue from 10 to 14 days. As new foliage appears, systemics must be reapplied as most do not move through the plant. Contact fungicides are protectants that remain on the leaf surface and act by inhibiting invasion at the surface, much like armor plating. Contacts wear off quickly, from five to seven days in the elements, and don't protect new growth.

SYSTEMIC FUNGICIDES have a weak spot in the form of potential disease resistance developing with continuous use. Program rotation reduces the chance of disease resistance to the specific fungicide by interjecting a different fungicidal family with a different mode of action. Rotation from *Triforine* to *Banner Maxx* to *Cleary's 3336* interrupts the pattern, preferably on an every-other-month basis.

CONTACT FUNGICIDES are less susceptible to resistance development than systemics and can safely be used continuously. Standbys are derivatives of *Manzate* and *Daconil*, but combining a systemic with a contact material provides even better protection against pathogen resistance.

COMBINATIONS provide protection *in* the leaf and *on* the leaf. Blackspot penetrates deep into the tissue and grows inside. Powdery mildew is more of a surface pathogen and can be blocked on the leaf surface. Contacts work quicker on powdery mildew; systemics work harder on blackspot. It makes good rose sense to use combination sprays, rotating the products from time to time.

SPREADER-STICKERS help both systemic and contact fungicides, and most fungicides available have some spreader-sticker already built in. However, use of a "buffer" to make water "wetter" enhances the effectiveness of the fungicides and prolongs the activity of insecticides. A buffer like *Indicate-5* lowers the pH of the spray solution, wets, spreads, penetrates, aids compatibility and reduces volatility. It gets the fungicides into working position. Another "super-wetter" is *Surf-King Plus*, similar in action to *Indicate-5* but without the pH color indicator. Both are very effective in an ongoing spray program, and are essential when using a miticide like *Avid*. Better coverage, better kill, longer lasting.

FLOWABLE FUNGICIDES, fungicides already in solution, are easier to use. Examples are *Manzate 200DF* (dry flowable), *Daconil 2787WFG* (water dispersible granules), *Maneb Flowable*... all go into the spray solution readily and stay there.

RAMBLER GIVEAWAYS... The Rambler is offering three great sheets on sprays and spraying, going into detail impossible in these columns. For a spray set, drop a line to the Rambler, at the address above. Enclose a stamped, self-addressed, business (#10) envelope, and I'll turn your request around by return mail... may even answer a question or two. Would love to hear from you.

IT TAKES RAIN AND SUNSHINE to make a rainbow… and roses. With a little help from you, these rosy rainbows will brighten up your rose garden.

BASAL BOOSTER… Now's the time to launch a major thrust for more basal and low breaks with a readily available source of nitrogen followed by *Epsom Salts* applied just after the initial bloom cycle while roses are at their peak of vigor. *Epsom Salts* (magnesium sulfate) works best when available nitrogen is present (a nitrate form is best). Use a soluble 20-20-20 the first week, 1/4 cup of *Epsom Salts* the second week, with successive applications of 20-20-20 weeks three and four. Cut the 20-20-20 concentration in half due to the frequency of application. New basals require lots of energy in the root zone for results, driven by lots of water.

IT'S THRIPS TIME… coming into rose gardens in waves looking for light-colored, fragrant blooms. Thrips appear to migrate from grasses and field flowers, at least they appear at the same time. *Orthene 75% SP* (soluble powder) is the Rambler's favorite control, systemic and safe for the most tender blooms. Use *Orthene SP* at 2 teaspoons per gallon of buffered solution. Get good coverage of buds and blooms with a pistol-pump sprayer every other day, making up a fresh batch of *Orthene* each time. The thrips fog will dissipate in a few weeks, and you can go back to occasional use of *Orthene* only when there is severe thrips pressure. Too much *Orthene* will set up the garden for spider mites, having destroyed the mites' natural predators.

MAY AND POWDERY MILDEW go together in many parts of the country. But there's hope for clean foliage and good blooms with early application of *Rubigan EC* at 2 teaspoons per 5 gallons of buffered water. Can be combined every other week with *Triforine*. *Systhane* is another good mildewcide (also known as *Nova, Eagle* or *Rally*) in a 40 WP formulation. It is the active ingredient in *Immunox*, a home-garden formulation. *Banner Maxx* works rather well on a 14-day schedule. Since these products are systemic, get protection *into* the tissue before powdery-gray appears. Powdery mildew hits new growth, get good coverage.

BUFFERED WATER? That's the Rambler's term for spray solution that has been treated with *Indicate-5* or *Surf-King Plus*, lowering the pH of the water and making it wetter. See the full description in the April Rambler.

FRESH HORSE MANURE? Should it be reported to the EPA? No, keep it a secret and treat your roses with all that you can haul. Use it on the rosebed, in the rosebed… wherever organic matter and bacterial action are needed. No need to compost horse manure/shavings/alfalfa hay/straw mixtures before using on roses. Some of the "good stuff" is lost by waiting for the "well-rotted" stage. Let the microbial action rejuvenate the beds, feeding the soil. Use manure from stalls rather than horse lots to reduce weeds. The Rambler's roses think it's a special treat to get an inch or two of horse manure mulch just a week out of the horse.

NO ACCESS TO A HORSE? Then make up some "Fragrant Formula" with fish meal, cottonseed meal, alfalfa meal and some form of roughage like fine-ground bark shavings and leaves. By volume, use four times as much roughage as meal. Add some blood meal if you like, maybe bone meal. Make a big pile, mix the dry ingredients with a pitchfork, moisten lightly and allow to digest for a week. Turn again. The finished product will be just like manure without having to run it through a horse. Use a big pitchforkful per bush and lots of water. Your soil organisms and roses will love it. Your neighbors will love the roses, too, when the sharp ammonia odor dissipates in a day or two. Try some!

SUMMER TONICS by the Rambler next month. You'll want these recipes.

JUN.
1999

THOUGHT FOR THE MONTH: Never invite a rosarian to an evening of wine, women and roses. He'll want to know what kind of roses.

RAIN AND SUNSHINE make a rainbow… here's how to use both for a pot of gold in your rose garden.

TONICS for all sorts of problems are in vogue these days, but the Rambler's favorite is alfalfa tea, used in the rose garden whenever the bushes look a little droopy. The "secret" ingredient is Triacontanol, a growth hormone occurring naturally in alfalfa. It just makes the whole soil/nutrient process work better. Brew up a batch of tea in a 32-gallon plastic trash barrel, using about 12 cups of alfalfa meal or pellets per barrel. Fill with water, stir and then cover for several days while the brew steeps. Be sure to cover the elixir — it smells. Stir with a broom handle now and then to convince yourself that it's working.

GIVE A FINAL STIR and then pour about a gallon of tea for each bush, about half that much for miniatures. The leaves will green up and growth recommence. The Rambler's roses like to take tea in early spring, mid-summer and again in late summer.

FORTIFIED TEA may be even better, depending on your feeding program. To the finished tea, add 1/3 cup of chelated iron (*Sequestrene*), 1/2 cup of *Epsom Salts*, and one cup of 20-20-20 soluble fertilizer with trace elements. Stir well and stand back. The roses are going to grow.

GO TO THE FARM SUPPLY STORE for alfalfa, cottonseed, fish and other natural meals. These are friendly folks who will get what you need if it's not in stock in the back. And they may throw in a "gimmie cap" that says "Hank's Horse Feed." You have just become a member of a gardening fraternity.

GOURMET FARE for roses includes *Osmocote,* timed-release nutrients that roses like and are great on convenience, which rosarians like. There are several formulations but most growers like the action of *Osmocote* 15-11-13 with trace elements, good for three to four months. And there's a 16-8-12 that works for about eight months. A good menu to consider.

SPIDER MITES WILL BE ACTIVE as summer heats up, multiplying furiously and sucking the life right out of rose leaves. Head off severe infestation by keeping mite populations under control early as well as throughout the season.

Water-washing is a good practice, directing a strong, fine water spray underneath the leaves. In many cases water-washing is all that's needed as an ongoing summer routine. If water-washing is impractical or the mites get ahead of you, get going with *Avid* FAST! Wash as best you can with lots of water, spray underneath the leaves with the *Avid* enhanced with *Stirrup-M*, the sex-attractant pheromone. *Avid* is used at 1/4 teaspoon per gallon, *Stirrup-M* at three drops per gallon. Repeat the process in four days to catch the hatch.

PAY ATTENTION AND ACT FAST as spider mite season arrives. Watch dense, low growing roses for leaves that turn gray-green. Pull some suspicious lower leaves and look for salt-and-pepper specks with traces of webs. You won't see the mites without a glass, but the tell-tale signs are evident. With just a little close observation and practice, you can spot spider mites at work from 20 feet away. *Avid* works best when not combined with other insecticides or fungicides… and has greater residual and systemic action in a "buffered" spray solution, i.e. lower pH with a spreader. Need a cheap buffer? To alkaline tap water, add from 1-2 tablespoons of white vinegar per gallon plus a few drops of dishwashing liquid. The spray solution will spread evenly on leaves, even underneath. Done right, the leaves will "glisten" with spray.

NEW GROWTH STARTED at the end of the cane but died? Probably not series, the cane just could not support the growth, and when stressed it shriveled up and died. Pruned canes have stored-up nutrients, and when they are not replaced, the emerging growth stops. Trim back and don't worry.

GIVEAWAYS. The Rambler has run some more giveaways covering Alfalfa Tea, Fragrant Formula, Glossary of Rose Terms and Index of Rose Control Fungicides. Want a pack? Send a SASE (#10 size) to the Rambler. Happy to share.

HAVE YOU NOTICED… The hardest thing to open is a closed mind. But you can open up on these summer ideas.

A SUMMER DIET is healthy on organics, releasing nutrients and building soil without boosting excessive growth. Broadcast a cup or so of alfalfa meal or pellets per bush (right on top of the mulch) and follow up with lots of water. Manures, compost, fish meal and mixtures of all these maintain green leaves followed by bushels of roses. Miniatures like the same thing… just in smaller quantities.

MINI ORGANIC TONICS include fish emulsion or *Mills EasyFeed*. Minis love both. About a tablespoon of *EasyFeed* per 2- to 3-gallon container or medium-size mini is both easy and a good feed. Just sprinkle the *EasyFeed* mixture (sort of a moist coffee grounds consistency) on top of the soil and let water pick up the food and deliver to the roots. Also fairly soluble in water if you would rather use a bucket.

FEED THROUGH MULCH, not underneath. A good mulch is loose and porous (remember it is an insulator) that lets nutrients and water flow through readily. Pellets and meals and compost crumbs work into the mulch, breaking down and becoming soluble as water comes through. Nutrients are released like coffee comes from coffee grounds, ready to perk up growth.

SUMMERTIME may seem like an odd time to talk about cold frames, but you'll see some new version in "advanced gardener's" yards. They're good for starting seeds in the spring and rooting cuttings during summer and fall. Exotic '90s cold frames are treated-lumber boxes with *Lexan* windows, which open and close with solar-powered vent openers. Works by thermal expansion of liquid in a cylinder arm… opens up when it's warm, closes when it's cool. Creates a mini greenhouse environment… and cheap. Located in light shade, rose cuttings take right off in a soilless rooting mix. Add a mister and valve control if you're really high tech. We're going to see MANY more roses on their own roots in the future. A cold-frame propagation box speeds up the process.

MINI VIEWS… The Rambler has finally given in to BIG miniature rosebushes… in certain applications. This season was the clincher. The Rambler trimmed back the miniature plantings in front of the house last December taking them down overall to about 18 to 24 inches. At pruning time in March the bushes were already putting out so much new growth that it would have been cruel to cut them any more. Just nipped out a few bad canes here and there. The Rambler was rewarded with hundreds of blooms in each bed about mid-April on bushes averaging 3 feet high, and still growing. Plan to shear the bushes overall in late May for another crop. They stop traffic with their size and color. Try a light trim in your garden.

TRADITIONALLY-TRIMMED miniatures (shorter, better-groomed, grown for competition) make great accent flower beds and are also useful in the foreground of large-rose plantings. Minis are compatible with large roses — just hold off on the feed and let them have what's left over from the large roses. And the Rambler has always liked the effect of minis planted UNDER tree roses in a frame pattern. Blooms below, blooms above. Just keep the minis carefully groomed and you'll have a striking combination.

WHISKEY BARRELS make beautiful miniature rose planters. Half-barrels cost about $18, can be filled with $4 worth of soilless mix and three miniatures for a mound of color accent. Minis like the drainage and the feeding control of barrels, and the grower likes the easy stand-up care. Set the barrel on a tripod of bricks to keep the bottom dry and the oak wood will last for years and years. The Rambler's minis like *Jack Daniels* barrels, but almost any good bourbon will do.

ENJOY your summertime projects… and roses.

THE ROSARIAN who never changes his mind never corrects his mistakes. August is a good time to pick up on these tips prompted by questions in the Rambler's mail bag.

CHIPS... as in wood chips, ARE good for rosebeds as a mulch, soil conditioner, weed preventer... just like nature intended. With rare exception, hardwood or pinewood chips work well in the garden. Just add some supplemental nitrogen to support the decomposition process; the cheapest lawn fertilizer you can find, broadcast over the mulched area. Same for pine needles. The Rambler recently lost a couple of trees to ice storms and overcrowding. The resulting chips left a huge pile in the driveway — a springtime bonanza. Now if I just had someone to spread them.

INSECTICIDES AND SPIDER MITES. Can't have one without the other. The Rambler used more *Orthene* than usual this season to cope with a world-class invasion of thrips. Had good, clean blooms during the spring bloom flush and now have spider mites from all over the galaxy. Too much insecticide kills off the beneficials, and the spider mites have come back with a vengeance. It would have been much better if less *Orthene* had been used in general spraying and more frequent applications applied to buds with a small hand sprayer. When a grower tries to bend the rules, the rules usually prevail.

JAPANESE BEETLES have been unusually severe in the Eastern United States this season, and we still don't have a control that doesn't set up some other undesirable reaction. *Liquid Sevin* works, but leaves residue, kills beneficials and needs frequent application. *Sevin Dust* with the *Dustin-Mizer* has to be used three times a week, calm day, dry foliage. Picking is impractical for most growers. But the Rambler is encouraged by the use of *Milky Spore* last season over the whole yard and overlapped some of the neighbors with a SIGNIFICANT decrease this year, in spite of living on a golf course. Don't tell me that the beetles don't travel. Given another year or two, and the *Milky Spore* may make June pleasant again as far as beetles are concerned. But control is relative; as far as the Rambler is concerned, you have control when there are some roses and most of the foliage left after the beetle invasion.

HANDY SPRAYER... the new *Black & Decker* 3-gallon power sprayer that's just right for small gardens. Rechargeable battery powered, the canister is mounted on a light two-wheel tripod frame like a golf-bag buggy. Works on air pressure rather than liquid pump, has an adjustable nozzle for droplet size and coverage. It sure beats a hand pump; costs about $100 and is easy to use, easy to wash out. One charge will put out 6-8 gallons of spray without getting tired. The Rambler prefers a heavy-duty rechargeable for large gardens, but this rig is pretty good. Look up a *Black & Decker* outlet in your area; the dealer here even has a demo and will let you spray into a bucket. Check it out.

FOLIAR FEEDING... The Rambler has always been cautious about foliar feeding, questioning just how much good it did and concerned about leaf burn if used improperly. But now the Rambler concedes that sea-mineral supplements make a difference, even when an otherwise good feeding program is in place. *Response* is a good one, and the Rambler has used it in combination with all sorts of fungicide-insecticide mixes with good effect. *Response* and similar elixirs are regularly advertised in these pages.

COMPATIBILITY of spray materials continues to concern rosarians, and rightly so. Do we really want to treat rosebushes to a chemical cocktail? Most fungicides/insecticides are compatible, i.e. *Funginex* and *Orthene*. A good example is *Orthenex*, a combo of *Funginex, Orthene,* and *Vendex*. Rule of thumb: combine as few materials as possible and ALWAYS try out a new combination on a small number of bushes and visit with other growers in your area. That's what this rose hobby is all about.

SUMMER SCHEDULE: Feed the soil, water, spray, wait for cooler weather.

EXPERIENCE IS LIKE MANURE... it's only good when spread around. These September Ramblings mark 29 years of chatting with you good rose folks each month, sharing ideas and experiences to enjoy roses more. You've been loyal, responsive readers... the Rambler appreciates the opportunity to be with you in these pages.

HANG ONTO THE LEAVES. Your roses are going to need them for fall and winter. Healthy, happy leaves are doing most of the work producing roses. September is NOT the time to "wait for next year." There's still plenty of time to grow some more leaves (and roses)... and be sure to keep the leaves you already have. If you have had a blackspot outbreak, double up on the spray schedule for the next two weeks and get good coverage. The Rambler likes *Funginex* and *Manzate* or *Daconil*, used in combination. You'll be rewarded with fresh, clean leaves in no time.

ZAP THE INSECTS. Fall is a good time to put up an insect lamp/electric grid to get the moths that lay bud worm eggs... before they have a chance to lay them. It's easier to control bud worms BEFORE they bore into the buds. BUG ZAPPERS make life far more pleasant for the rosarian in the garden as well, knocking down an amazing volume of stinging, biting bugs. They're usually on sale in the fall. Get one.

AMAZING RESPONSE... It sounds too good to be true, but organic-based liquid feeding brought beetle-damaged roses back into new leaf and production in two weeks. The formula was something like the Rambler "fortified tea" without the alfalfa. The basis was *Mills EasyFeed* with a little extra *Epsom* salts and chelated iron. Also made up a batch (32-gallon barrel) with *Mills Magic Mix*. Let these concoctions brew for a couple of days, then bucket or pump out on the roses. Amazing really applies when used on miniatures in containers.

FISH MEAL in the planting hole also brings new life to transplanted container roses. The Rambler had some 30 big roses in 3-gallon containers that HAD to be set out in mid-summer... and the roses were struggling. Planting holes were dug in prepared beds with the containers "tried out" for size and depth. In a hands-and-knees operation, the pots were lifted out and the bottoms cut out with a linoleum knife. About a half-cup of fish meal was stirred into the bottom of each hole with a little on the sides. Then the pots were carefully placed in the holes, making sure that the soilless mix didn't fall out. Began the backfill with another cup of fish meal mixed in, cutting away the sides of the pots. Tamped in gently by hand and flooded with LOTS of water. In spite of very high temperatures, no rain and lack of daily attention, these transplanted roses rebounded immediately and are thriving. And you can be sure that the roots of those roses are happy and spreading throughout the fish-mix.

LUGGING BUCKETS of water with soluble fertilizers, tonics and elixirs is not the Rambler's idea of a good time in the garden. The EASY solution is to use a *Little Giant* submersible pump to deliver measured amounts to roses in beds or containers. *Little Giant* is a pump common to small fountains and ponds — cheap and virtually trouble-free. Works great in a 32-gallon plastic garbage can, limited only by the length of a grounded electrical cord. Can also be mounted outside the barrel with an intake hose (and strainer) dropped into the mix. Even works with alfalfa tea mixes provided the intake does not go into the sediment on the bottom. The sediment can be diluted with water and applied by bucket or the barrel refilled for another brewing.

WANT FAST COMPOST? Add some gypsum to the pile along with some dolomite lime. If the pile is low on green material, throw in some cheap lawn fertilizer to heat up the process. You'll notice an immediate improvement in the overall action. Air, moisture and a source of soil bacteria will go to work on garden debris with even more vigor with these supplements.

WHEN YOUR WORK speaks for itself, don't interrupt. But the Rambler is going to break in this month with some "clarifications" that may make rose growing more fun.

NAME BRANDS vs. GENERIC... When the Rambler writes enthusiastically about the wonders of *Mills EasyFeed*, it doesn't mean that some other organics won't perform just as well when used properly. Look at the benefit to be derived and act accordingly for your situation. It's foolish to ship heavy "name brands" across the country when a local or regional sources can supply your needs. That's the beauty of rose society "country stores" that buy in quantity and sell to members at a discount.

DACONIL... Much maligned but also very effective when used correctly. *Daconil*, especially the EC formulations, will BURN in hot weather. Better for spring and fall when temperatures are lower. Or, to reduce the risk, use the WDG (Water Dispersible Granules) type. *Daconil* is a good contact fungicide for blackspot or powdery mildew when used in combination with a systemic like *Funginex, Banner Maxx* or *Cleary's 3336*.

BANNER MAXX... Touted to be the product of choice replacing *Triforene* in the fungicide arsenal. It is a good choice, but not a miracle. In most applications, *Banner Maxx* will keep a normal rose garden fungus-disease free for 14 days, particularly when used with a contact fungicide. But even this highly effective systemic cannot be stretched to 21 days when fungus pressure is high or if the roses have wet leaves for long periods. These situations require greater frequency and alternate fungicides. But the Rambler enjoyed blackspot-free roses of all types with a two-week schedule using *Banner Maxx* with *Manzate*, both used at label strength. Check plantings with *Triforene/Manzate* were equally clean with weekly spraying.

WATER... It doesn't make much difference HOW you get the water to the roses, but how much. The Rambler likes the *Dramm* nozzles that put out a flat spray and evenly water an area, mostly because I use organics and granular feeds on the surface of the mulch and want the water to percolate through the bed applications like coffee grounds. That way I get water, air, nutrients and soil working together in a "natural" way. But the porous hose (*Moisture Master*) also delivers water reliably and without waste, just oozing away and getting water to the roots. The Rambler's park garden has *Moisture Master* laid under the mulch in each bed, which has kept the roses growing and blooming during the hottest dry spell that Greenville has seen in years. And this garden is fed exclusively with pelletized fertilizer (16-8-6 with trace). With just one feeding in March (about 2 cups per bush), the roses average 5-6 feet tall.

SHEARING MINIS... A good idea for lots of growth and bloom with minimum work. But there eventually comes a time when growth has to be contained. That time came in early August when normally manageable miniatures exceeded 4 feet high and 3 feet across. A mini jungle. So... borrowing from a previous storm, mite and neglect damage, the Rambler pruned back as if the calendar read early March... down to about 12 inches, cleaning up the middle and stripping all the leaves. As of this writing (mid-August), the minis are rebounding with a vigor, lots of new growth, buds and breaks. I expect to have a bumper crop mid-September. Tip: this works on big roses, too. Don't try this in October, but keep in mind for a "new start" in the future.

WATER AGAIN... Roses want to slow down in the fall, getting ready for winter dormancy. But don't slow down the water. Hold back feeding, keep up the spray program... healthy roses handle winter better. NOTHING happens unless there is plenty of water available to support the processes. Some dramatic changes are taking place in the plant and water is the catalyst. You'll be rewarded with late fall bloom and a stronger plant next spring.

NOW THAT YOU UNDERSTAND these "clarifications," I'm sure that you'll take modest credit for them. Talk with you next month.

ROSARIANS know that you have to do a job to really learn how. The Rambler hopes that you'll learn a lot this month from these early-winter tips.

WINTER seems like a dormant, inactive period in the garden, but there's really a lot going on. For example: freeze/thaw will work for you all winter in mechanical as well as biological processes. Loosen the bed you want to improve with a spading fork and pile on lots of organic material and leaves. As moisture freezes and expands, tissues break down in the same way as decomposition in the summer. Nature has been building soil this way for a long time.

CHEMICAL things are happening as well... a good time to adjust the pH of the soil with application of agricultural lime (if needed). Top application is not as effective as lime is relatively insoluble. The process is a REACTIVE one when soluble lime comes into contact with soil crumbs. Lime, in the presence of hydrogen ions (the indicator for pH), reacts with those ions to form water. By reducing the hydrogen ions, the pH goes up. It's a fairly slow process; use the winter months to advantage.

A STRONG BACK AND SPADING FORK will do the mechanical thing if the rosebed needing lime can't be tilled or spaded. Use the fork to open up holes to take the lime (the Rambler likes pelletized dolomite lime). Broadcast the lime, then lightly scratch the soil back to let nature and chemistry work.

TO GET IN BALANCE/STAY IN BALANCE, about 6.5 to 6.8. A good rule of thumb is to add a pound of dolomite lime for every pound of nitrogen used during the season. Example: a 5-10-5 ammonium sulfate fertilizer, 50-pound bag, contains 2.5 pounds of nitrogen. Use 2.5 pounds of lime for the same area. And ALWAYS TEST before adjusting. For NEW beds in heavy clay soil, work in about 25 pounds of lime per 100 square feet of bed and let it work all winter.

HEALTHY BUSHES make it through the winter: weak ones struggle to survive. Roses that gradually go dormant are protected with a sort of natural "anti-freeze" in the cells, a solution that does not freeze and expand to the degree that growing plant fluids do. Pay attention to nature's call to slow down.

FROST ON THE PUMPKIN means it's time to winter protect appropriately for your climate. Thanksgiving weekend seems to be the time that most rosarians favor for winter protection rather than rushing out a few hours before a cold front. The whole idea is to insulate... to maintain a fairly constant temperature, avoiding freeze/thaw situations in the tissues. Combinations of loose materials do this best, held in place with fences, boughs, wire cones, paper collars or what have you. Leaves and loose "stuff" act like thermal blankets. When the insulation is organic, there's an extra benefit in the spring as it adds humus to the soil.

MODERATE CLIMATES call for some winter protection, too. Some soil/leaf combinations over the bud union help avoid sudden temperature changes... roses may think that it's time to grow after a warm spell. A shovelful of insulation material over a bud union has saved many rosebushes.

REALLY COLD CLIMATES require more soil protection, mounded 6 to 8 inches over the canes, then covered with leaves. Bring in soil rather than taking soil from between the bushes in the beds. Soil/mulch combinations are great... they breathe better.

WINTER FEEDING is a practice worth considering, something like composting in place. Growers in severe as well as milder climates put down a layer of leaves in the rosebed, broadcast a cupful of pelletized fertilizer (13-13-13) per 10 square feet, then add some more leaves. By spring the lower layer of leaves will have broken down into a rich humus, threaded with white mycelium. The nitrogen works on the leaves, not on the soil, breaking down the organic material and setting up the soil for better activity in the spring. You may select to leave all of the leaves in the bed when springtime arrives, broadcasting more fertilizer on top. Advocates of winter feeding report no untimely new growth in either the fall or winter when roses are put to bed with this "nightcap."

CHAT with you again in Y2K. Have a HAPPY ONE!

EXPERIENCE IS LIKE MANURE... it's only good when spread around. So the Rambler is busy spreading whatever, having had LOTS of experience (good and bad).

NO TIME FOR A LONG WINTER'S NAP... Now's the time to take a good look at HOW and WHY your roses are coping with winter. Then you'll know how to respond. Pay particular attention to the amount of good wood on some bushes and loss on others. Difference in protection? Less wind, more moisture, insulation able to breathe, more gradual dormancy... all could be factors in survival. Make it a good practice to observe, and then put this new understanding to work. Rosarians can't just shut down for the winter.

PRUNING PRACTICES... Every rosarian has a pet theory. Some growers whack off the tops with hedge shears or loppers, even with a chain saw (depends on how much cane you have and where you live) and still get lots of blooms with little or no dieback. The Royal National Rose Society (UK) has reported a number of trials comparing mass sheared plantings with conventional pruning. Contrary to popular belief, roses that were sheared had more blooms and bloom-producing canes than bushes done the old-fashioned way. This OBVIOUSLY does not apply to roses in cold climates where every inch of cane is precious, but does have application in milder areas. The point is: pruning may not be as critical as "experts" lead us to believe.

VALENTINE'S DAY is almost here... a perfect opportunity to present your favorite rosarian with a truck load of horse manure. Horse manure from a riding stable (stalls), steaming and fragrant on delivery, just needs a red ribbon on top to get spring off to a good start. Apply a cozy 5-inch blanket at a time appropriate for your area and spring will not be far behind.

TOXIC CONCERNS... planting roses where roses have been before? Need NEW soil? Not to worry. The problem is very rare and just gives rosarians something new to worry about. There's a big word for it: ALLELOPATHY, the suppression of growth of one plant species by another due to a release of toxic substances. The Ramber has NEVER observed this in roses after planting and replanting for years and years. Most growth slow-down is from "tired soil" that needs some organic matter to make it alive again. Hauling soils and mixes in and out just does not make sense in most cases. But you will ALWAYS get dramatic results by replacing with a large quantity of GOOD MIX, but the growth area can also be rejuvenated with a shot in the humus area.

THINK HUMUS THIS YEAR, most any kind will do. Humus is simply partially decomposed organic matter that acts like a glue to bind clay and silty particles together into granules or crumbs. This causes the soil to become quite porous, allowing air and water to move readily. Combined clay and humus act together to hold water as well. And crumb structure allows excellent gas exchange so the soil has sufficient oxygen capacity to support the microorganisms converting nutrients into forms available to the plants.

A DINING TABLE. Humus derived from organic matter builds a "table" from which rose roots can absorb water and nutrients. This crumb-making capability holds nutrients up to three or four times more than clay or silty soils alone. Nutrients don't leach out as readily.

KEY TO BETTER GROWING. Humus IS the key to good rose growing. It helps hold and make available water and nutrients, increases porosity of the soil and supports the "living" process. Need any more reasons to have up to 25 percent organic matter in your rosebed? Just check out the loads of roses enjoyed by growers who have understood this wonder of nature all along.

MAKE YOUR OWN, use leaves, straw, manures, sphagnum peat or whatever else you can find in nature that breaks down. Then you will have discovered the "secret" of happy growers.

WILL TELL YOU how to make "artificial manure" next month. Just in time for springtime soil feeding. What a way to start the New Year.

WITH SOME ROSARIANS, it's hard to tell if they are contributing to the solution or adding to the problem. Here are some solutions you can claim for your own.

ARTIFICIAL MANURE... What will they think of next? This is for the rosarian who doesn't want a horse or have a farm friend (and pickup truck) for the real thing. Guaranteed to grow grass on fence posts and roses in rocks. It's a good soil amendment, top dressing, basic feeding formula... especially in the spring.

MIX UP A BATCH in your own back yard. Combine 3 ample yards of compost materials or leaves, 100 pounds of coarse organic stuff, 100 pounds cottonseed meal, 100 pounds alfalfa meal (or pellets), 50 pounds bone meal, 50 pounds fish meal and 50 pounds gypsum. You can vary the mix a bit if you like. Make a pile in an area suitable for composting, adding lighter ingredients a little at a time, turn with a pitchfork, mix well. Then moisten lightly and turn with a fork twice a week for two weeks. As the pile works you will smell a sharp *ammonia* odor. If the pile is too wet or lacking coarse material, it will smell *dead* and turn into a slime. Ready in three weeks, use two garden shovelfuls per bush in the spring, and in the summer. You'll be feeding the soil that ultimately feeds the roses. Use generously — it really works.

DIRTY-KNEES ROSARIANS... Hands and knees planting is easier on bad backs and roses than bending over. Use a short shovel, like the old foxhole tool. In a prepared bed, it's easy to scoop out a hole and rebuild a cone to support the roots and bush, then let water and soil do the rest. Roots and shank should be stable without holding. Scoop soil over the roots lightly and begin to let water run slowly into the hole. Add more soil, then more water. No need to tamp or pack. *Mud* them in.

COVER UP YOUR WORK. Hill up newly planted roses with loose, protective cones of mulch or other insulating material until just the tips of the canes stick out. Make a real *mound*, a couple of big shovelfuls per bush. Moisture conservation in the canes is important, not sunshine and wind. Moisture in the canes (and new growth) is supported by new root has; hilling keeps canes from drying out until roots have a chance to deliver.

CLEANUP SPRAY is a good practice for newly pruned bushes, getting ahead of the spores and overwintering insects without damaging cane tissue. Cold-weather rosarians like dormant oils or oil/sulfur/lime combinations, but must be applied when canes are still dormant. Most of these combinations make a terrible mess on the side of the house or fence. The Rambler likes to use the same controls cold or warm weather: a contact fungicide/insecticide combo with a little extra spreader-sticker, used at label strength. There is *no need* to increase the concentration. Spray climbers and ramblers particularly well; infected bushes can spread spores like wildfire when conditions are right.

REBUILDING? Dormant roses can be dug and set aside for a week or two while rebuilding an existing bed, giving both a new lease on life. Or, new bare root roses can be held over while a bed is in construction. Dig carefully with a spading fork; don't worry about soil. Handle like bare-root. Trim up as needed. Discard the weak ones. Set the bushes aside and bury or cover with soil, sacks, mulch, bark or any other material that will keep the bushes cool and moist. A shallow trench with soil to cover is ideal. My dad referred to this as "heeling in" since the bushes were slanted in a trench. But dirt and manure types like the Rambler say that the bushes are "healed in" and thus protected until planting. Whatever you call it, it works.

IT'S TIME TO BREAK DORMANCY and get ready for spring. Get into your own garden as well as other gardens; you'll be surprised what you can learn out there in the dirt. Dirty knees, dirty hands... a great way to live.

ONLY A MEDIOCRE ROSARIAN is always at his or her best. To be the best you CAN be (U.S. Army ad), move out with these spring suggestions.

A NON-TRADITIONAL planting technique for potted roses is worth considering. Use on POTTED roses only, and with a little rose sense. Contrary to traditional rose wisdom, a time-released fertilizer can be used when planting a well-developed potted rose. Roses which have been confined to pots for a month or so have developed a fairly good system of fine, new roots. The rosarian wants these roots to expand into the planting bed as soon as possible. The roots can be lured with some strategically placed, time-released fertilizer like *Osmocote*... a sort of carrot in front of the horse.

CONCENTRATION AND LOCATION are important. Dig the hole to the right depth and try the rose (still in the pot) for fit. Then mix one ounce of *Osmocote* with some soil an inch or so below the root level. Cut out the bottom of the pot with a sharp knife and position in the hole. Slit the sides and lift away (there should be all kinds of white feeder roots on the outside). Backfill the hole with a few inches of soil and mix another ounce of *Osmocote* around the perimeter. Add more soil/mix and FLOOD with water. Hill up slightly and keep moist. Use NO MORE than 3 to 4 ounces of time-release per bush. You'll see new top growth throughout the early season, knowing the roots are growing also.

WANT MORE BASALS? Safely available with a one-two punch using *Epsom* salts (magnesium sulfate) and a readily-available source of nitrate-form nitrogen. Works at pruning time as well as after the initial blooming cycle. Magnesium, so essential in the rose tissue process, leaches readily, as does nitrogen. Kick off the process with 1/4 cup of *Epsom* salts per established bush, following every-other-week with applications of soluble high nitrate. Two feedings should do it. New basals need LOTS of energy Get the energy into the root zone with PLENTY of water for good results.

FISH EMULSION is the rose starter of choice. Think of fish emulsion to soil as lighter fluid is to charcoal: it gets everything going An ounce or two of fish emulsion per gallon of water applied generously to just-planted roses gets the soil organisms working in a won't-burn way. This can't be said for all of the "stimulators." Soak again in a month with fish mix. Use LOTS of water. Miniatures like fish, too... about one-third as much.

TREE ROSES ought to be enjoyed in more parts of the country, even in areas where they need to be buried for the winter. Some rosarians are hesitant, saying the trees are "hard to start" and cost a lot of money. Just give the emerging buds and small canes the same kind of "humidifying" that hilled-up bush roses enjoy. Add a couple of handfuls of very wet sphagnum moss to the bud unions and small canes, much like "air-layering." Work some moss throughout the canes and then loosely secure a plastic bag over the whole head, creating a miniature greenhouse. This keeps the canes moist from drying out until the new roots have a chance to deliver moisture up the long tree standard. Cut some small air holes in about two weeks. Gradually uncover, depending on weather.

MUSHROOM MAGIC. Watch for a new family of fungicides called "strobilurins," which are naturally occurring materials found in mushrooms. Novartis is bringing out *Compass*, a 50 percent water dispersible granule formulation that appears to be an excellent preventive for blackspot, powdery mildew and rust... effective for 14 days. *Compass* is a "mesostemic" fungicide, characterized by a high affinity of the fungicide for the waxy layers of the leaf surface. It penetrates the leaf surface but does not move through the plant's vascular system. It binds tightly to the leaf and is very weather resistant. Used at 1/8 teaspoon per gallon, it is leaf-safe (does not burn). However, users may need to take out a loan at the bank as the initial purchase is costly, about $200 for 8 ounces. Lots of good things are happening for rosarians.

APRIL is the month when rose fun really begins… keeping in mind growing roses isn't hard work unless you'd rather be doing something else.

WARM ROOTS ARE HUNGRY… Fertilizers applied to cold soils won't do much good until the root zone warms up, explaining why some rosarians think the fertilizing program isn't working. The canes, warmed by sunshine, may be waking up, but the roots are waiting for a clear signal that spring has arrived. To illustrate: check new roses in black plastic pots set on a warm, reflective surface. In just a week or two, tiny new roots have spread throughout the pot and the rose is off to a fast start. For rosarians in a hurry, apply diluted, readily available foods like alfalfa tea and fish emulsion, soaking the root zone.

GROW ROOTS, THEN ROSES applies to miniatures in particular. Small, newly-rooted miniature plants perform much better if first repotted in 1-gallon plastic pots and allowed to develop a real root system before planting in a new bed. Use a light, friable mix with some organics like compost, placing the pots in filtered light for a week or so. Feed lightly (weak fish emulsion) on a weekly basis, and the lightest miniatures just jump out of the pots. Set out when some small roots come out of the side holes.

FISH STORY… A Rambler family member not noted for his horticultural expertise decided to try some roses at a newly-constructed home (formerly an alfalfa field) near Boulder, CO. With the Rambler's help, some 50 bushes got into the decomposed-granite, sandy soil… all in a row, trench irrigated. Water disappeared as if connected to a drain pipe but reached the last bush at the end of a long day. Good lake water, pumped from a nearby pond. After the first bloom, it was suggested that some manure might increase the fertility of the gravel. Another food source came from the nearby pond: buckets and buckets of bluegills caught by willing grandchildren. Shallow furrows were scratched with a mattock, filled with fish and covered. Fresh cow manure (this was in the country) was heaped on the bushes also, a grain-shovelful at a time. Filled the irrigating trench with pond water every other day for a while. Result: No burn and growth to 5 feet by fall, no small task in that short growing season.

BLACKSPOT 101 REFRESHER… Lush leaves make roses and also make great hosts for a variety of pathogens bent on multiplying. Add free water and specific temperatures for continuous, spreading infection. A maintenance problem.

PROTECTIVE VS. REACTIVE… Best results come from a protective-preventive spray program; start spraying BEFORE the pathogen is likely to be active. Preventive spraying is regular and cyclical in nature, knowing when to start and when to reapply, depending on the fungicide of choice. Reactive spraying, waiting until the disease is present and then attempting to control, results in irreparable damage and foliage is lost. Lost foliage means lost roses.

SYSTEMIC AND CONTACT fungicides have specific approaches. Systemics are absorbed by the leaf tissue, protected from the elements and effective within the sprayed tissue for 10-14 days. As new foliage appears, systemics have to be reapplied as most do not move through the plant. Contact fungicides are protectants that remain/bond on the surface of the leaf, inhibiting pathogen penetration, much like armor plating. But contacts wash off quickly in the elements and must be applied every five to seven days.

COMBINATIONS are best, providing protection IN the leaf and ON the leaf. It makes good rose sense to use combination sprays, rotating products from time to time.

EVERY ROSE GARDEN looks good in the spring. Enjoy it while you can. The hard work is coming up.

ROSARIANS are prone to applying pounds of cure, when a few ounces of prevention would do the job. There's the Integrated Plant Management (IPM) theme… work with all parts of nature.

INTEGRATED PLANT MANAGEMENT focuses on the factors which contribute to damage by disease or insects rather than on the problem itself. IPM is a triangle with three major factors always present: HOST (plant), PATHOGEN (disease or insect) and ENVIRONMENT (growing conditions). These factors are further influenced by TIME. Let's look at some examples:

HOST… some roses are more disease resistant than others. Many are mildew-prone, others blackspot easily. If these diseases are prevalent in your area, select resistant varieties or be prepared to battle diseases all season. And some roses are gracious insect hosts, too. Spider mites like certain varieties and types, particularly dense-growing miniatures with tiny leaves. Thrips like light-colored, fragrant blooms; darker blooms attract less and show less damage. Either live with some damage or wage an aggressive war; select varieties that are more tolerant.

PATHOGEN… The fungus disease or insect needs to be clearly identified and then controlled by a variety of specific means. Alternating spray materials or combining single-site and multi-site fungicides reduces the chance of resistance. Surface-protective materials like *Maneb* or *Daconil* inhibit leaf penetration. Systemics like *Funginex* and *Banner Maxx* block pathogen reproduction in the leaf. Combined, they have a one-two punch with better fungus control. Insects build up resistance, too. As in the case of spider mites. Water-wash to reduce spider mite populations, alternate miticides if they get out of hand. And LESS use of broad-spectrum insecticides spares mite predators which act as a control. Example: less *Orthene* equates to fewer spider mites.

ENVIRONMENT… It surrounds us all the time and is easy to observe. Roses in full sun have less trouble with fungus diseases than roses in partial shade or subject to periods of wet leaves. Sun and good air circulation inhibit powdery mildew. Damp conditions promote blackspot; dry climates with cool nights and warm days are more likely to support powdery mildew. Rosarians have some de-

gree of control over the growing environment. Example: most lawn irrigation systems spray leaves and keep them wet for long periods, resulting in blackspot. Change the water environment. Even resistant varieties like 'Bonica' can be covered with blackspot when grown in partial shade. Reason: the leaves stay wet longer because of morning dew. Location is important in insect control, too. Miniature roses planted next to a foundation are perfect breeding grounds for spider mites. Mites breed in any location with a warm incubator effect. Location is a consideration when planting otherwise-resistant roses near fungus hosts like ramblers (although we don't call them that any more). You're also in trouble with roses in any area that is hard to spray… climbers over a trellis.

TIME impacts all of the IPM factors. A timely spray schedule is absolutely essential. Given time, spores will reproduce… as will spider mites. Understand the time that it takes in your environment to reproduce spores or insects. Control BEFORE spores emerge, then continue on a timely basis. Weeks of warm, humid weather support blackspot; dry spells slow down the process. Hot, dry weather brings on spider mites; water-wash more frequently then. The TIME factor is important to host, pathogen and environment.

CONSIDER ALL THE PARTS of the IPM equation. Ignore one factor and you'll have to work harder elsewhere to overcome the consequences. That's the whole ides of INTEGRATED. Consider and work with ALL of the parts of the triangular puzzle to produce roses satisfactory you.

IPM isn't just easy… it's a necessity.

A SUMMER SUGGESTION... Roses like lots of water... mostly sweat. Do your share (but not TOO much) with a couple of these hot-weather tips...

FERTILIZER BURN. How does it happen? It's simple: too much nitrogen and not enough water. But why does it happen? Roses are made up of cells whose activity is supported by water, just like human skin and tissue. Burn occurs when water is removed or displaced from the cells. Most fertilizers use ammonium sulfate or ammonium nitrate as a nitrogen source, synthesizing the element found in nature. These compounds are HYGROSCOPIC in nature, that is, have the tendency to take up water. If the compounds (fertilizers) in the soil are too concentrated, moisture is absorbed from the soil, and even the roots, thereby destroying or otherwise interfering with the moisture support system for the cells.

NATURE LIKES BALANCE. Concentrated solutions want to add water and will perform this trick through osmosis, pulling moisture through the cell walls. The solution to fertilizer burn is to apply appropriate amounts and ALWAYS with plenty of water. That's the reason for the advice: water first, feed, water again. If in doubt, water some more.

COMBO CONTROL for fungus disease control should be part of your rose vocabulary. Combinations of systemic and contact fungicides provide protection IN the leaf and ON the leaf for a one-two punch. Examples are *Funginex* and *Manzate*, or *Funginex* and *Daconil 2787*... a good weekly program. Or try another combo of *Banner Maxx* and *Manzate* (or *Daconil*) on a 14-day cycle. The new family of fungicides called "strobilurins" has a combo-like action that is "mesostemic," penetrating the leaf surface but not into the vascular system. *Compass* and *Heritage* are members of this new family derived from mushrooms. As with all fungicides, materials should be rotated to avoid build-up of resistant fungus strains.

ALPHABET ACRONYMS... Check out these indentifiers that make spraying easier and better. You know that EC (as in *Orthene 9.4% EC*) means emulsifiable concentration, a solvent carrying the active ingredient. Another, SP, indicates a soluble powder, (as in *Orthene 75% SP*). The active ingredient is soluble, goes right into solution.

Manzate 200DF labels the compound as dry flowable, especially treated to go into water suspension easily, much better than the greasy, talc-like stuff that used to settle out in the spray tank. *Daconil Ultrex* is a water dispersible granule (WDG) that goes right into the spray mix without difficulty. It's the Rambler's opinion that *Daconil Ultrex* is far superior to the *Daconil* in a solvent carrier. Security puts out a formulation of *Daconil* called *FungiGard*, a very convenient FLOWABLE mix which they call *Aqua-Blend*. The stuff is already in water solution. Wetable powders (WP) are the hardest to handle, often refusing to disperse in the spray solution. The next time you buy, look for SP, DF, WDG or flowable formulations for easier handling.

LEAVES SHOULD GLISTEN. How much is "enough" spray on leaves? Most advice calls for "good coverage," whatever that is. A better definition suggests application of the spray material to a "glistening" stage, not to run-off. When a leaf glistens, the material has spread evenly over the leaf without gaps or droplets. Spreader-stickers and spray "buffers" make water somewhat "wetter" and able to spread and adhere to the leaf, something like dishwasher detergents that buffer water without leaving spots on glassware. Spray effectiveness is a function of spray mix, pressure and nozzle setting. PLUS the care of the rosarian. "Glistening" saves materials and does an effective job. Take a good look next time you spray to see just how well your leaves glisten. If they don't, make some changes in your program.

AS A ROSARIAN, if you must open up a can of worms the compost pile seems a likely place. Here are some ideas you may want to compost this summer...

COOL ROSES... and cool rosarians, both good objectives when the temperature tops out. Nature's air conditioner is mulch, an insulating blanket that saves water, controls weeds and adds to the richness of the soil at the same time. Just a few inches of loose organic mulch dramatically reduces soil temperature and moisture evaporation. Most "home mix" mulches are combos of wood chips, ground bark, leaves, straw, compost or what have you. Skeptics say these mulches "leach" nitrogen from the soil, but all it takes is an extra handful of any cheap nitrogen source to release soil-building humus. Nitrogen is used in the process, replace it.

OLD MULCH? What if mulch doesn't break down right away? Leave it in place, use for winter protection and just add some more next season. Old wives' tales hold that mulches harbor insects and fungus spores. This is only partially true; these living bits of nature live in many environments; control with an extra insecticide/fungicide spray pass.

WHAT HAPPENED TO THE BLOOMS? In many parts of the country rose midge is the culprit this time of year. Blackened tips where a tiny bud should emerge is the evidence left behind. Blind growth only; no blooms. A good control is granular *Diazinon* broadcast in and around the rosebeds just after the first bloom cycle. This gets the soil-borne insect at the source. *Diazinon* liquid misted over the tops of bushes also helps. Midge season is short; two applications should do the trick.

WATCH OVERKILL. Take it easy on insecticides. Excessive use of *Orthene* (or any other broad-spectrum insecticide) kills off the beneficials, and rosarians wind up with spider mite infestations that defoliate bushes. When thrips are a "real" problem, spray just the blooms and buds. For those "special" blooms, mist the buds with a "*Windex*-type" sprayer, mixing up a fresh batch of *Orthene* each time. Insecticides become addictive — once you're hooked, it's hard to quit. Kick the habit if you can.

READY TO SWITCH? *Funginex* costs too much? Switch to *Banner Maxx* for fungus disease control, particularly if you have a large rose garden. *Banner Maxx* is a very effective control for blackspot and powdery mildew, and can be applied every two weeks rather than weekly. It is a persistent fungicide that loses effectiveness slowly. Used at just 1/3 teaspoon per gallon of buffered water, it is also cost-effective. Combine with a contact-type like *Manzate* for the best protection. Start with a clean garden, go on a *Banner Maxx* schedule, and you'll enjoy better roses with less work. A bit pricey initially (about $100 a quart), but a little goes a long way, and it has a long shelf life.

SUMMERTIME TONIC... Best summer cooler is some alfalfa tea, fortified with a touch of *Epsom* salts and trace elements. Refreshing for roses, summer relief for rosarians. For a tea recipe and other good summer stuff, drop the Rambler a note with a self-addressed business envelope.

SOME GOOD STUFF worth sharing. The Rambler encourages you to get a *Gardens Alive* catalog... the current catalog sells all sorts of stuff, but also is an excellent guide to common diseases and insects in the garden. You can get a catalog by calling (812) 539-8650 or get on your computer with www.gardens-alive.com. You may or may not buy into all of the organic products that *Gardens Alive* touts, but this is a really good informational piece. Especially look at the *Dustin-Mizer* duster, a great way to get dusts of all sorts into the garden.

A SUMMERTIME TREAT is the Moore Miniature Roses catalog (Sequoia Nursery). It's a lifetime history of roses of all types by Ralph Moore, father of miniature roses. For a catalog, call (559) 732-0309 or log onto www.miniatureroses.com.

STAY COOL. We'll talk about water systems next month.

NOTHING SEEMS IMPOSSIBLE to the rosarian who doesn't have to do it himself… but this month is an updated do-it-yourself water systems short-course.

THE WATER AWARD goes to *DripWorks*, the "We make it simple" source of irrigation products. Loyal readers may recall that the Rambler field-tests irrigation systems in new rosebeds from time to time: *DripWorks Emitters, Dramm Stix, Dramm Nozzles* (rigid pipe) and *Moisture Master,* the porous hose made from recycled automobile tires. The BEST report is that ALL of the systems worked well, were relatively inexpensive, delivered water to roses in sufficient quantity and were adaptable to many common garden situations. BUT, the flexibility and ease of installation of the adjustable flow emitters of *DripWorks* continues to win the praise of the Rambler.

ADJUSTABLE FLOW EMITTERS are on 5-inch plastic stakes, fed with 1/4-inch spaghetti tubing plugged into 1/4-inch polyvinyl tubing with transfer barbs. The poly tubing connects to a hose end or faucet. Turn it on and each emitter (adjustable) delivers 4-5 gallons of water per hour over a 12-inch radius. Thin streams of water come out in an octagonal pattern, spreading and soaking. No waste, very little evaporation. The watering area can be increased or decreased by turning the top of the emitter. The spaghetti tubing allows placement of the emitter stake well away from the supply tubing, just where the grower wants it.

A STARTER KIT called *Glorious Gardens Rose Kit* in the *DripWorks* catalog sells for about $50. The Rambler installed it for 18 roses along a fence in just 45 minutes. Used a garden hose *Quick-Coupler* for water supply. To order a catalog with ALL kinds of great garden stuff call 1-800-522-3747.

DRAMM STIX works in a similar manner, fed through spaghetti tubing inserted into polyvinyl flexible pipe. The *Dramm* nozzle puts out an umbrella-like spray up to an 18-inch radius, delivering varying amounts of water. The wire "*Stix*" on which the nozzles are mounted come in lengths from 10 to 30 inches long. Just push the *Stix* in the ground where water is needed. Each *Stix* comes with 24 or more inches of tubing. The *Dramm* requires an 11/64-inch drill bit to make a hole.

Friction holds it in place, even at high water pressure. The *Dramm* delivery is particularly good for miniatures, directing a fine water spray under the foliage (drown the spider mites). *Dramm Stix* sets up just as quickly as *Glorious Gardens* IF you use transfer barbs instead of drilling… not every rosarian has an 11/64-inch drill bit and the urge to run power to the rosebed. A really GOOD system, suitable for many rose growers. Information sheets on *Dramm* are available by calling 1-800-258-0848.

DRAMM NOZZLES used in rigid *Schedule 40* PVC pipe should not be overlooked for neat, professional installations. The system accepts fertilizer injection systems, timers and what-have-you for reliable delivery. However, the rigid PVC pipe does not adapt well to curved installations, requires more time to lay out and build, and the holes for the nozzles must be carefully drilled. In a formal straight bed, you can build it and forget it for years and years. If you would like installation instructions for *Dramm Nozzles* or *Stix*, drop the Rambler a note with a SASE.

MEANTIME, MOISTURE MASTER keeps on oozing away with slow water delivery that is as flexible as a garden hose. Just snake the porous hose in, around and through the rosebeds or plants, hook up to a garden hose and let it run for an hour or so… depending on water pressure and the size of the delivery hose. The Rambler's 125-foot line weaves in and out of a large bed of miniatures, a couple of shrub roses, and a climber… about 45 plants in all. It takes about three hours to soak the bed with 50 pounds water pressure. It is installed on TOP of the mulch, pinned in place with stiff wire. On top it is easy to see what is happening and watch the spread of the water. Easy to work, patch, couple. Good!

CHECK THE NUMBER: The phone number for GARDENS ALIVE in the July issue was incorrect. Call (812) 537-8651 to get a SPRING 2000 catalog full of good stuff and guide to common insects and diseases.

A GARDEN IS A THING OF BEAUTY and a job forever... it seems like forever... this column marking 30 years of the Rambler in *American Rose*. Even the "Thought for the Month" comes from September 1970. But enough of the old stuff, here are some NEW ways to enjoy better roses.

SEEING SPOTS? Blackspot gets our attention this time of year as conditions are just right for fungus growth: warm temperature and high humidity. Add an irregular spray schedule or extra moisture, and the bushes lose their leaves. But it does not have to be this way. There's still time to control infection, grow some new leaves and enjoy some great roses.

PROTECTIVE/PREVENTIVE SPRAYING controls fungus infections best with a weekly program during periods of high stress. If that line of defense has some gaps, go to a reactive program with a combination of systemic and contact fungicides like *Funginex* and *Manzate* applied at shorter intervals, perhaps twice a week for two or three weeks. Also pull off all the infected growth you can and practice good garden hygiene. You'll be able to go back to a more normal schedule within a month. Increase frequency, not concentration of material.

PROGRAM ROTATION is important to head off disease resistance from continuous use of one systemic material. Rotation reduces the chance of resistance to a given fungicide by introducing a different fungicidal family, i.e., *Funginex, Cleary's 3336, Banner Maxx, Immunox* or *Compass* (one of a new family called "strobilurins"). And there are various contact materials, i.e. *Manzate 200, Mancozeb* or *Dithane* (there are several variations in the *Manzate* family) or one of the forms of *Daconil 2787*. Carefully mixed and matched with systemics, these fungicides are a match for the most virulent spores, provided you get them on the leaves.

GOOD COVERAGE is often overlooked. Use of a spreader-sticker in addition to the built-in surfactant is usually in order. The Rambler recommends *Indicate-5*, buffering the spray solution and making the water wetter for even leaf coverage. *Indicate-5* even has its own pH indicator to confirm a slightly acid condition in any water. Makes spraying easier and more effective.

WET LEAVES SET UP HIGH STRESS. Leaves that remain wet for extended periods, maybe due to shade or evening overhead watering, are going to show infection. Check both water and shade. The Rambler noted blackspot on some container-grown miniatures while nearby roses on the same spray routine were clean. Reason: the container minis were watered in the evening with a wand water breaker; the leaves stayed wet all night. Cleared up the problem by watering in the morning before going to work. Solved a shade problem by cutting off the sprinkler system in that area.

EXTENDED PROTECTION. One garden the Rambler looks after is in full sun all day. It has been consistently clean of both blackspot and mildew with a *Banner Maxx* spray program at 1/3 teaspoon per gallon every 21 days. A *Manzate*-type contact fungicide was combined every other spraying. During a prolonged rainy period, *Manzate 200 DF* was sprayed by itself every two weeks. It is important to note that this garden has DRY leaves unless it rains.

SEVERE BLACKSPOT STRESS in another garden required *Banner Maxx* every 14 days, again with a contact material every other spraying. Equally effective was *Funginex* and *Manzate* in combination weekly. *Cleary's 3336* and *Mancozeb* also did a good job on a weekly basis and could be stretched to 10-14 days with just a trace of blackspot showing up.

OPENING UP THE BUSHES helped in all growing situations, trimming out blind and twiggy growth from the center of the plant. Getting the sunshine in to dry the leaves made a big difference. It also seemed to encourage low breaks and stronger remaining canes.

LET SOME SUNSHINE IN... get on a spray program and enjoy great roses this fall.

ROSE IDEAS that work are those you put to work. Here are a few to work on as winter approaches…

ALMOST TIME TO WINTERIZE roses and rosarians, insulating living material to survive cold and dry. The idea of insulation is to maintain a fairly constant temperature, avoiding freeze/thaw situations. Combinations of materials do this best, held in place with fences, boughs, cones or what-have-you. Roses like "thermal blankets" just like rosarians. When organics are used as insulators, there's an extra benefit as they add humus to the soil. And humus is much lighter than hauling soil in and out.

REALLY DEEP COLD requires more protection with soil mounded 6 to 8 inches over the canes, then covered with leaves. Bring in soil rather than taking from between the bushes in the beds. Soil/mulch combos are great… they breathe better.

ANTI-DESICCANT SPRAYS also help in the winter protection process, particularly with climbers and ramblers. Anti-desiccant sprays like *Wilt-Pruf* and *Cloud Cover* retain moisture that is otherwise lost to cold, dry winds… with an added plus of fungus protection. Lets the natural anti-freeze in the canes stay in the canes instead of evaporating out. When bushes drop their leaves, trim up to suit the situation and thoroughly spray the canes before wrapping or covering. Remember that canes are round and the backside needs some coverage too. More canes are lost to drying out than to actual cold; a liquid blanket can make a difference.

DIG A TRENCH, BURY FOR THE WINTER… the ultimate protection, but the maximum work. Roses received in late fall are much better off buried than potted and moved in and out of protection all winter. It's a natural sort of dormancy, sometimes called the "Minnesota Tip" buying method. The "Tip" calls for a trench up to the bush that is wide and deep enough to accommodate the bush with bundled canes. Loosen soil on one side of the bush and tip into the trench. Fill with soil and leaves. Tip back up next spring.

A DORMANCY VAULT can protect new bushes, miniatures or yearling plants. Pick a spot where it is easy to dig a trench 18 inches or so deep. Set aside soil. Line the vault with soil and leaves. Tie the bushes with twine, then bundle. Tuck into the vault and cover with leaf/soil mix. Tie a rope on the bundle so you'll know where to dig next spring. Cover area with leaves and wait for spring. Easy.

WINTER FEEDING/COMPOSTING IN PLACE. Many rosarians in severe as well as milder climates put down an 8-inch layer of leaves in the rosebed, broadcast a cupful of 10-10-10 pelletized fertilizer per 100 square feet, then add several more inches of leaves. By spring, the lower layer of leaves has broken down into a rich humus threaded with white mycelium. Don't disturb the lower layer of leaves any more than necessary at pruning time, or you may elect to leave all of the leaves in the bed, broadcasting more fertilizer on top. Rosarians who winter feed report no untimely growth in fall or spring when roses are put to bed with this "nightcap."

SAVE AND USE THE LEAVES. Most winterizing includes leaves in one form or another. Loose, leafy mixtures work best and don't pack. Uncomposted leaves that are shredded can shed water and are stingy on insulating air space. Shredded leaves work best when blended into soil. Or leaves can be composted in place over the "garden" area, piled into a windrow, dumped into a rick… anything to return nature's nutrients to the soil. To speed the process, add some dolomite lime to sweeten the pile and gypsum to keep it open and aerated. Broadcast five pounds or so of each onto and into a substantial pile, windrow or rick.

OR JUST SAVE THE LEAVES over winter to use as "bulk" in making up artificial manure next spring. The Rambler will share a time-tested fragrant formula with you at the appropriate time.

ENJOY THE FALL, but get ready for winter. Even warm-climate rosarians have some work to do to stay in step with Mother Nature.

EXPERIENCE is yesterday's answer to today's problems. Here are some shared experiences this season that will make your 2001 roses even rosier.

MINI-FLORA roses are finally taking off, being grown and enjoyed in many parts of the country. Now that they are "legitimate," rosarians are using them more and more in the landscape. If you haven't grown any of these "larger size" minis, you should do so next season.

NEW PRODUCTS are coming into the market that make life with roses more fun and less work. The Rambler has written about some of these for years, but availability was spotty. In your garden plan for next year, include some pH test strips to KNOW the balance in your rosebeds. Very easy to use, cheap, reliable. The merits of pH test strips are being widely touted in the newsletters everywhere. And *Indicate-5* is being used more and more as a conditioner/acidifier/spreader for spray materials. It really does make water "wetter" and spray materials more effective. With a built-in color indicator, the user can't go wrong.

SEAWEED EXTRACTS are also coming into their own. The Rambler likes *Response* added to every spray mix. Just takes a touch, but there is a noticeable difference in leaf substance and color. And the same thing must be happening with the blooms. There are a couple of exotic concoctions available like "Australian Red Kelp"... Australian or not, worth a try, just don't use too much.

WATER CRYSTALS, a hydrophilic (water and nutrient storing) polymer has a great application in container-growns of all kinds. You can expect savings of 30 percent to 50 percent of normal watering amounts of watering intervals. Translated this means watering container roses two or three times a week rather than daily during hot summer weather. Good in coarse sandy soils also. The polymer crystals absorb up to 200 times their weight in water and the roots grow right into them. Just hydrate and incorporate into any soil-less or sandy soil mix. The Rambler has used water crystals in barrels and pots for years (like *Broadleaf P4*) with consistent results.

ALFALFA TEA... still the best tonic around. Rave reviews come in every month on how roses (big ones and minis) perked up and bloomed. Alfalfa tea releases a growth hormone that makes all the processes work better. As a tea, it goes to work right away, you'll see a difference in seven to 10 days. Some additives like *Sequestrene 330 Fe* (chelated iron), *Epsom* salts (magnesium sulfate) and *Mills Easy-Feed* make it even better. Brew up a batch in a 32-gallon trash can with 10-12 cups of alfalfa pellets or meal, fill with water, stir occasionally for a week and give big roses a 1-gallon treat of the smelly elixir, minis about a half-gallon. Tea does NOT replace the normal feeding routine, just makes it work better.

POWER SPRAYERS... if you have any number of roses, you should get one. Now widely used and in every price range, rosarians are enjoying spraying with less work, less material and better results. While the Rambler uses a *Spot Shot*, he recommends the 3-gallon *Black & Decker* battery sprayer for smaller gardens. Keep it clean and maintained and it will give years and years of service with a $100 investment. TIP: Use a little silicone grease on the on-off piston now and then and spray away.

FUNGICIDES... every rosarian has a favorite or is looking for a new one. But the consensus of rosarians as reported in newsletters (and from the Rambler's experience) is that *Banner Maxx* combined with a contact material like *Fore* (manzate) or *Daconil Ultrex* will keep most rose gardens clean on a two-week schedule. Also have good reports and experience with *Cleary's 3336* as the systemic fungicide. *Compass* is also getting good reviews, but is a bit pricey for the average rosarian.

SHARED EXPERIENCE is what the Rambler does best. And as a year-end gift, I'll send you a whole pack of giveaways (how-to sheets and formulations) if you'll drop a note with a couple of 33-cent stamps. You'll get a big envelope of stuff that you'll be able to use. Just reprinted... just for you.

HAVE A HAPPY ONE and get ready for a Rosy 2001.

Howard Walters, 2001.

**JAN.
2001**

*THOUGHT FOR THE MONTH: Gardeners will be interested to know that
the government says it is the soil that's overworked.*

ROSE WISDOM abounds during this semi-dormant time… there's not a thing to be proved in the rose garden or on the show table. And have you ever noticed how roses get bigger and better with retelling?? A resolution for 2001: Tell the Queen of the Show story only when asked. Anyway, here are some Ramblings worth talking about…

GROW SOME SOIL… and you'll grow more and better roses. It's a relatively simple process when you understand the basics. Much like the Rambler's advice to grow leaves, then roses. You can't have one without the other.

SOIL SCIENCE… Soils are made up of mineral particles, among other things. These particles vary in size from gravel and rocks to sand to silt to clay in a decreasing size gradient. Clay is so small, for example, that it barely settles out in water because the force of friction between the clay particle and water is greater than the pull of gravity. In a soil, these flat-surfaced clay particles hold water and elements so that rose roots can pick them up. Clay surfaces carry a negative charge, much like a magnet, and attract positively-charged particles to them. The positively-charged particles that are attracted are ions of potassium, calcium, magnesium, et al. Attracted to clay, the ions can then be absorbed by the roots through water.

THE ROLE OF HUMUS… Humus is partially decomposed organic matter. It acts like a "glue" to bind clay and other soil particles into granules or crumbs. Soil crumbs (loamy) tend to be quite porous, and water and air enter the soil readily. Clay and humus act together to hold water, giving the "soil" a high water-holding capacity. It also allows excellent gas exchange so the roots have a sufficient supply of oxygen to support microorganisms converting minerals into forms the roots can pick up.

WORKING HUMUS… Humus derived from organic matter builds a "table" where roots can feed. As part of the soil granules or crumbs, humus has tremendous ability to hold positively charged ions, up to three or four times better than clay. It is the "holding" capability that slows leaching of nutrients from the rosebed. Humus is the key to good rose growing. It helps hold and make available water and nutrients, increases porosity of the soil, supports living organisms and keeps soil pH in balance. Need any more reasons to have up to 25 percent organic matter in your rosebed? Just check out the loads of roses enjoyed by growers who have understood this wonder of nature all along.

OWN-ROOT ROSES BETTER? It depends. Some own-root roses are better performers when budded; others are not. But roses on their own roots are gaining in popularity and availability in many parts of the country. Suckers from understock are things of the past. Well-adapted own-root varieties usually produce more canes and have less winter damage. They also seem to live and thrive longer, too. Of course, there is an offset. Own-root roses take somewhat longer to get to rose production size. Even a well grown own-root is not going to make it to the trophy table very often the first season. But, once established, watch out.

TOXIC CONCERNS about planting roses where roses have been before? Need new soil?? The Rambler says, "not to worry." There's a big word for it, ALLELOPATHY, the suppression of growth of one plant species by another due to the release of toxic substance. The Rambler has NEVER observed this in planting and replanting for years and years. If there is a growth slow-down, it's from "tired soil" that just needs to some organic matter to make it alive again. Of course a new mix for a planting hole is going to be full of all kinds of stuff, and roses will take right off. But in most cases, just give the soil a shot in the humus area.

EASY PRUNING next month, something all of us look forward to. For 2001, think POSITIVE for a short winter, long spring.

THE GOOD NEWS is that the bad news is wrong. Growing good roses isn't nearly as hard as we make it. Relax a bit this season and let Nature do her thing.

ARTISTIC PRUNING... Pruning is a highly overrated art. Rosarians anguish over where to cut and how to cut, but more roses will grow well in sport of the pruning technique. Practice and observation are the best learning tools, a sort of on-the-job training. Just visualize what you want the bush to look like this season and apply a little rose sense. Get out the dead wood, shape to please and prune to an outside eye. Get out to a pruning demonstration, if you can find one, and then into the rose garden when the time is right.

THINK OUTSIDE THE BOX... The Royal National Society conducted trials at St. Albans and found that roses trimmed with hedge shears had more leaves and more roses than roses pruned conventionally. The Rambler suspects the "Rose Truth" is somewhere in the middle.

CLIMBERS are cussed and discussed at pruning time, trying to come up with more blooms from an uncooperative bramble of thorns. Variety selection, identification or productive wood and training of the canes are the most important considerations. True climbers are bred for vigorous growth and lots of blooms. Climbing sports of hybrid teas are not in the same class. These sports can put out an impressive flush in the spring (if the canes are trained horizontally) followed by an occasional repeat. Untrained sports throw canes 10 feet long with one bloom on top.

TRAIN CLIMBING CANES to a horizontal support, a gradual process. Bloom laterals will emerge at each leaf axil, reaching for the sun. Each bloom lateral can be cut and enjoyed (or spent bloom removed) just like a hybrid tea. Some climbers cascade naturally, blooming all along the cane. Don Juan is a classic example- a rich, velvet red with great fragrance. Altissimo, Handel and Dortmund are also good choices. Canes can be trained up and over a trellis or arbor, weaving the canes for a lateral movement. Canes wound around a pillar achieve the same result... blooms all over.

HEAL 'EM IN... When rebuilding beds, dormant roses can be dug and set aside for a week or two, giving both a new lease on life. Dig carefully with a spading fork, don't worry about taking a ball of soil. Check the root system for galls and dead roots. Trim out or discard, depending on the severity. Don't bother with a weak bush; it takes more work than a healthy one. Set the dug bushes aside and cover with soil, sacks, mulch, bark or any other combo that keeps the bushes cool and moist. My dad referred to this as "heeling in," since the bushes were slanted in a trench. But dirt and manure types like the Rambler refer to this as "healing in." Whatever you call it, it works.

GROUND PINE BARK is much maligned by the uninformed but growingly praised by those who have enjoyed the benefits of this cheap, readily available soil improver. Short compost, leaves, peat moss? Try working about 25 percent fine-ground pine bark (by volume) into the soil, even more if the soil is really hard or depleted. The newly-worked area becomes friable almost overnight. Offset acidity with about 10 pounds of dolomite lime per 100 square feet, plus 5 pounds of 5-5-5 fertilizer to support the decomposition process. Or the Rambler likes cottonseed meal/alfalfa meal to feed the microorganisms working on the bark.

VALENTINE SPECIAL for rosarians. Instead of candy, ask for/deliver a load of horse manure to top-dress rosebeds or rejuvenate old ones. Find a friend with a horse, visit a stable, take riding lessons... whatever. This horse gold is worth its weight in roses. The Rambler's roses have enjoyed many a Valentine gift, which officially opens the rose season. Try some.

SPRINGTIME TONICS next month. We'll look at some chemical/organic combinations to please the most discriminating rose palate.

FEED STORE FRENZY strikes rosarians about now as they stock the rose pantry for the season. Here are some menus your roses will enjoy…

ROSES HAVE BIG APPETITES… but are also finicky eaters, so you'll want some things on the menu they like. Start with an appetizer, follow with three squares a day (and lots of water) and finish up with a dessert. Rosarians like this kind of menu, too.

FISH APPETIZER is a good starter (fish emulsion, of course). Fortify with a little urea in solution. Get this mix into the root zone, even if the soil is a little on the cold side. Fish emulsion or combinations of fish, alfalfa or cow tea feeds the soil which supports the organisms converting nutrients into forms available to plants. There's some food value in these teas, but the primary boost comes from cultivating the soil organisms going after the urea.

WARM ROOTS dine heartily. Fertilizers applied to cold soils don't do much good until the soil warms up, explaining why some rosarians think the program isn't working. The canes, warmed by sunshine, are waking up, but the roots are waiting for a clear signal that spring has arrived. Have you ever noticed how quickly roots grow when newly-potted in black plastic pots are set out on a warm, reflective surface? Same thing happens with electric bench blankets in a greenhouse, warming seedlings from the bottom up.

STICK-TO-THE-RIBS FOOD to sustain growth is next. The ribs (canes) are doing a lot of work. Organics do this very well, releasing slowly with all the right stuff for growth. Timed-release fertilizers may also be on your menu, releasing slowly and evenly. Organic enthusiasts, like the Rambler, like to mix up a batch of organic potpourri with a seasoning of 10-10-10 plus trace elements… making up a hundred pounds or so at a time.

FEED STORES sell the staples in this recipe. Mix about 50 pounds each of alfalfa meal (or pellets) and fish meal, 25 pounds each of cottonseed meal and blood meal, 25 pounds of bone meal, 10 pounds of triple superphosphate and finally about 50 pounds of 10-10-10 with trace (coated release). Blend these dry ingredients in a couple of big wheelbarrows or in a big pile… but keep it dry as it will begin to work. Analysis will be about 8-8-8; use about three heaping cups per bush, a scant half-cup for miniatures. Scratch in the soil a bit and flood with LOTS of water. Repeat this mostly-organic feast about mid-August.

TOP OFF WITH DESSERT about two weeks before peak bloom (or perhaps two weeks before a rose show or event). A typical dessert is a soluble mix of *Peter's 20-20-20* with fish emulsion, about 2 tablespoons of each per gallon of water, 1 gallon per large rose.

SNACKS ARE ALSO TASTY from time to time and relished by roses. The Rambler likes a tonic of alfalfa tea, cow tea or a similar brew laced with an iron chelate like *Sprint* (sequestrene) and *Epsom* salts. Use whenever foliage pales or growth slows. Depending on the climate, this may be two or three times during a season, delivering a growth hormone as well as iron. *Epsom* salts (magnesium sulfate) can also be broadcast to encourage basal breaks (small handful per bush), particularly right after the first bloom flush when roses are at their peak of vigor. Broadcast some available nitrogen at the same time. Make sure the bushes have plenty of water to drink during heave growth. Water is good all the time, but absolutely essential when feeding and growing.

CONVENIENCE FOODS… There are some good ones available regionally like *Mills Magic Rose Mix*, convenient and organic and liked by all kinds of roses. No mixing, no muss, no fuss. *Mills Easy-Feed* is an even more convenient soluble material. Look around your region for *Mills* or a similar product, remembering the organic sources. Alfalfa pellets are convenient also. Just broadcast and let water do the work.

SPRAY PROGRAMS are on the agenda next month, just in time for new leaves and fungus disease.

SPRING is the time to spring into action to manage fungal disease in your garden. Here's BLACKSPOT 101 for your garden quiz.

GROW LEAVES, THEN ROSES... lush leaves make great hosts for a variety of pathogens bent on finding a home. Add free water and specific temperatures for continuously spreading infection. Obviously a maintenance problem.

PROTECTIVE OR REACTIVE... the best approach is a protective-preventive spray program BEFORE the pathogen becomes active. Preventive spraying is regular and cyclical in nature, knowing when to start and when to reapply, depending on the fungicide of choice. Reactive spraying, waiting until the disease is present and then attempting to control, results in irreversible damage and lost foliage. Lost foliage means lost roses.

SYSTEMIC AND CONTACT fungicides are readily available to the hobby grower, and each type has a specific approach. Systemic fungicides are absorbed into the leaf tissues. In the tissue, systemics are protected from the elements and effective within the sprayed tissue from 7-14 days. As new foliage appears, systemics must be reapplied as most do not move through the plant. Contact fungicides are protectants that remain on the leaf surface and act by inhibiting invasion at the surface, a sort of armor plating. Contacts wear off quickly, in 5-7 days and don't protect new growth.

SYSTEMIC FUNGICIDES have a weak spot in the form of potential disease resistance with continuous use. Program rotation reduces the chance of resistance by interjecting a different fungicidal family and mode of action. Rotation from *Funginex* (Triforine) to *Banner Maxx* to *Cleary's 3336* interrupts the pattern, preferable on an every-other-month basis.

CONTACT FUNGICIDES are less susceptible to resistance than systemics and can be safely used continuously. Trusted standbys are derivatives of *Daconil* and *Manzate*. But COMBINING a systemic with a contact material provides even better protection against pathogen resistance.

COMBINATIONS provide protection *in* the leaf and *on* the leaf. Blackspot penetrates deep into the tissue and grows inside. Powdery mildew is more of a surface pathogen and can be blocked on the leaf surface. Contacts work quicker on powdery mildew; systemics work harder on blackspot. *Rubigan* is an exception, a very good systemic for powdery mildew.

SPREADER-STICKERS help both systemic and contact fungicides, and most fungicides already have some spreader-sticker built in. However, use of a "buffer" to make water "wetter" enhances effectiveness of fungicides and prolongs the activity of insecticides. A buffer like *Indicate-5* lowers the pH of the spray solution, wets spreads, penetrates, aids compatibility and reduces volatility. It gets the fungicides into working position. Another "super-wetter" is *Surf-King Plus*, similar in action to *Indicate-5* but without the pH color indicator. Both are very effective in an ongoing spray program and are essential when using a miticide like *Avid*.

FLOWABLE FUNGICIDES, fungicides in aqueous (water) solution, are easier to use and less likely to burn. Examples are *Manzate DF* (dry flowable), *Daconil 2787 WDG* (Water Dispersible Granules) and *Maneb Flowable* all go into the spray solution readily and stay there.

GOOD SPRAY EQUIPMENT delivers the goods. Buy the best sprayer to fit your needs (and finances).

MAGIC POTIONS are not the answer in blackspot prevention. However, a new family of fungicides called "Strobilurins" are close to the magic class. A mushroom derivative called *Compass* is 50 percent water dispersible granule formulation that appears to be an excellent preventive for blackspot, powdery mildew and rust and effective for 14 days. *Compass* is a "mesostemic" fungicide with high affinity for waxy leaf surfaces but also penetrates the leaf system. Binds tightly to the leaf and very weather resistant. It's expensive, about $200 for 8 ounces, but used at 1/8 teaspoon per gallon. Cost per spray gallon is comparable to *Cleary's* and *Banner Maxx*.

APRIL SHOWERS BRING MAY FLOW-ERS ... especially roses. Here are some tips to work with the showers sure to come your way...

IT'S THRIPS TIME... coming into rose gardens in waves looking for light-colored, fragrant blooms. Thrips appear to migrate from grasses and field flowers, at least they appear at the same time. *Orthene 75% SP* (soluble powder) is the Rambler's favorite control, systemic and safe for the most tender blooms. Use *Orthene SP* at 2 teaspoons per gallon of buffered solution, get good coverage of buds and blooms and hit the beds, too. Spot-spray developing buds and blooms with a pistol-pump sprayer every-other day, making up a FRESH batch of *Orthene* each time. The thrips fog will dissipate in a few weeks and you can go back to occasional use of *Orthene* ONLY when there is severe thrips pressure. Too much *Orthene* will set up the garden for spider mites, having destroyed the mite's natural predators.

MAY AND POWDERY MILDEW go together in many parts of the country. But there's hope for clean foliage and good blooms with EARLY application of *Rubigan EC* at 2 teaspoons per 5 gallons of buffered water. Can be combined every-other-week with *Triforine*. *Systhane* is another good mildewcide (also known as *Nova, Eagle* or *Rally*) in a 40 WP formulation. It is the active ingredient in *Immunox*, a home-garden formulation. *Banner Maxx* works rather well on a 14-day schedule. Since these products are systemic, get protection INTO the tissue before powdery-gray appears. Powdery mildew hits new growth; get good coverage.

BUFFERED WATER? That's the Rambler's term for spray solution that has been treated with *Indicate-5* or *Surf-King Plus,* lowering the pH of the water and making it wetter. Start EVERY spray session by treating the water, then adding the active materials. You'll see a difference even in the mixing process.

BASAL BOOSTER... Now's the time to launch a major thrust for more basal and low breaks with a readily available source of nitrogen followed by *Epsom* salts applied just after the initial bloom cycle while roses are at their peak of vigor. *Epsom* salts (magnesium sulfate) works best when AVAILABLE nitrogen is present (a nitrate form is best). Use a soluble 20-20-20 the first week, 1/2 cup of Epsom salts the second week, with successive applications of 20-20-20 weeks three and four. Cut the 20-20-20 concentration in half due to the frequency of application. New basals require LOTS of energy in the root zone for results, driven by LOTS of water.

FRESH HORSE MANURE??? Should it be reported to the EPA?? No, keep it a secret and treat your roses with all that you can haul. Use it on the rosebed, in the rosebed... wherever organic matter and bacterial action are needed. No need to compost horse manure/shavings/alfalfa hay/straw mixtures before using on roses. Some of the "good stuff" is lost by waiting for the "well rotted" stage. Let the microbial action rejuvenate the beds, feeding the soil. Use manure from stalls rather than horse lots to reduce weeds. The Rambler's roses think it's a special treat to get an inch or two of horse manure mulch just a week out of the horse.

NO ACCESS TO A HORSE?? Then make up some "Fragrant Formula" with fish meal, cottonseed meal, alfalfa meal and some form of roughage like fine-ground bark shavings and leaves. By volume, use four times as much roughage as meal. Add some blood meal if you like, maybe bone meal. Make a big pile, mix the dry ingredients with a pitchfork, moisten lightly and allow to digest for a week. Turn again. The finished product will be just like manure without having to run it through a horse. Use a BIG pitchforkful per bush and lots of water. Your soil organisms and roses will love it. Your neighbors will love the roses, too, when the sharp ammonia odor dissipates in a day or two.

JUN.
2001

THOUGHT FOR THE MONTH:
My garden was great last week. Sorry you missed it.

ROSE IDEAS are much like children... our own are wonderful. Here are some that the Rambler thinks are great.

TIME FOR TEA... in vogue these days of tonics and magic elixirs. Alfalfa tea is still the best, used in the rose garden whenever the bushes begin to look a little droopy. The "magic" is triacontanol, a growth hormone naturally occurring in alfalfa. It makes the whole soil/nutrient process work better. Brew up a batch in a 32-gallon trash barrel, using about 12 cups of alfalfa pellets or meal per barrel. Fill with water, stir and cover for several days while the brew steeps. Be sure to cover the barrel — it smells. Stir with a broom handle now and then. Ready in about a week.

TREAT THE ROSES with about a gallon of brew, about half as much for minis. The leaves will green up and growth will recommence. The Rambler's roses like to take tea in early spring, mid-summer and late summer. Fortified tea may be even better, depending on your feeding program. To the finished tea, add 1/3 cup of chelated iron, 1/2 cup of Epsom salts and 1 cup of 20-20-20 soluble fertilizer with trace elements. Stir well and stand back. The roses are going to grow.

VISIT THE FARM STORE for alfalfa, cottonseed, fish and other natural meals. These friendly folks will get you what you need if it is not in stock in the back. You'll become a member of an exclusive gardening fraternity when you relax in a feed store.

GOURMET FARE for roses includes *Osmocote*, timed-release nutrients that roses like and are great on convenience, which rosarians like. There are several formulations, but most growers like the action of *Osmocote* 15-11-13 with trace elements, good for three to four months. And there's a 16-8-12 that works for about eight months. A good menu to consider.

SPIDER MITES WILL BE ACTIVE as summer heats up, multiplying furiously and sucking the life right out of rose leaves. Head off severe infestation by keeping mite populations under control early as well as throughout the season. Water-washing is a good practice, directing a strong, fine water spray underneath the leaves. In many cases, water-washing is all that's needed as an ongoing summer routine. If water-washing is impractical, or the mites get ahead of you, get going with *Avid* FAST! Wash as best you can with lots of water, spray underneath the leaves with *Avid* enhanced with *Stirrup-M*, the sex-attractant pheromone. *Avid* is used at 1/4 teaspoon per gallon, *Stirrup-M* at three drops per gallon. Repeat the process in four days to catch the new hatch.

PAY ATTENTION AND ACT FAST as spider mite season arrives. Watch for leaves that turn gray-green. Pull suspicious lower leaves and look for salt-and-pepper specs with traces of web. You won't see the mites without a glass, but the telltale signs are evident. With a sharp eye, you can spot spider mites at work from 20 feet away. *Avid* works best when not combined with other insecticides or fungicides... and has greater residual and systemic action in a "buffered" spray solution, i.e., lower pH with a spreader. Need a cheap buffer? To alkaline tap water, add from 1 to 2 tablespoons of white vinegar per gallon plus a few drops of dishwashing liquid. The spray solution will spread evenly on leaves, even underneath. Done right, the leaves will "glisten" with spray.

TAKE IT EASY ON INSECTICIDES. Excessive use of *Orthene* (or any other broad-spectrum insecticide) for thrips also kills off the beneficials and rosarians wind up with spider mite infestations that defoliate bushes. When thrips are a real PROBLEM, spray just the blooms and buds. For those "special" blooms, mist the buds with a spray bottle, mixing up just a quart of fresh solution each time. There's no need to use an insecticide with each application of fungicide. Insecticides become addictive — like drugs. Once you're hooked, it's hard to quit. Kick the habit if you can.

ROSARIANS who know all the answers haven't asked all the questions. Here are some Q&A's for July...

JAPANESE BEETLES continue to plague eastern United States rosarians, and we still don't have a control that handles all situations without some drawbacks. *Liquid Sevin* works, but leaves residue, kills beneficial and needs frequent application. *Sevin Dust* with the *Dustin-Mizer* has to be used three times a week on calm, dry foliage. Picking is impractical for most growers. But the Rambler is encouraged by the effectiveness of *Milky Spore*, even without treating the whole neighborhood. The Rambler applied *Milky Spore* two years ago over the whole yard and overlapped some of the neighbors last season. Have seen a SIGNIFICANT decrease in beetle population this year, in spite of living on a golf course. Don't tell me the beetles don't travel. Given another year or two to spread, the *Milky Spore* may make June pleasant again.

GOOD FOLIAGE, NO BLOOMS? Midge is probably the culprit if your garden is in the eastern United States. Blackened stem tips where a tiny bud should emerge is the evidence left behind. Blind growth may push out, but no blooms. A good control is granular *Diazinon* broadcast in and around the rosebeds like fertilizer, applied just after the first bloom cycle. This gets the soil-borne insect at the source. And mist the tops of the bushes with diazinon liquid. Since the midge season is short, two applications should do the trick.

BATTERY-POWERED SPRAYER not meeting expectations? Maybe you need a system upgrade to take full advantage of the power and pressure that makes the job easier. The Rambler suggests that you upgrade to a system, such as *Spray Systems*, with interchangeable parts and accessories. Start with a good control handle (looks like a paint spray gun). Then add a 24-to-30-inch wand and adjustable or fixed nozzle for your particular application. For roses, the Rambler likes a 30-inch wand curved on the end, fitted with a *Tee-Jet 8004* nozzle. This combination puts out a flat, fan-shaped spray pattern that covers 24-30 inches of a rosebush at a pass. *Spray Systems Tee-Jet* has a wide assortment of nozzles from adjustable to cone shape to flat, with a coarse or fine spray. Check out a spray equipment dealer or exterminator supply store for *Spray System* parts.

HANDY SPRAYER... The recently introduced *Black & Decker* 3-gallon power sprayer is just right for small gardens. Rechargeable battery-powered, the canister is mounted on a light, two-wheel tripod frame like a golf bag buggy. Works on air pressure rather than a liquid pump, has an adjustable nozzle for droplet size and coverage. It sure beats a hand pump; costs about $100 and is easy to use, easy to wash out. One charge will put out about 6 to 8 gallons of spray without getting tired. The Rambler prefers a heavy-duty rechargeable for large gardens, but this light rig is very good. Look up a *Black & Decker* outlet in your area; the dealer here even has a demo and will let you spray into a bucket.

KEEP ANY SPRAYER CLEAN by running a weak vinegar solution through it, then flushing with clear water. Get rid of old spray (safely). Partially clogged sprayers are neither effective nor fun to use. Use the vinegar purge every second or third use, flush with water EVERY time. The Rambler has a *Spot Shot* that hasn't failed or clogged in 15 years and a *Hudson* pump-up that is even older than that... just by taking good care of them.

AIR CONDITION rosebeds with a cooling, water-saving soil-conditioning mulch this time of year... if you haven't done so already. You'll spend fewer hours in the hot sun pulling weeds and more time enjoying your roses. Lots of choices are cheap: ground bark, pine needles, compost, leaves and mixtures of all of these. Use liberally, replace nitrogen used in the decomposition process with a light broadcast of any lawn fertilizer. No need to pull back mulch when feeding roses, broadcast on top or pour through, just like water through coffee grounds. Mulches add to, not rob soil.

SUMMER SCHEDULE: Feed the soil, water, spray... wait for cooler weather.

ROSES NEED A LOT OF WATER... mostly in the form of sweat. But for REAL water, here's an updated do-it-yourself water systems short course... just in time for hot, dry weather.

WATER, WATER, ANYWHERE... and the Water Award goes to *DripWorks*, the "We make it simple" source for irrigation products. Loyal readers may recall that the Rambler field-tests irrigation systems in new rosebeds from time to time: *DripWorks Emitters*, *Dramm Stix*, *Dramm Nozzles* (rigid pipe) and *Moisture Master*, the porous hose made of recycled automobile tires. The BEST report is that ALL of the systems worked well, were relatively inexpensive, delivered water to roses in sufficient quantity and were adaptable to many common garden situations. BUT, the flexibility and ease of installation of the adjustable flow emitters of *DripWorks* continues to win the praise of the Rambler... wanting to spend more time with roses and less time in construction.

ADJUSTABLE FLOW EMITTERS are on 5-inch plastic stakes, fed with 1/2-inch spaghetti tubing plugged into 1/2-inch polyvinyl tubing with transfer barbs. The poly tubing connects to a hose end or faucet. Turn it on and each emitter (adjustable) delivers 4 to 5 gallons of water per hour over a 12-inch radius. Thin streams of water come out in an octagonal pattern, spreading and soaking. No waste, very little evaporation. The watering area can be increased or decreased by turning the top of the emitter. The spaghetti tubing allows placement of the emitter stake well away from the supply tubing.

A STARTER KIT called Glorious Gardens Rose Kit in the *DripWorks* catalog sells for about $50. The Rambler installed it for 18 roses along a fence in just 45 minutes. Used a garden hose *Quick-Coupler* for water supply. To order a catalog with ALL kinds of great garden stuff call 1-800-522-3747.

ANOTHER WATER-WINNER is *Moisture Master*, which keeps oozing away with slow water delivery that is as flexible as a garden hose. Just snake the porous hose in, around and through the rosebeds or plants, hook up to a garden hose and let it run for an hour or so... depending on water pressure and the size of the delivery hose. The Rambler's 125-foot line weaves in and out of a large bed of miniatures, a couple of shrub roses, and a climber... about 45 plants in all. It takes about three hours to soak a bed with 50 pounds of water pressure. It is installed on TOP of the mulch, pinned in place with stiff wire. Easy to work, patch, couple. Good!

DRAMM STIX works in a manner similar to adjustable flow emitters, fed through spaghetti tubing inserted into polyvinyl flexible pipe. The *Dramm* nozzle puts out an umbrella-like spray up to an 18-inch radius, delivering varying amounts of water. The wire "Stix" on which the nozzles are mounted come in lengths from 10 to 30 inches long. Just push the Stix in the ground where water is needed. Each Stix comes with 24 or more inches of tubing. The *Dramm* requires an 11/64-inch drill bit to make a hole. Friction holds in place, even at high water pressure. The *Dramm* delivery is particularly good for miniatures, directing a fine water spray under the foliage (drown the spider mites). *Dramm Stix* sets up just as quickly as Glorious Gardens IF you use transfer barbs instead of drilling... not every rosarian has a 11/64-inch drill bit and the urge to run power to a rosebed. A really GOOD system, suitable for many rose growers. Information sheets on *Dramm* are available by calling (414) 684-0227.

DRAMM NOZZLES used in rigid schedule 40 PVC pipe should not be overlooked for neat, professional installations. The system accepts fertilizer injection systems, timers and what-have-you for reliable delivery. The Rambler has used *Dramm* nozzles for many years with great results. However, the rigid PVC pipe does not adapt well to curved installations requires more time to layout and build and the holes for the nozzles must be carefully drilled. In a formal straight bed, you can build it and forget it for years and years.

WATER IS A PRECIOUS COMMODITY and in short supply in many parts of the country. A good system saves resources, money and effort while supporting bumper crop of roses.

ROSARIANS know of many troubles, but most of them never happen. Here are some timely tips to make worrying easier...

MERIT, a relatively new insecticide with great promise, is high on the Rambler's chart for effectiveness... aphids, thrips, even Japanese beetles. At first, *Merit* seemed too good to be true, but after a full season of trials and comparisons, there is nothing else on the market like it. Imagine, thrips control for seven to 10 days, no leaf or bloom damage, compatible with fungicides, caution label and cost effective. As an illustration of effectiveness and safety, *Merit* is used in plantscape and greenhouse situations, where insect populations are very difficult to control.

APPLICATION RATE for *Merit* is 1/4 teaspoon per gallon, preferably in a solution conditioned with *Indicate-5* or *Surf-King Plus*. It is also reported to be even more effective when combined with a nitrogen source. Several very knowledgeable rosarians report that *Response*, the foliar seaweed fertilizer, appears to enhance the systemic qualities of *Merit*. Best of all, *Merit* DOES knock out adult Japanese beetles and maintains a good residual. Rambler's advice: give *Merit* a trial in your garden for a season — you'll become an advocate, too.

SOME ROSE JARGON you need to know: the phrases "multi-site" and "single site" are used to categorize fungicides. The definitions are very simple, but appear contradictory. A "muti-site" fungicide is a surface protectant which does not enter the leaf itself; the active ingredient remains on the surface. Examples are *Manzate 200*, *Fore*, *Mancozeb*, *Fungi-Gard*, *Daconil*, etc. These fungicides attack fungus (inhibit growth) in more than one way. "Single site" fungicides like *Triforine*, *Cleary's 3336*, *Rubigan*, *Immunex*, etc., enter the leaf and act against one site (or function) in the fungus. The locally systemic fungicides do not translocate to new growth, but are effective in treated tissue.

BEST OF BOTH WORLDS is a combination spray solution of "multi-site" and "single-site" *Fore* and *Cleary's*. One works on the leaf; the other works in the leaf. And, by switching off products from time to time, resistance to the fungal action is avoided. A good consideration when selecting a fungicide spray program.

CORN EAR WORMS begin drilling small holes in choice buds this time of year, but they can be headed off before the drilling starts. Alert rosarians can squash the tiny, cream-colored eggs laid in the stems of the sepals. Or, destroy the moth that lays the eggs with a *BUG ZAPPER*, the Rambler's name for the luminous lamp, electric grid cage. Small gray moths emerge from the soil to lay the eggs; get them on the way to the buds. Hang the zapper about 8 feet off the ground, away from the rosebeds. Depending on the wattage of the lamp(s), a zapper will protect a wide area. Usually on sale in the fall, a zapper is a good investment to fry flying bugs.

INSECTICIDE of choice for bud worms is *Mavrik*, long lasting and effective. But many rosarians are respiratory-sensitive to this product, even when using a mask. If you elect to spray, wear a mask, read and follow label instructions carefully and you'll be all right.

Oct. 2001

THOUGHT FOR THE MONTH: *Let nature and the rosebush alone as much as you can… they are more experienced than you are.*

EXPERIENCE is like manure… it's only good when spread around. RAMBLINGS this month shares a really BAD summer experience and outlines a GOOD recovery, sustained by an old bit of rose wisdom, "I already KNOW how to grow better roses than I do."

DROUGHT, DISEASE AND NEGLECT combined to devastate two rose garden plantings under the Rambler's care. No fungicide protection, off-and-on watering, and a weed crop heavy enough to be baled for cattle feed. The beds looked like lush pasture grass with an occasional rose sticking up. Really bad. RECOVERY called for some strong and backbreaking measures. First, the weeds had to go — pulled by hand being careful to get the roots. The weed crop was hauled off to the compost pile by the wheelbarrow-ful, with heavy watering before and after. Next came a broadcast application of alfalfa pellets in the beds, followed with 3-4 inches of ground pine bark mulch. The Rambler treated the miniature, floribunda and hybrid tea beds the same. About 400 roses of all types were affected.

GROOMING followed with trimming of bloom canes, removal of spent blooms and beetle-damaged foliage. The miniatures got a combined shearing and pruning of dead wood. About a third of the rose foliage was lost. An attempt was also made to pull the diseased blackspot leaves, but this proved to be an almost impossible task. Leaves were dropping anyway, so repeated applications with the water-wand blew off most of the stragglers, and probably colonies of spider mites. By this time, the beds looked pretty sparse.

FUNGUS CONTROL was the next order, a combination spray of *Funginex* and *Manzate 200DF*. Spray solution was buffered with *Indicate-5*. Really good coverage was applied twice a week for two weeks. Then *Banner Maxx* with *Daconil 2787WDG* every second week. *Maneb Flowable* was sprayed alone at midpoint of the *Banner Maxx/Daconil* routine.

LEAVES began to grow, emerging clean and undamaged with disease apparently checked. New growth came from a soluble, available feeding program that applied floods of water. The program was similar to quick-growth routines used by avid exhibitors getting ready for a show.

A SIPHON SYSTEM called *E-Z Gro* was the key to recovery. The roses received a light feeding twice a week applied with a water-breaker wand. The soluble mix of *Peters 20-20-20* came through the siphon canister attached near the hose bib. With the flexibility of the garden hose, it was easy to fertilize an entire garden in 30 minutes or less. *E-Z Gro* really is an automatic fertilizing system, as the manufacturers claim, and is endorsed by a good many very successful and busy rose growers. The secret: *E-Z Gro* applies fertilizer in liquid form, allowing roses to absorb nutrients immediately through the leaves and roots (with immediate results).

SOLUBILITY is the key, *Miracle-Grow* and *Mills Easy-Feed* worked equally well. Fill the canister, dial in the setting, and a 50-1 ration is automatically dispensed. It sure beats the bucket and pour system. Several rates/settings can be dialed in. The hose bib connector should be attached to a water-breaker so there is no danger of siphoning back into the water supply.

HAVE THE GARDENS RECOVERED? Absolutely. After seven weeks into the process, all of the bushes are well-leafed, free of disease and forming good buds. The bloom will not be as lush as first spring bloom, but certainly satisfying. The Rambler attributes recovery to an intensive spray program with AVAILABLE plant nutrition, thanks to the *E-Z Gro* system. If you are interested in a holiday gift to yourself or a gardening friend, check out the Rosemania products list in these pages. Or call 888-600-9665. You (and your roses) will be happy that you did.

WITH ROSES, it's what you learn after you know it all that counts. Here are some items that were "relearned" this season that will make your rose growing even more fun in 2002...

NEW PRODUCTS are coming into the market that make life rosier than ever. Availability is much greater, and in quantities appropriate for hobbyists. pH test strips are now almost rosarian-proof; they are easy to use, cheap and reliable. More and more hobbyists are using test strips to monitor and control pH, as evidenced by newsletter notes all over the country.

INFORMATION ADS are expanding in these pages, a healthy sign that suppliers understand the grower's need to know. Many product promotions offer easy-to-follow instructions on product use, as well as on-line and 800-number assistance. The Rambler encourages you to take advantage of this enterprise in your garden effort.

INDICATE-5 continues to be used more and more as a conditioner/acidifier/spreader for spray materials. It really does make the water "wetter" and spray materials more effective. With a built-in color indicator, the user can't go wrong.

SEAWEED EXTRACTS are also gaining new credibility. The Rambler likes *Response* in the regular spray mix, a deviation from his usual stance to avoid foliar "wonder foods." Just a little with every spray mix brings a notable difference in leaf substance and color without burn. Blooms appear to be deeper in color and substance as well. There are a number of exotic concoctions on the market, just use carefully and cautiously (read the directions).

ALFALFA TEA... still the best tonic around. Rave reviews continue to come in month after month on how roses (big ones and minis) perked up and bloomed after a tonic treatment. Alfalfa tea releases a growth hormone that makes all the processes work better. As a tea it goes to work right away; you'll see a difference in a week. Some additives like *Sequestrene 330Fe* (chelated iron), Epsom salts (magnesium sulfate) and *Mills Easy-Feed* make it even better. Brew up a batch in a 32-gallon trash can with 10-12 cups of alfalfa pellets or meal, fill with water, stir occasionally, steep for about a week. Then apply about 1 gallon of this smelly elixir (one half as much for minis). Tea does not replace the normal feeding routine, just makes it work better.

FUNGICIDES... we're always looking for a new miracle. But the consensus of rosarians as reported in newsletters across the country (and from the Rambler's experience) is that *Banner Maxx,* combined with a contact material like *Fore* (manzate) or *Daconil Ultrex* will keep most rose gardens clean on a two-week schedule. *Cleary's 3336* also gets good reviews as the systemic fungicide; also *Compass*, a good material but a bit expensive for the average rosarian.

HYDROPHILIC WATER CRYSTALS, a water and nutrient-storing polymer has great application in container-growns of all kinds. You can expect savings of up to 50 percent in water amounts and intervals. This means watering container roses two or three times a week rather than daily during hot summer weather. Really good in coarse, sandy soils also. These polymer crystals absorb up to 200 times their weight in water, and the roots grow right into them. Just hydrate (load with water) and incorporate into any soil-less or sandy soil mix. The Rambler has used water crystals in barrels and pots for years with consistently good results. *Broadleaf P4* is relatively new on the market and is available and affordable. The Rambler recommends that you enjoy the water benefits in your containers next season.

GET A POWER SPRAYER... if you have 25 or more roses, you should ask Santa for one this year. Now widely used and in every price range, rosarians are enjoying (?) spraying with less work, less material and better results. While the Rambler uses a *Spot Shot*, he recommends a 3-gallon *Black & Decker* battery sprayer for smaller gardens. Keep it cleaned and maintained and it will give years of service with an investment of $100. Maintenance is important with ANY sprayer: clean and rinse with every use, use a little silicone grease on pressure controls and spray away. A really good rose tool.

ROSARIANS know that you have to do a job to really learn how. Here are some rosy items the Rambler learned the hard way…

WHAT'S HAPPENING OUT THERE? Now's the time to take a good look at HOW and WHY your roses are coping with winter. This is not the time for a long winter nap. Check out the winter protection; add some more insulation if needed. And note the amount of good wood on some bushes and loss on others. Is the difference in protection? Less wind, more moisture, insulation able to breathe, more gradual dormancy… all could be factors in survival. Make it a good practice to observe, and then put this new understanding to work.

GET A PRUNING PLAN… Every rosarian has a pet theory. Some just cut off the tops with hedge shears or loppers and let nature take its course. Hedge roses in mild climates can even be cut with a chain saw and still get lots of bloom with little or no die back. Trials in the United States and United Kingdom compared sheared mass plantings with conventional pruning practices, i.e., one cane at a time, careful to cut to an eye. Contrary to what you might expect, sheared bushes had more blooms and bloom-producing canes than bushes done the old-fashioned way. This *does not* apply to roses in cold climates where every inch of cane is precious, but does have application in milder areas. The moral: pruning may not be as critical as "experts" lead us to believe.

THINK HUMUS THIS YEAR. Almost any kind will do. Even in winter you can tell if your soil is crumb-like enough to allow air and water to enter the soil readily. Crumbs in the presence of air and water support the microorganisms that convert minerals and nutrients into forms that roots can pick up.

HUMUS is simply partially decomposed organic matter that acts like a glue to bind clay and silty particles together into granules or crumbs. Combines, clay and humus act together to hold water as well.

A DINING TABLE. Humus derived from organic matter builds a "table" from which rose roots can absorb water and nutrients. Crumbs hold nutrients, up to three or four times more nutrients than clay or silty soils alone. An added plus, hu-mus tends to level out pH swings. It acts as a sort of "conditioner" for nutrient availability.

TOXIC CONCERNS? Some rosarians worry about planting roses where roses have been planted before. Need NEW soil? The Rambler says, "Not to worry." The problem is very rare and just gives rosarians something new to worry about. There's a big word for it: *allelopathy*, the suppression of growth of one plant species by another due to the release of toxic substances. The Rambler has NEVER observed this in roses after planting and replanting in the same rosebeds for years and years. Most growth slow-down is from "tired soil" that just needs some organic matter to liven it up again.

HAULING NEW SOILS in just does not make sense in most cases. It is much easier to amend the soil in place by activating the fresh organics with cottonseed meal and allowing it to mellow for a week or so. You will *always* get dramatic results by replacing soil with a *good mix*, but this takes a good deal more work.

MANURE IN THE WINTER? No better time. Manures and other organics (compost, meals, humus mixtures) are primarily soil builders rather than fertilizers. Manures won't cause too-early spring growth, but set the stage for soil organisms to go to work converting nutrients when the soil warms up.

VALENTINE TREAT… A dump truck load of horse manure from a riding stable… steaming and fragrant on delivery. All that's needed is a red ribbon on top. Rosebeds under a 5-inch blanket of manure really come alive when spring arrives. How about a gift for your garden?

BREAK DORMANCY with some rose catalogs… and then break out into the garden with some of the Rambler's season-openers.

CUSTOM PLANTING… the Rambler's gourmet preparation for some new rose plantings. It's really a one-hole-at-a-time approach to planting roses rather than a prepared "rosebed." Sometimes it is impractical to build a new rosebed or you just want to carefully place some rose strategically in the garden. It's easy. Just make sure the one-hole custom planting doesn't create a bathtub that holds water. Dig out a bushel-basket-size area. Get rid of the old soil, maybe on the compost pile. Loosen the soil in the bottom and on the sides, work in some gypsum and organic stuff. Then fill in with a light, well-prepared soil mix to a level well above the lawn or planting area for better drainage. Raise the custom planting unless you KNOW the drainage is good. With a rich, friable planting medium, your rose(s) will love the new home.

HANDS-AND-KNEES ROSE PLANTING is much easier on bad backs (and on roses) than the bend and twist. Dirty-knees rosarians get better results with less work. Use a short-short shovel, something like the old foxhole tool. If the soil has been well prepared, it's easy to scoop out a hole, rebuild a cone to support the roots and then let water and soil do the rest. Properly placed, the roots and shank will be stable without holding. Cover the roots lightly with soil mix and begin to let water run slowly into the hole. Add more soil, then more water. No need to tamp or pack. In short, MUD them in. If mud bothers you, wear some vinyl gloves…

COVER UP YOUR WORK. Hill up newly planted roses with loose, protective cones of mulch or other insulating material. Not just a little hill but a real MOUND. Conservation of moisture in the canes is important, not sunshine. Moisture in the canes is supported by new root hairs; hilling keeps canes from drying out until the roots have a chance to deliver.

A LITTLE ROOT PRUNING? It's a good practice for most bare-root roses. Lightly trim the ends of the roosts and cut out the broken ones based on the premise that root tips are the most prone to drying out. Trimming exposes healthy tissue for new root hairs to develop. The Rambler also likes to dip bare-root roses in a bleach solution to head off galls. Make a dip solution of 1 cup of bleach to 5 gallons of water in a tall canister or trash can. Dip the rose, roots and canes, for a half-minute or so and then plant as usual. The BEST overnight soaking solution is fish emulsion and water with about 1 cup of emulsion to 5 gallons of water.

ROSES IN BOXES, ready to plant, confuse many growers. Plant in the box or take it out? The box plant has probably arrived at the garden center fresher and better than the packaged roses and may get better handling than the roses potted on site. The Rambler likes to cut the box away if the plant is still dormant and treat it much like a bare-root, spreading out the short roots. If the box-rose is beginning to leaf, cut away the box very carefully without disturbing the new roots. For well-advanced growth, slice the box hoping that the roots will quickly find their way out of confinement. Box roses WILL GROW, with some extra care.

CLEANUP SPRAY for newly-pruned bushes is a good idea to get ahead of spores and overwintering insects, provided that cane tissue is not damaged. Rosarians in really dormant cold regions like oil and sulfur or lime/oil/sulfur combinations, but they MUST be used while canes are still dormant. Oil plus bright sunshine plus tender growth means burn. The Rambler prefers a cleanup which mixes safely in cold or warm weather with a fungicide/insecticide combination at label strength with a little extra spreader-sticker. There is NO NEED to boost the concentration. *Triforine/Manzate* with *Malathion* is about as good as you can get. Spray climbers and shrub roses particularly well as carryover spores on green tissue can spread like wildfire when conditions are right.

MAR. 2002

THOUGHT FOR THE MONTH:
If a rosarian were to enter the Garden of Eden, he would order fertilizers right away.

WHAT'S FOR DINNER? It's time to make out a rose menu that lasts all season. Try this FIVE-STAR special…

ROSES ARE HUNGRY… but also are discriminating eaters, so you'll want to have some things on the menu they like. Start with an appetizer, follow with three squares a day (and lots of water) and finish up with dessert. Rosarians like this kind of menu too.

BEGIN WITH A FISH APPETIZER, fish emulsion, of course, fortified with a bit of urea-type 36-6-0 in the solution. Get this mixture into the root zone at pruning time, even if the soil is a bit on the cold side. Fish emulsion or combinations of fish, alfalfa or cow tea feed the soil, supporting the organisms converting nutrients into forms available to plants. There's some food value in these mixtures, but the primary boost comes from activating the soil organisms, which will go right after the urea.

WARM ROOTS develop appetites. Fertilizers applied to cold soils don't do much good until the root zone warms up; this explains why some rosarians think the feeding program isn't working. The canes, warmed by sunshine, are waking up, but the roots are waiting for a clear signal that spring has arrived. Have you ever noticed how quickly roots grow when newly planted roses in black plastic pots are set out on a warm, reflective surface? Same thing happens with electric bench blankets in a greenhouse, warming seedlings from the bottom up.

THE NEXT FEEDING SHOULD STICK TO THE RIBS (CANES) and support sustained growth. Organics do this very well, releasing slowly with all the right stuff for growth. Timed-release fertilizers also release slowly and evenly and may be a part of your menu. But organic enthusiasts and the Rambler like to mix up a batch of organic stew with a seasoning of 10-10-10 with trace elements, a hundred pounds or so at a time.

FEED STORES sell the staples in this recipe. Mix about 50 pounds of 10-10-10 with trace (coated release), 50 pounds of each of alfalfa meal and fish meal, 20 pounds each of cottonseed meal and blood meal, 25 pounds of bone meal and 10 pounds of triple superphosphate. Blend these dry ingredients in a couple of big wheelbarrows or in a big pile, but keep it dry as it will begin to work. Analysis will be about 8-8-8; use about 2 heaping cups per bush, about a 1/2 cup for miniatures. Scratch into the soil a bit and flood with lots of water. Repeat this organic feast about mid-August.

ROSE DESSERT follows about two weeks before peak bloom, or perhaps two weeks before a rose show. Typical is a soluble mix of *Peters 20-20-20* and fish emulsion, about 1 tablespoon of each per gallon of water, one gallon per large rose.

SNACKS are also good from time to time. The Rambler likes a tonic of alfalfa tea, cow tea or similar brew laced with an iron chelate like *Sprint* whenever foliage begins to pale or growth slows. Fortified tea is even better, adding *Carl Pool Instant, Miracle-Gro* or *Mills Easy-Feed* to the mix. Depending on the climate, this may be two or three times a season, delivering a growth hormone as well as iron. Epsom salts (magnesium sulfate) can also be broadcast to encourage basal breaks (small handful per bush), particularly right after the first bloom flush when roses are at their peak of vigor. Just make sure they have plenty of water to drink during heavy growth. Water is good all the time but absolutely essential when feeding and growing.

CONVENIENCE FOODS… There are some good ones available regionally, like *Mills Magic Mix*, convenient and organic and liked by all kinds of roses. No mixing, no muss, no fuss. Look around your region for Mills or a similar source; but remember that you can make up your own mix from scratch, the old fashioned way.

RELAX AFTER DINNER in late fall, knowing that the roses have been well fed and are happy.

WITH ROSES, it's what you learn after you know it all that counts. Here's a refresher on spray programs that the Rambler learned the hard way.

POWDERY MILDEW AND BLACKSPOT get our attention this time of year, depending on where you live. Cool nights, warm days, low humidity and dry leaves bring on powdery mildew. Conversely, warm temperatures, high humidity and wet leaves bring on blackspot. But we don't have to live in fungus fear. Rosarians have the materials and methods to maintain a clean garden… provided they are willing to get on a spray program and stick with it.

PROTECTIVE VERSUS REACTIVE SPRAYING… Best results in controlling (not eradicating) fungus disease are obtained with a protective/preventive spray program started when bushes are pruned and leaves first appear. Don't wait for powdery mildew to show… it's too late to save those leaves and buds. Spray when conditions are right for mildew, knowing there are spores out there just waiting to set up new colonies on tender, new growth. If the protective program falls short (or if you miss the schedule), fall back to a reactive program with a combination program of systemic fungicides like triforine and daconil applied at shorter intervals. In reactive spraying, increase the frequency, not the concentration.

PROGRAM ROTATION is important to head off disease resistance from the use of one systemic material. Reduce the change of disease resistance by interjecting a different fungicial family with a different mode of action. Examples are triforine (*Funginex*), *Cleary's 3336*, *Banner Maxx, Compass* or *Systane*. There are a number of contact (protectant) fungicides that remain on the leaf surface. Examples are variations of the manzate family, i.e., *Manzate 200, Fore, Mancozeb,* and an old standby, *Daconil 2787*.

RAMBLER ROTATION… The Rambler likes a combination of *Rubigan, Banner Maxx* and *Daconil 2787* sprayed every two weeks for the first month of the growing season. When mildew threat drops and blackspot increases, switch to *Cleary's 3336* and *Fore*. If triforine (*Funginex)* is your systemic of choice, spray weekly, adding *Rubigan* every other week the first month of the season.

IN HOT WEATHER, stop the daconil as a contact, and stick with one of the manzates. Daconil can burn, especially the petroleum distillate (EC) version. Whenever possible, choose a WDG (water dispersible granule) or DF (dry flowable) formulation of contact materials. These are easier to mix and spray, much less likely to burn.

In the fall, concentrate on powdery mildew again, adding *Daconil* or *Systhane* every other week. Continue rotation of systemics and protectants much like spring/summer.

COVERAGE IS IMPORTANT, and often overlooked. Use of a water-conditioner, spreader-sticker in addition to the built-in surfactant is usually in order. The Rambler regularly uses *Indicate-5* to lower the pH of the spray solution and make the water wetter. You can easily see the results on the leaves. *SurfKing Plus* is another good one, but I'm reassured with the color indicator built into *Indicate-5*. Condition the spray water FIRST, then add the systemic, contact fungicide and insecticide (if needed). Swirl the solution between each addition, pour into the sprayer and dilute. Spraying has never been any better.

A SPRAYER TO COVET… the *Black & Decker* rechargeable, battery-powered, 3-gallon model. Light-weight, simple, easy to clean out and quick to recharge, this is a gem of a sprayer for a medium-size rose garden, up to about 200 bushes. It's the best $100 garden investment you can make this season. It rolls around the garden easily — up steps, over flagstones, through thick grass. Has plenty of power for 5 to 6 gallons, appropriate droplet size and adjustable spray patter.

THINK FUNGUS-FREE. With a good program and sprayer, it's something you can enjoy this season.

THE BEST THING ABOUT SPRING is that it always comes when it's most needed. Here are some spring breaks for a rosy season... good for roses and rosarians...

BASAL BREAKS... Just after the first bloom cycle is the time to launch a major thrust for more basal and low breaks. That's when the bushes are at their peak of vigor. Feed with a readily available source of nitrogen followed by *Epsom* salts (magnesium sulfate) and lots of water. Epsom salts work best when a soluble nitrate form is in the root zone (check your fertilizer analysis to see how much is ammonium form and how much is nitrate form). I suggest using a 20-20-20 soluble the first week, 1/4 cup of *Epsom* salts the second week with successive liquid applications of diluted 20-20-20 weeks three and four. New basals and low breaks require LOTS of energy in the root zone for results, driven by LOTS of water.

WAVES OF THRIPS blanket gardens this time of year looking for light-colored, fragrant blooms. They come from field grasses and flowers, drifting along on humid spring breezes. *Orthene SP* (75 percent) is a universal favorite to control the bruising damage; it's safe and systemic for the most tender blooms. Use *Orthene SP* at 2 teaspoons per gallon of *buffered* spray solution, and get good coverage of buds and blooms once a week. Spot spray emerging blooms with a pistol-pump sprayer every other day, making up a fresh batch each time. The thrips fog will dissipate in a few weeks and you can go back to an *occasional* use of *Orthene* ONLY when there is severe thrips pressure. Too much *Orthene* will set up the garden for spider mites, having destroyed the mites' natural predators.

MERIT 75 PERCENT WP is a thrips and sucking insect control that is gaining popularity with rosarians who do not want to spray as often. Used at 1 teaspoon per 10 gallons of buffered spray solution, *Merit* is highly systemic — no flower damage and no leaf damage when used properly. Best of all, *Merit* is a control for Japanese beetles, the summertime scourge of rosarians in the Eastern United States. It has no residue like *Liquid Sevin* and spares many beneficials. Use *Merit* ONLY as required. It is compatible with fungicides like *Manzate, Daconil* and *Cleary's 3336. Merit* is due to become the successor to *Orthene* in thrips control.

SAVE THE FOLIAGE this time of the year, grooming spring bushes and cutting roses or spent blooms with the shortest possible stems. Leaves are the manufacturing processes for the bush. Gather all the possible sunshine and leaves for overall better growth and blooms throughout the season.

SHELF LIFE and saving spray chemicals from week to week provoke inquisitive argument among rosarians. Simply put, most formulations available to gardeners have a shelf life of at least three years without appreciably losing their effectiveness. Keep from freezing, excessively high temperature, preferably in a dark place. Tightly seal containers with wettable and soluble powders. It's usually the carrier that goes first, then the chemical degrades. If it is really old, the material will curdle in the spray solution or won't go into solution at all. Saving a mixed solution is an absolute "NO." Water activates the chemical, and it degrades rapidly. Dispose of leftover spray solution appropriately, preferably in the ground where there is no danger of runoff.

A SPRING TONIC? Roses like a tonic now and then, maybe a sip of alfalfa tea to green up the leaves further. It's a great growth hormone booster. Steep 12 cups of alfalfa pellets or meal in a 32-gallon trash can, fill with water, stir occasionally for a week and apply a gallon of this elixir per established bush, half as much for miniatures. You might also add a seaweed supplement like *Response* (1/4 cup per 32 gallon) or some chelated iron like *Sprint*.

BUFFERED WATER? That's the Rambler's term for spray solution that has been treated with *Indicate-5* or *Surf-King Plus*, lowering the pH of the water and making it wetter. Start EVERY spray session by treating the water, then adding the active materials. You'll see a difference even in the mixing process.

JUN. 2002

THOUGHT FOR THE MONTH:
Relax a little. Roses have been growing for a long time in spite of rosarians.

OPPORTUNITY NEVER COMES. It's here. June is a great time to continue the springtime flush of rose success. Here are a couple of garden tips to consider…

COMBO CONTROL for fungus disease should be a rule rather than an exception. Combinations of systemic and contact fungicides provide protection IN the leaf and ON the leaf for a one-two punch. Examples are *Funginex* and *Manzate* or *Funginex* and *Daconil 2787*… a good weekly program. Or try another combo of *Banner Maxx* and *Manzate* (or *Daconil*) on a 14-day cycle. When *Daconil* is appropriate (spring and fall) use the WDG (water dispersible granule) form for less burn. The WDG form is marketed as *Daconil Ultrex*, which goes right into the spray mix without difficulty.

A NEW FAMILY OF FUNGICIDES called "Strobilurins" has a combo-like action that is "mesostemic," penetrating the leaf surface but not into the vascular system. *Compass* and *Heritage* are members of this new family derived from mushrooms. The "Stros" claim to emit a vapor-like control for contact protection as well. As with all fungicides, materials should be rotated to avoid buildup of resistant fungus strains.

FERTILIZER BURN… widely misunderstood. Burn is simple: too much nitrogen and not enough water. Why does it happen? Roses are made up of cells whose activity is supported by water, just like human tissue. Burn occurs when water is removed or displaced from the cells. Most fertilizers use ammonium sulfate or ammonium nitrate as a nitrogen source, synthesizing the element found in nature. These compounds are HYGROSCOPIC in nature, that is, they have the tendency to take up water. If the compounds (fertilizers) in the soil are too concentrated, moisture is absorbed from the soil, and even the roots, thereby destroying or otherwise interfering with the moisture support system for the cells.

NATURE LIKES BALANCE. Concentrated solutions want to add water and will perform this trick through osmosis, pulling moisture through cell walls. The solution to fertilizer burn is always to apply appropriate amounts (organic or inorganic) and ALWAYS with plenty of water. That's the reason for the advice: water first, feed, water again. If in doubt, water some more.

SPIDER MITES are already on the make and will erupt in a severe infestation if some alert, preventative steps are not taken. Keep a sharp eye out for gray-green foliage near the ground. Infested leaves quickly lose color and drop off. Get busy at the VERY FIRST signs. To confirm, check undersides of leaves for tiny specs and webs. Wash UNDERNEATH leaves with a strong, fine spray of water, using a water wand (not a water breaker) if you have one. If washing with water two to three times a week doesn't do the trick, switch to *Avid*, a specific miticide that has great knockdown and fair residual. Mites do not appear to build up a resistance to it. Water-wash, spray *Avid*, and then repeat process in four to five days. Addition of a mite-attracting pheromone called *Stirrup-M* to *Avid* works even better. Use *Avid* at 1/4 teaspoon per gallon of buffered spray solution and a couple of drops of *Stirrup-M* per gallon to clean up most infestations. Then go back to water for control. It's rare that *Avid* has to be used more than twice a season.

FIND A FEED STORE to make rose growing more fun. Garden shops are all right, and nurseries carry lots of things that rosarians need, but it's hard to beat a good feed store. They will have all sorts of organics and fertilizers and sacks of stuff like alfalfa pellets, fish meal, cottonseed meal, bone meal and gypsum to warm the heart… not to mention the rose roots. Find the real thing… a place that smells like alfalfa and pasture with a couple of cats sleeping on the feed sacks. My feed store also sells (or gives away) rabbits, deserving a five-star organic rating. While you're there, pick up a "gimmie cap" that says "FRED'S FEEDS," the mark of a real dirt gardener.

GROWING GOOD ROSES should be as easy as falling off a diet. Maybe you'll fall for some of these suggestions to make summer roses easier and more fun.

LET THE AIR IN... that's essential to the soil processes. How does air move in the soil anyway? Water pulls it along. Water disperses throughout the soil media, attaching to soil particles and partially filling air spaces. In this form, water becomes available to the roots, carrying along nutrients in the process (having been processed by micro-organisms into forms that roots can take up). Deep soaking starts the process by coating the soil particles. As water is taken up, air fills the voids. Water actually drives nutrient solutions to the root zone, pulling along air to support the bacteria. Simple, isn't it? It's the reason that soils should be well-aerated or "friable"... so that water, air and soil can work together.

DRY, COOL AIR CAN KILL... classic winter kill, even without severely low temperatures. Dead can material is still showing up in midsummer in a Rambler garden severely dehydrated in early spring. The canes looked pretty good at pruning time, but later either dried up or produced one last gasp of growth before shriveling. A nearby planting with LOTS of water throughout the winter and early spring took right off and is still growing vigorously. Problem: A buried irrigation system that was not putting out. Lesson: Roses need (confirmed) water throughout the year.

HOT WEATHER DRILL... water-wash the bushes every chance you get. Water-washing reduces (and often controls) spider mite populations, cools the plants and adds an extra bit of refreshing water in hot weather. Really helps just before spraying, washing off spray residue, dust and all the junk that falls out of the air. If you are on a good spray schedule, water on the leaves won't hurt a thing.

RESPONSIVE... That's the way to describe how leaves react to micro-supplement foliars. The Rambler is generally skeptical of foliars that promise miracles, but the foliar *Response* really brings out the best in leaves. It is a liquid concentrate of Red Australian Kelp, applied at about a half-teaspoon per gallon of spray mixture. Leaves are more lush, better color and typical of the best the variety can produce. No "fake" look here. In *very*

hot climates, spray early in the morning and watch carefully. Discontinue if leaf coarseness appears. *Response* is *only* a micro-nutrient supplement, not intended as a major food source. Several good organic foliars are available; it doesn't have to be "red kelp." Try some.

TO FEED OR NOT TO FEED... that's a summertime question. The Rambler believes that roses like a good regular diet, even in mid-summer when blooms are sparse. Continue to grow *leaves*, which in turn will produce roses. Healthy bush, healthy roses. No need to go on a summer diet. That's the reason the Rambler likes timed-release foods like *Osmocote* as a steady, even diet, regardless of the overall feeding program. Particularly good is *Osmocote* 15-11-13 with trace elements, good for three to four months. Or 16-8-12 for 6 to 8 months. Even coated, slow-release lawn fertilizers help in the summertime.

KEEP THE LEAVES and build the bush. In hot weather, cut the shortest stems possible, leaving all the leaves you can. The leaves are the real food producers of the bush. When cooler weather arrives, the bush will be ready to push out better and larger blooms. Grooming and shaping is always important; just keep in mind that you're cutting off hard-earned growth.

COMPOST PILES are fun and friendly to the environment, and can be much more than piles of leaves in the fall. Recycle all of the stuff that has been poured or scattered on the lawn and garden to make it grow. The Rambler has been adding gypsum and dolomite lime to a compost pile of leaves, lawn clippings, weeds and what-have-you (except kitchen scraps) and notes that the wind-row pile breaks down faster, makes a mellow soil additive and is easy to work. For a row or pile of stuff about two cubic yards, mix in about 10 pounds of lime and 10 pounds of gypsum; turn now and then and keep lightly moist. You'll be surprised at the great soil-additive that comes out.

SUMMER DOLDRUMS?? Here are some tips on how to make roses move along to better blooms. The resident rosarian will feel better, too.

COOL ROSES... and cool rosarians, both good objectives when the temperature tops out. Nature's air conditioner is mulch, an insulating blanket that saves water, controls weeds and adds to the richness of the soil at the same time. Cheap, too. Just a few inches of loose organic mulch dramatically reduces soil temperature and moisture evaporation. Most "home mix" mulches are combos of wood chips, ground bark, leaves, straw, compost and what have you. Pine needles are also very popular in the South, although they don't break down as well. Skeptics say these mulches "leach" nitrogen from the soil, but all it takes is an extra handful of any cheap nitrogen source to release soil-building humus. Nitrogen is released in the process. Replace it.

OLD MULCH? What if old mulch doesn't break down right away? Just leave it in place for winter protection and add some more next season. Old wives' tales have it that mulches harbor insects and fungus spores. Only partially true; these living bits of nature live in many environments; control with an extra clean-up spray in the spring. Ask your roses this summer; they'll want mulch.

WOOD CHIPS from the tree service are gifts from nature. Several years ago the Rambler got a *free* load from a tree service working in the neighborhood. Used a pitchfork to cover several large beds 4 to 5 inches deep. Then broadcast pelletized lawn fertilizer and kept the beds good and moist. Walking in the beds did not compact the soil, moisture was conserved, and in two seasons the otherwise poor soil had improved to a mellow loam. Have since used chips on hard red clay with similar miraculous results. Good news this season: the tree service is now dumping chips in an obscure lot not a half-mile from the house, advertising "Free Mulch." Needless to say, the chips disappear as fast as the trucks can dump. Besides, it's good exercise to load by hand.

COOL, DRY, WINTERKILL REPORT
The Rambler garden suffering from drought and cold temperatures has staged a strong comeback with *lots* of water and deep-feeding liquid fertilizer. Also groomed to keep maximum leaves for food production. By fall the bushes should be back in good condition. Lesson learned: keep roses well watered year-round.

TOUGH LESSON LEARNED: If you are going to use herbicides, use carefully. An over-enthusiastic volunteer in the "shared garden" thought that the easy way to get rid of a healthy crop of nutgrass in the rose beds was to spray "carefully" with *Roundup*, a very effective herbicide that is absorbed by the leaves and translocated to the roots. The problem is that it works on *all* green leaves. Spreads of rose leaves developed. Typical dwarfing and yellowing in days. Some canes died back within a week. Fortunately, the overspray didn't get on many leaves. The clean portions of the bushes developed and grew normally. *Except* for the bed with newly planted roses that were well leafed out. These young plants could not handle the toxic shock and all died over a period of two weeks.

HERBICIDES can be used under and around mature plants if applied carefully. Use a dedicated herbicide sprayer with a long wand, holding the nozzle no more than 3 or 4 inches above the weed growth to be sprayed. Spray pattern should cover about 5 inches. Carefully control the application, *never* during breezy conditions. *Roundup* is a good product when used with caution, saving lots of work for gardeners. But it is a garden disaster when used carelessly.

SOMETHING DIFFERENT? Get a Moore Miniature Roses catalog (Sequoia Nursery). It's a historical document on roses of all types by Ralph Moore, father of miniature roses. Moore has all sorts of interesting things going on with mannerly shrubs, new colorations, roses for every application imaginable. See Moore's ad in the classified section. It's a true rose experience to enjoy his "old and new" write-ups.

SEPT. 2002

THOUGHT FOR THE MONTH: It matters not what goal you seek. It's secret here reposes; You've got to dig from week to week to get results or roses. —Edgar A. Guest

SOME OLD AND SOME NEW blend this month as the Rambler notes 32 years on these pages. It's remarkable how little rose growing has changed since 1970, but read on for some NEW ways to enjoy better roses.

SEEING BLACK SPOTS before your eyes? Blackspot gets our attention this time of year as conditions are just right for fungus growth: high humidity and warm temps. Add an irregular spray schedule or extra moisture, and the bushes lose their leaves. But it doesn't have to be this way; there's still time to control the infection, grow some new leaves and enjoy some great roses.

PROACTIVE/PREVENTIVE SPRAYING usually controls blackspot with a weekly program, usually *Funginex*, or a two-week program with *Banner Maxx*. If that line of defense fails, go to a reactive program with a combination of systemic and contact fungicides like *Funginex* and *Manzate* applied at shorter intervals, maybe twice a week for two or three weeks. Also pull off all the infected leaves you can and practice good garden hygiene. You'll be able to go back to a more normal schedule within a month. Increase frequency, not concentration of material.

PROGRAM OF ROTATION is important to head off spore resistance from continuous use of one systemic material. Rotation reduces that risk by introducing a new fungicidal family, i.e. *Cleary's 3336*, *Banner Maxx* or the very newest fungicide *Compass* (one of a new family called "strobilurins"). And there are choices of contact materials, i.e. *Mancozeb, Maneb, Dithane* (there are several variations in the *Manzate* family), or one of the forms of *Daconil 2787*. The Rambler likes *Daconil Ultrex*, a dry flowable formulation with less tendency to burn leaves. Contacts matched with systemics are a match for the most virulent spores, provided that you get them on the leaves.

GOOD COVERAGE is often overlooked. Use of a water conditioner in addition to the built-in spreader-sticker is usually in order, reducing the pH of the solution. The Rambler likes *Indicate-5*, buffering the spray solution and making the water wetter (like *Bufferin* is to aspirin). This promotes even leaf coverage without beading. *Indicate-5* even has its own pH indicator to confirm a slightly acid condition. Makes spraying easier, more effective.

WET LEAVES SET UP HIGH STRESS. Leaves that remain wet for long periods, may be due to shade or overhead watering, are going to show infection. Check both water and shade. The Rambler noted black spot on some container-grown miniatures while nearby roses on the same spray routine were clean. Reason: the container minis were watered in the evening with a water-wand breaker; the leaves stayed wet all night. Cleared up the problem by watering in the morning before going to work. Solved shade infection stress by cutting off the sprinkler system in that area.

EXTENDED PROTECTION. One Rambler garden is in full sun all day. It stays consistently clean of both black spot and powdery mildew with a *Banner Maxx* program at 1/3 teaspoon per gallon at 14- to 21-day intervals. A *Manzate*-type fungicide is combined with the systemic every-other spraying. During prolonged rainy periods, *Manzate* is applied every two weeks, coinciding with cutting of spent blooms. Takes just a few minutes, pays big dividends. It is important to note that this garden had DRY leaves unless it rains.

SEVERE BLACK SPOT STRESS in another garden required *Banner Maxx* every 14 days, always combined with either *Manzate* or *Daconil 2787*. *Funginex* and *Manzate* in combination were equally effective on a weekly basis. Same protection with *Cleary's 3336* and *Mancozeb* on a 14-day schedule.

LET SOME SUNSHINE IN. Opening up the bushes helped in all the situations, trimming out blind and twiggy growth from the center of the plant. Getting the sunshine in to dry the leaves made a big difference. Sunshine also encouraged low breaks and stronger remaining canes. Sun is the energy source for more and better roses.

CLEVER MEN make quips, and clever columnists repeat them... and they also repeat some of the more clever advice... because it works. Here are some thought-provokers that have been tested by time...

OCTOBER is the time for rose growth to slow down in most parts of the country. Roses go through a natural process of getting ready for winter as hours of sunlight shorten and temperatures drop. Roses want to mature, make rose hips and store nutrients in the canes and roots. Rosarians, on the other hand, want "just a few more blooms." Trimming and feeding tell the plant it is time to grow.

A SLOW-DOWN PERIOD gives roses and woody shrubs time to manufacture natural antifreeze that protects the cells... fluids with reduced capability of expanding when frozen. Late or over-enthusiastic application of fertilizer weakens plants as compared to bushes that are allowed to go to sleep naturally. It's still best to work with nature.

WINTER FEEDING is another matter and a practice worth considering. A better description might be "composting in place." Growers in severe as well as milder climates put down a thick layer of leaves in the rose bed, broadcast a cupful of pelletized fertilizer (10-10-10) per 10 square feet, then add some more leaves. By spring, the lower layer of leaves is broken down into a rich humus threaded with white mycelium. The fertilizer works on the leaves, not on the soil, breaking down the organic material and setting up the soil for lively activity in the spring. Don't disturb the lower layer any more than necessary when pruning in the spring in the event that feeder roots have reached for the compost. Advocates of winter feeding report no untimely new growth in either fall or spring when roses are put to bed with this "nightcap."

INSULATING WRAP for tree roses is cheap insurance for live bushes next spring, at least in milder climates. Fiberglass rafter or duct insulation, the "Pink Panther" blanket with foil backing, works well. Loosely wrap the standards from bottom to top, foil side out, and tie with cord. Flare out just under the bud unions and bundle wrap the major canes. The insulation protects from sudden freeze-thaws and drying winds and is certainly easier than burying the entire tree rose. In VERY severe climates, use the "Minnesota Tip" by trenching and tipping, effectively burying the entire plant until spring.

FOOL MOTHER NATURE with antitranspirant applications for freeze-prone climbers in exposed locations. Water loss (transpiration) is substantially reduced by spraying canes and remaining leaves at the onset of dormancy with *Cloud Cover*, *Wilt-Pruf*, et al. These products form a transparent, flexible film that is semi-permeable to moisture, but still permits the normal breathing process. The film retails the natural antifreeze in the canes and tissues. Major winter damage occurs from drying out (dessication), and it is usually more severe than pure cold. Anti-transpirants are easy to apply with ordinary spray equipment, taking extra care for good coverage. Be sure to clean the sprayer thoroughly, sprayer parts as well as canes are coated. The technique is a natural for climbers on fences and walls. Apply at dormancy, repeat later in the winter during a mild spell.

INSULATING LEAVES are still the most popular form of winter protection. Begin with a mound of soil or compost over the bud union (not from the rosebed), then add lots of leaves in a loose blanket. Keep leaves in place with wire baskets, rabbit-wire fences, evergreen boughs or even short snow fence. Some very cold climate rosarians use combinations of rose cones and leaves or bean baskets and leaves, the leaves serving as a protective insulation for the covers while maintaining more even temperature and moisture.

TESTIMONIAL: "I don't have time or energy to build boxes or bury roses, so I throw some dirt from the garden area on the bud unions and pile on the leaves as high as they will go. Even get some leaves from the neighbors. It's not very fancy, but the roses always go through the winter all right."

NO ONE can build a rosebed by turning it over in his mind. Now's the time to turn some soil and use the leaves harvested in the suggestions to follow.

FREEZE/THAW, a mechanical as well as a chemical process, will do much of the work this winter. Loosen the rosebed you want to improve with a spading fork, breaking the crust just a little. Then pile on lots of organic materials and leaves. As moisture freezes and expands, tissues break down in the same way as decomposition in the summer. Winter action reduces and blends the organic matter and soil into the "loam" that roses and rosarians like. Extra work with the fork speeds the process. Nature has been building soil this way for a long, long time.

WINTER is a good time to adjust the pH of the soil with an application of agricultural lime (if needed). Top application is not particularly effective as lime is relatively insoluble. The process is a reactive one in contact with soil crumbs. Lime, in the presence of hydrogen ions (the indicator for pH), reacts with those ions to form water. By reducing the hydrogen ions, the pH goes up. It's a fairly slow process.

SPADING FORK WORKS BEST. Use the fork to open up holes (rock back and forth) to take the lime (the Rambler likes pelletized dolomite lime). Lightly scratch soil back, let nature and chemistry work. To stay in balance (about 6.5), a good rule of thumb is to add a pound of dolomite lime for every pound of nitrogen used during the season. EXAMPLE: A 5-10-5 ammonium sulfate fertilizer, (50 pound bag), contains 2.5 pounds of nitrogen. Use 2.5 pounds of lime for the same area. And always test before adjusting. For new beds in heave clay soils, work in about 25 pounds of lime per 100 square feet and let it work all winter.

SOME BROWN, SOME GREEN, keeps the pile hot and clean. Referring, of course, to composting the harvest of leaves descending on us. Nature has been storing up all sorts of nutrients for us all season... a bounty that shouldn't be wasted. Leaves are the basis of nature's recycling effort which keeps soils alive and working. It's a simple process; don't worry about the nitrogen-carbon ratios. Just pile up a mixture of leaves and yard stuff, moisten and turn so that air is readily available. Bits and pieces of green materials act as starters; sift on some soil for extra working organisms. Cottonseed meal speeds things up, or add some manure. Gypsum also seems to make a pile work faster. By spring you'll have rich compost ready to go to work.

WINTER PROTECTION with leaves is a kind of composting process also. Rosebeds covered with leaves or cages with leaves are small-scale composters. And most of these insulating materials can be worked into the beds next spring, greatly reduced in volume and partially broken down. Other soil amendments like gypsum and perlite can be added at the same time, gradually working all winter.

ORGANIC ENTHUSIASTS with limited space break down leaves in plastic bags, adding just a bit of fertilizer to a bag of leaves and securing the top. A heavy mill bag works best as the composting process eats on the bag as well. Noting how nature breaks things down, fish meal stored in a plastic trash can will eat pinholes through the sides in just a few months. Fish meal needs to be in the ground or the compost pile, not in a can.

EXPERIENCE IS LIKE MANURE... it's only good when spread around. So the Rambler is busy spreading whatever, having had *lots* of experience (good and bad).

GROW SOME SOIL... and you'll grow more and better roses. It's a simple process when you understand the basics. Much like the Rambler's advice to grow leaves, then roses. You can't have one without the other.

THE STUFF IN SOIL... Soils are made up of mineral particles, among other things. These particles vary in size from gravel and rocks to sand to silt to clay in a decreasing size gradient. Clay is so small, for example, that it barely settles out in water because the force of friction between the clay particles and water is greater than the pull of gravity. In a soil, these flat-surfaced clay particles hold water and elements so that rose roots pick them up. Clay surfaces carry a negative charge, much like a magnet, and attract positively charged particles to them, ions of potassium, calcium, magnesium, et, al. Attracted to clay, the ions can then be absorbed through the roots through water.

THE ROLE OF HUMUS... Humus is partially decomposed organic matter. It acts as a "glue" to bind clay and other soil particles into granules or crumbs. Soil crumbs (loam) tend to be quite porous and water and air enter the soil readily. Clay and humus act together to hold waster, giving the "soil" a high water-holding capacity. The crumbs allow excellent gas exchange so that roots have a sufficient supply of oxygen to support micro-organisms converting minerals into forms the roots can pick up.

FOOD TABLE... Humus derived from organic matter builds a "table" where rose roots can feed. As part of the soil "crumbs," humus has a tremendous ability to hold positively charged ions, up to three or four times more than clay alone. It is this "holding" capability that allows slow leaching of nutrients. Humus is the *key* ingredient in good rose growing. It helps hold water and nutrients, increases porosity of the soil, supports living organisms and tends to keep soil pH in balance. Need any more reasons to have up to 25 percent organic matter in your rosebed? Just check out the loads of roses enjoyed by growers who have understood this wonder of nature all along.

THE OLD RELIABLE FORMULA is a rose bed mix that *you* would like to grow in, using the best of soil science. The Rambler's recommendation calls for about one-third soil, one-third sand and one-third organic matter of some kind. Old Reliable works no matter where you live. Don't worry too much about the proportions, but if in doubt, add some more organics. A good soil has a "friendly" feel; you should be able to work your fingers into a settled bed without a trowel.

ORGANICS should be partially broken down, beginning to form humus. Animal manures break down rapidly and condition the soil in the process. Compost, manures, ground bark, leaves and combinations of all these materials work to keep the mix friendly for roots and organisms. Many growers like sphagnum peat, the more fibrous the better. Fine-ground pine bark works just as well. Mixtures last longer with particles of different sizes making up the soil crumbs.

GOURMET MIXES are seasoned with fish meal, alfalfa meal, gypsum and some bone meal. In acidic areas, add some dolomite lime. For a 100-square-foot rosebed, add 15 pounds of fish meal, 20 pounds of alfalfa meal (or pellets), 20 pounds of gypsum (calcium sulfate) and 15 pounds of bone meal. Mix well, let settle for a week or so, and it is ready for roses. Manure or cottonseed meal will activate the process, especially with lots of leaves.

THE TROUBLE WITH GOOD ADVICE is that it usually interferes with our plans. Pick up on these plans and make them your *own* good advice to launch the 2003 rose season.

MANURE WITHOUT A HORSE... What will they think of next? This is for the rosarian who doesn't want a horse or have a farm friend (and pickup truck) for the real thing. Guaranteed to grow grass on fence posts and roses in rocks. Horseless manure is a good soil amendment, top dressing, basic feeding formula... especially in the spring.

ARTIFICIAL MANURE can be made in your own backyard. Combine about three ample yards of compost material or leaves, 100 pounds of coarse organic stuff (like ground pine bark), 100 pounds of cottonseed meal, 100 pounds of alfalfa meal (or pellets), 50 pounds of bone meal, 50 pounds of fish meal and 50 pounds of gypsum. Mix can be varied to suit your taste. Make a pile in an area suitable for composting, adding lighter ingredients a little at a time. Turn with a pitchfork, mix well.

TO ACTIVATE DIGESTION PROCESS, moisten *lightly* and turn with a fork twice a week for two weeks. As the pile works, you will smell a sharp *ammonia* odor. If the pile is too wet or lacking coarse material, it will smell *dead* and turn into a slime. Add some more coarse material and keep turning. The new manure will be ready in about three weeks. Use two garden shovelfuls per bush in the spring and another one in mid-summer with mulch. You'll be feeding the soil that ultimately feeds the roses. Use generously, it really works.

DOWN IN THE MUD... hands and knees planting is easier on bad backs and roses than bending over. Use a short shovel, like the old foxhole tool. In a prepared bed it's easy to scoop out a hole and rebuild a cone to support bare roots and bush. Then let water and soil do the rest. Roots and shank should be stable without holding. Scoop soil mix over the roots lightly and begin to let water run slowly into the hole. Add more soil, then more water. No need to tamp or pack. *Mud* them in.

COVER UP YOUR WORK. Hill up newly-planted roses with loose, protective cones of mulch or other insulating material until just the tips of the canes stick out. Make a real *mound*, a couple of big shovelfuls per bush. Moisture conservation in the canes is important, not sunshine and wind. Moisture in the canes (and new growth) is supported by new root hairs; mounding keeps canes from drying out until roots have a chance to deliver.

RETHINK ROSES IN BOXES. We see lots of them in garden centers. Plant the box or take it out? The box plant has probably arrived at the garden center fresher and better than the packaged roses and may get better handling than the roses potted on site. But box roses have *very short* roots. The Rambler likes to cut the box away if the plant is still dormant and treat it much like a bare-root bush, carefully spreading out the roots. If the bush is beginning to leaf, cut away the box very carefully without disturbing the roots. If box rose is well advanced, slice the box hoping that the roots will quickly find their way out of confinement. Box roses will grow, with some extra care.

GROUND PINE BARK is an early-season essential. Much maligned by the uninformed, but glowingly praised by those who have enjoyed the benefits of this cheap, readily available soil improver. Try working about 25 percent fine-ground pine bark (by volume) into the soil, even more if the soil is really hard or depleted. The newly worked area becomes friable almost overnight. Offset possible acidity with about 10 pounds of Dolomite lime per 100 square feet, plus 5 pounds of 5-5-5 fertilizer to support the decomposition process. Or the Rambler likes cottonseed meal/ alfalfa meal to feed the microorganisms working on the bark. Pine bark lasts a long time and encourages root growth. Results have to be seen to be believed. Why do you think there is so much ground bark in the "soil-less" potting mix?

SPRINGTIME TONICS next month. We'll look at some chemical/organic combinations to please the most discriminating rose palate.

WITH ROSES, it's what you learn after you know it all that counts. Here's a refresher on spray programs that the Rambler learned the hard way.

PROTECTIVE VERSUS REACTIVE SPRAYING... Best results in controlling (not eradicating) fungus disease are obtained with a protective/preventative spray program started when bushes are pruned and leaves first appear. Don't wait for powdery mildew to show... it's too late to save those leaves and buds. Spray when conditions are right for mildew, knowing there are spores out there just waiting to set up new colonies on tender, new growth. If the protective program falls short (or if you miss the schedule), fall back to a reactive program with a combination program of systemic fungicides like triforine and daconil applied at shorter intervals. In reactive spraying, increase the frequency, not the concentration.

PROGRAM ROTATION is important to head off disease resistance from the use of one systemic material. Reduce the chance of disease resistance by interjecting a different fungicidal family with a different mode of action. Examples are triforine (*Funginex*), *Cleary 3336* and *Banner-Maxx*. There are a number of contact (protectant) fungicides that remain on the leaf surface. Examples are variations of the *Manzate* family and an old standby, *Daconil 2787*.

RAMBLER ROTATION... The Rambler likes a combination of *Rubigan, Banner-Maxx* and *Daconil 2787* sprayed every two weeks for the first month of the growing season, then, as blackspot increases, change to *Funginex* or *Cleary 3336* as your systemic of choice, adding *Rubigan* every other week the first month of the season.

IN HOT WEATHER, stop the *Daconil* as a contact, and stick with one of the *Manzates*. *Daconil* can burn, especially the petroleum distillate version. Use *Ultrex* granule formulation instead. It is easier to mix and spray, and much less likely to burn. In the fall, concentrate on powdery mildew again, adding *Daconil* or *Systhane* every other week. Continue rotation of systemics and protectants much like spring/summer.

COVERAGE IS IMPORTANT, and often overlooked. Use of a water-conditioner, spreader-sticker in addition to the built-in surfactant is usually in order. The Rambler regularly uses *Indicate-5* to lower the pH of the spray solution and make the water wetter. You can easily see the results on the leaves. *SurfKing Plus* is another good one, but I'm reassured with the color indicator built into *Indicate-5*. Condition the spray water FIRST, then add the systemic, contact fungicide and insecticide (if needed). Swirl the solution between each addition, pour into the sprayer and dilute. Spraying has never been any better.

A SPRAYER TO COVET... the *Black & Decker* rechargeable, battery-powered, 3-gallon model is light-weight, simple to use, easy to clean and quick to recharge. This is gem of a sprayer for a medium-size rose garden, up to about 200 bushes. It's the best $100 garden investment you can make this season. It rolls around the garden easily — up steps, over flagstones, through thick grass. It has plenty of power for 5 to 6 gallons, appropriate droplet size and adjustable spray patter. The Rambler added a longer wand to make it easier to get into thick bushes, but that is not needed in most applications. Remember when setting up any spray program, be sure to include the safety equipment — especially a respirator with replacement cartridges.

THINK FUNGUS-FREE. With a good program and sprayer, it's something you can enjoy this season.

THE BEST THING ABOUT SPRING is that it always comes when it's most needed. Here are some spring breaks for a rosy season... good for roses and rosarians...

BASAL BREAKS... Just after the first bloom cycle is the time to launch a major thrust for more basal and low breaks. That's when the bushes are at their peak of vigor. Feed with a readily available source of nitrogen followed by Epsom salts (magnesium sulfate) and lots of water. Epsom salts work best when a soluble nitrate form is in the root zone (check your fertilizer analysis to see how much is ammonium form and how much is nitrate form). I suggest using a 20-20-20 soluble the first week, 1/4 cup of *Epsom salts* the second week with successive liquid applications of diluted 20-20-20 weeks three and four. New basals and low breaks require LOTS of energy in the root zone for results, driven by LOTS of water.

WAVES OF THRIPS blanket gardens this time of year looking for light-colored, fragrant blooms. They come from field grasses and flowers, drifting along on humid spring breezes. *Orthene SP* (75 percent) is a universal favorite to control the bruising damage; it's safe and systemic for the most tender blooms. Use *Orthene SP* at 2 teaspoons per gallon of *buffered* spray solution, and get good coverage of buds and blooms once a week. Spot spray emerging blooms with a pistol-pump sprayer every other day, making up a fresh batch each time. The thrips fog will dissipate in a few weeks and you can go back to an *occasional* use of *Orthene* ONLY when there is severe thrips pressure. Too much *Orthene* will set up the garden for spider mites, having destroyed the mites' natural predators.

MERIT 75 PERCENT WP is a thrips and sucking insect control that is gaining popularity with rosarians who do not want to spray as often. Used at 1 teaspoon per 10 gallons of buffered spray solution, *Merit* is highly systemic — no flower damage and no leaf damage when used properly. Best of all, *Merit* is a control for Japanese beetles, the summertime scourge of rosarians in the Eastern United States. It has no residue like *Liquid Sevin* and spares many beneficials. Use *Merit* ONLY as required. It is compatible with fungicides like *Manzate*, *Daconil* and *Cleary's 3336. Merit* is due to become the successor to *Orthene* in thrips control.

SAVE THE FOLIAGE this time of the year, grooming spring bushes and cutting roses or spent blooms with the shortest possible stems. Leaves are the manufacturing processes for the bush. Gather all the possible sunshine and leaves for overall better growth and blooms throughout the season.

SHELF LIFE and saving spray chemicals from week to week provoke inquisitive argument among rosarians. Simply put, most formulations available to gardeners have a shelf life of at least three years without appreciably losing their effectiveness. Keep from freezing, excessively high temperature, preferably in a dark place. Tightly seal containers with wettable and soluble powders. It's usually the carrier that goes first, then the chemical degrades. If it is really old, the material will curdle in the spray solution or won't go into solution at all. Saving a mixed solution is an absolute "NO." Water activates the chemical, and it degrades rapidly. Dispose of leftover spray solution appropriately, preferably in the ground where there is no danger of runoff.

A SPRING TONIC? Roses like a tonic now and then, maybe a sip of alfalfa tea to green up the leaves further. It's a great growth hormone booster. Steep 12 cups of alfalfa pellets or meal in a 32-gallon trash can, fill with water, stir occasionally for a week and apply a gallon of this elixir per established bush, half as much for miniatures. You might also add a seaweed supplement like *Response* (1/4 cup per 32 gallon) or some chelated iron like *Sprint*.

BUFFERED WATER? That's the Rambler's term for spray solution that has been treated with *Indicate-5* or *Surf-King Plus*, lowering the pH of the water and making it wetter. Start EVERY spray session by treating the water, then adding the active materials. You'll see a difference even in the mixing process.

Made in the USA
San Bernardino, CA
31 August 2014